MONETARY ECONOMICS

consulting editor
RICHARD THORN
University of Pittsburgh

MONETARY ECONOMICS

controversies in theory and policy

edited with Introductions
by Jonas Prager
University College, New York University

RANDOM HOUSE NEW YORK

 Published in the United States by Random House, Inc., New York, and simultaneously in Canada by Random House of Canada Limited, Toronto.
ISBN: 0–394–30827–1

Library of Congress Catalog Card Number: 70–124130

Manufactured in the United States of America.
Composed by Cherry Hill Composition, Inc., Pennsauken, New Jersey. Printed and bound by Halliday Lithograph Corporation, West Hanover, Massachusetts.

Design by Jack Ribik

First Edition

987654321

To Joel and Sharon

WITHOUT WHOSE HELP
THIS BOOK WOULD
HAVE BEEN COMPLETED
LAST YEAR.

PREFACE

Product differentiation is characteristic of an imperfectly competitive market such as the one in which college texts are sold. Quality more than price determines the choice of a text. Thus, the appeal of a specific work must be based on its distinctiveness and uniqueness. What need does the present book of readings fill that is not satisfied adequately by one of the numerous basic money and banking texts? What distinguishes this book of readings from other similar anthologies currently available? Or, to put these questions most directly: Why bother with a supplementary text at all? And, if a supplementary anthology is desired, why should the present one be selected?

The answer to these questions lies in the considerations that guided the organization of this book and the choice of articles. Three major criteria differentiate this book from others.

1. *The focus on controversy.* In the past two decades monetary economics has risen phoenixlike from the premature grave to which it was relegated by the Keynesian revolution. Monetary policy and theory have become increasingly crucial both to the professional economist and to the policy makers in Washington. However, the fact is that the agreement extends no further than that monetary policy is important; how important it is or why it is critical is still at

the source of many major disagreements concerning analysis and the practical conduct of monetary policy. Since monetary analysis and policy are closely allied to the banking industry, it is no surprise that banking, too, has become embroiled in a number of theoretical and practical controversies. Basic texts for the money and banking course, by virtue of their comprehensiveness and their need to explain the fundamentals in their historical context, do not adequately treat the most pressing current controversies. Nor do the available anthologies focus their attention systematically on current controversies. The present book of readings, however, attempts to fill that gap.

2. *The integration of theoretical analysis and empirical verification.* Theoretical disputations have long been the characteristic of economists. As the old saying gloomily notes, "If you could lay all the economists in the world end to end, you would never reach a conclusion!" In this century, however, and with ever-increasing intensity, economists are trying to resolve divergent theories by submitting them to formal empirical tests. Indeed, the judges who awarded the first Nobel prize in economics saw econometrics—the science of formulating testable economic models and supporting or rejecting them by statistical procedures—as the most notable contribution of contemporary economists. The prize went to two men responsible for "discovering" this methodology—Sweden's Ragnar Frisch and Holland's Jan Tinbergen. The present volume attempts to integrate economic theory and statistical analysis; in many sections econometric articles are juxtaposed to analytical ones. For example, three of the four articles in Part VIII discuss various theoretical aspects of the rules versus discretion debate; the fourth selection presents an attempt to answer empirically the question, Would rules have worked more effectively than discretion? Basic texts and other anthologies rarely attempt to achieve this integration.

3. *A balanced representation of the Chicago School.* Although many economists disagree with University of Chicago Professor Milton Friedman's analysis and even more object to his policy recommendations, few would contend that he has not enriched and enlivened the field of economics. Indeed, were it not for Professor Friedman, many controversies would not have been aired. Yet only a limited number of the current basic money and banking texts have paid sufficient attention to Friedman's views, despite his impact both on economists and on the public at large. Other supplementary texts have not been as complete in presenting the Chicago School and its critics as the present one.

Two additional considerations played

a role in the design of this anthology. Although theory and its verification loomed important, a conscious attempt was made to include a number of articles that would appeal to the institutionally oriented economist. For example, almost all of Part IV can be thought of as descriptive rather than analytical, and so, too, to a degree, can Part III. Secondly, each section is preceded by an editorial introduction and each selection is preceded by a headnote. The introduction has as its objective the setting of the articles in their proper context as well as pointing out the interrelationships between the various articles. Thus, each section constitutes an independent unit. The articles also retain their independence; they can be read separately from adjacent selections.

A word is now appropriate about the most crucial editorial decision: the trade-off between breadth and depth. Since comprehensive coverage of each topic would have required a gargantuan book, a decision was made to aim for deeper coverage of a few vital issues rather than complete coverage that was lacking in substance. This goal has required the editor to exercise judgment over the topics to be included; he expects that few will agree totally with all his choices. In some instances, for example, issues were omitted not because they lacked significance or interest but because they were overly complex and required a degree of sophistication beyond that of the average, and often the superior, student. Other issues, however, were omitted because of a subjective decision of the editor concerning importance. Subjectivity also is evident in the selection of articles within each section. The goal set for inclusion was simple: which articles best serve the purpose of the text, given the ability of the student as a constraint? Obviously, however, a divergence of views is possible regarding the articles that meet the criterion most effectively.

The articles themselves were edited, despite the initial repugnance of the editor to so proceed. Sections, paragraphs, and, in a few instances, even sentences that were not germane to the topic at hand were eliminated. This policy necessitated the insertion of appropriate notation; however, it has made possible the inclusion of many more articles than otherwise would have been possible. Space considerations also dictated the elimination of footnotes in many instances; the cost here is marginal, since footnotes are usually designed to pick up the finer points, which, although appropriate to the professional reader, are not critical for the student. However, footnotes containing citations for references found in the body of the articles were retained.

To conclude this Preface, it is no more than appropriate to recite the usual litany of gratitude. As with the economy, my debts in preparing this volume grew as I proceeded, and I fear that my credit is reaching its limit. Truly many people contributed to this book, from my late mother, of blessed memory, and father, without whom this book would never have been conceived, to my numerous teachers and friends, who, each in his own way, added noteworthy contributions, and to my students, who have served over the past few years as unpaid but hopefully not unrewarded guinea pigs. I cannot thank each one individually here, but nonetheless they have earned my gratitude. I include in this collective "thank you" all the economists and non-economists who wrote the articles reprinted here, for they unwittingly wrote this book for me. The following, however, must be singled out for special kudos: Richard Thorn of the University of Pittsburgh helped shape the manuscript from its inception, read it with great care, and gave unstintingly of his advice and time. Benjamin Klebaner of the City University of New York read the introductions; I have benefited greatly from his many suggestions. My colleague at New York University, Simon Whitney, and my good friend, Charles Siegman, who is on the staff of the Board of Governors of the Federal Reserve System, read and significantly improved key portions of the manuscript. Over the years Benjamin J. Katz, now Chairman of the Department of Economics, University College, New York University, has been a friend, teacher, and counselor, lavish with encouragement and a constant source of sound advice. The Random House staff, especially Jeanne Singeisen and Barbara Conover, contributed more than their share. But, of course, the sound advice was not always heeded, the sage counsel at times was disregarded. It is therefore no more than right that responsibility for the final product devolves upon the editor. Finally, Helen has suffered the most from the ordeal of putting this book together; her husband often seemed to be wedded to this text rather than to her. Yet her encouragement never faltered; she knew, I guess, that ultimately her husband would return to his first and only love. He has.

New York
Spring 1970 JONAS PRAGER

bibliographical key

The chart on the following pages correlates Monetary Economics with the leading textbooks listed below. Selections are to be read in the order listed.

Harold Barger, *Money, Banking and Public Policy,* 2nd ed. (Chicago: Rand McNally, 1968).

Lester V. Chandler, *The Economics of Money and Banking,* 5th ed. (New York: Harper & Row, 1969).

John A. Cochran, *Money, Banking, and the Economy* (New York: Macmillan, 1967).

William E. Dunkman, *Money, Credit, and Banking* (New York: Random House, 1970).

William J. Frazer and William P. Yohe, *Analytics and Institutions of Money and Banking* (Princeton, N.J.: Van Nostrand, 1965).

Walter W. Haines, *Money, Prices and Policy,* 2nd ed. (New York: McGraw-Hill, 1966).

C. Lowell Harriss, *Money and Banking,* 2nd ed. (Rockleigh, N.J.: Allyn & Bacon, 1961).

Albert G. Hart et al., *Money, Debt and Economic Activity,* 4th ed. (Englewood Cliffs, N.J.: Prentice-Hall, 1969).

Paul M. Horvitz, *Monetary Policy and the Financial System,* 2nd ed. (Englewood Cliffs, N.J.: Prentice-Hall, 1969).

Harry D. Hutchinson, *Money, Banking and the United States Economy* (New York: Appleton-Century-Crofts, 1967).

John J. Klein, *Money and the Economy,* 2nd ed. (New York: Harcourt Brace Jovanovich, 1970).

Clifton H. Kreps and O. S. Pugh, *Money, Banking and Monetary Policy,* 2nd ed. (New York: Ronald Press, 1967).

David T. Lapkin, *Money, Banking, and the Nation's Income* (Homewood, Ill.: Dorsey Press, 1969).

#Thomas Mayer, *Elements of Monetary Policy,* The Random House Series in Money and Banking (New York: Random House, 1968).

———, *Monetary Policy in the United States* (New York: Random House, 1968).

*Paul Nadler, *Commercial Banking in the Economy,* The Random House Series in Money and Banking (New York: Random House, 1968).

Boris P. Pesek and Thomas R. Saving, *Foundations of Money and Banking* (New York: Macmillan, 1968).

Charles L. Prather, *Money and Banking,* 9th ed. (Homewood, Ill.: Irwin, 1969).

John G. Ranlett, *Money and Banking: An Introduction to Analysis and Policy,* 2nd ed. (New York: Wiley, 1969).

Harlan M. Smith, Random House Series in Money and Banking; see Mayer; Nadler, Smith.

**———, *Elementary Monetary Theory,* The Random House Series in Money and Banking (New York: Random House, 1968).

°———, *The Essentials of Money and Banking,* The Random House Series in Money and Banking (New York: Random House, 1968).

Eli Shapiro et al., *Money and Banking,* 5th ed. (New York: Holt, Rinehart & Winston, 1969).

Charles R. Whittlesey et al., *Money and Banking,* 2nd ed. (New York: Macmillan, 1968).

KEY	Barger	Chandler	Cochran	Dunkman	Frazer & Yohe	Haines	Harriss	Hart et al.	Horvitz	Hutchinson	Klein	Kreps & Pugh	Lapkin	Mayer, *Monetary*	Pesek & Saving	Prather	Ranlett	Smith, *The Random House Series in Money and Banking*	Shapiro et al.	Whittlesey et al.
Part I: The Controversy over the Definition of Money	1	1	1,19	1,17	2	1	1	1	1	Intro.	1,22	1	1		1, 5-8	1	1	[0]1	1,4	1
Part II: Issues in Commercial Banking Section A: Portfolio Analysis and Its Application	12,7	8,7	7-10	12,13	3	10,9	7,2	3,4	7,4	2,5	5-7 15	4, 6,9	4,5	App. A	12,13	12,3	4,2	* [0]7,5	6,7	8,7
Section B: Bank Size and The Structure of the Banking Industry	13	26	6		12	15	3	2	29	2	4	13	3		15	10		*	5	9
Part III: The Structure of the Federal Reserve System Section A: Federal Reserve Independence	28	9	28	16	11	33	25	23	31	20	10	32	19		30	20	6	[0]14	9	11
Section B: The Bank Supervision Controversy	13	9	5	12	11	15	8	23	30	2	10	10	3		3	10	6	* [0]2	6,9	6,9
Part IV: The Money Market and the Federal Reserve	9,14, 19,30	11,3, 25,24	16, 12,13, 21,23	16, 24,19	8,14, 4,20 (App. B), 13	13, 10,29	11,6, 15,25	5,23	20, 6,26	6,1, 12,19	10,13 7,20	27,5, 8,32	8, 4,9	2, App.	10,16, 18,30	8,18, 6,14	7,16, 14,19	[0]6, #10	11-14, 20	12,5, 18,21
Part V: Keynes Versus the Quantity Theory	20,10	16,11	17,20, 15,16	5,6, 3,17	20, 5,24	30, 23,14	16, 13,14	10, 8,23	16, 13,20	13, 9,19	20,21 22,13	22, 20,26	17, 18,8	4,3	22, 24,14	4,19, 16,18	18, 10,13	** 3-7, [0]10	18,16, 21,10	18, 14,7

	Barger	Chandler	Cochran	Dunkman	Frazer & Yohe	Haines	Harriss	Hart et al.	Horvitz	Hutchinson	Klein	Kreps & Pugh	Lapkin	Mayer, *Monetary*	Pesek & Saving	Prather	Ranlett	Smith, *The Random House Series in Money and Banking*	Shapiro et al.	Whittlesey et al.
Part VI: The Tools of Monetary Policy Section A: Reserve Requirements and Open-Market Operations	8	11	14	18	25	32,34	11	5	19,20	6	12,13	28	8	2	10,24	16,18	17	#6	10,11	12
Section B: Discounting and the Discount Rate	9	11	14,15	18	8,25	32,34	11	5	19	6,20	12	28	8	2	10	15,18	17	#6	11	12
Part VII: Problems of Monetary Policy Section A: Time Lags	29	24	22	20	26	33	23	23	31	19	27	33	19	6	25	17,18	18	#14	21	20
Section B: The Discriminatory Impact	29	24	22	20	26	33	23	23	31	19	27	33	19	5	25	17,18	18	#14	21	20
Part VIII: Rules Versus Discretion	29	11	22	20	26	33	21	23	23	19	27	33	19	7	16	16	18	#15	10	20
Part IX: Inflation: The Phillips Curve Controversy	33	13	25	20	16	31	22	19	27	17,21	21	19	19	1	25	20	15	#14	19	19,24
Part X: International Monetary Economics	25	20,18	27	22,24	22,23	37,39	19,20	18	12	15,16	25	18	19	1	32,34	27,28	24	o12	24,25	26,27

CONTENTS

PART ONE

the controversy over the definition of money

What is "money"? The accepted answer, long rehearsed in money and banking texts, is found by concentrating on the functional aspects of money rather than stressing its physical properties. The "medium-of-exchange" function ranks high among the characteristics of money; indeed, in the eyes of most contemporary economists this function is a sufficient criterion. Other properties of money are its use as a unit of account, as a standard of deferred payments, and as a store of value.

When a single commodity provides all these functions, little doubt can arise concerning the appropriateness of naming it "money." The cigarette, used by British war prisoners in Nazi prison camps, was money in all four of these senses. This fact is most vividly portrayed by R. A. Radford, who describes his own experiences in the opening selection.

When the multifaceted functions of money are provided by a variety of objects, however, identification of the money asset becomes far more difficult. Is an item that possesses either some of the functions of money or all the functions of money only some of the time to be considered "money"? What about a medium of exchange that is limited to a specified range of transactions—is it "money"? Is an article to be deemed "money" if it does not function as an impersonal exchange medium but is used only if the participants in the exchange themselves meet certain criteria? Some examples may help to visualize these questions. The value of certain prestige goods—slaves and cattle —is expressed in terms of brass rods by the Tiv of Nigeria, making the rods standards of value. Moreover, slaves and cattle are exchanged for brass rods, and thus the rods must be considered media of exchange. But the exchange of brass rods for foodstuffs and other subsistence goods is rare and involves a loss of status in the community. Similarly, consider the *ndap* shell money of the Rossel Islanders. There are twenty-two denominations of *ndap,* but, unlike a modern currency, where all denominations are related to one another mathematically (twenty $5 bills are the equivalent of and exchangeable for two $50 bills or one $100 note or 100 singles), conversion of one denomination of *ndap* to another is limited. The highest denominations are used only for special occasions. Class number 20, for example, "is a necessary indemnity payment to the relatives of a man ritually murdered and eaten, a transaction which is part of [the] mortuary rites for the death of a chief."[1] Two 10 *ndap* will not serve the same purpose, although, as among the Tiv, the lower denominations are used extensively for daily commercial transactions. Professor George Dalton has asked for a reconsideration of the definition of money and argued that what may be a proper concept of money in modern economies may not be appropriate for communities that still live in the Dark Ages of economic existence.[2]

The issue raised by the anthropologist-economist is, to a large extent, one of semantics. Similar questions asked about modern economies are often questions of substance, however. The quantity of money influences spending in one way or another. Moreover, because the decisions of a central bank affect the national economy by influencing the supply of money, central banks require a definition of money that is suited to their policy intentions. Only few objects typically serve as media of exchange (coin, paper currency, and demand deposit accounts in the United States). But many assets—savings deposits, various types of securities, and commodities—can substitute as stores of value. The critical question to be answered is, Which of these two functions is more closely related to or more certainly determines spending decisions? Professor James Tobin, in the second selection in this Part, discusses and criticizes a definition of money that would encompass not only commercial bank demand deposits and currency, but time deposits at commercial banks as well. He finds both the logic and the policy implications of this expanded "money"—which is based on the store-of-value function of money—deficient.

The Gurley-Shaw thesis, outlined in the succeeding article, answers at least one of Tobin's objections. Gurley and Shaw argue that bank money is not unique and that indeed the whole array of liquid assets supplied by financial intermediaries—commercial banks, savings banks, government institutions, and so on—are money substitutes. The growth of intermediation between savers and investors by institutions other than commercial banks thus reduces the importance of bank money in the economy and makes far more tenuous the relationship between money and economic activity.

Three views, then, are presented in answer to the question, What is money? Tobin opts for the definition of money as the medium of exchange and includes only assets that perform as exchange media—namely, currency and commercial bank demand deposits. Milton Friedman and Anna Schwartz, whose position is outlined in the Tobin article, broaden the concept by defining money as a "temporary abode of purchasing power" and would add other commercial bank deposits to the traditional listing. Gurley and Shaw go still further, contending that no unique identity ought to

---

[1]G. Dalton, "Primitive Money," *American Anthropologist*, 67, p. 56.

[2]*Ibid.*, pp. 44–62.

be given commercial bank liabilities; liabilities of other financial institutions are also stores of value.

For policy purposes, it is crucial to know the relationship between money, however defined, and economic activity. Richard H. Timberlake and James G. Fortson test the various definitions and conclude that the transaction role of money stands up extremely well against the newer alternatives.

The humorous selection by the late Professor Denis H. Robertson that concludes Part I provides a great deal of insight into the basically irrational characteristic of paper money and an inconvertible paper standard. Nonetheless, as irrational as such a standard may be, it has worked tolerably well for the advanced economies of the world. Indeed, the remaining important vestige of a commodity standard—the modified gold standard used in international trade—is evolving into an inconvertible standard (see Selection 57).

1 MONEY IN A PRISONER-OF-WAR CAMP

R. A. RADFORD

A pure exchange economy is often a theoretician's playground; rarely does it describe reality. He uses such a concept, however, to analyze essentials. But first principles can become even more graphic when they can be viewed in a realistic setting, as R. A. Radford does so ably in this selection. Note the relationship between the quantity of cigarette money and prices, and the advantages and disadvantages of a supplementary paper currency. A commodity money poses special difficulties. In this case, cigarette money, being consumable, literally went up in smoke, causing prices of other commodities to fall. New shipments of cigarettes, arriving at unknown intervals, caused prices to rise. Can you see the relationship between a cigarette standard and a gold standard? Would you recommend the adoption of a gold standard as an instrument of national policy?

• • •

THE CIGARETTE CURRENCY

Although cigarettes as currency exhibited certain peculiarities, they performed all the functions of a metallic currency as a unit of account, as a measure of value and as a store of value, and shared most of its characteristics. They were homogeneous, reasonably durable, and of convenient size for the smallest or, in packets, for the largest transactions. Incidentally, they could be clipped or sweated by rolling them between the fingers so that tobacco fell out.

Cigarettes were also subject to the working of Gresham's Law. Certain brands were more popular than others as smokes, but for currency purposes a cigarette was a cigarette. Consequently buyers used the poorer qualities and the Shop rarely saw the more popular brands: cigarettes such as Churchman's No. 1 were rarely used for trading. At one time cigarettes hand-rolled from pipe tobacco began to circulate. Pipe tobacco was issued in lieu of cigarettes by the Red Cross at a rate of 25 cigarettes to the ounce and this rate was standard in exchanges, but an ounce would produce 30 home-made cigarettes. Naturally, people with machine-made cigarettes broke them down and re-rolled the tobacco, and the real cigarette virtually disappeared from the market. Hand-rolled cigarettes were not homogeneous and prices could no longer be quoted in them with safety: each cigarette was examined before it was accepted and thin ones were rejected, or extra demanded as a make-weight. For a time we suffered all the inconveniences of a debased currency.

Machine-made cigarettes were always universally acceptable, both for what they would buy and for themselves. It was this intrinsic value which gave rise to their principal disadvantage as currency, a disadvantage which exists, but to a far smaller extent, in the case of metallic currency—that is, a strong demand for non-monetary purposes. Consequently our economy was repeatedly subject to defla-

From R. A. Radford, "The Economic Organization of a P.O.W. Camp," *Economica*, 12 (November 1945), 194–198. Reprinted by permission.

tion and to periods of monetary stringency. While the Red Cross issue of 50 or 25 cigarettes per man per week came in regularly, and while there were fair stocks held, the cigarette currency suited its purpose admirably. But when the issue was interrupted, stocks soon ran out, prices fell, trading declined in volume and became increasingly a matter of barter. This deflationary tendency was periodically offset by the sudden injection of new currency. Private cigarette parcels arrived in a trickle throughout the year, but the big numbers came in quarterly when the Red Cross received its allocation of transport. Several hundred thousand cigarettes might arrive in the space of a fortnight. Prices soared, and then began to fall, slowly at first but with increasing rapidity as stocks ran out, until the next big delivery. Most of our economic troubles could be attributed to this fundamental instability.

PRICE MOVEMENTS

Many factors affected prices, the strongest and most noticeable being the periodical currency inflation and deflation described in the last paragraphs. The periodicity of this price cycle depended on cigarette and, to a far lesser extent, on food deliveries. At one time in the early days, before any private parcels had arrived and when there were no individual stocks, the weekly issue of cigarettes and food parcels occurred on a Monday. The non-monetary demand for cigarettes was great, and less elastic than the demand for food: consequently prices fluctuated weekly, falling towards Sunday night and rising sharply on Monday morning. Later, when many people held reserves, the weekly issue had no such effect, being too small a proportion of the total available. Credit allowed people with no reserves to meet their non-monetary demand over the week-end.

The general price level was affected by other factors. An influx of new prisoners, proverbially hungry, raised it. Heavy air raids in the vicinity of the camp probably increased the non-monetary demand for cigarettes and accentuated deflation. Good and bad war news certainly had its effect, and the general waves of optimism and pessimism which swept the camp were reflected in prices. Before breakfast one morning in March of this year, a rumor of the arrival of parcels and cigarettes was circulated. Within ten minutes I sold a treacle ration for four cigarettes (hitherto offered in vain for three), and many similar deals went through. By 10 o'clock the rumor was denied, and treacle that day found no more buyers even at two cigarettes.

• • •

PAPER CURRENCY—BULLY MARKS

Around D-Day, food and cigarettes were plentiful, business was brisk and the camp in an optimistic mood. Consequently the Entertainments Committee felt the moment opportune to launch a restaurant, where food and hot drinks were sold while a band and variety turns performed. Earlier experiments, both public and private, had pointed the way, and the scheme was a great success. Food was bought at market prices to provide the meals and the small profits were devoted to a reserve fund and used to bribe Germans to provide grease-paints and other necessities for the camp theatre. Originally meals were sold for cigarettes but this meant that the whole scheme was vulnerable to the periodic deflationary waves, and furthermore heavy smokers were unlikely to attend much. The whole success of the scheme depended on an adequate amount of food being offered for sale in the normal manner.

To increase and facilitate trade, and to stimulate supplies and customers therefore, and secondarily to avoid the worst effects of deflation when it should come, a paper currency was organized by the Restaurant and the Shop. The Shop bought food on behalf of the Restaurant with paper notes and the paper was accepted equally with the cigarettes in the Restaurant or Shop, and passed back to the Shop to purchase more food. The Shop acted as a bank of issue. The paper money was backed 100 percent by food; hence its name, the Bully Mark. The BMk. was backed 100 percent by food: there could be no over-issues, as is permissible with a normal bank of issue, since the eventual dispersal of the camp and consequent redemption of all BMk.s was anticipated in the near future.

Originally one BMk. was worth one cigarette and for a short time both circulated freely inside and outside the Restaurant. Prices were quoted in BMk.s and cigarettes with equal freedom—and for a short time the BMk. showed signs of replacing the cigarette as currency. The BMk. was tied to food, but not to cigarettes: as it was issued against food, say 45 for a tin of milk and so on, any reduction in the BMk. prices of food would have meant that there were unbacked BMk.s in circulation. But the price of both food and BMk.s could and did fluctuate with the supply of cigarettes.

While the Restaurant flourished, the scheme was a success: the Restaurant bought heavily, all foods were saleable and prices were stable.

In August parcels and cigarettes were halved and the Camp was bombed. The Restaurant closed for a short while and sales of food became difficult. Even when the Restaurant reopened, the food and cigarette shortage became increasingly acute and people were unwilling to convert such valuable goods into paper and to hold them for luxuries like snacks and tea. Less of the right kinds of food for the Restaurant were sold, and the Shop became glutted with dried fruit, chocolate, sugar, etc., which the Restaurant could not buy. The price level and the price structure changed. The BMk. fell to four-fifths of a cigarette and eventually farther still, and it became unacceptable save in the Restaurant. There was a flight from the BMk., no longer convertible into cigarettes or popular foods. The cigarette re-established itself.

But the BMk. was sound! The Restaurant closed in the New Year with a progressive food shortage and the long evenings without lights due to intensified Allied air raids, and BMk.s could only be spent in the Coffee Bar—relic of the Restaurant—or on the few unpopular foods in the Shop, the owners of which were prepared to accept them. In the end all holders of BMk.s were paid in full, in cups of coffee or in prunes. People who had bought BMk.s for cigarettes or valuable jam or biscuits in their heyday were aggrieved that they should have stood the loss involved by their restricted choice, but they suffered no actual loss of market value.

• • •

2 WHAT IS MONEY?

JAMES TOBIN

When the primary characteristic of money is its medium-of-exchange function, any item generally used as a medium of exchange is money. If Professor Milton Friedman's definition of money as a "temporary abode of purchasing power" is accepted, however, a Pandora's box is opened. In the following selection, Professor James Tobin criticizes the Friedman definition and implicitly affirms the exchange function of money as its distinguishing characteristic.

• • •

What is money? The "money" whose stock F&S[1] trace and explain consists of currency and commercial bank deposits held outside the federal government and the banks. The main questions raised by this definition are these: Why are time and savings deposits in commercial banks, which are not means of payment, included? If they are included, why are similar claims on other financial institutions—notably deposits in mutual savings banks and shares in savings and loan associations—excluded?

On the first question, a decisive practical answer is that it is evidently impossible to distinguish time from demand deposits in commercial banks prior to 1914. But F&S do not stand on this answer. They do not think that their inability to exclude deposits not subject to check impairs the utility or relevance of their series for the stock of money. They cannot contend, of course, that their *M* measures the stock of means of payment, but they do not regard this as a defect.

More basic, in their view, is a concept of money as "a temporary abode of purchasing power enabling the act of purchase to be separated from the act of sale." I am not sure what this means; on its face the concept seems to allow all forms of wealth, all stores of value, to qualify as money. Clearly purchasing power can find temporary abodes other than currency and commercial bank deposits, for example in other savings institutions.

F&S recognize that, once the means-of-payment criterion is dropped, drawing the lines that define "money" is a matter of expediency. What statistical quantity works best? That is, what measure bears the closest and most predictable relationship to measures of economic activity? This is fair enough scientific procedure. But such open-minded pragmatism in the concept and definition of money is an unconvincing prelude to policy conclusions which stress the overriding importance of providing money in precisely the right quantity. Sometimes Friedman and his followers seem to be saying: "We don't know what money is, but whatever it is, its stock should grow steadily at 3 to 4 percent per year."

• • •

From James Tobin, "The Monetary Interpretation of History," *American Economic Review*, 55, 464–467. Reprinted by permission.

[1]Milton Friedman and Anna Jacobson Schwartz, *A Monetary History of the United States 1867–1960.* National Bureau of Economic Research, Studies in Business Cycles, No. 12. Princeton: Princeton University Press, 1963.

The central place which F&S give their money stock in theoretical analysis, historical interpretation, and policy recommendation invites critical scrutiny. Imagine a balance sheet expressing on one side the financial claims of the rest of the economy on the federal government (including the Federal Reserve) and the commercial banking system and on the other side the debts of the public to the government and the banks. (The balancing item is that amount of private net worth represented by the net debt of the central government to the public.) Both the government and the commercial banks have demand liabilities to the public, currency and demand deposits. Both have time liabilities to the public, securities and deposits. The total on which F&S focus is the sum of the government's demand liabilities to the public and all of the commercial banking system's deposit liabilities, time as well as demand. In their view, this seems to be the only feature of the consolidated balance sheet which matters.

Do F&S really think that the composition of this magnitude is of no consequence? Do they, for example, expect the velocity of a given *M* to be the same after a shift from demand to time deposits? And is their answer to this question the same whether such a shift is the autonomous result of a change in preferences or the induced effect of an increase in time-deposit interest rates? In special cases they recognize that compositional shifts are not neutral. They argue, for example, that shift to currency induced by bank failures will raise velocity—that is, it will reduce the demand for money because currency is an imperfect substitute for the safe deposits it replaces. But this attention to special cases suggests that there may be general and systematic compositional effects which the authors have ignored. . . .

What about the liabilities omitted from *M*, the interest-bearing government debt held by the public? Are its size and composition of no monetary consequence? F&S tend to take an extreme either/or black-or-white view. Generally they do not regard this debt as money or as affecting the significance for economic activity of the liabilities that are money. But there is an important exception. In 1942–51, Federal Reserve support of government security prices made them the equivalent of money, indeed of high-powered money. The true money stock should include these securities, valued at their support prices. By the same logic the 1951 Accord would abruptly shrink money to its usual constituents.

I think most readers will agree with me that this is farfetched. There is uncertainty about government security prices in normal times, but it does not prevent them from being good substitutes for bank deposits. This is especially true of short maturities, but it is true of any maturities the holders can match with their own future-payments schedules. Uncertainty was doubtless reduced, but it was not eliminated, by the Fed's wartime support commitment. There was considerable doubt, justified in the event, that the policy would be permanently continued. There is no evidence—either in interest rates on government obligations or in velocity figures—of such radical and abrupt revisions of public attitude towards government securities.

Moreover, I cannot see the logic which makes F&S so anxious to assimilate completely to money marketable government securities temporarily supported at par, and so reluctant to assimilate to money the liabilities of thrift institutions which are always "supported at par."

Finally, are F&S justified in neglecting the asset side of the consolidated balance sheet of the government and the commercial banking system? The authors are strongly opposed to giving attention to "credit" as against "money."

• • •

Does the composition of bank assets make no difference? Will the effect on economic activity be the same whether a given increase in the money stock reflects (a) commercial loans by banks to private-business borrowers, or (b) exchange of bank certificates of deposit for Treasury bills previously held by the public? The monetization of commercial loans (or really indirectly of the inventories of goods which they finance) seems to me to be alchemy of much deeper significance than semimonetization of Treasury bills. By this I mean simply that I would expect (a) to stimulate more spending on GNP than does (b). If so, the same *M* packs a bigger wallop if it is the counterpart of operations like (a) than if it is the result of asset swaps like (b). You will never detect the difference if you confine your attention to the liabilities of the banking system.

• • •

3 A RECONSIDERATION OF BANKING THEORY

JOHN G. GURLEY
AND EDWARD S. SHAW

The policy implications of the broadest definition of money, which includes a wide but unspecified variety of liquid assets, deserve special mention. Since "moneyness" is shared by a number of financial intermediary liabilities, central bank control over commercial banks is discriminatory. Indeed, continued control over commercial banks may only inhibit their growth relative to that of other intermediaries and thus erode the base of Federal Reserve control. It follows, then, that the Federal Reserve must voluntarily either deprive itself of its monetary controls or, through legislation, obtain the necessary weapons designed to exert some measure of influence over other financial institutions. A third view is also possible: Do nothing now, but, should serious difficulties arise, extend the controls. This latter position was adopted by the prestigious Radcliffe Commission, which investigated the British monetary system in the late 1950s. Which view do you think is appropriate for the United States?

• • •

A traditional view of the monetary system is that it determines the supply of money: it determines its own size in terms of monetary debt and of the assets that are counterparts of this debt on the system's balance sheet. Other financial intermediaries transfer to investors any part of this money supply that may be deposited with them by savers. Their size is determined by the public's choice of saving media.

As we see it, on the contrary, the monetary system is in some significant degree competitive with other financial intermediaries. The growth of these intermediaries in terms of indirect debt and of primary security portfolios is alternative to monetary growth and inhibits it. Their issues of indirect debt displace money, and the primary securities that they hold are in some large degree a loss of assets to the banks.

Bank deposits and currency are unique in one respect: they are means of payment, and holders of money balances have immediate access to the payments mechanism of the banking system. If money were in demand only for immediate spending or for holding in transactions balances, and if no other financial asset could be substituted as a means of payment or displace money in transactions balances, the monetary system would be a monopolistic supplier exempt from competition by other financial intermediaries.

But money is not in demand exclusively as a means of payment. It is in demand as a financial asset to hold. As a component of balances, money does encounter competition. Other financial assets can be accumulated preparatory to money payments, as a precaution against contingencies, or as an alternative to primary securities. For any level of money payments, various levels of money balances will do and, hence, various sizes of money supply and monetary system.

From John G. Gurley and Edward S. Shaw, "Financial Intermediaries and the Saving-Investment Process," *Journal of Finance*, 11, 260–262. Reprinted by permission.

The more adequate the non-monetary financial assets are as substitutes for money in transactions, precautionary, speculative, and . . . diversification balances, the smaller may be the money supply for any designated level of national income. For any level of income, the money supply is indeterminate until one knows the degree of substitutability between money created by banks and financial assets created by other intermediaries. How big the monetary system is depends in part on the intensity of competition from savings banks, life insurance companies, pension funds, and other intermediaries.

Financial competition may inhibit the growth of the monetary system in a number of ways. Given the level of national income, a gain in attractiveness of, say, savings and loan shares vis-à-vis money balances must result in an excess supply of money. The monetary authority may choose to remove this excess. Then bank reserves, earning assets, money issues, and profits are contracted. This implies that, at any level of income, the competition of non-monetary intermediaries may displace money balances, shift primary securities from banks to their competitors, and reduce the monetary system's requirement for reserves. In a trend context, bank reserves cannot be permitted to grow as rapidly as otherwise they might, if non-monetary intermediaries become more attractive channels for transmission of loanable funds.

Suppose that excess money balances, resulting from a shift in spending units' demand away from money balances to alternative forms of indirect financial assets, are not destroyed by central bank action. They may be used to repay bank loans or to buy other securities from banks, the result being excess bank reserves. At the prevailing level of security prices, spending units have rejected money balances. But cannot banks force these balances out again, resuming control of the money supply? They can do so by accepting a reduced margin between the yield of primary securities they buy and the cost to them of deposits and currency they create. But this option is not peculiar to banks: other intermediaries can stimulate demand for their debt if they stand ready to accept a reduced markup on the securities they create and sell relative to the securities they buy. The banks can restore the money supply, but the cost is both a decline in their status relative to other financial intermediaries and a reduction in earnings.

The banks may choose to live with excess reserves rather than pay higher prices on primary securities or higher yields on their own debt issues. In this case, as in the previous two, a lower volume of reserves is needed to sustain a given level of national income. With their competitive situation improved, non-monetary intermediaries have stolen away from the banking system a share of responsibility for sustaining the flow of money payments. They hold a larger share of outstanding primary securities; they owe a larger share of indirect financial assets. They have reduced the size of the banking system at the given income level, both absolutely and relatively to their own size, and their gain is at the expense of bank profits.

. . .

4 TIME DEPOSITS IN THE DEFINITION OF MONEY

RICHARD H. TIMBERLAKE AND JAMES G. FORTSON

Professors Timberlake and Fortson found that the simple correlation coefficient relating currency and demand deposit changes to changes in money income exceeded that of money more broadly defined, for almost all years, including the period 1953–1965. On the basis of their tests, they concluded that the additional explanatory value obtained by broadening the definition of money is small relative to that yielded by the narrow definition. A few reservations may be noted, however. First, annual data may not have been the most desirable form for testing the hypothesis; quarterly data, which are available at least for the last twenty years, might have been more appropriate. Second, the claim can be made that neither the Gurley-Shaw nor the Friedman-Schwartz hypothesis was tested adequately. In the case of the former, perhaps the inclusion of other near-moneys in the tests might have modified the results. Indeed, this conclusion has been drawn by G. S. Laumas, who fitted quarterly data to the Timberlake-Fortson equation and introduced other money substitutes. His results are far more favorable to the views of Gurley and Shaw.* Finally, it is puzzling that the coauthors of the present selection did not test the Friedman-Schwartz definition with their regression equation.

The original study by Milton Friedman and David Meiselman[1] on the competitive abilities of a stock of money and autonomous expenditures to predict money income in the United States has been subjected recently to an intensive reappraisal and review. The essence of the arguments seems to be that the accuracy of autonomous expenditures in predicting money income or consumption depends critically on the definition of autonomous expenditures chosen as a predictor. To a lesser extent this same issue can be raised about the various possible inclusions made in constructing "the" quantity of money used for testing purposes. Essentially, the question boils down to the "moneyish" influence time deposits exert on the "narrow" stock of money (currency and demand deposits).

The analysis presented below purports to develop a pragmatic answer to this question by allowing annual first differences in three diverse stocks of money to compete at predicting annual changes in money income. In order to check the results of the simple correlations, annual first differences in the narrow stock of money and annual first differences in all time deposits are then structured in the form of a multiple correlation to estimate annual changes in money income. The multiple correlation analysis also tests the data for a significant coefficient of moneyness in time deposits.

The raw data for currency, demand deposits, and time deposits may be used to construct an infinite number of money stocks. Each stock would include the first

---

From Richard H. Timberlake and James G. Fortson, "Time Deposits in the Definition of Money," *American Economic Review*, 57, 190–193. Reprinted by permission.

*G. S. Laumas, "The Degree of Moneyness of Savings Deposits," *American Economic Review*, 58, 501–503.

[1] Hereafter, references to the work of these authors is abbreviated to "F-M" [see Part V, selection 29—ed.]

two of these items plus some percentage (weight) of all time deposits. F-M chose to include in their money stock the percentage of time deposits in commercial banks. Both expediency and logic recommended this choice. It is expedient because reliable estimates for this definitional stock of money can be obtained for a much longer time period than can be obtained for other money stocks; and it is logical because of the distinct possibility that time deposits and demand deposits may be held as close substitutes for each other when they are claims against the same commercial bank. However, the case can also be made that the narrow stock of money is the only one that can be used for transactions and is, therefore, the only stock that influences spending. Yet another and contrary view sees *all* time deposits generating liquidity in the monetary system, and thus making more efficacious the spendability of the narrow money stock. Each of these concepts is logical, and each has intuitive plausibility. The choice, however, must be made in terms of the empirical relevance shown by the various stocks in predicting money spending.

The groundwork for this study required time series data of the three most relevant stocks of money: the narrow stock, M_1, the F-M stock, M_2, and the narrow stock plus all time deposits in commercial and savings banks, M_3. Data for money income from the spending side, Y, were taken from the original work by F-M and supplemented to 1965 using their definition. Annual first differences in the various money stocks were then correlated with annual first differences in money income for the reference cycle periods defined in the original F-M study. The results of this series of tests are summarized in the first four columns of Table 1.

The correlation values shown here make possible some interesting inferences that are obscured when only the values for longer periods are computed. First, the correlation coefficients for all the money stocks in most of the subperiods covered show extremely high degrees of association between changes in money and changes in income. Second, while the F-M money stock, M_2, has the highest correlation value over the entire period, the narrow money stock, M_1, has higher values in more of the years than either M_2 or M_3. This seeming anomaly results from the inclusion of data from the war years (1942–46) in the tests, and the much poorer performance of M_1 in that period. Third, time deposits improve the correlation values only in the 1933–38 period.

The first inference—that any of the stocks of money influences spending—needs no interpretation beyond that given by F-M. Second, the irregular values for the periods embracing the war years obviously result from biases in the raw data and confirm Donald Hester's observation on the original F-M study, viz.: "Indeed it is remarkable that the monetary model failed to reflect these conditions [in the 1942–46 period] more vividly."** The raw data associations for the various money stocks and money income do not reflect wartime discrepancies because of the dominance of trend in the series. First difference correlations do emphasize the warpings of normal spending relationships by abstracting trend. Price controls, rationing, much higher taxes, and exhortations not to spend, dammed up money in people's pockets or caused "under the table" spending, the effects of which could not be measured. This alteration continued to some degree through most of the Korean War. The 1953–65 correlation values indicate a gradual return to more normal relationships.

Third, the better performance of M_3 during 1933–38 can be attributed to two "real" factors also not measurable cardinally. First, very low interest rates on time deposits discouraged their attractiveness as investments and encouraged their

**"Keynes and the Quantity theory: A Comment on the Friedman-Meiselman CMC Paper," *Review of Economics and Statistics,* 46 364–68.

Table 1. Simple Correlations of First Differences in Three Conceptual Stocks of Money on First Differences in Nominal Money Income, the Percent of All Time and Savings Deposits in Commercial Banks, and Coefficients for a Multiple Regression of First Differences in Narrow Money and Time Deposits on First Differences in Nominal Money Income

Period Annually	$r_{Y.M_1}$ (Narrow)	$r_{Y.M_2}$ (F-M)	$r_{Y.M_3}$ (All Time)	Percent All Time Deposits in Commercial Banks (Average for Period)	b_1	b_2	b_2/b_1	$R_{Y.M_1}$	$R_{Y.M_1,T}$
(1)	(2)	(3)	(4)	(5)	(6)	(7)	(8)	(9)	(10)
1897–1908	[a]	.890	.820	[a]	[a]	[a]	[a]	[a]	[a]
1903–1913	[a]	.788	.813	[a]	[a]	[a]	[a]	[a]	[a]
1908–1921	[a]	.766	.726	[a]	[a]	[a]	[a]	[a]	[a]
1913–1920	.796	.786	.727	63	3.086	−1.131	− .3664	.796	.803
1920–1929	.775	.700	.702	70	4.939	−1.035	− .2096	.775	.779
1921–1933	.883	.801	.772	68	6.922	−1.128	− .1630	.883	.894
1929–1939	.891	.882	.865	58	3.170	.4467	.1409	.891	.893
1933–1938	.785	.766	.865	53	1.224	9.791	7.997	.902[b]	.987
1938–1953	.028	.006	−.145	63	.3812	−1.620	−4.249	−.419[b]	.471
1939–1948	−.019	−.009	−.171	63	.3681	−1.660	−4.510	−.410[b]	.458
1948–1960	.495	.408	.285	64	1.162	− .4902	− .3032	.496	.514
1953–1965	.667	.609	.633	68	1.919	.2903	.1521	.667	.692
1929–1960	.398	.501	.427	62	.8945	−1.146	−1.281	.401[b]	.504
1897–1960	[a]	.573	.517	54	1.004	.7277	.7251	[a]	.518

SOURCES: Original data for M_1 and T to 1957 were taken from U. S. Bureau of the Census, *Historical Statistics of the United States, Colonial Times to 1957,* Washington, D.C., 1960, Series X, p. 646. Data for M_2 and Y to 1957 were taken from [M. Friedman and D. Meiselman, "The Relative Stability of Monetary Velocity and the Investment Multiplier in the United States, 1897–1958," Commission on Money and Credit, *Stabilization Policies* (Englewood Cliffs, N.J.: Prentice-Hall, 1963), pp. 259–260, Table II-B—ed.]. Data for the period 1953–1965 were obtained from current issues [i.e., 1953–1965—ed.] of the *Survey of Current Business* and the *Federal Reserve Bulletin.* Percentages in Column (5) were computed by the authors.

[a] Separate estimates for demand and time deposits in commercial banks before 1913 are not reliable.

[b] These values are for the correlation coefficient of *time* deposits on income. The computer kicks out only the higher of the two values in a multiple correlation (without regard to sign). To compare the simple coefficient of the narrow stock of money on income, see Column (2).

use as quasi-transaction balances. Probably more important, however, was the influence of the bank debacle in the early 1930s on deposit holdings. Demand deposits lost some of their moneyness due to the additional risk imputed to them by depositors after the monetary blood-letting of 1932–33. Time deposits seemed less risky to both banks and their depositors, so the deduction reasonably can be made that moneyness was lost by demand deposits and gained by time deposits.

To test these conclusions further, and also to test for a significant monetary coefficient of time deposits, a multiple regression analysis was conceived using first differences in the narrow stock of money, M_1, and in all time deposits, T, to predict changes in money income, Y. The form of the testing equation is:

$$\Delta Y = a + b_1 \Delta M_1 + b_2 \Delta T, \qquad (1)$$

or

$$\Delta Y = a - b_1[\Delta M_1 + (b_2/b_1)\Delta T]. \qquad (2)$$

If time deposits have some degree of moneyness, the ratio (b_2/b_1) should be greater than zero but less than one. A value of one for this fraction would imply that time deposits had moneyness equal in degree to the items in the narrow stock of money. A negative value for (b_2/b_1) implies that time deposits serve more in the nature of investments: that people actively reduce their transactions balances to "buy" time deposits.

As can be seen from Table 1, the fraction (b_2/b_1) is between -1 and 0 except for the period 1933–38. In this period the ratio jumps up to 7.997! Furthermore, bringing time deposits into the picture as a multiple correlate to the narrow stock of money does not add significantly to the simple correlation coefficient in any of the periods except 1933–38. [See Columns (9) and (10).] But in this period first differences in time deposits are better predictors of changes in money income than are changes in the narrow money stock, and the multiple correlation coefficient becomes a whopping .987! Such dramatic results confirm the supposition that time deposits gained appreciably in moneyness due to the depreciation in confidence people had in demand deposits.

The value for (b_2/b_1) then becomes large and negative for the periods that include the war years, emphasizing the efforts of people to keep purchasing power they were enjoined from spending in a form that obtained some return. Only in the last 12 years does the ratio of (b_2/b_1) become a positive fraction of a magnitude that would give some credence to the theory of moneyness in time deposits, and even in this case the additional predictability gained from including time deposits in the analysis is insignificant (.667 to .692).

5 A SOCRATIC DIALOGUE

DENIS H. ROBERTSON

Why are reasonable people willing to accept pieces of paper in full payment for services rendered, for commodities sold, or for debts canceled? Why do they not demand items of intrinsic value? Read "Socrates' " penetrating questions.

• • •

The British monetary system . . . is . . . on the face of it a somewhat eccentric contraption. Between some enquiring Socrates from another planet and an economist instructed to explain its nature some such dialogue as the following might well take place:

Socrates: I see that your chief piece of money carries a legend affirming that it is a promise to pay the bearer the sum of one pound. What is this thing, a pound, of which payment is thus promised?

Economist: A pound is the British unit of account.

Socrates: So there is, I suppose, some concrete object which embodies more firmly that abstract unit of account than does this paper promise?

Economist: There is no such object, O Socrates.

Socrates: Indeed? Then what your Bank promises is to give me another promise stamped with a different number in case I should regard the number stamped on this promise as in some way ill-omened?

Economist: It would seem, indeed, to be promising something of that kind.

From Denis H. Robertson, *Essays in Monetary Theory* (London: Staples Press, 1940), pp. 173–174. Reprinted by permission.

Socrates: So that in order to be in a position to fulfil its promises all the Bank has to do is to keep a store of such promises stamped with all sorts of different numbers?

Economist: By no means, Socrates—that would make its balance sheet a subject for mockery, and in the eyes of our people there resides in a balance sheet a certain awe and holiness. The Bank has to keep a store of Government securities and a store of gold.

Socrates: What are Government securities?

Economist: Promises by the Government to pay certain sums of money at certain dates.

Socrates: What are sums of money? Do you mean Bank of England notes?

Economist: I suppose I do.

Socrates: So these promises to pay promises are thought to be in some way solider and more sacred than the promises themselves?

Economist: They are so thought, as it appears.

Socrates: I see. Now tell me about the gold. It has to be of a certain weight, I suppose?

Economist: Not of a certain weight, but of a certain value in terms of the promises.

Socrates: So that the less each of its promises is worth, the more promises the Bank can lawfully make?

Economist: It seems, indeed, to amount to something of that kind.

Socrates: Do you find that your monetary system works well?

Economist: Pretty well, thank you, Socrates, on the whole.

Socrates: That would be, I suppose, not because of the rather strange rules of which you have told me, but because it is administered by men of ability and wisdom?

Economist: It would seem that that must be the reason, rather than the rules themselves, O Socrates.

• • •

issues in commercial banking

portfolio analysis and its implications

In analyzing the commercial banking system, sight is often lost of its individual components, the banks. Yet in order to understand the functioning of the banking system, it is necessary to understand the microeconomics of the banking firm. One way to approach the workings of a banking firm or, for that matter, any financial institution, is to examine analytically the portfolio policies of the individual enterprise. The interest rates of the bank operating in a competitive market are not subject to its determination. A bank does have some degree of influence over the total quantity of funds available to it, however, because it can vary the terms it offers its depositors. It controls the disposition of funds once obtained, subject only to regulatory limitations that constrain a bank's freedom of allocation, both in terms of the percentage of assets that can be utilized at the bank's discretion and the types of assets that may be held. But the area of discretionary action is broad, indeed.

In its narrowest sense, portfolio analysis is concerned with the allocation of bank assets, given the quantity of funds available to the bank and the policy goals of the bank's management. Alternatively, but less frequently, portfolio analysis deals also with the theory of obtaining the financial resources that provide the bank's working capital. The first four selections in this Part limit themselves to the narrow definition of portfolio analysis; the fifth considers the broader interpretation.

What are the aims of portfolio management? A reasonable presumption to make is the usual one of profit-maximization for the firm, subject to the qualification of maintaining adequate safety for its stockholders' capital and sufficient liquidity to meet its deposit obligations. Roland I. Robinson, in the first selection in this Part, suggests that safety and liquidity are primary criteria and ought to be secured first. Earnings are necessary, of course, but are allotted secondary priority.

Suggestions along the lines mentioned are helpful but lack specificity. In applying them to the contemporary commercial banking institution, consideration of the different sources of funds must be taken into account. The modern bank holds demand, savings, and other time deposits together with its own capital funds. In the second selection, Fred G. DeLong declares that because the liquidity needs against each liability differ substantially, it is desirable to treat the individual bank as a composite of a number of banks. In the asset-allocation procedure he outlines, the liquidity needs of each type of deposit are considered separately, a procedure followed to some extent by Federal Reserve Bank examiners.[1]

Both Robinson and DeLong, by stressing the liquidity aspects of bank asset management, neglect the costs of the decision. Although banks maintain liquid assets to meet the withdrawal demands of depositors, rarely, if ever, are these demands known with any degree of accuracy. Bank management operates in the gray area of uncertainty and can at best hazard educated guesses about future events. The range of possible withdrawals suggests, however, that economic calculus ought to be applied. The benefits of any given liquidity position should be compared with the costs of that portfolio. For each possible portfolio allocation, the following question can be asked: Do we stand to gain or lose by shifting our portfolio, decreasing our liquid assets, and thereby increasing the risk of being caught short, even though we increase our earning assets and thus enhance our profit position?

Neither Robinson nor DeLong is concerned with this type of reasoning. But George R. Morrison centers his analysis around questions of this sort. His "expected loss function," which is used to determine the optimum cash position of a bank, explicitly introduces interest rates and the discount rate as costs of liquidity. In his model, liquidity will be sacrificed if the cost of attaining a little bit more liquidity exceeds the benefits resulting therefrom.

The theory of the money multiplier (that the banking system can create deposits greater than the reserves it possesses), as stressed by the money and banking texts, assumes a constant reserve ratio. More developed models assume constant cash and time deposit ratios as well. Portfolio analysis implies that banks can and should vary their reserve ratios, however. The public presumably acts similarly with respect to its deposit and cash holdings. The rigid multiplier concept must then be abandoned. Jonas Prager sets out to do so in his article on the "true" multiplier, which, unfortunately, can be calculated with far less accuracy than the textbooks imply. The money multiplier is shown to be a function of the interest rate. Consequently, a monetary policy designed to achieve a given reduction in the quantity of money or a specific rise in interest rates is shown to be partially self-defeating. Moreover, the value of the money multiplier will differ as general economic conditions change.

John H. Kareken explores the implications of portfolio analysis in a different context. Although commercial banks in the United States are enjoined from paying explicit interest rates on demand deposits, the author builds a model of bank portfolio selec-

---

[1]See Federal Reserve System, "Form for Analyzing Bank Capital."

tion based on the presumption that a demand deposit rate is payable. By then constraining the model (by removing demand deposit rate flexibility), he is able to contrast the equilibrium positions. Implicit in his model, however, is the ready willingness to trade off liquidity for earnings, and so Professor Kareken ends up at the opposite end of the spectrum from Robinson and DeLong.

Thus the old view of portfolio conservatism, a result of a concentration on the safety-liquidity aspects of portfolio management, stands in clear contrast to the "new" view, which sees the bank as a decision-making unit, weighing the costs and the gains of any proposed action. Economists on the whole are sympathetic to the latter view, and the more progressive banks, indeed, are abandoning rules-of-thumb management for more calculated and precise decision-making procedures.

6 PRIORITIES IN THE USE OF BANK FUNDS

ROLAND I. ROBINSON

In the following classic statement of bank asset management, Professor Robinson leans heavily on the safety or liquidity aspects of the portfolio. "When there is conflict between safety and profitability, it is better to err on the side of safety." That the "safety" bought may be costly and the risk perhaps small does not matter; liquidity needs predominate. This unwillingness to measure the cost of any action in terms of gain is reflected in statements made elsewhere in the following selection. Can you find them? A special kind of ethic seems to possess this excerpt; Robinson implies, for example, that a bank "ought" to lend rather than to engage in even more profitable investment. Is this a sensible policy?

• • •

. . . The essential banking problem is to resolve the conflict between safety and profitability in the employment of bank funds. Why is there a conflict? In its simplest form it can be seen by comparing the holding of cash with any form of investing funds. Since bank liabilities are payable in cash, it is obvious that cash is the premier banking asset. Any way in which the funds are otherwise used is not quite so good in the sense of immediate safety. Some investments of funds leave them in such shape that a recovery of cash can be both prompt and without chance of material loss. Such obviously superior assets involve a sacrifice: a lower interest income. Some forms of investment offer only a remote return of cash and the chance of loss both during the life of the investment instrument and at its maturity, but a particularly great chance of loss if an asset must be converted into cash (sold) before maturity. Here is the conflict: it is within this category of assets that the best interest returns are normally available. So the conflict between safety and profitability is the conflict between liquidity (the nearness to cash form) and the size of the interest return.

The division of banking assets between cash assets and earning assets and the division of earning assets between loans and investments is the practice commonly followed in publication of banking statements. Unfortunately, it is not the most meaningful division possible. The degree of liquidity within earning assets, a vastly more important distinction, is left obscure. Occasionally individual banks show more than is required in published statements but not often or regularly.

The division between "loans" and "investments" is more conventional than logical. The usual concept of a loan is a credit transaction between a borrowing customer and the bank. Loans are frequently but not regularly short-term in maturity. An investment is an impersonal or open-market credit and, more often than not, of longer term than a loan. However, this distinction tends to break down under close examination. Some

---

From *The Management of Bank Funds,* by Roland I. Robinson, pp. 11–18.

loans are syndicated among a number of lenders and are very nearly open-market obligations. Some investments turn out to have almost no market and are like long-term loans. Rather than involve ourselves with complex distinctions, we shall, throughout this treatment, speak of loans as being customer credits, negotiated directly by the bank holding them and not ordinarily subject to sale; we shall consider investments to be credit not always but primarily of longer maturities placed through the open markets and ordinarily subject to resale in these markets.

Our reason for making this distinction is that the institutional nature of commercial banks has been traditionally adapted to "lending" rather than to "investing" and, even though investments have come to occupy a large role in commercial banking, there is still much good sense in this traditional distinction. Because there are so many commercial banks, they tend to be close to the lending markets, closer than most other financial institutions. For the same reason, they are not so close to the central investment or capital markets.

THE SCHEDULE OF PRIORITIES

Having addressed ourselves to the question of safety versus profitability and also to the question of types of credit to which the commercial banking system is adapted, we are now in a position to suggest an order of priority for the employment of commercial-bank funds, an order which will dominate the discussion of the remainder of this study. Our sole guides in establishing this priority are two rules: (1) When there is conflict between safety and profitability, it is better to err on the side of safety, and (2) the commercial banking system should prefer the types of credit for which it is institutionally well adapted and should avoid those types for which it does not enjoy a natural advantage.

The Highest Priority: Primary Reserves

Before any other use of funds is considered, a commercial bank must provide itself with enough cash, that is, adequate primary reserves. Part of the reason is traditional. Commercial banks have the legal obligation to pay out their demand deposits without notice and "on demand," and "paying out" here means providing legal-tender currency—cash. Since the habit of the community is to depend on the commercial banks for its cash needs, a steady and expected inflow and outflow of cash is experienced by every bank. As we shall find, the amount of till cash kept by commercial banks is small, but it is nevertheless important. A further reason for keeping primary reserves is legal; for banks are required to hold some proportion of their deposits in cash form, depending on the legal jurisdiction in which a bank operates. In modern times the banks that are members of the Federal Reserve System keep their "required reserves" as deposits in a Federal Reserve bank, and, until very recently vault cash did not count as reserves. A further reason for keeping cash or primary reserves is the practical operating need of providing a means of paying or clearing checks and other credit obligations among banks. While a part of this clearing function is performed by the Federal Reserve System, much of it is still outside the System and is performed by the great city correspondent banks. Since there are other reasons for the existence of the correspondent banking system and the maintenance of balances with such banks, the full treatment of this part of our inquiry will be presented later; our purpose now is to note the position of such balances in the priority of employments.

Although our reason for putting cash or "primary reserve" needs at the top of the list is mainly that of safety, we must immediately note that there is much more than safety to this order. A great share of it is pure legal compulsion. While there have been cases in which bankers have depended on large cash holdings to make their banks safe, this is usually neither necessary nor even wise. To forgo income altogether may not be real safety in the long run. In other words, while cash enjoys the top position in priorities, we shall find that the usual rule of prudence is to keep as small a cash position as the law and ordinary standards of operation permit. In other words, the central provision for banking safety comes not in primary but in secondary reserves.

A moment's reflection on the nature of the central share of primary reserves—the required legal reserve—will make evident the reason why this seemingly contradictory fact is true. Since these reserves are required, they may not be depleted for any extended period to meet cash demands. In other words, only cash in excess of legal requirements or assets that can be converted into cash give a bank real flexibility in meeting its legal obligations.

The Second Priority: Protective Investment (Secondary Reserves)

We have already disclosed a major reason for our second priority. To plan for all possible and remote contingencies of cash needs by adequate cash holdings requires a bank to forgo earnings needlessly; indeed for reasons of long-run safety, banks should have adequate earnings. It may be "safer," in all reasonable senses of the word, for a bank to provide for contingent cash needs by the investment of funds in a form which is fairly close to cash or which can be turned to cash without material impairment of the principal sum invested, than just to carry the actual cash. In such investment of funds, the primary purpose is that of safety. Amount of return takes second place. In some periods the amount of income conceded for this safety has been small, but in recent years when funds have been in active demand, the income on protective uses of funds has usually been considerably below that available on other uses of funds.

• • •

The Third Priority: Customer Credit Demands

Once a bank has made itself safe, it should devote itself to the business for which it is best fitted. Traditionally, banks were primarily direct lenders to their customers. They invested in open-market securities only to the extent that safety required. If this were still possible, it would be a good practice.

A clear recognition of this priority will help in making one point of our later discussion abundantly clear. We shall argue that, in credit, the standards applied by commercial banks to loans do not need to be so high as those applied to investments. We shall argue that commercial banks often are required to take material risks in lending and should take them. We shall also argue that in open-market investments commercial banks seldom have any business taking more than minimum risks. Commercial banks are strategically located for lending. They know a great number of moderate-sized customers intimately; they can extend loan credit and collect it where other lenders could not. In the investment market they are not so strategically located. For example, face to face with insurance company competition a commercial bank is vastly better equipped to make customer loans; working through loan agents and with few offices the insurance companies just could not do so well. When it comes to open-market investment, insurance companies, greater in size and with more stable liabilities, have an advantage over most commercial banks.

Thus we introduce our fourth and last priority with a note of caution.

The Fourth Priority: Open-Market Investment for Income

When a commercial bank has provided the liquidity needed for safety and has satisfied in full the local customer demand for loans, it can enter the investment markets with any remaining funds; indeed, in some cases it must do so in order to earn a minimum living. The emphasis on income need will come up for much discussion later on; this much we can anticipate. Income need of and by itself cannot be a good excuse for taking many investment chances. Banks which cannot make a satisfactory income from customer loan credit and safe—very safe—open-market investment of funds should seriously consider liquidation. When there is a need for income, this need cannot but have weight in investment policy. A bank which has a pretty satisfactory income from loans but still has some funds left over for income investment might forgo trying to maximize investment income and decide that the value of flexibility is worth more than a slightly higher current income. In other words, an adequately high income may be the foundation for opportunities for even higher income. By the same token, the bank which is hard pressed for income may, under some circumstances, bargain away its prospects for improved income in exchange for slightly better current income.

We have already argued that commercial banks are none too strategically located for operation in the open investment markets. We might add that a modern circumstance compounds this difficulty. The investment markets now reflect the heritage of two great wars and a great depression; public debt obligations are important in these markets. Commercial banks, because of their monetary significance, are subject to rather more direct and detailed influence by public monetary and fiscal authorities. The commercial bank that leans heavily on the open investment markets for income will probably tend over the long run to live on a much more variable income and one that will tend to be quite skimpy if this nation should ever again suffer a prolonged period of slack economic activity.

7 LIQUIDITY REQUIREMENTS AND EMPLOYMENT OF FUNDS

FRED G. DeLONG

What distinguishes one bank from another? Part of the answer lies in the composition of liabilities, which, as the following selection proposes, should lead each bank to allocate its assets according to its unique liability–net worth structure. But note that this attempt to separate functions may nullify the flexibility that is created by the unification of all the banks—demand, time, and savings—under one roof. Furthermore, for DeLong, liquidity considerations are overriding; he ignores the fact that exact liquidity needs are rarely known. Contrast this viewpoint with that of George R. Morrison in the selection that follows.

Commercial bankers have traditionally employed their funds in the several types of assets without regard to the sources of the funds, following what is now termed the pooled-funds philosophy. This has in the past produced what appeared to be satisfactory results, largely because most of the funds were demand deposits. In the ten years ending in December, 1963, however, demand deposits increased only 24 percent while time deposits rose by 152 percent. As a result, time deposits are now 40 percent of total deposits, and it is predicted that they will account for over 50 percent of the total by 1970.

This raises the question of liquidity. For too long a time liquidity has been determined on a total basis, without regard for the fact that liquidity has two separate and mutually exclusive purposes. One need for liquidity is to provide funds to meet net declines in deposits. The other is to have funds available to meet increases in loans when they are rising faster than deposits. Because no two banks will have identical requirements, it is impossible to establish any total liquidity ratio applicable to all banks.

The change in deposit mix has also operated to make total liquidity ratios invalid. It is commonly accepted that time deposits require less liquidity than do demand deposits. Mutual savings banks and savings and loan associations have customarily carried less than half the liquidity of commercial banks. Part of the difference is attributable to the commercial loan requirements of the commercial banks; but the remainder arises from the fact that the mutual institutions have nothing but time deposits. Furthermore, regulatory authorities recognize the difference, in that they use time deposits as one measure of the maximum investment permitted in long-term mortgages. Since the deposit mix as between time and demand varies from bank to bank, any ratio which ties liquidity to total deposits is not only invalid but can be quite detrimental if applied to banks generally.

Liquidity for loans is no more standard for banks than that for deposits. The mix of loans is a major determinant of the amount of liquidity required. Commercial and industrial loans are much more vola-

Reprinted with permission from K. J. Cohen and F. S. Hammer (eds.), *Analytical Methods in Banking* (Homewood, Ill.: Richard D. Irwin, Inc., 1966), pp. 39–45.

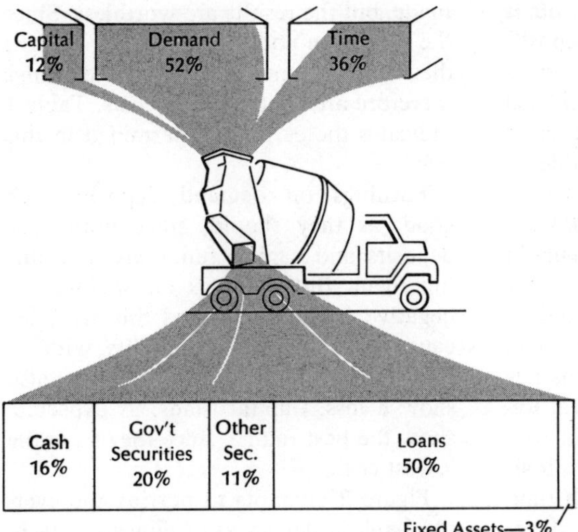

Figure 1 Average Commercial Bank in the United States, December 20, 1963

tile than consumer loans, which include both mortgages and installment credit. Each bank must determine according to the structure of its loan portfolio what secondary reserves it needs for loan purposes. Loans have increased more than 130 percent in the last ten years, while deposits have risen only 56 percent. This points up the fact that liquidity for loans has been a real problem, much more than that for deposits.

The pooled-funds approach to asset management makes difficult, if not impossible, the proper recognition of the differing liquidity requirements of the several sources of funds. Figure 1 attempts a graphic illustration of this approach.

Funds come in from demand and time deposits and from capital funds. These are poured into a pool in which they lose their identities. Loans and investments are made from this pool, but in making them, it is impossible to know the source of the money. Thus it follows that each dollar in the pool is used ratably in the different assets, or conversely, each dollar in an asset comes ratably from the several sources. The percentages used for assets and liabilities are the averages for all commercial banks in the United States as of December 20, 1963.

Now trace a dollar of capital funds. Of this dollar, 16 cents is held in cash. Since capital funds are not subject to withdrawal, no liquidity is required, and keeping 16 percent in sterile cash is absurd. Another 20 cents is in government securities, which are also considered as liquid, and although carrying some earning power, they yield less than any asset other than cash. Only 11 cents is invested in other securities, which yield about the best net return of any asset. The 50 cents in loans will provide a good return also. But only 3 cents is invested in fixed assets —buildings, equipment, etc.—thus making it necessary to put other kinds of funds in such assets. This is ridiculous, for all fixed assets should be provided by capital funds.

Now look at a dollar of demand money. The Federal Reserve requires that either 12 or 16½ cents, depending on the location of the bank, be kept on deposit with it. In addition, uncollected funds, or float, run from 6 to 10 cents per dollar of demand deposit. Thus the cash (which includes float on the statement) requirement for demand money runs from 18 cents to 26½ cents—but only 16 cents is thus carried. As a result, demand deposits are not carrying their full cash requirement, and are therefore being subsidized by other funds. Again 20 cents is carried in governments, which is reasonable in view of the low cash, but would be excessive if the proper amount of cash were carried. And the investment of 3 cents in fixed assets is totally inappropriate, for demand deposits should not be used to buy bricks and mortar, computers, etc.

Time deposits require only 4 cents per dollar for cash kept with the Federal Reserve. Although there can be float in connection with time deposits, it is nominal. Thus the fact that 16 cents of each time dollar is kept in cash is a serious detriment to the earning power of time deposits—what we have here, of course, is the time function providing reserves for the benefit of the demand function. With the excessive sterilization of time deposits in cash, the holding of another 20 cents in governments is an additional burden on this function. Very little liquidity is required for such funds, and this secondary reserve is much too high.

Determination of earnings by source of funds used in the pooled approach is made, but the results are worthless. Since the funds are pooled, each dollar returns the same income, and the net earnings therefore are controlled by costs. Table 1 indicates the earnings determined in this way.

Earnings on demand deposits look good, as they should, since both time deposits and capital funds are subsidizing them. But earnings on savings are negative when determined this way, because of the excessive liquidity with its low return. Other time deposits also show a loss. Capital funds, as expected, show the best return, since they have the lowest cost.

Figure 2 attempts to portray the average bank under an asset allocation technique.

Funds have been grouped into four "banks," based on liquidity requirements and relative turnover. The Demand Bank is now carrying not only its necessary cash requirement, but also some secondary reserves for loan purposes. The Time Bank has been set up because of the rapid growth of Negotiable CD's* about which

*Certificates of Deposit—ed.

Table 1. Average Commercial Bank in the United States

All yields stated on a fully taxable equivalent basis (50% tax rate), and are net of lending or investing costs

Assets	%	Yield
Cash and due from	16	0
U.S. gov't securities	20	3.89%
Other securities	11	5.61
Loans	50	4.59
Fixed assets	3	0
	100	3.69

Liabilities	%	Cost
Demand deposits	52	.91%
Savings deposits	27	4.13
Other time deposits	9	3.85
Capital funds and other liabilities	12	.74
	100	2.02

Earnings by types of funds		
Demand	3.69 – .91 =	2.78%
Savings	3.69 – 4.13 =	– .44
Other time	3.69 – 3.85 =	– .16
Capital funds	3.69 – .74 =	2.95

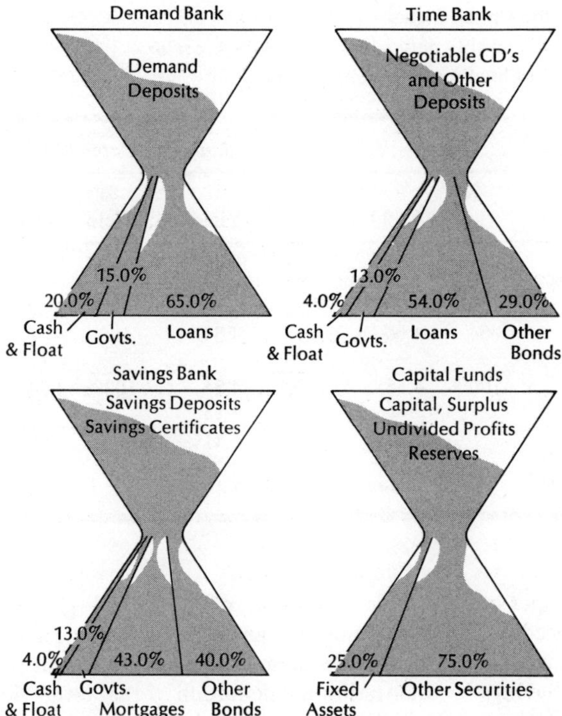

Figure 2 Average Commercial Bank in the United States, Pro Forma Asset Allocation Diagram as of December 20, 1963

much is still to be learned and hence performance should be closely observed. Until experience enables us to determine liquidity requirements, some governments are carried, the same as in the Savings Bank. The Other Bonds have maturities ranging out to five years, with the average life between two and three years. There is some risk here, since the CD's average much shorter life, but it is expected that maturing CD's can be replaced by new ones. Even if the CD market dries up through lack of funds or by interest rate limitations, it is expected that enough time will have run so that the bonds in this portfolio will have been reduced to an average life so short that they could be liquidated with little if any loss.

The Savings Bank looks very much like a mutual institution, except for the "Other Bonds," which they do not carry to any extent. All long-term mortgages are assigned to this bank as being appropriate to the types of deposits in the bank. All the funds in excess of the cash and governments are available for mortgages, but to the extent not so needed are invested in a bond portfolio having the same range of maturities carried by the mortgages.

Capital Funds are first invested in all of the fixed assets, with the remainder being invested in other securities running as long in maturities as investment judgment dictates. In the event of an increase of commercial loans beyond the capacity of the Demand Bank and Time Bank to support them, it would be appropriate to assign the longest term loans to Capital Funds. Maturities in the bond portfolio should be spread so that funds will become available each year, for either reinvestment in bonds or to be used for loans.

Table 2. Average Commercial Bank in the United States

All yields stated on a fully taxable equivalent basis (50% tax rate) and are net of lending or investing costs

	Demand Bank		*Time Bank*		*Savings Bank*		*Capital Funds*	
	% Held	Yield	% Held	Yield	% Held	Yield	% Held	Yield
Cash and due from	20	0	4	0	4	0	—	—
U.S. gov't securities	15	3.81%	13	3.81%	13	4.09%	—	—
Other securities	—	—	29	4.79	40	6.30	75	6.32
Loans	65	4.60	54	4.60	43	4.54	—	—
Fixed assets	—	—	—	—	—	—	25	0
	100%	3.56	100%	4.36	100%	4.54	100%	4.74
Cost of funds		.91		3.85		4.13		.74
Profit		2.65%		.51%		.41%		4.00%
Comparable profit as pooled funds		2.78%		−.16%		−.44%		2.95%

Table 2 shows the earnings by types of funds under the allocation procedure. Earnings on Demand Deposits have decreased, but are real earnings. Savings and Other Time Deposits now show profits as contrasted to losses under pooled funds, and capital has increased its profit even though carrying all the fixed assets at no earning power.

There is no magic in this. By separating the several sources of funds we have been able to apply appropriate liquidity requirements. This has resulted in a reduction of cash and a switch in investments, increasing the overall yield from 3.69 percent to 4.16 percent. This is an increase in net earnings of almost 13 percent. Following is a comparative statement of assets, reflecting the changes made under asset allocation:

The reduction of cash and governments may bother some bankers because of the decreased liquidity ratio—using the traditional definition of that term—in which only cash and governments are considered liquid. But we have provided adequate liquidity according to the types of funds, and in addition established a secondary reserve to meet increasing loan volume. As indicated earlier, the practice of measuring liquidity by the ratio of cash plus governments to total deposits is no longer valid, because of the changing deposit structure. In addition, the old formula assumed that all governments were liquid, regardless of maturity. When the famous "accord" was reached in 1951, government prices became subject to fluctuation according to the money market. There have since been many losses taken

	Under Pooled Funds	Under Asset Allocation
Cash and due from	16%	12%
U.S. governments	20	13
Other securities	11	22
Loans	50	50
Fixed assets	3	3
	100%	100%

on the longer maturities of governments. Recognition is now becoming general that assets other than governments have real liquidity. Among such assets would be commercial paper, bankers acceptances, Federal Agency paper, and municipal securities maturing within a year.

An asset allocation program cannot be fully effective unless there is a system of forecasting deposits and loans, such as is developed in a profit planning procedure. Based on the forecasts, liquidity problems can be anticipated and provided for, and the remaining funds can then be most gainfully employed. Conversely, a profit planning procedure will be just an exercise unless it is accompanied by a program for analyzing the forecasts and a determination made as to how the funds will be employed. By whatever name, the principles of asset allocation can contribute significantly to the earnings of banks.

• • •

8 LIQUIDITY PREFERENCES OF COMMERCIAL BANKS: THE THEORY

GEORGE R. MORRISON

Although this selection will appeal more to the mathematically inclined, the ideas expressed here are not difficult to comprehend. The model maintains that the desired cash-to-deposit ratio of a bank depends on the yield expected on alternative uses of its assets and the cost of not holding adequate reserves. The other elements that are likely to enter into the portfolio allocation decision (the mix of deposits, the liquidity of loans, the relative size of the bank, to name just a few) may be added to the model. They complicate it, but they will not change its essentials. The model as it stands is impossible to subject to empirical testing. (It is transformed into a testable entity further on in George R. Morrison's book.) But this deficiency should not detract from the theoretical interest of the model, which is considerable.

• • •

This [article] presents the model of bank behavior. . . . It will be shown that a bank's demand for cash assets can be regarded as an application of the static theory of profit maximizing inventory policy under conditions of uncertainty.

In the existing formal theory of banking, the basic assumptions are: (a) banks maximize expected profits (or minimize expected losses), (b) banks construct probability distributions of gains and losses from investment in assets, and (c) . . . profit maximization takes place subject to a specified distribution of cash drains during the planning period.

The salient features of the static theory of banking can be illustrated by means of the following elementary model. Assume that a bank can hold two types of assets —non-interest bearing cash and fixed-interest bearing loans—and can issue three types of liabilities—non-interest bearing deposits repayable in cash on demand, short-term interest bearing debt, and equity securities. Suppose the bank attempts to minimize its expected losses during the planning period by appropriate allocation of its assets between cash and loans. Assume further that the return per dollar of loans over the planning period is composed of an interest component, y, known with certainty at the beginning of the period, and an expected capital gain or loss component, g, whose probability density is $\phi(g)$, where g is distributed over the range $-1 \leq g < \infty$. The bank is also faced with the prospect that there will be a cash drain or inflow. This expected change in cash will be expressed as a proportion, v, of initial deposits.[1] Let us suppose that the probability density of v is $f(v)$, where v is uniformly distributed over the interval $c \leq v \leq b$, and $c \geq -1$. For simplicity, assume that the cash

From George R. Morrison, *Liquidity Preferences of Commercial Banks* (Chicago: University of Chicago Press, 1966), pp. 8–11. Reprinted by permission.

[1]In this model it is taken for granted that all deposits created by lending are drawn down by the borrowers simultaneously with the granting of loans at the beginning of the period. Thus "initial deposits" refers to deposits remaining after loan-created deposits have been removed. Thus the model follows the usual textbook exposition of the deposit expansion multiplier process.

drain or inflow always occurs at the end of the period after all returns have been accrued on loans but before any of the loans are repaid. Finally, let us suppose that all cash deficiencies (i.e., all cash drains over and above the amount that can be covered by drawing down initial cash assets to zero) must be met by borrowing at short term or by sale of loans, and that the penalty per dollar of cash deficiency is n, a cost that is known with certainty at the beginning of the period. This penalty cost is equivalent to the interest rate on borrowed funds, or to the transactions cost on forced sale of loans, which might be interpreted as a brokerage fee or as the spread between the bid and the asked price on securities. The bank is assumed to operate in perfectly competitive markets so that y, n, and g are independent of the bank's own decisions.

Defining ρ to be cash as a ratio to initial deposits, the expected loss function $E[L(\rho)]$ can then be written as follows:

$$E[L(\rho)] = y\rho + \rho \int_{+1}^{\infty} g\phi(g)\,dg + \int_{c}^{-\rho} n(-v-\rho)f(v)\,dv \qquad (1)$$

where the first two terms taken together represent the expected alternative cost of holding cash instead of loans, and the third term represents the expected penalty cost of cash drains exceeding ρ. It is assumed that only \$1 of loans can be created by the individual bank, per dollar of excess reserves, because of a loss of all deposits created in the process of making loans. This is the simplest, but not necessarily the most descriptively accurate, assumption about the loan-deposit loss function.

Substituting $f(v) = 1/(b-c)$ in (1) and evaluating the integrals in the expression gives

$$E[L(\rho)] = y\rho + \bar{g}\rho - \frac{n\rho^2}{2(b-c)} + \frac{nc^2}{2(b-c)} + \frac{n\rho^2}{b-c} + \frac{n\rho c}{b-c} \qquad (2)$$

where $\bar{g}$ is the mean of g.

The first- and second-order conditions for a minimum are found by successive differentiation of (2) with respect to ρ.

$$\frac{\partial E}{\partial \rho} = y + \bar{g} + \frac{n\rho + nc}{b-c} = 0 \qquad (3)$$

at a minimum or maximum.

$$\frac{\partial^2 E}{\partial \rho^2} = \frac{n}{b-c} > 0$$

since $n > 0$, by assumption.

The demand for cash by the bank is derived from the minimized expression (3).

$$\rho = \frac{(c-b)(y+\bar{g})}{n} - c \qquad (4)$$

If we set $b = c + k$, where $k > 0$, (4) can be rewritten as

$$\rho = \frac{-k(y+\bar{g})}{n} - c \qquad (5)$$

Since the mean of the uniform distribution over the range $c \leq v \leq b$ is

$$\bar{v} = \int_c^b \frac{v}{b-c}\,dv = \frac{b+c}{2}$$

and

$$b = c + k$$

we have

$$\bar{v} = c + \frac{k}{2}$$

Thus an expression for c in terms of $\bar{v}$ can be derived:

$$c = \bar{v} - \frac{k}{2} \qquad (6)$$

Substituting (6) in (5) yields a demand equation in terms of y, $\bar{g}$, n, $\bar{v}$, and k:

$$\rho = k\left[\tfrac{1}{2} - \frac{(y+\bar{g})}{n}\right] - \bar{v} \qquad (7)$$

Differentiating with respect to the parameters, y, $\bar{g}$, n, $\bar{v}$, and k gives:

$$\frac{\partial \rho}{\partial y} = -\frac{k}{n} < 0$$

$$\frac{\partial \rho}{\partial \bar{v}} = -1 < 0 \qquad \frac{\partial \rho}{\partial \bar{g}} = -\frac{k}{n} < 0$$

$$\frac{\partial \rho}{\partial k} = \tfrac{1}{2} - \frac{(y+\bar{g})}{n} \qquad \frac{\partial \rho}{\partial n} = \frac{k(y+\bar{g})}{n^2} \geq 0$$

The demand for cash varies directly with the penalty cost of a cash deficiency and inversely with the interest rate on loans, the expected capital gain on loans, and the expected cash inflow. The sign of the change in cash with respect to a small increase in k, the range of the distribution of expected cash flows, cannot be determined without more precise knowledge of the values of y, $\bar{g}$, and n. The demand for cash varies directly with k if $n \geq 2\,(y+\bar{g})$, and inversely if $n < 2(y+\bar{g})$. This may appear to be strange result, but its reasonableness can be shown on an intuitive level. Suppose, to begin with, that $k=0$, so that the amount of cash drain, v, is certain to be equal to $\bar{v}$. In this event, the optimal cash ratio will be exactly equal to $-\bar{v}$. This much is clear from (7). Now suppose that we hold the expected cash drain, $\bar{v}$, constant while increasing k slightly. Should the bank hold a higher or lower cash ratio now that the exact amount of the cash drain, v, is not known with certainty? Surely the answer will depend on the costs of erring by holding a higher or lower cash ratio than the actual cash drain outcome would require. The unit cost of holding too much cash will be the foregone expected return on loans $(y+\bar{g})$. The unit cost of holding too little cash will be the penalty incurred in borrowing or forced liquidation of assets (n). The higher the expected return on loans relative to the penalty the more likely it is that an increase in k will encourage a bank to take a large risk of holding too little cash, by reducing its cash ratio below $-\bar{v}$. Conversely, if the return on loans is low relative to the penalty, an increase in k will lead the bank to avoid the risk of being short of cash by increasing its cash ratio. This ambiguity in the effect of a change in the dispersion of expected cash drains should therefore cause no surprise; it is a consequence of attempting to minimize expected losses by balancing the opposing earnings risks of having too much or too little cash.

• • •

9 PORTFOLIO ANALYSIS AND THE MONEY MULTIPLIER

JONAS PRAGER

The rule of thumb is a thought-saving device that has found widespread acceptance in the conduct of a variety of enterprises and situations. Economy of thinking, however, often leads to acceptance of the rule of thumb as intrinsically correct rather than merely convenient. Such faulty logic appears to have been applied to the money multiplier, which often has been presented as an elementary concept, simply explained and simply calculated. In reaction to this representation, Jonas Prager demonstrates that the multiplier is a functional concept and suggests that the concept and its implementation are more complex than the simple formulation implies.

Although the following exposition does not deal with the relationship between variations in the required reserve ratio and the multiplier, such an analysis is easy to make and can be rewarding, especially when the conclusions are compared with those reached by Joseph Aschheim in Part VI. Similarly, the later discussion of discounting and the discount rate in Part VI may be viewed in the light of the present selection. Finally, test your understanding by answering the following questions. How would the banking system react to a payment of interest by Federal Reserve Banks on member bank deposits? How would this reaction affect monetary policy?

Analysis of the money multiplier has typically been couched in mechanistic formulations rather than subjected to analysis on the basis of economic forces. Most money and banking textbooks assume that the basic elements of the multiplier—the reserve ratios, the currency ratio, and the ratio of time to demand deposits—are constants and that on being plugged into the money-supply expansion formula, they yield the money supply. Federal Reserve officials in official publications and in appearances before Congressional committees have adopted this view and suggest that a dollar's worth of reserves supports approximately six times its weight in money. To be sure, both textbook authors and reserve officials realize that the formulas are oversimplifications. Yet the qualifications typically made involve the addition of other constants, rather than a revision of the basic theory.

On the other hand, a number of recent works on portfolio behavior explain the allocation of bank assets among the various asset categories on economic rather than institutional grounds.* The implications of contemporary asset allocation theory for multiplier analysis will be discussed here.

This article will demonstrate that the typical multiplier formula requires extreme and unrealistic assumptions and that under more moderate assumptions, the amount of money created or destroyed by the banking system will be less than the amount predicted by the institutional

This article was written especially for this volume.

*See the previous selection—ed.

multiplier formula. More important, however, is the fact that the value of the multiplier is unknown and can vary with changing circumstances. The first section of this article develops a simple theory of bank asset allocation that provides the background for aggregate analysis. The second section analyzes the reaction of the whole banking system to a change in reserves and derives some implications for this aggregate. The phenomena of internal or induced reserve flows are treated in the third section of the article. The model developed is a short-run, comparative-static one that is limited to the financial sector.

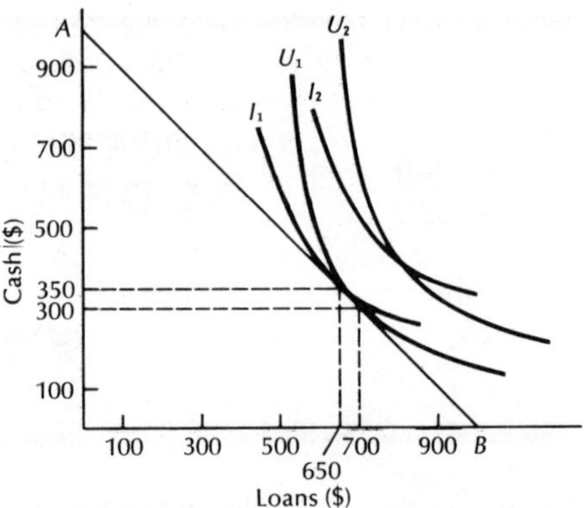

Figure 1 Iso-pro-li Curves and Portfolio Equilibrium

THE INDIVIDUAL BANK

The dilemma of bank management—how to maximize profits while maximizing liquidity—needs little exposition. One hundred percent liquidity and 100 percent nonliquidity are equally direct paths to bank failure. The liquidity-profit dilemma must be resolved by each banking firm, and no two banks need come to the same solution. In arriving at a decision, the bank's management will consider such objective information as the bank's deposit mix, size, interest rates, and the liquidity of its loan portfolio, as well as such subjective influences as management's willingness to run the risks associated with inadequate liquidity or its degree of reluctance to borrow from the district Federal Reserve Bank. The problem facing management may be analyzed in a manner similar to the theory of consumer choice, using a scheme analogous to the consumer's indifference map. Points on an individual curve, such as U_1 in Figure 1, represent equal combinations of profitability and liquidity, seen as a joint product of a given combination of earning assets (loans) and liquid assets (cash). Other things being equal, a banker will willingly sacrifice some quantity of liquid assets and thereby reduce his liquidity, provided the compensation in the form of profits—read additional loans—is, to his mind, adequate. Obviously, the more of his portfolio that is already devoted to loans, the more difficult it will be to induce him to sacrifice additional liquidity, and thus the shape of the U_1 curve, which we shall call an iso-pro-li (for iso-profit-liquidity) curve, is convex from below. The previously mentioned changes in the objective or subjective circumstances induce shifts in the curve. For example, a bank whose increasing proportion of stable time deposits is accompanied by a reduction in the relative weight of more volatile demand deposits can operate with a smaller liquid asset ratio and should be more willing to trade off liquid assets for loans. This effect changes the slopes of the iso-pro-li curves, as is demonstrated by contrasting the U curves to the I curves in Figure 1. Similarly, a decrease in the interest rate on loans, which reduces the profitability of a given loan portfolio, makes bank management less willing than previously to switch loans for liquid assets and again shifts the slope of the iso-pro-li curves.

As in the theory of consumer choice, the iso-pro-li curves in Figure 1 represent possibilities: points on a given iso-pro-li yield equal amounts of the profit-liquidity combination, whereas higher iso-pro-lis reflect a larger payoff. The actual allocation of funds, however, will depend not only on the conceptually possible, but also on the attainable. This datum is given by the volume of demand deposits available to the bank, which we assume to be the only liability of the bank, whose net worth is zero. Given these deposits, the banker can maintain an equivalent amount of cash reserves, or he can lend out an equivalent amount and so maintain zero reserves, or he can allot the total amount between cash and loans in a variety of combinations; in Figure 1, this choice is represented by the asset-boundary line, *AB,* whose slope equals one and whose intercepts equal the deposit total. Equilibrium, the actual decision, is found at the tangency of the asset boundary with an iso-pro-li. In Figure 1, the banker will decide, on the basis of the tangency of *AB* with U_1, to allocate his $1000 total assets into $300 cash and $700 loans.

How will the banker react to a fall in the interest rate on loans? As noted earlier, a fall in the interest rate shifts the iso-pro-li curves; their slopes become shallower, and a new tangency, *AB* with I_1, results. In equilibrium, a larger share of the portfolio will be in liquid assets and a smaller portion will be in loans. The reason for this shift is obvious: liquidity has become relatively less expensive, and its opportunity cost—the interest rate—has fallen; it has become a "better buy," and so more of it is "bought."

We can now develop a supply-of-loans curve, portraying the amount of loans any given bank wishes to lend at various interest rates. By changing the interest rate and thus shifting the iso-pro-li curves, new tangencies are obtained. When the quantity of loans supplied is plotted against the interest rate, a supply curve, such as S_1 in Figure 2b, results. One point deserves special mention at this juncture. The supply curve becomes totally inelastic before all assets are placed in the loan category, because the bank must always maintain some minimal amount of liquidity and/or more conventionally, because the required reserve ratio prohibits a 100 percent loan/deposit ratio.

THE BANKING SYSTEM

Because the banking system can create liabilities and because the system has a

Figure 2 Adjustment to an Increase in the Reserves of the Banking System

Figure 2a Adjustment by an Individual Bank to an Increase in Reserves

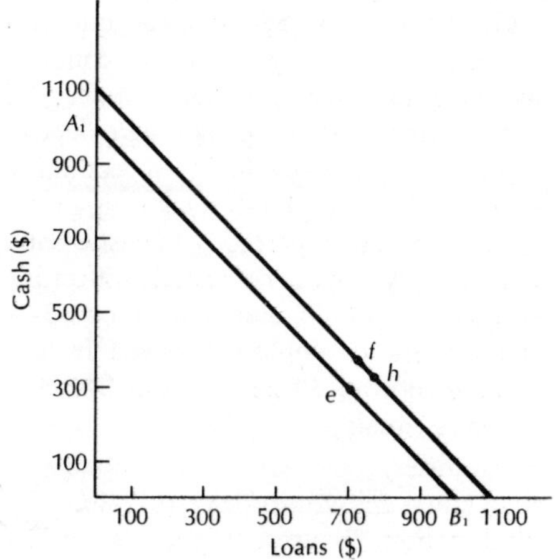

Figure 2b Adjustment of the Banking System to an Increase in Reserves

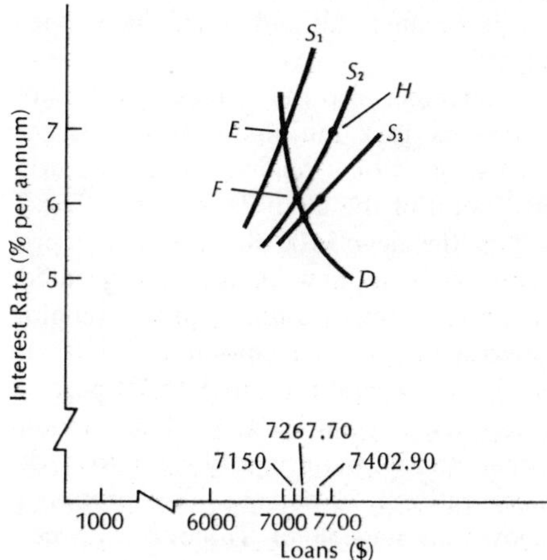

hand in determining interest rates, we now turn to an analysis of the banking system as an aggregate.

The supply of bank loans, together with other supply factors and the demand for credit—these latter shall be assumed unchanging—determines the interest rate on bank loans. This interest rate is reflected back to the individual banking institution in the same manner that a market price becomes a datum to the typical competitive firm studied in price theory.

Figure 2b illustrates the aggregate loan supply curve, S_1, derived by summing up the individual loan supply curves, the demand curve, and a competitively determined interest rate of 7 percent. This rate, being the market rate, determines the shape of the iso-pro-li map for the individual bank and, with the given asset boundary, A_1B_1, its optimum asset structure. (See point *e* in Figure 2a; for clarity, the iso-pro-li curves have been omitted.) The equilibrium position for the individual bank and the banking system are illustrated in the balance sheets of stage 1, Table 1.

Begin with the equilibrium state and introduce an autonomous increase in reserves, say, a $1000 open market purchase or a foreign inflow, such that each of the ten banks in this system receives an additional $100 in demand deposits. Presume, again for simplification, that before new loans are issued or new deposits created, all old loans have been repaid.

Remember also that the deposit loss of one bank in a multibank system is the deposit gain of a second bank. The critical point of the analysis is now at hand. When the new $100 flows into a representative bank, new loans can be granted, and if the bank assumes an unchanging interest rate—7 percent—it will wish to lend out an amount equal to 70 percent of its new deposit level, $770, an amount consistent with its equilibrium loan/deposit ratio of 70 percent. This process is shown in stage 2 of Table 1. The new loan supply curve for the banking system appears as S_2 in Figure 2b. The amount the system wishes to lend at 7 percent equals the distance from the vertical axis of Figure 2a to point *H*. But note that *H* is not an equilibrium point; with S_2, equilibrium is reached only at an interest rate of 6 percent and total loans of $7150 for the system, not $7700. At the lower interest rate, banks wish to lend relatively less, their iso-pro-lis shift, and the bank equilibrium is at *f* (Figure 2a; see also stage 3 of Table 1). Briefly, then, an increase in loanable funds reduces the interest rate, which forces a reevaluation of portfolio holdings toward relatively fewer loans and more reserves.

The end is still not at hand, however. Each bank now has created an additional amount of deposits ($15 more than in stage 1), which flows from one bank to another and vice versa. In this simple model, the $15 anticipated drain does occur, but an unanticipated inflow of $15 (deposits obtained by this bank's depositors from other banking institutions) also takes place so that no net reserve loss is experienced. Thus new loans and deposits can be created once again; stages 3 and 4 represent this process, which ends when the interest rate falls to 5.8 percent, the loan/deposit ratio is 64.5 percent, and no bank wishes to undertake additional loans.

Contrast now the results of this admittedly simplified and hypothetical case with the equally hypothetical but still more naïve assumption of a constant money multiplier. If interest rates did not matter and if bank loan/deposit ratios were always fixed—a condition that implies a perfectly elastic loan demand curve, or a perfectly inelastic bank loan supply curve, or exactly offsetting shifts of the supply and demand curves—the amount of deposits derived from a reserve ratio of 30 percent and $4000 of reserves equals

$$\frac{\$4000}{.30} = \$13{,}333.33$$

Table 1. Adjustment to an Increase in the Reserves of the Banking System

Stage	Event	*Balance Sheet of the Representative Bank* Assets		Liabilities		*Balance Sheet of the Banking System* Assets		Liabilities	
1.	Equilibrium; interest rate on loans (i) = 7%; loan/deposit ratio = 70%.	Reserves	$300	Deposits	$1000	Reserves	$3000	Deposits	$10,000
		Loans	700			Loans	7000		
		Total	$1000	Total	$1000	Total	$10,000	Total	$10,000
2.	Inflow of $100 in each bank; creation of additional deposit of $70 *if* i=7%. (N.B. This interim stage does not materialize. Instead, see stage 3.)	*R*	$400	*D*	$1170	*R*	$4000	*D*	$11,700
		L	770			*L*	7700		
		T	$1170	*T*	$1170	*T*	$11,700	*T*	$11,700
3.	New supply depresses i to 6%, induces portfolio reevaluation; new loan/deposit ratio falls to 65%.	*R*	$400	*D*	$1115	*R*	$4000	*D*	$11,150
		L	715			*L*	7150		
		T	$1115	*T*	$1115	*T*	$11,150	*T*	$11,150
4.	Outflows to other banks equal inflows from other banks. Loan policy evaluated at i=6%. D=$400/.35= $1140.29. (N.B. This stage also will not materialize. See stage 5.)	*R*	$400.00	*D*	$1140.29	*R*	$4000.00	*D*	$11,402.90
		L	740.29			*L*	7402.90		
		T	$1140.29	*T*	$1140.29	*T*	$11,402.90	*T*	$11,402.90
5.	$i \neq 6\%$, instead falls to 5.8%; new loan/deposit ratio equals 64.5%.	*R*	$400.00	*D*	$1126.77	*R*	$4000.00	*D*	$11,267.70
		L	726.77			*L*	7267.70		
		T	$1126.77	*T*	$1126.77	*T*	$11,267.70	*T*	$11,267.70

On the other hand, admitting some elasticity of the supply and demand curves for loans, as seems far more realistic, total deposits expand only to \$11,267.70, a smaller amount. Of course, the greater the elasticity of the loan supply curve and the slope $(\partial L/\partial i)$ of the demand curve, the larger will be the impact of a fall in the interest rate and the greater the discrepancy between the fixed loan/deposit multiplier and the functional multiplier. Indeed, the supply elasticities are not known, and, even if known for one situation, are unlikely to remain unvarying in a different situation. Obviously, the demand curve varies as well, so that no precise conclusion concerning the value of the multiplier is in order.

Similar theorizing is appropriate for a decrease in reserves, especially if banks hold an amount of reserves exceeding the legal reserve requirement. Money supply and loans will fall, but because a fall in loan supply increases interest rates, banks will reduce the cash/loan ratio. Therefore, demand deposits and loans fall by less than the extent predicted by the rigid multiplier formula. This statement holds true even if the bank (or the banking system) already has exhausted its excess reserves, because discounting at the Federal Reserve Bank permits banks to increase their loan/deposit ratio despite inadequate reserves of their own. In this instance, however, the relative cost of discounts versus loan yields becomes critical, a subject that is discussed more fully in Part VI.

Use of the discount window by member banks introduces the general topic of liability management. Banks obtain their funds from a variety of sources; liability management is concerned with arranging for an optimal distribution of these sources in much the same way that asset management deals with devising an optimal allocation of bank assets. A brief discussion of the implications of liability analysis is certainly germane at this juncture.

In recent years, American banks have sought to attract funds by a host of promotional schemes. Free blankets and alarm clocks, silverware and suitcases are offered new depositors. Higher interest rates are advertised, and even maximum interest rates specified by the regulatory authorities are circumvented by such perfectly legal stratagems as more frequent interest compounding. Banks also have actively searched for nondeposit sources of funds and have devised or revitalized some interesting arrangements. The federal funds market, where the excess reserves of one bank are lent to a second bank seeking reserves, has been reactivated after having remained dormant since the 1930s. Borrowing Eurodollars from foreign banks and, in many cases, from their own foreign branches has become common for the larger banks. Moreover, by issuing such certificates as capital notes, the banks borrow directly from the public.

The importance of liability management to the individual bank is evident; it is a means of increasing profits. Banks will pay for funds as long as the return from their use exceeds the cost of obtaining them. But these very actions by banks demonstrate the need for integrating the impact of liability management into the theory of the money multiplier. Without attempting to achieve full-scale integration—the student might wish to do this on his own, using Figures 2 and 3 as the basis—the following case does suggest the likely outcome. Suppose the Federal Reserve sells securities on the open market and thereby succeeds in reducing money supply and loans and raising interest rates. Liability management theory suggests that the banks, now finding lending more profitable, will offer to pay higher rates to suppliers of funds. Under the plausible assumption that the supply of funds to the banks is not entirely interest inelastic, banks will receive additional fund inflows and can reverse and partially offset the effects of the open market sale.

In short, higher interest rates not only increase the proportion of loans in the asset portfolio of the banks but, because of liability management, induce the banks to find new fund sources. The impact of liability management on the money multiplier is thus quite analogous to that of asset management. Rational bank decision-making procedures, both on the asset and liability sides of the balance sheet, lead to the inevitable conclusion that money multiplier theory cannot assume either a constant reserve ratio or a constant money multiplier.

In concluding this section, we wish to emphasize the importance of integrating the theoretical behavior of the banks into the multiplier analysis and of avoiding the naïve belief that a rigid formula is valid. Of course, the preceding model is far from complex, but it points out the way toward the development of a more sophisticated analysis. The next section, indeed, does suggest some further modifications.

DRAINS AND THE MONEY MULTIPLIER

The Time Deposit Drain

The simple banking multiplier does not express adequately the relationship between reserves and money supply even to those who accept the constant multiplier formulation. In an attempt to increase its relevance, the time deposit drain factor is often included, so that the denominator of the multiplier formula includes the reserve requirement against time deposits and the proportion of time to demand deposits. But this formulation fails to mention the causal factors that determine the drain and therefore suffers from the same weakness as does the simple multiplier.

In order to increase the sophistication of the analysis, let us explore the impact of a change in the interest rate on loans. One possible reaction is that the public will vary its holding of each type of deposit in accordance with the interest rate change. The public may be represented by a community iso-pro-li map as in Figure 1, showing now the public's relative preferences for demand and time deposits. The slope of the curves depends on preferences for liquidity and revenue and also on such objective factors as wealth and the utilities associated with the two deposit forms. The asset boundary line is assumed to be equal to the stock of saving, which can be allocated among demand deposits or time deposits. The tangency point is the equilibrium point, of course.

Liability management theory suggests that a change in interest rates paid on bank assets will cause a variation in the interest payments that a bank makes on its liabilities. A fall in loan rates will induce a fall in rates paid on time deposits, especially on certificates of deposit. In turn, the consumer iso-pro-lis will shift, bringing about a reduction in the proportion of time to demand deposits that consumers hold. The result is to increase the multiplier.

Banks' liquidity-profitability positions will also vary as a result of the public's reaction to an interest rate change. As time deposits fall relatively to demand deposits, a bank's desired cash/deposit ratio can be expected to increase. The increase causes a tightening in the propensity to lend and brings about a decrease in the multiplier.

The net effect of the fall in interest rates depends, then, on the elasticity of the public's liquidity preference curve and the sensitivity of bank response to a change in its deposit mix. The net effect is not predictable a priori, but this fact should not be taken to imply that there is no effect. Again, the effect may change with economic circumstances and thus become difficult to handle.

The Currency Drain

Because currency is no more liquid than a demand deposit and because its rate of return is zero, demand deposits and currency may be treated as substitutes. This statement ought to be qualified only to the extent that banks charge for servicing demand deposits, but the qualification is not relevant unless a causal relationship can be found to exist between service charges and loan rates. Service charges on deposits have not responded quickly to interest rate changes and have been of marginal importance, in any case. Interest was paid on demand deposits in the United States prior to 1933 however, and still is paid in other countries where, insofar as it varies, it has results similar to those of changes in time deposit rates.

Thus the elements of the formal multiplier that are assumed to be constant for purposes of analysis and policy are not constant. Theoretically, they are subject to the same market forces that provide the framework for any economic decision. Banks allocate assets between liquid and earning assets, and individuals do the same. The net result of a given change in reserves by the central bank depends on the various reactions and interactions, and about all that is certain is that the total impact on the money supply cannot be predicted accurately on the basis of any simple formula.

We conclude this article by noting two points of interest. First, the concept of a multiplier predicated upon economic relationships rather than an inflexible formulation has found expression in some econometric models. For example, in the model of the United States' financial markets developed by Frank de Leeuw,[2] interest rates such as the Treasury bill rate

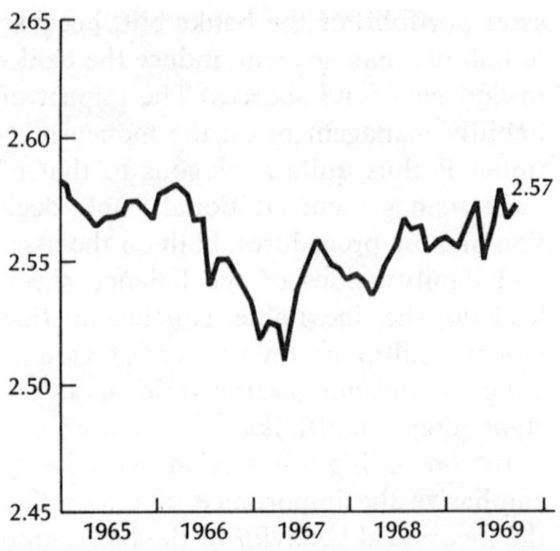

SOURCE: Jerry L. Jordan, "Elements of Money Stock Determination," Federal Reserve Bank of St. Louis, *Review*, 51, No. 10, p. 15. Reprinted by permission.

Figure 3 The Money Multiplier, 1965–1969

and the Federal Reserve discount rate enter explicitly as determinants of the money multiplier. They also help determine the portfolio behavior of the commercial banks. Interest rates on time deposits as well as yields on private securities also enter into de Leeuw's model; they contribute to a determination of changes in the public's demand for currency and demand deposits.

Secondly, the conclusion of this study, that the multiplier will not be constant but will vary as economic conditions are modified, is borne out by a study appearing in the October 1969 *Review* of the Federal Reserve Bank of St. Louis. By the simple expedient of dividing demand deposits by reserves, the money multiplier is derived. Figure 3 reproduces a segment of that calculation. Note the substantial fall in the money multiplier during the credit "crunch" of 1966 and its erratic but nonetheless clear rise since then.

[1] "A Model of Financial Behavior," J. S. Duesenberry, *et al.* (eds.), *The Brookings Quarterly Econometric Model of the United States* (Chicago: Rand McNally, 1965), pp. 465–532.

10 COMMERCIAL BANKS AND THE SUPPLY OF MONEY: A MARKET-DETERMINED DEMAND DEPOSIT RATE

JOHN H. KAREKEN

Professor Kareken sees the portfolio problem of the individual bank as a dual one. First, out of any given deposit stock, a bank must divide its assets between reserves and loans. Secondly, the bank must decide on the total volume of deposits it wishes to hold. By specifying revenue and cost functions, an equilibrium position that satisfies both desires is found. The model is then expanded to the macroeconomic level, where it determines deposit and loan rates as well as total loans and deposits. This macroeconomic model permits Professor Kareken to analyze what will happen when certain constraints are introduced into the analysis.

In opposition to other economists whose articles appear in this section, Kareken implicitly dismisses liquidity as a criterion in portfolio determination. Also, insofar as banks pay implicit interest rates on demand deposits (for example, by not charging depositors fully for the cost of servicing their checking accounts), the analysis expounded in the final section of this article becomes less than compelling. Finally, note that Kareken's results derive from the specific formulations of his equations—for example, increasing marginal costs of deposits (equation 9). What will happen if marginal costs decrease?

U.S. commercial banks have for a long time been prohibited by law from making explicit interest payments to demand creditors. They have never been prohibited, however, from making implicit payments; U.S. banking laws and administrative regulations have never ruled out a market-determined demand deposit rate. Possibly U.S. banks have all along been paying interest on their demand loans, if in unconventional ways; it could even be that the rate implicitly paid to owners of demand deposits has changed through time, much as other rates have. Whatever our casual impressions may be, we simply do not know. There is no basis in established fact for thinking it frivolous, even for someone preoccupied with the U.S. economy, to develop a financial sector model that determines an equilibrium demand deposit rate. Which is what is done in this [article].

In the first section the desired balance sheet of a profit-maximizing bank is derived. One of the components of this balance sheet is a desired stock of demand liabilities; as is shown there, this desired stock or scale of operations changes, not only when one or another of the bank's lending rates changes, but also when the demand deposit rate changes.

In the second section the model of the financial sector is specified. Among the equations of the model are the aggregate counterparts of the bank balance sheet equations of the first section.

How the equilibrium solution of the model of the second section is affected when the central bank alters its portfolio

From John H. Kareken, "Commercial Banks and the Supply of Money: A Market-Determined Demand Deposit Rate," *Federal Reserve Bulletin*, October 1967, pp. 1699–1708. Reprinted by permission.

of securities is investigated in the third section. It is shown there that with a freely fluctuating demand deposit rate the equilibrium stock of demand deposits may increase or decrease when the stock or supply of bank reserves is, say, increased.

In the fourth section the equilibrium or unconstrained solution of the model of the second section is compared with the disequilibrium solution which results when a demand deposit rate ceiling is imposed.

• • •

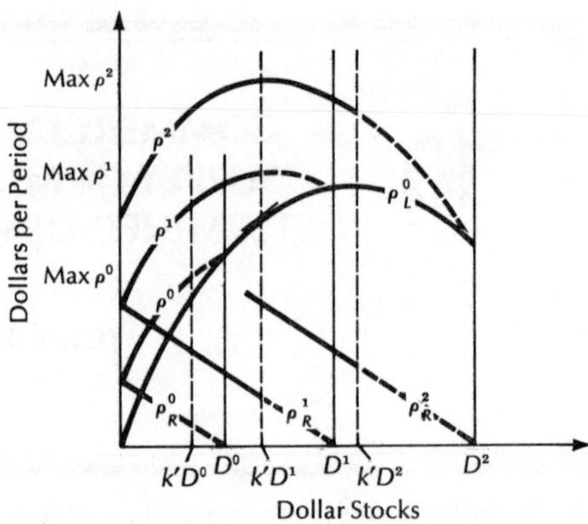

Figure 1

I. A DESIRED BALANCE SHEET

In this section a number of simplifying assumptions are made. It is not argued that they are realistic, only convenient. More realistic assumptions could have been made (for example, about bank costs), but no good purpose would have been served.

It is assumed that the individual bank holds as assets only reserves and one-period loans and has demand liabilities but no net worth. Its balance sheet constraint is therefore

$$R+L\equiv D \tag{1}$$

where R, L, and D are, respectively, the dollar totals of reserves, loans, and deposits. The constraint on its stock of reserves is

$$R\geq kD\,(0<k<1) \tag{2}$$

where k, the familiar legal reserve requirement, is given. The bank maximizes current-period profit, then, subject to the equality (1) and the inequality (2). This the bank does by choosing the appropriate stocks of assets and liabilities. It can be thought of, however, as first determining its optimum stocks of reserves and loans for any given stock of demand liabilities, and as thereafter determining its optimum stock of liabilities or scale of operations.

By assumption, some dollar return

$$\rho_L\equiv(r_L-c_L)\,L \tag{3}$$

is earned by the bank on its current-period stock of loans; r_L, which it takes as given, is the rate of return on loans and c_L is the average cost of making a loan. For $c_L=aL$, where a is some positive technological constant,

$$\rho_L=(r_L-aL)\,L \tag{4}$$

This is the equation of a family of loan-revenue curves. With every value of the loan rate there is associated a particular loan-revenue curve. The one associated with the rate r_L^0 is given in Figure 1; it is labeled ρ_L^0, and shows that as the bank's stock of loans increases the revenue from loans first increases but at some point reaches a maximum and thereafter declines.

By assumption, the dollar return

$$\rho_R=r_R R \tag{5}$$

is earned by the bank on its current-period stock of reserves; r_R, which it also takes as given, is the rate of return on reserves. From equation 1, however,

$$\rho_R=r_R\,(D-L) \tag{6}$$

This is the equation of a family of straight-line reserves-revenue curves. With every set of values of the rate of return on reserves and the stock of demand deposits there is associated a particular reserves-revenue curve, which shows how the revenue from reserves decreases as the stock of loans increases from zero to the assumed deposit stock. Three reserves-revenue curves are given in Figure 1. For the first, $\overset{0}{\rho}_R$, the assumed deposit stock is D^0. For the second, $\overset{1}{\rho}_R$, the assumed stock is D^1. And for the third, $\overset{2}{\rho}_R$, the assumed stock is D^2. For all, the assumed rate of return on reserves is $\overset{0}{r}_R$.[1]

Total revenue is by definition the sum of the revenue from loans and the revenue from reserves; that is,

$$\rho = \rho_L + \rho_R$$

or

$$\rho = r_L D + (r_L - r_R) L - aL^2 \qquad (7)$$

This is the equation of a family of total revenue curves, and with every set of values of the deposit stock and the rates of return on loans and reserves, there is associated a particular total revenue curve. In Figure 1 three total revenue curves are given. The first, ρ^0, is that associated with the deposit stock D^0 and the rates $\overset{0}{r}_L$ and $\overset{0}{r}_R$. It can be thought of as having been constructed by summing (vertically) the revenue from loans, as given by $\overset{0}{\rho}_L$, and the revenue from reserves, as given by $\overset{0}{\rho}_R$, at every stock of loans in the interval from zero to D^0. It shows, of course, how total revenue from loans and reserves changes as the stock of loans increases from zero to D^0, and more particularly that with the deposit stock D^0 and the rates $\overset{0}{r}_L$ and $\overset{0}{r}_R$, the maximum total revenue, Max ρ^0, is obtained with the largest possible stock of loans, $L^0 = k'D^0 = (1-k)D^0$, and the smallest possible stock of reserves, $R^0 = kD^0$.

Since the net rate of return on loans $(r_L - c_L)$ decreases as the bank's loans increase, it is not invariably true, though, that the asset portfolio consisting of the largest possible stock of loans and the smallest possible stock of reserves yields the maximum total revenue. For deposit stocks greater than D^1, the limiting portfolio is not the optimum portfolio. The total revenue curve ρ^1 of Figure 1 reaches a maximum at the stock of loans $L^1 = k'D^1$—or, with D^1 given, at the largest possible stock of loans. But at L^1 total revenue is also an unconstrained maximum. Even without a reserves constraint, L^1 would be optimal. At this stock of loans, the slopes of the loan-revenue curve $\overset{0}{\rho}_L$ and the reserves-revenue curve $\overset{1}{\rho}_R$ differ only in sign, and the slope of the total revenue curve ρ^1 is therefore zero. And although there is for every stock of deposits a different reserves-revenue curve, the slopes of these curves, being equal to the rate of return on reserves, are the same. It follows that for any given deposit stock greater than D^1, maximum total revenue is obtained with the stock of loans L^1.

Given the rates of return on loans and reserves, there is then an optimum portfolio for every stock of demand liabilities, and some maximum total revenue as well. How maximum total revenue varies with the deposit stock is shown by the appropriate maximum revenue curve. For the rates $\overset{0}{r}_L$ and $\overset{0}{r}_R$, the maximum revenue curve is Max ρ^0 of Figure 2. It shows that as the deposit stock increases from zero to D^1, maximum total revenue increases but at an ever decreasing rate, and additionally that as the deposit stock increases beyond D^1, total maximum revenue increases at a constant rate.

The shape of the maximum revenue curve of Figure 2 is easily explained. As the stock of demand liabilities increases from zero to D^1, successive increments are allocated in constant proportions between loans and reserves. But because the net rate of return on loans, that is

---

[1]An assumption of Figure 1, it should be noted, is $r_L > r_R$.

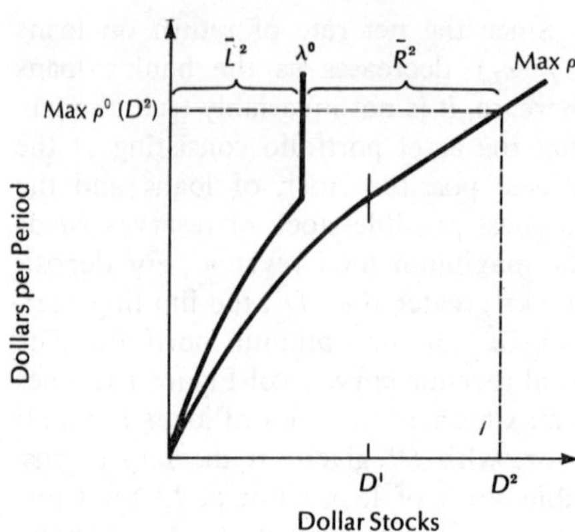

Figure 2

$(r_L - c_L)$, decreases as the stock of loans increases, maximum total revenue increases at a decreasing rate. As the stock of demand deposits increases beyond D^1, successive increments are allocated entirely to reserves, for with a loan stock greater than $k'D^1$ the rate of reserves exceeds the net rate of return on loans. And because the rate of return on reserves does not depend on the bank's portfolio, total maximum revenue increases at a constant rate beyond D^1.

There is another curve in Figure 2—namely, λ^0, the optimum-loan curve associated with the maximum revenue curve Max ρ^0. It is used to determine the portfolio of assets that yields the maximum total revenue obtainable from any given stock of deposits. Consider the stock D^2. Maximum total revenue, as shown in Figure 2, is Max $\rho^0(D^2)$. And the asset portfolio that yields this revenue? Along the horizontal line which intersects Max ρ^0 at D^2, the distance from the y-axis to the λ^0 curve gives the revenue-maximizing stock of loans $\bar{L}^2$; and the remaining distance, from the λ^0 curve to the Max ρ^0 curve, gives the revenue-maximizing stock of reserves, $\bar{R}^2$.

The profit-maximizing bank does not stop, though, once having determined its optimum portfolio of assets for any given stock of deposits. It goes on and determines its optimum stock of deposits, or optimum scale of operations.

Having demand deposits costs the individual bank something. By assumption, the total cost is

$$\gamma = (r_D + c_D) D \tag{8}$$

where r_D, taken as given by the bank, is the rate paid demand creditors and c_D is the average cost of servicing deposits, accepting and recording in-payments, clearing checks, and so on. For $c_D = bD$, where b is another positive technological constant,

$$\gamma = (r_D + bD) D \tag{9}$$

The total cost of deposits increases at an increasing rate. This is what the total cost curves of Figure 3, γ^0 and γ^1, show.

For the demand deposit rate $\overset{0}{r_D}$, the relevant cost curve in Figure 3 is γ^0. Given this rate, the loan rate $\overset{0}{r_L}$ and the reserves rate $\overset{0}{r_R}$, the profit-maximizing stock of demand liabilities is $\hat{D}^0$. By construction, it is at $\hat{D}^0$ where marginal cost and marginal revenue are the same. The maximizing stock of loans is $\hat{L}^0$ and the maximizing stock of reserves is $\hat{R}^0 (= \hat{D}^0 - \hat{L}^0)$.

Figure 3

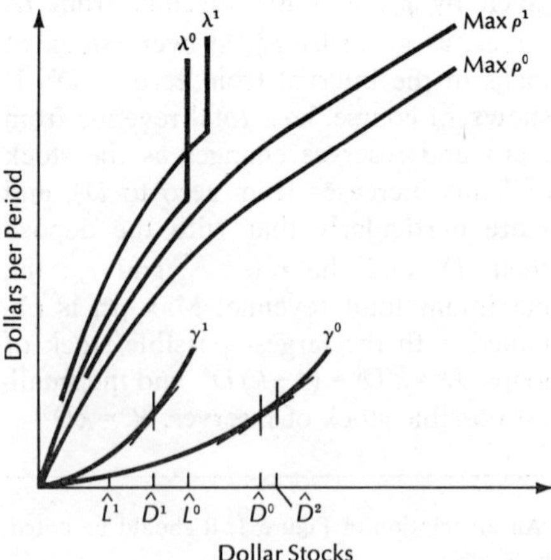

The desired or profit-maximizing balance sheet of the individual bank has then been determined, although only for one set of rates of return; and when a rate of return changes, the bank's desired balance sheet changes. Consider a *ceteris paribus* increase in the demand deposit rate, from $\overset{0}{r}_D$ to $\overset{1}{r}_D$. For the higher deposit rate, γ^1 of Figure 3 is the relevant cost curve; so the desired or profit-maximizing stock of demand liabilities is $\hat{D}^1$ not $\hat{D}^0$. The new desired stocks of loans and reserves are, respectively, $\hat{L}^1$ and $\hat{R}^1$ $(=\hat{D}^1-\hat{L}^1)$.

As a general rule, the bank's desired balance sheet also changes when either the loan rate or the reserves rate changes. Suppose that initially the rates of return are $\overset{0}{r}_L$, $\overset{0}{r}_R$, and $\overset{0}{r}_D$. The desired stock of demand deposits is therefore $\hat{D}^0$ (Figure 3). With a *ceteris paribus* increase in the loan rate, from $\overset{0}{r}_L$ to $\overset{1}{r}_L$, the maximum revenue and optimum-loan curves shift. For $\overset{1}{r}_L$, the relevant maximum revenue curve is Max ρ^1 and the relevant optimum-loan curve is λ^1. The desired stock of deposits is then $\hat{D}^2$. Also, with the higher loan rate, the desired stocks of loans and reserves are not what they were.

More could be done with the diagrammatic apparatus developed here. But perhaps enough has already been done to make clear that the profit-maximizing bank has a desired balance sheet—and, more particularly, a desired stock of demand liabilities—which in the main changes when rates of return change. How the individual bank's desired balance sheet might vary with the demand deposit rate is shown in Figure 4. Of special interest is the curve labeled $\hat{D}$, which shows how the bank's desired stock of demand liabilities varies with the deposit rate. It is the bank's demand deposit (money) supply curve and, as such, the curve for which there is no analogue in traditional models of bank behavior.

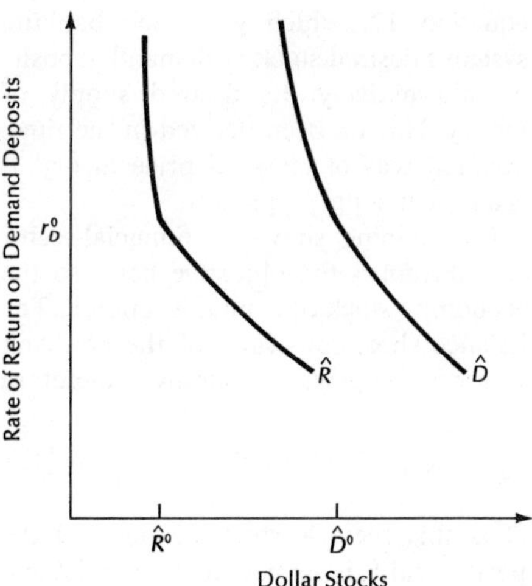

Figure 4

II. A SIMPLIFIED FINANCIAL SECTOR

After what has already been said, it would seem reasonable to suppose that

$$\hat{R}=R(r_L, r_R, r_D) \quad (10)$$

$$\hat{L}=L(r_L, r_R, r_D) \quad (11)$$

$$\hat{D}=D(r_L, r_R, r_D) \quad (12)$$

where now $\hat{R}$, $\hat{L}$ and $\hat{D}$ are, respectively, the entire banking system's desired stocks of reserves, loans, and demand liabilities.[2] Together, equations 10, 11, and 12 determine the desired balance sheet of banks as a group. Of special interest is

[2]These equations are obtained in an essentially straightforward way, in the first instance by aggregating over the individual units of the banking system. Actually, what the analysis of section I suggests is that

$$\hat{R}^i=R^i(r_L, r_R, r_D, k, Y, D)$$

and so forth where, as before, Y is aggregate money income and D is the total of demand deposits. But after summing, $D(=\hat{D})$ can be eliminated as an independent variable, and k and Y are here regarded as constants.

equation 12, which gives the banking system's desired stock of demand deposits or, alternatively, its desired supply of money. Having been derived in the time-honored way of classical price theory, it is a proper supply equation.

Determining short-run financial-sector equilibrium is the objective here; so the economy's stock of capital is ignored. The balance sheet constraint of the nonbank sector of the private economy is therefore

$$\mathfrak{D} \equiv \mathfrak{L} \qquad (13)$$

$\mathfrak{D}$ is this sector's stock of demand deposits, and $\mathfrak{L}$ is its net stock of indebtedness, or in other words its stock of indebtedness to private banks and the central bank. (There are no claims against the government; the central bank deals in private claims.) Since aggregate money income is taken as given, it is assumed that

$$\hat{\mathfrak{D}} = \mathfrak{D}\ (r_L, r_D) \qquad (14)$$

where $\hat{\mathfrak{D}}$ is the nonbank sector's desired stock of demand deposits.

For financial-sector equilibrium, there must be equality between the supplies of and demands for reserves, loans, and demand deposits. The equilibrium conditions are then

$$R\,(r_L, r_D, r_R) = R \qquad (15)$$

$$L\,(r_L, r_D, r_R) = \mathfrak{D}\,(r_L, r_D) - R \qquad (16)$$

$$\mathfrak{D}\ (r_L, r_D, r_R) = \mathfrak{D}\,(r_L, r_D) \qquad (17)$$

where R is the supply of bank reserves, fixed by the monetary authority. As indicated by equation 16, the stock of loans which in equilibrium the banking system must desire is $\mathfrak{D}(r_L, r_D) - R$. By equation 13, the public's desired stock of demand deposits is also its desired net stock or supply of loans; but to get the stock available to the banking system, the stock desired by the monetary authority, which of necessity is equal to the supply of bank reserves, must be subtracted.

There being only two independent market-clearing equations, one rate of return must be regarded as exogenously determined. Since it seems the natural thing to do, it is assumed here that the monetary authority fixes not only the actual stock of bank reserves, but the rate of return on reserves as well. For $R = R^0$ and $r_R = r_R^0$ the equilibrium conditions are

$$L\,(r_L, r_D, r_R^0) = \mathfrak{D}\,(r_L, r_D^0) - R^0 \qquad (18)$$

$$D\,(r_L, r_D, r_R^0) = \mathfrak{D}\,(r_L, r_D^0) \qquad (19)$$

By the usual macroeconomic criteria, these two equations can be said to determine the equilibrium values of the rates of return on loans and deposits. More generally, the system of equations 16, 17, and either 12 or 13 can be used to obtain the equilibrium values of the rates of return on loans and deposits and the equilibrium value of the deposit stock as functions of two policy parameters, the supply of bank reserves, and the rate of return on reserves.

Financial-sector equilibrium is illustrated in Figure 5. The curve $\hat{D}^0$ shows the banking system's desired stock or

Figure 5

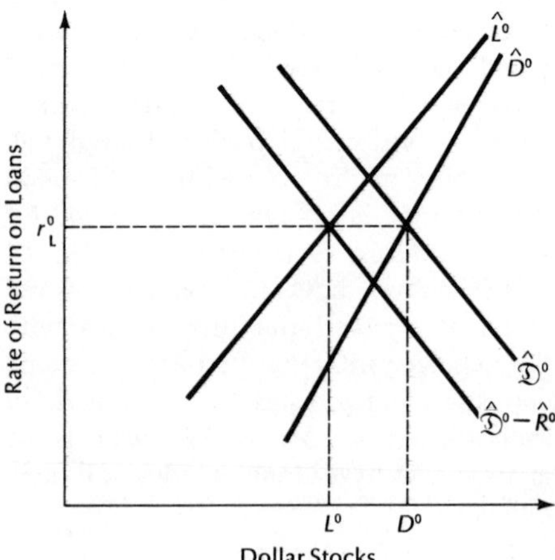

supply of demand deposits for the given reserves and deposit rates $\overset{0}{r}_R$ and $\overset{0}{r}_D$. The curve $\hat{L}^0$ shows its desired stock of loans, again for the rates r_R and $\overset{0}{r}_D$.[3] The curve $\hat{\mathfrak{D}}^0$ shows the nonbank sector's desired stock of demand deposits and, also, its desired net indebtedness. The remaining curve, $\hat{\mathfrak{D}}-\hat{R}^0$, shows the supply of loan claims to the banking system. ($\hat{R}^0$ is the official demand for the loan claims of the nonbank sector of the private economy.) At the loan rate $\overset{0}{r}_L$, the stock of loans desired by the banking system and the central bank together equals the nonbank sector's desired net indebtedness; and the banking system's desired stock of demand deposits equals the nonbank sector's. Then, too, the banking system's desired stock of reserves equals the actual stock or supply. The distance from the $\hat{\mathfrak{D}}^0$ curve to the curve labeled $\hat{\mathfrak{D}}^0-\hat{R}^0$ gives the actual stock of reserves; and the distance from the $\hat{D}^0$ curve to the $\hat{L}^0$ curve gives the banking system's desired stock of reserves.

For the stock of reserves R^0 and the rate of return on reserves $\overset{0}{r}_R$, the equilibrium loan rate is therefore $\overset{0}{r}_L$ and the equilibrium deposit rate is $\overset{0}{r}_D$. The equilibrium stock of loans is L^0. The equilibrium stock of deposits is D^0. In a world without currency, D^0 would be the equilibrium stock of money.

III. OPEN MARKET OPERATIONS

It has long been accepted that when the monetary authority makes, for instance, an open market purchase, thereby increasing the stock of bank reserves, the equilibrium rate of return on loans decreases, at least initially, and the equilibrium stock of money increases. Within the confines of traditional models, these are necessary results. In the language of diagrams, the money supply curve, si-called, shifts rightward when the supply of reserves is increased. But because the public's desired stock of money depends, with aggregate money income given, only on the loan rate, the money demand curve does not shift. And because the public's desired stock of money increases as the loan rate decreases, an increase in the stock of reserves cannot do other than decrease the equilibrium loan rate and increase the equilibrium stock of money.

Within the confines of the financial-sector model of section II, however, an increase in the stock of bank reserves does not inevitably produce an increase in the equilibrium stock of money. Stability does imply that the equilibrium loan and deposit rates decrease when the stock of reserves is increased and increase when the stock is decreased. But even if the financial sector is stable, the equilibrium stock of money will not necessarily increase when the stock of reserves is increased or decrease when it is decreased.

Resorting again to the language of diagrams, it is simply that the money demand curve shifts to the left when the supply of reserves is increased. This shift of the curve is not in itself enough to insure a decrease in the equilibrium stock of money, for the banking system's money supply curve shifts rightward. The shift of the money demand curve to the left is necessary, though, for the untraditional result.

To increase the stock of reserves, the monetary authority must initially create an excess demand for loan claims—or, equivalently, an excess supply of loanable funds. This is shown in Figure 6. With an increase in the stock of reserves, from R^0 to R^1, the loan-claims supply curve shifts to the left. For the rates of

[3] The analysis of section I suggests that

$$D_1(r_L, r_D, r_R) > 0$$

where D_1 denotes the partial derivative of $\hat{D}$ with respect to the first argument, that is, r_L. It also suggests that $L_1(r_L, r_D, r_R) > 0$. With the curves $\hat{D}^0$ and $\hat{L}^0$ as drawn in Figure 5, though, the assumption, admittedly strong, is that

$$D_1(r_L, r_D, r_R) - L_1(r_L, r_D, r_R) = R_1(r_L, r_D, r_R) < 0$$

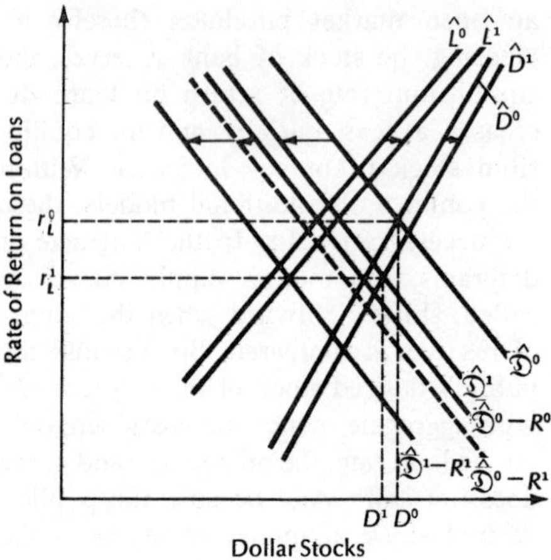

Figure 6

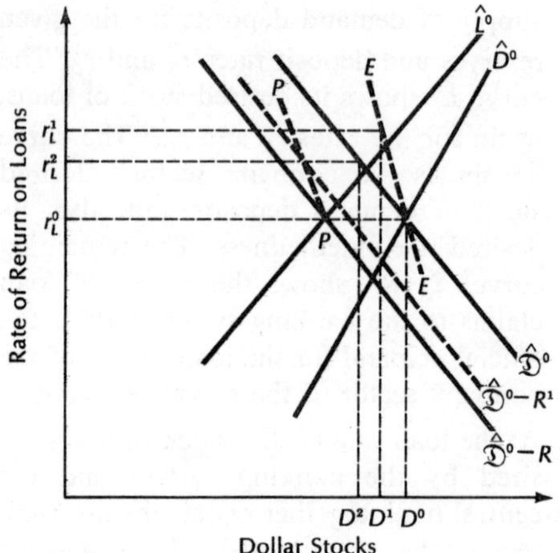

Figure 7

return on reserves and deposits r_R^0 and r_D^0 and the stock of reserves R^0, the relevant loan-claims supply curve is labeled $\hat{\mathfrak{D}}^0 - R^0$. But for these same rates of return and the stock of reserves R^1, the relevant loan supply curve is labeled $\hat{\mathfrak{D}}^0 - R^1$.

Presumably, then, an increase in the stock of reserves implies a decrease in the loan rate, and a decrease in the deposit rate as well. As will be clear from Figure 6, the loan rate cannot decrease without excess demand developing in the market for deposits. Moreover, with a decrease in the deposit rate, the deposit demand curve shifts to the left, so the loan-claims curve shifts to the left again; and the deposit supply curve shifts to the right, as does the curve giving the banking system's desired stock of loans.[4] With a decrease in the deposit rate, therefore, excess demand develops in the market for loan claims.

Still, if the financial sector is stable, rates do not go ever lower. In Figure 6 the new equilibrium solution, that associated with the rate of return on reserves r_R^0 and the stock of reserves R^1, is shown. The new equilibrium loan rate is r_L^1 and the new equilibrium deposit rate is r_D^1. The new equilibrium stock of money is D^1. The equilibrium stock of deposits has thus been shown as decreasing when the supply of reserves increases; it could have been shown, however, as increasing.

IV. A DEMAND DEPOSIT RATE CEILING

Just as an increase in the stock of bank reserves creates an initial excess demand for loan claims, so a decrease creates an initial excess supply. With a decrease, the equilibrium loan and deposit rates increase. Depending on what values are assigned certain parameters, the equilibrium stock of money either increases or decreases. In Figure 7 it is shown as decreasing. The curve labeled E gives the path along which the equilibrium stock of money and the equilibrium loan rate change as the stock of reserves changes. For the stock of reserves R^0, the equilibrium money stock is D^0 and the equilibrium loan rate is r_L^0; and for the stock R^1, which is less than R^0, the equilibrium values are D^1 and r_L^1. Of course, as the equilibrium money stock and equilibrium loan rate change along the E curve, the

---

[4]The analysis of section I suggests that

$$D_2(r_L, r_D, r_R) < 0$$

and the natural assumption is $\mathfrak{D}_2(r_L, r_D) > 0$.

equilibrium deposit rate changes too. With a decrease in the stock of reserves from R^0 to R^1, the equilibrium deposit rate increases from $\overset{0}{r}_D$ to $\overset{1}{r}_D$.

The change in financial-sector equilibrium just described is to be compared, though, with that which results when, with the demand deposit rate prevented from adjusting upward by a rate ceiling, the stock of bank reserves is decreased from R^0 to R^1. Suppose there is a restriction, $r_D \leq \overset{0}{r}_D$, on the deposit rate. To begin, the financial sector is in equilibrium.

The new (constrained) equilibrium is $\overset{0}{r}_L$. The deposit rate is $\overset{0}{r}_D$, so whatever happens to the stock of reserves it cannot increase. Now, then, with a decrease in the stock of bank reserves from R^0 to R^1, the loan-claims supply curve shifts to the right; for the new stock of reserves the relevant loan-claims supply curve in Figure 7 is that labeled $\hat{\mathfrak{D}}^0 - R^1$. Again, there is an initial excess supply of loan claims created, and so the loan rate increases. But the deposit rate does not increase, although an excess supply of loan claims is created by the increase in the loan rate. Thus, with an effective rate ceiling, the deposit demand and deposit supply curves do not shift. As the loan rate increases, the stock of money decreases along the original deposit demand curve, $\hat{\mathfrak{D}}^0$, not the curve labeled E.

But if the banking system is prevented by a deposit rate ceiling from going as much in debt to households and firms as it would like, its loan-claims demand curve, $\hat{L}^0$, is of no relevance. With an effective rate ceiling, the banking system allocates a given stock of deposits between loans and reserves. In Figure 7 the curve labeled P gives this allocation. The horizonal distance from the y-axis to this curve gives the stock of loans which, under constraint, the banking system desires; and the remaining distance, from the P curve, that is, to the $\hat{\mathfrak{D}}^0$ curve, gives what can only with qualification be called the banking system's desired stock of reserves.

The new (constrained) equilibrium loan rate is therefore $\overset{2}{r}_L$, and the new (constrained) equilibrium stock of deposits is D^2. At the loan rate $\overset{2}{r}_L$, the stock of loan claims which, under constraint, the banking system desires is equal to the stock made available; and the stock of reserves which, under constraint, it desires is equal to the actual stock.

The point would seem to be that the banking system, if bound by a rate ceiling, will desire a smaller stock of reserves than it otherwise would. In Figure 7 the distance at the loan rate $\overset{1}{r}_L$ from the curve labeled P to that labeled $\hat{\mathfrak{D}}^0$, which gives the constrained desired stock of reserves, is less than the distance from the curve labeled $\hat{\mathfrak{D}}^0 - R^1$ to that labeled $\hat{\mathfrak{D}}^0$.[5] It is

---

[5]Recall that with no effective rate ceiling $\overset{1}{r}_L$ is the equilibrium loan rate. At this rate therefore the banking system must desire the stock of reserves supplied, which is given by the horizontal distance from the curve labeled $\hat{\mathfrak{D}}^0 - R^1$ to that labeled $\hat{\mathfrak{D}}^0$. The banking system's desired stock of reserves can be written as

$$\hat{R} = \hat{R}_e + R_r = F(r_L, r_R, \hat{D}) + k + k\hat{D}$$

where $\hat{R}_e$ is the desired stock of excess reserves and R_r is the stock of required reserves. With the rate of return on reserves given $(\overset{0}{r}_R)$, then,

$$\hat{R} = F[r_L, \overset{0}{r}_R, D(r_L, r_D, \overset{0}{r}_R)] + kD(r_L, r_D, \overset{0}{r}_R)$$

If there is an effective rate ceiling, however, the banking system's stock of deposits is given by the public's demand, so

$$\hat{R}_c = F[r_L, \overset{0}{r}_R, \mathfrak{D}(r_L, r_D)] + k\mathfrak{D}(r_L, r_D)$$

where $\hat{R}_c$ is the stock of reserves which, under constraint, the banking system desires. But since

$$\mathfrak{D}(\overset{1}{r}_L, \overset{0}{r}_D) < D(\overset{1}{r}_L, \overset{1}{r}_D, \overset{0}{r}_R)$$

it follows that

$$R_c(\overset{1}{r}_L, \overset{0}{r}_D, \overset{0}{r}_R) < R(\overset{1}{r}_L, \overset{1}{r}_D, \overset{0}{r}_R)$$

if the desired stock of excess reserves increases as the stock of deposits increases. This is what the analysis of section I suggests and what has typically been assumed. (Very often the desired stock of reserves has been taken as homogeneous of degree one in the stock of deposits.)

therefore inevitable, at least within the confines of the financial-sector model of section II, that the equilibrium loan rate increases less when there is an effective rate ceiling than when the deposit rate can adjust.[6]

[6]In Figure 7 the equilibrium stock of money is shown as decreasing more when there is an effective rate ceiling than when the deposit rate can adjust. This would seem necessary, but I have not proved it is.

bank size and the structure of the banking industry

The concentration of the commercial banking industry into fewer and fewer hands constitutes a trend that has characterized American banking since the second decade of the present century. In the twenty years since 1948, the number of commercial banks has fallen from 14,164 to 13,679. In contrast to the years preceding World War II, however, the reduction in bank numbers has not been a consequence of bank failures; of the 609 banks that failed between 1934 and 1968, 80 percent did so before 1943.[1] Instead, the attrition is a direct result of the merger movement on the one hand and the relatively smaller number of new banks being chartered on the other hand. Simply put, the mortality rate has exceeded the birth rate, so that the net increase has been negative.

Why have fewer bank charters been obtained? Why have bank mergers been actively pursued? An understanding of developments in commercial banking demands answers to these questions.

Part of the explanation of the concentration movements lies in the statutes regulating the banking industry. The attitudes and interpretations of the authorities appointed to implement these laws are also important, indeed critical, elements.

New charters are regulated de facto by the Banking Act of 1935. That statute prohibits a bank from obtaining federal deposit insurance unless the Federal Reserve Board, the Comptroller of the Currency, or the directors of the Federal Deposit Insurance Corporation (FDIC) certify that banking criteria, such as the "financial history and condition of the bank" and its capital structure, and the "convenience and needs of the

---

[1]Federal Deposit Insurance Corporation, *Annual Report* (Washington, D.C., 1969), p. 230.

community"[2] aspects, have been considered. This need to meet specified conditions was one element responsible for limiting the number of new bank charters. But far more important was the interpretation of these criteria by the authorities, itself a consequence of the experience of bank failures during the 1920s and 1930s. The memory of massive liquidations—some 4000 in 1933, the peak year—led to a policy of self-restraint on the part of the chartering authorities. They believed that the stability and safety of the banking system could be preserved best by preventing new banks from entering communities already served adequately by established institutions. This attitude has led to such apparently incomprehensible administrative regulations as the one issued by the Comptroller of the Currency relating to the character of the organizers—they must be "forceful, sincere, intelligent or otherwise"; or another relating to the motives of the promoters—"Whether it would appear that his desire to organize a new bank is primarily for personal reasons (borrowing opportunities, unjustified personal animosity toward existing banks, prestige, or immoderate personal gain), rather than as a sound investment opportunity which will result in fulfilling a community need."[3]

Legislation, too, has played its role in determining the shape of the merger movement. Bank mergers since 1960 have been conducted according to the broad outlines of the Bank Merger Act of that year. Conditions for merging are fundamentally similar to those for chartering, with the additional requirement that the merger's impact on competition must also be considered. Various regulatory agencies are delegated approval power over bank mergers, a situation that naturally has raised questions of jurisdiction and coordination. The Act leaves to the judgment of the implementing authorities the importance to be assigned to each of these various elements—banking, need, and competition—in the final decision.

Note the contradiction between the restraint exercised in the chartering of new banks, an action that has limited competition, and the criteria of competitiveness explicit in the Bank Merger Act. The regulatory authorities are well aware of this inconsistency, and, since the early 1960s, measures have been proposed and occasionally taken to eliminate the paradox. First, whereas only 335 National banks were chartered in the quarter century between 1936 and 1960, Comptroller James J. Saxon's liberal policy led to the granting of 513 charters from 1962–1965.[4] Second, a new attitude has been urged, representative of which is the first selection in this Part. Federal Reserve Governor George W. Mitchell explores the reasons banks prefer to merge rather than open new branches and concludes that bank mergers ought to be judged on the basis of "competitive" criteria alone. He goes on to suggest a "hands-off" policy with regard to mergers unless it can be clearly demonstrated that competition will be hindered substantially upon the consummation of the merger. Governor Mitchell applies this "procompetitive" policy to bank chartering as well—let new banks enter at will.

---

[2] 12 USC 1816.

[3] U.S. Congress, House of Representatives, Committee on Banking and Currency, *Conflict of Federal and State Banking Laws: Hearings* (Washington, D.C.: Government Printing Office, 1963), p. 304.

[4] An interesting essay that supports this conclusion is S. Peltzman, "Bank Entry Regulation: Its Impact and Purpose," *National Banking Review*, 3, 163–177, reprinted in Administrator of National Banks, *Studies in Banking Competition and Bank Structure: Articles Reprinted from the National Banking Review* (Washington, D.C.: 1966), pp. 285–299.

Because a judgment concerning competitiveness is required of the regulatory authorities before they approve mergers, and *a fortiori* if Governor Mitchell's points are to be adopted, a workable definition of competition, or, alternatively, of guidelines for determining when competition is being interfered with substantially, becomes mandatory. The Supreme Court, by applying section 7 of the Clayton Antitrust Act to banking in the *Philadelphia National Bank-Girard Trust Corn Exchange* merger litigation, found itself face-to-face with this precise question. Although the Court avoided reaching a conclusive judgment on the issue, it did advance a criterion. When it discovered that the combined bank would control 30 percent of the market, the Court ruled that this percentage was unduly large and that the merger would result in "a significant increase in the concentration of firms in that market." Thus, 30 percent control violates competitive conditions, and one could anticipate that henceforth any merger resulting in no less than 30 percent control would be unlawful.

Yet even this conclusion is premature, for the ruling itself was subjected to intensive criticism. Some of the discussion surrounding the case is treated by Edward S. Herman in the second selection. Although he concludes that the Court ruled sensibly, the issue remains shrouded in controversy. In an attempt to settle the matter legislatively, Congress amended the Bank Merger Act in 1966. A merger may be approved, declared Congress, even though it results in a degree of concentration that would otherwise be in violation of the Clayton Act if "the anticompetitive effects of the proposed transaction are clearly outweighed in the public interest by the probable effect of the transaction in meeting the convenience and needs of the community to be served."[5] Instead of resolving the issue, however, Congress has managed to complicate matters even more. Without defining competitiveness or even appointing a single agency to administer the Act, Congress has accepted the confused status quo, leaving a number of authorities—the three regulatory agencies and the Antitrust Division of the Justice Department—to define the intent of the legislative branch. Moreover, banking and convenience, as well as competitive factors, remain as criteria. Thus, there is neither a single regulatory body whose rulings are binding nor an objective criterion for weighing the disparate considerations of competition, banking, and need.[6]

Litigation under the amended Bank Merger Act has already reached the Supreme Court. In 1968 the Court ruled against a merger of two large Nashville, Tennessee, banks, which had merged after obtaining regulatory agency approval but whose action had been contested by the Justice Department. The Court held essentially to the line it had declared in the *Philadelphia National Bank* decision. It found the Bank Merger Act amendment cited previously as inapplicable, for the defendants had not clearly demonstrated that the "merger was essential to secure this net gain to the public interest." In other words, for an anticompetitive merger to be permitted, the banks must first prove that no alternative solution other than merger could be found for the community. After *Nashville,* it appears clear that the competitive criterion is still to be given substantial weight. How much weight it is to be assigned, however, is not evident.

The economist, less interested in legal aspects, tends to take the view that public policy toward mergers must be based largely on the economic justifications under-

---

[5]Public Law 89–356, 89th Cong., Sec. 18, c, 5B.

[6]See Part III for further consideration of the general issue of conflicting responsibilities.

lying mergers. Firms often merge to take advantage of cost economies, which enable them to provide the same service at lower cost or an expanded service line at slight additional cost. Other firms merge to gain control over their markets and thereby enhance their profits. Still others do so because they find that in this way they can best accomplish diversification, which leads to more stable profits. Economists have tended to look with suspicion on mergers in which cost economies could not be obtained. When economies of scale are significant, however, a dilemma may result. Although taking advantage of the efficiencies of large-scale production lowers costs, it increases concentration and the possibility of market manipulation. The public policy called for in such a situation is indeed perplexing. Permitting concentration leads to a more efficient allocation of resources, but consumer welfare may be maximized only when competitive conditions are maintained. With regard to the public utilities, the issue has been resolved through comprehensive government regulation; the benefits of large size are obtained, whereas exploitation of the consumer is prevented.

What is the situation in banking? Do economies of scale exist, and if they do, are they sizable? Or do bank mergers bring about a reduction in the responsiveness of the industry to its customers? These questions must be answered if antitrust or antimerger policy is to be applied sensibly to the banking industry. A positive response to the first question would indicate the desirability of a promerger policy, whereas a positive response to the second one would suggest that an antimerger policy is more appropriate.

The first step, then, is to discover the presence of scale economies. Special problems arise in determining the extent of economies of scale in an industry characterized by multiproduct firms. The crucial question here is, What "output" does a bank produce? Many of the studies implicitly answer this question and then proceed to relate cost to output. Stuart I. Greenbaum reviews such studies in the third selection and contrasts them with some of his own.

A general conclusion that appears with regularity is that very small banks, those with assets of less than $5 million or even $10 million, are grossly inefficient and that significant economies of scale could be achieved by their consolidation via merger. There is little agreement, however, whether the merging of two middle-sized or large banks, each with assets of, say, $250 million–$300 million or $1 billion, would increase efficiency and reduce average costs.

Similar problems are faced when one tries to measure the impact of concentration or mergers on the interest rates charged or services provided. Although studies are numerous, conclusions are often contradictory. Some surveys have indicated that concentration and the interest rates charged on business loans vary directly, although one researcher has found an inverse relationship. Two studies have shown that consumers have gained from mergers. These conclusions, however, may prove to provide unreliable foundations for a general promerger policy, because special circumstances are likely to explain the favorable results. Thus the question of whether or not bank mergers are advantageous to the economy remains unresolved, and the arguments of both the proponents and the opponents of larger-sized banks have ample support.

The bank merger question is closely related to another one: Is branch banking a more or less desirable form of bank structure than unit banking? Indeed, where branching is prohibited by law, mergers tend to be infrequent, for the understandable reason that one of the two locations of the merged bank must be vacated. Unit bankers, seeking to preserve their territory against invasion by their "big" brothers, often point out the (spurious) association between unit banking and competition; a large number of individually owned banks is deemed to provide a less costly and a broader range of services, a direct consequence of competition. These protagonists of unit banking fail to point out that in many markets, the prevention of branch banking preserves a monopoly for the unit bank.

A judgment on merits would proceed by examining the relationship between banking structure and the costs and benefits of operation. Given two banks with equal total assets, one operating only from a single office and the other having, in addition to the main office, several branches, the relevant question is: Which bank will provide less costly and broader services to the community? This issue must be kept distinct from another one—namely, the relationship between size and structure. Just because the average size of the bank with branches is larger than the unit bank and the bank is therefore capable of taking advantage of whatever economies of scale may be present does not in itself prove the superiority of branch banking. A unit bank with equal total assets may be even more efficient. Such a comparison is justifiable only if a causal relationship exists between size and structure. In the next-to-last selection, George J. Benston contributes to a resolution of the conflicting claims by analyzing quantitatively both of these aspects but limits himself to the cost side. He investigates the costs of servicing deposits and loans of various sorts by branch banks and by unit banks. He also inquires whether or not the consolidation of certain unit banks into a main office with branches would reduce or increase costs. Benston's conclusions certainly shed light on the controversy, because they find some justification for the defenders of unit banking; yet once again many questions remain unanswered. Aside from the difficulty of combining the various disparate cost-difference estimates into a meaningful average, the cost side alone, as Benston notes, cannot serve as the sole criterion for public policy.

A broader survey of the issues is excerpted in the final selection. Jack M. Guttentag and Edward S. Herman, in a study written originally for the Pennsylvania Banking Law Commission, examine the benefits as well as the costs of branch banking versus unit banking. The conclusions arrived at lack finality, but the evidence cited tends to favor branch banking. Guttentag and Herman find less cause than Benston does for concern about the claimed disadvantages of branch banking; competition is encouraged when branching is permitted, interest rates tend not to be higher, and services to the community are not reduced—indeed they may even be broadened.

Most Western economists have tended to favor laissez-faire policies, with the burden of proof on the proponents of government intervention. This attitude would imply a policy of unrestricted entry into banking coupled with permissiveness toward mergers. Although the banking system has been closely regulated at least since the 1930s, the tenor of the selections in this section, as well as a great deal of the contemporary writings by economists, has been to suggest loosening the regulatory bonds. With depositors protected by the FDIC, these economists ask, Why control entry into banking and the structure of the banking industry more carefully than entry into or the structure of any other industry? Why, indeed?

11 MERGERS AMONG COMMERCIAL BANKS

GEORGE W. MITCHELL

"Banks merge because they find it profitable to do so." This simple and obvious dictum is the basis for a reform of the attitudes of regulatory authorities toward commercial banking and, implicitly, toward legislation as well. Do you agree with the author that "banking" considerations ought not to be a criterion in mergers? Is it realistic to identify the needs of the community and the profit interests of banks? Also, contrast the role attributed to nonbank competitors in this selection with that in the succeeding one.

INTRODUCTION

Recent developments in the structure of banking markets have caused concern in Congress, in the several agencies responsible in one way or another for the regulation and supervision of banks, and —belatedly—in the academic community. The concern of the 1930's, centered primarily in the ambiguous notion of an "overbanked" economy and in the inadequate safeguards to the safety and liquidity of the banking system, have shifted in the past decade to concern over growing concentration, a lessening of competition and—in some quarters, at least—a fear that regulation is too encompassingly confining to permit banks adequately to respond to changing requirements of a growing economy.

The view of banks as *sui generis* implicit in the policies designed to regulate and supervise them fails to recognize the change and rapid growth of highly competitive financial markets and alternative financing devices that have occurred in recent years and, hence, creates the impression of a body of policy rather badly out of step with the times. In the multi-stage and institutionally specialized financial markets of today, commercial banking is an important element but not the unique element it was in earlier times. This increasingly competitive environment has caused bankers to become more like the managers of any other profit-seeking enterprise.

It is my view that despite superficial differences between banking markets and those for other goods and services the market mechanism and the decisions made in the market place ordinarily can and should be relied upon to protect the interests and needs of individual communities and the general welfare of the country. Historic worries about bank safety and liquidity—which often ignore the vital distinction between safety and liquidity for depositors as contrasted with that of stockowners—and the chronic fears of "overbanking" have, I think, led to an overzealous regulation, overly restrictive policies on the entry of new banks, and inescapably to monopolistic and collusive practices. These practices have brought on too much suspicion

---

From *Perspectives on Antitrust Policy,* by A. Phillips, pp. 225–226, 230–243. Omission of footnotes.

of size, and too little faith in the integrity of the profit motives in assessing the benefits of mergers among banks. In short, it seems to me that what might be described as "procompetitive" policy toward banking would produce more, better, and cheaper banking services for the public than a policy of shelter and sanctuary.

• • •

THE REASONS FOR BANK MERGERS

. . . A good deal of the existing discussion of the reasons banks merge treats banks as a special kind of firm with special kinds of problems. Reasons having fairly wide currency are that banks merge because: (1) one of them has a management problem; (2) they wish to obtain capital more readily; (3) they wish to increase their loan limits; (4) they wish to offer a more complete range of banking services; (5) there are inevitable imperfections in the market for the stocks of small banks which causes both undervaluation and lack of liquidity; or (6) there is social prestige and political power associated with "bigness." I do not wish to imply that analysts who interpret bank motives for mergers in these terms are committing grievous error. They are needlessly complicating matters and taking the long way round to a rather simple proposition: banks merge because they find it profitable to do so.

I would suggest that if the tendency of banks to seek profits is examined closely enough, we shall have come a long way toward understanding the forces that lead to bank mergers. Detailed analyses of the implications of the profit motive for mergers have been presented by George Stigler and Edith Penrose.[1] It is an interesting and, I think, revealing exercise to apply their analyses to the case of banks.

Both Stigler and Penrose argue that an important reason why merger is a natural consequence of profit-seeking is that the dominant form of business organization in the economy is the corporation. This means that capital, market position, and good will once created are durable in time and separable from any particular set of owners. It means that there is a choice between purchasing what already exists or building anew. The choice between these alternatives will depend on which course for expansion is the more profitable. A bank can build new facilities and/or develop new markets on its own or it can acquire the facilities and markets of already existing banks. If a planned expansion is considered profitable regardless of the competitive implications for existing position of other banks or for the distribution of control over existing bank assets, then the bank will expand through acquisition only if acquisition is cheaper than doing so *de novo*. But if the change sought is in the market position of existing banks—through, say, a reduction in competition or a change in control over existing assets (the legal charter and established deposit relationships)—then merger may be the *only* way of achieving these objectives. In either case, acquisition will occur only if there are banks willing to part with their assets, including good will, and all other parts of their "establishment" that command a price, at a price equal to or less than their value to potential buyers. For an acquisition to occur, that is, there must be a buyer *and* a seller, both of whom expect to gain by the transaction. There must be a negotiable difference between "bid and asked."

I can provide only a general sketch of the way the profit motive, for both the buying and selling bank, tends to encourage mergers rather than *de novo* branching and internal expansion. In a reasonably perfect market, it should be noted, the purchase price of existing banks should correspond closely to the

---

[1]George J. Stigler, "Monopoly and Oligopoly by Merger," *American Economic Review,* vol. 40, no. 2 (May, 1950); Edith Penrose, *The Theory of the Growth of the Firm* (New York, 1960).

outlay necessary to build and develop a new bank, including in the latter the cost of forming the depositor good will, loan channels, and knowledge of the market which the existing bank stands ready to sell with its physical and financial assets.

One source of market imperfection which encourages acquisition of existing banks is the differential uncertainties involved. The intangible assets of existing banks can be accurately valued compared with the very uncertain cost of creating the same assets for a *de novo* branch. The reduction of uncertainty involved in acquisition would, by itself, cause the buying bank to offer what might appear to be an excessive premium over book or market valuation of the selling bank. In such circumstances, the buyer is paying what amounts to a risk insurance premium and the seller is receiving a larger discounted present value of future income from the sale than would be received from continued operations. Each is profit-maximizing.

Another reason for the existence of a negotiable difference between bid and ask might be thought of as a "management problem," but it is again a form of individual gain-seeking. It cannot be assumed that all bank owners view the future in the same way. That is, allowance must be made for different utility-risk-income-effort preferences among alternative prospective owners of the bank that would lead them to value the bank's assets in different ways. An example would be the case in which the owners of a bank in a rapidly growing new area find the problems of growth of the bank overwhelming. In order to meet its potential, the owners may have to install formal management techniques and deal with complexities such as an elaborate personnel training and development program and electronic customer accounting. In sum, life may become too complicated for and require too much effort from the present owners simply to maintain current income. A premium on the book value and market value of their shares may seem quite attractive, permitting the retention of income and a reduction of responsibility, time, and effort.

A negotiable difference in the valuation of the bank by its current and prospective owners may arise because of what might be called "differential loan capacities." The notion of a bank's loan capacity might be stated informally as follows: A bank operates under three constraints in its efforts to maximize net earnings. Two of these constraints are precisely defined. They consist of the balance sheet requirement (assets must equal liabilities plus capital) and the reserve requirement (a given percentage of deposits must be held as reserves). The third constraint is a complicated and informal limitation on the extent to which a bank may "lever" its portfolio. The constraint consists of a classification scheme which orders assets according to their quality and liabilities by their exposure to withdrawal. The upper limit on the leverage of the balance sheet becomes progressively more stringent as assets become more risky and liabilities more exposed.

If the capital and deposit position of the bank is given, then an upper bound on the set of proportions of a bank's portfolio in loans and investments is given. This upper bound is the bank's loan capacity. If yield rates on loans and investments can be forecast, then the bank can compute the addition to earnings an increase in capital (or deposits) can produce. A bank will find it profitable to expand if the addition to earnings from an increment to capital exceeds the cost of the increment to capital.

A bank's loan capacity, it must be emphasized, cannot be defined so precisely in practice. The leverage limit is not a formal constraint which imposes penalties for infraction but is at most a "guideline of prevailing practice." Most bank managements have independent judgment about capital adequacy, shaped by their own understanding about the stability of their deposit structure and modified by the investment alternatives that appear most attractive. The loan capacity of a bank operating in the "real world" is not a single boundary but a flexing band.

Differential loan capacities among banks may afford opportunities for joint profits which are larger than the sum of the independent profits before merger. If one bank, call it A, has "excess loan capacity" because it has specialized in loans (e.g., business loans) the demand for which has declined relative to other types of loans (e.g., consumer loans), it will be anxious to increase its earnings by developing a new line of loans. Bank A then has the choice of, say, branching into an area in which these types of loans are important, or purchasing a bank making such loans which it may develop. A negotiable difference between bid and ask will exist because banks already in the area must revise downward their estimates of the loans and deposits they can command should A decide to enter *de novo*. And Bank A will be willing to purchase other banks if they are cheaper than developing a new location.

Two banks, each of which has excess loan capacity, may be confronted with a local market in which the expansion of either would be at the expense of the other. If either or both attempt to expand, the profitability of both may be jeopardized by competitive effects on loan rates and costs. A joint venture in the form of a merger could be profitable to both sets of owners—though it should be noted that this type of profit-seeking through merger is at the expense of a reduction in competition.

It is also true that two banks, neither of which has excess loan capacity, may increase combined profits through a merger, even without a reduction in capital costs, an increase in yields on particular loans and investments, or economies of overhead in combined operations, if the ratio of incremental costs of placing particular loans and investments to the incremental revenue gained by these loans and investments is different between the two banks. The increase in profit which results from merger in these conditions is a rather peculiar case of gains from specialization.

I repeat that the above is no more than suggestive of an analysis of mergers through use of the profit motive. But, limited as it is, it appears to me to have more analytic promise than continued dependence on general assertions that banks merge because of management problems, imperfect capital markets, increased loan limits, et cetera. So long as emphasis on the profit motive is stressed, banks seem much less like a special kind of firm and seem amenable to conventional economic analysis.

THE NEED AND REQUIREMENTS FOR COMPETITION IN BANKING

An economic and political case for a procompetitive policy in banking, like the case against sin, is an easy one to make. But thinking through the full implications of such a policy is another matter.

Competition is important in banking for precisely the same reasons it is important in other industries. On the technical level, competition is the regulator that assures that each bank will combine resources in the "best" proportion to produce the "best" output. It will assure that monetary rewards reflect relative efficiencies and not positions in a power hierarchy. On a less abstract level competition in banking is a desideratum because it is *the* policy among feasible policies most likely to exploit differences of opinion among bankers on what is "an adequate return" and what constitutes "a maximum of risk." Without such differences of opinion, the banking system is much more likely to avoid than accommodate the marginal and innovative undertakings which become brilliant successes in service and profit. What is worse, the dead hand of monopoly administering credit is an exceedingly strong bulwark for the status quo in business organization and an exceedingly strong agent for those who would "keep competition within reasonable bounds" in other industries.

Only two basic objections can be raised against making competition the appropriate policy goal for our monetary system. The first is that economies of scale are such that competitive results are impossible to achieve. . . . I do not believe the facts support this argument.* The second is that banking, because of the need for safety and liquidity in the monetary system, must be supplemented by such extensive regulation that competition cannot operate even though the structure of the industry is conducive to competition. Put another way, the argument is that competition in the absence of regulation would cause extensive bank failures and seriously damage the public interest.

In the guise of protecting the public interest, many policies inconsistent with competition have arisen. Chief among these are barriers to entry—restrictions on the chartering of new banks and restrictions on *de novo* branching and branching by merger. The rationale is that without such barriers an "overbanked" situation would degenerate into a rash of bank failures.

It is difficult to give overbanking an operational meaning. Counting the number of banks in an area is an imperfect guide to whether the area is overbanked. For one thing, not all banks do the same kind of business. This is analogous to deciding that a city contains "too many" restaurants without checking to see which of these are lunch counters and which night clubs. Then too, a city with 10 banks can be seriously underbanked if these 10 banks are operating as a perfect cartel. A more workable index of overbanking may be bank earnings. If a group of banks in an area are earning less than a given percentage on capital, one might conclude that the area is overbanked. If these banks are earning more than a prescribed percentage on capital, one might conclude that the area is underbanked. The troublesome problem with such a measure is deciding whether low earnings are a result of too much competition or too little competence and aggressiveness.

It is important, I think, to be very clear about the nature of the conflict between a procompetitive policy and bank safety. If we mean by bank safety the safeguarding of the stockholders' equity then this conflict is present. Competition among banks, like competition among drug stores and lumber mills, does risk stockholders' equity. This, however, is the essence of an enterprise system where the entrepreneur is literally a "risker of capital." If, on the other hand, we take bank safety to mean *depositor safety,* then competition is *not* inconsistent with bank safety. The depositor can be, and in most circumstances is, insulated from bank failure through the capital cushion and insurance.

I am not saying that I seek a system that might lead to more bank failures. I do not think that anyone does. I am saying that we ought to have a hard second look at the basis for the conflict between competition and sound banking. The logical distinction of bank safety and depositor safety is part of such an appraisal.

Barriers to entry certainly do keep down the number of banks but it is not clear that they do much to help the bank lead a monastic existence. Banks face a variety of aggressive, expanding nonbank competitors in major components of their loan product lines. Entry barriers do little or nothing to insulate banks from competition for Government securities or tax exempt obligations; except in geographically isolated pockets of limited extent, they are ineffective against the nonbank competition for mortgages and consumer credit. These barriers can, however, contribute very significantly to keeping down the number of alternatives small business possesses. It is indeed questionable

---

*See, Selection 13—ed.

whether such an effect is a desirable one. Barriers to entry also strictly limit the alternatives of demand deposit account holders and the users of a variety of miscellaneous services conveniently packaged by banks—all in all vital services to the public.

It is difficult to avoid the conclusion that entry restrictions and other regulations have created opportunities for the growth of other financial intermediaries and that these have made substantial inroads on markets formerly served by banks. There is much to be said for an easier policy that would do more to allow banks to judge what is and what is not an overbanked area on the basis of what they think bank customers need and what they think they can earn. It is time, I think, for a stronger procompetitive stance on the part of the banking regulatory bodies.

A PROCOMPETITIVE POLICY FOR BANK MERGERS

Statutory authority is given to the banking agencies to approve or disapprove of merger and holding company cases in the Bank Holding Company Act of 1956 and the Bank Merger Act of 1960. The Supreme Court, in the recent *Philadelphia National Bank* case, construed the Clayton Act to cover bank merger cases.* The impact of the latter is, at best, uncertain but it is clear that under the Clayton Act the standard used is a competitive one—the determination of whether there is likely to be a substantial lessening of competition in any line of commerce in any relevant market.

The acts under which the banking agencies operate do not limit consideration to the competitive factor. On the contrary, the agencies must consider a *list* of factors, *one* of which is competition. The agencies are directed to examine the "banking factors"—character of management, financial history, prospects —and "the competitive factor." Congressional sponsors explicitly stated that neither of these factors would control decisions and "each must be considered in relation to the other." Congress clearly had in mind that the agencies should attend to a "weighted sum" of banking and competitive implications of a merger and that it may be necessary to substitute among them in particular instances.

This is a difficult assignment since both the interpretation of and weight given to each of the factors will vary from individual to individual. A procompetitive policy, however, would clarify some of the issues. Under such a policy, there would be a deliberate refusal by the regulatory agencies to collect and sift evidence which it can use to weigh motives. Mergers among banks, as we have seen earlier, can occur for a variety of reasons —most of them ultimately traceable to the profit motive. Banks do good but they are not "do-gooders." Moreover, motives are modified by changing circumstances. Banks may merge in an attempt to establish monopolistic dominance. They may merge to get out of business or quickly to reach into new lending activities or to follow a shift in the location of deposits. I do not know how one could go about untangling these motives, nor do I think that much in the way of a principle—or even a rule of thumb—could be developed to do so. Even if it could, good motives should hardly excuse a merger if monopolistic effects are present.

It suffices to assume the motive to merger is profit. In fact, if we really take the enterprise system seriously, we *must* assume that it is the profit motive that assembles resources to meet needs and that it is ordinarily an efficient and workable apparatus for this purpose. If this is accepted, regulating agencies need not enter into vastly complicated deliberations on whether the motives for a given merger are in the "public interest." If the regulatory body cannot demonstrate a significant reduction or potential reduction in

---

*See Selection 13—ed.

competition—a significant reduction in the alternatives of bank customers—it should conclude that the merger is not repugnant to the public interest. Such an approach would have the virtue of avoiding *ex cathedra* judgments on whether the profit motive ought or ought not to be allowed scope in particular merger cases. It also has the virtue of assuming that banks are best able to judge their stockholders' interests.

But what of the interests, convenience, and needs of the public? Will these also be served by this posture? In large part the answer to this question is implicit in the answer to the question "Do banks pay attention to their community's demand for bank services?" I think they do. A successful bank will be one which is able to determine or forecast its community's needs and shape the array of its service offerings to the pattern of demand. An unsuccessful bank will be one which does not attempt to determine or continually fails to forecast demand. A bank that persists in error or stubbornly refuses to adapt its service line, will experience declining earnings (customers will go elsewhere) and will become a failing rather than a going or growing concern. If other banks feel that this bank is not realizing the earnings potential of the area, they will have reason to consider the bank as a valuable piece of property and bid for it or attempt to enter the area *de novo*. In short, if the banking system is competitive, and if regulation is not misguided, a community's convenience and needs are not long unserved. This is the same as saying that earnings result from satisfying demand, not from not satisfying it. If there is a rule of thumb to be observed, it might be stated as follows: allow banks the judgment of their own best interest; the public's interest will best be served by vigorously promoting and maintaining competition.

The key to promoting and maintaining competition is a merger policy which explicitly recognizes the nature of the bank as a multiple-product, multiple-market firm. . . . Banks do not sell *a* product in *a* market but rather sell a range of products in a series of markets to borrowers having differential borrowing mobilities. The effect of mergers among banks must, thus, be judged in terms of the merger's impact on the structures of the multiple markets in which the banks participate—a judgment which, so far as I can see, reduces in the typical case to an assessment of the impact of the merger on the alternatives of the consumer and small business seeking demand deposit services and small loan accommodations. In any event, a sound merger policy must await empirical researches attempting to specify workable product and market concepts. Remarkably little energy has been spent in this direction.

Some feel that the regulatory agencies are incapable of a proper assessment of the problems in bank competition and merger. Perhaps they are right. I am, however, more optimistic because I believe that the considerations irrelevant to merger questions will largely vanish on proper exposure and that the durable consideration of competition can become the core of a consistent merger policy.

12 THE PHILADELPHIA BANK MERGER DECISION AND ITS CRITICS

EDWARD S. HERMAN

It is crucial in antitrust cases to delineate the relevant industry and market. For example, a firm manufacturing 90 percent of the aluminum siding used in the country may avoid monopoly classification if the proper industry is deemed to be the construction materials industry. Similarly, a corner grocery store may be subject to antitrust prosecution if the "market" is considered to be the immediate neighborhood. The courts in the *Philadelphia National Bank-Girard* case had to deal with both these issues before the question of the effect of the merger on competition could even be raised. All these problems are discussed in the following selection. In some cases litigated since the revision of the Bank Merger Act in 1966, lower courts have rejected the narrow Supreme Court definition of commercial banking. In one such ruling, mutual savings and savings and loan associations were deemed to be part of the banking industry.

Two unanswered questions remain: (1) Would a merger that tends to give a firm a 10 or 20 percent share of total bank assets in the relevant market be illegal? (2) Will the prevention of bank mergers in one market inhibit competitiveness in other markets? Because national banks may not lend to one customer a sum in excess of 10 percent of its capital, the application of antimerger regulations may prevent two medium-sized banks from competing in the market for large loans.

This article is focused on [three] issues raised in the PNB-Girard merger case.[1] . . . The issues discussed below are (1) the appropriate product line or "line of commerce" in the PNB-Girard case; (2) the scope of the market for banking services, particularly as it pertains to the proposed bank merger; [and] (3) the probable competitive effects of the merger in the Philadelphia area. . . .

I. THE LINE OF COMMERCE

A crucial problem in antitrust cases is establishing the product-market complex within which the forces of competition may be expected to operate. A "line of commerce" relates to the product aspect of this complex. From an economist's standpoint, a meaningful line of commerce would be an output type which is sufficiently differentiated from other outputs in the minds of buyers to make other products appear distinctly inferior substitutes. The greater the magnitude of the "gap in the chain of substitutes," the greater the potential monopoly power consequent on an increase in the concentration of sellers of a given product.

Commercial banks produce many different types of output, so that there are a considerable number of potential lines of commerce engaged in by this single institutional type. It is clearly possible for some of these lines of commerce to be en-

From Edward S. Herman, "The Philadelphia Bank Merger Decision and its Critics," *The National Banking Review*, 3, 391–400.

[1]*U.S. v. The Philadelphia National Bank, et al.*, 374 U.S. 321 (1963).

gaged in solely by commercial banks, and others to be supplied by banks along with non-banking institutions. Where this is the case, the relevant producers (or "industry") will be confined to commercial banks for some products and will extend beyond banks for others. From the standpoint of rational application of economics to antitrust problems, it would be perfectly sensible to limit the relevant producers to commercial banks if the outputs which they supply uniquely (or almost so) are of substantial importance in their own right. With the industry so defined, of course, little could be said about the competitive impact of structural change in that industry on a line of commerce in which non-banking institutions were major producers.

The Government contended that the outputs of non-banking financial institutions could be disregarded in evaluating the proposed merger, because such institutions do not provide serious competition to commercial banks in major product lines, particularly in the provision of checking account facilities and unsecured short-term business credit. The Government argued before the Supreme Court that "commercial banking" was itself the most relevant line of commerce, because all large banks provide a wide array of interrelated services in competition with one another, and "the most important elements of the service of commercial banks are supplied only by them." The District Court and the Supreme Court both accepted the view that commercial banking was a distinct line of commerce. The District Court laid stress on the interdependence of the various activities of commercial banks; the Supreme Court emphasized the uniqueness of bank services, some of which were alleged to be "so distinctive that they are entirely free of effective competition from products or services of other financial institutions; the checking account is in this category."

Messrs. Shull, Carson and Horvitz, and Motter* are almost uniformly critical of the Government and Court conception of the line of commerce appropriate to the merger case. But they tend to reject banking as a meaningful industry, not by explicitly denying that a large body of commercial bank customers is without effective substitutes for strategic banking services; they dispose of it more or less by implication on the grounds that other things, of somewhat uncertain importance, would be taken into account in an ideal treatment of these matters.

Consider the question of provision of demand deposit facilities. Carson and Horvitz note that commercial banks have no direct competition from other financial institutions in handling demand deposits, but they go on to point out that currency, travelers checks, register checks, and postal money orders are substitutes for demand deposits. Do they draw any conclusions as to whether these substitutes for checking accounts are sufficiently important for the bulk of demand deposit customers to limit seriously the potential monopoly power of commercial banks in this area? They do not: they conclude their discussion with the not very helpful statement that an appropriate economic analysis would take account of the substitutability among financial services.

Shull argues that demand deposits are held as a store of wealth, as well as a means of payment. Insofar as demand deposits serve the store of wealth function, they have important substitutes, and even active balances can be utilized more efficiently if the pressures are great. He calls attention to the economizing of demand deposit balances which took place under the tight money conditions of the last decade. Shull continues, "If bankers find they are losing demand deposits, or

*D. C. Motter, "Bank Mergers and Public Policy," *The National Banking Review,* 1, 89–100; D. Carson and P. M. Horvitz, "Concentration Ratios and Competition," *ibid.,* 1, 105–110; B. Shull, "Commercial Banking as a 'Line of Commerce,' " *ibid.,* 1, 187–206—ed.

not gaining demand deposits at a rate comparable to the growth of their communities, they will find little comfort in recalling that they have a monopoly of deposits in their 'means of payment' function." This is a rhetorical statement of little value in evaluating the implications of exclusive commercial bank provision of checking account facilities to the public. If a rise in price of a monopolized wonder drug induced doctors and patients to economize in its use, and even to replace it with other drugs in some uses, its producer might still "find comfort" in his generally strong monopoly position.

Shull's reference to the possibility of bankers finding that "they are losing demand deposits," points to another flaw in his discussion. If we are evaluating demand deposits as a distinctive *line of commerce,* it is not legitimate to count losses of such deposits to other commercial banks as relevant evidence of limits on bank monopoly power. Furthermore, if an asset holder shifts from demand deposits to a savings bank account, or to a claim against any other private financial institution, or to market assets, commercial bank demand deposits will not ordinarily be reduced. It is true that the demand deposits of individual banks may be affected by such shifts, but the extent to which this is true will depend on the commercial banking structure, not on the availability of substitutes for demand deposits.

In order to consider properly the issue of demand deposits as a line of commerce, we should ask: If commercial banking were completely monopolized (or were monopolized in Philadelphia and the three adjacent Pennsylvania counties), would this single bank possess substantially increased monopoly power in fixing service charges in its demand deposit function, or would this be prevented by the substitutability of currency and other asset alternatives? Unquestionably monopoly power would be significantly enhanced. The gap in the chain of substitutes as between demand deposits and other assets, for both payment and wealth-holding purposes, is substantial. It would seem evident (and it is not seriously questioned by Shull) that substitutes for demand deposits in carrying out the payment function are inadequate for many depositors now using checking accounts. The case with respect to demand deposits held as a store of wealth is more complicated and obscure, but people holding wealth in this sterile form are doing so either because of ignorance and inertia, or (more important) because they wish to remain completely liquid to be able to meet contingencies or to take advantage of expected future changes in asset prices. If these motivations are predominant, then it is unlikely that demand deposits held as a store of wealth will be very elastic to changes in service charges on checking accounts. This conclusion is reinforced by the fact that banks can discriminate in service charge adjustments by size of customer and type of service (and thus, to a degree, according to the availability of alternatives).

Motter, Carson and Horvitz, and Shull are also highly critical of the Court for overlooking other sources of short-term business credit. Motter mentions insurance companies as the overlooked competitors; Carson and Horvitz are particularly attentive to trade credit; and Shull stresses the growth of finance companies and open market credit. Again, none of these authors come to grips with the question—are these alternatives sufficiently important so that a significant body of bank borrowers would not be affected by a reduction in bank competition?

It is a well-known fact—unmentioned by Carson and Horvitz—that trade credit is frequently more expensive than bank credit, and is therefore regarded by those with the option of bank borrowing as a distinctly inferior alternative. It is also well established, and reiterated by members of the industry and the banks, that finance companies mainly lend to a special high risk small borrower whom banks tend to avoid. In the Federal Reserve System study, *Financing Small Business,* commercial finance companies and factors are described as follows:

> Their customers are estimated to number in the neighborhood of 15,000 business firms [whereas in October 1957 member banks had outstanding to small business 685,000 individual loans]. The clients of commercial finance companies and factors, by and large, are firms whose creditworthiness is such that they find it difficult to secure bank loans in the amounts needed. Generally, the form of credit extended by commercial finance companies involves substantial handling costs and above-average risk, so that the rates which they charge for their services are considerably higher than rates applicable on bank loans. . . . Commercial financing and factoring are particularly significant in a study of small business financing because credit is made available to small businesses that do not have access to bank credit or to the markets for equity and long-term debt funds.

Shull handles this by saying that "It could be argued that these other institutions are operating in a separate market—the higher-risk small loan market. But, in actuality, they have been chewing away at a larger loan market which formerly had been dominated by commercial banks." This is a questionable mode of expressing the facts of the case—the "It could be argued . . . But, in actuality, . . ." makes it sound as if the bulk of finance company business is competitive with bank lending, which is not so. The "chewing away" is still a fringe aspect of the commercial finance business, and the qualifications required by the growth of this sector are still quite small.

After noting that commercial banks now meet "a sizeable proportion of the needs of business for short-term funds," Shull concludes that "Given the trend in the short-term business loan market, it hardly seems safe to classify it, *a priori,* in any one particular local area, as a market in which commercial banks 'have little effective competition.' " Why the *trend* in the market should be more important than the *level*—which clearly indicates commercial bank predominance—is not shown. Furthermore, Shull does not establish that there is a trend away from the commercial bank as a supplier of short-term business credit, and certainly not for small businesses whose access to the open market is indirect. He seems to be relying heavily on Selden's finding of a rapid expansion in the commercial paper market in the last decade. But Selden also shows that the number of borrowers in the commercial paper market declined fairly steadily, from 4,395 in 1920 to 349 in 1961, while the average size of borrowing between 1920 and 1961 was rising from $255,000 to $4,481,000. Selden also notes that "Except for finance companies, every major group of borrowers has declined numerically since 1922."[2] Clearly, direct use of the open market by small commercial and industrial borrowers has been subject to a *falling* trend.

Since most of the expansion of commercial paper is accounted for by sales finance companies, which compete with banks almost exclusively in the financing of durable goods purchases (largely motor vehicles) by consumers and dealers, it is hard to see how this can be regarded as having major implications for the short-term business loan market. The "competitive threat" which such development presents to banks is the threat of alternatives available to specialized groups of large borrowers; the smaller business borrowers remain heavily dependent on commercial banks.

It should also be noted that Shull does not say that commercial banks have substantial effective competition in the Philadelphia area; he merely says that it would not be safe to say *a priori* that they do not. The implication is that the Court's

---

[2]Richard T. Selden, *Trends and Cycles in the Commercial Paper Market,* Occasional Paper 85, National Bureau of Economic Research, 1963, pp. 8 and 16–17.

statements on this matter were *a priori*. This disregards the fact that the Court's conclusions were presumably based on an extensive record in which these alternatives were considered at numerous points.

In conclusion, it is reasonable to regard commercial banks as sufficiently distinctive both in range of services rendered and in services uniquely offered to constitute a line of commerce, or a meaningful "industry." This follows mainly from their unique position in providing checking account facilities to the public and their special importance in making short-term credit available to business—particularly small and medium-size business. There are other services rendered by commercial banks in which their special position might justify ignoring outside competitors (e.g., the provision of personal trust services), but these two seem clearly in this category. And they are sufficiently important to justify looking at commercial banking as a distinct industry, although overlapping with other industries in many of its activities.

II. THE MARKET FOR BANKING SERVICES

In considering the appropriate "section of the country" the Supreme Court stated:

> The proper question to be asked in this case is not where the parties to the merger do business or even where they compete, but where, within the area of competitive overlap, the effect of the merger on competition will be direct and immediate. . . . This depends upon "the geographic structure of supplier-customer relations."

The Court recognized that designation of any specific area would be arbitrary and imperfect, but it concluded that, since banking is predominantly a local business, servicing individuals and businesses in the vicinity of the bank who would find it inconvenient to go elsewhere, the four-county area in which the merging banks do most of their business is the relevant market area. The Court acknowledged that banks outside the four counties may afford effective alternatives to customers within it, but it argued that "competition from outside the area would only be important to the larger borrowers and depositors. If so, the four-county area remains a valid geographical market. . . ."

The Court's position on the scope of the market for banking services is essentially sound. It is widely accepted by students of banking structure that a substantial part of the business of commercial banks, particularly small deposit and loan business, is derived from the immediate vicinity of the office and from customers with very restricted alternatives. Moreover, the record in the PNB-Girard case indicates not only that a large proportion of the small loans and deposits of the defendant banks originates in the four-county area (in dollar volume, 74% of the loans under $100,000; 89% of real estate loans under $50,000; 96% of the savings deposits of individuals; 89% of the demand deposits of individuals), but that, with the exception of large deposits and loans, bankers view their market as mainly local. For example, the testimony of an officer of Girard Trust indicated that in planning branch expansion in residential areas it is common to choose a radius of one mile in determining the geographic area from which a bank would be expected to draw the bulk of its business. A typical response to the question of the geographic area from which existing branch offices generate business is "(a)bout a mile radius to the location." The reason for the narrowness of this view of the prime service area of a banking office is that "(c)onvenience is an extremely important thing, and it is one of the reasons you establish a branch." When banks apply for branches, and the matter reaches the Banking Board of Pennsylvania, "They invariably submit to the Board, substantiated by maps and so on, what they call the particular local area from which they expect to draw the bulk of their business; and in practically every case which has appeared before the Board that area has a diameter of not more than a mile and a half or so." The testimony of Mr. Potts, president of PNB, is also illuminating for its frank minimization of the extent of competition between banks separated by more than a few miles (excepting, of course, competition for large loans and deposit accounts). Speaking of the Morrisville Bank, three to four miles from branches of PNB, Mr. Potts stated that competition between them would exist "to a limited degree, if at all." And referring to a bank that is five or six miles from a branch of PNB, Mr. Potts felt that "(t)he competition would be de minimis." These statements could be multiplied.

This evidence undoubtedly understates the extent to which nearby banks provide at least potential alternatives to bank customers; but it suggests that a substantial part of bank business is solicited and drawn locally, with convenience of location to customers a crucial factor in determining the service area of a bank. It also suggests that while the four-county area is smaller than the relevant market for some facets of bank business, it may also exaggerate the geographical scope of banking markets for other services and customers. Motter's conclusion that concentration statistics based on a four-county market are likely to overstate the degree of concentration in banking in the Philadelphia area does not take into consideration the existence of such intra-four-county submarkets.

Motter criticizes the Court, in part, for its reliance on the fact that "state law apparently recognizes [the four-county area] as a meaningful banking community in allowing Philadelphia banks to branch within it. . . ." Motter comments that "It is anomalous that a court so concerned with competition in banking should rely upon branching restrictions, which often act to stultify competition, as a factor in determining the proper 'section of the county.'" This seems to me a just criticism, although Motter gives it more attention than should be applied to what appears to be a parenthetical clause. The more important phrase following this clause, "and which would seem roughly to delineate the area in which bank customers that are neither very large nor very small find it practical to do their banking business," is given short shrift.

According to Motter, "(i)n the Philadelphia case, choice of *any one* section of the country, to the exclusion of others, can hardly lead to a realistic picture." If we substitute the word complete for realistic this statement would be true, but without operational significance. A really complete treatment would have to consider the product and market options of each actual and potential user of each service offered by commercial banks, clearly not a feasible project. Nor is it necessary; the Government and Court can legitimately select some facets of the banking business and some group of bank customers as likely to be affected by increased concentration in banking. If these services and customers are important, the market involving these services and customers is a relevant market.

III. THE COMPETITIVE IMPACT OF THE PROPOSED PNB-GIRARD MERGER ON THE PHILADELPHIA AREA

In the Philadelphia area the merger process sharply altered the banking structure between 1947 and 1960. In that period the number of banks with head offices in Philadelphia county (coterminus with the city) declined from 39 to 17, or by 44%. The number of banks with head offices in Delaware, Bucks and Montgomery counties declined from 69 to 26, or by 62%. For the four counties together the decline was from 108 to 43 banks, or 60%. At the same time the number of branch offices in the four counties increased from 70 to 240

(243%), and the total number of banking offices in the area increased from 178 to 283 (59%).

In 1947, the then largest bank in Philadelphia (PNB) controlled 23% of bank assets in the city and 20% of bank assets in the four-county area. The four largest banks held 57% of Philadelphia bank assets and 49% of bank assets in the four-county area. In 1960 the largest bank in Philadelphia (First Pennsylvania) controlled 25% of bank assets in Philadelphia and 23% of bank assets in the four-county area. The four largest banks controlled 76% of bank assets in Philadelphia and 69% of bank assets in the four counties.

The merger of PNB and Girard, if effected in 1960, would have reduced the number of banks in Philadelphia from 17 to 16 and the number in the four counties from 43 to 42. It would have increased the proportion of bank assets held by the largest bank in Philadelphia from 25 to 39%, and in the four counties from 23 to 36%. And it would have increased the fraction of bank assets held by the four largest banks from 76 to 85% in Philadelphia and from 69 to 78% in the four-county area.

The merger of PNB and Girard also would have altered sharply the relative size distribution of banks in Philadelphia. At the time of the trial the relative size of the six largest banks in Philadelphia (measured by total deposits) was: 100 (the largest bank), 97, 65, 45, 42, 24. If the merger had been consummated, the relative sizes would have been: 100, 62, 28, 26, 15, 8. The Government argued that the merger would give the new bank a competitive edge over its rivals, and might well induce defensive mergers by the remaining banks.

In evaluating these facts the Supreme Court stated:

> Specifically, we think that a merger which produces a firm controlling an undue percentage share of the relevant market, and which results in a significant increase in the concentration of firms in that market, is so inherently likely to lessen competition substantially that it must be enjoined in the absence of evidence clearly showing that the merger is not likely to have such anti-competitive effects. . . .
>
> Such a test lightens the burden of proving illegality only with respect to mergers whose size makes them inherently suspect in light of Congress' design in §7 to prevent undue concentration. Furthermore, the test is fully consonant with economic theory. That "competition is likely to be greatest when there are many sellers, none of which has any significant market share," is common ground among most economists, . . .
>
> The merger of appellees will result in a single bank's controlling at least 30% of the commercial banking business in the four-county Philadelphia metropolitan area. Without attempting to specify the smallest market share which would still be considered to threaten undue concentration, we are clear that 30% presents that threat.

The economic underpinning of these remarks is weak. As Abramson suggests in his Comment,[3] the Court's reference to the desirability of *insignificant* market shares is irrelevant to the Philadelphia case—both PNB and Girard (and several of their rivals) had significant market shares without merger. This was not a question of atomistic numbers versus oligopoly; it involved the issue of somewhat more or less concentrated oligopoly. Furthermore, not only is oligopoly the typical market structure of banking in urban centers in the United States, but Philadelphia also is (and, after the merger, would have been) relatively low on the scale of urban concentration. On the basis of 1956 data for concentration in the 53 reserve cities, after the merger Philadelphia still would have ranked only 32nd and 43rd in proportion of assets held by the largest and five largest banks, respectively.

It is true that a major and large capacity alternative would have been removed from the Philadelphia banking scene;

---

[3]V. Abramson, "Private Competition and Public Regulation," *The National Banking Review,* 1, 101–105—ed.

that the number of large banks (those with deposits over $100 million) in the Philadelphia area would have been reduced from 7 to 6 (in Philadelphia) and 8 to 7 (in the four counties); and that this reduction, plus the substantial edge in size which the new bank would possess over its rivals might be conducive to more effective leadership (and less effective competition). Further merger activity to rectify the heightened inequality in size might well have followed. Any adverse competitive effects or induced merger activity are conjectural, however, as there are no known strategic properties attaching to the changes in numbers or size distribution consequent on the proposed merger, or the 30% market share cited by the Court. Although there is a well grounded expectation that *drastic* reductions in numbers and increases in concentration will reduce competition, there is no scientific basis for predicting any significant effect on competition that would have resulted from the proposed merger of PNB and Girard.

The Court's reply to this line of reasoning was that Congress was so concerned with the rising tide of concentration that Section 7 of the Clayton Act was enacted to permit intervention in the process of concentration without "elaborate proof of market structure, market behavior, or probable anticompetitive effects." The Court went on to say that a merger which significantly increases market concentration "is so inherently likely to lessen competition substantially" that it must be enjoined in the absence of evidence to the contrary. Now these are separable lines of argument that have no necessary connection. The first is that in Section 7 Congress has attempted to ease the burden of the Government in proving mergers illegal. The second is the proposition that significant increases in concentration (used in a non-tautological sense), such as that involved in the proposed PNB-Girard merger, have a high probability of impairing competition seriously. The second proposition, as indicated above, must be rejected as unproven. The first statement is apparently valid, and involves the Government, defense, and the courts in the difficult problem of decision-making under conditions of inadequate information.

Congress has instructed the Executive and courts to halt monopolies "in their incipiency and before consummation," but it has provided no criteria to facilitate this. Economics has little to contribute to predictions of this sort, and even that little would require inquiries so time-consuming that the law would be stultified by delay. The courts, with some legislative sanction, have consequently tended to adopt arbitrary rules (such as the 30% market share benchmark suggested in the PNB-Girard decision), with rebuttable presumptions that mergers which carry market shares beyond certain limits will have anti-competitive effects. Such rules have a crude underlying economic rationale, but they are arbitrary, and can be defended only as pragmatic necessities to implement a philosophy of decentralized power. Whatever the merits and survival power of such rules, they have clearly shown the capacity to affect merger activity in the short run.

• • •

13 RETURNS TO SCALE IN COMMERCIAL BANKING

STUART I. GREENBAUM

Look for the methods and conclusions reached by a variety of investigations into the question of economies in scale in banking. It is not surprising that areas of disagreement exist. However, note with care the general conclusion that very small banks are inefficient, despite the fact that the relative efficiency of such banking giants as California's Bank of America, with assets of some $20 billion, or the immense New York City banks remains unexplored.

• • •

The following discussion will focus on the cost studies of David A. Alhadeff, Irving Schweiger and John S. McGee, Lyle E. Gramley, Paul M. Horvitz, Stuart I. Greenbaum, and George J. Benston.* These studies are rich in detail and subtleties reflecting the complexities involved in analyzing bank costs. This brief survey cannot do complete justice to the authors. The following will sketch the approach employed in each study, the data used, and the findings obtained. The significance and position of each study within the collection of works will be indicated, but a detailed criticism of each study will not be attempted.

Recent bank-cost studies attempt to infer returns to scale from estimated long-run cost-function parameters. Although common threads are found running through these studies—resulting largely from common data-availability problems—they are strikingly diverse in terms of model specification. Yet, with one exception [Gramley], all are aimed at shedding light on public-policy questions. All of these studies employ concepts of private, as opposed to social, costs, and possible divergences have not been carefully considered. For example, the relationship between bank size or concentration and the cost of public regulation has been ignored, as has the fact that bank reserves are a scarce resource to the banking system but practically a free good to the community.

Alhadeff's *Monopoly and Competition in Banking* was seminal. However, the empirical aspects of his analysis are vulnerable to criticism. Based on operating-

From Stuart I. Greenbaum, "Competition and Efficiency in the Banking System—Empirical Research and Its Policy Implications," *Journal of Political Economy,* 75, 465–474. Reprinted by permission.

*David A. Alhadeff, *Monopoly and Competition in Banking* (Berkeley: Univ. of California Press, 1954); Irving Schweiger and John S. McGee, "Chicago Banking," *Journal of Business,* 34, 203–366; Lyle E. Gramley, *A Study of Scale Economies in Banking* (Kansas City: Federal Reserve Bank of Kansas City, 1962); Paul M. Horvitz, "Economies of Scale in Banking," in Commission on Money and Credit, *Private Financial Institutions* (Englewood Cliffs, N.J.: Prentice-Hall, 1963), pp. 1–54; Stuart I. Greenbaum, "Banking Structure and Costs: A Statistical Study of the Cost-Output Relationship in Commercial Banking" (Ph.D. dissertation, Johns Hopkins University, 1964); George J. Benston, "Branch Banking and Economies of Scale," *Journal of Finance,* 20, 312–332 [reprinted in part as the following selection]; and George J. Benston, "Economies of Scale and Marginal Costs in Banking Operations," *National Banking Review,* 2, 507–549—ed.

ratio data for 1938–50 published by the Federal Reserve Bank of San Francisco, Alhadeff found that:

> If unit costs for different size banks were plotted on a scatter diagram with unit costs on the ordinate, and size of bank (or level of output) on the abscissa, a curve drawn by least squares would decline fairly sharply in the early ranges [up to perhaps $5 million in total deposits], remain fairly constant over a wide intermediate range [up to $50 million or more in total deposits], and then decline again in the range of the largest banks [over $275 million in total deposits].

... Using tabular inspection, Alhadeff related operating expenses to a host of variables, the most important of which was total earning assets—loans plus investments. The signal importance of the earning-assets variable derives from Alhadeff's identification of it as his measure of bank output. In fact, however, Alhadeff relates the ratio of operating expenses to earning assets to still another variable—total deposits—in order to derive his cost curves.

The problem of output definition pervades the literature and, therefore, justifies special consideration. If the ultimate findings of bank-cost studies are to have cogency, the measures of output employed must be related to community well-being. . . . Output measures that cannot be interpreted in terms of the socially relevant services produced by commercial banks should be considered suspect.

The use of earning assets to measure output, as suggested by Alhadeff, implies that lending is the primary productive activity of commercial banks. This view finds support in the fact that in recent years approximately 90 percent of the banking system's current earnings were directly attributable to lending activity. However, the use of earning assets as an output measure also implies that all forms of bank credit are perfect substitutes to the community, that is, a $100 consumer loan is the same as a $100 business loan, which is the same as a $100 interbank loan. The earning-assets measure may be thought of as a price-weighted index in which all the weights are of equal value. Observed differences in interest rates on various types of bank credit argue against the use of this type of output measure.

Because earning assets is a balance-sheet variable—as are deposits and total assets—still other doubts are raised regarding its use as a measure of bank output. Although the use of stock variables to represent flow concepts is not uncommon, when flow measures are readily available the reasons for substituting stocks should be explicit and reasonably compelling. Such arguments have not been made. In their absence, income-statement variables, such as current operating earnings, would appear to be preferable.

Emphasis on the selection of an appropriate output measure has been questioned by those who have argued that earning assets, deposits, total assets, and current operating earnings are so highly correlated that the issue is more apparent than real. This contention is demonstrably false. In regressing current operating expense on the various suggested measures of output, I obtained adjusted coefficients of determination ranging from 0.015 to 0.701. Moreover, the estimated total cost equations were linear, quadratic, or cubic depending on the measure used.

Horvitz employs essentially the same methods and model used by Alhadeff. However, he uses Federal Deposit Insurance Corporation data on all insured banks for the period 1940–60 and data provided by the Federal Reserve System on all member banks for 1959. Not surprisingly, Horvitz' findings are similar, in many respects, to those of Alhadeff.

> Over most of the range of bank size the decline in costs is very small and only in the largest size class was the decline substantial. This result bears out the description of costs . . . in Alhadeff's work. . . . The important

point . . . is that once a bank reaches the relatively small size of $5 million of deposits, additional size does not result in reduced costs to any great extent until the bank reaches the giant size of over $500 million. This indicates that a small bank can compete on even terms with very large banks.

. . . The Horvitz study is perhaps best viewed as an attempt to check Alhadeff's findings with data of broader geographic and temporal coverage. Consequently, it suffers similar shortcomings. . . .

The Schweiger-McGee study, "Chicago Banking," differs from those of Alhadeff and Horvitz because it uses regression analysis and, perhaps more important, because it employs a different cost-equation specification. The dependent variable in the Schweiger-McGee cost equation is the ratio of current operating expense to total assets, and the primary independent variable—the output measure—is total deposits. The regression equations are calculated using transformed data—which may cause serious estimating problems—for all member banks for the year 1959. In addition, costs of member banks in the Chicago Federal Reserve District for 1959 are analyzed using tabular inspection. The authors summarize their findings as follows: "Banks of less than $50 million in deposits can realize marked cost savings by growing. Cost savings from larger size are very sharply reduced for banks larger than $50 million in deposits." . . .

In *A Study of Scale Economies in Banking,* Gramley went one step beyond Schweiger and McGee. It will be remembered that Alhadeff and Horvitz drew their inferences directly from tabular data while Schweiger and McGee employed regression analysis in conjunction with transformed deposit data. Gramley applied regression analysis to data from individual-bank earning and condition reports, perhaps the richest source of banking information. The data are a sample—approximately stratified randomly—of 270 Kansas City District member banks, and each observation was an average of annual data for the years 1956–59. The banks in the sample were virtually all unit banks. Gramley also differed from his predecessors in his specification of the cost equation. The ratio of current operating expense to total assets was his dependent variable, and total assets served as the primary independent variable.

Gramley is one of the few who displays serious concern about the output problem. He states that the primary argument of his cost function—total assets—is not to be interpreted as a measure of, or proxy for, bank output. Gramley's inability to handle the output problem to his own satisfaction led him to circumscribe carefully the interpretation of his findings. He states that "the study . . . does not seek to determine whether, from the standpoint of achieving maximum social efficiency, the banking system should be composed of small or large units."

Gramley indicates that the cost-asset ratio is best expressed as a negative linear function of the logarithm of assets. Thus, average costs decline sharply with size increases among small banks, but the cost curve flattens out as banks become larger. A subsequent acceleration in the decline of costs among larger banks is not observed, but the largest banks in Gramley's sample are considerably smaller than those in Horvitz' sample.

Although my study of bank costs was under way before the publication of Gramley's work, it can be viewed as an attempt to fill a gap in his study. To quote Gramley:

The Nation's economic welfare depends very much on how efficiently resources are employed in the banking industry as a whole as well as in other lines of activity. That is why many studies of scale economies are directed specifically toward the social concept of efficiency in resource allocation.

But to attempt an evaluation of scale economies in banking from so broad a perspective would entail a much more extensive investigation than is undertaken in the present study. The question of what constitutes "output" of banks, and how the various dimensions of output should be given weights representing social valuations, is quite profound; an attempt to answer it would involve an excursion into areas of economic theory and theories of social welfare.

These are the questions that define the focus of my study. Dissatisfaction with the measures of output used in earlier studies prompted the development of a new alternative designed to impart greater public-policy relevance to the findings of bank-cost studies. The new measure initially divides output into two components: lending and all other. Lending output was defined as the gross yield-weighted sum of the diverse earning assets in each bank's portfolio. Yield weights were obtained by experimenting with least-squares regression equations of the following general form:

$$\frac{Y_i}{A_i}=b_0+\sum_{j=1}^{n}b_j\frac{Z_{ij}^{\wedge}}{A_i^{\wedge}}+\sum_{j=n+1}^{m}b_jX_{ij}+u_i$$

where Y_i is the ith bank's gross operating income directly attributable to lending; A_i is total assets of the ith bank; Z_{ij} is the ith bank's holding of the jth type of earning asset; X_{ij} are variables designed to isolate systematic interfirm price variation attributable to imperfect output markets; $b_0, b_1, \ldots, b_m$ are calculated net regression coefficients; and u_i is a stochastic term. Experimentation indicated that sixteen classifications of earning assets provided ample disaggregation and satisfactorily homogeneous earning-asset groupings.

Output of the ith bank was defined as:

$$Q_i=\sum_{j=1}^{16}b_jZ_{ij}^{\wedge}+W_i$$

where W_i is a measure of non-lending output—defined as the ith bank's current operating revenue minus Y_i. The less elegant treatment of non-lending output was the result of difficulties in finding quantity measures for non-lending services, but, in aggregate, less than 10 percent of current operating revenue was directly attributable to these sources. The chief merits of this output measure include its explicit recognition of: (1) the multiproduct nature of commercial bank output, (2) interbank price differences resulting from imperfect markets, and (3) production as a flow process. The principal shortcoming of the Q_i output measure is its failure to treat transaction size as a product characteristic. It is prima facie implausible to assume community indifference to variations in average transaction size of bank services: a \$10,000 loan is not a perfect substitute for twenty loans of \$500. If average transaction size is positively related to bank size, ignoring average transaction size will probably result in overstating economies of scale.

The basic data were obtained from 1961 earning and condition reports for 745 individual member banks in the Kansas City Federal Reserve District and 413 member banks in the Richmond Federal Reserve District. The Kansas City District is almost entirely a unit-banking area, whereas the Richmond District has a substantial number of branch systems. Regressing current operating expense on the output measure indicated U-shaped average cost curves in the Kansas City District, with optimal-size banks of approximately \$300 million in deposits. In studying the Richmond subsample of branch banks, evidence of independent plant and firm effects on cost was found. Not only are there savings attendant to increases in plant size, but, in addition, cost reductions accompany increases in firm size when output per plant is held constant. . . .

Benston's study has a number of attributes that set it apart from earlier works. Perhaps most interesting is the eschewal of a single-valued measure of output; "each bank was divided into six separate units—'producing' demand deposits, time deposits, mortgage loans, instalment loans, business loans, or securities." Each type of output is measured in terms of numbers of loan or deposit accounts with the average dollar volume of transactions included among the arguments of the cost functions. Therefore, Benston avoids one of the major shortcomings of my formulation. However, Benston's approach has a number of questionable aspects.

Consider that elements from both sides of the bank's balance sheet—deposits and earning assets—are treated as types of output. From the viewpoint of the individual bank, deposits reflect borrowing while earning assets reflect lending. Banks pay others to hold deposits, not the reverse. In effect, deposits reflect the bank's purchase of the services of money. They may be thought of as a substitute for capital to the individual bank. These considerations suggest that deposits are more usefully thought of as a factor input to the bank.

The rejection of a unidimensional or single-valued index of output also introduces difficulties. If an over-all assessment of returns to scale is desired, some combinatorial scheme must be introduced. The stage of the analysis at which the output mapping should take place is open to question, but Benston presents disparate and unreconciled findings. Without additional bases for interpreting the findings, generalized interfirm comparisons are impossible, and the analysis stands incomplete.

Benston's data are generated by the *Functional Cost Analyses* published annually by the Federal Reserve Bank of Boston. Taken from questionnaires submitted by eighty to eighty-three banks, the data apply to operations in 1959, 1960, and 1961. The surveyed banks range in asset size from $3.4 million to $55.0 million. It should be noted that Benston's results depend upon the individual banker's allocation of his expenses—according to prearranged guidelines—to the various output categories.

Benston finds that although "there are economies of scale of direct cost with respect to the number of deposit accounts or loans, these are not great: efficiency of operations is not largely a function of bank size." . . .

If the recent bank-cost studies are judged on the basis of whether they have supplied the reliable information necessary for evaluating regulatory policy, they have failed. But this is a harsh standard, especially since the first of these studies was published but twelve years ago. The gradual improvement among these studies and the nature of the shortcomings in the most recent works suggest that continued effort can yield handsome dividends in terms of the sought-after information. The increasing attention devoted to conceptual problems is especially noteworthy. This is evidenced in the later studies by advances in defining bank output. . . . Improvements in the techniques of bank-cost analysis are especially significant in light of the imminence of automated payments, which will inevitably alter the underlying production function. Only the scope of this change remains in doubt, and those who have studied the question argue that automation of payments will have a profound impact. Therefore, current findings relating to economies of scale are likely to be obsolete in the near future. The transitory quality of such findings is in contrast to the probable transferability of advances in the techniques of cost analysis. The practical irreversibility of banking-structure policy changes and the imminence and estimated impact of automated payments might well counsel against policy changes based on convincing cost-study findings, even if they were available.

• • •

I have emphasized that firm findings regarding economies of scale are not at hand. However, study of the literature cannot fail to convey some impressions on this question. My review of this literature has led me to the view that small banks—say $10 million or less in assets—are probably grossly inefficient. It seems likely that significant economies of scale prevail beyond the $10 million asset size, but they are probably of a smaller order of magnitude. The conditions under which banks of more than $300 million in assets operate are much more difficult to judge. The studies done have run the gamut, observing rising costs, falling costs, and essentially constant costs. Thus, the optimal bank size is unknown.

The inefficiency of smaller banks may be attributable to their inability to spread overhead costs, limitations to specialization among employees, high transactions costs of moving funds in small amounts, loan risk interdependencies, and limitations on risk pooling. Some of these problems can be overcome by correspondent banking facilities, but the impression is that they are not overcome. This suggests that correspondent facilities leave much to be desired.

• • •

In the absence of regulation of entry, merger, and branching, and further assuming no improvement in correspondent banking facilities, small banks probably would be eliminated gradually and replaced with branches of larger institutions. The extent of consolidation that would occur is uncertain, but international comparisons suggest that the industry might ultimately be composed of fewer than one hundred firms, perhaps fewer than fifty. Such a consolidation might result in real savings on the order of $1 billion per year.* The distribution of such savings among factor services in banking, consumers of bank services, and the community at large would remain to be resolved. In any case, the $1 billion per year may be viewed as the cost of the present regulatory framework and should be weighed against the advantages inherent in present policies.

• • •

*This estimate is based on research conducted by Professor Greenbaum—ed.

14 BRANCH BANKING AND ECONOMIES OF SCALE

GEORGE J. BENSTON

The author of the following selection concentrates on small and medium-sized branch and unit banks. Because the data available to him were limited, he was forced to neglect the giants. In this limited endeavor, however, he finds, not surprisingly, that a given amount of business can be accomplished more cheaply under one roof than under many. The slight economies of scale that appear to exist for middle-sized banks are insufficient to overcome the additional costs of branch banking; even merging a few unit banks into a branch system will not lower the costs of doing business. On the other hand, the costs are not substantially higher, either; thus there seems to be little justification in supporting unit banking by restrictions on branching because of the cost aspects. Moreover, the additional convenience of being able to bank at a variety of locations is undeniable.

I. INTRODUCTION

Which organizational form, unit or branch, for the banking industry best serves the public welfare? This question has prompted much of the recent research on the organization of the banking industry. This [article] focuses on one unresolved aspect of this larger question; namely, which form is most efficient with respect to private costs and benefits. The empirical findings reported here hopefully will complement the recent, excellent research done on the relative ability and desire of branch and unit banks to serve local communities.

The controversy between unit and branch banking supporters would be simplified if entry into the banking industry was not restricted; then we could say, "let the best bank win." However, even with free entry and no limitations on the form of organization of banks, it still would not be clear whether the successful banks were those that operated most efficiently or those that were able to maintain oligopolistic market arrangements. Therefore, it is important to determine whether the branch or unit form of bank organization is inherently more efficient.

This [article] focuses on the costs of banking operations. Excluded from consideration are differences between branch and unit banks that might arise from differences in fund acquiring and fund using opportunities, capital requirements, and ability to get approval from the regulatory agencies to establish new offices. Rather, my inquiry is limited to the costs of processing deposits, loans and securities, of administration, business promotion and occupancy—in short, the costs of operating banks.

Differences in operating costs between branch and unit banks may arise from two sources. First, branch banks, *per se*, may be more or less costly to operate than unit banks of the same size. Second,

From George J. Benston, "Branch Banking and Economies of Scale," *Journal of Finance,* 20, 312–318, 326–328, 330–331. Reprinted by permission.

branch banks may be able to grow larger than unit banks and take advantage of economies that may come from large-scale operations.

The claims and counter-claims about relative operating efficiencies usually have been supported by descriptive reasoning. For example, opponents of branch banking claim that branch banks have higher operating costs than unit banks that possess the same output because it is costly to coordinate the operations of more than one banking office. Branch banking proponents counter with the assertion that branch banks tend to employ more "progressive" branch managers who operate their branches more efficiently than the department managers of unit banks operate their departments. Economies of large-scale operations are claimed for branch banks because they usually are larger than unit banks. That economies of scale do exist has been generally assumed rather than demonstrated.

My study is directed towards providing empirical evidence (1) on the operations costs or cost savings associated with branch banking, *per se,* (2) on the economies or diseconomies of scale excluding consideration of branch banking and (3) on the joint effects of (1) and (2). Thus answers are provided to the following questions:

1. Is a unit bank of a given size more efficient than a branch bank of the same size, *ceteris paribus,* and, if so, how much are these costs and in which specific banking services are they found?

2. If a bank should increase its demand deposits, installment loans, or other banking service by, say, ten percent, by what percentage will its costs increase, irrespective of its being a unit or branch bank?

3. If branch banks, *per se,* are more expensive to operate than unit banks, but if there are economies of scale, will merging several unit banks into one branch bank result in lower or higher operating costs, and in which banking services will these net costs or cost savings be found?

The data and method of analysis used for this study are described in Section II. The findings derived from these data are presented in detail in Section III and summarized in Section IV. . . . A brief conclusion follows.

II. DATA AND ANALYSES USED

I analyzed the operating cost and output data from sample of 83, 82, and 80 New England member banks for the years 1959, 1960 and 1961. Because the banks ranged in size from $3.5 to $55.0 million in total assets, these samples are not fully representative of the population of United States banks although over half of the number of commercial banks in the United States are within this range. Further, the largest branch bank in the sample operated twelve branches, far short of such giant branching systems as the Bank of America or Chase Manhattan. In spite of these limitations, this study can serve as a useful supplement to the broader-based data noted below.

The data upon which the study is based were gathered by the Federal Reserve Bank of Boston. The Bank has conducted a cost analysis service for member banks in the First Federal Reserve District since 1957. Staff from the participating banks attend a seminar in which they are given detailed instructions on filling in the cost analysis forms. They allocate direct costs to the banking services of demand deposits, time deposits, mortgage loans, installment loans, business loans and securities. Many costs are easy to allocate: savings tellers work only on time deposits and specific loan forms are related to the loans made. However, some costs, such as the salary of an officer in a small bank who makes all types of loans, had to be allocated. These allocations of salaries are based on time sheets. Other costs are allocated by means of specific analyses. Most of the banks included in the samples had several years of experience in filling in the forms, and the data they reported were carefully checked by the staff of the Federal Reserve Bank of Boston.

The costs of banking operations were analyzed as a function of output, product mix, branch and unit banking, factor prices, mergers, and other variables that affect costs.

Output is defined as the average number of deposit accounts or loans outstanding during the year. An average of the number outstanding at each month end was computed to reduce the effect of randomness and to approximate more closely the flow of work processed rather than the stock of work on hand at a particular time. This variable, instead of the dollar volume of loans and securities, was used because the operations work of banks, and hence costs, is closely related to the number of deposit accounts and loans they process. Had output been defined as the dollar volume of loans and securities, a finding of lower costs per dollar that results from a bank's having processed accounts and loans with larger outstanding balances might have been mistaken for operating efficiency.

The effect of product mix on operations costs was controlled by analyzing relatively homogeneous banking services individually. Six banking services were distinguished: demand deposits, time deposits, mortgage loans, installment loans, business loans, and securities. Intercorrelations among these services were controlled and accounted for by three methods: (1) indirect costs, which affect all of the banking services, were not included with direct costs but were analyzed separately, (2) "total assets" or a similar variable was included in each of the banking service regressions to estimate the effect of over-all bank size on individual services, and (3) variables that specified outputs of banking services that are related to the one analyzed were included in the regressions where specific interrelations of possible joint cost situations were thought to exist. Indirect costs were separated into three categories: administration, business development, and occupancy expenses. These were analyzed individually.

Analysis of each banking service and type of indirect cost separately enables a determination of the specific banking function with which economies of scale and/or branch banking costs are associated. This identification should be helpful for policy decisions.

Approximately half of the sampled banks are branch banks, as Table 1 shows. The effect of branch banking on costs was estimated by including one of three possible variable forms in the regressions: (1) the number of banking offices (*NO*); (2) a dummy variable where 1 = branch bank and O = unit bank (B_0); and (3) a dummy variable matrix where:

$B_1 = 1$ for banks with one branch, 0 for other banks,
$B_2 = 1$ for banks with two branches, 0 for other banks,
$B_3 = 1$ for banks with three branches,

Table 1. Percentage Distribution of Unit and Branch Banks

			Number of Branches				
Year	Unit Banks	Branch Total	One	Two	Three	Four	Five to Twelve
1959	55%	45%	17%	17%	7%	4%	0%
1960	45	55	17	15	12	4	7
1961	44	56	18	14	11	5	8

0 for other banks,
$B_4 = 1$ for banks with four branches, 0 for other banks,
$B_5 = 1$ for banks with five or more branches, 0 for other banks.

The form used was the one that caused the greatest reduction in the adjusted standard error of estimate.

The dummy variable matrix, which in most instances fits the data best, has several advantages over the other forms. This form requires the least specification of the functional relationship between branch banking and costs. . . . The dummy variable matrix also provides data on the consistency of the relationship between costs and branching. For example, a finding of significant coefficients only for the four-branch (B_4) but not for the other dummy variables would lead one to suspect the validity of conclusions drawn from the data. Finally, the additional costs of operating different-sized branching systems can be computed readily from the coefficients of the dummy variables.

Other determinants of operations costs, such as the average size of deposit and loan balances outstanding, factor prices, the rate of change and variability of output, mergers, the number of transit items, checks and deposits processed per demand deposit amount, etc., were accounted for by inclusion of additional independent variables in the regressions.

The variables were transformed to common logarithms for several reasons. First, this procedure resulted in approximate homoskedasticity among the residuals from the regressions. Second, *a priori* reasoning suggested a multiplicative rather than an additive relationship among the variables. This is especially important for the branch banking variable, because any additional costs should be a function of the size of banks, rather than a constant amount. . . . Third, when the squares of the logarithms of the number of deposit accounts or loans were included as independent variables, the equation was capable of estimating any theoretically recognized cost curve. In this manner, the linearity assumption, for which cost studies often are criticized, was avoided.

III. THE FINDINGS FOR INDIVIDUAL BANKING SERVICES AND TYPES OF INDIRECT EXPENSES

The results of the analyses of the demand deposit, installment loans, time deposits, mortgage loans, business loans and securities banking services and the indirect expenses of administration, business promotion and occupancy are given in this section.* Substantial additional costs of branch banking were found for demand deposit, installment loan and occupancy expenses, and small additional costs for indirect administration expenses.

Two types of tables are presented. One (such as Table 2 below) shows the additional direct operations costs of the banking services of branch banks with various numbers of branches over unit banks, where all other factors (such as the level of output) are accounted for. The percentage increase in cost and the dollar amount computed at the geometric means of the output and other variables are given. These tables provide answers to the first question posed above: Is a unit bank more efficient than a branch bank of the same size, *ceteris paribus*, and if so, how much are these costs and in which specific banking services are they found? The additional costs of a four-branch bank over a three-branch bank, for example, also can be computed from these tables by simple subtraction.

The second table (such as Table 3 below) combines the effects of cost savings due to economies of scale with the additional costs of branch banking to answer

---

*Only the analysis for demand deposit service, which is representative of the technique used for the others, is reproduced here—ed.

the question: Will merging several unit banks into one branch bank result in lower or higher operating costs, and in which banking services will these net costs or cost savings be found? This table also shows the cost savings that are derived from economies of scale and the additional branch banking costs that are expected at the greater level of operations that a newly merged branch bank might experience. These estimates are given in terms of percentages of direct costs. Thus, for example, one can observe in Table 3 that a consolidation of five unit banks into a branch bank with four branches is estimated to result in additional direct demand deposit costs of 9.7 percent from the 1960 sample. This percentage increase is the difference between the additional costs of branch banking that would be incurred at the new scale of operations of 24.1 percent (28.2 percent from Table 2 times 85.6, the elasticity of costs with respect to output at the new level of output) and the cost savings due to the increased scale of operations of 14.4 percent.[1]

Demand Deposit Service

Demand deposit operations expenses average 35 per cent of the total operating expenses of the banks sampled. These expenses (in common logarithms) were analyzed as a function of the following independent variables (all of which are in common logarithms):

N_d = Average number of demand deposit accounts outstanding.

A_r = Average balance of regular checking accounts only.

SC_r = Service charge rate on regular checking accounts only.

WIN = Weighted activity items—checks, deposits, and transit items—per account.

RN_d = Ratio of the number of regular to the total number of accounts, in percentages.

W = Relative wages per employee in each bank's county.

B_1, B_2, B_3, B_4, B_5 = Matrix of branch dummy variables described above, where $B_1 = 1$ for a bank with 1 branch and 0 for banks with other than one branch, etc.

The squares of the number of accounts (N_d), average balance of accounts (A_r) and weighted activity items per account (WIN) variables were included in the regression along with the non-squared forms, but they were subsequently omitted because they were not significant or were collinear with the unsquared terms.

The one-branch variable (B_1) regression coefficient was smaller than the standard error of its coefficient and thus is not considered to be significant. The additional cost over unit banks of performing the same volume of operations with two, three or four, etc., branches was computed from the regression coefficients of the branch banking dummy variables, all of which were at least two and one-half times the size of their standard errors. These are summarized in Table 2.

It is interesting to note that the increase in additional branch banking costs is less than proportional to the increase in the number of branches operated. Hence, it appears that additional branch banking costs *per banking office* decrease with the number of banking offices oper-

[1]These calculations also can be shown by considering the following relationships. Let C_i = the operations costs of unit bank i. Then $\sum_i^n C = S =$ the sum of the costs of the unit banks that merged to form a branch bank. The new branch's costs are subject to economies of scale by the percentage E, and thus are equal to $S \cdot E$, but also are higher due to the additional costs of branch banking by the percentage A. Thus, the branch bank's additional costs are equal to $S(E \cdot A)$ and its costs savings due to economies of scale are $S(1-E)$. $E \cdot A$ is the percentage increase due to branch banking and $1-E$ the percentage decrease due to economies of scale.

Table 2. Demand Deposit Service, Additional Direct Operations Cost of Branch Banking Over Unit Banking[a]

Number of Branches	Additional Cost Computed at Geometric Means 1960	Additional Cost Computed at Geometric Means 1961	Percentage Increase in Cost 1960	Percentage Increase in Cost 1961
2 (B_2)	$22,400	$16,000	21.6	15.9
3 (B_3)	17,300	23,700	16.7	22.4
4 (B_4)	27,200	43,200	28.2	40.9
5+ (B_5)	39,100	38,200	37.7	36.2

[a]The regression run on the 1959 data is not useful because the data available are not comparable to those used in 1960 and 1961. Probably as a result, none of the forms of the "branches" variable are "significant" for the 1959 regression, though they are positive. (For this study, a "significant" coefficient is one that is at least as large as the standard error of the coefficient.) The one branch variable (B_1) is omitted because it is not "significant."

ated. Also the costs of banks that operated only one branch differed little from those of unit banks.

The elasticities (E) (and their standard errors) of direct operations costs with respect to output (N_d) estimated are .856 (.044) in 1960 and .809 (.052) in 1961. Table 3 summarizes the joint effect of the additional costs of branch banking presented in Table 2 and the elasticities.

Thus the findings indicate that if two units banks combine to form a branch bank with one branch, they would only experience cost savings due to economies of scale. It is not until five or more unit banks form a branch bank with four branches that net additional costs are experienced.

• • •

IV. A SUMMARY OF THE FINDINGS

Higher costs for branch banking were found consistently among the samples for the demand deposits and the installment loans services and for occupancy expenses. Higher costs were also found for indirect administration expenses and for the time deposits services, but the coefficients from which these are estimated had relatively large standard errors or were inconsistent in magnitude among the samples. Business loans, mortgage loans, securities and indirect business development expenses appear to be unaffected by the branch or unit form of organization.

Economies of scale were found for all of the banking services and indirect

Table 3. Demand Deposits, Additional Costs of Branch Banking (A) and Cost Savings Due to Scale of Operations, in Percentages

Number of Branches	Additional Cost of Branch Banking at New Scale of Operations ($A \times E$) 1960	Additional Cost of Branch Banking at New Scale of Operations ($A \times E$) 1961	Cost Savings Due to Scale of Operations ($1-E$) 1960	Cost Savings Due to Scale of Operations ($1-E$) 1961	Net Addition to Costs ($A \times E$) − ($1-E$) 1960	Net Addition to Costs ($A \times E$) − ($1-E$) 1961
1 (B_1)	.0	.0	14.4	19.2	−14.4	−19.2
2 (B_2)	18.5	13.6	14.4	19.2	4.1	− 5.6
3 (B_3)	14.3	19.2	14.4	19.2	− 0.1	.0
4 (B_4)	24.1	35.0	14.4	19.2	9.7	15.8
5+ (B_5)	32.3	31.0	14.4	19.2	17.9	11.8

Table 4. Net Percentage Increase or Decrease in Operations Costs Due to the Joint Effect of Branch Banking and Economies of Scale

Bank Service or Type of Indirect Expense	*Number of Branches* One	Two	Three	Four	Five and Over[a]
Demand deposits					
1960	.0	1.4	.0	3.4	6.3
1961	.0	−2.1	.0	5.9	4.4
Average	.0	−0.4	.0	4.7	5.4
Installment loans					
1959	−0.4	0.5	1.1	1.6	
1960	−0.5	0.1	0.6	1.0	2.0
1961	−0.5	0.4	1.1	1.6	3.1
Average	−0.5	0.3	0.9	1.4	2.6
Occupancy expenses					
1959	.0	1.3	3.2	18.3	
1960	1.0	2.4	3.0	9.4	6.4
Average	0.5	1.9	3.1	13.9	6.4
Sub-total, percentages computed from "reliable" coefficients	.0	1.8	4.0	20.0	14.4
Administration expenses					
1959	1.0	1.1	2.1	2.5	
1960	−0.3	1.0	2.0	2.8	4.4
1961	0.7	1.2	1.6	1.8	2.4
Average	0.5	1.1	1.9	2.4	3.4
Time deposits					
1959	−1.3	0.2	−0.5	−1.3	
1960	−0.2	−0.2	0.8	−0.2	−0.2
1961	−0.6	−0.6	0.7	1.5	−0.6
Average	−0.7	−0.2	0.3	.0	−0.4
Mortgage loans					
1959	−0.3	−0.3	−0.3	−0.3	
1960	−0.3	−0.3	−0.3	−0.3	−0.3
1961	−0.4	−0.4	−0.4	−0.3	−0.3
Average	−0.3	−0.3	−0.3	−0.3	−0.3
Securities					
1959	−0.3	−0.4	−0.4	−0.5	
1960	−0.2	−0.5	−0.2	−0.6	−0.5
1961	−0.3	−0.3	−0.1	.0	−0.3
Average	−0.3	−0.4	−0.2	−0.4	−0.4
Total	−0.8	2.0	5.7	21.7	16.7

[a]Where the number of offices variable (*NO*) was used, the computation is for banks with eight branches. None of the banks in the 1959 sample had more than four branches.

expenses except for business loans and indirect business promotion expenses. However, the elasticities measured were not much less than unity, in most cases.

The over-all effects on total bank operations costs of branch banking and economies of scale are summarized in Table 4. The percentages tabulated were determined by (1) computing for each sample, at the geometric means, the percentage of total operations expenses due to each banking service and type of indirect expense, and (2) multiplying the percentage by the net percentage increase or decrease in costs due to the joint effects of additional branch banking costs and economies of scale [for example, as in Table 3—ed.]. The product is the net estimated percentage increase or decrease in operating costs caused by branch banking and economies of scale. These percentages are given for each of the samples so that the reader can judge the stability of the estimates.

Except for occupancy expenses, Table 4 shows the average net increase or decrease in the sum of their operating expenses that two or more unit banks would experience if they merged to form a branch bank (not including the temporary costs of merging and assuming, of course, that their experience would be that measured for the sampled banks). Thus, if five unit banks merged to form a branch bank with four branches, the total demand deposit operations expenses of the new branch are expected to be 4.7 percent higher than the sum of these expenses of the five unit banks. However, this reasoning does not apply to occupancy expenses. Table 4 shows only that the occupancy expenses of the four-branch bank, to continue the example, are 13.9 percent higher than those of a unit bank that processes the same volume of output. The 13.9 percent increase, then, is the additional cost of serving the same number of customers from five locations instead of one—it may be more or less than the sum of the occupancy costs of the five original unit banks.

The distinction just mentioned between occupancy expenses and the other groups of operations expenses is important when banking policy is considered. Given that banking is a regulated industry with restricted entry, it is necessary to determine whether the net increases in operations costs that branch banks experience are offset by the convenience benefits to the public of being served by more than one banking office. The additional cost of occupancy is different from other additional operations expenses because it is the cost of providing additional convenience. Further, the average percentage increase in expenses due to occupancy expenses [is] 49 percent of the total gross increase found for branch banks with four and over branches. The demand deposits service accounted for 26 percent, installment loans for 10 percent, and administration expenses for 15 percent of the total gross increase, on the average, for banks with four and more branches.

Another important finding is that one- and two-branch banks have costs that are not much different from those of unit banks. This is an interesting finding, considering that researchers most often label banks as unit or branch, on the assumption that this dichotomy is useful. It appears better to group one- and two-branch banks with unit banks, at least for cost studies.

• • •

VI. CONCLUSIONS

Because the population from which the samples were drawn is limited to medium-sized banks, one hesitates to draw conclusions that may be applied to the entire banking system. With this understanding, the following conclusions are offered.

The study shows that branch banking does entail additional costs that are not offset by economies of scale. Analysis of these costs reveals that (1) branch banks with one and two branches do not have costs that are very different from those of unit banks, (2) approximately half of the additional costs are due to occupancy expenses, and (3) the marginal cost of additional branches beyond eight probably is very small. The additional occupancy expenses may be excluded as "extra" costs for policy considerations, because there is no evidence that the total costs expended on occupancy by, say, five unit banks would be greater than those expended by one branch bank with four branches, assuming that it processed the same volume of output as the unit banks. With additional occupancy expenses omitted, the costs of branch banks with three branches do not appear to be very different from those of similar-sized unit banks and branch banks with four and over branches experience additional costs that average approximately 9 percent of total operating expenses.

It does not necessarily follow from these findings that charges would be higher to depositors and borrowers of branch banks. Other differences between branch and unit banks, such as ability and desire to take risks, may offset or reinforce differences in operating expenses.

Thus, the conclusions that can be reached must be limited to a statement of the fact that, exclusive of occupancy costs, additional operating expenses for the banks sampled average approximately 9 percent. Whether these costs are offset by the convenience to the public of having more offices at which to bank, or by other factors, or whether the magnitude of the costs are different for larger banks than those sampled, remain questions for policy makers and future research.

15 BANKING STRUCTURE AND PERFORMANCE

JACK M. GUTTENTAG
AND EDWARD S. HERMAN

The following selection, a summary of numerous monographs on the branch versus unit banking controversy, reinforces the conclusion reached previously, namely, that little support can be marshaled to justify restrictions against branching. With 72 percent of the states permitting some form of branch banking, there are still sixteen states that strictly prohibit branching entirely. Moreover, branching across state lines, even when the market area exceeds a single state—the economy of Camden, New Jersey, is more allied with that of Philadelphia, Pennsylvania, than it is to Elizabeth, New Jersey, which is in turn closer, geographically and economically, to the New York City community than it is to Camden—is also restricted. Would the arguments presented in this selection make a case for interstate branching?

• • •

BANKING STRUCTURE AND COMPETITION

Competition is a behavioral concept, relating to how firms adjust to and interact with one another in the process of doing business. Competition so defined is conceptually distinct from *market structure* or *economic performance.*

Banking covers a wide range of market situations. In some banking markets, competition is intense; in others it is virtually nonexistent. In almost all phases of banking, competition is restricted in some ways at least. These restrictions are, in considerable part, the consequence of government regulation of entry, interest rates, and portfolio composition. They also reflect the traditional conservatism of many bankers, the complexity and relatively long-term character of many important bank-customer relationships, and the relatively small number of banks in many local markets. Small numbers of rivals in a market tend to create an interdependence of reactions that limits competition, with or without explicit collusion.

• • •

Regarding competitive techniques, price competition is employed by commercial banks mainly in areas where banks have nonbank rivals, including time and savings deposits, loans to Government securities dealers, and to some extent consumer and real estate loans. In markets where there is little competition from nonbank sources, mainly demand deposits and short-term business loans, bank competition more often is of the nonprice variety. . . .

The nonprice competition that pervades much of the banking business (as well as much of American business in general) stresses advertising and other forms of promotion, as well as new types and superior quality of services. This has its uses in stimulating new bank services, which are frequently socially advantageous innovations. But insofar as nonprice competition merely involves ad-

---

From J. M. Guttentag and E. S. Herman, *Banking Structure and Performance* (New York: Institute of Finance of the Schools of Business, New York University, 1967), pp. 15–19, 21–29. Reprinted by permission.

ditional advertising expense, larger numbers of "new-business" executives, or additional services of little real value to customers, nonprice competition may involve undesirable increases in social costs. It may also reinforce other factors tending to limit price competition, since it involves efforts to attach customers more firmly to banks by means of product differentiation.

There is some limited and inconclusive evidence that nonprice competition is more intense under branch than under unit banking. Evidence on the effects of the entrance of the New York City banks into Nassau County after 1960, the spread of the Philadelphia banks into adjacent counties after 1950, and the growth of branch banking in California after 1910, all suggest some resultant intensification of competition. A study of competition in the Third Federal Reserve District also found that the intensity of competition was usually highest under statewide branching and was always lowest under unit banking.

Competition through new entry, either actual or potential, is likely to be more intense under branch banking than under unit banking. The establishment of new offices has long been an area of vigorous competition among branch banks. In the interests of safety, regulatory authorities are likely to be more cautious in granting new bank charters than in giving branch permits to well-established institutions. They are also likely to be under less pressure to restrict entry under branch banking, since the branch banks wish to preserve their own freedom to open new offices. Branch banks are also generally able—because of superior resources, personnel, experience, and familiarity with local conditions—to move more rapidly to exploit opportunities to establish new banking offices. There is evidence, furthermore, that branch banks can maintain offices in urban locations where unit banks would not be economically feasible.

It has been argued that competition by branch banks has at times been predatory, and that they have used their size and power to intimidate, coerce, and destroy their smaller competitors. There is little evidence, however, to substantiate these charges.

In sum, there is some evidence of an intensification of nonprice competition associated with branch banking, and little or no evidence that such competition reaches destructive proportions. It should be noted that this finding is drawn from an environment in which financial centers within branch banking states, with few exceptions, still contain five or more banks and in which predatory competition would involve possible law violations.

It is sometimes argued that with liberal branch banking laws, restraints on predatory competition will not prevent branch banks from gaining a complete ascendancy at some indeterminate future time. But the goal of preserving a decentralized banking structure cannot be identified with the preservation of unit banking *per se*. Although large banks are usually branch banks, most branch banks are small (in 1959 more than half had deposits of less than $25 million). Public policy can permit branching and still exert strong influence toward preventing or eliminating any undue concentration of banking resources. The recent liberalization of entry conditions, for example, undoubtedly contributed to the marked rise in the formation of new banks in statewide branching states during 1963–1964. Assuming the maintenance of relatively easy conditions of entry, and some regulatory restraint on banking concentration, relatively small banks (branch and unit) should maintain a significant place in the banking structure.

BANKING STRUCTURE AND THE PRICE OF BANKING SERVICES

The impact of alternative banking structures on prices and other aspects of performance is their ultimate and most decisive test. Unfortunately there are very substantial difficulties involved in obtaining dependable evidence on relative performance. One problem is the great variation in structure (size, office numbers, etc.) within both unit banking and branch banking jurisdictions. It is extremely difficult to know *a priori* which of these diverse elements of structure might be strategic in affecting various aspects of performance. The second problem is that many factors besides bank structure, such as population density, income levels, and degree of urbanization affect bank performance (including the prices of banking services). The third problem is that some bank services are sold as part of an interdependent "package," so that it is difficult to isolate the impact of structure on one dimension of the package. This is notably the case with business loans. Since banks tend to compete for business customers mainly in terms of services offered rather than rate, we would not expect the business loan rate to be a sensitive measure of any differential pressures on transactions associated with differences in banking structure. The fourth problem is that transactions with banks often involve some element of bargaining, so that the price may fluctuate within a range dependent on the aggressiveness of the contracting parties. The fifth problem is the hazard of generalizing results covering specific markets at a particular time to other markets and other times.

• • •

A number of recent inquiries have examined the effects of branch banking on the prices of specific banking services. Some of these studies are of the cross-section type; others are of the time-series type, where samples are taken of structure and prices at different points of time. The latter method has been used most extensively in "before-and-after" investigations of the effects of bank mergers. Most of these studies do not attempt to separate the effects of branch banking *per se* from the effects of size.

Recent investigations do not show that branch banking has any marked or consistent effect on the rates of interest charged on unsecured small business loans. With regard to rates charged by branch and unit banks under settled market conditions, separate studies covering New York State and New England yield conflicting findings. Evidently any tendency for rates to be higher at either branch or unit banks is not pervasive or very pronounced. There are indications that branch bank *expansion* puts some downward pressure on small business loan rates. The evidence on this pertains largely to the spread of branch banking into non-metropolitan areas, however, where branch banking may reduce concentration. In the metropolitan areas, where branch banking may tend to increase concentration, the same price results will not necessarily follow.

The pattern of rates on consumer installment loans defies easy generalization. In some cases unit banks seem to charge lower rates and in other cases the opposite is true. Evidently consumer ignorance and other peculiarities of this market make possible wide diversities even within the limits of what would ordinarily be considered a "single market," and this obscures whatever variation might be associated with differences in branch-unit structures. Mergers may increase or decrease rates, depending on the circumstances, but as often as not rates are unaffected. Again there is some indication that branch bank expansion into non-metropolitan areas tends to reduce rates.

There are indications that the expansion of branch banking outside the metropolitan core areas has tended to reduce interest rates on mortgage loans. However, metropolitan areas in unit banking states do not appear to have higher rates than areas in branch banking states, when account is taken of regional rate differences. The effects of branch banking in the metropolitan core areas have not been investigated with sufficient precision to support any inferences.

The available evidence indicates that branch banking tends to be associated with lower savings deposit interest rates in metropolitan areas, and higher rates outside these areas. Various studies have found that, following a merger, rates are frequently raised and seldom reduced at new branch offices. In communities newly entered by a branch bank via merger the remaining unit banks sometimes raise their rates to match those of the new entrants. It has also been found that among banks in isolated non-metropolitan communities, those located in states where branching is permitted pay higher rates than those in states where branching is prohibited.

Thus, the spread of branch banking into non-metropolitan areas tends in many cases to generate more favorable terms to the public, putting downward pressure on loan rates and upward pressure on time deposit rates. With regard to service charges on demand deposits, however, this generalization is reversed. The extension of branch banking into suburban and rural areas tends to increase the level of service charges. The larger banks have higher service charges, and when they move out to the countryside, either through merger or through *de novo* expansion, they bring these charges with them. These high charges appear, however, to be a product of financial centers and large banks rather than branch banks as such. There is no indication that branch banking tends to raise service charges within metropolitan areas.

Among the factors that may play some role in explaining the anomalous behavior of service charges are differences in pricing policies followed by large and small banks. The former appear to be heavily influenced by average costs; small banks, on the other hand, may be more heavily influenced in their pricing decisions by the rate they can earn on additional loanable funds, which might be high if it is measured by the loan rate. Small banks may also face stronger resistance to higher service charges from customers with relatively inactive accounts, for whom the advantages of demand deposits are marginal and who might switch into currency or time deposits. The force of tradition may also play a role in retarding adjustments by small banks to rising cost levels.

BANK ORGANIZATION, SIZE, AND OPERATIONAL EFFICIENCY*

Bank operating efficiency refers to the real cost of producing a given financial service. Four separate although interrelated questions have been raised regarding the comparative operating efficiency of branch and unit banks. The first question is: (1) Are branch or unit banks more efficient, accepting the fact that branch banks are usually much larger? This question hinges in good part on whether there are significant scale economies in banking, *i.e.,* whether average costs fall as bank size increases. The available evidence on scale economies is unfortunately of limited value. This is because the measure of operating efficiency that is generally used, the ratio of current expenses to total assets, is influenced by many factors that are not related to efficiency. These factors include the proportion of various types of assets in bank portfolios (consumer installment loans, for example), the proportion of time deposits in bank liability structures, and the importance of noncredit services which increase expenses but are not reflected in total assets. In general, the existing literature does not succeed in making adequate allowance for such influences.

When the effects of size are sorted out from the other diverse influences on expense-to-asset ratios, it does appear that

*The preceding two selections also deal with this issue—ed.

scale economies exist in the bank size range up to $10 million. (This range includes about three-fourths of all commercial banks in the United States.) The magnitude of these economies is impossible to measure, but there are strong indications that it is substantially less than a decade ago, perhaps as a result of the elimination (mainly by absorption) of some of the least efficient of the smallest banks. In the intermediate-size range (say $10–$200 million) there are some indications of very modest economies of scale, although the margin of statistical error is quite large and this finding is by no means certain. For the larger banks (above $200 million) nothing is known about scale economies.

Even if findings on economies of scale were definitive their implications for the relative efficiency of branch and unit banking would be obscure. If the data employed in assessing these economies cover both unit banks and branch banks, as they do in some cases, the effects of scale are intermingled with the effects of organization. If the data cover only unit banks, as in other cases, it could imply that scale economies observed for unit banks were available to branch banks, which need not be the case; growth through branching may be expensive. Data on scale economies for branch banks alone are very sparse, and they are also of dubious significance because of the difficulties in taking account of the great differences in the number of branch offices among branch banks of a given size.

In order to disentangle the effect of scale economies from the effect of organization *per se,* most recent studies have asked another question: (2) Are branch banks more efficient than unit banks of the same size? They are unanimous in finding that branch banks invariably have higher expense-to-asset ratios in given size classes than unit banks. Some studies suggest that this finding refutes the alleged cost superiority of branch banks. However, since branch banks provide an additional convenience output in the form of more office facilities than unit banks in the same size class, we would expect their expense ratios to be higher. In addition, other factors unrelated to efficiency also artificially inflate the expense ratios of branch banks relative to unit banks of the same size. For example, branch banks make more consumer installment loans. From a policy standpoint, furthermore, branch and unit banks of the same size are not realistic alternatives.

In an effort to obtain greater policy relevance, several recent studies ask a third question: (3) Would the consolidation of a number of unit banks into a branch system increase or decrease costs? This question is most germane to an overall evaluation of the relative operating efficiency of branch as opposed to unit banking. Since a large proportion of unit banks have deposits of less than $10 million, and would therefore benefit from scale economies with further growth, there is a presumption that consolidation of smaller unit banks at least would raise efficiency. The results of one recent study, which compared average costs of branch banks with collections of unit banks having the same output and number of offices, support this presumption. The branch banks involved in this investigation, however, were relatively small. Thus, because of the limited coverage and other limitations of the study this conclusion is not solidly grounded. Further research on this question is badly needed, particularly with reference to consolidations involving large branch systems.

A final question (4), which is directly relevant to public policy regarding bank mergers in a mixed (branch and unit) banking system, is whether a given bank office could be operated more efficiently as a unit bank or as an office of a branch bank. This question involves a comparison of the marginal cost of an additional office to a branch bank with the cost of operating the same office as a unit bank.

The study referred to above provided some evidence that branch banks of the modest size included in the sample can operate an additional office more economically, but the limitations noted in the preceding paragraph apply to this finding as well.

BANK STRUCTURE AND ALLOCATIONAL EFFICIENCY

The extent to which resources are directed into appropriate uses from the standpoint of the overall community is termed allocational efficiency. One of the most important issues in resource allocation is whether branch or unit banks do a better job in meeting local credit demands. Local credit demands have a high social priority, since there may not be any nonbank sources of credit in the local community, or such sources may be substantially more expensive than bank credit.

There is clear evidence that branch banks have higher loan-to-asset ratios than unit banks, even in given bank size categories. With some important exceptions (mainly in the large business loan category), higher loan ratios imply larger credit extensions to the local community. Since branch banks are more heavily concentrated in the rapidly growing western states, interstate differences in loan demand may explain part of the differences in loan-asset ratios, but this is by no means the entire explanation. The higher loan ratios of branch banks also appear to result from their wider network of offices, which places them in closer proximity to local customers; from a willingness to maintain a less liquid position than unit banks; and from the greater ability of branch banks to maintain more offices in specialized locations in urban areas, which generate only selected types of business. Branch banks also possess an automatic mechanism for channeling funds from offices where loan demand is light to offices where it is heavy. This is reflected in the much wider range of loan-deposit ratios for individual branch offices than for individual unit banks.

Under unit banking, funds can be shifted to areas of strong loan demand through the correspondent system, by means of interbank deposits, interbank loans, the sale and purchase of assets, and participations. The available evidence suggests that the flow of loanable funds through transfers of interbank deposits tends to be perverse, *i.e.,* funds flow from outlying localities, where interest rates are high, to urban centers, where they are low, while regionally, they flow from the high-rate western states to the low-rate eastern states. Reverse flows arising from interbank borrowing and sale of assets are very small. Only participations are of quantitative importance as a vehicle for transferring funds. This vehicle, however, is used mainly by the larger unit (and branch) banks. Since presumably the need for participations is greatest among the smaller banks, frictions within the correspondent system evidently impede the free flow of funds to and from the smaller unit banks. Such frictions may include the high transactions cost involved when two independent decision-making units must concur on each loan; a fear by the smaller client bank that it may lose its customer to the correspondent bank; and the unwillingness of the correspondent bank to lend more than a fraction of the amount of a client's deposit balance to the customer of a client bank.

Recent studies do not support the oft-repeated charge that branch banks neglect nonurban areas in favor of the city where the head office is located. The evidence shows that out-of-town branches of major branch banks often have loan-deposit ratios exceeding those of the head office.

It also has been alleged that larger banks neglect small business customers. Such neglect is inferred from the fact that the share of their business loans going to small business (as opposed to the share going to large business) is smaller than it is for small banks. Since large banks make loans to both large and small firms, however, while small banks are largely limited to small firms, this is statistically inevitable and does not imply that bank growth would result in a reduced share of loans to small business. While bank growth does reduce the ratio of loans to small business to total business loans, it raises the ratio of total business loans to total assets. Some tentative calculations we have made suggest that bank growth to as high as $250 million of deposits would tend to increase the share of loans to small business, while growth beyond that level would have the opposite effect.

It also has been asserted that the decision-making machinery of branch banks is inferior to that of unit banks. However, little evidence is available on this issue. If the local unit banker is sometimes better informed about local borrowers and conditions than the local branch manager, the latter may have broader perspective and greater knowledge of industrywide conditions. Unit banks do make more unsecured loans than branch banks but whether on balance this is desirable is questionable. The unit banker, because of his close connection to the local community, may find some good loans that go "against the book" and which would not be made by the branch bank, but the unit banker may also make bad loans for the same reason. Recent studies suggest that branch office managers do not have less discretionary authority to make loans than unit bankers.

A second important issue is whether branch or unit banks provide the larger number of office facilities. It has often been argued on *a priori* grounds that branch banking would generate more offices because a branch bank can profit from special purpose offices in locations that could not support a unit bank. It has only been recently, however, that this hypothesis has been tested statistically.

The evidence is clear that in metropolitan areas branch banking results in the provision of more offices. In 1959 the largest 26 metropolitan areas in statewide branch banking states had one banking office for every 10,500 persons while the largest 26 areas in unit banking states had 19,500 persons per office. Both the central city and suburban communities have more offices under branch banking. Evidently metropolitan areas generate a heavy demand for "convenience" facilities (mainly checking and savings accounts, and consumer loans) at scattered locations which can be better met by limited service branch offices than by unit banks. In addition, the regulatory authorities may be more liberal in approving new branch and bank applications when the existing competitor in the area of the proposed new office is a branch office of a large bank than when it is a unit bank.

Studies of office facilities under branch and unit banking that use entire states as the unit of analysis do not show branch banking as superior, but these investigations do not surmount serious technical difficulties associated with use of state data. None of them take account of the marked differences between states in patterns of population dispersal, which must exercise a strong independent influence on the number of bank offices.

Banking facilities in non-metropolitan communities are sparse as compared with metropolitan areas, and differences in the relative provision of office facilities under branch and unit banking are consequently of great importance. The available studies show that after allowing for regional effects, branch banking provides appreciably more offices than unit banking in the larger non-metropolitan communities. In communities of less than 10,000 persons, however, the advantage of branch banking is quite narrow, for reasons that are not completely clear.

A third issue is whether branch or unit banks provide more auxiliary services such as special checking accounts, foreign exchange, trust services, revolving credit, payroll services to business, and the like. The evidence is abundantly clear that large banks, which are commonly branch banks, offer a wider range of services than smaller banks. This is true of each of the services cited above. Smaller branch systems (less than $25 million) generally offer more services than unit banks in the same size class.

Larger branch systems, of course, offer a much wider range of services than small unit banks, and the absorption of the latter into branch systems through merger generally results in some enlargement of the range of services offered. This fact is now heavily documented by a number of "before-and-after" studies of merged banks. These studies by their nature probably tend to exaggerate the extent to which valid demands for services are met that previously had been neglected. Information is not ordinarily gathered on the use made of the newly provided services, or the extent to which they might have been provided before merger through third parties, e.g., correspondent banks. Nevertheless, the evidence suggests that the spread of branch banking results in some expansion in the number of banking services offered the public.

PART THREE

the structure of the federal reserve system

federal reserve independence

The statutory independence of the Federal Reserve System from the executive branch of government and the relatively loose bonds connecting it to the legislative branch are a unique feature of American central banking. Aside from the power to appoint the Governors of the Board of Governors, the President of the United States cannot exert any legal influence over the Federal Reserve officialdom. And even that power is constrained in the sense that rarely is the majority of the Board likely to be appointees of a single President—the fourteen-year tenure of Governors being responsible for that. Indeed, the Supreme Court-executive relationship is the most proper analogue to the status that Board members enjoy vis-à-vis the Chief Executive.

Congressional control over the Reserve System is stronger, because the System is a child of Congress. But the power of the purse, that major and perhaps penultimate weapon for ensuring that agencies comply with Congressional directives, is absent; the Federal Reserve is self-financing.

One of the many controversies concerning the structure of the Federal Reserve—and this debate can be traced back even to the period prior to the passage of the Federal Reserve Act in 1913—relates to the linkage between the executive and the Federal Reserve. For example, the 1913 Act made the Secretary of the Treasury the ex officio chairman of the Federal Reserve Board to ensure a strong voice for the administration, a move objected to by many responsible individuals. The controversy smoldered for a time, flared up again in the early 1930s, and was seemingly extinguished with the removal of the Secretary from the Board in 1935. But the acrimonious public debate between the Board of Governors and the Truman Administration between 1950 and 1951 demonstrated that the issue possessed the regenerative powers of the phoenix.

The excerpt from the report of the authoritative Commission on Money and Credit (CMC), which opens this section, notes that the present degree of Federal Reserve independence from the executive is excessive. Yet voluntary cooperation cannot provide the close ties that a coordinated set of economic policies demands. The commission members advocate the establishment of closer ties through reforms in the appointive process, although they cherish some amount of independence.

Milton Friedman disagrees with this viewpoint. He shows independence to be inefficient; his reasons are to be found in the second selection. At least two conclusions can be derived on the basis of the anti-independence views expressed therein. First, and this is the view espoused by Professor Friedman and his disciples, a monetary rule ought to be substituted for discretionary control, obviating the need for a Board of Governors. The pros and cons of this statement are debated in Part VIII.

But a second tack is no less legitimate, and that is total subjugation of the System to the executive, say, by making it a subdepartment of the Treasury. Although few economists or public officials espouse this extreme position of Treasury ascendancy, fewer objections are raised to the suggestion that closer Presidential supervision be assured. The privately owned central bank, not at all responsible to the government, is an anachronism; the last one, the Bank of England, fell under total public control in 1946. On this point, all three economists represented in this section are unanimous. Instead, the independence question hinges on the degree of central bank autonomy within the government.

The proponents of independence contend that further government encroachment on the territory of the central bank would bring untoward consequences in its wake. These contentions are disregarded by the proponents of reform, who suggest that closer ties would be advantageous, indeed. Jonas Prager, in the concluding selection, allows the proponents and opponents to argue their cases for themselves. The CMC proposal, he claims, is not likely to achieve even its limited aims, and he questions these aims, too. Can national macroeconomic policy be coordinated even if the President becomes responsible for monetary policy? Although Prager does not accept the arguments voiced in favor of the status quo, he rejects the points raised by persons favoring closer executive ties. If change is unlikely to bring any meaningful improvement in the execution of national policy, why bother? Indeed, this has been the attitude of Congress, which has not modified the structure of Federal Reserve-executive relations since 1935, the many objections, Congressional hearings, and committee reports notwithstanding.

16 THE ORGANIZATION OF THE FEDERAL RESERVE SYSTEM

COMMISSION ON MONEY AND CREDIT

The broad review of American monetary policy presented by the Commission on Money and Credit in 1959 was praised by some and rejected by others. The many highly respected men who served on the Commission hailed from numerous fields—industry, labor, education—and the consensus arrived at represents a good appraisal of the possible rather than the ideal. A brief glimpse into their views is afforded by the following excerpt. In particular note (1) the two distinct uses of the term "independence" and (2) the position voiced by the Chairman of the Board of Governors. By 1964 that view had been modified, as will be evident from the third selection in this Part.

The Federal Reserve System is charged with the formulation as well as the execution of monetary policy. Its mandate and structure are therefore of first importance in appraising governmental means of achieving national economic goals. . . . This section deals with its structure, which is a joint product of legislation and practice.

The basic questions are both administrative and political. They center on the degree of independence of the System from the other organs of the government on the one hand, and from the banking community on the other.

THE PRESENT STRUCTURE

The System has a regulated private base, a mixed middle component, and a controlling public apex. The mixture of public and private elements is unique among the closely regulated sectors of our national economy, and unique too among central banking systems around the world. It reflects in part the changing conceptions of the role of central banking over a half-century and in part the shift in interests and influences that has attended the System's evolution.

At the apex stands the Board of Governors (FRB). Its seven members are appointed by the President with the consent of the Senate for 14-year terms, one term expiring on January 31 in each even-numbered year. Members may be reappointed, and they are removable "for cause"; but the removal power has not been exercised. Because of the length of the term, most new appointments are to fill vacancies in unexpired terms. In making appointments the President must give due regard to "fair representation of financial, agricultural, industrial, and commercial interests, and geographical divisions of the country," and not more than one member can be appointed from any one Federal Reserve District.

The Chairman and Vice-Chairman of the Board are designated from among the Board members by the President for

---

From The Commission on Money and Credit, *Money and Credit: Their Influence on Jobs, Prices, and Growth,* pp. 81–87.

four-year renewable terms which do not, unless by accident, coincide with the President's.

The independence invited by long, staggered terms is reinforced by the System's complete exemption from the controls of the budget and congressional appropriations. Board operating funds come from semi-annual assessments on the twelve Federal Reserve banks; the assessments, like the operating expenses of the banks, are a prior charge on their earnings before surpluses are transferred to the Treasury. Nevertheless, Board members' salaries are fixed by law and the Board in practice observes government salary scales for its staff in Washington.

At a level of authority equivalent to the Board's, but in the public-private category, is the Federal Open Market Committee (FOMC), by law composed of all seven FRB members and five of the twelve Federal Reserve bank presidents. The President of the Federal Reserve Bank of New York is always one of the five; the others serve in annual rotation. In practice, all twelve Reserve bank presidents regularly attend FOMC sessions and participate in the discussions, though only five of them vote.

The Presidents of the Reserve banks are not government appointees; they are elected for five-year terms by the boards of directors of their respective banks, subject to the approval of the FRB. Their compensation is fixed by their boards of directors, again subject to FRB approval. In the early years they were usually commercial bankers, but as the System has developed, recruitment from within has become more characteristic. The positions have attracted capable men.

The annual reports of the Board of Governors, in setting out the minutes of meetings, decisions, votes, and reasons therefor, as the law requires, record FOMC and FRB proceedings in separate sequences. This appearance, however, scarcely mirrors the realities, for FOMC and FRB actions are regularly discussed together.

• • •

THE DISTRIBUTION OF POWER

Of the System's three instruments of general monetary policy—changes in member bank reserve requirements, changes in the rediscount rate, and open market operations—the first is lodged clearly with the FRB. The second, the rediscount rate, is "established" every two weeks by each Reserve bank, but "subject to the review and determination" of the FRB. In practice this appearance of a measure of regional autonomy has largely yielded to the national nature of the money market. But the Board explores regional sentiment in discussions of possible changes in the rate at meetings of the FOMC, and conclusions usually emerge from discussion and consensus. By determining changes before their announcement the FRB avoids occasions when it might have to disapprove regional preferences publicly.

The control of open market policy, the third and most flexible instrument, is formally vested not in the Board but in the FOMC. The meetings of the FOMC, held at least every two or three weeks, have become, in Chairman Martin's words, "a forum, a clearing-house for all the aspects of policy determination in the System, not failing to recognize the statutory responsibility of the Board of Governors for reserve requirements." The System coordinates its policies and actions, that is to say, in sessions that intermingle its public and private elements completely, and fuses all its powers in support of decisions reached there.

In concluding this description it is appropriate to notice that things have not always been as they are. In a half-century the size and composition of the Board have undergone several changes. It began with five appointed members (two of whom had to be experienced in banking or finance) providing representation of industrial, commercial, financial and regional interests (but not agriculture or labor), together with two *ex-officio* members, the Secretary of the Treasury and the Comptroller of the Currency. The term of office was 10 years. In 1922 the Board was enlarged to bring in an agricultural representative, while the requirement of financial experience for two members was dropped. The term of office was extended in 1933 to 12 years, and again in 1935 to 14 years. At that time, at Senator Glass' insistence, the *ex-officio* memberships were terminated, and the appointive members increased to seven. At that time too, the Board was given a majority of the membership of the FOMC, which had first been given statutory recognition in 1933. Two trends are discernible in these changes, notably in the 1935 legislation: one toward centralization of control over banking and monetary policy through the System, and the other toward increased independence of the System from the rest of the government.

Independence and decentralization remain matters of dispute. What is beyond dispute is the change in the primary function of the System, and in the general awareness of that function. What was thought of in 1913 as essentially "a cooperative enterprise among bankers for the purpose of increasing the security of banks and providing them with a reservoir of emergency resources" has not ceased to be that. But it has also become one of the most potent institutions involved in national economic policy.

FEDERAL RESERVE BOARD CHANGES

It is a matter for argument and judgment whether and in what directions, and how far, the System's governing structure should be altered in the national interest. The basic issue is the degree of independence of the Federal Reserve from other parts of the government and from the banking community it both serves and regulates. A strong advocate for the claims of monetary stability is needed within the government, and the central bank is the natural home of such advocacy. A measure of independence from the Treasury with respect to support of the Treasury securities market is a requisite too, if the central bank is to exercise effective monetary control. Disagreements turn on how far insulation from the President and Congress and from the other agencies concerned with economic policy helps or hinders the expression of the central bank's viewpoint; and on whether a clear locus of authority is needed to secure coordination and prevent conflicts from deteriorating into stalemates.

Some arguments for independence are more or less frankly antidemocratic in their premises. For example, it is said that anti-inflationary measures are unpopular though necessary, and therefore the best assurance of their being taken is by "endowing the Board of Governors with a considerable degree of independence," or that "hard" decisions are more acceptable to the public "if they are decided by public officials who, like the members of the judiciary, are removed from immediate pressures." Others assert, instead, that the accountability of the System is achieved through its responsibility to Congress, and call the Federal Reserve an "agent of Congress," invoking then the doctrine of the separation of powers to argue that this requires independence for the Federal Reserve from the executive. It has been argued, however, that the FRB is less accountable to Congress than the line departments in the presidential hierarchy. It does not depend on appropriations for its funds and so is freed from the most potent of congressional controls over administrative agencies. And Congress has been notably circumspect in even suggesting its policy views to the Board, let alone incurring responsibility for its decisions. All agencies, line departments like the Treasury no less than the FRB, are "creatures of Congress" in the sense of owing their existence and powers to legislation. And agencies with single heads are more easily held accountable by Congress or by anyone else than those with boards at the top.

No doubt there are occasions and types of pressures that need to be guarded against. But the telling arguments for independence are less protective than positive: independence spells opportunity; it is an invitation to vigor; it attracts able people.

The need for coordination, however, is very important. Isolation may mean weakness, and presidential support can be very helpful at times. The real ability of the System to influence national economic policy might well be increased rather than diminished if its ties to the President were closer. The Commission believes that somewhat closer ties are advisable.

Of the means to this end, one has already been tried and discarded: the *ex-officio* memberships of the Secretary of the Treasury and the Comptroller of the Currency on the Board. This tended rather to subordinate the System to the Treasury, and it is not simply a Treasury view but an over-all perspective that is wanted.

A presidential power to issue published directives to the Board has also been suggested, on the principle that if presidential influence is to be brought to bear, it had better be out in the open. The objection to this is not its visibility but the clumsy nature of the instrument. No one wants every Board action to require presidential clearance. Nor is a mechanism desirable that would tend to dramatize differences in views. The need is for closer working relationships and greater unity of purpose and outlook.

The mildest suggestion, amounting to no change, was urged by Chairman Martin in 1952, after the "Accord": he granted the need for coordination but argued that it could be met through informal consultation. If congeniality of temperament and outlook among agency and department heads could always be counted on, the Commission would have looked no further for solutions. But in the interests of government-wide coordination of economic policy the Commission . . . recommends some steps to provide a consultative forum and to increase the incentives toward concert. To the same end, and because of the exceptional degree of the FRB's independence, the Commission makes the following recommendations here.

The FRB Chairman and Vice-Chairman should be designated by the President from among the Board's membership, to serve for four-year terms coterminous with the President's.

This strikes a balance in formal status between tenure at the President's pleasure, which some of the Commissioners would prefer, and no change, which other Commissioners advocate.

The FRB should consist of five members, with overlapping ten-year terms, one expiring each odd-numbered year; members should be eligible for reappointment.

This would assure the President of one vacancy to be filled shortly after his inauguration, while retaining the general stability of Board membership. The reduction in numbers should enhance the status of members, and the ten-year term combines a sufficient protection for independence, with some safeguard against superannuation.

• • •

17 AN INDEPENDENT CENTRAL BANK

MILTON FRIEDMAN

Professor Friedman lists four objections to the independence of the central bank from the government. Three of them are applicable even when the government exercises some control over the central bank. Are his arguments equally applicable to relationships between two departments, say Treasury and Commerce, where jurisdiction may also overlap? If so, how are we to proceed?

• • •

The device of an independent central bank embodies the very appealing idea that it is essential to prevent monetary policy from being a day-to-day plaything at the mercy of every whim of the current political authorities. The device is rationalized by assimilating it to a species of constitutionalism. The argument that is implicit in the views of proponents of an independent central bank—so far as I know, these views have never been fully spelled out—is that control over money is an essential function of a government comparable to the exercise of legislative or judicial or administrative powers. In all of these, it is important to distinguish between the basic structure and day-to-day operation within that structure. In our form of government, this distinction is made between the constitutional rules which set down a series of basic prescriptions and proscriptions for the legislative, judicial, and executive authorities and the detailed operation of the several authorities under these general rules. Similarly, the argument implicit in the defense of an independent central bank is that the monetary structure needs a kind of a monetary constitution, which takes the form of rules establishing and limiting the central bank as to the powers that it is given, its reserve requirements, and so on. Beyond this, the argument goes, it is desirable to let the central bank have authority largely coordinate with that of the legislature, the executive, and the judiciary to carry out the general constitutional mandate on a day-to-day basis.

• • •

A first step in discussing this notion critically is to examine the meaning of the "independence" of a central bank....

A . . . basic meaning is . . . that a central bank should be an independent branch of government coordinate with the legislative, executive, and judicial branches, and with its actions subject to interpretation by the judiciary. Perhaps the most extreme form of this kind of independence in practice, and the form that comes closest to the ideal type envisaged by proponents of an independent central bank, has been achieved in those historical instances where an organization that was initially entirely private and not formally part of the government at all has served as a central bank. The leading ex-

From Milton Friedman, "An Independent Central Bank," in Leland B. Yeager (ed.), *In Search of a Monetary Constitution* (Cambridge, Mass.: Harvard University Press, 1962), pp. 224–230, 232–239.

ample, of course, is the Bank of England, which developed out of a strictly private bank and was not owned by or formally a part of the government until after World War II. If such a private organization strictly outside the regular political channels could not function as a central monetary authority, this form of independence would call for the establishment of a central bank through a constitutional provision which would be subject to change only by constitutional amendment. The bank would accordingly not be subject to direct control by the legislature. This is the meaning I shall assign to independence in discussing further whether an independent central bank is a desirable resolution of the problem of achieving responsible control over monetary policy.

It seems to me highly dubious that the United States, or for that matter any other country, has in practice ever had an independent central bank in this fullest sense of the term. Even when central banks have supposedly been fully independent, they have exercised their independence only so long as there has been no real conflict between them and the rest of the government. Whenever there has been a serious conflict, as in time of war, between the interests of the fiscal authorities in raising funds and of the monetary authorities in maintaining convertibility into specie, the bank has almost invariably given way, rather than the fiscal authority. To judge by experience, even those central banks that have been nominally independent in the fullest sense of the term have in fact been closely linked to the executive authority.

But of course this does not dispose of the matter. The ideal is seldom fully realized. Suppose we could have an independent central bank in the sense of a coordinate constitutionally established, separate organization. Would it be desirable to do so? I think not, for both political and economic reasons.

The political objections are perhaps more obvious than the economic ones. Is it really tolerable in a democracy to have so much power concentrated in a body free from any kind of direct, effective political control? What I have called the "new liberal" often characterizes his position as involving belief in the rule of law rather than of men. It is hard to reconcile such a view with the approval of an independent central bank in any meaningful way. True, it is impossible to dispense fully with the rule of men. No law can be specified so precisely as to avoid problems of interpretation or to cover explicitly every possible case. But the kind of limited discretion left by even the best of laws in the hands of those administering them is a far cry indeed from the kind of far-reaching powers that the laws establishing central banks generally place in the hands of a small number of men.

I was myself most fully persuaded that it would be politically intolerable to have an "independent" central bank by the memoirs of Emile Moreau, the governor of the Bank of France during the period from about 1926 to 1928, the period when France established a new parity for the franc and returned to gold. Moreau was appointed governor of the Bank of France in 1926, not long before Poincaré became premier after violent fluctuations in the exchange value of the franc and serious accompanying internal disturbances and governmental financial difficulties. Moreau's memoirs were edited and brought out in book form some years ago by Jacques Rueff, who was the leading figure in the recent French monetary reform.

The book is fascinating on many counts. The particular respect that is most relevant for our present purpose is the picture that Moreau paints of Montagu Norman, governor of the Bank of England, on the one hand, and of Hjalmar Schacht, at that time governor of the Bank of Germany, on the other; they were unquestionably two of the three outstanding central bankers of the modern era, Benjamin Strong of the United

States being the third. Moreau describes the views that these two European central bankers had of their functions and their roles, and implies their attitude toward other groups. The impression left with me—though it is by no means clear that Moreau drew the same conclusions from what he wrote, and it is certain that he would have expressed himself more temperately—is that Norman and Schacht were contemptuous both of the masses—of "vulgar" democracy—and of the classes—of the, to them, equally vulgar plutocracy. They viewed themselves as exercising control in the interests of both groups but free from the pressures of either. In Norman's view, if the major central bankers of the world would only cooperate with one another—and he had in mind not only himself and Schacht but also Moreau and Benjamin Strong—they could jointly wield enough power to control the basic economic destinies of the Western world in accordance with rational ends and objectives rather than with the irrational processes of either parliamentary democracy or laissez-faire capitalism. Though of course stated in obviously benevolent terms of doing the "right thing" and avoiding distrust and uncertainty, the implicit doctrine is clearly thoroughly dictatorial and totalitarian.

• • •

I turn now to the economic or technical aspects of an independent central bank. Clearly there are political objections to giving the group in charge of a central bank so much power independent of direct political controls, but, it has been argued, there are economic or technical grounds why it is nevertheless essential to do so. In judging this statement, much depends on the amount of leeway that the general rule governing the central bank gives to it. I have been describing an independent central bank as if it could or would be given a good deal of separate power, as clearly is currently the case. Of course, the whole notion of independence could be rendered merely a matter of words if in fact the constitutional provision setting up the bank established the limits of its authority very narrowly and controlled very closely the policies that it could follow.

• • •

One defect of an independent central bank in such a situation is that it almost inevitably involves dispersal of responsibility. If we examine the monetary system in terms not of nominal institutional organization but of the economic functions performed, we find that the central bank is hardly ever the only authority in the government that has essential monetary powers. Before the Federal Reserve System was established, the Treasury exercised essential monetary powers. It operated like a central bank, and at times a very effective central bank. More recently, from 1933 to 1941, the Federal Reserve System was almost entirely passive. Such monetary actions as were taken were taken predominantly by the Treasury. The Treasury engaged in open-market operations in its debt-management operations of buying and selling securities. It created and destroyed money in its gold and silver purchases and sales. The Exchange Stabilization Fund was established and gave the Treasury yet another device for engaging in open-market operations. When the Treasury sterilized and desterilized gold, it was engaging in monetary actions. In practice, therefore, even if something called an independent central bank is established and given exclusive power over a limited range of monetary matters, in particular over the printing of pieces of paper or the making of book entries called money (Federal Reserve notes and Federal Reserve deposits), there remain other governmental authorities, particularly the fiscal authority collecting taxes and dispersing funds and managing the debt, which also have a good deal of monetary power.

If one wanted to have the substance and not merely the form of an independent monetary authority, it would be necessary to concentrate all debt-management powers as well as all powers to create and destroy governmentally issued money in the central bank. As a matter of technical efficiency, this might well be desirable. Our present division of responsibility for debt management between the Federal Reserve and the Treasury is very inefficient. It would be much more efficient if the Federal Reserve did all of the borrowing and all of the managing of the debt, and the Treasury, when it had a deficit, financed it by getting money from the Federal Reserve System, and when it had a surplus, handed the excess over to the Federal Reserve System. But while such an arrangement might be tolerable if the Federal Reserve System were part of the same administrative hierarchy as the Treasury, it is almost inconceivable that it would be if the central bank were thoroughly independent. Certainly no government to date has been willing to put that much power in the hands of a central bank even when the bank has been only partly independent. But so long as these powers are separated, there is dispersal of responsibility, with each group separately regarding the other group as responsible for what is happening and with no one willing to accept responsibility.

In the past few years, I have read through the annual reports of the Federal Reserve System from 1913 to date, seriatim. One of the few amusing dividends from that ordeal was seeing the cyclical pattern that shows up in the potency that the authorities attribute to monetary policy. In years when things were going well, the reports emphasize that monetary policy is an exceedingly potent weapon and that the favorable course of events is largely a result of the skillful handling of this delicate instrument by the monetary authority. In years of depression, on the other hand, the reports emphasize that monetary policy is but one of many tools of economic policy, that its power is highly limited, and that it was only the skillful handling of such limited powers as were available that averted disaster. This is an example of the effect of the dispersal of responsibility among different authorities, with the likely result that no one assumes or is assigned the final responsibility.

Another defect of the conduct of monetary policy through an independent central bank that has a good deal of leeway and power is the extent to which policy is thereby made highly dependent on personalities. In studying the history of American monetary policy, I have been struck by the extraordinary importance of accidents of personality.

At the end of World War I, the governor of the Federal Reserve System was W. P. G. Harding. Governor Harding was, I am sure, a thoroughly reputable and competent citizen, but he had a very limited understanding of monetary affairs, and even less backbone. Almost every student of the period is agreed that the great mistake of the Reserve System in postwar monetary policy was to permit the money stock to expand very rapidly in 1919 and then to step very hard on the brakes in 1920. This policy was almost surely responsible for both the sharp postwar rise in prices and the sharp subsequent decline. It is amusing to read Harding's answer in his memoirs to criticism that was later made of the policies followed. He does not question that alternative policies might well have been preferable for the economy as a whole, but emphasizes the Treasury's desire to float securities at a reasonable rate of interest, and calls attention to a then-existing law under which the Treasury could replace the head of the Reserve System. Essentially he was saying the same thing that I heard another member of the Reserve Board say shortly after World War II when the bond-support program was in question. In response to the view expressed by some of my colleagues and myself that the bond-support program should be dropped, he largely agreed but said, "Do you want us to lose our jobs?"

• • •

The actions of the Reserve System depend on whether there are a few persons in the System who exert intellectual leadership, and on who these people are; its actions depend not only on the people who are nominally the heads of the System but also on such matters as the fate of particular economic advisers.

So far, I have listed two main technical defects of an independent central bank from an economic point of view: first, dispersal of responsibility, which promotes shirking responsibility in times of uncertainty and difficulty, and second, an extraordinary dependence on personalities, which fosters instability arising from accidental shifts in the particular people and the character of the people who are in charge of the system.

A third technical defect is that an independent central bank will almost inevitably give undue emphasis to the point of view of bankers. It is exceedingly important to distinguish two quite different problems that tend to be confused: the problem of credit policy and the problem of monetary policy. In our kind of monetary or banking system, money tends to be created as an incident in the extension of credit, yet conceptually the creation of money and the extension of credit are quite distinct. A monetary system could be utterly unrelated to any credit instruments whatsoever; for example, this would be true of a completely automatic commodity standard, using only the monetary commodity itself or warehouse receipts for the commodity as money. Historically, the connection between money and credit has varied widely from time to time and from place to place. It is therefore essential to distinguish policy issues connected with interest rates and conditions on the credit market from policy issues connected with changes in the aggregate stock of money, while recognizing, of course, that measures taken to affect the one set of variables may also affect the other, and that monetary measures may have credit effects as well as monetary effects proper.

It so happens that central-bank action is but one of many forces affecting the credit market. As we and other countries have seen time and again, a central bank may be able to determine the rate of interest on a narrow range of securities, such as the rate of interest on a particular category of government bonds, though even that only within limits and only at the expense of completely giving up control over the total stock of money. A central bank has never been able to determine, at all closely, rates of interest in any broader or more fundamental sense. Postwar experience in country after country that has embarked on a cheap-money policy has strikingly demonstrated that the forces which determine rates of interest broadly conceived—rates of return on equities, on real property, on corporate securities—are far too strong and widespread for the central bank to dominate. It must sooner or later yield to them, and generally rather soon.

The central bank is in a very different position in determining the quantity of money. Under systems such as that in the United States today, the central bank can make the amount of money anything it wishes. It may, of course, choose to accept some other objective and give up its power over the money supply in order to try to keep "the" or "a" rate of interest fixed, to keep "free reserves" at a particular level, or to achieve some other objective. But if it wishes, it can exercise complete control over the stock of money.

This difference between the position of the central bank in the credit markets and in determining the money supply tends to be obfuscated by the close connection between the central bank and the banking community. In the United States, for example, the Reserve banks technically are owned by their member banks. One result is that the general views of the banking community exercise a strong influence on the central bank and, since the banking community is concerned primarily with the credit market, central banks are led to put altogether too much emphasis on the credit effects of their policies and too little emphasis on the monetary effects of their policies.

In recent times, this emphasis has been attributed to the effects of the Keynesian Revolution and its treatment of changes in the stock of money as operating primarily through the liquidity preference function on the interest rate. But this is only a particular form of a more general and ancient tendency. The real-bills doctrine, which dates back a century and more, exemplifies the same kind of confusion between the credit and the monetary effects of monetary policy. The banking and currency controversy in Britain in the early nineteenth century is a related example. The central bank emphasized its concern with conditions in the credit market. It denied that the quantity of money it was creating was in any way an important consideration in determining price levels or the like, or that it had any discretion about how much money to create. Much the same arguments are heard today.

The three defects I have outlined constitute a strong technical argument against an independent central bank. Combined with the political argument, the case against a fully independent central bank is strong indeed.

• • •

18 AN ANNIVERSARY GIFT FOR THE FEDERAL RESERVE SYSTEM: THE 1964 PATMAN BILLS

JONAS PRAGER

Congress must deal with an immense number of issues, all involving the national interest, and it is humanly impossible for every Congressman to gain expertise in each area. Of necessity, then, a division of labor has evolved, and the expert gains an influence disproportionate to his single vote. Congressman Wright Patman is one of the legislative experts on the Federal Reserve, and the following article is based on the 1964 round of his continuing battle with the Board of Governors, chaired from 1951–1970 by William McChesney Martin. (In 1967 Congressman Patman introduced similar proposals once again, this time as H.R. 11 of the 90th Congress.) The view presented by this article opposes reform under present circumstances. Would this conclusion have to be modified if Congress were to permit limited Presidential discretion over tax rates?

The Federal Reserve System, organized in 1914, has recently ended its year-long fiftieth anniversary celebration. The fifty years have not been uneventful, and the Reserve System has been blamed more often for causing economic disasters than praised for preventing them. As a result, suggestions for modifications in the structure, tools, and operations of the System have flowed forth incessantly. A certainly unsolicited addition to this torrent came in the form of a series of bills introduced by the long-time opponent of Federal Reserve policies, Representative Wright Patman of Texas, Chairman of the House Committee on Banking and Currency.

Patman introduced six bills in 1964, three of them concerned with the structure of the Reserve System and three concerned with the monetary policy in a broad sense. One or two of the bills are not terribly important; the net effect of the others, however, would be a major revision of United States monetary policy. Two of the latter bills would reorganize the System and change its relationship to the President and to Congress. Another probably would destroy the effectiveness of monetary restraint during strong expansionary and inflationary periods. Still another would have serious implications for the structure of commercial banking in the United States as well as for monetary policy in general.

The objective of this article is to examine and analyze some of these Patman bills, the comments of the participants in the Congressional hearings called by the Subcommittee on Domestic Finance, and the conclusions of the legislators. Sections I and II survey the Patman bills concerning the relationship of the Federal Reserve to the executive and to Congress and examine the controversies surrounding these issues. Section III evaluates the recommendations of the witnesses and the subcommittee and suggests that both protagonists and antagonists of Federal Reserve independence have missed the point.

This article has not previously been published.

I

H.R. 9631, introduced by the Chairman of the House Committee on Banking and Currency, is perhaps the most revolutionary bill insofar as organization of the Reserve System and its relationship to the federal government is concerned. The purpose of this bill is to tie the Federal Reserve to the executive; in essence, Mr. Patman wishes to restore the pre-1935 organization of the Federal Reserve. The reversion to antiquity is implied in a very minor change: the appellation "Board of Governors of the Federal Reserve System" is to be replaced by "The Federal Reserve Board," the very name that appeared in the Federal Reserve Act of 1913 and that was changed in the "declaration of independence," the Banking Act of 1935.

This minor change is but a portent of other structural revisions. The Secretary of the Treasury, removed from the Board in 1935, is returned to the Board and is seated in the chair once again. The Reserve Board is to become the center of monetary policy making, with the abolition of the Open Market Committee and with the lodging of open market operations with the Board. Some Patman provisions go even further than the original Act in binding the System to the administration. Whereas the President could remove a member for "cause" only under the previous Acts, H.R. 9631 states bluntly: "The President may remove any appointive member from office." No "ifs," "buts," or other qualifications precede or follow this terse sentence.

The crucial issue raised by this Patman Bill is that of Federal Reserve independence. The major objective of the proposal is to reduce the System's autonomy from the executive. It is not surprising, therefore, that the major controversy that broke out time and time again during the "hearings" revolved around the independence argument.

Federal Reserve officials admitted that a central bank not responsible in any manner to the public—that is, a private central bank such as the Bank of England prior to its nationalization in 1946—was unthinkable. Still, they thought that central bankers should possess a marked degree of autonomy. The reasons given were numerous. Chairman Martin testified that monetary stability is the key to prosperity and that only an independent central bank can resist the pressures that constantly rise to subvert "sound" credit policy.

> The country cannot prosper without a sound basic economy and sound credit conditions. To maintain such conditions, it is essential that money—the "medium of exchange" by which goods and services change hands—must adequately and flexibly serve its purpose in a complex economy. . . . Because money so vitally affects all people in all walks of life as well as the financing of the Government, the task of credit and monetary management has unique characteristics. Policy decisions of an agency performing this task are often the subject of controversy and frequently of a restrictive nature; consequently, they are often unpopular, at least temporarily, with some groups. The general public in a democracy, however, is more apt to accept or tolerate restrictive monetary and credit policies if they are decided by public officials who, like members of the judiciary, are removed from immediate pressures.[1]

Governor J. L. Robertson went one step further in advocating the autonomy of the central bank: independence is necessary to prevent "the possibility of utilizing the money creating facilities of the Federal Reserve System for purposes of financing unsound operations on the part of the Government." President George H. Ellis of the Federal Reserve Bank of Boston raised the specter of international disaster as the possible result of a loss of Federal Reserve independence: "The sub-

---

[1]All citations unless otherwise noted are from U.S. Congress, House of Representatives, Committee on Banking and Currency, Subcommittee on Domestic Finance, *The Federal Reserve System After Fifty Years, Hearings* (Washington, D.C.: GPO, 1964).

stantial alteration in the structure of the Federal Reserve System as proposed in the bills under discussion might raise the serious prospect of loss of confidence in the dollar and lead to a rapid gold outflow."

The System received some outside aid as well. Professor Leo J. Raskind of Vanderbilt University suggested that advice from an independent agency is a virtue that ought to be preserved. Representatives of both the American Bankers Association and the Independent Bankers Association testified that the present system was working well and that there was no need for revising its structure.

The academic community was represented well at the hearings, both quantitatively and qualitatively. Despite the diversity of views, a consensus of sorts was evident in the testimony of these men. Almost all objected to the Patman provision which would place the Secretary of the Treasury on the Federal Reserve Board. The primary objection to this step lay in the fear of placing the power to create money in the hands of the officer responsible for financing federal government expenditures. Fear that "cheap finance" will take precedence over proper monetary policy is certainly not without historical evidence; too often minimizing interest charges on the national debt has been given priority over combating inflation by a tightening of the money supply and an increase in interest rates. Chairman Martin summarized the basic feelings on this issue when he said, "The question is whether the principal officer in charge of paying the Government's bills should be entrusted also with the power to create the money to pay them."

Similarly, there was a consensus that the Reserve System should be more closely allied to the President of the United States. The agreement extended to the very manner in which Presidential control would be exercised: the term of the Chairman of the Board of Governors should run concurrently with that of the President. This conclusion is rather a letdown, for most of the professors prepare for battle with a mighty opponent by pointing out the great need for the enemy's defeat and then combat the giant with peashooters. The two points usually made in opposing central bank independence—namely, the need for political responsibility by all public agencies and the requirement for a coordinated national economic policy – are expressed and reiterated throughout the hearings. Several interesting analogies are brought into play to make the points. Professor Dudley Johnson testified:

> In my opinion, the argument for an independent monetary authority is inconsistent with the principles underlying a democracy. To argue that the control over the money supply should be independent of the values of certain representatives of the citizenry in a democracy strikes me as ludicrous. It is as if Congress were to create a Department of War and Peace and the President of the United States would appoint a Board composed of seven members for terms of 14 years, with the terms arranged so that one expires every [other] year. Now the Board would have the exclusive jurisdiction to decide whether or not the United States would or would not go to war. Its decision would be binding irrespective of the wishes of the administration.

And Professor John G. Gurley stated:

> "Independence" is a good word, and so many people think that the independence of the Federal Reserve is a good thing. But it is not a good thing. It is like having two managers for the baseball team, each manager independent of the other. The managers could get together for lunches once a week —that might help. Or one of them could try to offset the actions of the other—that might work a bit. Nothing of this sort really would correct the basic situation—the intolerable arrangement of having two managers.

The implication of the witnesses is clear. The Reserve System is not responsible to the political authorities; it need not coordinate its policies with those of other government agencies. Something must be done. The Federal Reserve must be brought under control. Yet what reforms did the academicians suggest in order to make the System subject to government policy? The very proposals of the proponents of Federal Reserve independence were adopted. Giving the President appointive control over the Chairman, as suggested elsewhere by Chairman Martin, was the major recommendation.

It must be noted that the effectiveness of executive control over monetary policy by virtue of its power to appoint the Chairman, even by selecting a newly chosen member for the chair, is doubtful. Chairmen have often become independent of the administration, as can be documented amply. Martin himself was originally a Truman appointee. Yet he subscribes to a conservative monetary ideology, one associated with the Republican party rather than to the more liberal, loose-money views of the Democrats. Marriner Eccles, whose resignation from the chair was not accepted by President Truman, later thought little of defying the Chief Executive. Indeed, in the pre-Accord schism between the Reserve Board and the administration, Eccles came close to calling President Truman a liar. In Britain and Canada, where the government appoints the heads of the central bank, central bankers have pursued the policy that they have thought best, despite strong disagreements over their course of action by their respective executives. Why should this minor modification in the organization of the Federal Reserve Board solve the problem of coordination? One must suspect that this reform would not change the status quo. These suspicions are confirmed by recalling once more the Federal Reserve's support of this proposal side-by-side with its wholehearted espousal of independence.

In all justice it must be noted that some witnesses, notably Professors John Gurley, Abba Lerner, Michael Reagan, and Robert Strotz, and Nathaniel Goldfinger of the AFL-CIO, couple the Presidential appointment of the Federal Reserve Board Chairman with Presidential removal of this official at will. Although this power of removal surely strengthens the President's hand, it is doubtful whether coordination is achievable in this manner. The power of removal is an emergency power; the objective of coordination is to prevent emergencies. Thus if a structural change is necessary, it should not be a plan designed to remove an incompatible official; rather it should involve intervention or mutual consultation in the decision-making process. Indeed, from this point of view, and in spite of other serious deficiencies noted previously, the Patman proposal, which would place the Secretary of the Treasury in the Reserve Board chair, is a much more efficient tool for controlling the Board than is reliance on the appointment-removal power.

When the analysis underlying the testimony of the experts is followed to its logical conclusion, it is obvious that stronger measures are necessary to bring about a coordinated economic policy. Along these lines, Professor Henry M. Villard proposed the establishment of a National Economic Council (NEC), including the Federal Reserve System, the Treasury, the Council of Economic Advisers, and "other interested Government agencies." The NEC would serve in advisory capacity, much as does the National Security Council. But final decisions would be left solely to the President. Thus the Federal Reserve would be made responsible to the President in the same way that the Treasury is; it would become an agency within the administration rather than a body separate from the executive.

In short, the spotlight of the Patman investigation shone on the degree of central bank independence from the executive. Two divergent views were evident. Federal Reserve officials, representatives of the financial community, and Secretary of the Treasury Douglas Dillon felt that the extent of Reserve System autonomy was proper and desirable and that it had withstood the test of time. The representatives of the academic community, on the other hand, believed that both the tradition of representative democracy and the necessity for coordinated economic policy required closer ties with the administration. Yet in spite of these differing views on the proper relationship, both the advocates of independence and their opponents arrived at the same basic proposal. They agreed that the term of Federal Reserve Board Chairman be made coterminous with that of the President, so that the latter would be able to appoint a chairman congenial to him and in agreement with his economic policies. They further agreed that it would be wrong to replace the Secretary of the Treasury on the Reserve Board.

What did the subcommittee conclude? The subcommittee split up on the basis of partisan lines. The Democratic majority shared the views of most economists testifying before them and believed that closer executive ties were necessary. Policywise, the majority exceeded the limited changes suggested by the consensus of witnesses. Perhaps the most important recommendations were two that did not appear at all in the Patman bills:

1. Require that the President set forth in his periodic economic reports, in conjunction with his recommendations on fiscal and debt management policy, guidelines concerning monetary policy, domestic and foreign—including the growth of the money supply, as defined by him—necessary to attain the goals of maximum employment, production, and purchasing power of the Employment Act of 1946.
2. Express the sense of Congress that the Federal Reserve operate in the open market so as to facilitate the achievement of the President's monetary policy; and require that the Federal Reserve, if its monetary views and actions diverge from those recommended by the President, file with the President and the Congress a statement of reasons for its divergence, in form like the President's Economic Report.[2]

The President is to formulate monetary policy, and the Federal Reserve is to implement it, the subcommittee concluded. Should the Federal Reserve believe that policy to be improper, it has the right to act as it wishes. But it must justify its defiance of the President. Pressure is thereby placed on the Reserve System to accommodate the President. Of course, Board Chairmen have always been under some pressure to accommodate their policies to those of the executive. But they have also enjoyed a marked degree of freedom, which would be constrained further if these recommendations became law.

The subcommittee also recommended that the term of the Chairman run concurrently with that of the President. By other structural modifications, specifically the reduction of the Reserve Board to five, with the term of each Governor lowered to five years, the President would be able to appoint a Chairman soon after he took office. Moreover, after five years in office, he would have appointed all the current Board members. Certainly, these provisions are aimed at increasing executive control. The Democratic majority, however, did not proceed as far as it could, for the power to remove Board members, the Chairman included, is denied the President.

In conclusion, the subcommittee accepted the theory of democratic responsibility for the monetary authorities and saw the need for a coordinated economic policy. It acted on these bases to link more closely the central bank to the executive.

II

Wright Patman not only wished to increase Federal Reserve dependence on

[2]U.S. Congress, House of Representatives, Committee on Banking and Currency, Subcommittee on Domestic Finance, *The Federal Reserve System After Fifty Years: Proposals for Improvement of the Federal Reserve and Staff Report* (Washington, D.C.: Government Printing Office, 1964), p. vi.

the executive; he also saw a need for a tightening of the rather loose bonds between the System and Congress. This goal was evident in a section of H.R. 9631 and in another of the Patman bills, H.R. 9685.

The relevant section of H.R. 9631 would require General Accounting Office (GAO) audits of the Board and the Reserve Banks. To be sure, the System is presently audited annually—the Board by an outside firm and the banks by the Board's auditors. Yet the proposed modification is substantive, for GAO audits involve more than a simple review of accounts. The GAO is charged by H.R. 9631 with investigating and reporting "any program, financial transaction, or undertaking observed in the course of the audit which in the opinion of the Comptroller General has been carried on without authority of law." Thus the Reserve System would be subject to a continuous and close scrutiny over all its operations. Because the GAO reports directly to Congress, the System would be subject to direct Congressional inspection on a regular basis. Indeed, the special dispensation granted to the Federal Reserve for self-audit was most likely a result of the desire to protect the System from Congressional intervention.

Congressional control over the Federal Reserve would be strengthened further by the provisions of H.R. 9685, which would subject the Board and System to the appropriations procedure of Congress. Income earned by the System would be paid to the Treasury; expenditures would be derived from Congressional allocations. The Federal Reserve Act of 1913 had intended to make the System self-supporting, with the rediscount mechanism and the purchase and sale of securities serving as the major sources of earnings. The monetary authorities thus have been able to avoid Congressional control via the appropriations process. Because the power of the purse is still strong—it is perhaps Congress' strongest means of control over the governmental agencies—the Reserve System would, with the passage of H.R. 9685, no longer be as free of Congressional control as it formerly was.

The Federal Reserve's increased dependence on Congress, as implied by the reliance on Congressional appropriations to meet Federal Reserve expenditures, was opposed not unexpectedly by Reserve System officials. More surprising was the opposition to the bill voiced by most of the economists who ventured a comment on the issue. For example, Professor Harry Johnson of the University of Chicago approached the bill with mixed feelings. He argued on the one hand that the legislature should have the right to review expenditures and decide on appropriations. In this sense, the Federal Reserve should in no way be different from an executive department or any of the regulatory commissions. On the other hand, he felt that Congress has all too often economized in the narrow sense and has not foreseen the long-run consequences of its stinginess. One obvious example, it seems to me, is in the area of compensation. Salaries of the Reserve Board members are wholly out of alignment with those paid men of similar stature in the private sector of the economy; even their statutory inferiors are remunerated more handsomely. Perhaps the most glaring difference in salaries is between the Chairman of the Board of Governors, at $20,500 annually, and the President of the Federal Reserve Bank of New York, at $70,000 annually—more than three times as much. In fact, the Adviser to the Board of Governors, whose salary is determined by the Board, earns $7,500 more per annum than his superiors, the Governors, whose salaries are fixed by Congress.[3] If Congress were to

[3]A list of salaries paid Federal Reserve as well as other Federal officials may be found in the *Hearings,* pp. 921–923. The salaries of Governors have been increasing since 1964, but the obvious discrepancies have not been removed.

treat the Reserve System as niggardly as it does other agencies, a deterioration in the quality of personnel is a certainty.

Most of the economists, however, objected to closer Congressional control for another reason. Harold Barger of Columbia University lucidly expressed the consensus that was implied in much of the testimony:

> It is axiomatic . . . that in a democratic and self-governing society, monetary policy should be fully subordinated to control by the administration of the day, and that its coordination with other aspects of economic policy should be assured. But I do not believe that Congress is equipped to undertake such control and coordination of day-to-day monetary policy. In my opinion effective direction of the Reserve Board must come, not from Congress, but from the President.

The belief is that Congress is a legislating body and that it is too unwieldy to execute policy. The administration should administer, and, because the consensus was to tie the Reserve System more closely to the President, there was no need to provide for legislative control as well; indeed, such a practice might prove harmful.

The Democratic majority accepted both Patman proposals because they felt that there was no good reason to continue the Reserve System's unique status. Other so-called independent agencies—the ICC, FCC, etc.—must have their books audited by GAO and appeal to Congress for expenditures. Why should the Federal Reserve be different? Underlying this agreement with Patman was the majority's belief that the central bank should not be independent from Congress, that it must respond to the public as represented by Congress.

III

The anti-independence policy proposals that have been assessed thus far lean very heavily on the two grounds of democratic and coordinated decision making. The time has come to examine the validity of these grounds in their American context. Two questions must be answered: (1) Is the Federal Reserve System as presently constituted a democratic institution? (2) Does Federal Reserve autonomy prevent the coordination of national economic policy?

The answer to the question whether the Reserve System is democratic or not depends upon one's interpretation of democracy. To be sure, the question is not easy to answer. But certain points cannot be denied. In the sense that the Federal Reserve is a creation of Congress, is accountable to Congress, is dependent upon the graciousness of Congress for its existence, and can be modified by Congress—as is the objective of Representative Patman's bills—the Federal Reserve certainly cannot roll merrily along, disregarding all legal impositions. The Federal Reserve has never claimed that it could oppose the will of Congress, nor has it done so. It is an agency within the government; it is not a private institution.

Patman denied the democratic nature of the Federal Reserve in the following colloquy:

> *Mr. Shapiro:* . . . it seems to me that the notion of an independent Fed, that is to say, independent of everybody but their own willful desires, I would regard as technically inaccurate, for the Congress of the United States indeed can change this by legislation. . . .
>
> *The Chairman* [Mr. Patman]: . . . You know, in a democracy such as our own, there are a lot of people who have bottleneck positions, any one of whom can say "No" and make it stick, but there is not one person in the United States who can say "Yes" and be absolutely sure. They just cannot do it.
>
> Now, when you go to making legislative changes you first introduce a bill that is referred to a subcommittee. The subcommittee chairman can stop it if he wants to.

Then it passes out and it goes to the whole committee, and the whole committee chairman can have a lot of influence on it, and it can stop there.

Then it has to go through the leadership of the House and then the Rules Committee and those four bottlenecks—that is not all—just those four we see every day.

And then in the Senate it is the same way. So the chances of getting something really meaningful but opposed by an entrenched interest in this country, that is profiting so much by occupying a position that gives them special privileges, are rather remote because it takes only a few to stop things while a majority cannot always actually accomplish things.

So we have those deterrents to changes. So we should not speak of them glibly in that we can just go to Congress and get something done right quick. We just cannot do that.

It is too difficult in a democracy, as it should be. I am not saying that a change should be made. I think it is all right.

Another point is that the people, who handle the money, control the supply to a great extent and interest rates, perform the most important functions of our Government. The people who do that can veto the wishes of the President if they wish to.

They can also veto the will of Congress if they want to. They can veto the program of the administration in power regardless of the politics.

Thus Patman expressed an opinion that Congress is not always responsive to the will of the people, because various impediments prevent the passage of desired legislation. In all truth, no one can deny that these bottlenecks exist; certainly the Congressional system can be made more responsive to the populace. But just as certain is the fact that Congress, despite its cumbersome nature, does represent the people, does respond to the majority. Patman himself says in the statement just cited, "I am not saying that a change should be made. I think it is all right." The fact that the Federal Reserve's governors do not respond to the wishes of a group of Congressmen is not symbolic of an antidemocratic institution. It simply recognizes that Congress as a whole has not acted. And until Congress does act, the Reserve Board continues to function in accordance with its existing legislative mandate. Thus the System cannot be deemed a nondemocratic institution.

The major remaining issue, then, is the validity of the desire to establish closer ties with the executive. A coordinated economic policy is necessary, and the administration should be the coordinator, it was claimed. How valid is this conclusion?

The major weapons used in attaining the objectives of the Employment Act of 1946 are monetary and fiscal, with an occasional assist from Presidential moral suasion. Monetary policy lies primarily, but not exclusively, with the Federal Reserve. The Treasury, too, has monetary powers; for example, it can change the volume of government deposits held by the commercial banking system. The Treasury also sets the interest payment on government securities and thus can influence interest rates. It is evident that one reason for coordination stems from the need to assure that the institutions of monetary control do not work at cross-purposes. A recurrence of the 1950 debacle, when the Treasury set a rate on to-be-issued government securities and the Reserve Board permitted an increase in market rates that resulted in a negligible market absorption of the Treasury issue, should not be tolerated.

The problem of unifying the weapons of monetary policy under one head merits more than a brief appraisal. It is difficult, however, to see why the President of the United States, rather than the Federal Reserve, should be made the coordinator. The Treasury's monetary powers are ancillary to its main functions, the collection and disbursal of Government revenues. Congress has delegated monetary control to the Reserve System. Why not then add these Treasury monetary powers to the Reserve System tool kit? Alternatively, the Treasury could be ordered by Congress to accept Federal Reserve domination in monetary matters. The Douglas Subcommittee of the Joint Economic Committee accepted this second view in its 1950 *Report:*

> Congress by joint resolution [should] issue general instruction . . . that . . . it is the will of Congress that the primary power and responsibility for regulating the supply, availability, and cost of credit in general shall be vested in the duly constituted authorities of the Federal Reserve System and that Treasury actions relative to money, credit and transactions in the Federal debt shall be made consistent with the policies of the Federal Reserve.[4]

The main issue concerning coordination is not this one, however, but another —the unification of monetary and fiscal policy. This issue was implicit and sometimes explicit in much of the testimony before the Patman Subcommittee, and indeed most often when the "independence" question was debated. Two citations from the subcommittee hearings may be presented to demonstrate this point. Professor Abba Lerner, in his written testimony, claimed, "Independence of the monetary authority from the Executive in matters of policy, even if both do the best they can in the public interest, leads to fiscal and monetary policies working at cross-purposes, defeating each other's objectives." Professor Leo Raskind implied as much when he stated, "When the President, who has authority to make decisions involving nuclear war, is barred by statute from responsibility for the monetary component of economic stabilization policy, the need for change is apparent." Patman, in a widely circulated address originally delivered in the House of Representatives (August 3, 1964) and entitled "The ABC's of America's Money System," stated, "Monetary policy has been formulated in a vacuum—uncoordinated a good deal of the time with our fiscal and economic policies and programs." Thus the major claim to be examined is that the President should be given control over monetary policy in order to assure its conformity to his fiscal policy.

The key words in the preceding sentence are "his fiscal policy." The basic assumption of the proponents of Presidential control over monetary policy is that fiscal policy lies in the President's hand. Yet such an assumption is so far from the truth that it is difficult to understand how so many intelligent and well-versed individuals have committed this error. Fiscal policy is synonymous with budgetary policy, and a brief review of the budget-making process will serve to demonstrate the small amount of Presidential discretion that is involved.

Three administrative agencies are concerned with the budgetary process—the Treasury, the Council of Economic Advisers, and the Bureau of the Budget. The Treasury collects revenues and pays for government expenditures. It also possesses informal recommendatory powers, because its head is the government's major financial officer. Similarly, the members of the Council, as the administration's economists, are concerned with fiscal policy, but they too have only advisory powers.

The Bureau of the Budget is the President's arm for expenditure control. It is charged with reviewing executive agency expenditure proposals and recommending to the President the sums it deems proper. Its judgments are weighed heavily by the President in the formulation of the administrative budget. The Bureau, however, is not all-powerful, because any agency can appeal directly to the President.

Once the administrative budget is completed, it is submitted to Congress. Here lies the real budgetary power. Congress dissects the budget, each House splitting it in twain and sending it to the respective appropriations and finance

---

[4]U.S. Congress, Joint Economic Committee, *Monetary, Credit and Fiscal Policies, Report* (Washington, D.C.: Government Printing Office, 1950), p. 2. [Coordination in this area is discussed in Selection 26—ed.]

committees. The appropriations committees then parcel out the expenditure proposals among the various subcommittees, which then examine, investigate, deliberate, conclude, and recommend. Thus the budget is chopped into minute pieces and then reassembled as though it were a jigsaw puzzle. When the budget is completed and passed by both Houses, its final shape is determined. Thus Congress, not the President, creates fiscal policy. Coordination of monetary and fiscal policy under the President achieves little in the way of unification, simply because fiscal policy is not subject to Presidential control.[5] It is also true that the President can exercise some discretion over expenditures, especially by refusing to spend all that is appropriated. He cannot exceed the maximum set by Congress, however, nor is it realistic to assume that the executive will spend less than is available to it. It follows that a conclusive case for amending the Federal Reserve's status on these grounds has not been demonstrated. The arguments made in favor of decreasing independence are simply not conclusive.

In short, in the United States, although the abstract idea of coordination is appealing, it is misleading. The "checks and balances" that lie at the basis of the tripartite division of the federal government prevent Presidential control over fiscal policy and thus destroy the plausibility of the "coordination" argument. The Federal Reserve System has defied the President of the United States more than once. In this way it may have caused ill feeling and perhaps even economic dislocation. But unless a major structural change that gives the President control over economic stabilization policy in general (such as Presidential discretionary fiscal policy) is promulgated, it is meaningless to expect much from attempts to modify Federal Reserve-administration relations.

[5] The fact that eighteen months passed before Congress, in 1968, acted on President Johnson's proposed tax surcharge and thirteen months elapsed before it passed the 1964 tax reduction bill should drive home this point.

the bank supervision controversy

"Fed Blocks [Comptroller of the Currency] Saxon on Foreign Stocks," read a headline in the New York *Herald Tribune* in July 1964; the Comptroller countered by impugning the motives of the Board. This controversy concerned the rights of national banks to purchase stock in foreign banks; it was but one of a number of issues in the early 1960s over which the different bank regulatory authorities did not see eye to eye. For example, disputes arose in the area of bank mergers (see the second section of Part II) and federal funds. With respect to the latter, the authorities quibbled over the question whether federal funds transactions were loans or sales. Because a national bank may not lend more than 10 percent of its capital to a single borrower, defining the disposal of federal funds as a loan would place a limit on such transactions. Alternatively, calling these transactions sales would permit complete bank discretion in the alienation of federal funds. The Federal Reserve Board of Governors adhered to the "loan" definition but in 1963 the Comptroller accepted the "sales" label and thus set himself at odds with the Board.

A more recent confrontation between the regulatory authorities has taken place over the issue of one-bank holding companies. Federal banking legislation regulates holding companies that own 25 percent or more of the stock of two or more banks but does not apply to holding companies that own only one bank. Although the one-bank holding companies do not represent a new feature on the banking scene—there were over 500 such firms incorporated by 1965—the majority of them were either small or primarily engaged in activities other than banking. The reason for the current

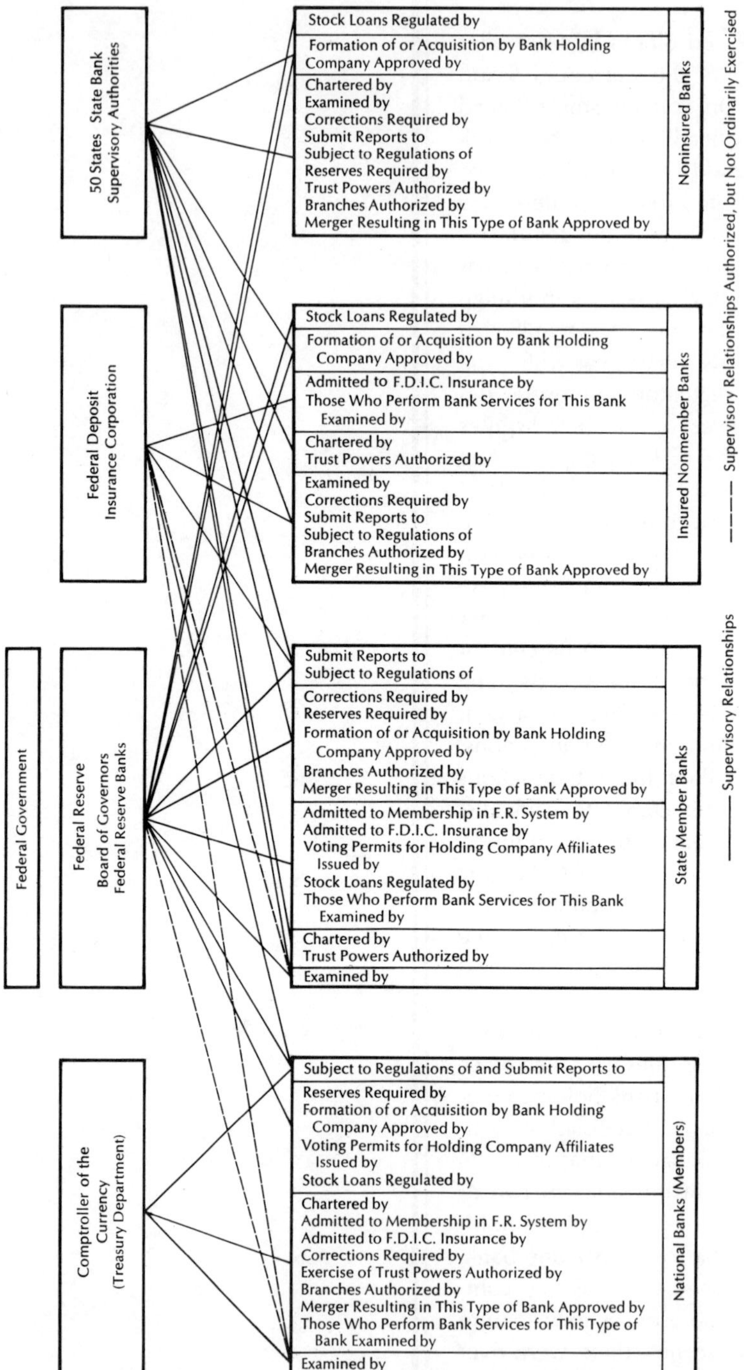

Figure 1 Supervision of the Commercial Banking System—Principal Relationships

SOURCE: J. C. Welman, Jr., "Allocation of Supervisory Responsibility Today," Federal Reserve Bank of St. Louis, *Bank Supervision* (1963), p. 18.

interest in the one-bank holding company lies in the nature of the newer corporations. The banking giants, who will play the dominant role in new holding companies, wish to adopt this organizational form in order to expand into activities otherwise closed to them by the banking authorities. More than forty of the 100—and eight of the ten—largest commercial banks had either formed or planned to form one-bank holding companies by the early part of 1970. Although the Comptroller has publicly favored this institutional reform, Federal Reserve officials have announced their opposition and have sought legislation designed to regulate and confine the one-bank conglomerates.

Central to this dispute is the fact that Congress has not clearly defined the authority of each regulatory agency. Figure 1 illustrates some of the areas of overlapping jurisdiction and includes state as well as federal supervisory authorities. It is unlikely that Congress could ever devise an ironclad division of responsibilities. The alternative suggested by some experts is to create a single agency, possessing authority to implement all federal banking legislation. This proposal might involve the establishment of a "Federal Banking Commission," or it might be accomplished by amalgamating two of the three existing regulatory bodies into the third. Indeed, in 1965 two bills were introduced in Congress to unify the federal supervisory authorities. One, H.R. 107, would have abolished the Comptroller of the Currency and the FDIC directorate and transferred their bank supervisory powers and those currently held by the Board of Governors of the Federal Reserve System to a newly created Federal Banking Commission, whereas the other, H.R. 6885, would have made the Secretary of the Treasury responsible for all supervision.

The two selections appearing in this section debate the merits of a monolithic regulatory agency. Howard H. Hackley defends the consolidation proposal; Carter H. Golembe, however, argues that the disadvantages of centralization outweigh its advantages.

19 IS THERE A CASE AGAINST A SINGLE FEDERAL BANK SUPERVISORY AGENCY?

HOWARD H. HACKLEY

In the earlier parts of the article of which the present selection is only the conclusion, Howard Hackley examines in detail more than twenty areas of differences in interpretation that represent only some of the centers of dispute among bank regulatory authorities. He writes that "many have been omitted, and new conflicts arise almost every day." That being the case, the opening sentence of the following selection does not come as much of a surprise. Hackley's arguments are directed at the federal supervisory authorities. Would you be willing to extend his conclusions to the state level as well, replacing the present fifty state banking authorities with one federal regulatory commission?

• • •

The sheer logic that underlies proposals for a single federal bank supervisory agency is so persuasive that arguments *against* such proposals deserve special analysis. For the most part, such arguments have been made in opposition to the establishment of a new Federal Banking Commission, but their reasoning, if valid, would apply also to the consolidation of supervisory functions in an existing agency, whether the Treasury Department, the Federal Reserve, or the FDIC.

In general, opposition to a single agency has been based on one or more of four grounds: (1) that a single agency would impair, if not destroy, the dual banking system; (2) that it would result in a "monolithic" concentration of power in one agency; (3) that it would eliminate a desirable element of initiative and innovation and thus tend to impede the development of a dynamic and progressive banking system; and (4) that the present system "works well" and should not be changed. Some of these grounds may overlap each other and they might be stated in different terms, but it is believed that they fairly embrace all of the principal arguments advanced against consolidation of federal bank supervisory functions in a single agency of the federal government.

Impairment of the Dual Banking System

The argument most frequently expressed is that consolidation of federal bank regulatory authority in one agency would impair, imperil, eliminate, or destroy our traditional dual banking system. This argument raises two pertinent questions: (1) what is meant by the dual banking system, and (2) regardless of the merits of that system, how would a single federal bank supervisory agency affect it?

Comptroller of the Currency James J. Saxon has very aptly observed that there is "no word in the lexicon of bankers which has been more susceptible of various understandings, but so little expressed in precise and concise definition

From Howard H. Hackley, "Our Baffling Banking System," *Virginia Law Review*, 52, 814–815, 817–828. Reprinted by permission.

as has the term 'dual banking system.' "[1] In general, the term has been defined simply as the "system by which state and federally chartered banks coexist." More specifically, this system has been described as resting upon three fundamental principles: (1) freedom of movement between the state and national bank systems; (2) a minimum of federal control over state banks; and (3) competitive equality between national and state banks.

These and many other attempts to define the dual banking system serve only to demonstrate the ambiguity of the term. It may even be questioned whether such a thing as a dual banking system actually exists today. One may plausibly argue that we have fifty-four banking systems—the fifty-one systems governed by the laws of the fifty states and the District of Columbia, plus the national banking system, plus the two hybrid state-federal systems that result from the voluntary membership of some state banks in the Federal Reserve System and the voluntary election by other state banks to obtain deposit insurance. In another sense, it may be argued that we actually have a quadruple banking system, consisting of national banks, state member banks, nonmember insured state banks, and nonmember noninsured state banks.

Assuming, however, that we have a dual banking system in the sense that every bank is free to decide whether it will operate under a state charter as a state bank, or under a federal charter as a national bank, one may question whether a dual banking system necessarily results in a minimum of federal regulation of state banks or complete competitive equality between state and national banks. State banks are subject to federal regulation (with one or two exceptions) *only* if they voluntarily subject themselves to such regulation, either by joining the Federal Reserve System or by obtaining federal deposit insurance. Again, if state and national banks were placed on a perfectly equal competitive basis, it is difficult to understand why any bank would have reason to convert from one system to the other; indeed, in such circumstances we would have, in substance if not in form, a single banking system.

In any event, the question here is whether consolidation of federal bank supervision in a single agency would impair the dual banking system as it has been defined above. Assertions that this would be the case have been made frequently and vehemently.

• • •

Presumably, much of the opposition to proposals for consolidation of federal bank supervision in a single agency has been based on the fear that it would necessarily involve expanded regulation of state banks by the federal government. Actually, such proposals would not in any respect change the *substantive* requirement of federal law; they would change only the structure of federal bank supervision. They would not extend to state banks any provision of federal law not now applicable to such banks. The fear that the mere establishment of a single agency would lead to encroachment on the powers of the states and thus imperil the dual banking system appears to have no logical foundation.

• • •

Concentration of Power

Frequently coupled with the assertion that a single federal bank supervisory agency would weaken the dual banking system has been the argument that such a single agency would concentrate "monolithic" power in that agency and eliminate the "checks and balances" that result from distribution of authority among three federal banking agencies. For example, it has been stated that the Federal Banking Commission proposal makes

---

[1]Address to the National Association of Supervisors of State Banks, Bretton Woods, N.H., September 18, 1962.

sense "if we intend to adopt the concept of the monolithic state"; that it represents a "monolithic approach"; and that it would result in an "undue, and potentially dangerous concentration of power in one Federal agency." It has been alleged that the present tripartite division of authority is "well adapted to the thesis that checks and balances and separation of power among these agencies . . . are decidedly in the public interest"; and that such consolidation of authority in a single agency would result in "one czar that becomes absolute in power and therefore it is contrary to what we like to think of as our checks and balances."

In reply to such arguments, Governor Robertson has urged that the proposed Federal Banking Commission bill simply would not create a federal "superagency" and that the proposed Commission "would have no new powers over the banking industry, but only those that are now exercised by one or more of the three agencies," except that the Commission would indeed have "one new and important power—the power to administer the Federal banking laws in a consistent, equitable, and efficient manner, to establish uniform ground rules that would aid, rather than impede, the progress of the entire banking industry and equalize competitive opportunities within it."[2]

The argument that a single federal banking agency would eliminate the "checks and balances" inherent in the present tripartite division of federal bank supervisory authority is patently based upon a fallacious analogy to the constitutional separation of legislative, executive, and judicial powers in the federal government. The two are not the same. The three federal banking agencies all perform functions of the same character in a single area of federal regulation pursuant to laws of Congress. Opponents of a single agency in this area apparently believe that the existence of three regulatory agencies precludes the assumption of arbitrary power over the banking industry by any one agency simply because a bank in any of the three classes of federally supervised banks is free to switch to one of the other classes if it feels that it may obtain more lenient treatment by the federal agency that supervises the other class of banks. Obviously, this sort of "checks and balances" is not desirable; on the contrary, it merely tends to encourage the "race in laxity" that Governor Robertson has deplored. As the Governor has stated, those who oppose a single agency "fight under a banner bearing the motto 'Divide and conquer' " and for that reason "*want Federal* bank supervision to be fragmented."

Stultification of Progress

Some who oppose a single federal banking agency have suggested that the present tripartite structure engenders a kind of "competition" among the several federal agencies that tends to stimulate new ideas and imaginative thinking and thus promotes a dynamic, progressive banking system.

For example, the Comptroller of the Currency has argued that the present system preserves a "variety of sources of initiative" and that a single agency would lead to "stagnation" and "eliminate the kind of diversity and innovation which is so essential . . . ." Indeed, when asked about the chaos resulting from the present tripartite federal banking structure, the Comptroller stated: "If this is chaos, this is the most profitable and useful chaos we have ever seen."[3] Similarly, Chairman Randall of the FDIC has expressed the view that differences among the federal banking agencies are desirable, since they are the "natural outcome of a system which is flexible enough to not only work in such an environment,

[2] *American Banker,* Feb. 28, 1963, p. 1, col. 1, at 2, col. 3; *id.,* June 26, 1963, p. 1, col. 3.

[3] *1965 Hearings on Consolidation of Federal Bank Supervisory Functions* 263.

but to develop new tools, new methods to serve the public."[4]

The answer to such arguments is similar to the answer to arguments that a single agency would result in concentration of power and elimination of checks and balances. It is undoubtedly true that three federal banking agencies may have different ideas as to what is most conducive to progressive banking; but, if the three agencies construe the same provisions of federal banking law in different ways, or if one of the agencies adopts policies more liberal than those of the others, the end result may not be progress but simply, again, a "race in laxity" that could threaten the soundness of the banking system.

Perhaps the best answer to such arguments was reflected in the following question put by Congressman Multer to Vice-President William F. Kelly of the American Bankers Association:

> Why have only three agencies of Government, why not have six agencies and let the group or the individual or the bank go to six different agencies and present his application each time until he finally gets one of the six who will grant his application?[5]

• • •

The Status Quo Argument

A standard argument against a single federal banking agency is that the present banking system has worked well and that there is no need for any alteration of the system. The argument is generally accompanied by the assertion that differences among the federal bank supervisory agencies can always be resolved by mutual agreement and coordination.

• • •

Unquestionably, the present system "works," but no unbiased student of the subject could honestly conclude that it "works well." Anyone who has read the 1963 and 1965 House hearings on bills to unify federal bank supervision cannot help but be convinced that the present federal bank regulatory structure is on the verge of chaos. Anyone who has carefully studied the unequal manner in which many federal banking laws apply to different classes of banks and the numerous interpretative, regulatory, and policy differences among the Comptroller of the Currency, the Federal Reserve, and the FDIC can only conclude that the present system involves a wasteful and inefficient duplication of functions and gross inequities among different classes of banks. Anyone who reads the financial papers and talks to commercial bankers cannot fail to get the impression that the present confusion in federal bank regulation, particularly over the last four or five years, has tended to generate public disrespect for the banking agencies and a gradual lowering of banking standards.

In brief, the case against a single federal banking agency cannot be supported on any logical grounds. On the contrary, it seems increasingly apparent that the only certain means of correcting the inequities in our banking system is through consolidation of federal bank supervisory functions in one agency. In 1940, long before Governor Robertson made his proposal for a Federal Banking Commission, a committee appointed by the Attorney General to study administrative procedures in government agencies came to a similar conclusion. That committee stated:

> In view of the inherent difficulties, it is highly probable that the solution lies not in makeshift voluntary "cooperation" between the various agencies but in the thoroughgoing coordination and unification of the several banking authorities, a possibility which is now being considered by the appropriate congressional committees and which is forcefully urged by the Board itself in its recent annual report.[6]

---

[4] *American Banker,* March 16, 1965, p. 1, col. 2, at 13, col. 1.

[5] *Hearings on Federal Banking Commission* 275.

[6] S. Doc. No. 186, 76th Cong., 3d Sess., pt. 9, at 41 (1940).

The same conclusion was reached twenty-five years later in a *Wall Street Journal* editorial which, after referring to current disputes among the banking agencies as "not only ridiculous but dangerous," stated: "The only effective way to end such disputes is to eliminate the built-in jurisdictional conflicts by combining bank supervisory powers in a single agency."[7]

SUMMARY AND CONCLUSIONS

From 1791 until 1836, with a five-year hiatus, our country had a single federally chartered bank, the Bank of the United States, along with state-chartered banks; but from 1836 until the Civil War, state-chartered banks flourished without competition from any banks organized under federal law and without regulation by the federal government. As a means of financing the Civil War, Congress in 1863 provided for the chartering of privately owned "national" banks that could issue currency secured by bonds of the United States and that operated under the supervision of the Comptroller of the Currency. With the apparent expectation that national banks would completely replace state banks, a prohibitive federal tax was levied on state bank notes. In self-defense, state banks solicited "deposits," instead of issuing notes as a means of obtaining loanable funds; later, they inaugurated new services, such as trust services, that were not then permissible for national banks. As a result, state banks survived and the "dual banking system" came into existence.

In 1913, as an outgrowth of the financial panic of 1907, Congress enacted the Federal Reserve Act, under which all national banks were required, and state banks were permitted, to become members of the Federal Reserve System, subject to specified reserve requirements and to certain limitations upon their operations. For the first time, state banks were brought under federal regulation, but only if they voluntarily submitted to regulation by joining the System. Such regulation was entrusted to a new federal agency, the Federal Reserve Board. Twenty years later, a nationwide banking crisis led to action which made federal deposit insurance available to all member banks, national and state, and to state nonmember banks that elected to obtain such insurance. As a result, federal regulation of state banks was further extended, but again only to state banks that voluntarily submitted to such regulation, and a third federal banking agency, the Federal Deposit Insurance Corporation, was vested with certain regulatory functions with respect to state banks that sought deposit insurance but not membership in the Federal Reserve System.

As the result of these developments, our country now has four classes of banks: national banks, chartered and regulated primarily by the Comptroller of the Currency but regulated in some respect by the Federal Reserve; state member banks, chartered and regulated by the states but voluntarily subject to certain requirements of federal law and regulations of the Federal Reserve; nonmember insured state banks, chartered and regulated by the states but voluntarily subject to certain requirements of federal law and regulations of the FDIC; and nonmember noninsured state banks, chartered and regulated (with a few exceptions) only by the states.

The net result is a banking system of almost unbelievable complexity. The banking laws of the fifty states are marked by countless differences. The powers of state banks and the limitations under which they operate are different in numerous respects from the powers of national banks and the limitations imposed on their operations by federal law —sometimes to the advantage of state banks and sometimes to the advantage of national banks. Restrictions of federal

[7]*Wall Street J.*, April 21, 1965, p. 18, cols. 1–2.

law on the operations of national banks, state member banks, and nonmember insured state banks are not uniform. Without rhyme or reason, some restrictions apply only to national banks, some apply only to national and state member banks, and some apply to all insured banks. Even where the same or similar provisions of federal law apply to different classes of federally regulated banks, they have not always been interpreted in the same manner by the three federal bank supervisory agencies.

Such a system has given rise, not only to great confusion, but, more important, to competitive inequalities among different classes of banks. Because membership in the Federal Reserve System usually subjects state banks to more severe restrictions than those applicable under state laws, particularly with respect to reserves, there has developed a trend on the part of the smaller state banks to withdraw from membership in the System. Because the Comptroller has applied federal banking laws to national banks more liberally than they have been applied by the Federal Reserve to state member banks, many state member banks, especially the larger ones, have converted to national charters. Theoretically, if these two trends continue, the day may come when there will be no state member banks.

What should be done to simplify our banking system and, particularly, to remove inequities among different classes of banks? In attempting to answer this question, one must start with two realistic, if not logical, assumptions: (1) the removal of all disparities among the banking laws of the various states cannot be expected; and (2) the dual banking system must be preserved. The second of these assumptions appears to mean that any bank must remain free to be either a state bank or a national bank; and this assumption rules out any idea of "nationalizing" our banking system, *i.e.*, subjecting all banks to regulation only by the federal government.

At the state level, there are two avenues that might be followed. First, without undermining the proper role of the states, it is possible that greater uniformity among state banking laws could be achieved in certain limited respects, such as, in the areas of capital requirements, limitations on loans to one borrower, and payment of interest on deposits. Second, there is clearly a need for action by the states to modernize their banking laws and to improve the caliber of their banking departments, particularly by upward revisions in salary scales.

At the federal level, there are several areas in which action might be taken to simplify our banking system and to eliminate inequalities among different classes of banks.

First, the logical basis for the advantages now enjoyed by national banks over state banks on constitutional grounds merits fresh consideration. It would seem worthwhile, for example, to reexamine the validity of the reasons for which national banks are immune from state taxation and "doing business" laws. Moreover, the applicability of state banking laws (*e.g.*, those regarding bank holding companies and the issuance of negotiable notes) requires clarification by Congress. It may even be questioned whether there is today any sound basis for exempting national banks from state regulation on the ground that they are instrumentalities of the federal government.

Second, consideration should be given to substantive changes in federal banking law which would more nearly equalize the applicability of such laws to different classes of federally regulated banks. For example, in order to insure effective implementation of national monetary policies, there are good reasons for extending reserve requirements of federal law, now applicable only to member banks of the Federal Reserve System, to all commercial banks or at least to all federally insured banks. Sound reasons also exist for extending to nonmember insured banks various other provisions of federal law that now apply only to members of the Federal Reserve System, such as restrictions on loans to affiliates, loans to executive officers, purchases of corporate stocks, and interlocking directorates.

Third, without regard to substantive changes in federal law, there is clearly a need for structural changes that would eliminate conflicts among federal bank supervisory agencies. Efforts in recent years to resolve such conflicts by coordination among the three federal banking agencies should be pursued. Efforts to resolve such differences by legislation as to specific issues should also be pursued to the greatest extent possible. However, attempts to settle differences through coordination procedures and specific legislation have borne little fruit. The only way in which such differences may be finally resolved seems to lie in the consolidation of federal bank regulatory authority in a single agency. At this point, one is confronted with questions (1) whether a single federal banking agency would impair the dual banking system, and (2) in which agency such authority should be consolidated.

As to the first of these questions, the writer believes that such a single federal banking agency would *not* threaten the dual banking system. The second question is more difficult to answer. On balance, the choice appears to be between the Federal Reserve Board and a new Federal Banking Commission. In favor of the Federal Reserve, the principal argument is that the effective performance of the Federal Reserve's monetary and central banking functions would be impaired by disassociating it from bank supervision and close contact with the commercial banking system. In favor of a new Banking Commission, the principal argument is that the Board of Governors should be free to devote all of its time to monetary and central banking functions and that the performance of these functions would not be impaired if the Board were given access to bank supervisory information, including bank examination reports.

Regardless of the agency chosen, three requisites are important. First, the agency selected should not be subject to political influence; it should be an independent agency, protected from pressures by Congress or the President. Second, it should be a board or commission rather than a single individual. Third, it should have express authority to delegate its functions within prescribed limits.

• • •

20 THE CASE FOR DECENTRALIZATION

CARTER H. GOLEMBE

The marked divergence of views between Carter H. Golembe and Howard Hackley can be readily seen by comparing the first sentence of the Hackley excerpt with one that appears in the following selection: "The logic that underlies the case for decentralized federal bank supervision is so persuasive that arguments *against* the system deserve special emphasis." Golembe believes that the historical development of the banking structure and legislative acts has not been haphazard and that, in any case, the divergent opinions among the authorities have not had any serious impact on banking.

• • •

The case for a decentralized bank regulatory structure necessarily depends upon weighing alternatives and concluding that one set of objectives is preferable to another. In simplest terms, this case entails acceptance of the assumption that two objectives are paramount: (1) a competitive commercial banking system comprised of a large number of independent units, and (2) the dispersion of control over that system. In this connection, it is important to take another look at the supervisory structure which Congress has assembled, and in particular to note its relation to the so-called dual system of banking.

Critics are quite correct when they point out that dual banking has become such an emotional issue or symbol that its meaning and functions are often obscured. Stripped of the excess verbiage which has accumulated like barnacles over the years, dual banking means two things, and just two things: (1) there shall be alternative routes of entry into the banking business, and (2) there shall be supervisory and statutory alternatives available to banks, arising out of the existence of a dual chartering system. The traditional or so-called "pure" dual system was based on federal and state duality—the entry and supervisory alternatives were provided by the states and the federal government. The "pure" system existed from 1863 to 1913, when federal supervision was extended to those state banks which chose to join the Federal Reserve System. Another substantial change occurred in 1933 when the FDIC was established, extending federal bank supervision to virtually all commercial banks.

Nevertheless, the basic ingredients of the dual system still remain. The genius of the present federal regulatory structure is that it ameliorates the problems caused by the pure dual banking system—most notably lax supervision, "overbanking," and bank failures—while it retains the benefits of the dual system.

Under the present system, the entry process still begins in the traditional fashion, by application for either a state or federal charter. However, success in obtaining the former no longer guarantees entry, since deposit insurance is

From Carter H. Golembe, "Our Remarkable Banking System," *Virginia Law Review,* 53, 1107–1114. Reprinted by permission.

needed if the bank is to operate successfully. But the need for virtually all new banks to obtain deposit insurance before entering the banking business does not mean that the FDIC is the sole decision-making body so far as entry is concerned. On the contrary, this power is shared by three federal agencies. This can be illustrated by considering the options available to a particular group desiring to start a bank. This group may obtain a state charter or a commitment for a state charter and may then apply to the FDIC for insurance. If the application is rejected, the organizers have the option of applying to the Federal Reserve Bank of their district for membership in the Federal Reserve System as a state bank. If this application is accepted, deposit insurance is automatically granted by reason of that membership, regardless of the earlier decision by the FDIC. Finally if the organizers are rejected by both the FDIC and the Federal Reserve Bank of their district, they may then apply directly to the Comptroller of the Currency for a national charter, which also includes the automatic grant of insurance.

It seems clear that provision for alternative entry routes is necessary to guard against the dangers inherent in concentrating in one agency the power to make entry decisions. If entry decisions are to be made by one agency, whether federal or state, there is always the possibility that a meritorious application will be rejected, either because a mistake has been made in appraising the prospects of and need for the new bank, or because existent commercial banks are able to exercise sufficient influence over the chartering agency to prevent organization of the new bank. Providing alternative entry routes may not be a complete solution, but it does in fact solve this problem in many cases. Anyone close to the procedure for organizing new commercial banks has personal knowledge of situations in which a new bank was organized and became profitable even though one of the chartering agencies had previously rejected the application either on the ground that there was no need for the new bank or that it might jeopardize existing banks.

Turning now to the supervisory alternatives, a bank may elect at any time to operate under either federal or state law, and may choose among three federal supervisors. In fact, each year there are a number of decisions to "convert" from state to national or national to state charter, or to retain the state charter and "convert" into or out of the Federal Reserve System. The motives in such cases vary. For many years there has been attrition in the number of Federal Reserve member banks as small banks leave to take advantage of generally lower reserve requirements for nonmember banks. Within the past several years there has been a noticeable shift, mostly within the Federal Reserve System, from state to national charter, due undoubtedly to the rulings of the Comptroller. And inevitably there are some conversions of all types which are motivated by the belief of a few bankers that the particular federal supervision they receive is either inadequate or unduly harsh. One of the surprising facts is that the number of conversions is so small. For example, in 1965 there were fifty-three conversions of one type or another, representing less than one-half of one percent of all commercial banks.

The important point to note, however, is that a commercial bank cannot avoid federal supervision, unless it is willing to give up deposit insurance. But despite the conflicts and difficulties described earlier, this federal supervision is neither inadequate nor unduly harsh, for the supervisory staffs of the three federal agencies are of particularly good quality and operate under high standards. Under the existing bank regulatory structure, the basic options available under the traditional dual banking system remain available. At the same time, federal standards and federal supervision have been used to ensure a highly competitive banking system, remarkably free from bank failures.

There is not the slightest doubt that centralization of federal bank regulation would kill the dual system. At this point it is essential to avoid semantics and concentrate attention on the effect that centralization would have on (1) entry and (2) supervisory alternatives. Under a centralized system, the right of entry into banking would be decided in one place—the Federal Banking Commission, or its equivalent. That a choice between state and federal charters would still be possible is irrelevant, since a group, whose application for a national charter had been rejected by the Commission, would stand little chance later, when it was required to appear before the same body to request insurance under a state charter. Similarly, the supervisory safety valve would be gone at the federal level. No matter how rigid or how stultifying supervision became, there would be no alternative available to a bank unless it chose to give up deposit insurance. Only a pale ghost of the dual system, statutory alternatives, would remain.

The logic that underlies the case for decentralized federal bank supervision is so persuasive that arguments *against* the system deserve special emphasis. Of course, the primary argument is that frictions and conflicts result from the tripartite system with its overlapping jurisdictions. However, the following arguments have also been advanced: the present structure is the result of historical accident; it leads to a "race towards laxity" in supervision; it is desired by bankers who, presumably, seek out the easiest supervisor; it is illogical to disperse federal authority among three agencies when one could do the job, and particularly when the single agency would not possess any more power than that which the federal government now exercises through three agencies.

The so-called "accident" of divided federal authority has already been discussed. However, additional comment is warranted by the arguments that there will be a "race towards laxity" and that bankers will seek out easier supervision. First, it must be stated categorically that the quality and ability of federal bank supervisory personnel, in all three agencies, is of the highest caliber. There simply is no evidence, in this writer's opinion, to show that federal supervisory personnel are becoming less diligent or less competent. Quite the contrary, standards are continuously being raised. If "race towards laxity" simply means the attraction which the national system has had for some banks in recent years because of the Comptroller's attempts to free national banks from restrictions, then the issue moves into other areas—for example, is the fact that the Comptroller authorized direct leasing for national banks sufficient by itself to support a charge of deterioration in bank supervision? The question as to whether a particular ruling or action was justified in terms of the Comptroller's statutory authority is largely irrelevant. To sustain a charge of "race towards laxity" it must be shown that the ruling will lead to unsafe or unsound banking practices. It is submitted that such a case has not been made.

Bankers may switch charters or supervision for a variety of reasons, but few are so naive as to think that easier supervision will somehow result. Generally, the reason for switching is simply the desire to operate under the set of laws which is most favorable to the particular business of the bank. Small state banks have been leaving the Federal Reserve for years in order to obtain lower reserve requirements, even though this move results in supervision by the FDIC, which has long been recognized as a particularly "tough" supervisory agency. Larger banks tend to join the Federal Reserve System when the advantages of the discount window and other Federal Reserve services become significant. For certain types of bank operations a national charter is desirable; for other types a state charter may be preferable. As indicated earlier, the actual number of conversions is remarkably small, but those which do occur suggest that the federal regulatory structure, without sacrificing high standards, has attained a degree of viability which might well be envied by other regulatory systems.

Perhaps the most difficult argument to understand is the contention that a division of regulatory authority is illogical, and that this "problem" can be solved by consolidating authority in one place. What is forgotten, or not mentioned, is that the powers which are to be combined are not the same. What is proposed is to combine not only regulatory power, but also the powers of bank insurance (FDIC), chartering (Comptroller), and supervision in general (all three agencies). To argue that the resulting single agency would really be no more powerful than the sum of the three is absurd. One might argue with comparable logic that to combine in the executive branch all the powers of Congress and the Supreme Court would not result in a "superagency," since the executive "would have no new powers . . . but only those that are now exercised by one or more of the three." The simple fact is that if one federal agency were to issue all national bank charters, decide on the insurability of all state banks, and supervise all insured banks (national and state), there would be a concentration of financial power unparalleled in American financial history.

A few final observations are called for on the matter of conflicts and friction which, if they were substantial, would result in a virtually unworkable system. If this were true, one would expect to find the banks and the agencies united and vehement in their demands for centralization. But time and again commercial banks have made it clear that they prefer the existing regulating structure, even though self-interest would seemingly call for the opposite position if the charges leveled at the present system were accurate. Of course, it is sometimes intimated that banks prefer this arrangement because it permits them to play one agency off against another. But this allegation is inconsistent with the fact that bank conversions are relatively few. Also, supervisory standards are far superior today than they were prior to 1933, when there were only two federal banking agencies, or prior to 1913, when there was only one.

The agencies' attitudes are more interesting. For reasons not entirely clear, the driving force behind criticism of the federal regulatory structure has long been centered in the Federal Reserve Board or among its staff. Neither of the other two federal agencies has seen fit to press the issue with such urgency and in such undeviating fashion as the Federal Reserve. As early as 1938, the Board of Governors directed a major portion of its annual report at what it saw as conflict and confusion arising out of the divisions of federal regulatory authority. It concluded, in words not unlike those used by Mr. Hackley almost thirty years later:

> The banking picture emerges as a crazy quilt of conflicting powers and jurisdictions, of overlapping authorities and gaps in authority, of restrictions making it difficult for banks to serve their communities and make a living, and of conditions making it next to impossible for public authorities to apply adequate restraints at a time and in conditions when this may be in the public interest.

In view of the sense of impending regulatory or banking disaster conveyed by the above analysis, it is not improper to ask how the banking system performed during the period from 1938 to 1967. The answer, of course, is found in the performance of the economy itself. A truly remarkable rate of economic growth has been financed in substantial part by a vigorous and dynamic banking system. To cite figures would be superfluous; the simple fact is that the economy could not have performed as it did if the banking system had been as restricted and hobbled as was claimed.

Another factor deserving mention is the immense change in banking during this thirty year period of regulatory "chaos." The expansion of physical facilities at a rate surpassing population growth, the swift manner in which banks have reacted to changing economic requirements, the development of new financing devices, and the spirit of innovation evident during the last decade all suggest that there is a vitality and ferment in commercial banking which is unlike that found in any other regulated industry. One can be mildly curious as to whether this would have been possible had there been a single federal regulatory agency during all of these years. Certainly there is little in the record of other industries so blessed—railroads, for example—to suggest that the single agency approach is deserving of emulation.

CONCLUSION

The fatal flaw in arguments for centralization of federal regulatory authority is that they rarely, if ever, are addressed to the basic issue: the structure of the American banking system. It is not difficult to demonstrate that the federal regulatory system is loosely constructed, that lines of authority overlap, and consequently the possibility is always present of conflicting rulings or unseemly disputes. Also, one could scarcely dispute the contention that centralization of federal authority in one agency would be a more efficient way of operating, and certainly a less frustrating one for the regulators.

The difficulty is that the regulatory system is inextricably linked with the structure of banking, and this structure, too, is illogical and inefficient in some respects. Can one justify the existence of more than 13,000 banks, 72 percent of which have less than 10 million dollars in deposits, and 18 percent of which have less than 2 million dollars? Would it not be much better to follow the lead of other nations and have only a handful of banks with nationwide branch systems, with entry virtually foreclosed, and with the few banks tightly regulated by a single federal agency? Perhaps so, but if this is what is desired, then the advocates of centralization at the federal level should recognize and deal with this issue.

Certainly, steps can be taken to reduce the possibilities of conflict without damaging the underlying regulatory structure. For example, a study could be made of the possibility of transferring Federal Reserve supervisory authority to the FDIC insofar as this authority relates to state banks, and to the Comptroller insofar as it relates to national banks. This simple step would eliminate a considerable area of overlap and duplication; it would free the Federal Reserve to concentrate on its primary task of monetary policy; and yet it would preserve duality of entry and supervisory alternatives.

The foregoing is only one illustration of improvements which can be made without undertaking the revolutionary step of centralizing all federal banking authority—chartering, insurance and regulation—in a single agency. Of course, this proposal is not characterized by the simplicity of the plan for centralization. However, those who find themselves irresistibly attracted to a neat, tidy, symmetrical bank regulatory structure might well keep in mind that in banking, as in other fields, substance should not be sacrificed for form. In a recent article on urban planning, Bernard Taper could well have been describing the American banking system when he commented:

> No planner could ever have created a scene so varied, so full of enterprise and vitality. Yet planners are perfectly capable of destroying or homogenizing such a scene—and all too often do so.

PART FOUR

the money market and the federal reserve

The money market, dealing in short-term negotiable instruments, plays a leading role in the economy of the United States for numerous reasons. First, short-term securities provide the major source of commercial bank liquidity, and the banks engage in money market transactions in their continuous search for the optimum portfolio. Second, and partially because the banks do operate in this market, Federal Reserve open market operations lean heavily to money market securities. A further reason for open market transactions in the short end of the financial market is the market's relatively large size, which permits constant and often large-scale intervention by the monetary authorities without inducing wide and upsetting swings in interest rates or a freezing up of trade on the market. Third, the market functions to bring together lenders of short-term funds with borrowers. Some borrowers require loans for a brief interval only and issue, for example, 6-month commercial paper. Others (the United States government, for example) continuously refinance short-term issues and in effect borrow for long and indeed apparently infinite periods. Thus the market serves to finance short- and long-term investment as well as to provide extremely liquid forms in which to hold savings.

The central theme of this Part is the relationship of the money market to monetary control. The opening selection presents the minutes of the Open Market Committee of the Federal Reserve System (FOMC). The twelve voting members and their staffs meet at three-week intervals to review economic conditions and to decide formally on the appropriate use of the open market instrument of monetary policy. Discussion is free and open during the meeting, but as it draws to a close the Chairman, who is also the Chairman of the Board of Governors, sums up the consensus of the participants. A directive to the Manager of the Open Market Account is drawn up and voted on; decision is by simple majority.

The minutes reproduced here can be divided into two segments. The first part deals with an analysis of present and prospective economic conditions, covering not only the financial sector but also the actions of the industrial sectors and the government and, in recent years, foreign activities as well. This analysis provides the foundation for the decision, formalized in the directive, that constitutes the second segment of the minutes.

The role of the Manager of the Open Market Account, who is a Vice President of the Federal Reserve Bank of New York, and his staff is to implement the directive. They must decide whether to purchase or sell government securities in the market and how much to buy or sell so that the objective of the directive is attained. In the second selection, Paul Meek portrays a typical day in the life of these officials and demonstrates how the decisions are made. Although some commentators have objected to the discretion permitted the manager in interpreting the FOMC's charges to him, his freedom of maneuver is limited. As Meek points out, daily telephone contact between the Manager and Selected FOMC members is routine. Moreover, the Account Manager undoubtedly is constrained by the knowledge that he must report to the FOMC at each meeting and explain his actions. A manager who perverts the directives of the Committee will not remain long in that critical position.

While the Federal Reserve acts to control the economy through the money market, the market itself is evolving. New instruments are devised, and others that have disappeared are resurrected. Indeed, the growth of short-term instruments, as described in the third selection by Robert W. Stone, former Manager of the Open Market Account, may have been encouraged by open market operations. Because restrictive open market actions drive interest rates upward and tend to reduce total bank reserves, borrowers will seek alternative and less expensive sources of funds. Stone surveys the spread of the federal funds market and the flourishing of negotiable time certificates of deposit (CDs) during a period of rising interest rates. A more recent innovation lies in the use of Eurodollars—dollars held outside the United States—as an additional source of liquidity. This is discussed by Fred Klopstock in the next selection. The credit "crunch" in the middle of 1966 forced banks to find new sources of funds, and in the half year beginning in July, 1966, Eurodollar holdings of domestic American banks, obtained from their overseas branches, more than doubled. Although Stone deals primarily with the impact of new instruments or renewed methods on interest rate stability, we may note the relevance of these changes to the implementation of monetary policy. Increased activity in the federal funds market enables a smaller volume of reserves to perform a larger job; it increases the velocity of reserves. A bank owning reserves in excess of its legal and business requirements may sell these excess reserves to another bank. If the latter bank is now more willing and able to increase its deposits or is enabled to prevent a fall in them, actions that it would have avoided in the absence of this infusion of reserves, then use of the federal funds market leads to a larger supply of money and credit than otherwise. The appearance of CDs and Eurodollar trading on the domestic banking scene also can increase money supply and velocity, as Klopstock notes with regard to the latter.

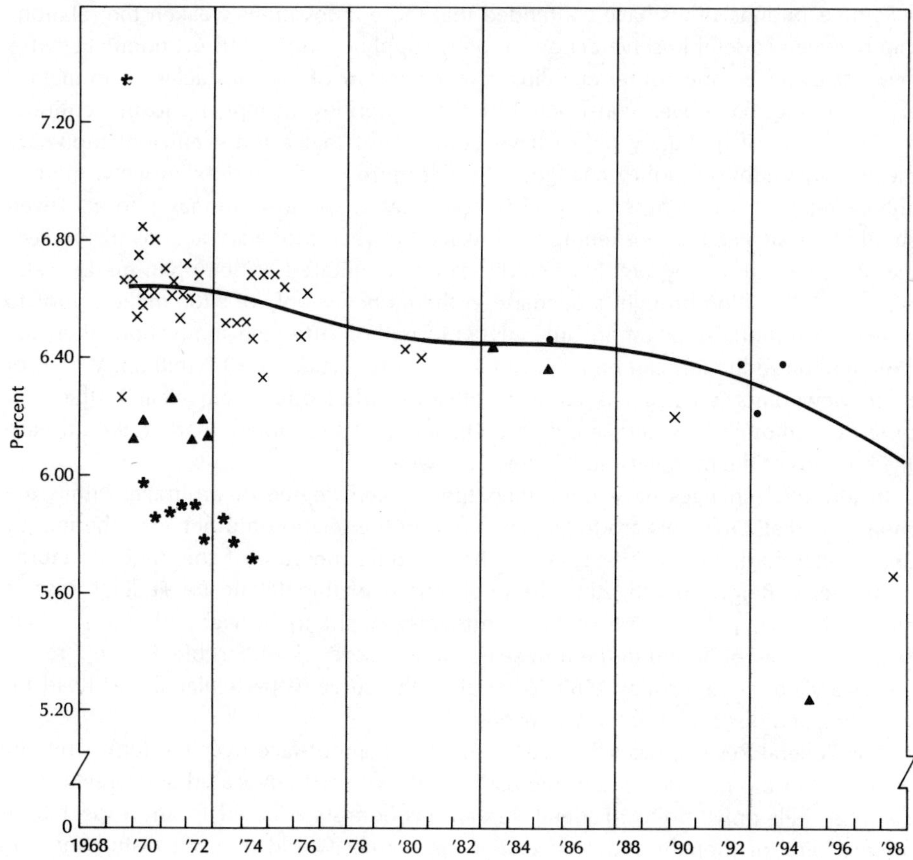

Figure 1 Yields of Treasury Securities, May 29, 1969, Based on Closing Bid Quotations

Legend:

Represented by the curve:

X Fixed maturity issues[1]

● Callable issues[2]

Disregarded in drawing the curve:

* 1½% 5 year exchange notes[3]

▲ Other deep discount issues[4]

SOURCE: U.S. Treasury Bulletin, June 1968, p. 71.

Note: The smooth curve is fitted by eye. Market yields on coupon issues due in less than 3 months are excluded.

[1]Treasury bills included are limited to maturities closest to 3 months, 6 months, and 9 months and to the longest maturity.

[2]Yields are plotted to earliest call date when prices are above par and to maturity date when prices are at par or below.

[3]Marketable notes issued in exchange for nonmarketable 2¾% Investment Series B bonds.

[4]Issues with coupon rates less than 3½%.

Some economists thus have contended that these innovations weaken the relationship between Federal Reserve actions, money supply changes, and economic activity; they act as an escape route, enabling circumvention of the obstacles to monetary expansion that have been constructed by the authorities. In replying to this critique, the defenders of monetary policy have pointed out that a more efficient monetary mechanism enables a policy change to be felt more rapidly and extensively, thereby enhancing its effectiveness. They also note that these institutional reforms, even should they succeed in weakening the linkage between monetary actions of the Federal Reserve and money supply or credit, can be countered. When open market sales of, say, $100 million brought a decrease in the money supply of $200 million prior to a new institutional innovation but only $150 million after the innovation, then the $200 million reduction can be achieved by security sales of $133.3 million. Which of these viewpoints is correct is far from obvious; what does seem clear is that less progress, although it would reduce the efficiency of the money market, would ease the burdens of the monetary authorities somewhat.

Institutional changes have intensified the marked degree of arbitrage within the money market. Does this arbitrage play a role in the relationship between the money and capital markets too? This question has become the core of the "rate structure" controversy. Before investigating the implications of this debate for Federal Reserve policy, however, the nature of the controversy ought to be clarified. An excellent exposition may be found in the fifth selection by Frederick M. Struble. Figure 1 reproduces a yield curve for May 1969. What gives the curve its particular slope? Read the selection and discover at least two divergent views.

The Federal Reserve has achieved a remarkable about-face over the term structure issue within the past decade. In the early 1950s, when it advocated and practiced its famous "bills only" policy, Federal Reserve economists adhered to an "expectations theory" line of thought and argued that the market would transmit disturbances in the short end of the market to longer maturities. They concluded that Federal Reserve operations in the money market would suffice to control not only the quantity of money but relative interest rates as well. By the early 1960s, the monetary authorities had rejected this view and, in "Operation Twist," placed the same full confidence in the "segmented market" theory. It was then claimed that the sale of short-term securities would cause money market rates to rise and would thereby ease the United States balance-of-payments position; similarly, the purchase of long-term government securities would keep the capital market rate low and would encourage domestic expansion. It seems appropriate to note that a synthesis of the two views is plausible, especially because supply factors may influence expectations.

The implications of the alternative theories of the yield curve affect a number of policy issues. First, when employing the open market weapon of monetary control, is the quantity bought or sold the only critical variable or does the maturity of the securities also matter? Second, should Treasury debt management policy be countercyclical, so that the average maturity of the debt is lengthened during expansionary periods and shortened during contractions? Third, should the Federal Reserve's policy of "even keel" be continued? Although this policy is analyzed in the final selection of this Part, briefly noted, it involves avoiding major central bank policy changes during periods of Treasury financing. Since this limitation on Federal Reserve flexibility occurs only when intermediate- or long-term Treasury debt is issued, the "do nothing" policy can be justified only if the lengthening of the average maturity of the debt or preventing a fall is itself stabilizing. If changes in the maturity of the debt have no impact on economic activity, however, this restraint on Federal Reserve maneuverability goes uncompensated by any virtues, and it is neither irreverent nor irrelevant to wonder whether even keel should be abandoned.

Current opinion among economists appears to favor the expectations hypothesis. For example, one econometric study, although it stressed the preliminary nature of its findings, concluded that Operation Twist was hardly successful and that "there is no evidence that the maturity structure of the federal debt, or changes in this structure, exert a significant, lasting or transient influence on the relation between the two [that is, short- and long-term interest] rates."[1] As is often true of econometric studies, however, the same information and indeed "proof" are subject to differing interpretations, and the conclusiveness of the results is open to question. In reference to the Modigliani-Sutch and similar studies, Professor Neil Wallace has written: "the difficulties encountered in such research . . . are such that the results are not likely to be given much weight in any revision of previously [held] notions about the effects on interest rates of changes in the maturity composition of the debt."[2]

The major contribution of the controversy over the term structure is, so far, not its resolution but the demonstration that an issue does exist and that conclusions thought self-evident are not.

Although this issue is of both theoretical and practical interest, the degree of its importance appears limited. As long as economists continue to debate the role of interest rates as determinants of economic activity (see Part V), the term structure controversy is surely secondary—the proverbial third wheel on the bicycle.

---

[1]F. Modigliani and R. Sutch, "Innovations in Interest Rate Policy," *American Economic Review*, 56, 178–197. Quote is from p. 196.

[2]N. Wallace, "The Term Structure of Interest Rates and the Maturity Composition of the Federal Debt," *Journal of Finance*, 22, 301–312. Quote is on p. 312.

21 MINUTES OF THE MEETING OF AUGUST 12, 1969, OF THE FEDERAL OPEN MARKET COMMITTEE

Aside from touching lightly on the issue of policy making, the following minutes are important because they are interrelated with many other articles in this text. Much can be gained by reading in conjunction with this selection the next one, which demonstrates the implementation of the directive, the articles by Fred Klopstock on Eurodollars and by Warren Gustus on even keel, which conclude this Part, the section of the article by Jonas Prager on integrating fiscal and monetary policy (Selection 18), and Governor George W. Mitchell's article (Selection 31). This last relationship is particularly interesting because the vote reproduced here shows that the members of the FOMC disagreed as to the appropriate steps to be taken. Their dispute stemmed from differing readings of the economic indicators, which is the subject of the Mitchell selection.

AUTHORITY TO EFFECT TRANSACTIONS IN SYSTEM ACCOUNT

According to preliminary Commerce Department estimates, real GNP had expanded in the second quarter at an annual rate of 2.4 percent, close to the 2.5 percent rate of the first quarter and somewhat slower than the 3.5 percent rate of the second half of 1968. However, substantial upward pressures on prices and costs were persisting; average prices, as measured by the GNP deflator, had increased at an annual rate of nearly 5 percent in both the first and second quarters. Staff projections suggested some further slowing of growth in real GNP in the second half of 1969 but only a moderate reduction in the rate of price advance.

Recent economic developments continued to present a mixed picture. Industrial production was tentatively estimated to have risen sharply further in July. On the other hand, weekly figures suggested that retail sales were about unchanged from June and no higher than they had been in February. Nonfarm employment expanded less than it had on the average in earlier months of the year, and the unemployment rate rose to 3.6 from 3.4 percent in June.

Average wholesale prices increased only slightly further from mid-June to mid-July. Average prices of farm products and foods, which had accounted for most of the rise in the wholesale price index in recent months, were unchanged. Price advances continued widespread among industrial commodities, but the average for such commodities rose only moderately because of further declines in prices of lumber and plywood. The consumer price index increased sharply in June with foods, particularly meats, accounting for much of the advance.

In the second quarter, according to the preliminary Commerce Department figures, expansion in real GNP had been sustained by a rise in inventory invest-

From *Federal Reserve Bulletin,* November 1969, pp. 880–887.

ment. Declines were recorded in residential construction expenditures and Federal outlays on goods and services, and the rate of increase was slower than in the first quarter for consumer spending and business outlays.

One uncertainty in the outlook for the second half of 1969 had been removed by the enactment in early August of legislation to extend the income tax surcharge at 10 percent through the end of the year. The mid-1969 Government pay raise was expected to lead to an increase in Federal outlays in the third quarter and to provide some temporary stimulus to growth in disposable income and consumer spending, but it seemed likely that the decline in Federal outlays would resume in the fourth quarter and that growth in consumer income and spending would again be moderating. Prospects were that residential construction activity would continue to decline in the third and fourth quarters. Further slowing in the expansion of business capital outlays was anticipated in both quarters, as suggested by the June Commerce-SEC survey of business plans and also by a special Federal Reserve survey of capital spending authorizations of about 200 large corporations conducted in late July.

With respect to the balance of payments, it appeared that outflows of U.S. capital remained sizable in July and that the very large deficits that had been recorded on the liquidity basis earlier in the year were continuing. The official settlements balance was still in surplus in the first half of July, a period in which the outstanding Eurodollar borrowings of U.S. banks increased considerably further. After mid-July, however, there was relatively little net change in such borrowings and the official settlements balance shifted toward deficit. Interest rates in the Eurodollar market declined from early July to early August but remained at relatively high levels.

On the Friday before this meeting the French Government announced an 11.1 percent devaluation of the franc. This action was taken against the background of recent substantial losses of international reserves by France and in the interests of avoiding a deflationary policy "that would impose unbearable sacrifices and massive unemployment on the country." Although certain Western European currencies had come under some selling pressure following the announcement, the initial reaction in foreign exchange markets appeared on the whole to be orderly. Earlier—around mid-July—the Bank of Canada had increased its discount rate and the German Federal Bank had announced an increase in reserve requirements against deposit liabilities of domestic banks; and around the end of the month discount rates had been increased by the central banks of Belgium and the Netherlands.

In its August refunding the Treasury offered a new 18-month, 7¾ percent note priced to yield about 7.82 percent in exchange for $3.4 billion of securities maturing on August 15. The new issue was well received and was quoted at a premium in the market. Of the $3.2 billion of maturing issues held by the public, about 14 percent were redeemed for cash. The Treasury was expected to raise about $1.5 billion to $2 billion of new cash later in the month through an offering of short-term securities.

The atmosphere in securities markets had improved recently—partly because of the enactment of legislation extending the income tax surcharge, of further indications that the rate of real economic expansion was gradually slowing, and of signs that credit demands from some sectors might be moderating. Yields on new long-term corporate bonds and municipal securities, which had been rising in the latter part of July, declined somewhat in early August. Municipal bond markets had been under particularly severe pressures partly as a result of congressional discussion of possible changes in the tax treatment of earnings on such bonds, and these pressures moderated after the House Ways and Means Committee modified certain earlier proposals in this area. Various short-term interest rates also had declined recently. For example, the market rate on 3-month Treasury bills, at about 7 percent on the day before this meeting, was down from a peak of 7.13 percent in late July, although it was little changed from its level 4 weeks earlier.

Commercial bank holdings of U.S. Government securities rose during July as a result of bank underwriting of the tax-anticipation bills sold by the Treasury at midmonth, but holdings of other securities decreased considerably. Business loans outstanding were about unchanged for the second successive month after expanding rapidly earlier in the year. To some extent the lack of growth in business loans since May reflected outright sales of loans to bank affiliates. Even with the inclusion of such loans, however, the increase in the last 2 months would have been at a rate only about one-third of that earlier in the year.

Total bank credit, as measured by the adjusted proxy series, was estimated to have declined at an annual rate of about 12 percent from June to July, as a large reduction in daily-average member bank deposits was only partly offset by a rise in the average level of Eurodollar liabilities of U.S. banks to their foreign branches. Banks increased their reliance on funds from other nondeposit sources, including funds obtained by selling assets to affiliates and to customers with bank guarantees. Rough estimates suggested that with a further adjustment for such funds the proxy series would have declined at an annual rate of 7 to 8 percent from June to July.

Private demand deposits and the money stock rose on the average in July—the latter at an annual rate of 6 percent—partly as a consequence of a large further contraction of U.S. Government deposits. The run-off of large-denomination CD's continued without abatement; since mid-December the outstanding volume of such CD's at weekly reporting banks had been reduced by more than $10.5 billion, or about 45 percent. There also were sizable outflows of other time and savings deposits following midyear interest crediting. Nonbank thrift institutions similarly experienced heavy outflows early in July.

In general, System open market operations since the previous meeting of the Committee had been directed at maintaining firm conditions in the money and short-term credit markets. Money market pressures had tended to ease for a time after mid-July as a result of a shift of reserves toward the money center banks. This tendency was not fully offset through System operations because bank credit appeared to be significantly below earlier projections. However, the extent to which operations were influenced by bank credit developments was affected by "even keel" considerations related to the Treasury refunding. Subsequently, a redistribution of reserves away from major banks had contributed to tighter money market conditions despite sizable reserve-supplying operations by the System. In the two statement weeks following the July 15 meeting, the effective rate on Federal funds had averaged about 8¼ percent—compared with a rate centering around 9 percent in earlier weeks—and since then had risen to a range around 9¾ percent. In the 4 weeks ending August 6, member bank borrowings had averaged $1,250 million, down somewhat from the previous period. A corresponding decline in excess reserves had left net borrowed reserves about unchanged on the average.

Prospective changes in the bank credit proxy and related variables were affected by the expected consequences of certain regulatory actions taken by the Board of Governors on July 24, 1969. These were (1) an amendment to Regulation D, effective July 31, requiring member banks to include in deposits used to compute reserve requirements all so-called "London checks" and "bills payable checks" used in settling transactions involving foreign branches*; and (2) amendments to Reg-

*For further clarification see Selection 24—ed.

ulations D and Q defining deposit liabilities subject to those regulations to include, beginning August 28, every bank liability on a repurchase agreement (RP) entered into on or after July 25 with a person other than a bank and involving any assets other than direct and fully guaranteed obligations of the United States or its agencies.

The first of these actions was expected to increase required reserves of member banks by about $450 million in the statement week ending August 20. The second action was not expected to have much effect on required reserves, since it appeared unlikely that a significant volume of newly written RP's of the types affected would be outstanding after late August. It was noted, however, that outstanding RP's were expected to decline as current agreements matured and that this decline would tend to reduce bank credit by an equivalent amount, other things equal. Moreover, it was considered likely that bank attitudes toward alternative sources of funds and toward their own lending and investing policies were already being affected by this action, and by the expectation that the Board would soon implement two other regulatory actions it had proposed near the end of June. The latter were proposals to amend Regulations D and M, among other things to place a 10 percent reserve requirement on borrowings by U.S. banks from their foreign branches, to the extent that these borrowings exceeded the daily-average amounts outstanding in the 4 weeks ending May 28, 1969; and a proposal to amend Regulations D and Q to bring a member bank's liability on certain Federal funds transactions within the coverage of those regulations.

The staff projections suggested that the adjusted bank credit proxy would decline at an annual rate of 9 to 12 percent from July to August if prevailing conditions were maintained in money and short-term credit markets. The projections allowed for only a small further rise in the average level of Eurodollar borrowings of U.S. banks. While no specific allowance was made in the projections for possible changes in the extent to which banks were utilizing funds from other nondeposit sources, it was noted that the outstanding volume of funds obtained from such sources probably would grow less rapidly than in July.

Among deposit categories, private demand deposits—and the money stock—were projected to decline moderately from July to August, and a further reduction in the average level of U.S. Government deposits was anticipated. Given prevailing levels of market interest rates, it was expected that large-denomination CD's would continue to run off, although less rapidly than earlier because the volume of maturing CD's was smaller. And it appeared unlikely that consumer-type time and savings deposits would show a marked expansion after the large net outflows of July.

In the Committee's discussion account was taken of the indications that the rate of expansion of over-all economic activity was moderating somewhat, of the recent legislation extending the 10 percent income tax surcharge through the end of the year, and of the substantial degree of monetary restraint already in effect. The Committee agreed that no further increase in monetary restraint would be warranted at present. In particular, it agreed that any tendencies toward firmer money market conditions that might result from recent regulatory actions by the Board of Governors or from other causes should be resisted through open market operations.

At the same time, a majority of the members thought that action to ease money market conditions would not be warranted now, in view of the persistence of inflationary pressures and the risk that such action would encourage a new surge of inflationary expectations. Some members of the majority expressed the view that System operations should not necessarily be undertaken to offset fully any easing tendencies that might be produced by market forces. On the other hand, it was suggested that the implementation of policy should not be unduly influenced by temporary swings in market psychology.

The Committee concluded that open market operations should be directed at maintaining the prevailing firm conditions in money and short-term credit markets. The proviso was added that operations should be modified if bank credit appeared to be deviating significantly from current projections. It was also agreed that operations should be modified if pressures arose in the aftermath of the devaluation of the French franc or in connection with the regulatory actions taken by the Board of Governors.

The following current economic policy directive was issued to the Federal Reserve Bank of New York:

The information reviewed at this meeting indicates that expansion in real economic activity slowed somewhat in the first half of 1969 and some further moderation is projected. Substantial upward pressures on prices and costs are persisting. Most market interest rates recently have receded slightly from their earlier highs. In July the money supply expanded as U.S. Government deposits decreased further; bank credit declined on average, after adjusting for an increase in assets sold to affiliates and to customers with bank guarantees. The runoff of large-denomination CD's which began in mid-December continued without abatement in July, and there apparently were net outflows from consumer-type time and savings accounts at banks and nonbank thrift institutions combined. The over-all balance of payments deficit on the liquidity basis remained very large in July; the balance on the official settlements basis was still in surplus in the first half of the month but subsequently shifted toward deficit as U.S. banks' borrowings of Eurodollars leveled off. Foreign exchange markets appear initially to be adjusting in an orderly fashion to the announced devaluation of the French franc. In light of the foregoing developments, it is the policy of the Federal Open Market Committee to foster financial conditions conducive to the reduction of inflationary pressures, with a view to encouraging sustainable economic growth and attaining reasonable equilibrium in the country's balance of payments.

To implement this policy, System open market operations until the next meeting of the Committee shall be conducted with a view to maintaining the prevailing firm conditions in money and short-term credit markets; provided, however, that operations shall be modified if bank credit appears to be deviating significantly from current projections or if pressures arise in connection with foreign exchange developments or with bank regulatory changes.

Votes for this action: Messrs. Martin, Hayes, Bopp, Brimmer, Coldwell, Daane, Robertson, Scanlon, Sherrill, and Swan. Votes against this action: Messrs. Maisel and Mitchell.

Absent and not voting: Mr. Clay. (Mr. Swan voted as his alternate.)

In dissenting from this action Messrs. Maisel and Mitchell indicated that they did not advocate lessening monetary and credit restraint. However, they did not want monetary policy to become more and more restrictive. It appeared to them that trends in monetary aggregates and the availability of credit were indicative of increased tightening that would be heightened if money market conditions were maintained at the levels called for in the directive favored by the majority. In order to guard against an undesired further tightening, they favored a directive calling for operations to moderate such contractive tendencies, if prospective declines in monetary aggregates should in fact occur, while maintaining the position of over-all monetary and credit restraint.

22 ALL PART OF A DAY'S WORK

PAUL MEEK

Although the impression is sometimes given that monetary policy has achieved the precision of the physical sciences, the truth is that much "seat of the pants" flying still goes on. The "feel" of the market is given operational meaning, whereas predictions of monetary conditions based on the record of the past provide background information. Judge for yourself in the following selection the relative weight assigned to research and to "feel." Note also how the Federal Reserve makes use of the "sources of funds" concept in conducting its operations. Finally, after reading this selection, consider the suggestion of some economists that Reserve policy ought not be concerned with money market conditions.

Each day presents a new challenge to the Manager of the Open Market Account. Yet each day has much in common with every other day. Let us go back to [the] Tuesday before Thanksgiving Day and follow the developments which led to the purchase of $242 million in Government securities. On such a day, as on all days, the Manager must bear in mind the current directive and the consensus of the last FOMC meeting. Let us suppose that the directive states that "open market operations should continue to foster money and credit conditions conducive to sustainable economic expansion," and that these broad objectives are to be pursued by maintaining about the prevailing conditions in the money market.

The main outlines of the task which lies ahead are at least roughly visible to the Manager early on Tuesday morning. He has before him the preceding day's projections of the behavior expected of the factors affecting reserves over the coming three weeks. Tuesday's projections will be available a bit later at about 10:45 a.m. The projections are based upon the behavior of reserve factors over the same calendar period during the past five years and take into account any special factors such as a foreign purchase of gold.

Yesterday's projections indicate that the decline in float at the month-end is expected to combine with the seasonal rise in currency in circulation during the next week to draw reserves in large volume from the banking system. A seasonal rise in required reserves associated with higher loan demands may add slightly to the drain on reserves. It thus appears that the Manager will have to supply reserves in substantial amounts just to maintain the existing degree of firmness in the money market. Indeed, the day before, Monday, the Manager provided $280 million in reserves by making $65 million in repurchase agreements with dealers early in the afternoon, after buying $215 million in Treasury bills outright for cash in the morning.

Useful as they are as a rough yardstick, the projections cannot be used as a precise guide to operations. Each year, for all its similarities to the past, produces a

From Paul Meek, *Open Market Operations* (New York: Federal Reserve Bank of New York, 1969), pp. 37–45.

pattern of financial flows that is all its own. The Manager and his experienced officers must look to the market itself for signals of the timing and magnitude of the reserve pressures actually at work on this particular day.

The new business day begins a few minutes after nine a.m. in the Trading Room of the Federal Reserve Bank of New York. The news ticker is pounding out the financial news that has accumulated since it closed down the night before. The securities traders scan the closing quotations recorded on the board across the open end of the U-shaped Trading Desk to reorient themselves before the new day begins. The traders concerned with the routine flow of Treasury, member bank and foreign transactions begin to check on the day's orders. Nearby, the officers of the Securities Department read research memoranda and engage in the routine tasks of office administration, which will soon have to be pushed aside.

DEALER CONFERENCE

At 9:15 a.m., two officers of the Securities Department hurry to a tenth-floor conference room to meet with one or two representatives of a Government securities dealer firm. Dealers confer every business day on a rotating schedule with the Reserve Bank officers directly responsible for the conduct of open market operations. At these conferences, the dealers comment on market developments and on any matter of interest to the firm. The Reserve Bank officers listen and ask questions.

This morning, representatives of three dealers are scheduled to appear, one after the other. At the first conference, a senior partner of a dealer firm observes that the market has been rather quiet during the last few days, and that he has been rather disappointed by the lack of corporate demand for Treasury bills. He finds that insurance companies and pension funds are holding off on bond purchases until the $100 million bond issue of the XYZ Corporation due to be offered on Wednesday hits the market. The dealer gives his views on whether the Treasury should issue short-term or long-term securities, or both, in meeting its cash needs, and indicates the kind of reception he thinks the market would give the new issues. After answering questions asked by one of the Reserve Bank officers, the dealer departs at 9:30 a.m.

Two representatives of a second dealer firm enter the conference room. Among other things, these representatives indicate that while the market as a whole has been quiet, their firm has handled some sizable transactions in the last few days. They feel that many investors have large cash positions and are merely waiting for more attractive yields. One also feels that conditions in the money market were a little tight yesterday afternoon even after the System's intervention; his firm had to pay a relatively high interest rate to obtain financing for its position through loans and repurchase agreements negotiated with banks and others. The second firm's representatives leave at 9:45 a.m., and the vice president in charge of the dealer operations of a New York City bank enters. The third conference covers much the same ground. The last dealer departs at 10 o'clock, and the Reserve Bank officers return to their offices to prepare for the daily call from the U.S. Treasury.

THE TREASURY CALL

Each morning shortly after ten, the Fiscal Assistant Secretary of the Treasury uses the direct telephone line linking the Treasury and the New York Reserve Bank to compare notes with the Manager or his deputy on the outlook for the Treasury's cash balance at the Reserve Banks. Their objective is to try to smooth out fluctuations in the Treasury's balance at the Reserve Banks and to minimize disruptive effects of changes in the balance on member bank reserve positions. They estimate the amount of funds that need to be transferred from the Treasury's Tax and Loan accounts at commercial banks to the Reserve Banks in order to maintain a fairly stable working balance in the face of checks they expect to be presented for payment at the Reserve Banks. (The Treasury channels a large part of its receipts from taxes and from sales of its securities through Tax and Loan accounts to reduce the sudden impact of these large flows on bank reserves.)

Today, the Assistant Secretary tells the Reserve Bank officer that his projections of daily Government receipts and expenditures indicate that the Treasury will need to transfer $100 million from Treasury Tax and Loan accounts at about 80 large commercial banks across the country (the Class C banks) to its account at the Federal Reserve Banks. This will be in addition to calls previously scheduled on Tax and Loan accounts at other commercial banks. The Reserve Bank official notes that projections of the New York Bank's staff point to a need to call about $140 million to maintain the Treasury balance at about the desired level. However, since bank reserve positions are expected to be under pressure from seasonal factors, the Reserve Bank officer and Assistant Secretary agree that the call be limited to 15 percent of the previous night's Treasury balances at the "C" banks—about $96 million.

The conversation over, the Reserve officer dials another officer in the Bank to inform him that the Treasury has decided to make a special call today on the "C" banks. By 11 a.m., the large banks will have been informed that they must transfer 15 percent of the Treasury's deposits with them at Monday's close to their district Reserve Banks. These transfers out of their reserve accounts are intended only to offset the bulk of the increase in member bank reserves expected to flow from the deposit of Treasury checks drawn on the Treasury's accounts at the Federal Reserve Banks. In practice, these checks are likely to be deposited widely over the country so that the big-city banks may find that the transfer of Treasury deposits from them to the Reserve Banks exceeds the amount of Treasury checks deposited with them. Typically, these banks will need to step up their overnight borrowing in the Federal funds market.

GETTING THE "FEEL" OF THE MARKET

In the meantime, the Government securities market has become active. At the Trading Desk, opening quotations are beginning to come in. Several of the traders around the Desk are talking to dealers to learn if any trend is developing. Other traders have a pretty good fix on orders to be executed for foreign accounts or for Treasury trust accounts. Reports have arrived from the research and statistics departments on dealer positions and on the previous day's reserve positions and Federal funds transactions of eight major banks in New York City and 38 banks in other cities. On hand also is a complete nationwide picture of the reserve positions of member banks as of Monday's close, including information on the distribution of reserves among money market banks and other reserve city and country banks.

Shortly after 10 a.m., two young ladies bring the quotation board up to date with "runs" of price and yield quotations obtained from telephone calls to securities dealers. The Federal Reserve's traders already know from their conversations with dealers what the board shows—that the market is steady with few changes either up or down. They also know that there has been little trading except for the professional activity of the dealers who are testing each other's markets by occasionally "hitting a bid"—selling securities at the price bid by another dealer. About 10:45 a.m., the Desk receives the first tentative quotation on Federal funds. The quote is 5¾ percent, a shade higher than yesterday's rate of 5½ percent, which exceeded the 5¼ percent discount rate at which member banks can borrow from their Reserve Banks.

One member of the staff calls each of the nonbank dealers to find out the volume of funds needed to replace loans maturing today or to finance securities for which payment must be made today. A few minutes before 11 a.m., his tabulation shows that the dealers need loans of about $750 million to finance their present securities holdings. Money was available at yesterday's close at 6 percent, but the dealers are not too sure about today. Several think money may be harder to get and more expensive.

The officer in charge of the Desk, who has just been joined by the Account Manager and another officer, summarizes for them the early morning market developments. Together they review the newest projection of the factors affecting bank reserves over the next three weeks—a report received only moments before from the Statistics Department. Today's projection indicates that the cash purchases and the repurchase agreements made by the System yesterday held Monday's decline in bank reserves to modest proportions. The outlook is for a sharp decline in bank reserves today and a further decline tomorrow, mainly because of a projected drop in float over the next two days of about $500 million and a very large increase in currency in circulation associated with the Thanksgiving holiday. A last-minute check with the traders reveals that banks and others are beginning to sell Treasury bills to the dealers in greater volume than buyers are coming to the dealers for bills. Treasury bill yields are beginning to rise—that is, prices are beginning to decline.

Meanwhile, a preliminary call is made to the Board of Governors in Washington and to the office of one of the Reserve Bank presidents currently on the FOMC. Information is provided on the full range of data available on bank reserves and the money and Government securities markets. Thus, the Reserve Bank president will have before him the data on which the Desk's plan of action is based. The officers hurry to an adjoining office to participate in a very important telephone conversation—the Federal Reserve conference call, which takes place at about 11:10 a.m.

THE CONFERENCE CALL

"Washington and Minneapolis are standing by," announces the telephone operator, completing the three-way telephone hookup that each morning enables the Account Manager to review developments with a member of the Board of Governors in Washington (or his representatives) and one of the Reserve Bank presidents currently serving on the FOMC. Sitting in on the conversation in New York today are the president of the Bank, the Manager of the System Account, and the officers of the Securities Department. One of the officers seated directly behind a telephone microphone speaks:

"Conditions have changed somewhat since we spoke yesterday. The Government securities market opened steady this morning with very few changes in prices and rates, and with little activity, but Treasury bills now seem to be in increasing supply so that yields are rising. There are some indications that long-term investors are holding off to see how the market will take the $100 million bond issue of the XYZ Corporation tomorrow. Our first tentative information on Federal funds showed a bid of 5¾ percent, ¼ percent above yesterday's closing rate, and word just received from the Trading Room indicates that funds have now begun to trade at 5⅞ percent. Dealer financing needs this morning are about $750 million. The banks have raised their call loan rates on dealer loans from 6 percent to 6¼ percent.

"Yesterday, bank reserves dipped slightly despite our action to supply reserves. The outlook is for a sharp decline in reserves today and tomorrow as currency in circulation increases and float declines. New York City and Chicago banks are under pressure and have been heavy buyers of Federal funds on each of the last three business days. Banks in several other major cities show reserve deficiencies. Today's call on the 'C' banks will withdraw $96 million and will probably add to pressure on the money-market banks."

The officer then reads the Manager's proposed plan for the day:

"In view of the expected stringency in reserves, the Account plans to purchase securities for cash. If the market continues to tighten, we may buy as much as $200 million of Treasury bills. Repurchase agreements with the dealers can be used to supply additional reserves if needed."

The conversation is, of course, more detailed than the above colloquy, and conclusions are supported by a marshalling of facts. Prospective developments in the next couple of days and weeks are discussed. Participants in Washington and Minneapolis may report additional information and express their views as to the appropriateness of the proposed action.

By 11:30 a.m., the call is usually completed. A member of the Board's staff who participated promptly summarizes the call in a memorandum sent to each member of the Board of Governors. A telegram from the Board provides each Reserve Bank president with a summary of the telephone discussion, within an hour or two after the call is concluded.

THE DECISION

Shortly before noon conditions in the market begin to jell rapidly, indicating a sharp increase in reserve pressures. The Federal funds rate jumps to the 5⅞ percent and dealers, New York City banks and other participants in the funds market report that funds are hard to find. Dealers report a pickup in commercial bank selling of short-term securities. Dealer portfolios have increased substantially even though the dealers have been lowering the prices they are willing to pay for bills (with a consequent increase in yields). At the same time, they have not been able to make any progress in meeting their financing needs by borrowing from their out-of-town contacts even though they have been offering to pay 6 percent for money. In fact, given the additional bills they have had to buy, they now need $850 million to pay off maturing loans and to pay for the securities they have bought.

The Manager reviews the evidence: "The market has really started tightening up. We had better move in right away in size to prevent this from getting out of hand. Let's go in and buy about $250 million in Treasury bills for cash today."

The Manager of the System Open Market Account has made his decision. Six securities traders gather around an officer of the Securities Department to receive instructions. . . . Within thirty minutes the Reserve Bank's traders purchase $242 million in Treasury bills for cash in a "go-around" of the market. A summary report from the New York Reserve Bank of the day's developments and System action will be on the desks of the Board members and all Reserve Bank presidents on the following morning.

The officers continue to watch the situation after the "go-around" is completed at around 12:20 p.m. The Federal funds rate eases back to 5¾ percent bid for a time, but then the brokers report that the bid appears to be building while the supply available remains limited. Given the persistence of tightness, the Manager approves the recommendation of the Desk officers that the System purchase about $300 million of Treasury and Federal agency securities under overnight repurchase agreements. By 1 p.m. the additional injection of reserves has been made—bringing the day's total to $542 million. A better balance returns to the Federal funds market, but the officers will not know until the next day whether the shortage of reserves reflected a sharper-than-expected drop in float or something else.

The market may debate whether the day's action was designed simply to head off the developing strain in the market or whether it had broader policy significance. The market may not be able to be sure on that score until it can look back on several weeks of action and see if a cumulative easing of bank reserves overlays the weekly fluctuations not ironed out by System operations. But for today it is sufficient that the reserve strains which threatened to become acute have disappeared. The crisis is over before it really got started.

Tomorrow is another day.

23 STRUCTURAL CHANGES IN THE MONEY MARKET

ROBERT W. STONE

Since Robert W. Stone wrote the following selection, the developments that he surveys have progressed further. For example, during 1969 the relationship between the rate on federal funds exceeded the discount rate, often by a wide margin. Why then did not the commercial banks resort to borrowing from the discount window of the Federal Reserve? One possibility is that the Reserve Banks simply limited the amounts they were willing to lend. The banks reacted by borrowing elsewhere; the profitability resulting from using federal funds presumably warranted paying a higher rate for them. This likelihood is evident, too, from the willingness of banks to pay high rates on time certificates of deposits—6¼ percent per annum, the maximum permitted by the Federal Reserve. The author also notes the increasing volume of arbitrage in the 1960s. Keep this in mind when reading the piece by Frederick M. Struble.

• • •

What I refer to as structural changes in the money market consist essentially of a growth in the kinds of money market instruments and the volume of each, and an associated growth in the number and the degree of aggressiveness and sophistication of money market participants. This combination has tended to damp short-run movements in rates on individual money market instruments relative to changes in rates on other money market paper and also, within the framework of the broad pattern of rate stability associated with the stable performance of the economy, to damp such fluctuations in all money market rates together as might nevertheless have occurred. I should add that, while some of the market changes discussed below are new, most of them consist of refinements and extensions of earlier practices. What are these changes?

From Robert W. Stone, "The Changing Structure of the Money Market," Federal Reserve Bank of New York, *Monthly Review,* February 1965, pp. 33–36.

THE GROWTH AND DEVELOPMENT OF THE FEDERAL FUNDS MARKET

The Federal funds market has undergone in recent years a rapid process of growth that as yet shows little sign of abatement. Currently published data on the transactions of 46 major banks across the country which tend to be the largest participants in the Federal funds market offer a partial glimpse of the volume of funds that passes through that market. Gross purchases and sales of Federal funds by those 46 banks during the eighteen statement weeks ended in July through October of 1964, for example, averaged about $3.0 billion per day. The staggering sums that move through the market daily reflect not only the more active, aggressive use of it by large banks, but also the participation of a growing number of medium-sized banks and even some relatively small ones. Indeed, several large regional money market banks across the nation have developed arrangements with their "country" correspondent banks under which they acquire and pool the excess reserves of the latter and keep them employed in the Federal funds market.

The size and efficiency of the funds market have helped make possible some of the highly aggressive and flexible market practices that in turn have tended to damp short-term fluctuations in rates on individual money market instruments. One of the more significant of these practices is the use by many bank money position managers of Federal funds and Treasury bills as virtual substitutes in the employment of money at short term. It is not new, of course, for banks with a margin of liquid resources available for investment to put those resources into bills when that rate is attractive relative to the funds rate and into Federal funds when the reverse is true. But the number of banks engaging in this "arbitraging" practice has increased markedly in recent years; and, in particular, there has been a sharp narrowing of the rate differentials that activate such switches of money between bills and Federal funds. To illustrate, a few months ago, when three-month Treasury bill rates were moving closely above and below the 3.50 percent level at which the Federal funds rate was almost always to be found, officials of several large banks informed me that it was their practice to move sizable amounts of money out of Treasury bills into sales of Federal funds when the three-month bill rate declined to 3.47 or 3.48 percent and to pull their money out of the Federal funds market and put it back into the bill market when the latter reached 3.52 or 3.53 percent. Furthermore, any particular bank's use of the Federal funds and Treasury bill markets in this way is not limited by the amount of its own resources that it may have available. A great many banks will buy Federal funds and immediately reinvest those funds in bills (and in other outlets, including loans to Government securities dealers) when worthwhile rate differentials appear. This kind of active money management tends to damp short-term fluctuations in Treasury bill rates.

The interaction that has developed between the Federal funds and Treasury bill markets is, of course, closest when the funds rate is generally stable—as it is when bank credit demand in relation to reserve availability is such as to put it at the discount rate most of the time. But it should be noted that the relationship between the Federal funds rate and the Treasury bill rate tends to be relatively close even when the funds rate is somewhat below the discount rate, as evidenced particularly by the experience of 1962 and early 1963, when the two rates seldom diverged by much, or for long, despite the fact that the funds rate was most often below the discount rate. While the Treasury bill and Federal funds rates tend to move closely together when the latter is at or somewhat below the discount rate, they have diverged for extended periods when the bill rate was above the discount rate. Under the reserve conditions that tend to prevail at such times, Federal funds are not a reliable source of supply of resources to carry a bill position—as they generally are under easier reserve conditions. Moreover, the discipline exercised at the "discount window" insures that Federal Reserve advances are also not a source of supply that is on call repeatedly. Very recently, some banks have begun to bid for Federal funds at rates above the discount rate, primarily for the purpose of acquiring a larger volume of resources for lending and investing. It is likely that such additional funds as are obtained by individual banks in this way will, in part, be re-loaned to Government securities dealers, who must, of course, borrow to carry their inventories of securities. If the banks willing to pay above the discount rate for Federal funds should develop fairly reliable sources of supply at that higher rate, it is likely that they will also use such funds to reinvest in bills if the spread in favor of the latter is attractive. This would tend to damp rate fluctuations in bills even when they are trading at levels above the discount rate.

THE GROWTH AND DEVELOPMENT OF OTHER MARKET INSTRUMENTS

Banks and other money market participants have long undertaken "arbitrage" operations in which they have switched money back and forth among the various short-term instruments, and rates on those instruments have therefore been linked and the markets for them interconnected. In recent years, however, the links have become stronger and the interconnections tighter. The strong urge of a growing list of economic units—banks, corporations, states, and municipalities, to name only the more prominent of them—to keep cash balances fully employed at the maximum return compatible with risk and liquidity considerations has, under the economic conditions that have obtained in recent years, produced an active demand for a large volume of short-term instruments and for efficient markets in which they can be traded. And those same economic conditions—and policy efforts to deal with our persisting balance-of-payments problem—have resulted in a larger and larger supply of liquid debt instruments to meet that demand. Thus the aggregate volume of Treasury bills has expanded by 39 percent to $55 billion since the end of 1960 (the volume held by the public increased by 32 percent to $47 billion). The volume of commercial paper outstanding has grown by 87 percent to $8.4 billion; bankers' acceptances have grown by 57 percent to $3.2 billion; short-term (within one year) paper of Government agencies has risen by 62 percent to $7.1 billion; and time certificates of deposit, which were relatively small at the end of 1960, have burgeoned to the point where the weekly reporting banks alone now have nearly $13 billion outstanding.

This impressive growth in the volume of money market instruments outstanding, and the rise in the number and level of sophistication of the economic units investing in them, have been accompanied by an increase in the efficiency of the markets in which the instruments are bought and sold—and, in the case of certificates of deposit, by the development of a broad new market. There are, of course, great differences in efficiency among the various markets, but each is more efficient than formerly. Hence, a given volume of any short-term instrument can now move through the market for that instrument with a lesser change in prices and rates than was formerly the case; or, to state the proposition inversely, for a given change in prices and rates, the amount of securities that can be traded is now larger than formerly. The growth of market efficiency, in the sense just indicated, has made it possible for market participants who wish to move funds back and forth among the various short-term instruments in response to shifting rate differentials to do so without encountering the kinds of frictions that would produce unacceptable price changes or undue delays. The result is an increasing volume of such "arbitrage" operations among the various market instruments and, of course, a concomitant tendency for short-term rate fluctuations in each of those instruments to be damped.

THE SPECIAL CASE OF NEGOTIABLE CERTIFICATES OF DEPOSIT

Since early 1962, banks have had leeway under Regulation Q interest rate ceilings to post rates on time deposits that are more fully competitive with other money market rates than formerly. Given that greater leeway, acceptance of time deposits from virtually all sources, including nonfinancial corporations, and the issuance of negotiable certificates evidencing such deposits have been major factors in producing the accelerated growth in commercial bank time deposits since the end of 1961; in particular, they have been major influences underlying the fact that a significant part of the recent time deposit growth has been in negotiable form. The rapid rate of growth of time deposits, and the development of a substantial margin of such deposits that is negotiable, have been accompanied by an increase in the interest sensitivity of such deposits. This is evidenced not only in the fact that ownership of existing deposits is actively transferred through the market from one owner to another as small shifts in rate differentials with other instruments appear; it is also evidenced by the ability of a bank to increase or decrease its volume of time deposits by very small adjustments in the rate it will pay to acquire such deposits. There have been several cases, for example, in which banks have attracted tens of millions of dollars of time deposits in less than a day merely by shortening by two or three months the maturity of deposits for which they were willing to pay a given nominal rate. Similarly, banks have been able to reduce their time deposits by making very slight downward adjustments in the rates they were willing to pay to renew maturing deposits.

The development of the time certificate of deposit, and the fact that banks can increase and decrease their time deposits with small shadings in rate, have significantly increased the flexibility with which the aggregate stock of money market instruments can expand and contract. The impact on rate fluctuations of this increased flexibility, however, depends on the nature of the factors that motivate banks to increase or decrease the supply of negotiable certificates of deposit. Let us assume, for example, that there occurs a given increase in the demand for money market instruments, perhaps in response to an increase in corporate cash flow. Other things being equal, this increase in demand would exert downward pressure on money market rates. At the lower rate level, there would presumably be some banks willing to issue negotiable certificates of deposit that would not have been prepared to issue such certificates at higher rates. The increased demand for money market instruments would thus elicit an increase in the stock of them; and the rate decline involved in the satisfaction of the increased demand would be less than if that demand converged upon the existing stock of money market instruments (or a less readily expansible stock). In cases of this kind, therefore, the time certificate of deposit has tended to reduce short-run fluctuations in rates in response to changes in demand for money market instruments.

The question may be raised whether there is any different impact on short-run rates when banks undertake to change the level of their negotiable time deposits in response to upward and downward movements in seasonal loan demand—as many banks do—as an alternative to changing their portfolios of money market instruments. If banks were to rely exclusively on changes in holdings of money market instruments as a response to seasonal changes in loan demand, they would, when faced with a rise in such demand, redistribute short-term instruments through the market to the nonbank sector. The desire of the banks to sell such instruments may be viewed as a reduction in demand for them; and other things being equal, some price decline, and rate increase, would be necessary to effect the redistribution. To the extent that banks choose to increase their negotiable time deposits in response to a seasonal rise in loan demand, they increase the supply of money market instruments, and this too involves some decline in their prices and increase in their rates. But the reduction in demand for such instruments that would have occurred had banks chosen the alternative of reducing their short-term portfolios does not, in this case, occur. Therefore, unless one is prepared to make asymmetrical assumptions with respect to the elasticities of supply and demand for money market instruments, one may conclude that whether banks choose to meet a seasonal rise in loan demand through liquidating short-term investments or through issuing new time certificates of deposit makes little difference in respect of the extent of the rate change associated with the rise in loan demand. To put the point another way, there seems to be no a priori reason for expecting an important difference in rate impact whether the rise in loan demand elicits an increase in the supply of money market instruments or a decrease in the demand for them.

To sum up the points made concerning negotiable certificates of deposit, the growth and development of these instruments have added an extra dimension of flexibility to the size of the stock of money market paper; and on balance it appears that the negotiable time certificate has tended, in some degree that cannot be quantified, to reduce short-run fluctuations in money market rates.

24 EURODOLLARS IN THE LIQUIDITY AND RESERVE MANAGEMENT OF UNITED STATES BANKS

FRED H. KLOPSTOCK

The Federal Reserve Board of Governors implemented a marginal reserve requirement of 10 percent against Eurodollar borrowing by United States banks effective September 4, 1969. This requirement, along with some other measures mentioned in Selection 21, have reduced the profitability of using Eurodollars. These reforms have contributed to the slowdown, indeed virtual cessation, of the rate of growth in Eurodollar borrowings by American banks from their foreign branches. Whereas near the end of August 1969 such borrowing stood at $14,658 million, by the end of November of that year it had reached only $14,897 million. Can you explain the relationship between the fall in the rate of growth of Eurodollar borrowing and the measures instituted by the Federal Reserve?

During the last decade, the large commercial banks in the United States have exhibited a remarkable degree of imagination and initiative in broadening their access to pools of liquid funds. Their success in attracting corporate and institutional balances through the issue of negotiable certificates of deposit (CD's) is a case in point. Other examples are their issue of "consumer" investment certificates and the flotation of unsecured notes and debentures in the capital market. More recently this increased readiness of banks to rely on what has become known as "liability management" in the adjustment of liquidity and reserve positions has been demonstrated by their large-scale use of balances acquired through their overseas branches in the Eurodollar market. The overseas branches became active in this market soon after it emerged in the late 1950's, and have gradually become the most important participants. But only since the midsixties have several of the major United States banks employed large amounts of Eurodollar balances for adjustments of their money positions in response to changing needs for funds, and more and more banks have opened overseas branches to gain access to the Eurodollar market.

For some of the large money market banks, Eurodollars have now become a major source of funds for loans and investments; in many instances, the head office's dollar liabilities to overseas branches exceed or closely approach its outstanding CD's. Altogether, liabilities of American banks to their overseas branches are now close to $13 billion. . . . The following pages examine the institutional and economic background of the practice of using Eurodollars in portfolio management, a practice that has greatly increased during the last two years.

From Fred H. Klopstock, "Eurodollars in the Liquidity and Reserve Management of United States Banks," *Essays in Domestic and International Finance* (New York: Federal Reserve Bank of New York, 1969), pp. 72–80.

THE EURODOLLAR MARKET AS A SOURCE OF FUNDS FOR UNITED STATES BANKS

The Eurodollar market, which centers on London with links in several other major financial centers in Western Europe and elsewhere, is a telephone and telex network through which many of the world's major banks bid for and employ dollar balances. By a generally accepted definition, Eurodollars come into existence when a domestic or foreign holder of dollar demand deposits in the United States places them on deposit in a bank outside the United States, but the term also applies to the dollars that banks abroad acquire with their own or foreign currencies and then employ for placement in the market or for loans to customers. Compared with other markets used by American banks for adjusting their liabilities, the Eurodollar market possesses distinctive features which both add to and detract from its usefulness as a source of funds.

By far the greatest merit of the market from the viewpoint of United States banks is that it offers the possibility of obtaining balances that are not subject to the regulatory restrictions applicable to demand and time deposits. Unlike United States banks, the overseas branches may pay interest on dollar call deposits and on time deposits with maturities of less than thirty days. Thus, United States banks can gain access, through the overseas branch route, to sizable amounts of funds that they are precluded by various regulations from acquiring directly from foreign depositors. In addition, balances payable at overseas branches are not subject to Regulation Q rate ceilings, a factor of great significance when rates for money market instruments in the United States or Eurodollar rates rise above the ceiling rates payable on deposits. And, finally, branch balances placed in head offices are not subject to member bank reserve requirements or to the fees of the Federal Deposit Insurance Corporation (FDIC). Indeed, especially during periods of tight money, the differential between Eurodollar rates and time deposit rates in the United States tends to reflect this saving.

Another advantage of the market is its broad scope. Actual and potential Eurodollar sources are diverse and widely dispersed geographically. They include countless banks and corporations in many parts of the world as well as monetary authorities and international financial institutions. When conditions in some countries restrict offerings by suppliers, conditions elsewhere typically free more resources for Eurodollar placements. Monetary authorities and international institutions may add to their offerings when commercial banks and corporations pull back theirs. In short, there is a high degree of supply flexibility in the Eurodollar market.

• • •

There are some negative aspects of the Eurodollar market from the viewpoint of money position management. The market is far away, and because of the time difference between London and New York (not to mention Chicago or San Francisco) opportunities for immediate and direct head-office communication with it are confined to a few hours during the morning. Moreover, due to the settlement and clearing periods involved, several days pass before a head-office decision to take on Eurodollars is reflected in available funds in the banks' reserve accounts. Meanwhile, conditions in domestic money markets may have changed significantly. Closely connected with the distance factor is the problem of adequate information. Because of the diverse conditions prevailing in the several major areas where dollar supplies originate, it is not always easy for the branches to obtain accurate knowledge of prospective market factors that might affect rates and amounts offered. And, in turn, head-office money position managers have not always found it easy to convey to their London offices their exact needs in terms of amounts and maturities, since their desire to draw on the market is partly conditional on the rates at which balances in various maturity sectors become available, and the rates change in response to market conditions.

• • •

MAJOR HEAD-OFFICE USES OF BRANCH BALANCES

Conceptually, the funds of overseas branches in head offices may be separated into three main categories: (1) balances borrowed by the head offices on a more or less continuous basis for the purpose of enlarging the banks' reserves, (2) balances acquired for short-term adjustments of reserve positions, and (3) working or operating balances to accommodate adjustments between head-office and branch accounts. The boundaries between the three categories are, at least for some banks, somewhat blurred; often the same balances serve all three functions, and clearly, whatever their maturity or the ultimate objective of their acquisition, they all add to the resources of the borrowing banks. Apart from these three categories, Eurodollars are also used by foreign banks and overseas branches for the purchase of loans from United States banks and to finance loans that otherwise would have been made directly by American banks.

Continuous Borrowing for Enlarging Reserves

The major motive of United States banks in using Eurodollar funds has been to obtain balances for enlarging or maintaining their credit potential. In their efforts to locate and solicit additional loanable funds, the banks have become increasingly attracted by the continuous availability in the Eurodollar market of very large amounts of funds in a broad maturity range. Although a large part of these funds are call and short-dated deposits, experience has demonstrated that over extended periods even the call component remains quite steady in the aggregate. Thus the presence in, or availability to, the Eurodollar market of very large interest-rate-sensitive funds provides the banks with an attractive alternative means of meeting demands on their liquidity positions and adding to aggregate deposit stability.

Rate advantages explain, of course, much of the heavy use of Eurodollar deposits. During recent years, they have been for extended periods less expensive, or at least not more expensive, than domestic deposits. Even when rates in the Eurodollar market are nominally higher than those in the CD market, it may be advantageous to increase holdings of branch balances, relative to sales of CD's, because of their exemption from reserve requirements and FDIC fees. A further saving associated with Eurodollar transactions through overseas branches arises from technical factors. When a bank engages in such transactions, it may benefit from reduced reserve requirements, while clearing the transaction, for at least one day—and for more if the date of the acquisition or repayment is followed by a holiday or a weekend. The reason is that the check received by a bank in connection with the transfer of a Eurodollar deposit increases cash items in the process of collection, which are deductible from demand deposits in computing reserve requirements even though the branch balance does not add to deposits subject to such requirements. This saving arises only if the Eurodollar deposit is either placed or repaid by the issuance of a so-called "bills payable" or "London" check. Unlike other outstanding officers' checks, such checks are typically not included in deposits subject to reserve requirements.

• • •

Borrowing to Finance Weekend Reserve Positions

United States banks seldom use Eurodollar balances for specifically adjusting day-to-day cash and reserve positions except over weekends. The Eurodollar market is generally not suited to immediate reserve adjustment needs. One reason is the distance factor: In the morning hours, London time, when the branch officers would need to obtain indications of immediate head-office needs in the light of current offerings, United States banks have not yet opened for business; by noon, New York time, when the evolving cash needs of banks are becoming evident, the London market is closing up shop. Of still greater significance is the fact that the normal delivery period for Eurodollars is two days, and even if arrangements can be made early in the morning London time to acquire dollars for same-day delivery in New York, these balances become available as bank reserves in Federal Reserve accounts only the next day (see below). Moreover, banks find it difficult to estimate changes in reserve positions for more than a few days in advance. For these reasons, banks generally consider the Federal funds market far superior to the overnight sector of the Eurodollar market for very short-term adjustments of reserve positions. Yet, because of the possible saving of required reserves noted above, many banks with overseas branches make continuous use of overnight deposits as a substantial core of relatively low cost funds.

An important use of the Eurodollar market as a tool of short-term reserve management is for the financing of weekend reserve positions. In fact, most of the banks with branches employ overnight deposits each Thursday as a partial substitute for Federal funds purchases on Friday. Because of New York check-clearing practices, overnight borrowing in the Eurodollar market value-Thursday for repayment on Friday can serve as bank reserves for three days—from Friday through Sunday. Eurodollar transactions are generally settled through checks on New York banks. Unlike Federal funds transactions, which are recorded in Federal Reserve accounts immediately, these checks must pass through the New York Clearing House, and it is not until the following business day that they become balances in the Federal Reserve accounts of member banks. Thus, a check drawn on bank A and deposited on Friday in bank B in repayment of a Eurodollar deposit does not draw down A's reserves until Monday; the same applies if the check is deposited on the day before a holiday.

• • •

No statistical information is extant on the volume of Thursday-Friday transactions by the overseas branches of United States banks. Aggregate branch balances in their head offices tend to increase on Thursday by amounts in the $100 million to $300 million range, depending in part on conditions in the Federal funds market. But the overall volume of Thursday-Friday transactions is in excess of this range, which does not reflect balances that mature or are called on Thursday and are placed again for one day.

• • •

Operating Balances of Branches

The third type of liabilities to overseas branches consists of balances carried with head offices for operating purposes. This item has no direct relationship to the branches' overall dollar liabilities. Actually there may be no necessity for a branch to carry an operating balance in its head office if it is authorized to overdraw its account at its head office in case of need, or if the various components of its assets carry maturities of the same length as those of its corresponding deposit liabilities. Moreover, branches are ordinarily able, at a price, to obtain additional balances in foreign currency deposit markets. But the voluntary credit restraint program has made it undesirable for head offices to expose themselves to sudden branch overdrafts for meeting deposit liabilities that cannot be replaced at the time of maturity without costly rate sacrifices. Some branches have been willing to build their asset portfolios on deposits that carry somewhat shorter maturities than loan and deposit placements abroad: it is not easy, and is at times impossible, to match dollar loans to corporations with dollar deposits of similar maturities. Branches also need operating balances to discharge obligations under letters of credit and to take care of a variety of payments orders by customers, and they need contingency reserves in view of their large outstanding loan commitments.

• • •

Eurodollar Financing of Loan Transactions

There is, finally, the special category of Eurodollar transactions represented by head-office loan transfers to branches. To some extent these entail the sale of outstanding loans under repurchase agreements. Until 1968, such sales appear to have arisen mainly from efforts of head offices to maintain their outstanding claims below the quota ceilings set by the voluntary credit restraint program. On occasion, though, even banks that had considerable credit leeway under the restraint program made sizable sales of loans to branches. Under these circumstances, however, the purpose appears to have been to enable individual branches to acquire earning assets with funds that they had taken in to accommodate important nonbank accounts on their books. More recently, sales of both domestic and foreign loans to branches have been employed on a fairly large scale as a device to obtain funds for additional domestic loans. Such sales wipe out any simultaneous increase in branch placements in head offices that have resulted from branch acquisitions of deposits abroad for the specific purpose of purchasing the loans. Of course, the head office does not acquire additional funds if the loan is paid for out of existing branch deposits.

Of greater importance than such sales, in terms of dollar amounts involved, are loans made by branches to meet loan demands on their head offices. For these loans to head-office customers the branches employ deposits obtained in the Eurodollar or other foreign currency deposit markets. It is, of course, possible that a branch would have increased its Eurodollar liabilities even in the absence of this particular loan demand and would have placed additional balances in its head-office account.

It should be mentioned again that many United States banks without branches sell substantial amounts of their foreign loans to foreign banks under repurchase agreements, primarily in order to hold their foreign claims below the credit restraint program ceilings; the foreign banks finance these loan purchases largely with Eurodollars. And there are indications that an increasing number of banks without branches have made arrangements to borrow Eurodollars directly from foreign banks. These two types of transactions are analogous to, and have the same liquidity and reserve effects as, the corresponding transactions between head offices and their overseas branches.

HEAD-OFFICE USE OF BRANCH BALANCES, 1964–68

Before 1964, relatively few of the banks with overseas branches made much use of the Eurodollar market for their head-office operations. Not until the summer of that year did aggregate head-office liabilities to branches remain continuously above $1 billion. Through most of 1965, they were substantially below $2 billion, as shown in [Figure 1]. The majority of the banks with branches apparently preferred other options for obtaining funds, either because of cost considerations or because head-office portfolio managements had not yet developed a close liaison with overseas branch managements.

During the first half of 1966, as Federal Reserve pressures on the banks'

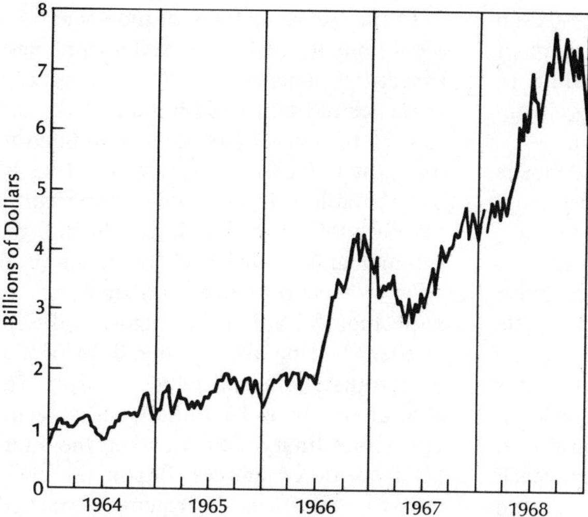

Figure 1 Liabilities of United States Banks to Their Foreign Branches
SOURCE: Board of Governors of the Federal Reserve System.

reserve positions mounted, borrowings gradually increased and the aggregate due to branches approached the $2 billion level. The increased resort to the Eurodollar market during this period represented primarily an attempt to obtain resources over and above those available in domestic deposit markets and thereby to lessen susceptibility to reserve pressures.

Toward the end of June 1966, the pace of borrowing through branches quickened even more. The large money market banks then used the Eurodollar market to cushion the effects of another weapon in the Federal Reserve's armory of credit control—administration of Regulation Q. With the Reserve System using Q as a deliberate means of reducing the rate of credit expansion, the banks were virtually priced out of the national CD market. But about four fifths of the loss in outstanding CD's suffered during the summer and fall of 1966 by the twelve banks with overseas branches was offset by increased Eurodollar takings from branches. Eurodollars at that time were in ample supply, partly because of large-scale shifts of funds out of sterling into dollars. By mid-December, aggregate redeposits in head offices, which had then reached $4.3 billion, amounted to substantially more than half of the twelve banks' outstanding CD's, compared with less than one fifth in mid-1966.

Thus, during the summer and fall of 1966, Eurodollar balances played an important role in banks' efforts to meet loan demands and commitments, offset losses of other resources, and reduce the need to liquidate securities at distressingly low prices. Moreover, the banks were then experiencing an increase in demand deposits relative to time deposits, and the resultant effects on required reserves were cushioned by the acquisition of balances not subject to reserve requirements.

Late in 1966 and early in 1967, when a large movement of foreign funds into the London money market coincided with a considerable easing of money market conditions in the United States, the use of branch balances by head offices fell rapidly, and by May 1967 it had dropped by about $1.5 billion from the peak level reached in December 1966. The figure then began to rise, however, and in November 1967 it began to exceed the amount outstanding during the 1966 credit crunch. During the short span of six months beginning in the middle of May 1967, aggregate borrowings from branches rose by about $2 billion.

This 1967 surge of branch deposits occurred in a market atmosphere quite different from that prevailing in the second half of 1966. During the latter part of 1967 the demand for business loans was relatively weak. The Federal Reserve supplied bank reserves quite liberally until late in the year, and banks were able to make considerable progress in improving their liquidity positions. There was little, if any, need to reach out for funds in Europe to compensate for shortages of funds in the United States. It appears, therefore, that there was a fundamental change in the banks' attitude with respect to taking Eurodollars from their branches. Before the summer of 1966, several of them approached the Eurodollar market with some hesitation, looking on it merely as a marginal source of funds. In general, they discovered the market's full potential only after having been virtually forced into it. As they became familiar with its breadth and depth, they lost their skepticism and came to regard the market as another normal source of funds to be tapped whenever the price was right.

Other factors also contributed to the surge in the use of Eurodollars during 1967. Foreign investors shifted substantial amounts of their short-term sterling investments into the Eurodollar market in response to the Middle East crisis in June and the weakening of sterling in the fall of 1967 prior to its devaluation. In addition, market relationships had been established, with considerable effort, and the banks desired to maintain them. Several felt that a withdrawal from the market because domestic funds could be easily substituted for Eurodollars would not serve their longer run interest, even if continued participation sometimes involved a rate sacrifice.

In the spring of 1968, as money market conditions in the United States tightened, aggregate balances held for overseas branches passed the $5 billion mark, and toward the end of June they amounted to more than $6 billion. Sizable dollar losses by the Bank of France added importantly to Eurodollar availabilities during the summer and contributed to the surge of "due to foreign banks" outstandings to more than $7 billion in August and September. During the closing days of the year, outstandings dropped sharply (to a total of about $6 billion) as a result of extraordinary demands on the market from other sources. But in the early months of 1969, borrowings reached new peaks as major United States banks turned to the Eurodollar market to relieve liquidity drains resulting from large runoffs of CD's.

IMPLICATIONS FOR MONETARY ANALYSIS AND POLICY

United States banks' initiative in attracting hitherto untapped liquid funds—their gradual shift from a passive to an active role in acquiring funds through incurring liabilities—has raised important issues for monetary analysis and policy. And their recently increased use of balances obtained by the overseas branches from foreign sources has added to both the number and the complexity of the issues with which analysts and policy makers need be concerned. The success of the banks' efforts to acquire additional funds abroad has implications that touch on many aspects of the financial mechanism, including the country's balance of payments, the distribution of bank reserves and the banks' response to reserve pressures, the foreign ownership of United States money market instruments, and monetary policy.

• • •

The transformation of demand deposits into branch balances in head offices does not change United States banks' total reserves, but it does reduce the level of their aggregate required reserves, since overseas branch balances in head offices are not subject to reserve requirements. This fact has to be taken into account if, as is often done, current changes in bank credit are estimated on the basis of changes in deposits subject to reserve requirements. Moreover, the banking system as a whole can carry a somewhat larger amount of earning assets on the basis of a given amount of reserves. Since the banks that obtain balances from their branches typically are in a net reserve deficiency position and tend fully to employ available funds, their additional reserves are likely to be reflected immediately in a bank credit increase or reduced borrowings from other sources rather than in larger excess reserves. In other words, these banks' acquisition of reserves through the Eurodollar operations of their branches increases the utilization of the banking system's reserve base, as do Federal funds purchases from those banks that are less fully invested.

The banks that have direct access to the Eurodollar market through their foreign branches are in a position to increase their share in total member bank reserves. If they were to abstain from absorbing Eurodollar balances, most of the underlying funds would be invested by foreign central banks in the United States money market and would therefore be more widely dispersed throughout the banking system. Of course, to the extent that foreign central banks place their dollar gains in time deposits with American banks, these balances would be largely held with the same banks that acquire funds through their branches. To be sure, banks without branches may borrow Eurodollar balances from foreign banks, and such borrowings are also exempt from Regulation Q ceilings and reserve requirements. But the branch route to Eurodollars is broader and more convenient and may well be less expensive in the long run. Moreover, it allows access to a much larger volume of funds than most banks can or would wish to secure through borrowings abroad. And only the larger banks in the United States have the credit standing that would enable them to obtain sizable dollar balances from foreign banks.

For individual banks with overseas branches, the availability of still another liability market of great breadth provides additional elbow room for portfolio and reserve adjustments. Inasmuch as the Eurodollar market is subject to influences emanating from prevailing climates in foreign money markets, its supply-demand balance at any one particular point in time may differ greatly from that in the New York money market. Money market tightness here may be accompanied by relative ease in the Eurodollar market. United States banks that find it undesirable or are unable to liquidate securities at such times, or are unable to add to their outstanding CD's because of interest rate limitations by the Federal Reserve, may find a ready alternative source of funds in branch balances. But, even in the absence of pressure or regulatory interference in domestic money markets, access to Eurodollars offers additional opportunities to minimize portfolio adjustment costs—as does resort to the national CD market. Moreover, the very knowledge that they are able to fall back on the Eurodollar market, and to use it in addition to or as an alternative to other liability markets, may induce portfolio managers to carry larger amounts of loans relative to aggregate deposits, and fewer liquid assets relative to aggregate assets, than they would otherwise consider prudent.

Monetary policy has had to take into account the buildup of overseas branch deposits in United States banks, and now continuously weighs the various implications and consequences of current and prospective changes in these placements. . . .

On the domestic side, the Federal Reserve System must be concerned with the redistribution of reserves arising from the access of banks with overseas branches to balances that other banks find it difficult or impossible to attract. It must also take into account shifts in the banks' aggregate demand for reserves as they acquire reserve-exempt balances. Furthermore, it must make allowance for the increased ability of the money market banks—the major source of business loans to large corporate borrowers—to fall back on the Eurodollar market whenever the interest rate ceilings impair the banks' ability to obtain funds in the national market for CD's. Indeed, now that some of the major commercial banks in the United States look beyond this country's borders for funds with which to make adjustments in their liquidity and reserve positions, a new and significant dimension has been added to central banking in the United States.

25 CURRENT DEBATE ON THE TERM STRUCTURE OF INTEREST RATES

FREDERICK M. STRUBLE

Frederick Struble does an excellent job in elucidating the various views and studies concerning the yield curve controversy. Consider, as you read this selection, the fact that economists tend to support the expectations hypothesis, while the financial community sticks to the market segmentation hypothesis. How can you explain this disagreement?

Can the monetary authorities—the Federal Reserve System and the U.S. Treasury—alter the relationship among maturity yields on Government securities by changing the maturity composition of Government securities outstanding? For many years, two different theories—the expectations theory and the segmented markets theory—have been used as a basis for answering this question.

The expectations theory contends that a change in relative supplies of securities with different maturities will not affect maturity yield relationships unless, in the process, it brings about a change in market expectations of future interest rates. On the other hand, the segmented markets theory argues that maturity yield differentials are caused by an imbalance between the maturity composition of debt demanded by lenders and supplied by borrowers. From this it follows that a shift in the maturity composition of supply will affect relative yields. The segmented markets theory acknowledges that market expectations of future interest rates may be changed as relative supplies in the various maturity sectors are altered, thus augmenting the change in yield differentials brought about by this operation. In general, however, most discussions of the segmented markets theory have emphasized the direct effects that changes in relative supplies will have on relative yields apart from any possible changes which might occur in expectations of future interest rates. Discussions of the expectations theory similarly have played down the possible effects that changes in the maturity composition of debt might have on interest rate expectations. As a result, the theoretical controversy has been clearly defined.

Although each of these theoretical positions has a long history, it seems a safe judgment that the segmented markets theory has been and continues to be the theory most generally accepted by market analysts. However, the degree of consensus on this question has been reduced considerably as a result of recent research. Older statements of the expectations theory have been reinterpreted incorporating more plausible behavioral assumptions and the more rigorous modern formulations have added clarity to the meaning of the expectations hypothesis. On an empirical plane, several of the more sophisticated tests have provided strong support for the expectations theory.

• • •

From Frederick M. Struble, "Current Debate on the Term Structure of Interest Rates," Federal Reserve Bank of Kansas City, *Monthly Review,* January–February 1966, pp. 10–16.

THE SEGMENTED MARKETS THEORY

Although the term, segmented markets, is used here to identify one theory of the term structure of interest rates, in other discussions this theory has been identified by several other terms, including institutional, imperfect substitutes, and hedging. Each refers to a type of balance sheet decisionmaking complicated by legal restrictions and traditional practices such as the matching of the maturity structure of one's assets with the maturity structure of one's liabilities—presumably in order to avoid risk. It is argued that because major groups of borrowers and lenders prefer to match assets and liabilities in this way, the market for credit instruments is partly compartmentalized, or segmented, according to the maturity of debt instruments. As a result, loans with different maturities are imperfect substitutes in the aggregate as well as for individual investor and borrower groups in the sense that different rates of return are required to hold securities with different maturities, and also, the size of the difference in rates of return varies with changes in the maturity composition of asset portfolios. This means that maturity yield differentials are determined by an imbalance between the maturity structure of debt demanded by investors and the maturity structure of debt supplied by borrowers.

Since the alternative theoretical position to be discussed in the next section of this article stresses the importance of interest rate expectations, it is worthwhile to note that discussions of the segmented markets theory generally have limited the influence of interest rate expectations to possible effects that *changes* in expectations of future interest rates can have on *current* interest rate relationships. This is quite different from the primary role assigned to expectations in the expectations theory. For, briefly, the expectations theory asserts that *current* differences in the maturity yields exist because the market expects interest rates to change over future periods of time. Moreover, it contends that it is possible to determine from a given yield relationship the pattern of future interest rates predicted by the market. Discussions of the segmented markets theory have either ignored this issue or have asserted that a current yield structure is not affected by interest rate expectations in this manner.

Several facts appear to provide strong support for the segmented markets theory. In particular, the behavior of many institutional lenders accords with the assumptions about investor behavior made by this theory. For example, commercial bank portfolios are heavily weighted with assets of short maturity while assets held in the portfolios of insurance companies and savings and loan institutions are predominantly long term. Many examples of borrower behavior also may be cited which conform to the assumptions underlying the segmented markets theory. Consumers usually finance purchases of houses with long-term mortgages and purchases of less durable consumer goods with shorter-term debt agreements. In a similar manner, business firms generally attempt to match the maturity of their liabilities with the durability of their assets—inventories are financed by short-term loans while plant and equipment investments are financed by longer-term loans. These examples clearly are far from exhaustive. Presumably, it is the pervasiveness of such practices that makes the segmented markets theory so compelling to many analysts, particularly those involved in the day-to-day operations of credit markets.

Against this evidence supporting the segmented markets theory, the results of recent empirical studies have been surprising. One study after another designed to measure the effects of the maturity composition of debt on maturity yield differentials was unable to discern a substantial relationship between these variables. Consequently, these findings have cast doubt on the segmented markets theory.

These empirical studies have not been entirely convincing, however. In attempting to estimate the implications of changing supply conditions, all but one study ignored the possible consequences of simultaneous shifts in demand. Most studies assumed that the demand for loans with different maturities remains relatively stable over time. If this is the case, then changes in maturity yield differentials can be attributed to changes in relative supply. If, however, conditions of demand change concurrently with changes in relative supplies, this would reduce the correlation between relative supplies and relative yields. The failure of most studies to consider this problem reduces their significance. The fact that the one study which did consider this problem came to essentially the same conclusions as the others, however, suggests that failure to consider this contingency may not have been an important deficiency. In addition, on an *a priori* basis, it seems unlikely that changes in demand would vary inversely with changes in supply so consistently that an actual relationship between relative supplies and relative yields would be entirely obscured.

THE EXPECTATIONS THEORY

The consistent findings that changes in relative supplies of securities with different maturities have only small effects on maturity yield differentials not only cast doubt on the segmented markets theory, they also provide indirect support for an alternative theoretical explanation of the term structure of interest rates. Both the pure expectations theory and the version of this theory which contends that liquidity preference is partly responsible for the establishment of maturity yield differentials, agree on one vital point: that the maturity structure of outstanding debt does not affect the maturity structure of yields.

The basic assertion of the pure expectations theory is that loans with different maturities, that are similar in all other respects, are perfect substitutes to investors in the aggregate. This means that the relationship among current prices and yields on securities with differing maturities are adjusted so that the rates of return on this debt—calculated to include capital gains and losses where applicable—are expected to be equal for any given period of time; and that the maturity composition of outstanding debt does not affect maturity yield differentials. From these assertions it follows that maturity yield differentials exist because the market is expecting interest rates to change over the future—to change in such a way that apparent differences in return which might be inferred from yield differentials are wiped out in the process—rather than because it expects the rates of return on loans with different maturities to differ. Moreover, any process which alters the maturity composition of investor portfolios, but does not change expectations of future interest rates, will not affect the existing structure of yields on loans with different maturities.

It should be emphasized that loans with different maturities may be perfect substitutes in the aggregate even though not every investor views them as such. Credit markets may be dominated by a relatively small but well-financed group of traders who treat loans of different maturities as perfect substitutes. If this is the case, the investors, whose actions are offset by these traders, would have no influence on security prices and yields. Security prices and yields would be established by traders willing to adjust their holdings of securities with different maturities until they expect the realized rates of return on the securities to be equal over any given period.

Still another possibility exists for rationalizing that certain securities in the aggregate are perfect substitutes. The preferences of different investor groups may overlap so that all securities within one maturity range may be perfect substitutes for one investor group, while securities in another maturity range may be perfect substitutes for another investor group. For example, banks may consider debt instruments over a certain range of short-term securities to be perfect substitutes while savings and loan associations, insurance companies, and other investors may view longer maturity dates as perfect substitutes. If the maturity ranges of different investor groups overlap sufficiently, the structure of yields would be adjusted as if each investor believed all securities to be perfect substitutes.

However one views the process which leads to loans with differing maturities being perfect substitutes in the aggregate, the essential point is that the yields and prices are determined by investors who expect the rates of return on these securities to be the same over any given period of time. It is necessary to qualify this statement moderately, since most presentations of the expectations theory do recognize that such factors as market impediments and transactions costs may result in some inequality in expected rates of return and may cause some distortion between actually established yield structures and those which would be established if these factors did not exist. In general analysis, however, it seems a valid practice to ignore these factors, for yield differentials change rather substantially over time, and it is highly unlikely that this behavior could be attributed in any significant way to changes in transactions costs or other market impediments.

There are two compatible ways to look at the equality of expected rates of return. An existing long-term rate can be considered equal, roughly speaking, to an average of a current short-term rate and the short-term rates which are expected to be established over time until the long-term loan matures. On the other hand, a current long-term rate can be viewed as standing in a specific relationship to a current short-term rate such that its price is expected to change just sufficiently so that its rate of return will equal the short-term rate over the period required for the short-term loan to mature.

In either case, any yield differential represents a market prediction that interest rates will change over the future. For example, consider two loans with 1 and 2 years to maturity that are selling to yield 2 percent and 3 percent, respectively. According to the pure expectations theory, this interest rate relationship indicates a market prediction that the price of the 2-year loan will fall by roughly 1 percent over the year. Or, it indicates that the market is expecting the yield on a 1-year loan to be roughly 4 percent 1 year in the future. This prediction is implied because the average of the current 1-year yield of 2 percent and the expected 1-year yield of 4 percent is roughly equal to the current 2-year maturity yield of 3 percent. In short, the expectations theory contends that differences in yields on loans with different maturities are established not because the market expects to receive a higher return on one security than on another, but instead, because the market expects the rates of return on the two securities to be the same over an equal period of time.

To view this conception from a broader perspective, consider the relationship among a whole range of yields on loans with differing maturities. This relationship is usually depicted by a yield curve, a curve which provides a general picture of the relationship among all maturity yields on a particular date. Three prevalent types of yield curves have been established during this century. The first is an upsloping curve with yields rising as maturity lengthens and then generally becoming flat in the range of longest maturity dates. The second is a downsloping curve with yields declining as maturity lengthens and then generally becoming flat in the range of longest maturity dates. The third is a flat yield curve with all maturity yields equal.

According to the expectations theory, the upsloping curve indicates that the market is expecting all yields to rise over future periods of time, with the greatest increases expected among short-term yields. The downsloping curve reflects market expectations that all yields will fall over future periods of time, with the greatest declines expected in shorter-term yields. The flat curve reflects market expectations that all yields will remain unchanged.

As might be expected, yield curves tend to vary over the business cycle and the types associated with the various phases of the business cycle lend plausibility to the expectations theory. For example, upsloping yield curves are usually observed during recessions and throughout the early part of a business expansion. It seems quite plausible that borrowers and lenders would be expecting interest rates to increase at such times. Conversely, downsloping yield curves generally have been established at or near the peaks of business expansion. With interest rates generally high historically, it is at least plausible that investors would be expecting to see yields decline in the future.

THE LIQUIDITY PREFERENCE VERSION OF THE EXPECTATIONS THEORY

Several discussions of the expectations theory have concluded that expected changes in yield relationships provide only part of the explanation for the existence of yield differentials. They have argued that lenders generally prefer to hold short-term loans as assets because the price of these assets tends to vary minimally. This preference is reflected in the willingness of investors to forego some expected return in order to hold short-term assets. As a result, longer-term assets generally provide a liquidity premium and their expected rate of return tends to be higher. To put this another way, it is asserted that the level of longer-term yields is always higher than it would be if the structure of yields was determined solely by market expectations. The fact that yield curves have sloped upward considerably more often than they have sloped downward since World War II often is cited as evidence of the existence of a liquidity premium on longer-term securities. It should be noted, however, that the predominance of upsloping yield curves is not necessarily inconsistent with the pure expectations theory. If the market generally had expected yields to rise over this period—and yields did rise—the larger proportion of yield curves would have had an upward slope. It will be remembered that at the outset of the postwar period interest rates were at historically low levels.

Although the liquidity preference variant of the expectations theory contends that rates of return on loans with different maturities are expected to differ, it does not view credit markets as being segmented. Instead, the size of the presumed liquidity premium is held to be unrelated, or essentially unrelated, to the maturity composition of outstanding debt. Thus, the position of the liquidity preference approach is the same as the pure expectations approach on this vital point. In addition, the liquidity preference theory asserts that, in general, changes in yield differentials imply that the market has changed its expectations about the future course of interest rates. Here, again, the liquidity preference approach is in accord with the pure expectations approach and in conflict with the segmented markets approach. For these reasons, it is possible to consider this position as a variant of the expectations theory.

IMPLICATIONS OF EMPIRICAL EVIDENCE

The expectations theory has never been widely accepted outside of academic circles. Until recently, one reason was the inability of analysts to develop a test which supported this theory. In fact, early studies which purported to test this theory concluded that it had no empirical validity. This conclusion was based upon the demonstration that yield predictions derived from a structure of yields in accordance with logic of the expectations theory were usually wrong. Recent presentations of this theory have made it clear, however, that this is not a valid test. A test of the market's ability to form accurate forecasts of future interest rates does not constitute a test of whether an existing yield structure depends upon market expectations of future interest rates. All that is asserted by the expectations theory is that yield differentials exist because the market expects interest rates to change. It is not claimed that the predictions of the market necessarily will be accurate. In addition to this clarification, recent studies have generated new evidence in support of the expectations approach. And, although these findings taken individually are not overwhelmingly compelling, as a group they do serve to increase the degree of acceptance of the expectations theory.

It is impossible in the short space available to describe these tests in detail, but their general approach may be outlined. First, hypotheses about how interest rate expectations are formulated at one point in time or how they are altered with the passage of time are developed. Maturity yield relationships established at various points in time and the subsequent changes in these relationships with the passage of time are then compared with this independent evidence of market expectations. A high degree of correlation has been found between these variables.

Another approach has been to draw inferences about the validity of the expectations approach by comparing actual interest rates established over a certain period of time with forecasted interest rates as implied by yield structures established in the past. The criterion used for judging the results was not whether market predictions always turned out to be correct, however, as it was in earlier tests of this kind. Rather, it was one of determining whether actual rates turned out *on the average* to be above or below forecasted rates. The presumption has been that if, on the average, actual rates were equal to forecasted rates, this suggested that the pure expectations theory was correct. The findings in several studies that forecasted rates generally exceeded actual rates has been the principal source of support for the assertion that a liquidity premium on long-term debt must be recognized as a factor in determining maturity yield relationships.

Although most recent empirical studies of the expectations theory have proceeded along the lines described above, it should be noted that some investigations have approached the problem from a different perspective and have found evidence which casts doubt on this theory. One piece of evidence of this kind has been the inability to identify a group of balance sheet units that behave like the hypothetical speculators assumed in some presentations of the expectations theory. Moreover, objections have been raised as to the possibility of the type of speculative activity ascribed to traders because of technical deficiencies in the market with regard to short-selling. Additional evidence, which would appear to be particularly damaging to the overlapping markets version of this theory, was the finding in one recent study that interest rate expectations were not uniform among different market observers. This conflicts with one of the assumptions usually made in presenting the expectations theory which is that interest rate expectations of all investors tend to be uniform.

SUMMARY AND CONCLUSIONS

The problem of explaining maturity yield relationships remains unresolved. The implications of recent empirical findings, although far from being one-sided, have shifted opinion away from the segmented markets theory and toward either the pure expectations theory or this theory modified to include the existence of a liquidity premium on long-term debt. Perhaps the most compelling evidence produced by these studies was the consistent finding that changes in the maturity composition of debt have little, if any, effect on the maturity structure of yields. This, of course, constitutes not only a direct challenge to the segmented markets approach but, in addition, provides indirect support for the alternative theory. Other direct tests of the expectations hypothesis have added further support for this theory. In fact, on the basis of the results of these two groups of tests, a strong argument has been made for rejecting the segmented markets theory and accepting the expectations theory. However, all the evidence does not point in one direction. The generally acknowledged fact that major groups of borrowers and lenders are constrained either by legal restrictions or personal preferences from viewing securities with different maturities as perfect substitutes, the inability to identify economic units performing as speculators, and the evidence of diverse interest rate expectations all serve to temper any inclination to discard the segmented markets approach and accept the expectations theory. Perhaps the best appraisal at this time is that, as a result of recent research, the expectations approach has won an important skirmish, but the outcome of the war remains in doubt.

26 THE POLICY OF EVEN KEEL

WARREN J. GUSTUS

Numerous issues are raised by the "even keel" policy of the Federal Reserve System. First, note again the relationship of even keel and the rate structure controversy pointed out in the Introduction to this Part. Note also that this policy represents voluntary cooperation by the central bank with the Treasury, and by a unilateral decision, the Federal Reserve could reverse its policy. Thus even keel can be considered in the light of the central bank's desire for independence as surveyed in Part III. The Federal Reserve has supported Treasury financing for almost two decades, so this problem seems to be of little immediate concern. But remember that the central bank permitted two Treasury financings to fail in 1950, and those who forget the past are forced to relive it. Finally, as a matter of record, because of even keel, the Federal Reserve was unable to announce or implement major policy changes in nineteen weeks during 1968, a third of a year in which inflation was becoming an ever-increasing menace and monetary policy was tightened continuously. Do you think that the advantages of even keel outweigh the disadvantages?

• • •

From the end of World War II down to 1961, the Federal Reserve was engaged in a series of steps to re-order priorities. In the process, it shook off the commitment to peg prices of Government securities—a policy which had hobbled its ability to regulate money and credit. But the Federal Reserve, like other central banks, has continued to feel a responsibility not to complicate the Treasury's job of managing the debt. This responsibility is expressed in the term "even keel." To quote from an official publication:

> While the System has believed that its power to create money should not be used to support these financings, it has recognized that concurrent monetary actions may affect their success. Consequently, the Federal Reserve has come to pursue whenever feasible what is known as an "even keel" monetary policy immediately before, during, and immediately after Treasury financing operations.

Although even keel dates back a number of years, its significance has increased recently. One reason is that with the growth of inflationary pressures many have been concerned with the constraint it may pose for monetary policy. In addition, the Treasury has had to come to the market to raise large amounts of new money to finance substantial budget deficits. A further complicating factor is the decline in average maturity of the federal debt, and the implications this may have for the frequency of refunding operations. Average maturity has been decreasing because the Treasury has not been able to sell long-term debt at interest rates above the 4¼ percent ceiling imposed by law.

In light of these considerations, questions have been raised about the need for even keel, its costs, and its benefits.

From Warren J. Gustus, "Monetary Policy, Debt Management, and Even Keel," Federal Reserve Bank of Philadelphia, *Business Review,* January 1968, pp. 5–7.

WHAT IS EVEN KEEL?

Both in definition and practice, even keel is an elusive concept. In general, most market participants understand that even keel is a policy by the Federal Reserve of avoiding actions during Treasury financings that would signify a shift in monetary policy. Even keel is a commitment to neutrality by the Federal Reserve, but this commitment is particularly important to the Treasury during periods of monetary restraint. Then a move toward more restraint might involve higher interest rates and capital losses to Government securities dealers underwriting the issue. It could even trigger a failure of the financing.

Under most circumstances, even keel means no change in the discount rate and no change in reserve requirements because these moves are visible evidence of a policy shift. It generally means that the Federal Open Market Committee will adopt neither a more nor a less restrictive policy, and that actual operations will be conducted in such a way as to suggest no policy change to the market.

Beyond these rather general concepts, even keel becomes more difficult to define. It depends to a great extent upon the market situation prevailing at the time. Although the aim is to keep reserve availability roughly the same, with free or net borrowed reserves and federal funds fluctuating in a fairly narrow range, a greater-than-normal (or less-than-normal) supply of reserves may be necessary to keep the money market steady. From an operational viewpoint, during periods of even keel open market operations are conducted so as to maintain a steady tone in the money market.

Even keel usually begins a few days before announcement of a Treasury financing and continues until a few days after payment and delivery of the securities. In the period before announcement of a financing and its terms, the Treasury is canvassing the possibilities. Any change in market conditions then would make it more difficult for the Treasury to tailor the issue to meet its own needs and those of the market. Between announcement and delivery, the market is deciding on its subscriptions. From the Treasury's viewpoint, this is the most critical period because the success of an issue is determined then. The period after the books close and while an issue is being distributed is important because of the implications for future Treasury financings. If dealers see the value of their holdings undermined as a result of a change in monetary policy, they may be reluctant to participate in future offerings, particularly if one comes along soon.

REASONS FOR EVEN KEEL

The Government securities market is a key market in the economy, with particular importance for the Federal Reserve and the Treasury. The Treasury raises new money there and refinances outstanding securities; private investors use the market to adjust their liquidity and as an investment outlet; and the Federal Reserve uses this market in conducting open market operations, one of the major instruments of monetary policy.

Most of the transactions are effected through dealers, one of whose functions is to make markets by buying and selling securities for their own accounts. These dealers must be willing and able to maintain inventories of securities to accommodate customers when there are no immediate offsetting transactions. They are a key element in a key market.

There are relatively few dealers, all of them operating with slender equity-to-total-funds ratios and handling very large flotations of securities. Without even keel, they might suffer windfall profits or losses as a result of changes in monetary policy during Treasury financings. For example, if an increase in monetary restraint and a sharp increase in interest rates were to occur before dealers had distributed an issue to investors, the markdown in their holdings could cause them serious financial difficulties as well as making them reluctant to underwrite succeeding issues. On the other hand, an easing of policy that brought about a decline in interest rates could result in windfall profits not justified by any economic function the dealers perform.

IMPACT OF EVEN KEEL

Government securities dealers have come to expect and depend on even keel. The Treasury relies on it in conducting its financings. The Federal Reserve recognizes even keel as part of its responsibilities as a central bank. Thus, there are strong reasons for its existence and continuation. Nevertheless, it is also important to consider the implications of even keel for monetary policy.

Economists agree that lags exist between a change in monetary policy and the full effects of the change. They do not agree on the duration and variability of the lags. In view of this uncertainty, it is hard to make a strong case that postponement of a change in monetary policy for several weeks does much harm. However, when the Treasury is in the market frequently, postponement of policy changes may have more serious consequences.

In considering the impact of even keel on timing of monetary policy, one must allow also for the interval needed to accomplish a shift in policy. About three free weeks between even-keel periods is the minimum necessary for the Federal Reserve to act. A week or two usually is required for the market to become aware that policy has been changed. Of course, if the policy change involves a change in the discount rate or in required reserves, recognition is instantaneous. Most of the time, however, open market operations are the policy tool used and they involve a lag between change in policy and recognition of the change. An additional week may be desirable to allow the market to adjust to a new policy; otherwise the Treasury could face considerable difficulty in financing in a market not fully adjusted to a shift in Federal Reserve policy.

Much of the time when even keel is in effect the Federal Reserve would not want to change policy anyway. To count up the duration of even keel and the time necessary to bring about policy shifts, therefore, may overstate the constraint on monetary policy. But even when a change in policy is not the issue, even keel may result in rates of growth in money and bank credit that are undesirable in terms of economic stability. The reason is that during even-keel periods the primary monetary policy objective is to maintain stability in money market conditions. As a result, bank reserves, money and credit have to be allowed to grow at whatever rate is consistent with money market stability. Sometimes these rates of growth will be consistent with those necessary to accomplish monetary policy goals but sometimes they will not.

Of course, the Federal Reserve can attempt to make compensatory changes in monetary policy outside of even-keel periods. For example, if a slowdown in growth of money and credit has to be postponed for, say, three weeks, policy can concentrate the desired changes at the end of the even-keel period. Sometimes, this is the case; and when it is, even keel poses no great problem for the timing of monetary policy. But when the Federal Reserve wishes to pursue a gradually more restrictive policy, sustained or frequent periods of even keel make it more difficult to compensate later for inaction. A danger is that sudden and sharp policy shifts will cause disruptions in money and credit markets.

• • •

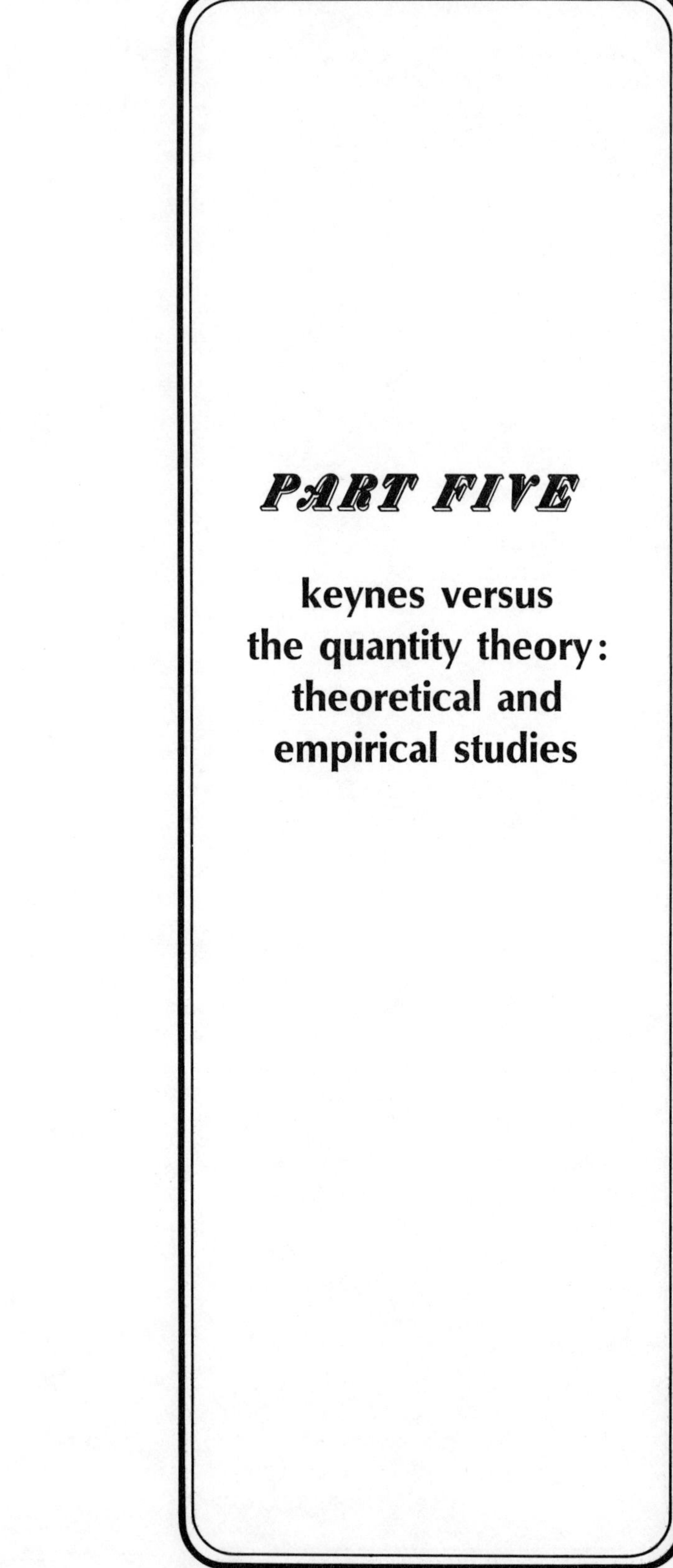

PART FIVE

keynes versus the quantity theory: theoretical and empirical studies

The pendulum, which swings from extreme to extreme but ultimately comes to rest in the center, aptly characterizes monetary theory during the past two centuries. In the beginning was the quantity theory of money, which can be traced back at least to the second half of the eighteenth century and David Hume. Quantity theorists believed that money-supply changes would bring in their wake changes in the price level but would not affect other variables such as the output of goods and services. Over the years, dissenters voiced their objections, but they were unable to marshal widespread professional support, and until the 1930s the quantity theory reigned supreme. Sudden death came in the decade following the appearance of Lord Keynes' monumental *General Theory of Employment, Interest and Money* (1936). His theoretical structure severed the direct link between money and prices and substituted instead a system in which money was linked only indirectly to economic activity and prices. Changes in the money supply might affect prices, but then again they might not. By the early 1940s, all except a few die-hard economists wholeheartedly embraced Keynesian theory and totally discarded the quantity theory. Indeed, as is often the case, the disciples expounded a more extreme and rigid formulation than did the master himself. In rejecting the view that money was all-important, they proclaimed that money was completely unimportant. Monetary policy was deemed ineffective and fiscal policy was enthroned. Only variations in government expenditures and incomes could do the job of stabilizing the economy.

Reaction to this extreme view was not long in setting in, but the pendulum did not swing all the way back to the opposite extreme. The quantity theory was revised, with the use of the Keynesian structure, by Professors Milton Friedman at the University of Chicago and Don Patinkin in Jerusalem. These two new versions of the quantity theory differ somewhat from each other as well as from the old theory. Patinkin concentrated on the "real balance effect," namely, that increases in the quantity of money at a given price level raise the amount of money people hold relative to the amount they wish to hold. This imbalance induces them to increase their spending until prices are forced up and restores the equality between desired and actual real balances. Thus a doubling of the quantity of money doubles real balances, and only when prices are doubled will the real value of the new balances be brought back to its original level. Friedman adopted a similar approach but focused his attention on portfolio changes induced by changes in the quantity of money. We shall return to the Friedman analysis at a later point in this Introduction.

Part V has two purposes: to display some of the Keynesian and post-Keynesian monetary analysis and to present some of the empirical work that has been advanced in support of one or another of the various approaches. In the first selection, Lawrence S. Ritter summarizes and contrasts a number of views on the role of money in the economy. Beginning with the naïve, money-doesn't-matter Keynesian model, he proceeds to the Hicksian version of Keynes, the familiar *IS-LM* exposition, which is the most commonly accepted version of Keynesian macroeconomics today. Then follows the Gurley-Shaw-Radcliffe view that liquidity and not money is the crucial variable in explaining aggregate demand. In essence, as was noted in the Introduction to Part I and in selection 3 of that Part, the uniqueness of money is denied. This theory, as well as the sophisticated Keynesian view of money, is contrasted with a brief exposition of the Friedman quantity theory.

In the second selection, Milton Friedman expounds primarily on his reinterpretation of the quantity theory. Although this neoquantity theory appears diametrically opposed to Keynesian theory, the two can be reconciled. Indeed, despite the major differences pointed out by Professor Ritter, logical amplification of Keynesian theory leads to the neoquantity theory. Consider the Keynesian liquidity preference theory: The demand for money depends, among other influences, on the rate of interest, the quantity of money demanded varying inversely with the interest rate. Keynes argued correctly that one of the elements in the decision of individuals and firms that bears on the amount of money they wish to hold is the opportunity cost of money, the amount of revenue they sacrifice when holding nonearning or low-earning money instead of higher-yielding other assets. Keynes referred to the interest rate on bonds as an appropriate measure of this opportunity cost; but he was not dogmatic and did not insist that the bond rate was the only proper measure. Indeed, we may presume not only that the Keynesian analysis can accept a variety of alternative asset yields—on bonds and stocks of a broad spectrum—but that different rates may be appropriate in differing situations. Moreover, there is no reason to restrict the barometer of alternative costs to financial asset prices; yields on real assets, too, can serve this purpose. Thus Keynesian theory, broadly interpreted, can accept a broad spectrum of assets, financial and real, whose yields are relevant in determining the demand for money. Now, if this view of Keynesian monetary theory is legitimate, then neo-Keynesians, too, can accept the adjustment process outlined by Professor Friedman on pages 198–199. Briefly summarized, Keynesian and neoquantity theories can be reconciled on the theoretical plane, both admitting asset prices in the demand for money function.

It is premature to conclude that this theoretical reconciliation leads to identical proposals for public policy. Nothing could be further from the truth. Whereas the neo-Keynesians espouse both discretionary fiscal and monetary policy, the Friedman school rejects the concept of discretionary policy (the subject of Part VIII) and the efficacy of fiscal policy. Disagreement occurs even on the issue of judging the tightness or looseness of monetary policy, a subject we shall turn to shortly. The parting of ways on policy comes from a divergence in emphasis—which of the adjustment processes is the more powerful and relevant one? The neo-Keynesians' view is that the primary impact of a change in the money supply is on interest rates, which exert an effect on investment spending, perhaps on expenditures for consumer durables, and probably on certain state and local government outlays. The neoquantity theorists reject the importance of this process and condemn public policies based on it. Instead, they adhere to the adjustment process outlined by Friedman and draw policy conclusions therefrom.

Much of the contemporary econometric work in macroeconomics is directed at confirming one view or the other. Professor Friedman reads the evidence of monetary history—and he is to be commended for the initiation of many major studies in this area—as favoring his interpretation of the monetary process. In the third selection, he and David Meiselman marshal further detailed evidence. Their article specifies two equations; one is representative of the Keynesian school and the other is a quantity equation. The two are then fitted to United States data, and the one more clearly demonstrating greater stability, meaning "expressing empirically consistent relations which can be depended on to remain the same from time to time" (p. 206), is deemed by the authors to be the more important and to confirm the usefulness of its specific theory. The results obtained by Friedman and Meiselman, together with the methodology that led them to their conclusions, are included in their article.

Neither their methodology nor their conclusions are left unchallenged, however. In a series of articles cited in the bibliography for this Part (see p. 428), they have been attacked for failing to specify correctly the function to be tested, for incorrectly defining the autonomous variables, and for including inappropriate data in fitting their equations. Perhaps the most telling criticism leveled against the study is that Keynesian theory cannot be represented by a single equation. By disproving that money does not matter, the authors have simply confirmed what Keynes had said all along. As Ritter demonstrates in Model B and as Friedman and Meiselman insist, money does matter; the difference between modern Keynesian theory and modern quantity theory lies in the degree of importance. (Recently, some neoquantity theorists have attacked another implication of Keynesian theory. They deny the efficacy of fiscal policy, claiming in effect that money *alone* matters. Few economists, however, accept this thesis.)

The Friedman-Meiselman model is merely one of a host of econometric models built—and still being constructed—to explain the workings of the American economy. Similar work characterizes the efforts of economists in a host of other countries. The Friedman-Meiselman study demonstrates that results can be achieved with relatively simple models. In the fourth selection, Robert H. Scott tests another simple model, showing equal confidence in naïveté. But the final selection is interesting for two other reasons as well. First, it does subject the Hicksian *IS-LM* model to the empirical test. The results are remarkably good in terms of their explanatory value as measured by the percentage of dependent variable explained by the independent variables, the coefficients of determination. Second, the article should prove to be a useful device in the learning process, because it puts flesh onto the skeletal macroeconomic theoretical structure.

How can both the outside observer and the policy maker determine the posture of monetary policy, its tightness or ease? This issue, known as either the indicator problem or the question of the proximate targets of monetary policy, is no more resolved than are the theoretical conflicts between the neoquantity and neo-Keynesian theories. Indeed, the differences in interpreting the monetary situation stem directly from the conflicting views of the monetary mechanism. Although theoretical niceties rarely demand immediate resolution, it is obvious that the central banking authorities, responsible as they are for monetary control, must ascertain the effect of their continuing policy decisions and the probable effect of specific operations currently in the planning stage.

In the 1950s, Federal Reserve authorities relied rather heavily on the free reserve position (excess reserves less borrowings) of the banking system. Fully realizing the limitations of this indicator, the monetary authorities nevertheless interpreted positive free reserve levels as indicating conditions of ease and negative levels as signifying tightness. In recent years, the authorities have limited their reliance on the free reserve concept, as it became evident that what mattered was not the absolute level of free reserves but the relationship between desired and available free reserves. The dethroning of free reserves meets with the general acceptance of most monetary economists, but little agreement prevails as to the choice of a new monarch or even the desirability of a monarchy. University of Chicago-trained quantity theorists advocate that the stock of money be selected as the unique indicator and would interpret the rates of growth of this variable as measuring either tightness or ease. Those who see the transmission process along Keynesian lines, whereby money affects economic activity through the medium of interest rates, would have us observe the movement of indicators measuring the price of credit. Still others suggest watching unborrowed reserves or a concept known as the monetary base, which is, with some additional adjustments, the "sources of reserves" side of the bank reserve equation.

Federal Reserve authorities feel that the stakes are too high to warrant reliance on one indicator and, as Governor George Mitchell explains in the final selection, adopt an eclectic view. Indeed, to do so would appear to be the most sensible way of running monetary policy. Because neither theory denies the existence of the other (and it is likely that money supply changes affect economic activity both directly and indirectly), a variety of economic seismographs, spotted strategically throughout the economy, will pick up disturbances not detected by any one individual indicator.

It is premature to expect that the Keynesian-quantity theory controversy will be resolved soon. Present empirical methods still cannot lead to generally accepted, conclusive results. On the theoretical plane, too, the debate will continue. And with the professionals engaged in continuing controversy, it is not surprising to find the public and our political leaders expressing dissatisfaction with the conflicting advice given them by leading economists.

27 THE ROLE OF MONEY IN KEYNESIAN THEORY

LAWRENCE S. RITTER

A broad spectrum of views concerning the impact of money on economic activity appears in the following selection, and the income form of the equation of exchange, $MV = PY$, can be used to summarize them all. Monetary theory deals with the causal relationship between M on the one side and nominal income on the other. Clearly, then, depending on the behavior of V, changes in money supply can have no effect or a small impact, or they can even induce changes in income that are more than proportional. Moreover, because velocity varies with the stage of the business cycle, money's impact varies too. Obviously, then, in controlling variations in the money supply, the monetary authorities must take into account induced or exogenous shifts in velocity. Indeed, the strength and effectiveness of monetary policy vary directly with the degree of predictability and/or control over velocity. See how the theories explained in the following selection fit into this framework.

In recent years it has frequently been asserted, primarily by Quantity theorists, that the main characteristic of Keynesian theory is that "money does not matter." The view that "money matters" is held to be the exclusive province of the Quantity theory, and extensive statistical tests are thereupon conducted to demonstrate that the supply of money has had an important influence on the level of economic activity. On this basis, Keynesian theory is, *ipso facto,* declared fallacious.

The purpose of this [article] is to examine carefully the role of money in Keynesian theory, in order to evaluate the thesis that in the Keynesian system "money does not matter." It turns out that the validity of this point of view depends in large part on which version of Keynesian theory one has in mind, just as the validity of many Keynesian criticisms of the Quantity theory depend on which version of the latter one has in mind.

Reprinted with permission from L. S. Ritter, "The Role of Money in Keynesian Theory," in *Monetary and Banking Studies,* D. Carson, ed. (Homewood, Ill.: Richard D. Irwin, Inc.), pp. 134–148.

I. KEYNES WITHOUT MONEY

The most familiar version of Keynesian economics, which we will call Model A, is the elementary simplification of Keynes in which the only determinants of the level of national income are the consumption function and a given volume of investment (including government) spending. Consumption spending is seen as depending mainly upon income, and investment spending is assumed to be given, determined autonomously. Occasionally, in order to include an accelerator effect, investment spending may also be made to depend partly upon income. Within this context, the equilibrium level of national income is found where realized income, resulting from consumption plus investment expenditures, equals anticipated income, on the basis of which spending decisions are made. Alternatively, equilibrium income is that level of income at which planned investment equals planned saving.

It is this simplified model which has been popularized by the widely known "Keynesian cross" diagram, in which either consumption and investment or saving and investment are plotted on the vertical axis, and anticipated income is plotted on the horizontal axis. Equilibrium income is determined where aggregate demand equals anticipated income or, alternatively, where planned investment equals planned saving. This particular analytical system has also been the basis for the bulk of orthodox Keynesian multiplier theory: a sustained increase in autonomous spending is assumed to raise equilibrium income by a multiple of the initial increment in spending. The specific value of the multiplier is determined solely by the size of the marginal propensity to consume. Such an uncomplicated formula for the value of the multiplier can only be derived from an equally uncomplicated frame of reference, such as that outlined above. For if the value of the multiplier depends solely on the size of the marginal propensity to consume, it must be assumed, implicitly or explicitly, that spending is insensitive to such increases in interest rates and tightening of credit availability as would normally accompany an expansion in income.

On the basis of this model, countless public policy recommendations, dealing almost exclusively with the implications of alternative fiscal policies, have been advanced over the years in the name of Keynesian economics. In this scheme of things, the Quantity theory's characterization of the Keynesian system as one in which "money does not matter" is quite accurate: national income is determined without any reference whatsoever to either the supply of or the demand for money, and public policy prescriptions are confined to the area of fiscal policy. Monetary policy is completely extraneous. That this model evidently commands considerable allegiance, even today, is attested to by the great amount of attention paid in 1962 and 1963 to alternative forms of tax reduction, and to the size of the resulting budget deficit, as compared with the relative lack of interest in how such a deficit should be financed, i.e., whether by monetary creation or otherwise.

II. KEYNES WITH MONEY

Although Model A is probably the most popular version of Keynesian economics, it is not the same economics to be found in Keynes' *The General Theory of Employment, Interest, and Money.* As far as Keynes himself was concerned, and as the title of his major work indicates, money plays a significant role in the determination of income and employment. Let us call the orthodox Keynesian system, as advanced in *The General Theory* and much subsequent literature, Model B.

Most important, Keynes did not assume that investment spending is exogenous, a given datum, but rather that it depends on relationships *within* the system, namely on comparisons between the expected rate of profit and the rate of interest. The rate of interest, in turn, depends on the supply of and demand for money. The demand for money, or liquidity preference, is viewed as consisting of two parts, the demand for idle money balances (with the amount demanded increasing as the rate of interest falls) and the demand for active or transaction balances (with the amount demanded increasing as the level of income rises).

In contrast to the partial Keynesian system, represented by Model A, the complete Keynesian system, Model B, requires that *two* conditions be fulfilled before income can be said to be in equilibrium. Not only must planned investment equal planned saving, as before, but in addition at any moment in time the amount of money people want to hold must equal the supply of money, the amount that is available for them to hold. If the second condition is not satisfied, the rate of interest will rise or fall, thereby altering the volume of investment and consequently changing the equilibrium level of income.

If, at a given interest rate and income, planned investment equals planned saving but the amount of money desired exceeds (falls short of) the supply, the interest rate will rise (fall), thereby reducing (increasing) investment spending and lowering (raising) the level of income. As the interest rate rises, the desired amount of idle balances contracts, and as income falls the desired amount of active balances contracts, until the amount of money demanded is reduced to the point where it is equal to the given supply. Thus, the equilibrium level of income eventually is reached, with both planned investment equal to planned saving and the demand for money equal to the supply, but the interest rate is now higher and income now lower than initially postulated.

Here there is room for monetary policy to operate: if the monetary authorities want to prevent upward pressure on the interest rate, and the consequent drop in income, they can increase the supply of money enough to satisfy the demand at the initial interest rate and income level. On the other hand, if they want to permit money income to fall, they can sit back and let nature take its course. Both of these are rather passive policies. More aggressive actions would call for increasing the money supply even more than enough to satisfy the initial demand, in order to stimulate an increase in income rather than merely prevent a decrease; or actually reducing the money supply, even though it is already less than the demand, to provide added impetus to the decline in income.

It is obvious that a policy of doing nothing is but one alternative among a spectrum of possibilities. The Federal Reserve at times seems to suggest that those changes in interest rates which occur when the central bank is passive are none of its doing. It is implied that changes in interest rates which take place when the central bank is holding the money supply constant are solely the result of "free market forces," and are in some sense preferable to changes which result from more active monetary policies. But as long as interest rates could be different if the central bank did something rather than nothing, it follows that interest rates are what they are in part because the central bank prefers them that way.

All this does not mean that the monetary authorities are omnipotent. In the orthodox Keynesian system, monetary policy is important but not always in the same degree. As a general principle, monetary policy is likely to be *less* effective the more interest-elastic the demand for idle balances (for then a change in the money supply will not succeed in altering the interest rate) and the less interest-elastic the investment and consumption schedules (for then a change in the interest rate will not induce a change in spending). This has typically been construed by most Keynesians to mean that monetary policy is likely to be less effective in combating depression than in stopping inflation. In a severe depression, the public may prefer to hold additional amounts of money at low interest rates rather than lend it out or buy securities, so that the rate of interest may reach a floor below which it will not fall; investment prospects may appear so bleak that reductions in interest rates become of negligible importance; and job prospects may appear so dismal that consumer spending on durable goods is severely inhibited, despite such additions to the public's wealth as are brought about by expanding the stock of money.

In formal Keynesian terms, during severe depressions the interest-elasticity of liquidity preference may become so great as to prevent increases in the supply of money from reducing the interest rate, as they normally would. And investment and consumer spending may become so unresponsive to changes in interest rates and in wealth as to preclude what would be expected to be their normal reactions. In terms of the equation of exchange, $MV=PT$, increases in the money supply would be offset by proportionate reductions in the velocity of money. Under such circumstances, money again "does not matter" in the Keynesian system, in the sense that increases in the money supply beyond a certain point will not affect the volume of spending, and for all practical purposes we are back in the world of Model A above.

It is important to realize, however, that severe depression is only a special case in the general Keynesian system. And even then, *decreases* in the money supply would not be looked upon as trivial. In other instances, the supply of money may be of crucial importance. From the beginning, for example, it has been a basic tenet of Keynesian doctrine that inflation cannot proceed very far without an increase in the supply of money. Rising incomes are seen as leading to larger demands for transactions balances, which in the absence of increases in the money supply must be drawn from formerly idle balances, inducing a rise in interest rates. This process can continue until idle balances are depleted, or perhaps somewhat further if there is some interest-elasticity in the demand for active balances at high interest rates. But, unless the money supply is increased, the expansion in spending is viewed as having to grind to a halt before too long, because rising interest rates and tightening monetary conditions in general will sooner or later choke off investment spending. Indeed, so strongly has this position been held by some orthodox Keynesians that they have at times objected to the use of monetary policy to stop inflation because of the fear that it is likely to be *too* effective. In brief, in the orthodox Keynesian system sometimes the supply of money is not very important, sometimes it is critically important, and most of the time it is somewhere in between, depending in each instance on the circumstances at hand.

It is rather ironic that Keynes should be the target of a blanket charge by Quantity theorists that he is responsible for propagating the view that "money does not matter." For in Keynes' own mind he was enlarging the scope of monetary theory, not narrowing it. Before Keynes, prevailing monetary theory in the form of the Quantity theory of money, had been concerned almost exclusively with the determination of the general level of prices, to the neglect of the influence of money on real output and employment. As expressed by Jean Bodin in 1569, through John Locke, David Hume, David Ricardo, John Stuart Mill, and Irving Fisher, the Quantity theory had always stressed that the supply of money determined primarily the absolute price level. The velocity of money was held to be an institutional datum and aggregate real output was assumed at the full employment level by virtue of Say's Law. In terms of the equation of exchange, $MV=PT$, V and T were assumed to be given so that changes in the money supply would result in proportionate changes in prices.

The policy implications of the pre-Keynesian Quantity theory were simple and paralyzing. Increases in the supply of money, even in periods of substantial unemployment, could never achieve any permanent benefit. They could only be harmful, by raising prices proportionately—a view that is deeply imbedded in popular folklore to this day. It is this framework, rather than the Keynesian, which in a fundamental sense views money as unimportant. Here money is seen as "neutral," a veil behind which "real" forces work themselves out just about as they would in the absence of money. In the Keynesian approach, on the other hand, money also plays a role in the determination of real output. For the first time money becomes more than merely a veil, and a monetary economy is seen as behaving very differently from a barter economy.

III. NEW DEPARTURES

Model C is a lineal descendant of Model B, but comes to rather different conclusions. Although Model C uses most of the orthodox Keynesian apparatus, it is so unorthodox in its handling of selected parts of that apparatus as to make it debatable whether it should be classified as a version of Keynesian theory. Perhaps it should be given a category of its own and called Radcliffism, since it has been most closely associated with the work of the Radcliffe Committee and Professors Gurley and Shaw.[1] In any case, in this model changes in the money supply are seen as no more likely to be effective against inflation than they were against depression in Model B!

The analysis of Model C differs from both previous models in that it does not ignore the liquidity preference function, as A does, nor does it stress the significance of its interest-elasticity, as B does. Rather than being ignored, the liquidity preference function is an integral part of Model C, *but the demand for liquidity is no longer viewed as identical with the demand for money.* And rather than stressing the importance of the interest-elasticity of the demand schedule for money, attention is directed instead to the likelihood of *shifts* in that schedule. While the orthodox Keynesian literature has a great deal to say about shifts in the investment demand function, through the influence of changes in expectations, it tends to ignore the possibility of shifts in the demand for money, and instead concentrates almost exclusively on its interest-elasticity.

In the orthodox Keynesian system, Model B, the demand for liquidity is synonymous with the demand for money. The ready availability of interest-yielding money substitutes, however, destroys that equation. Such near monies as time deposits, savings and loan shares, and Treasury bills are virtually as liquid as cash and in addition yield an interest return. Thus, the demand for money (demand deposits plus currency) may contract even though the demand for liquidity broadly conceived remains stable. Liquidity preference, in other words, may be satisfied partially by holdings of money substitutes in place of money itself.

There are two reasons for the demand for money in the orthodox Keynesian system. In the first place, active money balances are needed for transactions purposes. The demand for active balances is assumed to bear a more or less constant ratio to income, so that an expansion in income will lead to a proportionate increase in the amount of active balances desired. In the second place, idle cash is demanded because of uncertainties regarding the future course of interest rates. Idle cash is held primarily because of the fear that interest rates might rise (bond prices fall), imposing capital losses on bondholders. This is the main reason why Keynes believed that the amount of idle cash desired would increase as the rate of interest falls. The lower the rate of interest, the more it is likely to drop below what are considered "safe" or "normal" levels, leading to the expectation that its future course is likely to be upward, with consequent losses in capital values. Under such circumstances, it is prudent to get out of bonds and into a more liquid asset. In *The General Theory* the only liquid asset available is cash.

The existence of short-term money substitutes, however, provides an alternative to holding money for both of these purposes. With respect to *active* balances, there is no reason to assume that these need be held solely in the form of money. For immediate transactions purposes, there is little alternative to possessing the

---

[1]*Report* of the Committee on the Working of the Monetary System (London, 1959), and J. G. Gurley and E. S. Shaw, *Money in a Theory of Finance* (Washington, D.C.: The Brookings Institution, 1960). . . . [See also Selection 3—ed.]

medium of exchange itself. But for payments scheduled for several months in the future, there are many assets available which can serve as a substitute for holding cash without diminishing liquidity, and which at the same time provide an interest income. Firms with scheduled payments to make at particular dates in the future can hold Treasury bills, sales finance company paper, or repurchase agreements with government securities dealers, for example—all of which can easily be arranged to come due when the cash is needed. The very purpose of tax anticipation bills is to fill just such a need. Similarly, households can hold time deposits, paying interest from date of deposit to date of withdrawal, pending anticipated payments. For possible emergencies, lines of credit can be arranged on a standby basis in place of holding idle cash.

Many other methods exist through which both households and business firms can economize on their average holdings of transactions cash without impairing their liquidity positions. Indeed, there is ample evidence that high short-term interest rates in the postwar period have stimulated the expenditure of considerable ingenuity in the economical management of cash balances, with consequent reductions in the required ratio of active money balances to income. To the extent that this is accomplished, an expension in income will not lead to a proportionate increase in the amount of transactions cash desired.

With respect to *idle* balances, the existence of short-term money substitutes also provides an alternative to holding cash when it is feared that long-term interest rates might rise (bond prices fall). If it is thought that long-term rates are too low (bond prices too high) for safety, investors need not increase their holdings of idle cash to get liquidity, but instead can purchase Treasury bills or other interest-bearing liquid assets. With highly liquid money substitutes, the concept of a "safe" yield level is almost meaningless and the chance of suffering a capital loss close to nil; indeed, the very definition of a liquid asset is one which can be turned into cash on short notice with little or no loss in dollar value.

The concept of a "safe" yield level is crucial in decisions as to whether or not to buy *long-term* securities, because the existence of uncertainty regarding future long rates gives rise to the fear of taking substantial capital losses (or the hope of making capital gains). But the rationale behind buying *short-term* liquid assets is that if yields rise no loss need be suffered. The securities will mature shortly anyway, and thereby turn into cash at their face value. And, in any event, even if one has no choice but to dispose of them before maturity, the resulting capital losses (or gains) are likely to be small. Unlike long-terms, a rather large change in yields on short-term instruments involves but a small change in their price.

In brief, the amount of money desired may not increase when the rate of interest falls, even though the amount of liquidity desired does increase. At least part of the accumulation of liquidity is likely to take the form of interest-bearing near monies instead of nonearning cash. In comparison with Model B, the demand for idle cash balances will have contracted throughout the range of interest rates, even though the liquidity preference function may have remained stable. Under these circumstances, with both segments of the demand for money susceptible to leftward shifts, monetary policies confined to regulating the supply of money are not likely to be as successful in stemming inflation as orthodox Keynesian theory believes. Since the significant variable is not the supply of money, per se, but rather the supply relative to the demand, the flexibility of demand makes control of the supply, alone, an unreliable instrument through which to affect the level of economic activity. These results do not depend, as in orthodox Keynesian theory, on the short-run interest-elasticity of the demand for money, but rather on shifts in that demand.

In Model B, for example, if the economy is initially in equilibrium, with planned investment equal to planned saving and the demand for money equal to the supply, an exogenous increase in spending will raise money income and increase the amount of transactions cash desired proportionately. Limitation of the money supply—holding it constant—will then automatically result in an excess demand for money, which will raise interest rates, check investment, and thereby bring the expansion in income to a halt. There will probably be some slippage, as the rise in interest rates attracts some funds out of idle cash holdings into transactions balances, with the degree of slippage depending on the interest-elasticity of the demand for idle balances and the specific ratio between active cash and income. But that same rise in interest rates, and the related tightening of monetary conditions in general, will tend to discourage some expenditures. In any event, sooner or later idle balances will be depleted. If the monetary authorities want to accelerate the process, they can provide added impetus by actually reducing the money supply rather than merely holding it stable.

In the world envisaged by Model C, on the other hand, these results are not as likely to be realized. If the required ratio of transactions cash to income contracts as income rises, the expansion in income will not lead to a proportionate increase in the amount of active cash desired. It may not even lead to an absolute increase. Limitation of the money supply then may not produce very much of an excess demand for money, so that upward pressure on interest rates will be negligible, investment will not be checked, and the rise in spending will proceed unhindered. If, at the same time, the demand for idle balances has also shifted to the left, then—regardless of its interest-elasticity—formerly idle balances will become available for transactions use, again with minimal increases in interest rates. Instead of an excess demand for money, there might conceivably be an excess supply, with consequent *downward* pressure on interest rates. Even if the monetary authorities were to actually reduce the supply of money, they might be hard put to keep pace with the contraction in demand. And although idle balances must sooner or later be depleted, this will pose no obstacle to the continued rise in spending if the desired active cash to income ratio continues to contract.

Of course, the process need not be this straightforward. Models B and C need not be mutually exclusive, but may be combined over several cycles. Interest rates may indeed rise during periods of cyclical expansion, especially if the expansion is vigorous, as spending increases more rapidly than can be accommodated by contractions in the demand schedules for money. However, rising interest rates are likely to stimulate new financial techniques for economizing on cash balances.* These techniques of cash management, introduced during periods of tight money, are not likely to be abandoned when rates recede in the subsequent recession. As a result, the contraction in the demand for money may not be clearly evident until the *next* upturn in business conditions. When that upturn comes, the supply of money may be more than ample to finance it, even though, by past standards, it would appear to be less than adequate. In effect, liquidity is accumulated during the recession, in the form of money substitutes instead of money, and is then released when needed to finance expenditures when economic activity revives.

Presumably, the central bank could always reduce the money supply drastically enough to counteract the decline in the demand for money, and thereby produce the results it wants. But with business prospects cloudy, as they generally are,

---

*See Selections 23 and 24—ed.

and with past guidelines unreliable indicators of the current adequacy of the money supply, the monetary authorities are usually not sure enough of where they stand to take decisive action in *any* direction. This inaction is then rationalized by the invocation of moral principles, as ethical values are attributed to the determination of interest rates by "free market forces" and to "minimum intervention" in general.

It is for these reasons that Model C shifts attention away from the money supply narrowly defined to the significance of liquidity broadly conceived. Traditional monetary policy, which is confined to the control of the money supply, is seen as having to give way to a more broadly based liquidity policy if it is to successfully influence economic activity within the context of the present-day financial environment. It is thus Radcliffe monetary theory, rather than orthodox Keynesian theory, which poses the most fundamental challenge to the modern Quantity theory of money.

IV. SUMMARY AND CONCLUSIONS

The differences between orthodox Keynesian theory (Model B), Radcliffe theory (Model C), and the modern Quantity theory of money can be summarized most conveniently in terms of their implications for the behavior of velocity. This simultaneously affords a comparison of their respective evaluations of the effectiveness of monetary policy. For if monetary policy is to be effective—i.e., if changes in the money supply are to produce changes in aggregate spending, and thus in income—then velocity must either remain more or less stable or else move in the same direction as the money supply.

If the phrase "money matters" is to have any operational meaning, it must imply the existence of such conditions. In terms of the equation of exchange, if changes in M are to produce changes in MV and thus in PT, then V must necessarily remain rather stable or else reinforce the change in M. On the other hand, to the extent that velocity falls when the money supply is increased, or rises when the money supply is decreased, or changes in the absence of changes in the money supply, the effectiveness of monetary policy is correspondingly reduced. If these offsetting changes in velocity are so great that the influence of monetary policy is negligible, then "money does not matter." In between these two extremes lies a continuum of possibilities.

It should be noted that the modern Quantity theory is not precisely the same as the pre-Keynesian Quantity theory. As presented by Milton Friedman, the present-day version of the Quantity theory is no longer strictly an explanation of what determines the price level. Friedman uses the Quantity theory to explain major depressions as well as inflations, so that it is now, like the Keynesian approach, essentially a theory of income determination.

In addition, Friedman accepts variations in velocity as consistent with the Quantity theory. Unlike Irving Fisher, Friedman does not view velocity as an institutional datum, nor as a numerical constant, but rather as a functional relationship in which the demand for money is a function of a number of variables within the system, such as interest rates, income, wealth, and expected changes in the price level. Depending on movements in these variables, velocity may vary both cyclically and secularly. This also represents a major shift in emphasis by the Quantity theory in the direction of the Keynesian approach, wherein velocity has *always* been functionally related to such variables.

Nevertheless, the two are still rather far apart. In Friedman's view, under normal circumstances the demand-for-money function is so stable and inelastic that such changes in velocity as do occur will not be very bothersome. Velocity may fall somewhat when the money supply is increased, or rise somewhat when the money supply is decreased, or even change to some extent in the absence of changes in the money supply so as to produce minor fluctuations in income despite stability in the stock of money. But these changes in velocity are assumed to be small. Velocity is no longer seen as constant, but it *is* seen as fluctuating only very moderately. Thus, changes in velocity are not likely to appreciably offset changes in the money supply, and major fluctuations in income are not likely to take place in the absence of major fluctuations in the stock of money. As a result, the modern Quantity theory views monetary policy as highly effective. Aside from minor short-run fluctuations in income, monetary policy is seen as both necessary *and sufficient* for the attainment of economic stability.

Radcliffe monetary theory, on the other hand, looks upon monetary policy in a rather different light:

> Though we do not regard the supply of money as an unimportant quantity, we view it as only part of the wider structure of liquidity in the economy. It is the whole liquidity position that is relevant to spending decisions, and our interest in the supply of money is due to its significance in the whole liquidity picture. The fact that spending is not limited by the amount of money in existence is sometimes argued by reference to the velocity of money. It is possible, for example, to demonstrate statistically that during the last few years the volume of spending has greatly increased while the supply of money has hardly changed: the velocity of money has increased. We have not made more use of this concept because we cannot find any reason for supposing, or any experience in monetary history indicating, that there is any limit to velocity.

While the Quantity theory views traditional monetary policy as both necessary and sufficient, and Radcliffe views it as too narrowly conceived to be of much use, Keynesian theory lies in between these two extremes. Sometimes changes in velocity are seen as nullifying changes in the money supply, sometimes they are seen as reinforcing, and most of the time they are seen as somewhere in between. The crucial determinants of the behavior of velocity in the orthodox Keynesian system are the interest and wealth-elasticities of the spending and liquidity preference functions, and these are likely to vary depending on the particular historical, institutional, and expectational circumstances at hand. Since velocity is not something the monetary authorities can depend upon, in the sense of being able to reliably anticipate its behavior, monetary policy emerges from the Keynesian system as usually necessary but rarely sufficient for the attainment of national economic objectives.

. . .

28 THE POST-KEYNESIAN REFORMULATION OF THE QUANTITY THEORY OF MONEY

MILTON FRIEDMAN

Professor Friedman gives a comparatively unbiased view in expounding the new quantity theory and how it differs from the Keynesian analytic framework. Few economists will disagree with this analysis. Only a minority of economists today are convinced by the empirical proof outlined in this article, however. Moreover, they do not share Friedman's disdain of discretionary monetary policy. His own work has stimulated further research and has enriched our understanding of the monetary process and monetary policy. Especially important is his brief section headed "The Process of Adjustment," which provides the theoretical justification for his views on the lag in the effect of monetary policy, a topic reviewed extensively in Part VII.

• • •

The postwar period has also seen a return to analysis in terms of the quantity equation accompanied by a reformulation of the quantity theory that has been strongly affected by the Keynesian analysis of liquidity preference. The reformulation emphasizes the role of money as an asset and hence treats the demand for money as part of capital or wealth theory, concerned with the composition of the balance sheet or portfolio of assets.

From this point of view, it is important to distinguish between ultimate wealth-holders, to whom money is one form in which they choose to hold their wealth, and enterprises, to whom money is a producer's good like machinery or inventories.

Demand by Ultimate Wealth-Holders

For ultimate wealth-holders the demand for money, in real terms, may be expected to be a function of the following variables.

(a) Total wealth. This is the analogue of the budget constraint in the usual theory of consumer choice. It is the total that must be divided among various forms of assets. In practice, estimates of total wealth are seldom available. Instead, income may serve as an index of wealth. However, it should be recognized that income as measured by statisticians may be a defective index of wealth because it is subject to erratic year-to-year fluctuations and that a longer term concept, like the concept of permanent income developed in connection with the theory of consumption, may be more useful.

The emphasis on income as a surrogate for wealth, rather than as a measure of the "work" to be done by money, is conceptually perhaps the basic difference between the reformulation and the earlier versions of quantity theory.

(b) The division of wealth between human and nonhuman forms. The major asset of most wealth-holders is their personal earning capacity, but the conversion of human into nonhuman wealth or the reverse is subject to narrow limits because of institutional constraints. It can

---

From Milton Friedman, "Money: Quantity Theory," in David L. Sills (ed.), *International Encyclopedia of the Social Sciences,* X, 439–446.

be done by using current earnings to purchase nonhuman wealth or by using nonhuman wealth to finance the acquisition of skills but not by purchase or sale and to only a limited extent by borrowing on the collateral of earning power. Hence, the fraction of total wealth that is in the form of nonhuman wealth may be an additional important variable.

(c) The expected rates of return on money and other assets. This is the analogue of the prices of a commodity and its substitutes and complements in the usual theory of consumer demand. The nominal rate of return on money may be zero, as it generally is on currency, or negative, as it sometimes is on demand deposits subject to net service charges, or positive, as it sometimes is on demand deposits on which interest is paid and generally is on time deposits. The nominal rate of return on other assets consists of two parts; first, any currently paid yield or cost, such as interest on bonds, dividends on equities, and storage costs on physical assets, and, second, changes in their nominal prices. The second part will, of course, be especially important under conditions of inflation or deflation.

(d) Other variables determining the utility attached to the services rendered by money relative to those rendered by other assets—in Keynesian terminology, determining the value attached to liquidity proper. One such variable may be one already considered—namely, real wealth or income, since the services rendered by money may in principle be regarded by wealth-holders as a "necessity," like bread, the consumption of which increases less than in proportion to any increase in income, or as a "luxury," like recreation, the consumption of which increases more than in proportion to any increase in income.

Another variable, one that is likely to be important empirically, is the degree of economic stability expected to prevail in the future. Wealth-holders are likely to attach considerably more value to liquidity when they expect economic conditions to be unstable than when they expect them to be highly stable. This variable is likely to be difficult to express quantitatively even though the direction of change may be clear from qualitative information. For example, the outbreak of war clearly produces expectations of instability, which is one reason why war is often accompanied by a notable increase in real balances—that is, a notable decline in velocity.

We can symbolize this analysis in terms of the following demand function for money for an individual wealth-holder:

$$\frac{M}{P} = f\left(y, w; r_m, r_b, r_e, \frac{1}{P}\frac{dP}{dt}; u\right) \qquad (1)$$

where M, P, and y [are defined as the quantity of money, the consumer's price index, and real income respectively]; w is the fraction of wealth in nonhuman form (or, alternatively, the fraction of income derived from property); r_m is the expected rate of return on money; r_b is the expected rate of return on fixed-value securities, including expected changes in their prices; r_e is the expected rate of return on equities, including expected changes in their prices; $(1/P)\,(dP/dt)$ is the expected rate of change of prices of goods and hence the expected rate of return on real assets; and u is a portmanteau symbol standing for whatever variables other than income may affect the utility attached to the services of money. Each of the four rates of return stands, of course, for a set of rates of return, and for some purposes it may be important to classify assets still more finely—for example, to distinguish currency from deposits, long-term from short-term fixed-value securities, risky from relatively safe equities, and different kinds of physical assets from one another.

The usual problems of aggregation arise in passing from equation (1) to a corresponding equation for the economy as a whole—in particular, they arise from the possibility that the amount of money demanded may depend on the distribution of such variables as y and w and not merely on their aggregate or average value. If we neglect these distributional effects, (1) can be regarded as applying to the community as a whole, with M and y referring to per capita money holdings and per capita real income, respectively, and w to the fraction of aggregate wealth in nonhuman form.

The major problems that arise in practice in applying (1) are the precise definitions of y and w, the estimation of *expected* rates of return as contrasted with actual rates of return, and the quantitative specification of the variables designated by u.

Demand by Business Enterprises

Business enterprises are not subject to a constraint comparable to that imposed by the total wealth of the ultimate wealth-holder. The total amount of capital embodied in productive assets, including money, is a variable that can be determined by the enterprise to maximize returns, since it can acquire additional capital through the capital market. Hence, there is no reason on this ground to include total wealth, or y as a surrogate for total wealth, as a variable in their demand function for money.

It may, however, be desirable to include a somewhat similar variable defining the "scale" of the enterprise on different grounds—namely, as an index of the productive value of different quantities of money to the enterprise. This is more nearly in line with the earlier transactions approach emphasizing the "work" to be done by money. It is by no means clear what the appropriate variable is: total transactions, net value added, net income, total capital in nonmoney form, or net worth. The lack of availability of data has meant that much less empirical work has been done on the business demand for money than on an aggregate demand curve encompassing both ultimate wealth-holders and business enterprises. As a result there are as yet only faint indications about the best variable to use.

The division of wealth between human and nonhuman form has no special relevance to business enterprises, since they are likely to buy the services of both forms on the market.

Rates of return on money and on alternative assets are, of course, highly relevant to business enterprises. These rates determine the net cost to them of holding the money balances. However, the particular rates that are relevant may be quite different from those that are relevant for ultimate wealth-holders. For example, rates charged by banks on loans are of minor importance for wealth-holders yet may be extremely important for businesses, since bank loans may be a way in which they can acquire the capital embodied in money balances.

The counterpart for business enterprises of the variable u in (1) is the set of variables other than scale affecting the productivity of money balances. At least one of these—namely, expectations about economic stability—is likely to be common to business enterprises and ultimate wealth-holders.

With these interpretations of the variables, equation (1), with w excluded, can be regarded as symbolizing the business demand for money and, as it stands, symbolizing aggregate demand for money, although with even more serious qualifications about the ambiguities introduced by aggregation.

The Process of Adjustment

Emphasis on the role of money as a component of wealth is important because of the variables to which it directs attention. It is important also for its implications about the process of adjustment to a difference between actual and desired stocks of money. Any such discrepancy is a disturbance in a balance sheet. As such it can be corrected in either of two ways: by a rearrangement of assets and liabilities through purchase, sale, borrowing, and lending or by the use of current flows of income and expenditure to add to or subtract from some assets and liabilities. The Keynesian liquidity-preference analysis stressed the first and, in its most rigid form, only one specific rearrangement: that between money and bonds. The earlier quantity theory stressed the second to the almost complete exclusion of the first. The reformulation enforces consideration of both.

The process of adjustment is important in particular for its implications about the time that readjustment may be expected to take. Balance-sheet adjustments can in general be expected to take considerable time, especially when they take the form of adjustments through alterations in flows and especially when they concern the money balance, *M,* whose function is precisely that of serving as a temporary abode of purchasing power, thereby permitting purchases to be separated from sales.

It is plausible that any widespread disturbance in money balances—through, say, an unanticipated increase or decrease in the quantity of money by the actions of monetary authorities—will initially be met by an attempted readjustment of assets and liabilities through purchase or sale. But such attempted readjustments will alter the prices of assets and liabilities, leading to the spread of the adjustment from one asset or liability to another. Such changes in prices will also alter the relative prices of capital items and the services they yield and so establish incentives to alter flows of receipts and expenditures. If the monetary change has altered the total nominal value of wealth, not simply its composition, this will introduce an additional reason to change flows. The effect of any monetary disturbance will thus spread in ever-widening ripples, and some of its most important effects may not be manifest for many months after the initial disturbance.

EMPIRICAL EVIDENCE

Empirical evidence about the relation between changes in the quantity of money and in prices, although it was sufficiently extensive to produce a widespread belief in the quantity theory, has seldom been systematically collated and organized. Until modern times, money was mostly metallic—copper, brass, silver, gold. The most notable changes in its nominal quantity under such circumstances were produced by sweating and clipping, by governmental edicts changing the nominal values attached to specified physical quantities of the metal, or by great discoveries of new sources of specie. Economic history is replete with examples of the first two and their coincidence with corresponding changes in nominal prices. The most important example of the third is the great specie discoveries in the New World in the sixteenth century. The association between this increase in the quantity of money and the price revolution of the sixteenth and seventeenth centuries has been well documented.

The nineteenth and early twentieth centuries offer another striking example, despite the much greater development of deposit money and paper money. The gold discoveries in Australia and the United States in the 1840s were followed by substantial price rises in the 1850s. When the rate of growth of the gold stock slowed down, and especially when country after country shifted from silver to gold (Germany in 1871–1873, the Latin Monetary Union in 1873, the Netherlands in 1875–1876) or returned to gold (the United States in 1879), world prices in terms of gold fell slowly but fairly steadily for about three decades. New gold discoveries in the 1880s and 1890s, powerfully reinforced by the development of improved methods of mining and refining, particularly the development of commercially feasible methods of using the cyanide process to extract gold from low-grade ore, reversed the trend. The world gold stock started to grow at a much more rapid rate, and no additional important countries shifted to gold, so there was no increase in demand from this source. The price trend also reversed itself. From the mid-1890s to 1914, world prices in terms of gold rose by 25 to 50 percent, depending on the index used.

Evidence from Great Inflations

The most dramatic evidence about the role of the quantity of money comes from periods of great monetary disturbances, and among these the most striking are the periods of extremely rapid price rise, such as the hyperinflations after World War I in Germany, Austria, and Russia, those after World War II in Hungary and Greece, and the rapid rises, if not hyperinflations, in many South American and some other countries both before and after World War II. These twentieth-century episodes have been rather more systematically studied than earlier ones. The studies demonstrate almost conclusively the critical role of changes in the quantity of money.

These studies also enable us to sketch with considerable accuracy a rather typical profile of an inflation that follows a period of fairly stable prices. The inflation often has its start in a period of war, but it need not. What is important is that something, generally the financing of extraordinary governmental expenditures, produces a much more rapid rate of growth of the money stock. Prices start to rise, but at a slower pace than the money stock, so that for a time the real stock of money increases. The reason for this is twofold. First, it takes time for people to readjust their money balances. Second, initially there is a general expectation that what goes up will come down, that the rise in prices is temporary and will be followed by a decline. Such expectations make money seem to be a desirable form in which to hold assets, and therefore they lead to an increase in desired money balances in real terms.

As prices continue to rise, expectations are revised. People come to expect prices to continue to rise. Desired balances decline. People also take more active measures to eliminate the discrepancy between actual and desired balances. The result is that prices start to rise faster than the stock of money, and real balances start to decline (that is, velocity starts to rise). How far this process continues depends on the rate of rise in the stock of money. If it remains fairly stable, real balances settle down to a level that is lower than the initial level but roughly constant—for a constant expected rate of rise in prices there will be a roughly constant level of desired real balances; in this case, prices ultimately rise at the same rate as the stock of money. A decline in the rate of rise in the stock of money is followed by a decline in the rate of rise in prices, and this is followed in turn by an increase in actual and desired real balances as people readjust their expectations; the converse also holds. The result is that once the process is in full swing, changes in real balances follow with a lag changes in the rate of change of the stock of money. The lag reflects the fact that people apparently base their expectations of future rates of price change on an average of experience over the preceding several years, the period of averaging being shorter the more rapid the inflation.

In the extreme cases, those which have degenerated into hyperinflation and a complete breakdown of the medium of exchange, rates of price change have been so high and real balances have been driven down so low as to lead to the widespread introduction of substitute moneys, usually foreign currencies. At that point completely new monetary systems have had to be introduced.

A similar phenomenon has occurred when inflation has been effectively suppressed by price controls, so that there is a substantial gap between the prices that would prevail in the absence of controls and the legally permitted prices. This gap prevents money from functioning as an effective medium of exchange and also leads to the introduction of substitute moneys, sometimes rather bizarre ones like the cigarettes and cognac used in post-World War II Germany.

Evidence from the United States

Recent studies of the monetary history of the United States provide an especially full documentation of monetary relations. Some of the salient findings may be summarized briefly.

(a) The real stock of money, expressed in terms of months of income, has risen from about 3½ months' income at the end of the Civil War in 1865 to over 7 months' income by 1960—that is, velocity has fallen (money is defined as currency held by the public plus all adjusted deposits in commercial banks, income is defined as net national product). One interpretation of this trend is that the rise in real balances reflects the contemporaneous rise in real income per capita. From the end of World War II to almost 1960, velocity rose rather than fell. It is not yet clear whether this was a temporary interruption or a change of trend.

(b) If allowance is made for the trend in velocity, there has been a very close connection between the stock of money per unit of output and prices. . . .

(c) In the course of business cycles the stock of money has slowed up its rate of growth well before the date designated by National Bureau of Economic Research reference-cycle dates as the peak of the cycle and has increased its rate of growth well before the trough. In mild contractions these decelerations have generally produced not an absolute decline in the stock of money but only a lower rate of growth. Every severe contraction has been accompanied by an absolute decline in the stock of money, and the severity of the contraction has been in roughly the same order as the size of the decline in the stock of money. Although changes in the rate of growth of the stock of money have to some extent reflected the contemporaneous course of business, on many occasions they have quite clearly been the result of independent forces, such as the deliberate decisions of monetary authorities. The clearest examples are probably the wartime increases and the decreases from 1920 to 1921, 1929 to 1933, and 1937 to 1938.

(d) Velocity as usually measured has tended to rise during business expansions and decline during business contractions. One explanation offered is that this pattern reflects the use of measured income in computing velocity rather than a longer term concept, such as permanent income. Another explanation offered is that it reflects the effect of interest rates.

(e) It is agreed that velocity is related to interest rates, higher interest rates being associated with higher velocity, and conversely, but there is wide disagreement about the magnitude and significance of the relation. One view is that changes in interest rates are either the primary or a major source of all cyclical and secular changes in velocity. Another view is that changes in interest rates have been a minor factor, much less important than changes in real per capita income for secular changes in velocity and much less important than differences between measured and permanent income for cyclical changes.

• • •

Stability of Velocity and the Multiplier

The challenge to the quantity theory offered by Keynes rested entirely on differences in empirical presumptions, which can be summarized in terms of the stability attributed to the velocity of circulation, on the one hand, and the Keynesian multiplier (the ratio of changes in income to changes in autonomous expenditures), on the other.

A systematic comparison of the relative stability of velocity and the multiplier has been made for the United States from 1896 to 1958.* The results are striking: velocity is consistently more stable than the multiplier. These results have been challenged by other writers, showing that this question is still far from settled.

POLICY IMPLICATIONS

On a very general level the implications of the quantity theory for economic policy are straightforward and clear. On a more precise and detailed level they are not.

Acceptance of the quantity theory clearly means that the stock of money is a key variable in policies directed at the control of the level of prices or of money income. Inflation can be prevented if and only if the stock of money per unit of output can be kept from increasing appreciably. Deflation can be prevented if and only if the stock of money per unit of output can be kept from decreasing appreciably. This implication is by no means a trivial one. Monetary authorities have more frequently than not taken conditions in the credit market—rates of interest, availability of loans, and so on—as criteria of policy and have paid little or no attention to the stock of money per se. This emphasis on credit as opposed to monetary policy accounts both for the great depression in the United States from 1929 to 1933, when the Federal Reserve System allowed the stock of money to decline by one-third, and for many of the post-World War II inflations.

The quantity theory has no such clear implication, even on this general level, about policies concerned with the growth of real income. Both inflation and deflation have proved consistent with growth, stagnation, or decline.

Passing from these general and vague statements to specific prescriptions for policy is difficult. It is tempting to conclude from the close average relation between changes in the stock of money and changes in money income that control over the stock of money can be used as a precision instrument for offsetting other forces making for instability in money income. Unfortunately there are many slips between this cup and this lip.

One slip is that a very close relationship *on the average* is consistent with much variation in the individual instance. A high correlation between changes relative to trend in the stock of money and in money income over many business cycles —involving, say, an average increase of 2 percent in money income for every 1 percent increase in money—is entirely consistent with the corresponding ratio varying in individual years or over single cycles from zero or a negative number to, say, 4 or 5. But for policy in a particular cycle, what is important is the relation in that cycle, not the relation on the average.

A second slip is the length of time it takes for changes in the stock of money to have their effect—this is one of the reasons for the variability that constitutes the first slip. A change in the stock of money today will have most of its effects some months from now, perhaps on the average as much as 12 to 15 months from now. A policy of using monetary changes to offset other forces making for instability therefore requires an ability to forecast a considerable time in advance what those forces will be—an ability that has so far been conspicuous by its absence. Moreover, the time it takes for monetary changes to be effective undoubtedly varies rather considerably. Hence it would also be necessary to forecast how long the lag would be in the specific instance.

These two slips mean that monetary changes intended to be stabilizing may in

---

*See the next selection—ed.

fact be destabilizing; they may introduce a random and erratic influence into economic affairs. It is a sobering thought that both the stock of money and economic activity displayed greater instability in the first two peacetime decades after the establishment of the Federal Reserve System (1919 to 1939) than in any other pair of decades in the whole of United States history. The blind, quasi-automatic forces that controlled monetary matters in earlier decades produced a higher degree of stability than a system specifically established to promote monetary and economic stability. The greater stability of prices and employment since the end of World War II may be a sign that we have learned how to avoid the mistakes of the interwar decades, but it is much too soon to have any confidence in that comfortable conclusion.

Other slips have to do with the indirect effects of methods used to control the stock of money; with possible conflicts between the objective of stable prices and such other objectives as stable exchange rates, stable employment at a high level, and low interest rates on government borrowing; and with the possible desire to use inflation as a means of imposing a tax on money balances.

One negative implication of the quantity theory, implicit in the above, is worth spelling out because of the continued widespread acceptance of the belief that fiscal policy is the key to control of the level of money income. The quantity theory implies that the effect of government deficits or surpluses depends critically on how they are financed. If a deficit is financed by borrowing from the public without an increase in the quantity of money, the direct expansionary effect of the excess of government spending over receipts will be offset to some extent, and possibly to a very great extent, by the indirect contractionary effect of the transfer of funds to the government through borrowing. Furthermore, the deficit will primarily affect income only while it lasts; a cessation of the deficit will mean a cessation of its effects. If a deficit is financed by printing money, there will be no offset, and the enlarged stock of money will continue to exert an effect after the deficit is terminated. What matters most is the behavior of the stock of money, and government deficits are expansionary primarily if they serve as the means of increasing the stock of money; other means of increasing the stock of money will have closely similar effects.

29 THE RELATIVE STABILITY OF MONETARY VELOCITY AND THE INVESTMENT MULTIPLIER IN THE UNITED STATES, 1897–1958

MILTON FRIEDMAN
AND DAVID MEISELMAN

In the late 1950s, the Commission on Money and Credit sponsored a series of studies by leading economists relating to the monetary environment—institutions, theory, and policy—of the United States. The essay by Milton Friedman and David Meiselman was one of the studies that attracted widespread attention. The authors' major conclusion is that the supply of money is more closely and consistently related to aggregate income than are "autonomous expenditures," the critical variable in their version of Keynesian theory. Space limitations preclude presenting the empirical section of their study in detail—that would more than double the size of this selection. We should be remiss, however, if we did not reiterate the fact already stated in the Introduction to this Part, that many strong objections have been raised to this study, so much so that it is regarded by some as no more than an interesting exercise, lacking any significance.

I. THE PROBLEM

There has long been a striking division among students of economic affairs about the role of money in determining the course of economic events. One view is that the quantity of money matters little; the other, that it is a key factor in understanding, and even more, controlling economic change.

The view that the quantity of money matters little is typically held for either of two reasons: one, because the quantity of money is regarded as adapting to "the needs of trade," and hence is regarded as a passive element in the economic system, determined by and responsive to other economic and noneconomic factors, but incapable of being a source of disturbances; the other, because the ratio of money to other assets is regarded as variable and pliable, and hence the economic effects of changes in the quantity of money are regarded as highly unpredictable.

The alternative view holds that the quantity of money does matter, and for three reasons: one, because the quantity of money is capable of being controlled fairly accurately by deliberate policy; two, because changes in the quantity of money can produce substantial changes in the flow of income, prices, and other important variables; three, because the relationships between the stock of money and other assets are relatively stable and dependable.

The most recent version of this division stems from the Keynesian revolution of the 1930's. This intellectual revolution proceeded on two rather different levels. On one level it was concerned with the long-run equilibrium of an economic system. On this level its chief proposition was that an economic system in which prices were entirely flexible might not possess any position of long-run equilibrium involving full employment of all factors of production. There is a "flaw in the price system" so that a system of simultaneous equations which describes it may not have a solution. On this level the analysis is both long run and purely abstract or theoretical; it makes essentially no call upon empirical evidence or relationships. Disputes on this level raged for some years but must now be regarded as reasonably well settled. It is now widely agreed that the Keynesian proposition is erroneous on the level of pure theory, that there always exists in principle a position of full employment equilibrium in a free market economy, though of course prices and wages may not be sufficiently flexible, or other adjustments sufficiently rapid, for this position to be attained in fact in any specified period.

The second level of analysis, and the one with which we shall be primarily concerned, is very different. It has to do with short-run relations and is primarily empirical rather than theoretical in character. Here the chief assertion is that there is a highly stable and persistent relationship between "investment" expenditures and total expenditures, which is to say, between investment and income, so that short-run changes in income can be regarded as largely caused by and reflecting corresponding short-run changes in investment expenditures.

The effect of the Keynesian view of short-run relations was to propagate the view that "money does not matter." It is clear that the Keynesian analysis need not have produced this result. Keynes himself assigned an important role to the stock of money in determining the interest rate through liquidity preference, he gave the interest rate an important role in determining investment, and he regarded the so-called "transactions" demand for money as highly stable. Hence, it would have been perfectly consistent with the Keynesian theoretical apparatus to have regarded money as a crucial variable. In practice, however, many Keynesians have tended to regard investment as unresponsive to interest rates and to concentrate on the simplest version of the theory, and hence to assign the stock of money to the limbo, to regard it as a relic of past misconceptions. Instead, emphasis has been placed on the relationship between two flows, "investment" and "consumption," the connection between the two being regarded as the mainspring of changes in the community's income. The key concept is the investment multiplier, the number of dollars of income associated with each dollar of "investment."

The view that money does not matter was rudely shattered by postwar experience. Country after country that adopted a "cheap money" policy, partly as a result of Keynes' ideas, found itself plagued with inflation. Only after some control was established over the stock of money and after interest rates were allowed to have some degree of freedom was pressure on the price level relieved. On the basis of postwar experience, one could no longer maintain that money did not matter. The view then shifted to the variant already suggested—that money matters, but "only" insofar as it affects interest rates, thereby investment, and thereby consumption.

It is important to recognize that the difference between this view and the view that money is directly related to income is purely semantic. Suppose one were to find an antediluvian quantity theorist who stuck to the most rigid form of the quantity theory. His first impulse would be to say that changes in investment could not affect income, prices, or anything else. After all, he would say, what determines the level of income is the stock of money, on the one hand, and the velocity of circulation of money, on the other, and investment is not included in this catalogue. On further reflection he might, however, modify his stand. He might conclude that while changes in investment could not influence income directly, they might do so indirectly by altering the rate of interest and thereby influencing either money or velocity. An increase in investment tends to bid up the rate of interest. A higher level of interest rates tends to induce banks to reduce their excess reserve balances or to borrow additional reserves and thus might lead to a rise in the stock of money as banks created additional deposits by exchanging reserves for earning assets. Similarly, higher interest rates might lead other holders of money to try to economize further on their cash holdings and so result in an increase in velocity. He might therefore conclude that investment could influence income indirectly through influencing the rate of interest and through the rate of interest influencing both the stock of money and velocity.

This way of putting it perhaps makes it clear that the central issue in dispute is not theoretical but empirical. It is easy enough to construct an analytical system that embodies both the relations between investment and consumption and the relations between money and income, that is, both the multiplier relations and the velocity relations. Economists who regard monetary changes as primary are divided from those who regard them as secondary much less by different theoretical systems than by different empirical judgments, different judgments about which set of relations in the more generalized theoretical system is (a) critical in the sense of being in practice the primary source of change and disturbance and (b) stable in the sense of expressing empirically consistent relations which can be depended on to remain the same from time to time. In other words, the crucial questions are (a) whether investment or the stock of money can better be regarded as subject to independent change, and to changes that have major effects on other variables, and (b) whether the multiplier (the ratio of the flow of income or consumption to the flow of investment) or velocity (the ratio of the flow of income or consumption to the stock of money) is the more stable.

. . .

The aim of this [article] is to present some evidence bearing on the second of the two crucial issues—the relative stability of the multiplier and of velocity. The limited evidence we assemble here cannot, of course, be decisive. But we hope that it is at least relevant to the main issue that divides economists into two groups, and that it is sufficiently objective to be regarded as evidence by all economists whatever their initial suppositions. Perhaps the evidence here presented is not the most clearly relevant. But we ask each reader not to dismiss the evidence without first asking himself constructively the question, "If this evidence is not the most significant for deciding between the two alternative views, what evidence would be?" Experience in asking this question of many economists has persuaded us that it admits of no simple and obvious answer; that if we have overlooked more relevant tests of the two views, they are not of a kind that are plain as a pikestaff.

In seeking to examine the relative stability of velocity and the multiplier, we faced an initial choice between two major approaches. The issue can be investigated by a sophisticated analysis involving many variables. Such an analysis must inevitably be restricted to a narrow segment of space and time, both because the data needed are not available for many countries or for long periods and because the time and effort required for the analysis are so great. Alternatively, the issue can be investigated initially on a rather simple level for a wide range of space and time. Our choice has been the second. It is our view that the issue that divides economists is extremely basic and one that should lend itself to a common answer over a wide range of circumstances. If it does not, it means that the dichotomy posed is much too simple, that the key issue is not which view to accept but rather the circumstances under which the one or the other view is likely to be the more fruitful. Moreover, in an investigation of this kind, it seems better to rely initially on a wide range of evidence interpreted on a rather simple level than on the more indirect and longer chain of connections inevitable in a sophisticated analysis resting on a narrower base. In addition, the evidence on this simple level may contain important implications or suggestions for more elaborate investigations, or for the formation of tentative judgments so unavoidable in the making of public and private policy.

In Section II we shall discuss the two alternative hypotheses in their simplest forms, and in Section III, empirical tests relevant to distinguishing between them. We shall then examine data for the United States, initially to define more precisely the variables to be used (Section IV), then to employ the U.S. experience for testing the two substantive hypotheses (Section V).

• • •

II. ALTERNATIVE THEORIES

In their simplest forms, the two alternative hypotheses can be expressed as follows:

$$Y = a + V'M \tag{1}$$

$$Y = \alpha + K'A \tag{2}$$

In both equations, Y represents the community's income over some time period. The first equation expresses the level of income as a linear function of the stock of money, M. The coefficient, V', is income velocity, or more precisely, marginal income velocity. The second equation expresses income as a linear function of autonomous expenditures. K' (for Keynes and Kahn) is the marginal multiplier. . . .

In a more complicated and sophisticated theory, of course, these equations could coexist. For the present, however, we shall consider them as alternatives and not as supplements.

Instead of dealing with the level of the variables at a point in time or during a period, as in equations (1) and (2), we can rewrite these equations in terms of first differences:

$$\Delta Y = V' \, \Delta M \tag{3}$$

$$\Delta Y = K' \, \Delta A \tag{4}$$

This form of writing the equations is relevant for correlations among first differences.

Our main approach to exploring the relative stability of velocity and the multiplier will be to fit to the U.S. data equations such as (1) and (2) rather than parallel equations (3) and (4) (see Sections III and V, below), though we shall do some of both.

Equations (1) and (3) express the simplest form of the quantity theory and equations (2) and (4) express the simplest form of the income-expenditure theory.

The first thing to note about equations (1) and (2) is that neither is a complete theory of "income determination" or of the business cycle even if we take V' and K' to be known numerical constants, not subject to change. Equation (1), and corresponding to it equation (3), assert that changes in income mirror changes in the stock of money. But as it stands, the theory is incomplete because it does not tell what determines the quantity of money. Similarly, equations (2) and (4) assert that changes in the flow of income are determined by changes in autonomous expenditures, but again, they do not tell what determines autonomous expenditures. In both cases we have, as it were, one blade of the Marshallian scissors. Another blade remains unspecified and is taken for granted.

The second point to note is that both sets of equations have a major gap, and incidentally, the same gap. If Y is interpreted as money income, then a change in money income (ΔY) may be regarded as divided into two components: a change in real income or output, say ΔQ, and a change in prices, say ΔP. Neither set of equations says anything about the proportions in which change in income will be divided between output and prices. In some versions of the quantity theory, particularly the highly rigid old textbook versions of the quantity theory, this gap is filled by the supposition that other factors determine total output, and hence that total output is not affected by changes in the stock of money. In that case, any change in the stock of money and in money income would be reflected entirely in prices. Similarly, in some versions of the income-expenditure theory, again the rigid old textbook versions, the gap is filled by a different assumption about output; namely, that output is infinitely elastic with respect to a change in autonomous expenditures or income up to some limit—the point of "full employment"—and perfectly inelastic thereafter, so that the supply curve of output is a reverse L shape. Under this assumption, the change in autonomous expenditures and in money income would be reflected entirely in output so long as output is within the elastic segment of the curve, entirely in prices, when output is within the inelastic sector. Neither supplementary assumption is an essential part of the theory in question; both are *dei ex machina* superimposed on the two theories. The validity of the theoretical relations between the stock of money and the flow of income on the one hand and between the flow of autonomous expenditures and the flow of income on the other hand do not depend in any way on the validity of these supplementary assumptions.

Although these and other supplementary assumptions are not necessary parts of the theories in question, the division of an increase in money income between prices and output, and of an increase in output between the part expected to be permanent and the part expected to be temporary may have a significant effect on the numerical values of the multiplier and of the velocity and on their stability.

• • •

Further elaboration of the simple expressions (1) and (2) would involve introducing additional variables to explain the values of V' and K'; it is through the introduction of those variables that the two theories may be reconciled. . . .

The fact that we have done so makes it necessary to emphasize that our results cannot be decisive. On the simple level at which we propose to test the two theories, equation (1) might turn out to be better than equation (2), or conversely; whereas on a more sophisticated level, when additional variables are introduced, the relative advantage of the two might be reversed. This possibility cannot be ruled out, although it seems a reasonable presumption that the relationship which explains the most in its simplest version is the relationship that will be most fruitful to explore further and to convert into a more sophisticated form.

III. THE EMPIRICAL APPROACH

Our main approach to exploring the relative stability of velocity and of the multiplier will be to fit equations such as equations (1) and (2) to data for various periods of time in order to determine which of the two fits the data better.

In choosing the periods of time, we have taken several considerations into account. First, since the question at issue is mainly the short-term stability of the relations being compared, it seems desirable to make the comparisons for relatively short periods. Second, since the relations may differ at different phases of the cycle, it seems desirable that any one comparison should cover one or more complete cycles, so as to prevent the possibility of distortion from starting and ending the period at different phases of the cycle. Third, since most of the available data are annual, single business cycles generally provide too small a number of observations to yield statistically meaningful results. The compromise we have adopted among these somewhat conflicting considerations is to divide the period for which data are available into two sets of overlapping segments, one set marked out by the troughs of the major depressions during the period (1896, 1907, 1921, 1933, 1938) except for the post-World War II period, which we have marked off simply by the end of the war; a second set, by peaks intermediate between the troughs of major depressions, except again for dates separating out World War II. Though the selection of the particular peaks has been somewhat arbitrary, the aim has been to select the peaks that are fairly clearly marked and either correspond to the completion of the sharp rebound that follows a major depression or that immediately precede a major depression. The dates we have used are 1903, 1913 (to get a period excluding World War I), 1920, 1929, 1939 (to get a period excluding World War II), 1948, and 1957. We have made computations for the period as a whole as well as the separate segments.

A second statistical problem arises out of the computational connection between the variables on the two sides of equation (2). By definition, $Y=C+A$, where C is consumption (induced) expenditures and A is autonomous expenditures (concepts that are yet to be defined precisely). Hence, if the observations for Y and A are for the same period and from a consistent set of computations, correlation of Y with A involves correlation of Y with part of itself. Both the "true" value of A and any errors of measurement in A are also included in Y. The correlation produced by this arithmetically common component tells nothing about the stability of any economic relation. To put the point in another way, in order to use equation (2) to predict the value of Y for any particular period, one must first know or predict the value of A. But knowing the value of A means knowing part of Y. The multiplier analysis adds nothing to the prediction of this component of Y. The independent contribution of the multiplier analysis is to predict the other component of income, consumption, from the known (or predicted) autonomous expenditure component.

When the data are synchronous, that is, when no lagged responses are introduced, it therefore is preferable to replace equation (2) by one obtained by subtracting A from both sides of equation (2), namely,

$$C=\alpha+KA \tag{5}$$

where $K=K'-1$. When the data are not synchronous this difficulty does not arise and it is possible to use equation (2). However, since only annual data are available for most of the period 1897–1958, and since a year is an unduly long unit for studying lags, much of the analysis is necessarily for synchronous data. Quarterly data are available for the period after World War II and we have experimented with various lags for that period.

The use of equation (5) instead of equation (2) requires a corresponding change in equation (1), if the two relations are to be kept comparable. It may be that consumption, on the one hand, or income, on the other hand, is easier to predict, in which case a comparison of equations (1) and (5) would be misleading. It would be like comparing the time per mile it takes one man to run a half mile and another to run a mile. In order to determine which is the better runner, they must, of course, run the same race. One may be the better runner at the half mile, the other at the mile, in which case neither can be said unambiguously to be "the better runner." In consequence, we have been led to substitute for equation (1)

$$C=\alpha+VM \tag{6}$$

where V has no such simple arithmetic connection with V' as K with K'.

• • •

In addition to considering (5) and (6) separately, we can combine them in

$$C=\alpha+VM+KA \tag{7}$$

where, although we have used the same symbols, V and K may have very different numerical values than in (5) and (6). It is necessary to express the equation in this form in order to obtain a valid statistical test whether the correlation between C and M is significantly different from the correlation between C and A. The partial correlations on each of the variables, M and A, keeping the other constant, indicate the net contribution of each to the explanation of C. It should be noted, however, that the simple correlations and the partial correlations necessarily differ in the same direction, so that the partial correlations add to our understanding of magnitude of effect but cannot reverse a conclusion about which variable is more highly correlated with consumption.

It may be worth restating this point in terms that help to bring out the economic and not only statistical considerations involved. If M and A were entirely independent of one another, in the sense that there was no statistical correlation between them, then, on the average, the partial correlations would equal the simple correlations, and the values of V and K derived from the separate equations would equal the values derived from the joint equation. However, in practice M and A are positively correlated and that is to be expected under either of the theories under consideration. Under the quantity theory, changes in M involve changes in all components of income, including both consumption and other components. Under the income-expenditure theory, changes in M influence rates of interest and thereby affect investment and consumption; in addition, changes in investment may induce corresponding changes in M via their effect on banks. Hence, a positive simple correlation between A and C may simply be a disguised reflection of the effect of M on C; alternatively, a positive simple correlation between M and C may simply be a disguised reflection of the effect of A on C. Presumably, the disguised effect will be smaller and less consistent than the direct effect which is why a comparison of the simple correlations is relevant and will yield the same result with respect to direction as a comparison of the partial correlations. But only the partial correlation can indicate how much of either simple correlation is produced by the disguised effect of the other variable.

Thus far we have dealt with equations expressed in money terms alone. One problem in introducing prices into the analysis is what price index to use and whether to use the same one for each variable. Neither question admits of a clear and unambiguous answer. Primarily for reasons of simplicity, and because the relations in "real" terms are a strictly subsidiary part of our study, we have used a single price index. (See Section IV for the considerations governing our choice of the particular price index used.) Given a price index, one way to introduce prices into the analysis is to deflate all the variables and to express the same relationships we have been considering in terms of deflated values. To some extent we shall do this. However, dividing variables initially expressed in money terms by some common index of prices introduces spurious correlation, since errors of measurement in the price index are introduced alike into both sides of the equation.

An alternative procedure for introducing prices that seems preferable is to introduce a price index as an additional independent variable. This step gives the following equations:

$$C=\alpha+VM+BP \tag{8}$$

$$C=\alpha+KA+BP \tag{9}$$

$$C=\alpha+VM+KA+BP \tag{10}$$

where again, although we have used the same symbols, V, K, and B, their numerical values will not be the same in the several equations.

These equations involving real magnitudes may have very different implications than the equations involving money magnitudes. For example, in dealing with money magnitudes, it is plausible to suppose the major direction of influence to run from M to Y or C, that is, to suppose that a change in the stock of money induces a series of responses within the economic system which lead in turn to a change in Y. This is partly because M, the stock of money in nominal terms, is or can be under the control of the monetary authority, which can make it anything it wishes within very narrow limits. In this sense, M can be entirely independent of the actions of the other participants in the economic process. In dealing with real magnitudes, on the other hand, the major direction of influence might easily be precisely the reverse. The monetary authority cannot make the real stock of money anything it wishes. The public can determine the real stock of money by bidding prices up or down. If, at any given price level, the nominal stock of money is larger than the public wishes to hold, it will seek to exchange the excess for other forms of wealth. In the process the public will bid up prices and correspondingly reduce the real value of the existing stock of money. The process will continue until the real stock of money is whatever the public wishes it to be, and conversely if the nominal stock of money is smaller than the public wishes to hold. It therefore seems more plausible to regard the direction of influence as running from the level of real income or real consumption to the real stock of money rather than the other way.

A similar contrast may hold for the relation between consumption and autonomous expenditures. In principle, it would be possible for "real" autonomous expenditures to be fixed independently of other considerations, as for example, by a government policy of determining its magnitude; the relevant direction of influence might then be from real autonomous expenditures to real consumption. The money relation might reflect the opposite direction of influence. In time of war, for example, consumers seeking to raise real consumption might simply bid up prices, thereby forcing the authority to raise money autonomous expenditures to keep the real level of such expenditures at the desired level. But clearly, there are also other possibilities.

Although statistical correlations, especially correlations involving lags, may give some evidence on direction of influence, they cannot be decisive. For example, a close correlation between the quantity of money and money income is consistent with either monetary changes influencing income or income changes influencing the stock of money. Even if changes in the stock of money tend to precede changes in income, the direction of influence need not be from money to income. Both changes might be the result of a common third influence, but with money reacting more rapidly than income, and there are still other possibilities. In addition to statistical studies of the kind presented in this paper, therefore, other kinds of studies are needed to judge with any confidence the direction of influence. Historical studies of particular episodes are especially valuable in this connection. The reason is that, in many episodes, attendant circumstances give strong evidence that changes in one or more of the variables were independent in origin. For example, a change in the supply of money brought about by currency reforms, gold discoveries, and the like, can hardly be attributed to contemporary changes in income.

• • •

IV. DEFINITION OF THE VARIABLES

We turn now to the selection of the statistical series to correspond to the four variables under consideration: induced expenditures, autonomous expenditures, the stock of money, and the price level. Income has already been defined as the sum of induced and autonomous expenditures.

One by-product of this investigation was the discovery that there is neither clear-cut agreement on the specific statistical definition of autonomous and induced expenditures nor any well established criteria for choosing particular definitions for a particular problem or period or body of data. This state of affairs is rather surprising in view of the mountains of literature on income-expenditure relations, and the large extent to which the appeal of the relations has derived from the appearance that they can be expressed in immediately measurable and operational terms in data contained in the national income accounts. A parallel problem of long standing is the definition of *M*. Should money be defined as consisting of currency alone, or of currency plus deposits? This question was a major element in the famous currency-banking controversy in England more than a century ago. If money is to include both currency and deposits, should it include demand deposits alone, or should it include also commercial bank time deposits? Time deposits in mutual savings banks? Savings and loan association shares? And so forth.

The range of choice is similarly wide for autonomous expenditures. Should autonomous expenditures include consumer as well as producer durables? Exports alone or the net foreign balance? Government expenditures only or the government deficit? The social insurance accrual? Or various in-between versions?

In our actual empirical work, much the greatest amount of time was spent in trying to draw the appropriate boundary lines rather than in the calculations and analysis designed to compare and test the two hypotheses. We are by no means satisfied that we have used the appropriate criteria in drawing the lines. Neither are we satisfied with the precise lines we have drawn, some of which we regard as highly tentative. Much further work remains to be done on this fundamental problem, in particular in determining statistical tests for making the best choice.

The large amount of empirical work we have done has led us to definitions that correspond fairly closely to those that have been and still are widely used in theoretical and statistical work.

What criterion should be used to fix the boundary lines? One simple method is to correlate alternatively defined measures of the independent variable with the dependent variable and then select the concept which yields the highest correlation. The argument for this procedure is that the precise empirical definition of variables should be selected so as to put the theory in question in its best light. For example, since it is not possible *a priori* to make any judgment about whether commercial bank time deposits should be regarded as part of the money supply, it seems plausible to decide this question by correlating (a) currency plus demand deposits and (b) currency plus demand deposits plus commercial bank time deposits with one or more alternative definitions of income. If (b) should consistently be more highly correlated with income, then this criterion would suggest using the more broadly defined money supply in testing the stability of velocity.

Applying this criterion to the definition of autonomous reveals, however, that it is not satisfactory. Suppose the various alternative concepts of autonomous expenditures were correlated with *income.* The suggested criterion would then be vitiated by the existence of spurious correlation noted above. It is possible to get a correlation as close to unity as desired, simply by including all items of income that vary much over time in "autonomous," which is to say, by correlating these variable items with themselves. The procedure adopted above to evade the difficulties raised by the spurious correlation, namely, correlating the rest of income with autonomous expenditures, is no solution for the present problem, since each definition of autonomous would then be correlated with a different variable. For reasons already discussed, the resulting correlations would not be comparable. Lagged correlations are a possible way out, but which lag should be used?

An alternative approach can be illustrated by returning again to the problem of the treatment of commercial bank time deposits in defining "money." Suppose that the broader monetary total has a higher correlation with income than the narrower. The correlation between time deposits alone and income may then be (1) higher than either or (2) lower than one or both. Suppose it is higher than either. The higher correlation of the broader than of the narrower total with income may reflect simply the inclusion of an item highly correlated with income (namely, time deposits) rather than the inclusion of a substitute for the other items; it may reflect determination of the level of time deposits by the level of income and not the converse.

To put this point differently, the appropriate reason for including time deposits is not simply that they are highly correlated with income but that they are such close substitutes for the other monetary items that it is preferable to treat them as if they were perfect substitutes than to omit them. But if time deposits were perfect substitutes for the other items, shifting a dollar from time deposits to the other items would have no effect on Y. For example, consider shifts of deposits from banks with an even number of letters in their legal names to banks with an odd number of letters for a given total of deposits in the two together. Such shifts will clearly have no effect on the level of money income. This suggests that an appropriate criterion whether time deposits are sufficiently close substitutes for other items is whether income is more highly correlated with their sum than with each component separately; whether, that is, (2) of the preceding paragraph holds, in which case time deposits should be included, or (1) does, in which case they should not be.

The application of this alternative approach to the definition of autonomous expenditures can be illustrated by considering the question whether durable consumer goods should be included in consumption or in autonomous expenditures. Let D stand for consumption expenditures on durable goods, N on non-durable goods, C for their total, and A for autonomous, according to some tentative definition that excludes durable consumer goods but settles other doubtful items. The question to be decided is whether $D+A$ or A alone is a preferable definition for autonomous expenditures. If D and A were perfect substitutes as autonomous or income-generating expenditures, then a shift of $1 from D to A or from A to D would have no effect on N. Hence N would tend to have a lower correlation with either D or A alone than with their sum. Consequently, this approach implies that a necessary condition for the inclusion of D in autonomous is that

$$r_{N(D+A)} > \begin{bmatrix} r_{ND} \\ \text{and} \\ r_{NA} \end{bmatrix} \tag{1}$$

The requirement that the sum of autonomous and induced expenditures equal income gives rise to a similar test in the other direction, a possibility that did not arise for the simpler example of time deposits. Suppose (1) is not satisfied. If this occurred because D was a part of induced expenditure along with N, one might expect shifts between D and N to be independent of changes in A. Changes in A would affect only their sum. But this would imply that

$$r_{A(D+N)} > \begin{bmatrix} r_{AD} \\ \text{and} \\ r_{AN} \end{bmatrix} \tag{2}$$

This approach therefore yields the following criterion.

Possibility	Condition (1)	Condition (2)	Conclusion
(a)	Satisfied	Not satisfied	*D* autonomous
(b)	Not satisfied	Satisfied	*D* induced
(c)	Satisfied	Satisfied	Ambiguous
(d)	Not satisfied	Not satisfied	Ambiguous

There is nothing about the arithmetic of the relations among the correlation coefficients that requires either (a) or (b) to hold. It is entirely possible, and in our work has frequently happened, that either (c) or (d) should hold. In consequence, this criterion is not one that is necessarily decisive.

Unfortunately, however, we have been able to devise no criterion that seemed better to us. Consequently, we have employed the criterion just outlined. When the results have been ambiguous, we have followed the procedure that seemed more in accord with the general presumptions in the literature about income-expenditure relations.

In applying the criterion, we have in each case set up the problem as in the above example. That is, we have tentatively decided all questions of inclusion or exclusion except one, leaving us with a division of total income into three parts, the treatment of one of which is in doubt. . . .

The decisions reached on the basis of these tests were to define money and autonomous expenditures as follows:

Money = currency in public circulation
plus adjusted demand deposits
plus time deposits in commercial banks

Autonomous = Net private domestic investment
plus the government deficit on income and product account
plus the net foreign balance

One additional variable, prices, remains to be defined because in several sets of calculations we attempted to express the relationships among the variables in real rather than in money terms by introducing some index of prices. In all cases we have used an index of consumer prices. To test the stability of the multiplier in real terms is essentially to examine the response of consumers to changes in their real incomes brought about by changes in autonomous expenditures. The appropriate single deflator for this purpose is clearly an index of consumer prices. The same index of prices was used for the money-income relations, in part for purposes of consistency with the treatment of income-expenditure relations in real terms. In addition, most theoretical discussions of the demand for money relative to income focus on the household demand for money where again the appropriate deflator is an index of consumer prices.

We are by no means satisfied that we have throughout made the right decisions. We would welcome suggestions for a more satisfactory criterion, and plan further experiments with different definitions.

V. THE EMPIRICAL RESULTS FOR THE U.S.

The empirical results are remarkably consistent and unambiguous. The evidence is so one-sided that its import is clear without the nice balancing of conflicting bits of evidence, the sophisticated examination of statistical tests of significance, and the introduction of supplementary information that the economic statistician repeatedly finds necessary in trying to decide questionable points, and that is indeed a major source of pride and pleasure in his craft. . . .

Summary of Conclusions

The income velocity of circulation of money is consistently and decidedly stabler than the investment multiplier except only during the early years of the Great Depression after 1929. There is throughout, including those years, a close and consistent relation between the stock of money and consumption or income, and between year-to-year changes in the stock of money and in consumption or income. There is a much weaker and less consistent relation between autonomous expenditures and consumption, with the same exception, and essentially no consistent relation between year-to-year changes in autonomous expenditures and consumption. Moreover, such relationship as there is between autonomous expenditures and consumption seems simply to reflect the influence of money in disguise. The partial correlation between autonomous expenditures and consumption for a given stock of money is almost as frequently negative as positive but in either case is not very different from zero, again with the exception of a few years after 1929.

These statements hold both for the annual data available for a 62-year period and for the quarterly data available for the period after World War II. In addition, the quarterly data permit testing for leads and lags. Again the results are unambiguous. Money is more highly correlated with consumption two quarters later than with consumption in any earlier or later quarter. Autonomous expenditures are more highly correlated with consumption in the same quarter than with consumption in any later quarter. These results do not deserve much confidence because of the strong trends in all the series. But so far as they go, they argue that the direction of influence is from money to consumption or income. The synchronous correlation between autonomous expenditures and consumption may simply reflect the effect of the money stock on both magnitudes.

The results are essentially the same when prices are brought into the picture except, as noted above in Section II, that the direction of influence is probably reversed for money. Except for World War II, there is a close and consistent relation between the stock of money in real terms and the level of consumption or income; which is to say, there is a highly stable demand function for money. Except for the Great Depression, there is no stable and consistent relation between real consumption and real autonomous expenditures; the relation is as often negative—which is to be expected from the limitation of resources under reasonably full employment conditions—as positive; which is to say, the cyclical consumption function is unstable.

In other words, the simple version of the income-expenditure theory to which we have deliberately restricted ourselves in this [article] is almost completely useless as a description of stable empirical relationships, as judged by six decades of experience in the United States. Though simple, this version is substantially the one that is presented in almost every recent elementary economics textbook as the central element in the theory of income determination. Such results as we have so far obtained from analyses for other countries strongly confirm results for the United States. On the evidence so far, the stock of money is unquestionably far more critical in interpreting movements in income than is autonomous expenditures.

• • •

30 ESTIMATES OF HICKSIAN IS AND LM CURVES FOR THE UNITED STATES

ROBERT H. SCOTT

Read this selection and then examine Figure 1 carefully. Find the corresponding *IS-LM* diagram that appears in your textbook and compare it with Figure 1. Note the major differences, and explain them. (Hint: Is there a liquidity trap in Figure 1?) Because Figure 1 is based on empirical estimates, it ought to wield more authority than do textbook diagrams, which are only examples. What, then, are the policy implications of Robert Scott's diagram? Would you, as one of the monetary or fiscal authorities, place a substantial degree of confidence in these curves when formulating proper macroeconomic policies?

There are more facts around than there are theories capable of explaining. But, while a theory should be capable of explaining a large number of facts in order to be useful, it is generally supposed that theories should not try to explain *all* of the facts relevant to their domain. This is because the theory, if it permits of no exceptions whatsoever, is necessarily as complex as the set of facts it is designed to explain. Current developments in the field of macroeconomic model building provide a case in point.

On the one hand, there is the momental work of Professor Friedman on the influence of changes in the stock of money on the aggregate level of economic activity. It is testimony to his perseverance and the merit of his findings that many economists now protest that they never meant to imply that money didn't matter. The direct evidence that he has provided has undeniably made its mark, and the efforts of many economists are now directed toward uncovering evidence of variables other than the money supply that matter significantly.

On the other hand, a magnificent chain of developments following in the heritage of Tinbergen has led to the construction of large and elaborate macroeconomic models. It is a living tribute to the ingenuity and creativity of men like Klein, Goldberger, Suits, and others, that the Brookings-SSRC model of the economy of the United States has been constructed.[1] But, this model has not been constructed without some misgivings, misgivings that reflect serious concern over the problems of complexity that are bound to arise whenever a model contains hundreds of equations.

The model to be presented here, stemming from Hicks, could perhaps be called twice as big as Professor Friedman's inasmuch as it contains two equations rather than one.* The primary purpose is to test a theory, but elements of the model appear to be promising for forecasting purposes as well. Use in forecasting, however, awaits refinement.

Early empirical attempts to find a significant role for interest rates in the frame-

From Robert H. Scott, "Estimates of Hicksian *IS* and *LM* Curves for the United States," *Journal of Finance,* 21, 479–487. Reprinted by permission.

[1] J. S. Duesenberry, G. Fromm, L. Klein, and E. Kuh, editors, *The Brookings Quarterly Econometric Model of the United States,* Rand McNally and Co., Chicago, 1965.

*See the previous selection—ed.

work of a Keynesian system using simultaneous equations estimating techniques were not notably successful. In spite of this, widespread belief persists that monetary policy, to be effective, operated by way of its influence on the cost of credit. The empirical model which follows indicates that an index of *current* bond yields does indeed act as an inhibitor to *current* aggregate spending. It is, of course, only one bit of evidence, but it is suggestive of further investigation. Friedman and Meiselman wrote that ". . . it seems a reasonable presumption that the relationship which explains the most in its simplest version is the relationship that will be most fruitful to explore further and to convert into a more sophisticated form." In a certain sense the Hicksian model that follows represents a "more sophisticated form" of the Keynesian system. But, since the stock of money and interest rates also enter the model, in another sense it is a conversion that involves a synthesis of Keynesian and neoclassical views. Indeed, Keynes himself assigned an important role to money, and rather than dichotomizing the two points of view, as Friedman and Meiselman did, would it not be best to attempt to integrate them?

I. THE MODEL

The Hicksian *IS* and *LM* curves may be treated in a fashion analogous to the treatment of demand and supply curves. Proceeding along familiar lines, define the following variables:

- Y = Income
- C = Consumption
- I = Investment
- $\bar{G}$ = Government Spending plus Net Exports
- $\bar{M}$ = Money Supply
- M_1 = Transactions Balances of Money
- M_2 = Liquidity Balances of Money
- R = Long-term Interest Rate

Two of the eight variables, $\bar{G}$ and $\bar{M}$, are cxogenous.

The system contains two identities:

$$Y = C + I + \bar{G} \qquad (1)$$

$$\bar{M} = M_1 + M_2 \qquad (2)$$

It also contains four functional relations:

$C = C(Y)$, the consumption function (3)

$I = I(R,Y)$, the investment demand function (4)

$M_1 = M_1(Y)$, the demand for transactions balances, and (5)

$M_2 = M_2(R)$, the demand for liquidity balances (6)

To consolidate the six equations, a first step may be to substitute equations (3) and (4) into equation (1). This yields:

$Y = C(Y) + I(R,Y) + \bar{G}$, or simply (7)

$$Y = Y(R,\bar{G}) \qquad (8)$$

Next, by substituting equations (5) and (6) into equation (2), one finds that:

$\bar{M} = M_1(Y) + M_2(R)$, or simply (9)

$$R = R(Y,\bar{M}) \qquad (10)$$

Equation (8) resembles what Hicks called the *IS* curve, and equation (10) resembles what he called the *LL* curve (usually called the *LM* curve). Using these two equations, the model has four variables, two exogenous and two endogenous. Hence, it satisfies the *a priori* criterion for identifiability.

II. ESTIMATES OF THE PARAMETERS

Quarterly data for the period 1951 through 1964, seasonally adjusted where appropriate, were used in this experiment. Table 1 contains two stage least squares (2*SLS*) estimates of the structural equations. The estimate of the *LM* curve (equation [2], Table 1) contains

Table 1. Estimates of Hicksian IS-LM Curves for the U.S.*

2 Stage Least Squares Estimates	Coefficient of Correlation
(1) $Y = 2{,}019.65 \;-1{,}545.33\hat{R} \;+43.94G$ $\qquad\qquad\qquad(212.8)\qquad(5.48)$	.986
(2) $R = \;2.441 + \;.0233\hat{Y} - \;.0460M$ $\qquad\qquad\qquad(.0073)\qquad(.0195)$	.861

*Standard Errors in parentheses. Hats over Y and R indicate values estimated from reduced form in accordance with 2*SLS* estimating techniques. . . .

Y = Gross National Product, seasonally adjusted, annual rates, billions of current dollars.

R = Yield on AA corporate bonds, not seasonally adjusted, average for the quarter.

M = Currency, Demand Deposits and Time Deposits, seasonally adjusted, billions of current dollars. Quarterly figures were computed as the arithmetic average of the averages given for the first half of each month in the *Federal Reserve Bulletin.* (The latest revision of the money supply series was unavailable when this study was begun.)

G = Government spending and net exports, seasonally adjusted, annual rates, billions of current dollars.

N = 56, quarterly data from 1951 through 1964.

theoretically expected signs in front of the coefficients and the coefficients are significant as their standard errors indicate. The coefficient of M is especially interesting in view of the fact that the simple correlation between R and M is +.833. Thus, the addition of Y as a variable along with M to explain corporate bond yields serves to account for the superficial appearance of a positive relationship between R and M. It appears that an increase in the money supply, defined to include time deposits, of a billion dollars accompanies a reduction in the corporate bond yield of about 4 basis points.

The literature contains several other estimates of *LM* curves and liquidity preference functions that support in a rough way the evidence presented here. However, there are no other estimates of the *IS* curve. The coefficient of $\hat{R}$ in equation (1) indicates a very flat *IS* curve, but nevertheless with the theoretically expected negative slope. By inference this evidence supports the proposition that *current* interest rates hold investment spending below what it currently would be if interest rates were somewhat higher. The inference follows from the presumption that it is through $\hat{R}$ that private investment relates to Y in the equation for the *IS* curve. A myriad of earlier studies attempting to relate current investment spending to current interest rates, by and large, failed to succeed. Exceptions are found in certain industry studies. Most researchers, therefore, shifted to the use of lagged interest rates, or focused upon distributed lag functions. But disregarding the inference about investment spending as opposed to spending in general, this is evidence that an index of monetary conditions in the form of a series of *current* bond yields acts as an inhibitor to *current* aggregate spending.

If one looks at the coefficient of G in equation (1), approximately 44, and views this as the partial derivative of Y with respect to G, it appears that the so-called "government spending multiplier" approximates 44. This large figure is less surprising, however, if one notes that the government spending multiplier in this model depends not only upon the marginal propensity to consume but also upon the marginal propensity to invest since the investment demand function contains an income variable along with a rate of interest variable. Furthermore, this is an indication of the change in income that would accompany a change in government spending *only if* the monetary au-

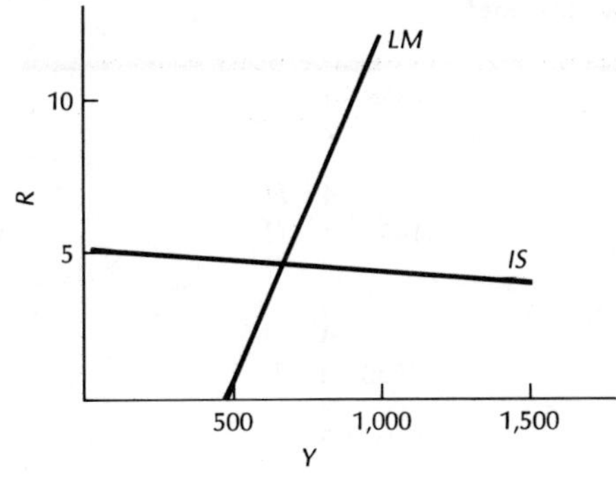

Figure 1

thorities were willing to provide the necessary increase in the money supply to keep interest rates unchanged. And, from equation (2) it can be shown that to keep interest rates unchanged in the face of an increase in income of $44 billion the monetary authorities would have to add $22.3 billion to the stock of money (inclusive of time deposits).

Figure 1 is a graphical presentation of the equations in Table 1 with arbitrarily chosen values for G and M of 140 and 300, respectively. If larger values were chosen, the respective curves would shift rightward.

III. THE HUDSON HYPOTHESIS

H. R. Hudson contends that the Hicksian *IS* curve should be U-shaped. He arrives at this position by introducing an asymmetrical "accelerator" type of effect. (It is not strictly an accelerator because of the absence of a lagged relationship.) Thus, investment is a function of the rate of interest, and of income, but the relationship of investment to income is nonlinear so that for low levels of income $\partial I/\partial Y$ is near zero, and for high levels of income it is large.[2] Contrasting the investment function with the savings function, he concludes that for low levels of income

$$\frac{\partial I}{\partial Y} < \frac{\partial S}{\partial Y},$$

and for high levels

$$\frac{\partial I}{\partial Y} > \frac{\partial S}{\partial Y}.$$

Following through with this proposition, it can be shown that it clearly implies that the *IS* curve is U-shaped. Of course, Hudson's analysis is much more elegant than this cursory statement of his position would indicate. At this point only his proposition that the *IS* curve is U-shaped is subjected to a test.

As of today there is little in econometric literature that could help one estimate structural parameters for a simultaneous equations system in the event that one of the equations is curvilinear. By transformation of variables into (say) logarithmic form, the entire system can be estimated, but this would be desirable only if one feels that the system is linear in logarithms. Therefore, for this simple model, estimates were made to see if the *IS* curve were V-shaped, instead of U-shaped, by simply taking that part of the sample for which income was thought to be "low" and that part for which income was thought to be "high." By looking at a graph showing G.N.P. in constant dollars, this selection was made arbitrarily according to the rule that income would be considered low if it were below the previous period's income and/or if it were below income attained during a prior cyclical peak. Thus, incomes for the entire "cup" of the cycle were considered "low." That is, incomes were "low" from the peak of the cycle until this peak was surpassed in a later period. All other periods were considered to be periods of "high" income. Table 2 [see page 220] shows this arbitrary division of periods.

[2]H. R. Hudson, "A Model of the Trade Cycle," *Economic Record*, Vol. 33, December, 1957, pp. 378–389.

Table 2. Designation of Periods of "High" and "Low" Income*

Year	Quarter		Year	Quarter	
1951	1	*H*	1958	1	
	2	*H*		2	
	3	*H*		3	
	4	*H*		4	*H*
1952	1		1959	1	*H*
	2			2	*H*
	3			3	
	4	*H*		4	
1953	1	*H*	1960	1	*H*
	2	*H*		2	*H*
	3			3	
	4			4	
1954	1		1961	1	
	2			2	
	3			3	*H*
	4			4	*H*
1955	1	*H*	1962	1	*H*
	2	*H*		2	
	3	*H*		3	
	4	*H*		4	
1956	1		1963	1	
	2			2	*H*
	3			3	*H*
	4			4	*H*
1957	1	*H*	1964	1	*H*
	2	*H*		2	*H*
	3			3	
	4			4	

*"High" income periods are designated by *H,* the remaining undesignated periods were treated as "low" income periods.

This arbitrary division of the data was the result of a visual inspection of the pattern generated by plotting GNP data in constant dollars. The rule was to treat income as "low" even when expanding if it was below the income achieved in the previous upswing. Thus, the entire "cup" of a dip was treated as low, and only periods of expansion above the previous highs were treated as highs.

Table 3. Estimates of Hicksian IS-LM Curves for "Low" Values of Income*

2 Stage Least Squares Estimates	Coefficient of Correlation
(1) $Y = 755.02 - \underset{(146.3)}{631.25\hat{R}} + \underset{(3.93)}{21.31G}$	.985
(2) $R = 2.558 + \underset{(.0092)}{.0204\hat{Y}} - \underset{(.0253)}{.0400M}$	.850

*$N=30$.

Table 3 shows the estimates of the structural parameters for "low" values of income and Table 4 shows them for "high" values. The coefficient of $\hat{R}$ in equation (1) of Table 3 is negative and statistically significant, a minus 631. This value is absolutely much smaller than the same value for high levels of income, found in Table 4, equation (1), a minus 1,473. By interpreting this information on a graph showing *IS* and *LM* curves, the *IS* curve would appear slightly L-shaped.

Table 4. Estimates of Hicksian IS-LM Curves for "High" Values of Income*

2 Stage Least Squares Estimates	Coefficient of Correlation
(1) $Y = 2{,}099.84 \; - 1{,}473.10\hat{R} \;\; + 40.68G$ $(276.3) \quad (6.88)$	.988
(2) $R = \;\; 2.156 + \;\; .0241\hat{Y} - \;\; .0466M$ $(.0108) \quad (.0278)$	.875

*$N = 26$.

It may be that, for the period covered by the data, 1951 through 1964, the U.S. economy did not reach "high" levels of activity; that is, it did not press into the range of income where the positive slope of the *IS* curve suggested by Hudson came into being. Or, perhaps the data should have been divided into three parts, "low," "medium," and "high," so that they would yield three sets of estimates. The problem of dividing the data becomes greatly more complex, however, the more divisions there are, and this was not attempted.

Figure 2 is a graphical representation of the results of dividing the data. The *LM* curve estimates for both high and low income values differed only slightly from that for the entire period, hence the *LM* curve is the same in Figure 2 as shown in Figure 1. The righthand portion of the *IS* curve was plotted from equation (1) in Table 4, and the lefthand portion was plotted from equation (1) in Table 3. In both instances it was again assumed that *G* and *M* were 140 and 300, respectively. The intersection point of the two estimates of the *IS* curve was arbitrarily chosen to represent the slight L-shape effect, and should not be taken to imply a particular level of income that would divide income into "high" and "low" levels.

Figure 2

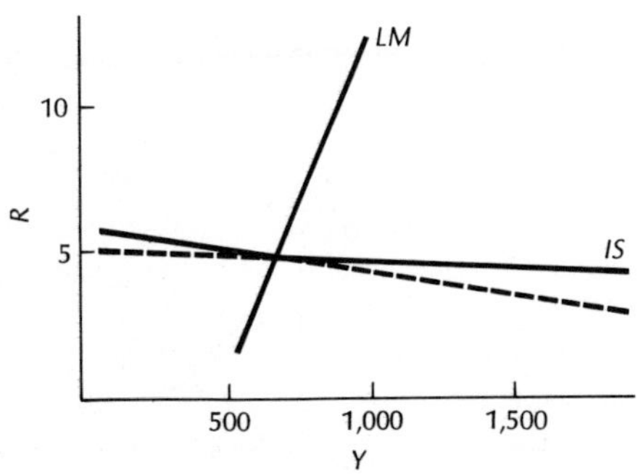

The vaguely L-shaped *IS* curve implies that monetary policy is more influential in periods of high income when the economy presses near full employment than in periods of low income and excess capacity. This proposition, while familiar, typically emanates from discussions of the *LM* curve and the inference from it of a "liquidity trap" in periods of low interest rates. Here, support for the proposition is found in the *IS* curve. From the data one might draw the inference that the original Keynesian investment demand function, in which investment is a function of the long-term interest rate alone, is somewhat more elastic in periods of high income than in periods of low income. This inference, consistent with the data, supports the Keynesian contention of an inelastic investment demand function during depressions.

But, a presumed asymmetrical "accelerator" type of effect (or, it might be called a curvilinear income effect on investment) is also capable of explaining the results of the experiment. For, even if the Keynesian investment demand function held its shape over swings in income, it is more important to watch monetary conditions carefully in periods of high activity than in periods of low activity. This is because a small change in investment generated by a change in monetary conditions may result in a large inducement to invest and large changes in income in an economy characterized by near full-capacity utilization of resources. Thus, monetary conditions are of far greater importance to stabilization objectives in periods of high-level activity than in periods of low-level activity not only because a "liquidity trap" may exist and lenders may hoard idle balances of money when income and interest rates are low, but also because in low-activity periods accelerator effects are nearly nonexistent since increases in demand can be easily met simply through greater use of currently existing excess capacity.

IV. CONCLUSIONS

All of the estimates of the structural parameters for this simple two-equation system have theoretically expected signs, and the data fit the model exceptionally well, especially in view of the amount of aggregation involved. It is refreshing to find, after years of teaching the Hicksian model, not only that interest rates are affected by the money supply and income as other studies have shown previously, but also that current income is affected by current interest rates and by autonomous expenditures. Hence, the evidence reaffirms the desirability of coordinating monetary and fiscal policies in the interests of economic stability.

Experiments run with divided data indicate that the *IS* curve is flatter when income is "high" than when income is "low." Hence each of our policy tools, fiscal and monetary, is more sensitive and should be handled with greater care in an economy pressing close to full employment. For if incomes are "high" changes in government spending will result in relatively large changes in income (or in interest rates if the monetary authorities do not alter the supply of money).

While it is fashionable among economists these days to create large and complex models and then subject them to empirical test, perhaps it would be better to experiment more extensively with simple models, and proceed to disaggregate and expand them only slowly, step by step. The Hicksian model developed in this [article] might be an appropriate base.

31 INDICATORS OF MONETARY POLICY

GEORGE W. MITCHELL

In the fourth quarter of 1968, the 3-month Treasury bill rate rose by more than one-half a percentage point, reaching an average of 5.94 percent per annum in December. Similar rate increases occurred in other short-term interest rates, as well as in capital market rates. Although the federal funds rate did not follow this pattern, it did exceed the bill rate throughout the quarter and averaged 6.02 percent per annum in the last month of 1968. During the same quarter, total bank reserves grew at an annual rate of 8.8 percent, whereas nonborrowed reserves rose by only 3 percent. Member bank deposits, on the other hand, grew by 12.2 percent. Except for nonborrowed reserves, in which a major decrease in the rate of increase was noticeable, the rates of increase in the other two variables fell only slightly below those of the previous quarter. Money supply, defined as demand deposits adjusted and currency outside the banking system, rose at an annual rate of 7.6 percent, more rapidly than the previous quarters' increase of 4.5 percent, but the reverse was true for commercial bank time and savings deposits. Although these nondemand deposit accounts increased by 15.7 percent in the final quarter of the year, they had grown by 17.9 percent in the previous three months.

These data, which come from the lead article in the February 1969 issue of the *Federal Reserve Bulletin,* demand interpretation. What is happening in the monetary sector of the economy? Was the fourth quarter of 1968 a period of increasing monetary tightness or is the opposite conclusion more correct? Governor George Mitchell addresses himself to these questions in this selection. After you have read the selection, try to answer the questions posed here.

Mr. MITCHELL. I am pleased to have this opportunity to appear before this committee to discuss the principles of conducting monetary policy as part of an overall economic stabilization program. My formal statement is addressed to a question that has been widely discussed in the past several years, and in which this committee already has demonstrated an active interest: what financial variable or variables should be used as intermediate targets of monetary policy? More specifically, in assessing whether monetary policy has been tight or easy, what interpretation should be assigned to the movements in the stock of money, as against movements in other financial variables such as broader measures of liquid assets, credit flows and terms, money market conditions, or the level and structure of interest rates?

On a question as complex and as controversial as this, there are bound to be differences in views among observers—even among those whose vantage points are very similar. Consequently, I could not hope to express adequately the judgments of the Board as a whole, nor shall I try to do so. The opinions to be expressed are my own.

From testimony of George W. Mitchell before the Joint Economic Committee of Congress, May 8, 9, 15, and 16, 1968, reprinted in *Standards for Guiding Monetary Action: Hearings* (Washington, D.C.: U.S. Government Printing Office, 1968), pp. 120–129.

The central question with which I shall be dealing—the intermediate targets of policy—has been debated extensively in the professional journals, although without sufficient agreement having been reached to provide any automatic guide for monetary policy decisions. Some economists affiliate exclusively, or primarily, with changes in the rate of credit expansion, either in terms of total credit expansion or some critical segment thereof, such as bank credit. Others look principally to changes in the economy's liquid assets, either in the aggregate or in some segment of the total, such as the money stock. Others look principally to the terms and conditions on which funds can be borrowed, regarding changes in the level and structure of interest rates as the basis for establishing the course of monetary policy.

To set forth the conclusion of my argument briefly, it seems to me that in our dynamic economy, no single variable—whether it be the money stock, money plus time deposits, bank credit, total credit, free reserves, interest rates, or what have you—always serves adequately as an exclusive guide for monetary policy and its effects on the economy. It follows from this that excessive concentration of our attention on any single variable, or even on any single group of related variables, would likely result in a potentially serious misreading of the course and intensity of monetary policy.

It may be helpful to establish the rationale for this conclusion in rather general terms first, and then appraise, in this context, the conduct of monetary policy in some recent critical periods. Monetary policies pursued by the Federal Reserve do have an important effect on the Nation's money stock. While our knowledge of the effects that reserve injections have on the time dimension of monetary expansion is imprecise, the Federal Reserve generally could make the money stock grow or decline in line with what was thought to be appropriate for economic stabilization purposes. But it is a mistake to assume that Federal Reserve policies are the only factor influencing the money stock. It is equally mistaken to assume that policy actions do not extend beyond the money stock to affect growth rates of other financial assets, expectations of market participants, and the terms on which borrowers in a variety of different credit markets find funds available to finance spending plans. Failure to appreciate the potentially disturbing effects of policy actions on aspects of the monetary and credit environment other than the money stock could easily lead to serious mistakes in monetary management.

We must, and do, guide Federal Reserve policies with a careful assessment of the effects those policies have on the money stock. But in interpreting movements in the money stock over time it is essential to recall that the movements are the result of the interaction of many forces: The behavior of the nonbank public, acting in response to its desire to hold money and other financial assets; the behavior of Federal Reserve in supplying bank reserves, and in setting discount rates, reserve requirements, and ceiling rates that banks may pay on time deposits; the behavior of the commercial banks in using the reserves supplied to them by the Federal Reserve; the behavior of all financial institutions in bidding for the savings of the public. It is erroneous to interpret changes in the money stock as though they represented exclusively the result of the operation of a guidance system for the economy administered by the central bank. Variations in money holdings over any period represent the supply behavior of the central bank acting together with the demand factors existing in the private sector of the economy.

A meaningful interpretation of changes in the growth rate of the money stock must try to take into account, therefore, the factors underlying the public's demand for money and its ability to substitute between money balances and other financial assets. It is particularly important to assess properly what is happening to growth rates of other financial assets that are likely to be close substitutes for money in the public's financial asset portfolio. Our monetary history, as I read it, does not indicate that there is any unique financial asset, or combination of financial assets, which satisfies the public's liquidity preference.

Indeed, over the past decade—and especially in the past 5 or 6 years—there have been significant changes in the public's preference for various types of liquid assets. For example, in the late 1950's we observed that the growth rate of time deposits of commercial banks was beginning to respond to changes in monetary conditions. Monetary policies that limited the overall supply of bank reserves and bank credit tended to raise rates of interest on market securities. Because rates paid on time deposits by commercial banks were generally less flexible, these deposits became less attractive to the public, relative to market securities, and their growth rate slowed. Expansive monetary policies, contrariwise, tended to accelerate time deposit growth.

Manifestly, a given dollar increment to bank credit associated with a rise in time deposits need not be any the less expansive, in terms of its effects on spending, than if the increase in bank credit were supported by a rise in demand deposits—and hence by a growth in the stock of money. Indeed, it might be more expensive, since banks might channel funds received through time deposit growth into types of uses more likely to stimulate economic activity. For some time, therefore, we have taken into account the growth rate of commercial bank time deposits, as well as the money stock, in trying to steer the course of monetary policy.

But the meaning to be assigned to any given growth of time deposits is not easily determined. It means one thing if rapid growth in time deposits reflects aggressive bidding for these deposits by the banking system, with the public responding to banks' efforts to obtain loanable funds through this route by reducing money balances. The meaning would be very different if the funds attracted to time deposits at commercial banks represented funds diverted from the close competitors of banks in the savings field—the mutual savings banks and savings and loan associations. Still a third meaning would be suggested if an increase in time deposits represented funds that someone would otherwise have invested in Treasury bills, while the banking system puts the funds into mortgage loans.

Thus, interpretation of the economic impact of changes in commercial bank deposits involves understanding the sources from which funds flow into these assets, and the reasons for these flows. And increasingly, it has become evident that the posture of monetary policy—as it affects yields on market securities and the desire and ability of banks to bid for funds—influences also the flows of funds to nonbank thrift institutions, and through them the supply of funds seeking long-term investment, especially in mortgages. When the effects of policy spread this pervasively through the financial structure, efforts at setting the course of policy by specifying a relatively inflexible pattern of behavior for a single financial variable, such as the money stock, could produce seriously disequilibrating changes in economic activity.

The problems we face are not likely to be solved by concocting alternate definitions of money, in hopes that by doing so we will find the magic statistical series whose behavior tells us just what we need to know to establish the posture of monetary policy. Undoubtedly, our understanding of monetary processes is improved by expanding our vision beyond the narrowly defined money stock and its immediate determinants, but we should not expect to find a magic divining rod for monetary management. What we need is a better understanding of the meaning of changes in money and in other liquid assets, not new definitions of what money is.

This point can perhaps be illustrated briefly by reference to the debate in the course of policy during the early 1960's, when growth in the money stock was quite moderate, but growth rates in total bank credit were relatively high. In 1962, particularly, growth of the money stock receded to only about 1½ percent, while the growth of bank credit—under the impetus of an 18 percent rise in commercial bank time deposits—increased to almost a 9 percent rate. Earlier in the postwar period, that high a growth rate of bank credit had been associated with strongly expansive monetary policies. The result was a critic's paradise; Federal Reserve policy could alternatively be criticized as exceptionally expansive, or unusually restrictive, depending on the monetary variable used by the critic.

I argued at that time—and I would still argue now, given the benefit of hindsight—that both of these interpretations of monetary policy were inaccurate. The growth of time deposits in 1962—and more generally, throughout the early years of the 1960's—reflected partly a reduction in the public's demand for demand deposits. This reduced demand for money was a response to both the higher rates banks paid on time deposits, and the spread in the use of negotiable CD's by large corporations as a liquid investment medium. Slow growth of the money stock was thus reflecting predominantly a reduction in the public's desired money holdings relative to income. But, in part, time deposit growth also reflected an increase in the banking system's role as an intermediary in the savings-investment process. Banks were bidding for funds that would otherwise have been channeled directly by savers to market securities, or indirectly through nonbank thrift institutions to the mortgage market. High growth rates of bank credit were in large measure a reflection of the increased intermediary role of the banks. On balance, I have always thought that the posture of monetary policy in 1962 was properly described as essentially accommodative, or perhaps moderately expansionary, rather than unusually stimulative or unusually restrictive.

The best evidence that this interpretation is the proper one stems from what was happening at that time to interest rates, and what happened subsequently to economic activity. If policy had been unusually restrictive, as the slowdown in money growth suggested, we should have expected to see a sharp rise in interest rates—followed by a subsequent marked slowing in GNP growth, or at least in those sectors of the economy most sensitive to monetary policy, such as residential construction. If policy had turned exceptionally expansive as suggested by the marked increase in bank credit growth, we should have expected to see a marked decline in interest rates, and a subsequent surge of spending, particularly in those areas most responsive to policy.

What in fact happened was neither of these. Long-term interest rates were gently declining through most of 1962, while short-term interest rates remained relatively stable throughout the year. GNP growth did slow down temporarily in late 1962 and early 1963, but this moderation in the rate of expansion could scarcely be attributed to tight money. The homebuilding industry—a good barometer of the effects of policy on spending—experienced a generally rising level of activity during the year, made possible by relatively ample supplies of mortgage money.

Interest rates, therefore, provide potentially useful information as to the course and intensity of policy, and can never be ignored in setting the targets of policy. Observing interest rate changes can help immeasurably in assessing the meaning of changes in money and other liquid asset holdings. Of course, given sufficient time, the impact of monetary policy on interest rates tends to disappear. Expansive monetary policies which initially lower interest rates will eventually increase spending, and the resulting rise in credit demands and income will tend to push interest rates back up again. Nonetheless, there are lags between monetary policies and their final effects on spending and incomes—and in the interim, the impact of monetary policies will be recorded in interest rates. Interest rate changes, consequently, are often of substantial value as indicators of the posture of monetary policy.

Of course, using changes in an interest rate or a matrix of interest rates as the sole guide for policy would be as misleading as depending solely on changes in the stock of money. For one thing, some of the important effects of monetary policy in credit markets do not show up in interest rates, but in other aspects of loan contracts—down payments, maturities, or the ability of a borrower to get credit at all. These changes in credit availability may well be as significant as interest rate movements in stimulating or restricting particular types of spending. More important, perhaps, is the fact that changes in interest rates result from changes in credit demands as well as supplies. As with the money stock, interest rate changes are partly the result of Federal Reserve policy, but they are partly a product of the behavior of the nonbank public, the commercial banks, and other financial institutions.

If we are to make use of interest rate movements as guides to policy, then, we clearly cannot assume simply that monetary policy is moving toward restraint every time interest rates rise, or conversely that falling interest rates always imply greater monetary ease. Interest rate movements have to be interpreted in the light of accompanying changes in such financial quantities as the money stock, commercial bank time deposits, and claims against nonbank savings institutions. Similarly, interpretation of changes in financial quantities, such as in the money stock, must be made in the context of changes in the prices and yields of a wide range of financial assets among which investors may choose to hold their funds. Thus, neither financial prices nor quantities alone tell us enough of the story to permit either to serve as an exclusive guide to policy.

Moreover, at each juncture the interplay of quantities and prices in financial markets takes on substantive meaning as a guide to policy only in light of developments in the real sectors of the economy. For it is only by disentangling the complex inter-relationships between financial markets and markets for real goods and services that we can hope to assess adequately the separate roles of both demand and supply factors in determining quantities and prices of financial assets.

This analysis does not lead to any obvious and simple prescription for gaging and directing the course and intensity of monetary policy. This is regrettable, not just because it maximizes the potential for disagreement among policymakers and observers evaluating the same set of facts, but also because it implies that we have found as yet no simple device for circumventing the arduous tasks involved in making judgmental decisions at every step of the game.

I would not want to pretend that our economic judgment—or that of any other economic policymaking body—is infallible. But I would argue that the procedures we do follow—blending judgment with comprehensive, quantitative analysis of current and prospective developments—have produced better results than would have been achieved by following any of the simple rules advocated by some economists. I have already described how misleading it was to have described the course of monetary policy in 1962 by relying solely on changes in the money stock. Let me turn to a more recent—and more controversial—period, the conduct of monetary policy since the middle of 1965. A frequently voiced criticism of policy in this period, as typically set forth by those who judge the posture of policy either exclusively or mainly on the basis of the growth rate of the Nation's money stock, is that monetary policy became excessively stimulative shortly after the middle of 1965, and remained so until the late spring or early summer of 1966. The high rate of growth of money balances during this period, it is contended, was a principal source of the inflationary pressures we suffered in 1966. Also, it is alleged that monetary policy became excessively restrictive in the late spring or early summer of 1966, and remained so until late in the year—as the monetary authorities characteristically overreacted, it is said, to their earlier mistake of excessive ease. This criticism goes on to argue that monetary policy once again swung too far in 1967, producing an unusually high rate of expansion in the money stock that set the stage for a revival of inflationary forces late in 1967 and on into the current year.

There is an alternative interpretation of monetary policy during this period, derived from a more careful and comprehensive view of developments in the real economy and in financial markets from late 1965 to date, that accords more closely with the unfolding facts of the situation. As this committee knows well, the problems of excess demand, economic instability and inflation that have plagued us for nearly 3 years first made their appearance in the summer and early fall months of 1965. Our defense effort in Vietnam had just begun to be enlarged, and defense orders were pouring out in volume. At the same time, growth in the stock of money accelerated from a rate of about 3 percent in the first half of 1965 to about 6 percent in the final 6 months of that year.

Whatever one's views on the relative importance of the defense buildup, as opposed to the rise in the monetary growth rate, as factors in the ensuing increase in the growth rate of aggregate demand, hindsight points clearly to the view that prompter and more vigorous efforts should have been taken to counter the inflationary head of steam that was developing in the latter half of 1965. By imposing measures of fiscal restraint then, and adapting monetary policies to the altered environment, we might have preserved the balanced, orderly growth that we had been enjoying over the previous 4 years. We did not, largely because the magnitude of the defense effort that was getting underway then, and the reverberations it was having in virtually every corner of the economy, were not fully recognized until late in 1965. Given the knowledge that we have presently—which was not then available—the course of monetary and fiscal policies in the latter half of 1965 looks inappropriate.

Once a program of monetary restriction was initiated in December of 1965, however, we moved to a posture of restraint much more quickly and decisively than the figures on the money stock alone would indicate. The accompanying [figure] shows the percentage changes, at annual rates, of the money stock, money plus time deposits at commercial banks, and savings accounts at major nonbank thrift institutions. (These percentage changes are calculated from 3-month averages to smooth out some of the erratic monthly movements in these series.) The chart indicates some rather critical differences in the timing of these three series in the period from mid-1965 to mid-1966. Thus, though the money stock continued to rise briskly over the early months of 1966, the growth of money and time deposits together began to decline in the late fall months of 1965. And the growth rate of nonbank savings accounts was already declining sharply by the end of 1965, as depositors of these institutions responded to the attraction of rising yields on market securities and on commercial bank time deposits.

Thus, the supply of credit represented by the growth of all these financial assets together began to decline well ahead of the downturn in the rate of expansion in money. This decline in supply, operating jointly with the heavy credit demands arising from rapid growth in current spending, underlay the marked and pervasive rise in interest rates we were experiencing in the first quarter of 1966. Monetary restraint was beginning to develop in financial markets early in 1966, even though rapid money stock growth continued.

If any doubt existed that monetary restraint was beginning to pinch before it became evident in the banking figures, those doubts should have been laid to rest by what happened to the volume of homebuilding during 1966. It is widely recognized that monetary policy affects spending for goods and services only with a variable and often a rather considerable lag, and that it has a larger impact on housing than on any other sector of the economy. In 1966, however, housing starts leveled out in the first quarter and then began to drop abruptly in the second, reaching a trough in October. This timing of the response of housing starts to financial restraint can be explained, I believe, only by recognizing that the principal indicators of monetary restraint in early 1966 were not recorded in the money stock, but in the steep decline in the inflows of funds to nonbank financial institutions. Had we guided policies solely by the money stock in early 1966, we could easily have overlooked altogether the strong effects on housing that monetary restraint was in fact producing.

But as the year 1966 progressed, an increasing intensity of monetary restraint was signaled by almost every indicator of monetary policy customarily observed. Growth in the money stock was halted for a period of 7 to 8 months and the expansion in commercial bank time deposits declined markedly after midyear. Large banks, particularly, were put under se-

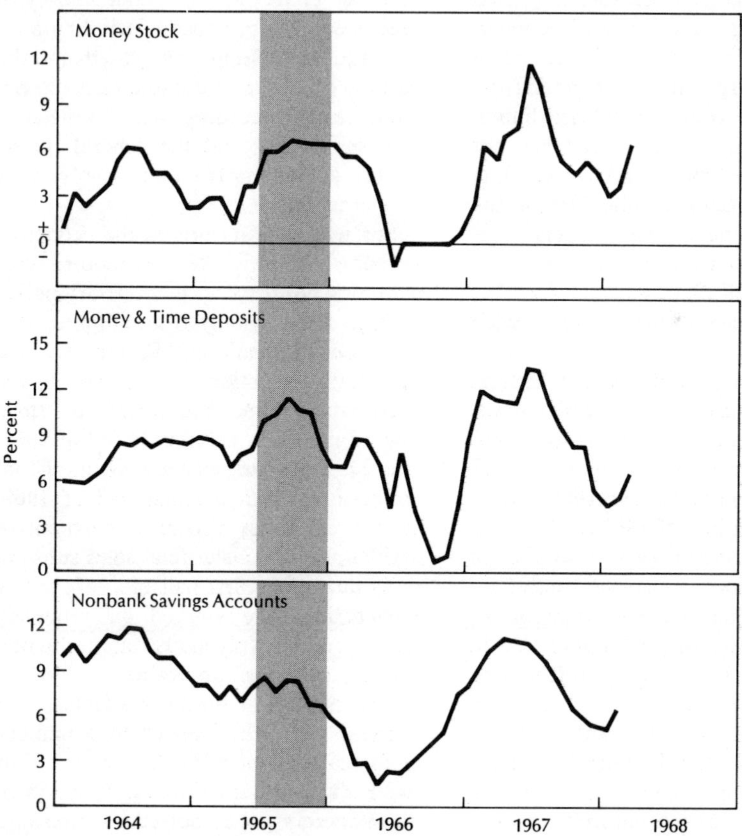

Figure 1 Financial Assets—Annual Growth Rates

vere strain, as the maintenance of ceilings on large CD's at 5½ percent—while yields on competing financial assets were rising rapidly—led nonfinancial corporations and other large investors to shift their funds out of the CD market. Inflow of funds to nonbank intermediaries, meanwhile, continued at low levels through the summer and early fall months. These signs of monetary restraint in the quantities were also reflected in interest rates, which rose rapidly during the summer of 1966 to the highest levels in about four decades.

Perhaps a case could be made for the argument that some of the financial indicators in the summer and early fall of 1966 overestimated the degree of monetary restraint generated by policy actions. Some of the financial pressure suggested by the declining growth rate of commercial bank deposits, for example, was being cushioned by large inflows of funds from abroad—in the form of increased liabilities of our banks to foreign branches. But the relief to the bank system as a whole was relatively limited. The fact of the matter is, I believe, that monetary restraint became quite severe in the summer and early fall of 1966, a conclusion that would have been drawn from a wide variety of indicators of monetary policy.

As noted earlier, some critics of Federal Reserve policy have concluded that monetary policy became excessively tight during this period and point to the slowing of real growth in output late in 1966 and on through the first half of 1967 as confirmation of their point of view. I would not question that some of the restrictive effects on spending of earlier tight monetary policies were still being recorded in the first half of 1967—although it may be noted that outlays for residential construction began to rise as early as the first quarter of that year. What I would question is the contention that the inventory adjustment of early 1967 was entirely, or even primarily, caused by tight money in 1966.

The undesired buildup of inventories that occurred in the last quarter of 1966 reflected mainly the inability of business to foresee the slowdown in final sales that resulted when consumers began to exercise more cautious buying attitudes. Personal consumption expenditures had been rising at a rate of about $8 to $9 billion per quarter in the year ended with the third quarter of 1966—and so far as anyone knew at that time, they might well have continued to do so. But consumer buying slowed materially in the fourth quarter, as a major increase occurred in the personal savings rate, and consumers continued to exercise caution in their buying habits throughout 1967. At best, this behavior of consumers can be contributed only in small measure to tight money in the summer and fall months of 1966. Many other factors were undoubtedly of fundamental importance—including a reaction to the rapid income growth and the buildup of stocks of durable assets in the immediately preceding years, resistance to rising prices, and the general uncertainties emanating from our involvement in Vietnam.

But whatever its origin, the economic slowdown of early 1967 did require compensating adjustments in monetary policy to keep the economy from slipping into recessionary conditions. Fortunately, the inventory correction of early 1967 was anticipated in time to take the initial steps toward monetary ease in the fall of 1966, and this helped to bolster residential construction through the first half of 1967. With fiscal policy also turning expansive and helping to bolster final sales substantially during the first half of 1967, excess inventories were worked off relatively quickly, and by July industrial production had begun to turn up again.

The pickup in business activity after midyear 1967 was foreseen by a number of forecasters, including our own staff at the Federal Reserve Board. Why, then, did monetary policy not take earlier and more decisive steps to reduce the rate of expansion in the money stock and in bank credit during the latter half of the year? There are two parts to the answer to that question.

First, the high rate of expansion in the money stock during the final 6 months of last year greatly overstates the actual degree of monetary ease promoted by monetary policy. What it represented was the supplying of funds through monetary policy to permit the satisfaction of a sharp increase in liquidity preference on the part of nonfinancial corporations. Their desires to rebuild liquid asset holdings stemmed only in part from the experience with tight credit policies in 1966. Of more fundamental importance were the trends in corporate liquid asset management over the previous several years, together with the heavy toll on corporate liquidity resulting from the acceleration of tax payments that began in 1966.

In the years immediately prior to 1966, businesses in the aggregate had little need to concern themselves with their liquidity positions or with the availability of bank loans or other sources of funds to meet their credit needs. Partly as a consequence of this, additions to liquid asset holdings were relatively modest. Thus, increases in liquid asset holdings of nonfinancial corporations were less than $1 billion in each of the years 1964 and 1965.

Businesses entered the period of accelerated tax payments, therefore, with little preparation for meeting a heavy excess of tax payments over accruals. For nonfinancial corporations, payments exceeded accruing liabilities by about $2 billion in the second quarter of 1966 and by about $5 billion in the second quarter of 1967. With credit markets taut during a large part of this period, liquid asset holdings were run down by nearly $3 billion in the year ended in mid-1967, in reflection of the heavy needs for funds for accelerated payments of taxes and other purposes.

Many businesses, consequently, took the opportunity afforded by more ample credit availability in 1967 to do something about their liquidity positions. Corporate long-term security issues began to rise rapidly in reflection of these increased liquidity demands during the spring of 1967, and they remained at exceptionally high levels until late in the year. Observers close to financial markets reported that an unusual increase in liquidity preference was responsible. The demand for money had thus risen for reasons not associated with intentions to spend for goods and services. This is the kind of increase in demand for money which monetary policy can meet, by permitting an increase in the supply, without inflationary consequences.

The behavior of interest rates during the latter half of 1967 provided the confirmation needed that this interpretation was on the right track. Interest rates on longer term securities had begun rising in the spring months in response to the rapidly growing supply of corporate long-term borrowing. Short-term rates, however, continued to decline until shortly before midyear. After midyear, however, interest rates began to rise drastically across the range of maturities, and the increases were much too rapid to be explained by the effects of rising incomes and economic activity generating increased demands for credit. They were reflecting increased demands for quick assets to restore balance sheet liquidity—demands that were not being fully satisfied by the rate of growth in money and time deposits permitted by monetary policy. It seems evident that monetary policy was much less expansive in 1967 than the high rate of monetary growth, taken by itself, might seem to imply.

Nevertheless, had it been known that timely fiscal restraint was not going to be forthcoming, monetary policy would have been less expansive over the summer and fall of 1967, in order to achieve a posture more consistent with a return to price stability. Earlier adoption of a program of monetary restraint would have been difficult, in light of the turbulent state of domestic and international financial markets but it would not have been impossible. Such a program was not adopted earlier, I believe, largely because those of us responsible for making monetary decisions found it almost inconceivable that this Nation would once again, following the painful experience of 1966, choose to rely exclusively on monetary policy to moderate the growth in aggregate demand and slow inflationary pressures. Let us fervently hope that the brightening prospects for fiscal restraint we presently see on the horizon provide justification for that expectation.

the tools of monetary policy

reserve requirements and open market operations

Experimentation and innovation, laced with a good measure of conservatism, is an apt description of the approach adopted by Federal Reserve officialdom with respect to the tools of their trade. Indeed, the history of the Federal Reserve can be traced out in terms of the monetary weapons available to and employed by the Federal Reserve. In the formative years and even earlier—the period of the passage of the Federal Reserve Act—the primary tool of the central bank was the discounting process. Philosophically attuned to the Act itself, the passivity of discounting—the initiative rests with the member banks—reflected the attitude that the Federal Reserve System was to encourage the smooth functioning of the banking system rather than actively influence the private economy. The Federal Reserve System was designed to see that a malfunction affecting certain banks did not snowball into a general crisis and panic. In the words of Harold Barger, the functions of the System were to be "therapeutic rather than prophylactic."[1]

The Reserve Banks, which were constituted as self-financing entities and were obliged to pay dividends to their stockholders, the member banks, had no guarantee that the discounting process would bring in an adequate amount of revenue. Accordingly, the provision of the Federal Reserve Act that enabled the Reserve Banks to buy and sell certain types of assets for their own accounts, reaping not only interest but perhaps even capital gains, was interpreted as providing a second source of revenue. The Roaring Twenties was a period of experimentation

---

[1]H. Barger, *The Management of Money: A Survey of American Experience* (Chicago: Rand McNally, 1964), p. 46.

with these open market operations; they evolved from their original role as a source of revenue to become part of the arsenal of the Federal Reserve System. With this new discovery, and under the forceful leadership of a few individuals, notably Benjamin Strong, Governor of the Federal Reserve Bank of New York from 1914 to 1928, came the realization that the Federal Reserve could and should control the money and credit markets. Thus the open market operation came into active use, and its development was recognized by Congress in the Banking Act of 1933.

The history of variations in the required reserve ratio follows a different course but again must be understood as a creative response to economic conditions. Already under the National Banking Act of the Civil War period, national banks were required to hold a certain portion of their deposit liabilities in a reserve account. The Federal Reserve Act embraced this idea and did not provide for discretionary control of the ratio. Not until 1933, in reaction to the shock of catastrophic bank failures, was the Board of Governors permitted to vary the ratio of required reserves to deposits. Then, in the Banking Act of 1935, the present format of this weapon was incorporated into law.

There is no need to elaborate on the host of minor weapons (including the only one now subject to Federal Reserve discretion, the margin requirement on credit for security purchases) that were given to the Federal Reserve, used by it, and then revoked as economic conditions varied. But we should take note of a new variation in reserve requirement policy—the dependence of the reserve ratio on the volume of deposits. Since July 1966 for time deposits and January 1968 for demand deposits, the first $5 million in deposits carry a lower reserve ratio than do deposits exceeding that sum. For example, as of September, 1970, the first $5 million of net demand deposits at reserve city banks must be backed by reserves equaling 17 percent of the total. This requirement rises to 17½ percent for sums in excess of $5 million. For time deposits other than savings deposits, the ratios are 3 percent and 5 percent, respectively. Thus "evolution" is the key term to use in describing the development of the three major weapons that Federal Reserve policy uses today.

The philosophy of "make haste slowly" is no less evident. For example, the open market weapon did not achieve its prominence until at least World War II, when it was used as the primary means of maintaining low-cost government borrowing. Another example has been the steadfast objection by the Federal Reserve's top echelons to numerous proposals advanced in the past decade that were designed to provide the System with certain stand-by selective controls. Finally, reserve ratios based on deposit size have been discussed at least since the 1940s, and although they were adopted in other countries, they came into use in the United States only in 1966.

Present monetary policy is conducted primarily through open market sales and purchases of government securities. Daily transactions are common, as described in Part IV. Less frequently do the Reserve Banks vary the discount rate, and least often is the legal reserve ratio modified. To be sure, different bodies within the Federal Reserve System are responsible formally for each tool, a situation worthy of raised eyebrows at the least. The discount rate is the primary responsibility of each Reserve Bank, the reserve ratio comes under the sole authority of the Board of Governors, and the Federal Open Market Committee is the legal organism charged with implementing the open market instrument. Less confusion exists than appearances indicate, however, and the complexity of authority is not the reason underlying the varied frequency of use of each tool. First, by virtue of its constituting a majority of the FOMC and as a result of its veto power over discount rates, the Board of Governors has the power to conduct monetary policy on its own. More important, however, is the *modus vivendi* that has evolved. It centers around the triweekly FOMC meeting, where all the Federal Reserve Bank presidents and senior staff join with the Board to evaluate economic conditions and to decide on the conduct of monetary policy. The consensus arrived at encompasses not only the policy to be followed but also which of the various tools are to be brought to bear.

Accompanying the ascendancy of the open market operation is the rather remarkable pattern of variations in the required reserve ratio. In the years between 1953 and 1968, for example, the ratio against demand deposits in central reserve and city banks was changed ten times, and in each case it was lowered. Similar statements can be made for other bank and deposit categories. This observation prompts us to ask two questions: (1) What advantage does the open market operation possess relative to modifications in the legal reserve ratio, thereby accounting for the former's frequent use? (2) Why has the direction of change in the reserve requirement ratio for more than a decade been unidirectional?

The first two selections in this Part deal directly with these questions. Conceptually, the money multiplier formula, which relates total reserves to demand deposits or money supply via the reserve ratio, makes the first question difficult to answer. Take the formulation in its simplest form where "reserves" divided by the legal reserve ratio yields total deposits. With reserves of $50 billion and a ratio of 10 percent, demand deposits of $500 billion can be supported. Suppose now that the monetary authority wished to lower the deposit level by $100 billion. Apparently, two equal alternatives present themselves: reduce reserves by selling $10 billion in government securities on the open market or increase the reserve ratio from its present level of 10 percent to 12½ percent.

The defense of the Federal Reserve to this challenge is presented in the opening selection, taken from former Chairman William McChesney Martin's testimony before the Joint Economic Committee of Congress in 1959. Various reasons are adduced by Martin to demonstrate the relative superiority of open market operations, especially as a means of restraining undesired economic exuberance. Not all economists are convinced by his reasoning, however. John H. Kareken, in the second selection, writes what is in essence a rebuttal of Martin's testimony. Professor Kareken's main point can be summarized as follows: No convincing argument has been advanced to justify the second-class status of frequent or positive reserve ratio changes. Moreover, a few side effects of reserve ratio increases may be desirable per se. Judge for yourself which of the two articles is more convincing.

A further comment is warranted. Many monetary economists have agreed with the position taken by the Federal Reserve on this issue, but for another reason. They claim that because the money supply can be controlled effectively through open market operations, there is no need to introduce a second weapon to do the same job. Some merit may be found in this view, but it cannot bear heavy weight because, if carried to the extreme, it is equally applicable to monetary policy as a whole. Why use monetary policy when fiscal policy can mold the economy in the desired form?

One practical result has emerged from this debate. The long-standing, one-sided Federal Reserve policy concerning the open market operation is at least partially responsible for a number of Congressional investigations into the conduct of monetary policy and the accompanying threats of reform. Indeed, it is quite likely that the new willingness to increase the reserve requirement ratio is the response of the monetary authorities to increasing political pressure.

Portfolio analysis sheds some light on the reserve requirement-open market operation controversy, and Joseph Aschheim formulates his model on that basis. A commercial bank, weighing liquidity and profit considerations, reacts differently to an increase in the reserve requirement, which reduces profitability as it increases liquidity, than it does to an open market sale, which does not change the ratio of liquid assets to earning assets. Consequently, more loans will be issued under the former circumstances, and although the money supply can be reduced by an equal amount by either method, the loan market will be affected differently.

Although Professor Aschheim's analysis is interesting, it has been criticized on a number of grounds. Questions of the appropriateness of definitions, of importance of the secondary impact, and of incompleteness have been raised. Moreover, one school of monetary economists, the neoquantity theorists, disregard his theory entirely, because it is the quantity of money that matters, they claim, and not the volume of loans. More empirical information is needed, however, before the Aschheim model can be dismissed as irrelevant.

In closing this introduction, a suggestion may be appropriate. Follow the actions of the Federal Reserve especially when conditions call for monetary restraint. Will reserve requirements be raised again? Will a new rationalization, emphasizing the efficacy of reserve requirement policy, be advanced? Will Congressmen urge the monetary authorities to implement reserve ratio increases more frequently? These questions are related to "political economy" perhaps more than to economics, but they are no less germane or critical.

32 RESERVE REQUIREMENT CHANGES VERSUS OPEN MARKET OPERATIONS

WILLIAM McC. MARTIN, JR.

The following article explains why America's central banking authorities have found changes in the reserve requirement to be a less useful tool than open market operations are and consequently have varied the requirement only infrequently. In other countries and under different circumstances, however, greater and often increasing reliance is placed on variations in the reserves that banks must hold idle with the central bank. In Great Britain, for example, a scheme of "special deposits"—interest-earning required reserves—was introduced in 1960 by the central bank. A "Notice" issued on April 11, 1967, attests to the manner in which the scheme is to be implemented. "The Bank [of England] . . . will stand ready to adjust the calls [for Special Deposits] more frequently than in the past to keep credit conditions continuously in line with the changing needs of the economy." In underdeveloped economies, where the money markets are underdeveloped too (if they exist at all), open market operations are ruled out from the start; thus the major burden of monetary policy is borne by reserve requirement modifications. In short, even if Martin's arguments are correct with respect to the United States economy, care must be taken before they can be applied elsewhere.

• • •

Theoretically the Federal Reserve System can supply reserves to, or withdraw reserves from, the money market on its own initiative either by purchasing or selling U.S. Government securities or by lowering or raising the reserve requirements of member banks. Technically the use of either instrument of policy can be adopted to achieve a desired level of net free or net borrowed reserves. It follows that after the operation has been concluded the mathematical expansionary effect and the mathematical restrictive effect on the money supply of the net free or net borrowed reserve position, so achieved, would be the same. Here the technical similarity ends.

From Joint Economic Committee of Congress, *Employment, Growth, and Price Levels: Hearings* (Washington, D.C.: U.S. Government Printing Office, 1959), Part 6A, pp. 1462–1465.

In a number of respects, use of changes in reserve requirements to effectuate monetary policy differs from resort to open market operations, as follows:

A. METHOD OF DIFFUSION

A major difference is that a change in reserve requirements affects every member bank directly and immediately with equal force, irrespective of differing individual situations or conditions whereas the effects of an open market operation are felt individually and gradually by the member banks through the operation of market forces. For example, sales of securities in the open market may be reflected in withdrawals of deposits at some banks by some customers. The banks' adjustment to these withdrawals may involve sales of securities, which lead to deposit withdrawals and reserve losses at still other banks. In general, the most extended banks will feel the additional pressure most, but it is not possible to trace meticulously the direct chain of impact of an open market operation.

B. SIZE OF OPERATION

Open market operations lend themselves much more readily than do changes in reserve requirements to achieving small changes in the availability of reserves. They can be used readily to provide or withdraw reserves on any given day in amounts that vary from as much as $100 million (and frequently very much larger amounts) down to figures as small as the denominations of the securities that are traded. Changes in reserve requirements, on the other hand, because they are made as percentages of very large sums, normally change the availability of reserves by very much larger amounts. In the future under the new legislation, any change in the percentage will apply, at the very least, to one of the four categories of deposits (using most recent figures as illustrations) [shown in the table below].

As a general rule, changes in reserve requirements, to be equable, must be generalized to include all net demand deposits or all time deposits. Even if such a change were as small as one-quarter of 1 percent, which is much smaller than has been used in the past, and it were applied to net demand deposits, it would supply or withdraw bank reserves in the amount of $257 million in one operation. If special circumstances permitted an adjustment to be made in reserve requirements of either Reserve city member banks or of country member banks alone (and this would not happen frequently), an adjustment as small as one-quarter of 1 percent would involve $165 million if it were confined to the new class of Reserve city member banks, and $92 million if it were confined to country member banks.

These illustrations are in terms of changes of one-fourth percentage points in reserve requirements, one-half is the smallest ever applied to date to member banks. One can, of course, by resorting to smaller and smaller fractions in theory make changes in reserve requirements appear capable of as minute adjustments as changes induced by open market operations. Very small fractional changes at relatively frequent intervals, however, would create very difficult problems of adjustment for member banks and would almost certainly be disruptive to the smooth flow of credit in the market.

This factor of size of impact is one reason why it is more difficult to use an increase in reserve requirements to contain a boom than it is to use a decrease to combat a recession. If an increase in reserve requirements is imposed at a time when member banks' holdings of excess reserves are low, or completely offset by borrowing at the discount window, there are only three options open to the banking system to achieve compliance: (1) by wholesale liquidation of loans in an amount several times the increase in reserves required (about six times at present), or (2) by sales of U.S. Government securities in comparable volume (i.e., about six times at present) to nonbank investors, or (3) by borrowing at the discount window a sum equal to the amount involved in an increase in reserve requirements. In the case of any combination of

Table 1. [In millions]

	Net Demand Deposits	Time Deposits
Reserve city (including central Reserve city) banks	$ 66,134	$28,481
Country banks	36,892	25,488
Total	$103,026	$53,969

these, lower prices for U.S. Government securities could be expected. From the moment of the announcement, there would be a strong tendency for potential buyers of U.S. Government securities to defer their bids, thus tending to provoke a disorderly market that would force intervention by the system open market account. Such intervention to restore orderly conditions might require purchases in greater amounts than were involved in the original increase in reserve requirements. As a result, the effort to combat overexpansion in a boom by reducing bank liquidity might induce disorder in the market for Treasury issues and, subsequently, a situation of even greater bank liquidity than had prevailed before the restraining action was initiated. These same problems do not arise when reserve requirements are reduced.

There are occasions when a lowering of reserve requirements may be superior technically to an open market operation. For example, one such occasion arose very suddenly in June 1953 when a series of unforeseen developments in connection with Treasury tax payments produced a situation which needed a very large injection of reserves in a very short period. The reduction in reserve requirements ordered at that time exactly met the technical requirements. It is doubtful whether purchases of securities in the open market would have achieved a similar result.

C. IMPERSONALITY OF OPERATION

It is important that operations undertaken to effectuate the broad purposes of monetary policy be as impersonal as possible in their impact on various segments of the economy. They should affect broadly the availability and cost of borrowing and the return obtainable on saving in general rather than any particular form of borrowing or any particular type of saving.

From the point of view of impersonality, changes in reserve requirements are, in one sense, more impersonal than open market operations which, in addition to changing the availability of reserves, also add to or subtract from the volume of particular types of securities in the market. To the extent, however, that open market operations are confined to short-term securities, these operations are also, in practice, quite impersonal in their effects.

Changes in reserve requirements are not at all impersonal in the extent to which they affect the competitive position of different types of banks. They affect directly only member banks of the Federal Reserve System. Nonmember banks which are subject only to State-imposed reserve requirements are left untouched unless the State requirements are varied automatically with those of member banks.

When resort is made to the open market instrument, the reserves are removed through an impersonal market transaction. The actual absorption of reserves from the market results from the sale of securities to a willing buyer. Thus, the first impact of an open market operation comes about because a transaction has been effected between a willing buyer and a willing seller, rather than as a result of a change in an official regulation. Apart from the publication of Federal Reserve statements, commercial banks are not aware of the absorption of reserves by Federal Reserve. Reserve losses to individual banks take the form of adverse clearing balances, which frequently occur in the normal course of business.

D. EXPECTATIONS

There is one major respect in which member banks seem to react differently during a recession to the provision of a given amount of excess reserves according to whether the stated excess is the result of a series of purchases of U.S. securities in the open market, on the one hand, or of a reduction in reserve requirements, on the other. This is in addition to the fact that a reduction in reserve requirements places additional lending power in all member banks simultaneously.

It seems to be expected generally that an increase in reserve availability brought about by a change in reserve requirements is likely to be more permanent and that the added lending power will not be quickly withdrawn. Member banks, consequently, are likely to react more positively to a reduction in reserve requirements by moving promptly to expand and also to incorporate additional permanently desirable assets in their asset structures. They will be more likely to expand their long-term assets by purchasing mortgages and also to make customer commitments extending longer into the future, commitments for term loans, for new lines of credit, and for future mortgage financing.

This differential response has both favorable and unfavorable characteristics. It undoubtedly facilitates the quick adoption by businessmen of plans that lead toward expansion and emergence from the recession. It may, at the same time, however, commit the commercial banks to future extensions of credit that they would later rather not have made.

For example, a great many of the bank lines of credit that financed the very rapid expansion of installment credit in 1955 were entered into during the third quarter of 1954 at roughly the same time that reserve requirements were lowered. It will never be possible to prove a cause and effect relationship between these two developments, but experience in both 1954 and again in 1958 suggests that this type of response on the part of member banks does accompany reductions in reserve requirements and that it may be quite dramatic on some occasions.

E. LONG-RUN REDUNDANCIES OR DEFICIENCIES OF RESERVES

In 1927, the long inflow of gold from abroad after 1920 and the low rate of increase in currency in circulation as the use of checking accounts became more general finally reduced the demand for Reserve bank credit to a point where there was a danger that the Federal Reserve banks would lose operating contact with the market.

Should such a contingency recur, it would constitute a clear technical case for increasing reserve requirements, the increase to be effectuated preferably in a period when reserves were redundant. Resort to the reserve requirement arm would be indicated as a technical matter because the Federal open market account would not be in possession of sufficient securities to operate effectively on the side of restraint in the market. The increases in reserve requirements in the midthirties represent an adjustment of this type.

A reverse technical situation would occur if growth in world output and correspondingly in world demands for gold as reserves should exceed additions to world gold stocks in such a way as to result in a deficiency of world gold supplies relative to needs for monetary reserves. Under such circumstances, a reduction in reserve requirements against deposits might be in order.

F. RELATION TO TREASURY OPERATIONS

With respect to the System's ability to act independently in pursuit of its statutory responsibilities, there is little difference between its use of open market operations and reserve requirements. The System does, in fact, take into account, in either case, Treasury financing activities, endeavoring to interfere with these as little as possible while pursuing its own objectives.

As pointed out earlier, however, because of their greater flexibility and the fact that their magnitude can be adjusted to current market developments, open market sales are less likely than reserve requirement increases to create market conditions unfavorable to a Treasury operation.

• • •

33 ON THE RELATIVE MERITS OF RESERVE RATIO CHANGES AND OPEN-MARKET OPERATIONS

JOHN H. KAREKEN

In an almost point-by-point rebuttal, John H. Kareken takes issue with William McChesney Martin's contention that open-market operations are preferable to reserve ratio changes, especially increases in the ratio. Of special interest is Kareken's allegation concerning the relationship between the reserve ratio policy of the Board of Governors and the profitability of member banks. Decreases in the ratio increase the proportion of earning assets that commercial banks may hold in their asset portfolio. And yet this discriminatory policy may be sound from the long-run point of view of monetary policy. Member banks can resign from the System at their own initiative and may be expected to do so if the costs of membership exceed the advantages. The Federal Reserve can retain its control over the monetary system only by ensuring substantial membership in the System, and therefore must convince the banks that it is no less advantageous to belong to the System than to leave it. Permitting higher bank profits certainly cannot help but serve as an inducement to the member banks to stay. In this situation, wouldn't compulsory membership in the System for all commercial banks or all insured commercial banks be desirable?

Federal Reserve officials, when trying to decide whether to change legal reserve ratios or to engage in open-market operations, do not simply get together and toss a coin. Instead they try to figure out which of these two ways of regulating bank lending best suits the circumstances of the moment; for they, like most economists, believe that the economic effects produced by a change in reserve ratios differ significantly from those produced by an equivalent open-market operation.[1] Nor can there be much doubt that System officials are right, at least in principle, in relying on judgment rather than on chance; since these approaches do differ in their effects, it does matter which one is used. What can be doubted, however, is that System officials have put their (collective) finger on the real differences between the reserve-ratio and open-market approaches. Their reasons for sometimes using one approach and sometimes the other do not ring true. Specifically, official reasons for making day-to-day adjustments in member banks' reserve positions by means of open-market sales and purchases will not stand up under close scrutiny (see Sec. I); and the same can be said of the official defense of the post-Accord record on reserve ratios (see Sec. II).

But let it be understood from the outset that the argument being made here is not that Federal Reserve officials have consistently erred in making their decisions about when to change reserve ratios and

From John H. Kareken, "On the Relative Merits of Reserve-Ratio Changes and Open-Market Operations," *Journal of Finance,* 16, 65–72. Reprinted by permission.

[1]An open-market operation and a change in legal reserve ratios are equivalent if they produce the same change in the ability of member banks to hold earning assets. (Other definitions of equivalence are possible.)

when to deal in Treasury securities. Rather, it is that if these officials have been right, they have been right for the wrong reasons; either this, or they have not been making their real reasons known.

I. DAY-TO-DAY RESERVE ADJUSTMENTS

It is an operating principle of the Federal Reserve that day-to-day changes in autonomous variables affecting member banks' reserves (e.g., float) should be offset by changes in System holdings of Treasury securities. To change legal reserve ratios, it is held, is to produce a remedy all out of proportion to the problem; most of the time, variables affecting reserves change only slightly in value from day to day, whereas "even *small* changes in reserve ratios, say of one or two percentage points, result in large changes in available reserves and liquidity positions of member banks." In words much favored by authors of money and banking texts, the effects of changes in legal reserve ratios are "too blunt and powerful."

But granted that even the traditionally used one-half percentage point changes in reserve ratios have considerably influenced member banks' ability to lend, this still leaves unanswered the quite pertinent question: Why cannot reserve ratios be changed by, say, one-tenth of one percentage point or by whatever fraction will produce the desired amount of excess reserves, however small? Merely to assert that "administrative" or "technical" difficulties stand in the way is not sufficient. What these difficulties could be is not easy for an outsider to determine.

There is another point which has been made by Federal Reserve officials in defense of the preference for making day-to-day reserve adjustments by means of open-market operations. Allegedly, member banks would find it extremely difficult, if not impossible, to adjust to frequent small changes in legal reserve ratios. ("Very small fractional changes at relatively frequent intervals . . . would create very difficult problems of adjustment for member banks and would almost certainly be disruptive of the smooth flow of credit in the market.") Again, though, why this should be so is not clear. Individual banks, even when operating in a world of unchanging reserve ratios, nevertheless have to deal with the possibility of deposit fluctuations. To introduce the possibility of small frequent changes in reserve ratios, however, is like increasing the dispersion of possible deposit fluctuations. This being so, then member banks, if they can manage when reserve ratios are fixed, can also manage when they change frequently. There would thus seem to be no reason to expect an interruption of the "smooth flow of credit."

If the emphasis on the disruptive effects of frequent changes in legal reserve ratios is considerably overdone, so is the official argument that stresses the difference between the way in which a change in reserve ratios affects individual banks and the way in which a change in System holdings of Treasury securities affects them. ". . . A change in reserve requirements," Federal Reserve officials have observed, "affects every member bank directly and immediately with equal force, irrespective of differing individual situations or conditions, whereas the effects of an open market operation are felt individually and gradually by the member banks through the operation of market forces." What is the implication? System officials have never said explicitly, but presumably it is that changes in System holdings of Treasury securities, in contrast with changes in reserve ratios, eliminate transient excesses and stringencies in the money market without disrupting the whole banking system. But whatever the (desired) implication is, it is based on a difference that is largely without substance.

Admittedly, when reserve ratios are altered, excess reserves of all member banks change by the same amount relatively, so that the initial impact is evenly distributed over the banking system. In contrast, when the System's portfolio of Treasury securities is altered, the initial impact is felt by the so-called money-market banks—by those banks which, as a matter of course, supply securities financing. But when the Federal Reserve engages in open-market operations, it must, in a manner of speaking, trust the market mechanism to carry out its intentions; if, for example, an official purchase of Treasury securities is made to offset, say, a temporary reserve stringency, it still remains for the market mechanism to get these funds into the hands of "needy" bankers. And yet, if the market mechanism, particularly the federal funds market, serves this purpose when the System buys Treasury securities, why should it not do the same when reserve ratios are lowered? Of course, some bankers may be tempted by a reduction in reserve ratios to expand their loan portfolios; others, though, will surely want to put their newly acquired reserves into the money market; indeed, this is the more likely response, assuming that bankers view the new reserve ratios as impermanent, as, in fact, they should.

The moral of the story is clear: if the analysis of the two approaches is carried beyond the initial impact stage, as it should be, there turns out to be little difference between them. (To deny this is to raise serious question about the wisdom of using open-market operations to adjust reserve positions elsewhere than in New York and Chicago.) Nor should the possibility of an even greater similarity in the future be ignored. Currently, some banks are undoubtedly not practiced in the art of money-market operations, so that reserves supplied them on a temporary basis probably would not get into "circulation" immediately. Were reserve ratios to be changed frequently, however, as a means of offsetting short-run influences on total bank reserves, many more banks would find it worthwhile to learn the tricks of the trade and take a more active role in the money market.

There is a final defense of the open-market approach which must now be considered. It is heard less often than those already reviewed, perhaps because the Federal Reserve Bank of New York, which favors it, speaks out less often than the Board of Governors, but it is not much more convincing. Briefly, it is that the open-market approach, besides being a way of adjusting bank reserves, is also a way of gathering information about money-market conditions and so about the need for reserve adjustments. In this latter respect, then, the open-market approach differs from the reserve-ratio approach. Also, the System, when willing and able to trade in Treasury securities, is in a position to keep its market informants (dealers in Treasury securities) honest.

There are ways other than by actually dealing in the open-market, however, of keeping informed about money-market conditions. System officials can always keep a watchful eye on the federal funds market. True enough, not all member banks participate in this market, so day-to-day changes in reserve positions may not be fully reflected in the federal funds rate. But banks unfamiliar with the federal funds market are familiar with the discount windows of their regional Reserve banks. And surely it is neither expensive nor time-consuming to collect information about member-bank borrowing. Nor is it apparent why the System, if it does not trade frequently in Treasury securities, will lose effective (reliable) contact with the money market. Is there really any good reason why informants (market participants) should give inaccurate information to the Federal Reserve? If the answer is "No," then System officials can, as it were, get the information they need simply by asking.

In sum, the usual arguments for preferring the open-market to the reserve-ratio approach for making day-to-day adjustments in bank reserves do not seem convincing.

II. CYCLICAL-SECULAR RESERVE ADJUSTMENTS

Since March, 1951, legal reserve ratios, though never increased, have been lowered on four different occasions; at present they are not so very different from what they were following the initial increases in mid-1936, although, of course, they are still considerably above what they were before the Federal Reserve first exercised the authority granted it under the Banking Act of 1935. But this latter fact has not tempered the criticism—of which there has been a good deal, particularly in Congress—of those who object to the post-Accord trend of reserve ratios. The question put to Federal Reserve officials by their critics is the obvious one: Why is it that these ratios can be reduced during periods of economic contraction but not increased during periods of economic expansion?

There is a reasonable answer for this question. It makes a difference, in terms of member banks' earnings and Treasury interest costs, whether the System engages in open-market operations or varies reserve ratios. Which approach favors bank earnings relatively and which the Treasury depends on whether bank reserves are to be reduced or expanded. If reserves are reduced, then bank earnings will be larger relatively if the open-market approach is employed; and Treasury interest costs will be higher than they would be, had reserve ratios been increased. If reserves are increased (the more realistic possibility), then supplying reserves by means of open-market operations rather than by means of reductions in reserve ratios decreases relatively both bank earnings and Treasury (net) interest costs. The reasons are apparent. First, the Federal Reserve is subject to a higher "tax rate" than are private economic units, so that a transfer of Treasury securities to the System reduces net interest payments by the Treasury. Second, if reserves are supplied by such a transfer of securities, the mandatory ratio of earning assets to total assets will be higher than otherwise it would be.

Of course, it is easier to note this difference than it is to figure out its significance for System behavior. What member banks' earnings and profits should be is not easily decided; the competitive position of member banks can be used as a basis for discussion, as can the adequacy of their capital positions, but debates along these lines have so far proved inconclusive. Here, however, the important point is that Federal Reserve officials, in defending their post-Accord record on reserve ratios, have not seized upon the bank earnings argument. Instead they have chosen to rest their case on an apparent asymmetry in the responses of the economy to increases and decreases in reserve ratios—an asymmetry which, if valid, makes the post-Accord record appear quite acceptable and understandable but which, in fact, does not appear to be valid.

During periods of economic expansion, System officials have argued, increases in reserve ratios cause severe and undesirable downward pressure on Treasury securities prices, partly because banks have to sell securities to gain reserves and partly because non-bank investors, anticipating a fall in prices, put off buying. Presumably, then, downward pressure on prices during periods of economic expansion is somehow less desirable than upward pressure during periods of contraction; otherwise this argument is hardly a defense of reductions in reserve ratios unmatched by increases. One wonders, though, reviewing developments of 1957–58, whether this is really so. These developments suggest that reductions in reserve ratios, if not initially offset by official open-market sales, carry the potential for "speculative" excesses—which, whether rightly or wrongly, worry a good many people. But, obviously, open-market operations can be used to lessen the impact of variations in reserve ratios, and it is this point that considerably diminishes the force of the argument of Federal Reserve officials. Neither does it do any good to argue in rebuttal that the same effect got from the use of reserve-ratio changes and open-market operations can be got from the latter alone; this ignores the possibility that one may want to gain an advantage associated with, say, an increase in reserve ratios.

System officials have also argued that reserves generated by a reduction in reserve ratios, besides being distributed immediately over the entire banking system, are viewed by bankers as more permanent than reserves gained through favorable clearing balances (which is where effects of official open-market purchases show themselves). And, being viewed as more permanent, these reserves are put to work directly and at once throughout the whole economy. Economic activity is thus stimulated more quickly.

This observation about bankers' responses is undoubtedly accurate; with the actual history of reserve-ratio changes to go by, bankers would be foolish to take a different view of reserves gained in this manner. But, again, it is hard to see why this observation is an argument in defense of the post-Accord record, which shows decreases in reserve ratios but no increases. Why should there be an asymmetry in bankers' responses? Are not bankers likely to view a loss of reserves due to an increase in reserve ratios, even if initially offset by System purchases of Treasury securities, as more permanent than clearing balances losses? This is surely a powerful argument in favor of cyclical increases in reserve ratios, for it suggests that there is an important "announcement effect" associated with such increases. (Bankers will immediately take steps to bolster their reserve positions, even though they do not—because of an accompanying temporary increase in the System's portfolio—feel the pinch right away.) This is of no small consequence, particularly since the System appears to have had some difficulty in making its influence felt quickly enough during periods of rapid economic recovery.

The arguments advanced by Federal Reserve officials in defense of the way they have managed reserve ratios in the post-Accord period thus do not appear adequate to the task. The first, concerning the relationship between reserve-ratio changes and the behavior of Treasury securities prices, is actually an argument in favor of non-variable reserve ratios or of smaller changes in these ratios than have been typical; it does not support the view that reserve ratios can be decreased in "normal" or non-emergency situations but not increased. The second argument, concerning the response of bankers to changes in reserve ratios, suggests that these ratios should vary cyclically, which again is not what was intended.

III. CONCLUSION

Federal Reserve analyses of the issues of monetary policy are characteristically of high intellectual quality. This is why the weaknesses in its opinions about the reserve-ratio and open-market approaches are so surprising. One can but wonder whether the official reasons for sometimes using one approach and sometimes using the other are not just a disguise. Perhaps the Federal Reserve's general preference for the open-market approach and its management of reserve ratios in the post-Accord period are to be explained by a considerable (and perhaps healthy) respect for the realities of politics, for the idea that the System can govern and so discharge its responsibilities only so long as it does not unduly antagonize too many member banks.

It is interesting that Federal Reserve officials should emphasize so much the difference between the ways in which the reserve-ratio and open-market approaches affect individual banks—especially since, from the narrowly economic point of view, this differencc is largely without substance. From the broader viewpoint of political economy, however, this difference may be very real. To engage in open-market operations is to hide the harsh hand of regulation in the "impersonal" workings of market forces; seemingly, individual banks are not controlled. But to use the reserve-ratio approach is to leave this hand completely exposed and, hence, to run greater political risks.

And what of the successive reductions in legal reserve ratios? Assuming that member banks' earnings have (or had) to be increased, this post-Accord trend makes sense. Perhaps, then, it is to be explained by a need to guarantee that member banks do not fare badly in the special position, as subjects of Federal Reserve control, in which they have been placed. No doubt System officials are under continuous pressure to help improve bank earnings; although many years have passed, bankers cannot have forgotten what reserve requirements were during the period 1914–35, before the Banking Act of 1935 was passed and before a wave of special circumstances carried them to much higher levels.

Of course, these explanations of mine may be dead wrong. But if they are, then still before us is the problem of satisfactorily accounting for Federal Reserve preferences and actions.

34 RESTRICTIVE OPEN-MARKET OPERATIONS VERSUS RESERVE REQUIREMENT INCREASES: A REFORMULATION

JOSEPH ASCHHEIM

Some economists have advanced the proposition that open-market operations obviate the need for the other weapons of monetary control. Reform is suggested along two lines: (a) a reversion to the status quo ante 1933, when the reserve ratios were stated in the Federal Reserve Act and not subject to Reserve Board discretion, or (b) a 100 percent required ratio, which would not only remove discretion but eliminate money creation by the commercial banking system. Joseph Aschheim's analysis would seem to support this general approach, because if open-market operations can control money supply no less successfully than can variations in the reserve requirement and are less upsetting to the securities markets, reserve requirement changes would be superfluous. Before accepting this conclusion, however, it would be desirable to increase the complexity of this model—for example, by incorporating the possibility of borrowing reserves, the subject of the next section. See if, after reading that section and having mastered the reluctance versus profitability theories of discounting, you can integrate a borrowing function into the Aschheim analysis. An additional reason for skepticism lies in the generally accepted idea that the achievement of multiple goals requires manifold instruments of control. Voluntary disarmament therefore may hinder the achievement of the full range of monetary targets.

• • •

Throughout the section, the case considered is that of commercial banks being loaned up as the monetary authority seeks to reduce the volume of bank deposits, assumed to be entirely demand deposits, by a given amount. The monetary authority is assumed to be contemplating the choice between a restrictive open-market operation and in increase of cash-reserve requirements as alternative measures for reducing bank deposits by the given amount. It is also assumed that bank assets consist of three types: (a) cash reserves, (b) Government securities, and (c) private loans; where, in liquidity per unit (a) > (b) > (c), while in income per unit (c) > (b) > (a). Furthermore, it is posited that bank income, as well as the moneyness of bank assets, has diminishing marginal utility, and that the two marginal utilities are independent of each other. Finally, it is assumed that bank assets equal demand deposits.

From Joseph Aschheim, "Restrictive Open-Market Operations *Versus* Reserve Requirement Increases: A Reformulation," *Economic Journal*, 73, 258–262. Reprinted by permission.

A. NUMERICAL ILLUSTRATION

Suppose the commercial banking system is subject to a cash-reserve requirement of 10% and that the monetary authority has just reduced demand deposits from 100 to 90 by means of a sale of 1 unit of Government securities in the open market. Balance Sheet 1 reflects the full commercial-bank adjustment to the reduction of deposits under open-market operations.

Balance Sheet 1

Assets		Liabilities	
Reserves	9	Deposits	90
Securities	25		
Loans	56		

By contrast, suppose that the same reduction of demand deposits has just taken place through an increase of reserve requirements from 10.0 to 11.1%, as indicated in Balance Sheet 2.

Balance Sheet 2

Assets		Liabilities	
Reserves	10	Deposits	90
Securities	24		
Loans	56		

Now consider Balance Sheet 2 by comparison to Balance Sheet 1. The ratio of loans to securities is higher in 2 than in 1, consistent with the different "income" effect of the higher reserve requirement. Yet Balance Sheet 2 cannot constitute a final adjustment to the higher reserve requirement, once the liquidity consideration is introduced. The liquidity of asset structure 2 is greater than that of 1. Since the marginal utility of the moneyness of bank assets is lower in 2 than in 1, banks will be induced to shift further from securities to loans than is reflected in 2. This additional shifting constitutes the differential "liquidity" effect of higher reserve requirements. Accordingly, Balance Sheet 2, in which the "liquidity" effect is missing, overstates the volume of securities and understates the volume of loans that banks will have incentive to attain.

Balance Sheet 3 illustrates a full adjustment to both "income" and "liquidity" effects of the higher reserve requirement.

Balance Sheet 3

Assets		Liabilities	
Reserves	10	Deposits	90
Securities	23		
Loans	57		

Comparison of 3 and 2 points to the further security liquidation that constitutes the "liquidity" effect. Comparison of 3 and 1 points to the combined outcome of the "income" and "liquidity" effects, which is a higher volume of loans under increased reserve requirements than under restrictive open-market operations.

B. FORMAL STATEMENT

To analyze formally the joint outcome of the "income" and "liquidity" effects, let us briefly recall what each of two effects implies on the basis of the assumptions spelled out in [A]. The "income" effect implies that the proportion of bank-held securities to banks' earning assets will be smaller after an increase of reserve requirements than after a restrictive open-market operation. The "liquidity" effect implies that the total liquidity of bank assets will be no higher after an increase of reserve requirements than after a restrictive open-market operation of equivalent magnitude.

Now we denote with respect to commercial banks:

D = deposits
o = after restrictive open-market operations
r = after an increase of reserve requirements
C = required cash reserves
S = Government securities
L = private loans
E = earning assets
Z = total liquidity of assets
Z_c = liquidity coefficient of cash
Z_s = liquidity coefficient of securities
Z_l = liquidity coefficient of loans

The definitional and behavioural relationships to be regarded as given can accordingly be set forth as follows:

$$D_o = D_r \quad (1)$$
$$D_o = C_o + S_o + L_o \quad (2)$$
$$D_r = C_r + S_r + L_r \quad (3)$$
$$C_r > C_o \quad (4)$$
$$E_o = S_o + L_o \quad (5)$$
$$E_r = S_r + L_r \quad (6)$$
$$Z_o \geqq Z_r \quad (7)$$
$$Z_o = Z_c C_o + Z_s S_o + Z_l L_o \quad (8)$$
$$Z_r = Z_c C_r + Z_s S_r + Z_l L_r \quad (9)$$
$$Z_c > Z_s > Z_l \quad (10)$$

From (7), (8) and (9) we get:

$$Z_l(L_r - L_o) \leqq -Z_c C_r - Z_s S_r + Z_c C_o + Z_s S_o \quad (11)$$

Therefore,

$$L_r - L_o \leqq -\frac{Z_c}{Z_l}C_r - \frac{Z_s}{Z_l}S_r + \frac{Z_c}{Z_l}C_o + \frac{Z_s}{Z_l}S_o \quad (12)$$

From (2), (3) and (12) we get:

$$L_r - L_o \leqq -\frac{Z_c}{Z_l}C_r - \frac{Z_s}{Z_l}(D_r - C_r - L_r) + \frac{Z_c}{Z_l}C_o + \frac{Z_s}{Z_l}(D_o - C_o - L_o) \quad (13)$$

Hence,

$$L_r - L_o \leqq \frac{Z_c}{Z_l}(C_o - C_r) + \frac{Z_s}{Z_l}(-L_o + L_r - C_o + C_r) \quad (14)$$

Now let: $C_r - C_o = C^*$
$L_r - L_o = L^*$

Accordingly, we rewrite (14):

$$L^* \leqq \frac{Z_c}{Z_l}(-C^*) + \frac{Z_s}{Z_l}(C^* + L^*) \quad (15)$$

Therefore,

$$L^* - \frac{Z_s}{Z_l}L^* \leqq \frac{Z_c}{Z_l}(-C^*) + \frac{Z_s}{Z_l}C^* \quad (16)$$

Hence,

$$L^*\left(\frac{Z_s}{Z_l} - 1\right) \geqq \frac{Z_c}{Z_l}C^* - \frac{Z_s}{Z_l}C^* \quad (17)$$

Therefore,

$$L^* \geqq \frac{C^*\left(\frac{Z_c}{Z_l} - \frac{Z_s}{Z_l}\right)}{\frac{Z_s}{Z_l} - 1} \quad (18)$$

From (4), (10) and (18) we get:

$$L^* > 0 \quad (19)$$

Thus, the joint outcome of the "income" and "liquidity" effects is necessarily a greater *total reduction* in bank loans after a restrictive open-market operation than after an equivalent increase of cash-reserve requirements.

From this outcome it necessarily follows that increases in reserve requirements will put more direct pressure on Government-security yields than will equivalent open-market operations. The proof is this:

We infer from (1) through (4), (5) and (6):

$$E_o > E_r \quad (20)$$

From (5), (6), (19) and (20) we get:

$$S_o > S_r \quad \text{Q.E.D.} \quad (21)$$

Now recalling that $E_o - E_r$ is equal to the amount of securities sold by the monetary authority in the course of restrictive open-market operations, while $S_o - S_r$ is the difference between the amount of securities which commercial banks liquidate under increased reserve requirements and the amount of securities they unload under restrictive open-market operations, we infer from (19), (20) and (21):

$$S_0 - S_r > E_0 - E_r \text{ Q.E.D.} \quad (22)$$

In other words, the total of securities unloaded by commercial banks under an increase of reserve requirements exceeds the sum of central-bank plus commercial-bank sales under an equivalent open-market operation. In brief, restrictive open-market operations have the comparative advantage of limiting the strain of unloading on the Government securities market as a by-product of their comparative advantage in curbing the shifting by commercial banks from securities to loans.

. . .

discounting and the discount rate

Some years ago a leading scholar reviewed the progress of Federal Reserve thought as it found expression in a booklet of the Board of Governors designed for the general public, but quite sophisticated nevertheless. His article compared four editions of *The Federal Reserve System: Purposes and Functions*—those of 1939, 1947, 1954, and 1961.[1] A new edition was published in 1963. The principle of discounting and the role of the discount rate, changing as it did under new and differing conditions, are two of the items traced in his article. In the years following the Great Depression, with member banks borrowing at near-zero levels, Reserve authorities expressed their willingness to lend to members for almost any purpose. In the next edition of *Purposes and Functions,* published in the early postwar years, a period characterized by excessive bank liquidity and the general sterility of restrictive monetary policy, discounting was deemed objectionable. Federal Reserve policy makers stressed that the use of the discount window was a privilege, subject to Reserve Bank discretion, and not a right granted automatically to the member banks at their request. The authorities could, if they so desired, regulate administratively the quantity of discounts. The booklet stressed that accommodation was to be discouraged through appropriate modifications in the discount rate, however. The efforts of the Federal Reserve to hold down discounts and thereby inhibit bank reserve expansion were aided presumably by the reluctance of mem-

---

[1]L. S. Ritter, "Official Central Banking Theory in the United States, 1939–1961: Four Editions of *The Federal Reserve System: Purposes and Functions*," *Journal of Political Economy*, 70, 14–29.

ber banks to remain in debt to the central bank, a reversion to the central banking theory of two decades earlier. More will be said about this reluctance theory later; it is enough to note here that its introduction at this point and its retention since 1947 in the defense of discounting have been most convenient indeed.

The next edition appeared a few years after the famous Treasury-Federal Reserve Accord of 1951, which released the Reserve System from Treasury dominance and from a loose money policy in general. The Federal Reserve stressed the administrative limit on discounting, whereas the influence of the rate was removed from the spotlight. Instead, the rate was found to serve another purpose, one already introduced in the preceding edition—it is a signaling device that informs banking circles in particular and the community at large in general of Federal Reserve policy intentions.

The 1961 and 1963 editions, although they differ somewhat from earlier versions, treat discounting almost identically. Indeed, the section on discounting in the 1963 edition is just about a verbatim copy of the 1961 text. Banks are thought to borrow from the Federal Reserve when discounting is cheaper or more convenient than other alternatives. Emphasis thus is placed, not on the discount rate per se, but on its relationship to other market rates such as the Treasury bill rate or the rate on federal funds. This concept forms the basis for the member-bank borrowings equations in a number of major econometric studies, including the SSRC-Brookings[2] and the Federal Reserve-MIT[3] models. In these studies, however, the relationship between borrowings and the spread between the discount rate and the Treasury bill rate—the variable adopted to represent the host of market alternatives—is presumed to be linear, so that the more market rates exceed the discount rate, the greater is the volume of borrowings at the discount window. This theory implies, then, that banks do not feel constrained in discounting, nor do the Reserve Banks limit borrowings. *Purposes and Functions* accepts neither assumption; banks do feel reluctant to borrow, and the Reserve Banks are free to refuse accommodation. It does seem likely that an upper limit on borrowing exists, as shown by the fact that through 1966 and the early part of 1967 and during more recent periods as well, the federal funds rate exceeded the discount rate. If borrowing reserves from the Federal Reserve is a perfect substitute for borrowing reserves from commercial banks, the former rate ought never to rise above the discount rate.

The announcement effect also finds expression in the newest editions, although its role, when compared with the 1954 edition, is put more modestly. The monetary authorities agree that although "discount rates [are] pivotal rates in the credit market," and a change is "an important indication of the trend of Federal Reserve policy" (1963 edition, p. 45), these statements are not always true. Often discount rate increases will follow market changes, so that the spread between the discount rate and market rates will be maintained. This practice can be interpreted, not as a tightening of monetary policy, but as the prevention of credit ease.

The function of discounting as a source of reserves, the relationship between the cost of borrowing and its profitability, and the announcement effect of discount rate changes are examined carefully by Warren L. Smith in the opening essay in this section. Although he presents both sides of each issue, he is critical of Federal Reserve

[2] J. S. Duesenberry, et al. (eds.), *The Brookings Quarterly Econometric Model of the United States* (Chicago: Rand McNally, 1965), Chap. 13.

[3] F. de Leeuw and E. Gramlich, "The Federal Reserve-MIT Model," *Federal Reserve Bulletin*, January, 1968, pp. 11–40.

discount policy for a number of reasons. First, the Federal Reserve does not vary the discount rate often enough to maintain a constant spread between its lending rate and money market rates. As a result, the profitability of borrowing varies, and despite the fact that the Federal Reserve believes its discount policy to be stable, the changing spread means that its beliefs fall short of its action. Second, the very operation of the discount window permits new reserves to be created, often during a period when open market operations work to reduce bank reserves. Finally, because of the uncertain and possibly perverse announcement effects, discount rate changes may do more harm than good. After reviewing various proposals directed at revising the discount mechanism, Professor Smith votes for a discount rate that is tied to the bill rate and that exceeds it by a given percentage.

Numerous objections can be raised against this suggestion, and many of them can be found in Smith's own essay. To be sure, the tied discount rate would avoid adverse announcement effects and would not lead to borrowing motivated by discount-bill rate differentials. But the escape mechanism criticism of discounting is not voided, because banks can continue to obtain reserves as long as they pay the rate. Moreover, consider the spread between money market rates and bank lending rates. If discounting is not to be limited administratively, profit considerations—based on lending at, say, 9 percent and rediscounting at 6 percent—might encourage continuous and heavy borrowing. An additional point to be made is that discretionary variations in the discount rate are useful in periods of balance-of-payments deficits. An increase in the rate serves to drive home to the international financial community the seriousness with which the monetary authorities view the situation and to proclaim by action that the central bank has actively moved to remedy the deficit. The desirability of such action from the domestic point of view might be questioned, but in the contemporary international financial system (reforms are considered in Part IX), increases in the discount rate combined with austere fiscal policies are expected. A modification of the Smith proposal has been advanced by some economists who would maintain a constant spread between the rates during normal times but would permit occasional variations in the differential. Notwithstanding, one may accept the diagnosis of discount policy advanced by Professor Smith and still reject his remedy. The reader himself will have to decide whether he accepts Smith as his doctor.

The profitability theory, whereby banks use the discount window when it is profitable to do so, is crucial to much of Smith's article, but is accepted only partially by Murray E. Polakoff, the author of the second selection. Although he accepts the theory that banks borrow more as the differential between market yields and the discount rate grows, Polakoff finds a dual constraint—bank tradition against outstanding indebtedness to the central bank and Federal Reserve administrative limits—acting to inhibit continuous borrowing by member banks. The profitability motive is slowly overcome by the reluctance motive. Marshaling his empirical evidence, Professor Polakoff notes that the marginal propensity to borrow *(mpb)* is negatively related to the bill-discount rate spread, a point that conforms with his theory but is at odds with the profitability theory.

The profitability-reluctance debate still goes on. Whether the *mpb* is negative or not is also unclear. One econometric tour de force found the *mpb* to be constant,[4]

---

[4]S. Goldfeld, *Commercial Bank Behavior and Economic Activity* (Amsterdam, The Netherlands: Humanities Press, 1966).

and further studies by both authors in collaboration with others have not as yet led to an agreed-on resolution.

One positive outgrowth of the debate on discounting has been the reevaluation of the discounting process by the Federal Reserve. In 1965 the Board of Governors established a top-level Steering Committee, composed of three Board members and four Reserve Bank Presidents, to review the whole borrowing mechanism and to design and recommend such reforms as were thought appropriate. A summary of the committee's report concludes this section. In essence, the report rejects the notion that the discount function ought to be abolished and disregards the argument that discounting provides a means of escaping the policies imposed through the other control mechanisms. It further rejects the notion of a constant link between the discount rate and some market rate. Finally, the committee opposes reliance on the discount rate to the exclusion of quantitative or administrative limits. On the other hand, the administration of the discount window was found to be uneven, and banks had stated some uncertainty about their chances of accommodation. This condition is to be changed. Moreover, the profitability thesis is accepted implicitly, because the discount rate is to be more closely related to market rates. Accordingly, more frequent changes of the discount rate are anticipated, and a modification is likely to reduce the undesired announcement effects as well. The basic philosophy of discounting, then, is retained, and its usefulness is expected to increase. Again, the Federal Reserve demonstrates a creative response to informed public criticism, but with a significant lag.

35 THE ROLE OF DISCOUNT POLICY

WARREN L. SMITH

Choose any recent period—the last six months will serve handsomely—and check current copies of the monthly *Federal Reserve Bulletin* for market interest rates and the Reserve Bank discount rate during that interval. The most convenient representative of market rates is the 3-month Treasury bill rate on the market yield basis; it may be found on an average monthly basis on the page headed "Interest Rates" in the statistical section of the *Bulletin*. Has the differential between the bill rate and the discount rate remained constant? Do not be surprised to discover that it has not. What, then, are the implications of this varying differential for both the portfolio policies of the individual banks and for monetary policy? Using the *Bulletin* once again, compare the most recent changes in the discount rate with the movement of market rates. Did discount rate changes occur prior to or after modifications in market rates? Is any pattern evident, or do the relative changes appear to be haphazard? What does it all imply?

• • •

A. THE DISCOUNT RATE AS A COST FACTOR

It is possible to distinguish two main facets of Federal Reserve discount policy. In the first place, the discount rate represents the cost of borrowed reserves, and the rate is changed from time to time for the purpose of regulating member bank borrowing. Changes in the rate for this purpose should be co-ordinated as closely as possible with open market operations. In addition, however, the discount rate at times plays an independent role in monetary policy, serving as a signal to the economy of changes in Federal Reserve policy. Let us first consider the discount rate as a regulator of member bank borrowing.

From Warren L. Smith, "The Instruments of General Monetary Control," *National Banking Review* (September 1963), pp. 49–55, 59–68.

1. Cost Versus "Reluctance" as a Regulator of Borrowing

Due to the organization of the banking and financial system in the United States, it has not been feasible to establish the discount rate as a "penalty rate" in the sense in which this has been the case in Britain. There a penalty rate has been possible because the discount houses rather than the banks have customarily done the borrowing from the Bank of England. Since the discount houses have made a practice of carrying quite homogeneous portfolios of commercial bills and, in recent years, Treasury bills, it has been feasible to keep the Bank rate above the yield on such bills, so that when the discount houses are "forced into the bank" (as the phrase goes), they lose money on their borrowings. Traditionally, this penalty rate has served to keep borrowing from the Bank of England to a minimum and to make the interest rate structure highly sensitive to monetary action carried out through the co-ordinated use of open market operations and the discount rate.

In the United States, member banks borrow directly from the Reserve banks, and since there are very many member banks operating in numerous local and regional, as well as national, credit markets and investing in a great variety of earning assets bearing a wide range of yields, it is not feasible to maintain a true penalty rate.

Since the 1920's, it has come to be widely accepted doctrine that use of the System's discount facilities is restrained by a tradition against borrowing on the part of member banks. As evidence in support of this view, which has come to be known as the "reluctance theory," it was pointed out that in the 1920's open market interest rates were more closely related to the amount of outstanding member bank borrowing than they were to the discount rate, suggesting that member banks did not like to be in debt and, when they were, tended to liquidate secondary reserve assets in order to repay their borrowings, thus forcing up open market interest rates.

Although the purposes for which banks borrow—to maintain their reserve positions in the face of customer withdrawals or clearing drains and to meet temporary (e.g., seasonal) increases in their customers' demands for loans—are commonly so pressing as probably to be quite cost-inelastic, it does not follow that member bank borrowing is insensitive to the discount rate. Banks have a choice of obtaining additional funds by borrowing at the Federal Reserve or by liquidating secondary reserves or other investment securities. Given a certain "reluctance to borrow," the major factor influencing the choice will presumably be the relevant cost of funds obtained by the various methods, and this depends chiefly on the relation between the discount rate and the yield on assets that the bank might liquidate. In principle, the relevant comparison is between the discount rate and the expected yield on the asset whose liquidation is being considered over the period of time for which the funds will be needed, taking account of any capital gains or losses that may be involved. For instance, if interest rates are expected to fall during the period, the relevant interest rate for comparison with the discount rate may be higher than the current interest rate on the asset. This factor will be more important the longer the maturity of the asset.

Thus, there is little doubt that commercial banks are "reluctant" to borrow in the sense that borrowing is felt to involve a form of disutility. However, the banks' reluctance can be overcome provided that the profits to be obtained from borrowing (as compared with other means of obtaining reserves) are sufficiently attractive—that is, banks balance the disutility of borrowing against the utility of further profits. Moreover, not all banks are equally reluctant to borrow: this is evidenced by the fact that the Federal Reserve has found it necessary to discourage "continuous borrowing" and to bolster the banks' reluctance in its regulations covering discounts and advances. In addition, the System keeps the borrowing practices of individual member banks under constant surveillance and in this way attempts to reinforce the banks' reluctance to borrow. At the same time, the System apparently does not unequivocally refuse to lend to member banks, despite the fact that it has authority to do so under the Federal Reserve Act.

2. Co-ordination of Open Market Operations and Discount Policy

It used to be said with reference to monetary policy in the 1920's that open market operations served the function of making the discount rate effective. In order to implement a restrictive monetary policy, the Federal Reserve would sell Government securities in the open market; this would put pressure on member bank reserve positions and cause them to increase their borrowings. At this point the discount rate would be raised, and the increase in borrowings was supposed to help to insure that the discount rate increase would be transmitted through into an increase in other interest rates.

In view of the primary role of open market operations under present conditions, it is better to look at the matter the other way around and to say that the discount rate can be used to support and strengthen the effectiveness of open market operations. Thus, when the System, for example, wishes to implement a restrictive policy during a period of inflation, it uses open market operations to keep down the supply of reserves in relation to the swelling demands for credit. As a result, interest rates rise and member banks, finding their reserve positions under increased pressure, tend to increase their borrowings from the Reserve banks. In order to discourage the creation of additional reserves through borrowing, the System can raise the discount rate in pace with the increase of other interest rates. Thus the discount rate can be used to supplement and strengthen open market operations. Conversely, when the System desires to ease credit conditions, it provides additional reserves through open market operations, and in order to discourage member banks from using a portion of the new reserves to repay indebtedness at the Reserve banks, the discount rate can be lowered.

A variant of this reasoning which stresses the reluctance of member banks rather than the discount rate has also been expressed by persons connected with the Federal Reserve System. According to this view, most member bank borrowing arises out of the fact that in a unit banking system such as ours with a very large number of banks, individual banks often find their reserve positions unexpectedly depleted as a result of unfavorable clearing balances associated with redistribution of reserves among the banks. Borrowing is a handy means of making temporary adjustments in reserve positions; if the depletion of a bank's reserve position lasts very long, the bank may later adjust by liquidating secondary reserves, using the proceeds to repay its borrowing at the Reserve bank. The pressure on banks to make prompt adjustments in portfolios in order to repay borrowing depends on the level of the discount rate in relation to other interest rates.

At times when monetary policy is tight and the Federal Reserve is maintaining pressure on bank reserve positions in the interest of limiting excessive growth of bank credit, more banks will be managing their reserve positions closely, reserve deficiencies will occur more frequently, and member bank borrowing will increase. Due to the fact that the banks are reluctant to borrow, the increase in borrowing causes them to adopt more cautious lending policies and to reduce the availability of credit. However, since banks balance the disutility of borrowing against the utility of increased profits, it is necessary to make successive upward adjustments in the discount rate as interest rates rise due to the effects of the restrictive policy, in order to stiffen the banks' reluctance to remain in debt and to encourage them to contract their loans and investments.

It may be noted, however, that short-term open market interest rates are subject to a considerable amount of random variation in the short run and that, under present arrangements, the discount rate is only changed at irregular and rather infrequent intervals. For this reason, the differential between the discount rate and other interest rates varies rather erratically. . . . As a result of the continuously shifting relation between the discount rate and other interest rates, the willingness of banks to borrow presumably undergoes considerable erratic variation.

3. Does Borrowing Reinforce or Offset Open Market Operations?

There has been some discussion as to whether the increase in member bank borrowing that occurs during a period of credit restriction is a factor which intensifies the restrictive effects or a loophole which weakens the effectiveness of monetary policy. It is almost certainly true that, as a result of the reluctance of member banks to borrow, banks tend to follow somewhat more restrictive and cautious policies as far as loans are concerned when they are in debt to the Reserve banks than when they are not in debt. However, the important thing to bear in mind is that if banks were constrained not to borrow when their reserve positions were impaired by a restrictive policy, they would have to adjust their reserve positions in some other way. This would ordinarily mean contraction of loans or investments. Thus, in the absence of borrowing, the adjustment would itself *consist in* restricting credit. On the other hand, to the extent that borrowing occurs, restrictive effects are postponed and banks are merely put in such a position that they are somewhat more likely to restrict credit at some future time. Moreover, it should be noted that borrowing by one member bank for the purpose of adjusting its reserve position adds to the *aggregate* reserves of all member banks and thus indirectly takes some of the pressure off other banks. Adjustment of reserve positions through liquidations of securities, on the other hand, does not add to the reserves of the system of banks.

Thus, it seems clear that the effect of increased member bank borrowing at a time when a restrictive policy is being applied is to offset rather than to reinforce the restrictive policy. The effect may not be very important in itself, since the induced increase in borrowing is not likely to be large enough to pose a serious problem for the authorities; it merely means that a somewhat more restrictive open market policy is required than would otherwise be necessary. However, there are a number of other offsetting reactions in the banking and financial system—such as shifts in the composition of bank portfolios from Government securities to loans, adjustments by financial intermediaries, and so on—and the addition of one more such reaction, even though not quantitatively very large, may not be wholly without significance.

Another point of view that has been expressed concerning the discount mechanism is that, while it has an offsetting effect, this effect is actually helpful to the monetary authorities, because it can be likened to a brake on an automobile. It is said that brakes, by making it possible to control the car more effectively, permit one to drive at a higher rate of speed than would otherwise be possible. Similarly, the discount mechanism, although seeming to weaken monetary controls, actually strengthens them by making it possible to use other controls (chiefly open market operations) more vigorouslv. However, this is not a proper analogy. If the automobile simile is retained, the discount mechanism is more like a defective clutch than a brake, and few would argue that a slipping clutch makes it possible to drive at a higher rate of speed. A brake is a discretionary weapon and not a device that automatically operates more intensively, the harder one pushes on the accelerator.

• • •

B. THE DISCOUNT RATE AS A SIGNAL

Thus far, we have been considering changes in the discount rate as an adjunct to open market operations, the purpose of which is to serve as a partial governor of member bank indebtedness by regulating the cost of obtaining reserves by borrowing as compared with sales of secondary reserves.

To some extent, the discount rate also plays an independent role in monetary policy by serving as a signal of the intentions of the monetary authorities. Particularly at turning points in business conditions, a change in the discount rate is often the first clear indication of a basic alteration in monetary policy. Discount rate changes of this kind are said to have psychological effects or "announcement effects," which may influence business conditions by altering the expectations of businessmen and financial institutions.

1. Difficulties of Interpreting Discount Rate Adjustments

It is commonly taken for granted that the announcement effects of discount rate changes are normally such as to strengthen the impact of monetary policy. However, those who advance the expectations argument have not explained in any detail the way in which the expectational effects are supposed to work. Actually, there are several different possible expectational effects, and in the case of each of them there is some uncertainty concerning even the direction (let alone the magnitude) of the effects.

One of the difficulties is that many changes in the discount rate are merely technical adjustments designed to restore or maintain an appropriate relationship between the discount rate and other rates of interest, as indicated above. Most of the periodic adjustments that are made during periods when interest rates are gradually rising or falling are of this nature. However, the interpretation placed on even these rather routine changes is sometimes unpredictable, because their timing may be affected by various considerations not directly related to stabilization policy. Sometimes, for example, discount rate adjustments may be accelerated in order to get the possible accompanying disruptive effects on the securities markets out of the way before an important Treasury debt management operation is scheduled. Or, on the other hand, action may be postponed until the repercussions of a forthcoming debt management operation are out of the way. Furthermore, the very fact that technical adjustments are sometimes interpreted by the public as having policy implications may affect System decisions concerning the timing of such adjustments. Such factors as these not only tend to make the interpretation of discount rate changes difficult, but are also partly responsible for the System's difficulties, referred to earlier, in adjusting the discount rate frequently enough to maintain a reasonably stable relation between that rate and other interest rates.

Partly as a result of erratic timing and partly due to the fact that the business situation is usually fraught with some uncertainty, discount rate changes that are in fact meant to be merely routine adjustments are sometimes endowed with importance as "straws in the wind" regarding System policy by the press and by students of financial and economic affairs. And sometimes even a *failure* to change the discount rate so as to maintain "normal" interest rate relationships is taken as a sign of a change of System policy. Moreover, it is quite common for different commentators to place different interpretations on System action—or even lack of action—with respect to the discount rate.

The truth is that changes in the discount rate constitute the crudest kind of sign language. Why this Stone Age form of communication should be regarded as superior to ordinary English is really quite difficult to understand. And, in this particular case, the use of such crude signals is subject to a special disadvantage arising from the fact that the signal itself has an objective effect on the situation in addition to serving as a means of communication. That is, changes in the discount rate combine action and communication, and there may be times when it is proper to act and not speak and other times when it is proper to speak and not act.

It is possible that some of the disadvantages of discretionary discount rate changes could be overcome, if the changes that were made were accompanied, at least under some circumstances, by statements explaining the reasons underlying the action. However, a change in the discount rate requires action by the boards of directors of the Federal Reserve banks and approval by the Board of Governors. As a result, a very large number of persons are involved and the reasons for the action may vary among the different participants—some of whom may not thoroughly approve of the action—thus making it difficult to agree upon a generally acceptable accompanying statement. This raises an interesting question: how can the general public and the business community help but be confused in their interpretations of a change in the discount rate when the persons who are responsible for making the change are not themselves entirely clear about the reasons for it?

2. Announcement Effects of Discount Rate Adjustments

In addition to the confusion resulting from the fact that some discount rate adjustments are meant to be signals of a change in monetary policy while others are not, there is a further question whether the resulting announcement effects, even when they are intended, will help to stabilize the economy. Announcement effects work through expectations, and the relationships involved are quite complex. It is possible to break down expectational reactions into reactions of lenders, reactions of borrowers, and reactions of spenders.

a. EXPECTATIONAL EFFECTS ON LENDERS AND BORROWERS. A discount rate change may cause shifts in lenders' supply curves of funds and/or in borrowers' demand curves, the nature of these shifts depending upon the kind of expectations prevailing among lenders and borrowers. If interest rate expectations are elastic, a rise (fall) in present interest rates creates expectations of an even larger proportionate rise (fall) in future interest rates, whereas, with inelastic expectations, a rise (fall) in present interest rates induces the expectation of a smaller proportionate rise (fall) in future interest rates.

Let us take the case of a discount rate increase and suppose that initially it causes a rise in market interest rates. If lenders have elastic expectations, they may reduce their present commitments of funds in order to have more funds available to invest later on, when interest rates are expected to be relatively more favorable. Conversely, if lenders have inelastic expectations, they may increase the amounts of funds they are willing to supply at the present time. Borrowers, on the other hand, may postpone their borrowing if they have inelastic expectations and accelerate it if they have elastic expectations. For a reduction in the discount rate, all of these reactions are reversed.

According to this view, the announcement effects of a discount rate adjustment will be clearly of a stabilizing nature if lenders have elastic expectations and borrowers have inelastic expectations, since in this case an increase in the discount rate will reduce both the demand for and the supply of funds, while a reduction in the discount rate will increase both demand and supply. On the other hand, if lenders have inelastic and borrowers elastic expectations, the effects will be clearly destabilizing, while if both groups have elastic or both have inelastic expectations, the outcome is uncertain and will depend on the relative strengths of the two reactions.

Thus, in order to get favorable reactions on both sides of the market, it is necessary for lenders and borrowers to have the opposite kinds of expectations—a phenomenon that does not seem very likely. However, the significance of all of these considerations is considerably reduced due to the fact that, in practice, their main effects may be confined to producing changes in the interest rate structure. That is, a lender who has elastic interest rate expectations is not very likely to reduce the total supply of funds offered in the market; rather, he is likely to reduce his supply of funds in the longer-term sectors of the market, putting the funds into the short-term sector, while he awaits the expected rise in yields. Or, if he has inelastic expectations, he may shift funds from the short- to the long-term sector. Conversely, a borrower who has elastic expectations may not accelerate his total borrowings, but instead merely increase the proportion of his borrowing in the long-term market. Or, if he has inelastic expectations, he may shift a portion of his borrowings from the long- to the short-term market. With our present limited knowledge concerning the effects of changes in the structure of interest rates on the level of expenditures, it is impossible to judge the effects of such shifts in the supply and demand for funds between the long- and short-term markets. It does seem safe to conclude, however, that the effects would not be very important.

b. EXPECTATIONAL EFFECTS ON SPENDERS. A discount rate adjustment may affect not only interest rate expectations of lenders and borrowers but also the sales and price expectations of businessmen on which spending plans are based. However, it is not entirely clear what the nature of these effects would be or how they would affect economic stability. Taking the case of an increase in the discount rate, two situations (doubtless there are many variants of these) may be distinguished to illustrate the possibilities.

First, if inflationary expectations were already widespread and quite firmly established, if the possibility of restrictive anti-inflationary action by the Federal Reserve had not adequately been taken into account in the formation of these expectations, and if there was widespread confidence that monetary policy was capable of bringing inflation promptly and firmly under control, then a rise in the discount rate heralding the onset of a vigorously anti-inflationary monetary policy might have a bearish effect on sales and price expectations and thereby cause cutbacks and cancellations of expenditure plans. In this case, the announcement effects would be helpful to the authorities.

Second, if the outlook was somewhat uncertain but shifting in an inflationary direction, if observers were aware of the Federal Reserve's concern about the situation and were waiting to see whether the System would act, and if—perhaps on the basis of past experience—it was felt that monetary policy (even though potentially effective) would take considerable time to be brought to bear effectively enough to check the inflation, then a rise in the discount rate might have a bullish effect by confirming the emerging view that the near-term outlook was inflationary. In this case the announcement effects would be destabilizing.

Similar alternative expectational reactions could be postulated in the case of a reduction in the discount rate for the purpose of stimulating business activity. Although it is difficult to generalize concerning such matters and the effects might differ considerably from one situation to another, the second of the possible patterns of reaction outlined above seems, in general, considerably more plausible than the first. That is, it seems likely that the announcement effects of discount rate changes on the expectations of businessmen may frequently be of such a nature as to weaken rather than strengthen the effectiveness of monetary policy. At the same time the actions of the Federal Reserve are only one of the factors—and ordinarily not a major one—on which business expectations are based, and it is therefore doubtful whether the announcement effects of discount rate changes are really very important one way or the other.

We may conclude that the "psychological" effects of discount rate changes on the domestic economy—like all expectational phenomena in economics—are highly uncertain and that the discount rate as a weapon of "psychological warfare" is of very dubious value to the Federal Reserve.

A change in the discount rate has traditionally been used as a "signal" by some countries in an entirely different connection. In time of balance of payments crisis, a sharp increase in the discount rate may be used to communicate to the rest of the world a country's determination to defend by whatever means may be necessary the external value of its currency. Britain has used discount rate changes for this purpose on occasion since World War II, and this was a major reason why Canada abandoned the "floating discount rate" system (discussed below) and raised the rate to 6 percent at the time of the Canadian balance of payments crisis in June 1962. While a long tradition has perhaps made discount rate increases a reasonably effective means of international communication in some situations of this kind, there are surely other equally satisfactory means available; e.g., English, French, Latin, or Zulu.

C. CONCLUSIONS CONCERNING PRESENT DISCOUNT POLICY

The above analysis suggests that the discount rate as presently handled is not a very effective element in Federal Reserve policy. At times when a restrictive policy is applied, the induced increase in member bank borrowing constitutes a minor "leakage" in the controls, since it permits member banks to postpone contraction of their loans and investments and also adds to the total supply of member bank reserves. For the purpose of controlling the amount of borrowing, the Federal Reserve relies on adjustments in the discount rate, together with a tradition against borrowing that prevails among member banks and System surveillance of the borrowing practices of the banks. Due to the fact that open market interest rates fluctuate continuously while the discount rate is changed only at somewhat unpredictable discrete intervals, the relation between the discount rate and open market rates (which largely determines the incentive to borrow) behaves in a very erratic fashion. . . .

Discretionary changes in the discount rate may at times have rather unpredictable effects on the business and financial situation, partly because it is often uncertain whether such changes are meant to be passive adjustments to keep the discount rate in line with other interest rates or whether they represent independent moves to tighten or ease credit. To the extent that changes in the discount rate do influence business conditions directly, they do so chiefly through psychological or "announcement" effects, the nature of which depend upon the kinds of expectations held by lenders, borrowers, and spenders. Although these announcement effects are quite complex and probably not of great importance in most cases, it seems likely that on occasion they may tend to increase economic instability.

D. POSSIBLE REFORMS IN DISCOUNT POLICY

A number of students of monetary affairs have expressed discontent with the present discount policy of the Federal Reserve, although some of them have not made specific suggestions for a change. However, at least three fairly specific proposals for reform have been suggested. Two of these would de-emphasize discount policy—one by getting rid of the discount mechanism entirely and the other by tying the discount rate to market interest rates and thereby eliminating discretionary changes in it. The third would move in the opposite direction by trying to reform the discount mechanism in such a way as to make the discount rate a much more powerful weapon of credit control. We shall discuss each of these proposals in turn.

1. Abolition of the Discount Mechanism

The proposal has been advanced quite forcefully by Professor Milton Friedman that the discount mechanism should be abolished altogether.* Friedman argues that the legitimate function of the central bank is to control the stock of money and that the discount rate is an ineffective instrument for this purpose. Many of his arguments are similar to the ones set forth above. . . .

One difficulty with the complete elimination of discounting is that the discount mechanism serves a useful function as a "safety valve" by which banks are able to make adjustments in their reserve positions and the Federal Reserve is able to come to the aid of the banking system—or individual banks—in case of a liquidity crisis. In order to provide a means for individual banks to make short-run adjustments in their reserve positions, Friedman proposes the establishment of a fixed "fine" to be assessed on reserve deficiencies; the fine to be set high enough to be above likely levels of market interest rates, in order to prevent the device from becoming an indirect form of borrowing from the Federal Reserve. As far as liquidity crises are concerned, he contends that, due to the success of deposit insurance in practically eliminating bank failures, such crises are now scarcely conceivable and that the "lender of last resort" function of the Federal Reserve is now obsolete, so that we need not worry about its elimination. It may be noted that if the discount mechanism were eliminated, it would be possible to use the repurchase agreement technique as a means of providing emergency assistance to the banking system in times of crisis.

2. Tying the Discount Rate to the Treasury Bill Rate

An alternative to the complete abolition of borrowing would be to change the discount rate at frequent intervals in such a way as to maintain an approximately constant relation between it and some open market interest rate, such as the Treasury bill rate. For example, each week as soon as the average rate of interest on Treasury bills at the Monday auction became known, the discount rate could be adjusted so as to preserve a constant differential between the two rates.

Under this arrangement, the discount rate would no longer be a discretionary credit control weapon, and the unpredictable and often perverse announcement effects on the expectations of businessmen and financial institutions would be done away with. To the extent that the Federal Reserve wanted to influence expectations and felt that it could manage such effects so as to contribute to economic stability, it could implement these effects through the issuance of statements concerning its intentions, the economic outlook, and so on. While the present writer is rather dubious about the value of such activities, it is surely true that to the extent that they can contribute anything useful they can be handled better by verbal means than through reliance on such a crude signal as the discount rate.

The major question involved in the adoption of an arrangement for tying the discount rate to the bill rate would be the choice of the proper differential between the two. Obviously, the discount rate should be above the bill rate; beyond this the establishment of the differential is a matter of judgment. The larger the differential, the smaller would be (a) the average amount of borrowing and (b) the swings in borrowing that would occur as credit conditions changed. In view of the wide variations among individual banks with respect to both portfolio composition and expectations, the present writer feels that a fairly large differential of perhaps one percent would be desirable, in order to keep down the amount of borrowing, which, for reasons discussed earlier, represents a minor leakage in monetary controls. But there does

*M. Friedman, *A Program for Monetary Stability* (New York: Fordham University Press, 1960), pp. 35–45—ed.

not seem to be any analytical principle that provides a basis for selecting the proper differential. Doubtless the best procedure would be to experiment with various differentials, retaining each one long enough to observe its effectiveness.

Under this arrangement, in contrast to the complete elimination of discounting, the discount mechanism would continue to be available to serve as a means of making temporary adjustments in bank reserve positions and as a "safety valve" that could be used in times of crises. If this approach were adopted, it would probably be desirable to give up the efforts to rely on such an intangible and unreliable means of controlling discounting as the traditional "reluctance" of member banks and the so-called "surveillance" of the Federal Reserve, recognizing borrowing as a "right" rather than a "privilege" of member banks, and relying entirely on the discount rate (in relation to the bill rate) as a means of controlling it.

A procedure of the kind discussed above was employed in Canada from November, 1956, to June 1962. During this period, the Bank of Canada adjusted its lending rate each week so as to keep it ¼ of 1 percent above the average rate on treasury bills at the most recent weekly auction. The reasons given for adopting such an arrangement in 1956 were similar to those set forth above. The policy was abandoned at the time of the Canadian balance of payment crisis in June 1962, when, as part of a program for dealing with the crisis, the discount rate was raised to 6 percent as a signal to the rest of the world of Canada's determination to defend the external value of the Canadian dollar. The traditional discretionary discount rate policy has been employed in Canada since that time.

3. Increasing the Effectiveness of the Discount Rate

A proposal for reform of the discount mechanism very different from the two discussed above has recently been advanced by Professor James Tobin.[2] Instead of dismantling the discount mechanism entirely or abolishing discretionary changes in the discount rate, Tobin would greatly increase the importance of the rate and turn it into a major weapon of credit control.

The Tobin proposal calls for two changes in present procedures:

1. The Federal Reserve would pay interest at the discount rate on member bank reserve balances in excess of requirements.

2. The prohibitions against payments of interest on demand deposits and the ceilings on the payment of interest on time and savings deposits would be repealed.

These changes would greatly increase the leverage of the discount rate by making it an important consideration for banks that are not in debt to the Federal Reserve as well as for those that are. The opportunity cost to a bank of increasing its loans and investments would be the return it could earn by holding excess reserves, and this cost would be firmly under control of the Federal Reserve. Moreover, the interest rate offered by the banks to holders of idle deposits would presumably be linked rather closely to the rate paid on excess reserves, since the bank could always earn a return on its deposits at least equal to one minus its reserve requirement times the discount rate. Thus, if the Federal Reserve wished to tighten credit, it could raise the discount rate, and this would increase the opportunity cost of lending for all of the member banks (whether they were in debt or not) and would, therefore, make them willing to lend only at higher interest rates than previously, while at the same time causing the banks to raise interest rates on deposits, thereby increas-

[2] James Tobin, "Towards Improving the Efficiency of the Monetary Mechanism," *Review of Economics and Statistics,* XLII (August 1960), pp. 276–279.

ing the attractiveness of bank deposits relative to other assets on the part of the public. The discount rate could be used independently to control credit, or it could be combined with open market operations. It is not clear, however, what principle should govern the division of responsibility between the two weapons.

The proposal is ingenious and would certainly be practical and capable of being put in operation without causing disruption. And it might have the incidental advantage that the payment of interest on excess reserves might encourage more banks to become members of the Federal Reserve System. What is not clear, however, is why a flexible monetary policy could be implemented more effectively by means of the discount rate under this proposal than is now possible by means of open market operations. It is true that the proposal would presumably permit the Federal Reserve to control the cost of bank credit very effectively, but this can already be done—in principle at least—by open market operations. In part, the problems of monetary policy seem to stem from the fact that the demand for bank credit is not very sensitive to changes in interest rates and other monetary variables, so that it has proved to be difficult to operate forcefully enough to produce prompt changes of the degree necessary for effective stabilization. Perhaps it would be possible to bring the forces of monetary policy to bear more rapidly by means of the Tobin proposal, but this is by no means obvious. If the proposal merely provides another way of doing what is already possible, it hardly seems worthwhile.

The repeal of the existing restrictions relating to payment of interest on deposits is in no way dependent upon provision for the payment of interest on excess reserves, and there is much to be said for the repeal of these restrictions, even if the remainder of the Tobin proposal is not adopted.

4. Conclusions

Of the three proposals for reforming the discount mechanism, the present writer feels that the strongest case can be made for the procedures of changing the discount rate each week in such a way as to maintain a constant spread between the discount rate and the Treasury bill rate. This would be a less drastic reform than the complete elimination of discounting, would eliminate the unpredictable effects of discretionary changes in the discount rate, would preserve the discount mechanism as a safety valve, and would eliminate the effects on credit conditions that now result from erratic variations in the relation between the discount rate and open market rates. The Tobin proposal for increasing the potency of the discount rate as a credit-control weapon is worthy of careful study, but it is not yet clear that the proposal would greatly strengthen the hand of the Federal Reserve.

If the present system of making discretionary adjustments in the discount rate at irregular intervals is retained, it would be desirable to reform the administration of the discount mechanism, perhaps by shifting the authority for making changes in the rate from the individual Reserve banks to the Federal Open Market Committee. The purpose of such a change would be to reduce the number of persons involved in decisions regarding the discount rate so that it would be easier to agree on the reasons for making changes. This would facilitate the issuance of explanatory statements at the time changes are made, in order to eliminate the confusion that often results due to the varying interpretations that are frequently placed on rate changes in the absence of explanations. It should then be feasible to make more frequent technical adjustments in the rate with less need to worry about the danger of disruptive effects on the credit situation, thereby permitting closer co-ordination of the discount rate with open market operations.

36 FEDERAL RESERVE DISCOUNT POLICY AND ITS CRITICS

MURRAY E. POLAKOFF

Regulation A, introduced in its present form in February 1955, is the Federal Reserve guideline on discounting. It reads in part, "In considering a request for credit accommodation, each Federal Reserve Bank gives due regard to the purpose of the credit and to its probable effects upon the maintenance of sound credit conditions, both as to the individual institution and *the economy generally*" (italics added). Despite the implication that discrimination will be practiced in the administration of the discount window, thus facilitating borrowing when expansion is desired and restraining it in times of excessive exuberance, Reserve officials have generally denied that their conduct followed this pattern. Murray Polakoff's thesis leads him to suggest eliminating this passivity and to endorse active administrative control over discounts. It does appear that the Federal Reserve has moved in that direction, because at the end of August 1966, a letter concerning discount operations was sent by the Reserve Bank Presidents to their district member banks. The critical portion said:

> Accordingly, this objective [slower rate of expansion of bank loans to business] will be kept in mind by the Federal Reserve Banks in their extension of credit to member banks through the discount window. Member banks will be expected to cooperate in the System's efforts to hold down the rate of business loan expansion . . . and to use the discount facilities of the Reserve Banks in a manner consistent with these efforts. It is recognized that banks adjusting their positions through loan curtailment may at times need a longer period of discount accommodation than would be required for the disposition of securities.

Greater reliance on qualitative regulation rather than on the price mechanism is objected to on general grounds by many economists. Joining them are members of the Joint Economic Committee, who have suggested that there be "minimum opportunity for differences in administration from one borrowing member to another. . . ."* With whom do you agree?

*U.S. Senate, 91st Cong., 1st Sess., Report No. 91-8.

• • •

RULES VERSUS DISCRETION IN DISCOUNT POLICY

While the System had been struggling during the decade of the 1950's for a viable posture related to discounting, academic criticism in the post-Accord period has tended, for the most part, to center around the issue of discretion versus non-discretion in the execution of discount policy. Many of the arguments favoring lack of discretion have ranged, frequently within the same individual, from technical criticisms of current policy to philosophic positions which eschew deliberate

Reprinted with permission from M. E. Polakoff, "Federal Reserve Discount Policy and Its Critics," in *Monetary and Banking Studies*, D. Carson, ed. (Homewood, Ill.: Richard D. Irwin, Inc., 1963), pp. 199–211.

intervention in a market economy coupled with a distrust of those in positions of power. Thus, Professor Simmons has voiced resentment against deliberate use of the discount window through "nonprice rationing to control the amount of lending done by the central bank" and, for the same reason, has stated that the "present discount mechanism seems poorly suited to serve as a monetary control in a market economy."[1] Similarly Professor Friedman has opposed continuance of System administrative action on the grounds that the "exercise of discretion is an undesirable kind of specific credit control that involves detailed intervention into the affairs of individual banks and arbitrary decisions by government officials."* Whatever the specific criticisms of official discount policy, the results have been reflected in a spate of suggestions ranging from advocacy of a nondiscretionary penalty rate to complete abandonment of the discount mechanism.

A leading advocate of a nondiscretionary discount policy is Professor Warren Smith.* While Smith accepts completely Turner's reasoning on the importance of the cost impact of discount rate changes** and, therefore, criticizes official discount policy in the expansion phase 1954–56 for its failure to maintain a penalty rate, he adds a new dimension to the controversy by concentrating on the so-called "announcement effects" accompanying discount rate changes. In so doing, he takes issue with the Fed that the market psychologically interprets discount rate changes in line with System intentions and reacts accordingly. In his opinion, frequent rate changes do tend to be destabilizing on both the supply and demand sides of the market. For example, increases in the discount rate during periods of expansion may misfire inasmuch as instead of supplying a note of caution they may accelerate optimism on the part of businessmen concerning the economic future and so lead to rapidly increasing demands for credit instead of inhibiting investment decisions. More important is the fact that lending institutions which do pay careful attention to System actions may become confused by discount rate changes and so react perversely, since, at times, they may attribute to upward changes a marked tightening of monetary policy, whereas such changes may merely represent technical adjustments to changes in other market rates. At other times, failure to make such adjustments may create expectations of a fundamental change in monetary policy, thereby enhancing credit availability and a decline in long-term rates. The result may be such as to bring forth a flood of capital issues previously kept off the market. On the other hand, a technical readjustment misinterpreted by market lenders as a sign of increasing pressure by the Fed may lead to sharply increasing long-term yields and credit rationing, thereby forcing the System to offset its current policy unwillingly through temporary easing of restrictive open-market operations. Given the failure of System policy to enforce a penalty rate augmented by potentially destabilizing "signal" effects, Smith advocates abandonment of discretionary discount policy and the establishment of a fixed relationship between the discount rate and the Treasury bill rate. The former automatically would be adjusted each week so as to maintain a constant differential of 1 percent or more between it and the auction rate on Treasury bills.

As Smith himself admits, changes in the discount rate are only one, and not a very important kind of information on which business expectations are formed. Furthermore, empirical data for the pe-

[1]Edward C. Simmons, "A Note on the Revival of Federal Reserve Discount Policy," *The Journal of Finance,* Vol. XI, No. 4 (December, 1956), pp. 414, 420.

*See the previous selection—ed.

**R. C. Turner in 1938 proposed the profitability hypothesis of reserve adjustment. See his *Member Bank Borrowing* (Columbus: Ohio State University Press, 1938)—ed.

riod 1955–59 would not tend to support the notion that discount rate changes lead to destabilizing actions on the part of businessmen. Thus, changes in business loans from commercial banks as well as public offerings and private placements of corporate security issues during that period tended to precede, rather than follow, initial changes in the discount rate. Again, there was little correlation between changes in the discount rate and registration of new corporate issues. On the supply side, it is difficult to believe that knowledgeable financial institutions, aware of the fact that changes in discount rates in recent years have followed, rather than led, changes in money market rates would react strongly and perversely to discount rate changes. Also, they necessarily make use of many other indicators in forming and confirming their expectations of prospective economic and financial developments, including other aspects of monetary policy such as the free reserve position of member banks. Finally, fluctuations in long-term rates are much more influenced by other forces than uncertainties associated with the discount rate. At the very least, systematic empirical research should be undertaken as to the likely effects of discount rate changes on the money and capital markets before the expectations argument is made the basis for abandonment of discretionary discount policy.

Quite apart from the validity of the expectations argument, a nondiscretionary penalty rate would prevent the System from altering the relative cost of borrowing at times when changing economic conditions might be such as to make it important to encourage a change in the willingness of member banks to borrow. Furthermore, to the extent that discount rate changes have any adverse psychological effects, deliberate manipulation of the discount rate by the System for the purpose of confounding market expectations would be impossible under a nondiscretionary policy.

An extreme variant of the nondiscretionary approach would go so far as to abolish discounting completely as a credit control weapon. While Professor Friedman is more aware than most of the potentially inhibiting effects on borrowing of System administrative action, nevertheless he opposes its continuance on philosophic grounds as well as on the grounds that it cannot be applied in a sufficiently sensitive manner in the short run so as to produce "predictable" results. So far as official discount rate policy is concerned Friedman, like Smith, agrees that frequent changes in the discount rate tend to be destabilizing in terms of market expectations. However, such changes are necessary if the System is to keep its monetary policy unchanged. This involves the Fed in changing the discount rate as open-market rates change, a purely technical adjustment but nevertheless one which is interpreted by the market as meaning a change in policy. Nowhere does Friedman evaluate the reluctance of banks to borrow as a possible deterrent to the excessive use of the discount window. Given his strictures against discount administration and discount rate policy, he would substitute for present practices a fixed fine "large enough to make it well above likely market rates of interest." Such a fine would be necessary to prevent discrepancies between required and actual reserves from becoming an indirect form of discounting. By setting the fine sufficiently high so that it would be punitive for those individual banks failing to meet their reserve requirements, it would then become the equivalent of a true penalty rate except that no collateral, eligibility requirements, or criteria of appropriate borrowing would be involved.

One of the arguments in favor of retention of the discount facility, whether on a discretionary or nondiscretionary basis, is that it serves as a safety valve for those individual banks temporarily in reserve arrears. Such banks can always obtain reserve accommodation provided they are willing to pay the going rate. Friedman, however, feels that the federal funds market already serves as an effective substitute for discounting. Moreover, other substitutes would become available under the push of profit incentives should rediscounting be discontinued. While there may be considerable merit to these contentions, nevertheless it must be remembered that market imperfections may continue to exist to an even greater degree among such substitutes than through direct access to the discount window. Some of the arguments which can be mustered against criticism of the "safety valve" feature of discounting are as follows: (1) The discount mechanism is particularly well suited to supplying a portion of reserves for seasonal needs and reserve losses and supplying them directly and immediately to the points where they are most needed. This is not true of open-market operations, the sole instrument of credit control which Friedman would have the Fed retain. (2) Given our unit banking system, it is inevitable that during periods of strong inflationary pressure the very mechanics of our check-payment mechanism would be such as to cause sharp swings in the reserve positions of individual banks as payments were accelerated. A punitive fine in place of the borrowing privilege and failure to borrow in other markets and from other banks faced with similar problems might only lead to abrupt curtailment of earning assets by the deficient banks, thereby resulting in disturbing effects in their local communities and in the money and capital markets. (3) It is a fact that frictions do exist in the credit markets. Thus, only a small minority, and those the larger banks in the System, are in a position to avail themselves fully of the federal funds market in order to tap excess reserves lodged elsewhere to meet their temporary reserve deficiencies. On the other hand, discounting serves as a safety valve for *all* member banks faced with an unexpected deficiency in their reserve positions.

IN DEFENSE OF DISCRETION

It is interesting to note that the Fed, as well as its critics, appeared to be agreed on one major issue during the debates of the 1950's: namely, that the spread was a critical variable in explaining member bank borrowing behavior and, further, that should it widen substantially during an expansionary period there would appear to be little or no ceiling to the volume of indebtedness incurred by member banks in the aggregate. Thus, Simmons, Aschheim, Friedman, and Kareken* assume that member bank demand for reserves borrowed from the System is highly or perfectly elastic with respect to market interest rates. Even Smith, who like Turner before him, recognizes a borrowing constraint in the form of the tradition against borrowing as well as the deterrent impact of the policing activities of the System upon bank borrowings, nevertheless fails to *integrate* such constraints with his least cost thesis. What he does is to compartmentalize "need" and "profits" in such a manner that the former is applied only to the goals of bank borrowing, whereas the latter becomes important simply as a means of attaining such ends. This assumed ambivalence in bank borrowing behavior leads him to ignore the reluctance motive when explaining the *extent* to which member banks make use of the discount window. When translated into prescription, it tends to exaggerate the importance of the cost element and to minimize the effects of nonprice constraints in affect-

*Simmons, *op. cit.;* J. A. Aschheim, *Techniques of Monetary Control* (Baltimore, Md.: Johns Hopkins Press, 1961), pp. 83–98; Friedman, *op. cit.;* J. H. Kareken, "Federal Reserve System Discount Policy: An Appraisal," Banca Nazionale del Lavoro, *Quarterly Review,* 12, 103–125 —ed.

ing the amount of discounting so that the only practical alternative appears to be the abandonment of discretion and a fixed penalty rate.

Similarly, the Fed during the 1950's, while continuing to emphasize the importance of the reluctance motive in influencing the course of member bank borrowing, nevertheless appeared convinced that, given increasing spreads during periods of inflationary pressures, the reluctance of banks in general to borrow from it tended to grow weaker relative to increasing profitability. The logic of the argument seemed to imply that unless the discount rate in such periods could be raised often and high enough so as to keep it in line with changes in the bill rate, borrowings would escape from the confines of being a safety valve and merely would become transformed into an engine of inflation. Hence, the inner agonizing within the System during the middle 1950's resulted in revision of Regulation A and the frequent use of discount rate changes. During the expansion phase 1955–57 the discount rate was raised on seven different occasions while it was increased five times during the period 1958–60.

A recent study made by the writer suggests that both the Fed and its critics may have underestimated radically the effectiveness of the reluctance motive and administrative action by the Fed in influencing the actual path of member bank borrowings.[2] Scatter diagrams for the period 1953–58 indicated that the general shapes of the borrowing curves clearly were not those that one would infer from the profitability and Fed hypotheses. Rather they showed either a tendency for borrowing to taper off as the bill rate rose relative to the discount rate or even the possibility of a downturn in the outstanding volume of indebtedness in the face of increasing spreads. Similar results were found for the expansion phase 1954–57. Subsequently, the writer fitted linear and second degree parabolic functions by the method of least squares to the data for 1954–57. Analysis of variance tests were then performed. At the 5 percent level of significance, it was found that a simple linear regression was inappropriate. However, when a second degree function was employed it was found to give an acceptable fit to the data. This tended to confirm the impression of nonlinearity of the borrowings path for 1954–57 found in the scatter diagram.

Figure 1 suggests the borrowings path for the expansion phase 1958–60. For the period as a whole there would appear to be the same tendency for the marginal propensity to borrow to decline as spreads increase followed by an absolute decline in indebtedness after a spread of −.2 is reached. However, the chronological distribution of the monthly averages of daily borrowings during 1958–60 was such as to indicate the possibility of a structural shift between the earlier and later phases of the period. Accordingly, it was broken up into two phases, that of April, 1958–March, 1959, and April, 1959–May, 1960. The data were then plotted in the scatter diagram to be found in Figure 2. They tend to confirm the upward shift in the borrowings curve. At the same time, however, both borrowing slopes appear to be curvilinear rather than linear. The early period shows an absolute downturn in indebtedness beyond a spread of .4. The later period indicates a tapering off of borrowings with a net borrowings ceiling established within a relatively wide range of spread values. The slopes of both curves do not appear to be consistent with either the profitability or Fed hypotheses.

A theoretical explanation which the writer believes is consistent with the empirical slopes of the expansion paths is one which, unlike the least-cost hypothesis, initially assumes *both* reluctance and relative cost to be mutually operative in

[2] "Reluctance Elasticity, Least Cost, and Member-Bank Borrowing: A Suggested Integration," *Journal of Finance,* 15, 1–18. . . .

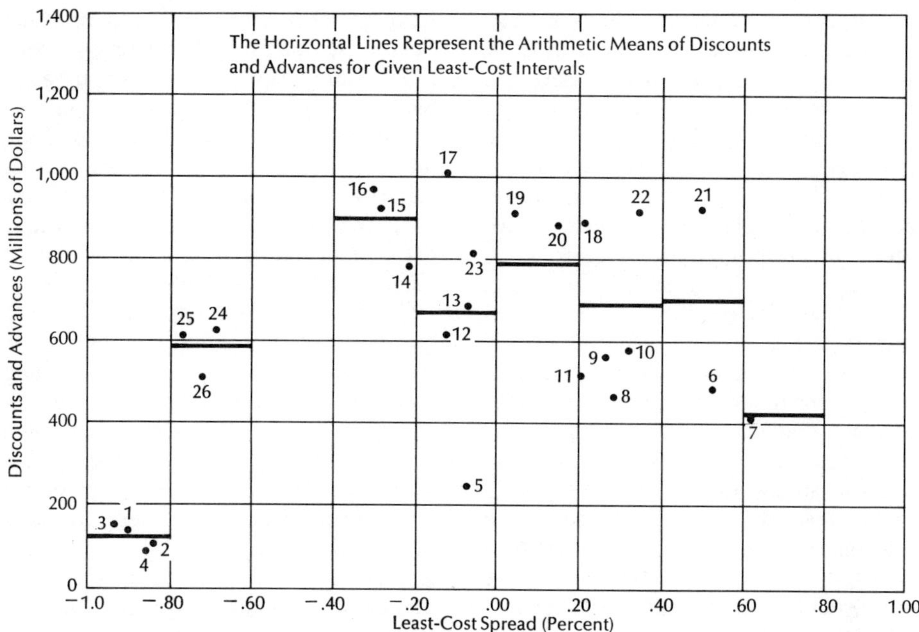

Figure 1 Relation of Member-Bank Borrowings to Least-Cost Spread, April, 1958, Through May, 1960—Monthly Averages of Daily Figures

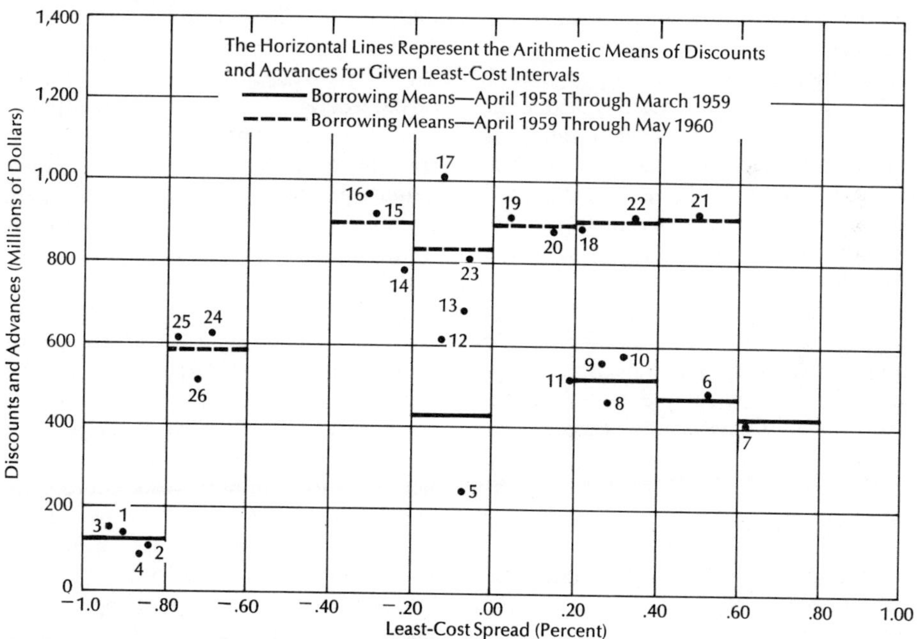

Figure 2 Relation of Member-Bank Borrowings to Least-Cost Spread, April, 1958, Through May, 1960—Monthly Averages of Daily Figures

the adjustment of member bank reserve positions. Given the end or ends of bank borrowing (i.e., need and/or profit), the extent to which they will avail themselves of the discount window rather than the open market in satisfying their desire for such funds depends on the relationship between the degree of reluctance or disutility involved in borrowing from the Fed, on the one hand, and the favorable cost differential or utility between borrowing at the discount rate and the opportunity cost of disposing of Treasury bills, on the other. Moreover, it is further assumed that not only are the banks reluctant to make use of the discount window as an avenue for obtaining additional loanable funds but that such reluctance tends to *increase* (rather than *decrease* as in the Fed analysis) relative to profitability as the differential widens and borrowings grow. Given both assumptions, it then follows logically that the nature of any empirical function depicting the relationship between spread and borrowings for member banks in the aggregate must be one which resembles the reaction curves found in Figures 1 and 2. For example, starting from an initially low level of discounts and advances, as the spread widens and borrowings increase, the degree of reluctance begins to exceed considerations of relative cost. As this occurs, the slope of the curve begins to taper off since the marginal propensity to borrow is declining. Further increases in the spread can only result in a situation where the borrowings curve flattens out completely as the demand for additional funds becomes perfectly inelastic followed perhaps by an absolute decrease in indebtedness as banks proceed to repay a portion of their outstanding liabilities to the System.

Under discount rate changes and open-market operations, administration of the discount window by the System is directed primarily toward avoiding undesirable operating practices on the part of each individual bank rather than toward controlling the overall volume of credit. As a former leading authority within the System has put it: "The stress [in discount administration] . . . is on good banking practices; no attempt is made to orient each borrowing bank's position into the broader aims of current Federal Reserve credit control." In spite of this "banking" approach, the tradition against borrowing implemented by discount administration was sufficient both in 1954–57 and 1958–60 to overcome "profitability" as spreads increased. As a result, an effective borrowings ceiling seems to have been established. Furthermore, unlike the 1952–53 period when quarterly averages of daily indebtedness rose to nearly $1.5 billions in two out of the eight quarters, no quarterly averages of daily borrowings in 1954–57 exceeded $1.0 billions. In fact, throughout the 36 month expansion phase 1954–57, monthly averages of daily borrowings barely exceeded $1.0 billions in four months while the record was even better in 1958–60 when monthly averages of daily indebtedness touched $1.0 billions in only one of 26 months. While part of this may be explained by increasing use of the federal funds market as an alternative to the discount window, it is a reasonable conjecture that much of the better performance in the 1958–60 expansion phase as compared with 1954–57 lies in the increase in the effectiveness of discount administration. While the revised Regulation A set out general borrowing criteria in February, 1955, it must have required some considerable time for the individual Reserve Banks to implement it by working out detailed criteria applicable to their districts and for their member banks to be informed, and thoroughly appreciative of, the limits of borrowing applicable to them. It would seem that the effectiveness of regulation and bank attitudes toward it have changed secularly. That the System currently faces the 1960's with more confidence in its ability to contain excessive borrowing demands with the discount tools now at its disposal may be inferred from one of its recent statements in which, while downgrading the relative importance of spreads, it elevates discount administration to a position roughly comparable with the tradition against borrowing.

Furthermore, should the range of borrowings at different spreads become too wide in the future for System tolerance, it should be possible to counteract it through administration of the discount window in a conscious contracyclical manner. Such a policy offers an alternative approach to "penalty rates" or complete abolition of the discount function and yet retains the many advantages associated with the discount window. It also avoids any of the "adverse expectational" effects posited for frequent discount rate changes. While the precise techniques would have to be studied in some detail, it seems reasonably clear that the System by increasing its degree of moral suasion as borrowings rose could, at the same time, increase the banks' aversion to discounting since such restrictive action would strongly reinforce their own tradition against borrowing. As a result, there would be a downshift in the borrowings path so that at each spread there would take place a smaller volume of borrowings than formerly. While the System appears to feel that it is impractical to use discount administration in an anticyclical manner, this is more in the nature of a pronunciamento than a serious attempt to study the possibilities of such a course of action should it be needed. As has been pointed out in a somewhat different connection, "there is no basis for thinking that nonprice rationing is in principle any less effective than price rationing in curbing unwanted expansions of System credit; . . . what has been wanting in Federal Reserve policy is a lack of will."[3] Certainly the will to innovate must be included along with courage and judgment if one is to justify the use of discretionary monetary policy.

[3]John H. Kareken, "Federal Reserve System Discount Policy: An Appraisal," Banca Nazionale del Lavoro, *Quarterly Review,* 48 (March, 1959), p. 119.

37 REAPPRAISAL OF THE FEDERAL RESERVE DISCOUNT MECHANISM

GEORGE W. MITCHELL

A recent study by Federal Reserve economists, reported in the August 1968 issue of the Federal Reserve Bank of Chicago's *Business Conditions*, sheds some light on the use of the discount window by Seventh District member banks. The 1966 data are most illuminating, because they represent a period of tight credit conditions. Only approximately a quarter of the banks borrowed during 1966. Dividing the banks into the larger reserve city and the smaller country banks shows that although 92 percent of the former were in debt at some time during that year, only 25 percent of the latter made use of the discount window. In terms of volume, the large city banks "usually account for a large part of the total amount borrowed," and "there is little indication . . . that many banks have applied for Federal Reserve loans to cover seasonal requirements. . . ." Keep these points in mind when reading the proposal for discount reform. Who stands to benefit most from these new suggestions?

MR. MITCHELL: Thank you, sir. It is a pleasure to be here and testify before you once again on this day to talk about our report on the proposed changes in lending facilities to member banks.

The studies and research on which the Report is based were undertaken to be sure our lending operations—properly called our discount mechanism—were appropriate to present-day banking institutions and environment. To be more effective in meeting changing community credit needs, commercial banks need central bank assistance as well as supervision. We are pleased to discuss our findings with you.

The redesign suggested by the Report would represent the latest in a whole series of evolutionary changes in Federal Reserve lending policies and procedures. When first established by the Federal Reserve Act in 1913, the discount mechanism was expected to operate by member banks presenting certain types of short-term customer notes—termed "eligible paper"—as collateral for borrowing at the Reserve banks. During most of the first 20 years of Federal Reserve operation, member banks borrowed a sizable proportion of their total required reserves on the security of such customer notes.

After 1934, however, member banks accumulated large amounts of Government securities and other liquid assets; accordingly, they did very little borrowing from their Federal Reserve banks, and collateralized such borrowing as they did with Government securities. This marginal role for the discount window was formally recognized in a change in 1955 in the Board's regulation A covering loans to member banks; under that revision, bank borrowings from the Federal Reserve were to be limited to assistance over the peaks of temporary, seasonal, or emergency needs for funds that exceeded the dimensions that the

From Joint Economic Committee of Congress, *Federal Reserve Discount Mechanism: Hearings*, September 11 and 17, 1968 (Washington, D.C.: U.S. Government Printing Office, 1968), pp. 3–9.

banks could reasonably be expected to meet out of their own resources.

In the last decade or so, however, credit demands on banks have grown and loan-to-deposit ratios are much higher, rising from 47 percent to 60 percent. Moreover, at many banks portfolio management has pared liquidity positions substantially, and borrowings from sources other than the Federal Reserve have expanded enormously. In addition, a small but growing number of banks has also been led to withdraw from membership in the Federal Reserve System, chiefly in order to avoid reserve requirements and thus enable them to invest a greater portion of their resources in earning assets. In view of these developments, the proposed redesign of the discount mechanism is aimed at relating Federal Reserve lending more clearly and closely to the changing banking and community needs.

Before I outline the new proposals which have been made for our lending facilities, it might be well for me to mention three longstanding basic principles of Federal Reserve lending that were reaffirmed by our study.

First among these is that Federal Reserve credit is extended primarily to accommodate bank asset and liability adjustments over limited time periods and to meet essentially short-term fluctuations in member bank needs for funds.

In short, no continuous borrowing.

The second principle reaffirmed, however, is that Federal Reserve banks always stand ready to lend to any of their member banks caught in special regional or local adversities—such as droughts, drastic deposit drains, or other emergencies—for as long as reasonably needed for the bank to work out of these circumstances.

Thirdly, the Report recognizes that the Federal Reserve serves as "lender of last resort" to buttress the entire financial system in the event of widespread emergency. Within the limits of existing law, and lending primarily through member banks as intermediaries, the Federal Reserve is prepared to supply liquid funds to other types of financial institutions when such assistance is not available elsewhere and is necessary to avoid major economic disruption.

Along with these continuing principles, the Report suggests several modifications of lending operations to better serve emerging needs. Let me summarize the main new suggestions briefly, and then outline each one in somewhat greater detail.

To provide more clear-cut access to Federal Reserve lending facilities, the Report proposes that each soundly operated member bank be given a "basic borrowing privilege," enabling it to borrow up to a specified limit from its Reserve bank upon request in as much as half of its weekly reserve periods.

In addition, it is proposed that any member bank foreseeing large seasonal bulges in its needs for funds would be able to arrange for loans from its Reserve bank to meet such needs in excess of a specified minimum. This arrangement, more explicit and more liberal than currently provided, is termed the "seasonal borrowing privilege."

Member banks experiencing drains of funds that are not of a seasonal or emergency nature, but that are bigger or longer in duration than can be accommodated under the new "basic borrowing privilege," could also arrange for additional credit pending an expected and timely reversal of their fund outflows or an orderly adjustment of their assets and liabilities. Such borrowings would be subject to essentially the same kinds of administrative procedures now applied to similar situations.

A final innovation proposed by the Report is to make the discount rate—the interest rate charged by Federal Reserve banks on their loans to member banks—more flexible than heretofore. It is recommended in the Report that the discount rate be changed considerably more frequently and by smaller amounts, keeping it reasonably closely in line with the movements in other money market rates.

Turning now to some of the major features of these recommendations, the most commonly used of the new lending provisions for member banks in sound condition would undoubtedly be the basic borrowing privilege. The size of each bank's basic borrowing privilege would be established as a proportion of some base drawn from the bank's balance sheet; the current proposal suggests capital stock and surplus. Required reserves could also be used.

Frequency of use of the basic borrowing privilege would also be limited. This is necessary because Federal Reserve credit is not properly a long-term or permanent addition to the loanable funds of individual member banks. The aim is to make credit available over a long enough period to cushion the bulk of short-term fluctuations or portfolio adjustments and in most cases permit orderly adjustment to longer term movements of funds.

The proposed frequency limitation would allow assured and virtually automatic access to credit so long as the bank is indebted in no more than half the reserve periods in the specified interval.

Before the plan is finally made effective, choices will be made in the light of comments received as to the particular percentages which would apply to the amount and frequency limitations. The controlling considerations will be that individual credit access should not be so small or so infrequently available as to be insignificant to the member banks, nor should total access be so liberal as to interfere with Federal Reserve open-market operations aimed at carrying out national credit policy objectives.

Borrowing within the basic borrowing privilege limitations could, as noted, take place virtually upon request, unless the Reserve bank had notified the member bank that its overall condition was unsatisfactory as determined by such factors as adequacy of capital, liquidity, soundness, management, or noncompliance with law or regulation and that such unsatisfactory condition was not being corrected to the Reserve bank's satisfaction. The only other circumscription on the actions of a qualified borrowing bank would be the avoidance of net sales in the Federal funds market during the reserve periods in which it was borrowing from the Federal Reserve. This administrative rule, already in force, is retained in the new proposal in the interest of precluding retailing operations in Federal Reserve credit obtained through the discount window.

It is recognized that the basic borrowing privilege as I have been describing it would not be large enough to encompass every member bank's needs for funds in all instances that justify the use of discount credit. This is particularly true in cases of the larger banks which borrow infrequently but for rather large amounts, but it is also true in cases of smaller banks faced with sharp temporary drains of funds. Arrangements are therefore recognized as necessary to permit member bank borrowings outside the basic borrowing privilege up to the limits of appropriate needs on as convenient and understandable terms as possible. These arrangements, referred to in the Report as "other adjustment credit," would be available pending an expected and timely reversal of fund outflows or an orderly portfolio adjustment. Such borrowings would be subject to essentially the same kinds of administrative procedures and surveillance now applied to similar situations, with the precise timing and nature of administrative actions determined as at present by the circumstances surrounding individual cases. Close contact among the Federal Reserve Board staff and the Federal Reserve banks' discount officials will be maintained in the interest of dealing uniformly with similar cases.

The third general category of credit which would be available to member banks at the proposed discount window is called the "seasonal borrowing privilege." A Reserve bank would be prepared to establish such a seasonal borrowing privilege for any member bank experiencing demonstrable seasonal pressures persisting for a period of at least 4 consecutive weeks and probably longer, and exceeding a minimum relative size. It is expected that this borrowing privilege would be of value principally to smaller unit banks in agricultural or resort areas in which seasonal swings have a substantial impact on the entire community and where access to the national money markets or other adjustment resources is not always readily available.

The existence of seasonal pressures would be judged on the basis of past years' patterns of loan and deposit fluctuations. The establishment of a qualifying seasonal swing in net availability of funds—defined as deposits minus loans to customers in the bank's market area—would ordinarily be fixed by negotiation once a year. Once the existence of a qualifying seasonal need was established, the reserve banks would agree to extend discount credit up to the qualifying amount and for the length of time the need was expected to persist, up to 90 days. The 90-day maximum is imposed by statute; however, should the need extend over a longer period than this, the reserve banks would regard renewals of credit as in accordance with the initial seasonal credit negotiation. Seasonal credit needs would normally be expected to last for several months, but in exceptional cases could range up to as much as 9 months, we believe.

Seasonal credit obtainable at a reserve bank would be limited to the amount of the borrowing bank's seasonal swing in excess of a specified percentage of its average deposits in the preceding year. This "deductible" principle, requiring a bank to meet a part of its seasonal needs out of its own resources, is designed to encourage individual bank maintenance of some minimum level of liquidity for purposes of flexibility. It would also serve effectively to limit the aggregate amount of credit extended under the seasonal borrowing privilege to an amount consistent with overall monetary policy, while allowing the Federal Reserve to provide this assistance to all those member banks with relatively large seasonal needs.

The proposed redesign of the discount window would provide that the Federal Reserve continue to supply liberal help to its member banks in emergency situations. So long as the member bank is solvent and steps are being taken to find a solution to its problems, credit would be available on the same basis as it currently is, and, within the limits of the law, special and flexible arrangements would continue to be made where necessary. Assisting a bank in an emergency situation would generally require credit extension for periods longer than would normally be allowed at the window, but this would be expected and regarded as appropriate.

The Federal Reserve, in its role as lender of last resort to other sectors of the economy, may find it necessary to extend credit assistance to institutions other than member banks. This action would be taken only when other sources of credit have been exhausted and failure of the troubled institutions would have a significant impact on the economy's financial structure. When lending to nonmembers, the Federal Reserve would act in cooperation with the relevant supervisory authority to insure that steps are taken to find a solution to their problems. The Federal Reserve Act authorizes direct advances to nonmembers, but only if collateralized by U.S. Government securities. Since most nonmember institutions of the types apt to require emergency credit assistance do not have sizable holdings of this asset, credit would normally be extended through a conduit arrangement with a member bank. Most types of nonbank financial institutions have borrowing relationships with their commercial banks as a matter of course and, ideally, this indirect lending by the Federal Reserve could fit in with such business practice. Such credit would be provided at a higher rate than the basic discount rate.

The proposed discount window does not include the provision of intermediate- or long-term credit to meet the needs of banks servicing credit-deficit areas or sectors—that is, areas or sectors where the opportunities for profitable investment continuously outstrip the savings generated locally. While this is recognized as a problem of some significance, it was concluded that its solution lies outside the proper scope of the discount window. The steering committee concluded that an appropriate and effective solution to this problem was most likely to be found in the improvement of secondary markets for bank assets and liabilities. Detailed studies of the feasibility of actions to promote such improvement are expected to begin in the near future.

I should emphasize that Federal Reserve open-market operations are still envisioned as the main tool of monetary policy. The proposed changes in discount operations, however, would alter to some degree the current relationship between these two methods of reserve injection, with the discount mechanism assuming a somewhat increased role. This would come about as a result of the accommodation of more of the day-to-day fluctuations of reserve needs at the window, the improved distribution of reserves brought about by injection of some reserves directly at the point of need, and more flexible and effective use of the discount rate as an influence on bank borrowing. The first and second of these benefits would entail a generally higher level of borrowing being done by a typically rotating group of member banks. But this is not conceived to mean a corresponding increase in total reserves or a loss of control in this area, since the Federal Reserve would retain the ability to bring about and maintain the desired level of overall credit availability, taking into account the relatively small increase expected in credit outstanding at the window, through purchases and sales of securities in the open market.

To simplify my oral remarks this morning, I have avoided citing specific numbers, technical conditions, or underlying statistical evidence associated with the proposed changes in the discount mechanism. For your convenience, I have summarized these details in ... Table [1]. ... If you have any questions about such matters, I will be glad to answer them either now or in subsequent correspondence.

Let me emphasize that all these details are provisional at this stage, and subject to review and modification in the light of our study of the comments and reactions received. The proposal at this stage represents a report of a Federal Reserve committee. The Board of Governors has not yet taken any substantive action on the proposals contained in the Report nor published any change in its Regulation A which governs borrowing. We have already received a good many comments on the Report from a variety of sources, including both bankers and banking organizations and others. We have had assistance from the reactions and suggestions of numerous academic scholars; several leading economists have contributed analytical papers on one question or another related to the discounting area; and the Board has scheduled two different seminars with a number of professors of economics at which ideas on this subject could be profitably exchanged.

I can assure you that the views expressed in these hearings also will be taken into account by the Board.

As we now see it, the shape of the proposal under consideration can be encompassed within the framework of existing legislation. It may be, however, that certain aspects of the studies and of comments received might make it desirable for the Board to request some amendments in the language of certain govern-

Table 1. Summary of Proposal for Redesign of Discount Mechanism

	Basic Borrowing Privilege (1)	*Other Adjustment Credit* (2)	*Seasonal Borrowing Privilege* (3)	*Emergency Credit to Member Banks* (4)	*Emergency Credit to Others* (5)
Definition	Member bank access to credit upon request, within precisely stated limits on amounts and frequency and on specified conditions.	Supplemental discount accommodation, subject to administrative procedures, to help a member bank meet temporary needs that prove either larger or longer in duration than could be covered by its basic borrowing privilege.	Member bank access to credit on a longer-term and, to the extent possible, prearranged basis to meet demonstrable seasonal pressures exceeding minimum duration and relative amount.	Credit extended to member banks in unusual or exigent circumstances.	Credit extended to institutions other than member banks in emergency circumstances in fulfilling role as lender of last resort of the economy.
Rate	Discount rate	Discount rate	Discount rate	Discount rate	Significant penalty above discount rate.
Quantity limitations	(20 to 40) percent of 1st $1,000,000 capital stock and surplus plus (10 to 20) percent of next $9,000,000 plus (10) percent of remainder.	None specified	Seasonal needs in excess of (5 to 10) percent of average deposits subject to reserve requirements in preceding calendar year.	None specified	None specified
Frequency or duration limitations	(6 to 13) of any (13 to 26) consecutive reserve computation periods.		Need and arrangement must be for more than 4 weeks. Maximum 9 consecutive months.		
Administrative procedures	None other than general discouragement of net selling of Federal funds by borrowing banks.	Appraisal and, where necessary, action broadly similar to procedures developed under existing discount arrangements.	Prearrangement involves discussion between discount officer and bank management concerning amount, duration, and seasonality of need. Administrative review maintained during borrowing to prevent abuse or misuse.	Continuous and thoroughgoing surveillance. Require that bank develop and pursue workable program for alleviating difficulties.	Continuous and thoroughgoing surveillance (may have to be through conduit). Require that institution develop and pursue workable program for alleviating difficulties.
Other restrictions	Must not have been found to be in unsatisfactory condition.	None specified	None specified	None specified	Required to use all other practicable sources of credit first.
Method of provision	Direct	Direct	Direct	Direct	(1) Through central agency; (2) direct; (3) conduit through member bank.

ing statutes in order to permit the revised discount mechanism to be as effective as possible. As you know, the Federal Reserve has already proposed a bill—S. 966—popularly termed the "eligible paper" bill—which would make certain changes in the provisions of the Federal Reserve Act relating specifically to lending to member banks. It would seem likely that most, if not all, of the changes suggested by our studies could be encompassed by the language in that bill. Of course, neither the eventual changes which might be made in the mechanism nor any resultant need for legislation can be finally settled at this stage, but at a somewhat later date we may need to address a communication to the Congress regarding the pending, or possibly additional, amendments to the statute.

All of us involved in this reappraisal recognize that, even after any of the suggested changes were introduced, a period of transition would undoubtedly be required before the full potential of the discount mechanism could be realized either by the Federal Reserve or the member banks. However, I believe that there is a good possibility that this redesign can bring this mechanism in closer touch with the prevailing economic climate and lead to a more effectively functioning banking system that is better equipped to serve evolving needs of the community.

PART SEVEN

problems of monetary policy

lags

Although static theory dismisses the time dimension from its analytic framework, economic dynamics is concerned not only with the equilibrium values of a model but also with the time path by which that equilibrium is achieved. The student of economics is introduced to an elementary form of dynamics early in the game when he learns the theory of the money multiplier: A change in reserves is followed through a series of stages and ends when some related variation in money supply has resulted (see, for example, Selection 9). The real world obviously is more closely approximated by dynamic analysis, and it is with practical matters that the monetary authorities are most immediately concerned. Thus a model that proves that central bank sales of securities on the open market will cause money supply to fall but fails to state how soon this decrease will occur—in one week, one quarter, one year, or even longer—is interesting but operationally valueless. This section deals with the time dimension of monetary actions and focuses on the critical question, How soon do monetary actions become effective? In the jargon of economists, this is the problem of the lag. Related to this issue is another—How long does it take the monetary authorities to act? This, too, involves a lag.

The lag issue can be handled most easily when subdivided into three interrelated yet somewhat distinct categories. The first deals with the length of the lag, the second with its variability, and the third with its distribution.

Measuring length requires defining a beginning and an end. An obvious statement, to be sure, and yet critical nonetheless. There is a substantial degree of unanimity concerning the conceptual dating of the initial period; either it is reckoned as the date when, by hindsight, a policy change was called for or, alternatively, when policy was implemented in fact. The former definition is pertinent to the discretion versus rule controversy (the second question asked in the previous paragraph and the subject of Part VIII); the latter is relevant for testing the effectiveness of a given policy and for predicting the outcome of a contemplated move. The criterion for terminating the lag also is agreed on—when the desired effect has been obtained. Unfortunately, there is little unanimity concerning the practical (as opposed to conceptual) method of defining initial and terminal dates. This subject is dealt with extensively in this Part. Because this issue is discussed later, attention will be focused on a different point here—the fact that not all lags are of equal length.

Lags are not uniform. Some are long, others are short, and still others range in the twilight zone. Length, then, must be defined as the average of all measured lags. Now, depending on whether the average length is short or long, the work of the central bank is made easier or harder. A short (say, 3-month) lag is likely to pose few problems for the monetary authorities; it can be ignored for all practical purposes. This conclusion is invalid, however, in the case of a lag of a year; from the initial date until the time the policy was judged effective 12 months have come and gone. Economic conditions probably will not be identical over a span of that magnitude; they may have changed quite drastically. Thus the policy called for a year previously is not the one desired today. Moreover, it would be presumptuous to claim that our present knowledge of forecasting yields accurate predictions of economic activity, so that even a long average lag poses no difficulty. The selections in the first section deal almost exclusively with the controversy over length, and it is again appropriate to avoid further discussion at this point but to return to it a bit later on.

The question of variability is no less critical or controversial, and only space limitations preclude adding a few selections on this important topic. Variability can be measured in many ways, but in essence it stands for the fact mentioned before, that lags are not of uniform duration. The average removes variation (as all summary measures do), and although its usefulness is not to be disparaged, the average obviously must sacrifice some information in order to provide the simplicity that is its key characteristic. With respect to the lag, a long average duration poses difficulties, as has been shown previously—but so does a short average lag if that average is associated with a marked degree of variability. Take, for example, a 5-month average lag, derived from three episodes: two 1-month lags and one 3-month lag. The monetary authorities may be pleased with the relatively rapid-acting effect of their policies as indicated by the 5-month lag. This satisfaction, however, is of an intellectual nature and is useful for public relations purposes; it does not effectively aid them in their policy-making tasks. But if the central bankers lack reasonable confidence in the outcome of their decisions—will these decisions become effective next month or in more than a year from now?—their ability to implement a sagacious policy is severely constrained and indeed may be an impossible task. Perhaps an analogy may prove helpful. Imagine you are driving a car with a faulty accelerator, so that depressing it firmly speeds the vehicle up by 20 mph on the average, but that sometimes acceleration is only 5 mph and at other times 35 mph. When you need that sudden burst of speed, knowledge of the 20 mph average is not at all consoling, and you should be less than confident that this time you will obtain the average acceleration. You may get it, of course—you may even reach the maximum possible, but chances are just as good that your speed will move upward by 5 mph. Contrast this episode with another where the decision is based on an average acceleration of 20 mph and a variability of ±1 mph. Then the average indeed is a sufficient indicator of the chances of success in almost all instances.

Because variability depends on the definition of the lag, the dating of the initial and terminal periods is critical here no less than in determining the average, and the debate on length is obviously applicable to variability too. Milton Friedman, using his methodology, concludes in an article, a portion of which is reproduced as the first selection in this Part, that an outside estimate of variability is 6 to 7 months, but admits considerable lack of confidence in this estimate. He refuses to concede, however, a small degree of variability such as less than one month. Thomas Mayer, again in an unreproduced portion of the article excerpted below, agrees with the tentative nature of Professor Friedman's findings but is less than certain of the improbability of a lag of near-uniform duration. He concludes with an agnostic viewpoint: "at present, there is no convincing evidence either way."

The third issue centers around the concept of a distributed lag. Any policy is likely to be cumulative, becoming more or less effective or perhaps becoming more and then less powerful as time passes by. This tendency is true of monetary policy no less than it is of other governmental or even private policies.

A new product—for example, felt-tipped pens—is likely to yield only few sales when first introduced; the public needs time to adjust to the new item. But then, if the item catches public attention, sales move rapidly upward until eventually the market is saturated and significant new sales become increasingly more difficult to achieve. Similarly, textbooks—the book you are reading—must successfully penetrate the market, and this procedure takes time; but as the text attains recognition, its sales move rapidly upward. Then, as the used textbook market thrives, new sales decrease. So, too, must there be a path by which monetary policy, now initiated through open market transactions, discount rate modifications, reserve requirement changes, or even just admonitions by central bankers, proceeds to exert its influence on economic activity. Whether it takes the form of a major impact at the beginning that falls off over time, as seems unlikely, or the reverse, a gradually increasing impact, as appears more plausible, or a rising and then falling pattern, as Professor Friedman suggests (see p. 297), and as seems sensible indeed, the fact is that we do not know which of these time paths, if any, is most appropriate. Notwithstanding Friedman's willingness to disregard this issue, the monetary authorities ignore it at their peril. A short average lag with a small variance and a diminuendo pattern would make monetary policy rapid-acting and leave negligible aftereffects. But a crescendo pattern may cause difficulties later on, because after the initial reason for the policy disappears, the policy itself continues to be felt. On the other hand, even a long average lag might not prove to be a critical stricture against managed money if the distribution is such that a substantial part of the effect is felt soon. Unfortunately, the current state of our knowledge in this area is one of almost total ignorance, and any conclusion is surely premature.

Length, variability, and distribution—all are elements in the crucial issue of lags, and all are either at the center of debate or shrouded in a proverbial London fog. As mentioned earlier, the present section is most concerned with the question of length. We turn now to that problem.

The total lag in policy can be divided into inside and outside lags, the lags preceding the implementation of a conscious policy decision and those succeeding it. The combined inside and outside lags are most relevant to the rules-versus-discretion debate discussed in the next Part, whereas the outside lag alone is appropriate when judging the time required for a given policy to become effective.

Subsumed under the inside lag are the recognition lag and the action lag. The former refers to the elapsed time between the actual need for implementing a policy change and the awareness of that need by the authorities. This lag is primarily a result of the time needed to gather and interpret information; for postwar monetary policy, the duration of this lag has been estimated by Mark H. Willes to be from 3 to 4 months.[1]

How quickly do the authorities react by modifying or reversing policy once the desirability of so doing is apparent? Perhaps the contrast between lags in monetary and fiscal policy is most noticeable here. Major fiscal actions require Congressional approval, which, as the year-and-a-half delay in passage of the 1968 tax surcharge amply demonstrated, can be difficult to obtain quickly. The flexibility of monetary policy, working through a consensus of less than a score of men and formally even fewer, is clearly evident. Dr. Willes calculated the monetary policy action lag to be zero and at times negative, as actions were taken in advance of cyclical turning points.[2] Thus, according to Dr. Willes' calculations, the inside lag ranges from 0–3 months.

The outside lag begins at the terminal point of the inside lag or when the new policy is initiated and continues to the terminal date of the total lag. The outside lag of monetary policy is divided by Professor Mayer into a credit market lag and an output lag.[3] The former refers to the period between the policy change and its influence on the credit market, in terms of modifications in the attitudes and actions of borrowers and lenders. Some scholars place this lag within 2 months, but this estimate is rejected as too low by others. The output lag occurs from the terminal point of the credit market lag to the time that the effect is ultimately felt, that is, output changes. Estimates here range widely, from 3 months to more than 1½ years. Totaling these various sublags leads to a range of from 4 months to approximately 2 years, a diversity of view that is certainly not consoling to the seeker of simple answers.

Professor Friedman is among those who stress the presence of long lags, and his most elaborate defense is included in this Part. Central to his position and to the lag controversy is his method of measuring the lag: The initial point of the lag is a peak or trough in the rate of change of money supply, and the terminal point is a business cycle peak or trough. His justifications are set out at considerable length here, because his detractors have rejected the validity of his measurement process. One member of the opposition is John M. Culbertson, who finds fault with both the initial and terminal dating procedure and states his conviction that the lag is of short duration. John H. Kareken and Robert M. Solow similarly object to Friedman's methodology; the excerpt that follows is from their major study of lags in monetary policy, and its

---

[1]M. H. Willes, "The Inside Lags of Monetary Policy: 1952–1960," *Journal of Finance*, 22, 591–593.

[2]The negative lag should not be taken to imply that the Federal Reserve predicted well. Rather, it is a consequence of acting for reasons unrelated to the cycle and that fortuitously led to the proper anticyclical move.

[3]T. Mayer, "The Inflexibility of Monetary Policy," *Review of Economics and Statistics*, 40, 358–374.

lucidity minimizes the need for editorial comment. The length of their study precludes reprinting here; however, a number of their conclusions appear in the fourth selection. A word about the Kareken-Solow methodology is relevant; although the negative task of demolition is performed in the third selection, a complete job requires the construction of a substitute framework. Kareken and Solow choose to decompose the lag into its component parts—action, recognition, and so on—and calculate the duration of each time interval. Not only are the lags distinguished, but individual calculations are performed for distinct economic sectors separately. These authors therefore eschew reliance on a single indicator to date the start and end; they believe that diversity can be more informative. Other points to note are that (1) money supply plays no direct role in the Kareken-Solow analysis; (2) regression analysis and a distributed lag method are used; and (3) the terminal date is not a turning point of the cycle but a change in production of one of the sectors. Thus, although Friedman is concerned with the outside lag and Kareken and Solow are concerned with the total lag, this difference is the least important one; the dispute is far more basic and therefore more significant.

Thomas Mayer and his cavalry gallop to the rescue of the beleaguered Friedman camp. In a critique of the Kareken-Solow study, Mayer demonstrates that his two fellow economists have not learned to add. However, to save the attackers, it is sufficient to point out once again that controversies in economics are not resolved so easily. The fact that Kareken and Solow work with a distributed lag means that monetary policy can be compared to a time capsule that releases its medication not all at once but over an interval. Professor Mayer takes as his cut-off point the interval in which 50 percent of the effect is felt, but this is merely an arbitrary decision; a lower cut-off point would have resulted in a correspondingly shorter lag estimate.

In the final selection, a defense of the short average lag is proposed. Logic, not econometrics, is the tool of Donald P. Tucker, and his conclusions will stand or fall on the validity of his assumptions. But given the facts that the banking market is not a perfectly competitive market and that price leadership and administered pricing work against rapid price reactions to changing market conditions, the assumption of an interest rate lag seems appropriate indeed. Thus, the pervasive conclusion of a long lag for monetary policy (see the last sentence of Professor Mayer's article) appears less than unanimous.

Two general points will bring this introduction to a conclusion. The first has to do with econometric testing of the lag and is somewhat appropriate to econometric testing in its entirety. Econometric models are based on historic data and, among other uses, attempt to measure the specific impact of individual variables. This method substitutes for the controlled experiment of the physical scientist; no one will permit the economic experimenter to monkey around with the economy or segments of it, contracting this part and encouraging that, in order to observe what will transpire. Consequently, he must rely on what has happened and interpret the past as best he can. Not surprising, then, is the fact, evident to all by now, that conclusive answers are not derived from econometric model building. Just as theorists can and do differ regarding what is plausible, so econometricians, even those who agree on the basic theoretical structure, can come to contrary interpretations of the historical experience.

Moreover, because only historical data can be subjected to testing, the question of what would have happened if a different course had been pursued is a moot one. And yet this is just what we wish to know. In the specific example of the lag, can any of the methods for measuring the lag answer the question of what would have happened to income or to the cyclical turning point if monetary policy had been different? To be sure, Professor Friedman and others have suggested that increasing the money supply by a constant percentage would have proved more successful, and if this policy will not eliminate the lag, it will avoid the instability that is its consequence. Without going into detail at this point (the task is fulfilled in Part VIII), it is enough to point out that this hypothesis is only speculation and has yet to be documented. Moreover, monetary actions are not the only causes of changes in economic activity, and thus the measured lag may reflect the overriding impact of some other variable.

Historical analysis has another weakness when it comes to measuring the outside lag. This weakness is the fallacy of computing the outside lag without considering the strength of the policy. It seems plausible to assume that a stronger policy, one that presses down harder on the banking community and other financial institutions, works not only more intensively but quicker, too. Past policies, the basis for the econometric work, can tell us no more than that for the strengths used heretofore—and the policy mixes used previously—the lag was such and such. A future-oriented policy maker may study the record, but he would be unwise to conclude that because the record of the past was spotty, the future must be no better. In short, econometrics as an aid should be used with care.

The second point to be made has to do with the efficacy of monetary policy even if we grant the supposition of a long lag. Not infrequently the economy is hanging in balance, uncertain whether to proceed on the same path or whether to reverse direction. A little nudge may do the trick, and a policy tool that can supply that impetus can prove most valuable. All agree that monetary policy does begin to work quickly; the average may be long, but no one denies the immediacy of some effect. The inside lag of monetary policy is short and, once implemented, brings some results soon. It is just the right tool for these delicate moments, immeasurably better than a do-nothing attitude. Confirmation of this attitude may be obtained from the published results of the Federal Reserve-MIT model. A simulation showed that a $1 billion increase in unborrowed reserves, which would take three years to push up GNP by more than $11 billion, would increase GNP by approximately $1 billion in one quarter.[4]

Take your choice now—short lag or long? An impediment to policy or an evil that can be lived with? Come to a conclusion after reading the following selections; your opinion on the rules-versus-discretion controversy in Part VIII hinges heavily on your interpretation here.

---

[4]F. de Leeuw and E. Gramlich, "The Federal Reserve-MIT Econometric Model," *Federal Reserve Bulletin*, January 1968, 11–40. This model has been criticized as improperly specifying relationships in a manner likely to overstate the lag by W. H. White in "The Timeliness of the Effects of Monetary Policy: The New Evidence from Econometric Models," Banca Nazionale del Lavoro, *Quarterly Review*, 86, 276–303.

38 THE LAG IN EFFECT OF MONETARY POLICY

MILTON FRIEDMAN

Quantity theorist Friedman has been at the center of the storm on many issues, presenting audacious theories and proofs and startling his fellow professionals with his iconoclastic views. Despite this fact or perhaps because of it, Professor Friedman has managed to gain a wide degree of popular support among the general public and economists too. The lag controversy is no exception; Friedman has called attention to this important issue and has written about it extensively. The following excerpt is from an article that represents his most complete statement on the topic. The editor has taken the privilege of omitting the theoretical framework that explains why the Chicago economist anticipates the lag to be long. The explanation, which is based on the neoquantity theory and its complex adjustment process, has already been made available (see Selection 28).

For some years now, I have been engaged in extensive empirical studies of the relation between the stock of money and economic activity. Though a full report on this work is not yet in print, and will not be for some time, I have had occasion to summarize some of the results in a paper submitted to the Joint Economic Committee, in subsequent testimony before that committee, and in a series of lectures on monetary policy. These necessarily condensed and preliminary statements of results without the full evidence underlying them have apparently given some readers a misleading impression of the exact content of the findings and of the kind and strength of the empirical evidence underlying them. I therefore welcome the opportunity offered by J. M. Culbertson's recent thoughtful criticism of my views in this *Journal* to clarify some of these issues.*

The central empirical finding in dispute is my conclusion that monetary actions affect economic conditions only after a lag that is both long and variable. Culbertson infers that the maior evidence leading me to this conclusion is the timing of peaks and troughs in the rate of change of the stock of money relative to peaks and troughs in general business. He regards this evidence as faulty on three grounds:

1. It refers to the rate of change in the stock of money and not its level.
2. It relates turning points in one series to turning points in business rather than to "the point at which things begin to go differently than they would have in the absence of the action."
3. It "implies that monetary change has been an exogenous variable and that causation runs only from monetary change to economic developments. In fact . . . causation also has run in the other direction."

As counterevidence, Culbertson argues that:

From Milton Friedman, "The Lag in Effect of Monetary Policy," *Journal of Political Economy,* 67, 447–449, 451–461. Reprinted by permission.

*J. M. Culbertson, "Friedman on the Lag in Effect of Monetary Policy," *Journal of Political Economy,* 68, 617–621—ed.

4. "The surprising moderateness of the economic fluctuations that we have suffered in the past decade" is direct testimony against a long and variable lag, since such a lag in the effects of policy actions would imply a similar lag in the "natural stabilizing forces."

His own conclusion is that:

5. "The broad record of experience . . . support[s] the view that anticyclical monetary, debt-management, and fiscal adjustments can be counted on to have their predominant direct effects within three to six months, soon enough that if they are undertaken moderately early in a cyclical phase they will not be destabilizing."

On policy issues Culbertson makes two main points:

6. Even if the lag were long and variable, this fact would not by itself determine appropriate stabilization policy. It would imply that "policies should not attempt to be actively anticyclical but should behave in a manner that is cyclically neutral. However . . . there would be considerable disagreement as to what constitutes "neutrality" in this connection."
7. He finds me "guilty of an inconsistency in reaffirming in connection with . . . the lag doctrine the automatic system [I] prescribed earlier for stabilization policy."

I shall consider first the questions of fact and then, more briefly, the policy issues.

The empirical conclusion that Culbertson questions consists of three separable parts, each important in its own right. The conclusion is that changes in the behavior of the stock of money (A) exert an important independent influence on the subsequent course of events with a lag that is (B) on the average sizable and (C) highly variable, relative to the usual length of cyclical movements.

It is important to distinguish these three parts for two reasons. First, the evidence for them is very different. For example, the items in Culbertson's critique I have numbered 1 and 2 refer primarily to Part B and have little or no relevance to either A or C; item 4 refers primarily to C. Second, their relevance to policy is also very different. Part A is a precondition for any effective monetary policy, and Culbertson clearly accepts it despite item 3. Given A, either B or C alone would suffice to cast serious doubt on the effectiveness of discretionary monetary policy. Suppose the mean lag were zero or the 4.5 months implied in Culbertson's item 5. If the lag were highly variable, this would still mean that monetary actions in large measure introduce a random disturbing element into economic affairs. On the other hand, suppose the standard deviation of the lag were the 0.9 months or less implied in Culbertson's item 5, but the mean lag were, say, 12 months. This would mean that effective monetary action requires an ability to forecast a year ahead, not an easy requirement in the present state of our knowledge.*

• • •

THE LENGTH OF THE LAG

Culbertson apparently takes it as self-evident that timing comparisons between peaks and troughs in the rate of change of the money stock and in general business are "misleading," and that the relevant comparison is between the rate of change of the money stock and the rate of change of general business or between the level of the money stock and general business. It has become a commonplace of economics as a result of discussion of the acceleration principle that the rate of change of a smooth cyclical series will tend to move in the same direction as the series itself roughly one-quarter of a cycle earlier. . . . Hence, says Culbertson, "on a more [*sic*] proper basis of comparison the 'lag' might largely disappear."

• • •

---

*The excerpts that follow deal only with Part B of the original article. The full article also considers in details Parts A and C—ed.

Four main points require attention: (a) The general considerations bearing on the comparisons that are likely to be the most meaningful are of three kinds: dimensional, statistical, and economic. These can at most be suggestive. For what they are worth, however, they suggest that comparison of the rate of change in the stock of money with the level of business is likely to be more meaningful for cyclical analysis than either of the comparisons Culbertson and others prefer. (b) Any single comparison by itself may not be sufficient for either scientific description or policy guidance. "The" lag is a sophisticated and complex concept. (c) We have in fact made a number of different comparisons, and recent experience has provided a particularly striking quasi-experiment, all of which are consistent with a long lag in the effect of monetary actions. (d) Consideration of the channels through which monetary policy may be expected to operate renders a long lag highly plausible.

A. Dimensional, Statistical, and Economic Considerations

We must beware of semantic traps. Because we speak of the "level" of business and also the "level" of the stock of money, it does not follow that these are necessarily comparable magnitudes. By the "level of business" we generally refer to a flow: the number of dollars of expenditures per year; man-hours of employment or unemployment per year; cars produced per year—all magnitudes having the dimensions of dollars or physical units *per unit of time.* The "level" of the stock of money refers to an amount at a point in time, to a stock not a flow. Its dimensions are simply dollars, not dollars per unit of time. The rate of change of the stock of money, on the other hand, does have the dimensions of dollars per unit of time and therefore has the same dimensions as the so-called level of business.

It may help to make the same point in terms of economic categories. Investment in inventories, which is a component of national income, is the derivative (or rate of change) of the stock of inventories; net investment in residential construction is the derivative of the stock of houses; and so on. Indeed, every item in the flow of income can be regarded as the derivative of a corresponding stock, though no doubt it is forcing matters to treat in this way such items as the rental value to the owner-occupant of the services of the land he occupies. From this point of view, the stock of money is comparable to the stock of housing or to the stock of durable goods, in short, to wealth rather than to income. The imputed value of the services rendered by the stock of money is comparable to such income items as the rental value of land; the rate of change of the stock of money is comparable to such items as residential construction, production of durable consumer goods, net investment in inventories, and so on. Similarly, the rate of change of business is a second derivative of a stock comparable dimensionally not to the rate of change of money stock but to the second derivative of the money stock.

These dimensional considerations are suggestive, but they are not the primary grounds on which one should determine what comparisons are most meaningful. The crucial question is not arithmetic but substantive: What relations are empirically stable and dependable? What form of expressing variables yields the simplest and most easily handled relations? For example, the quantity equation in its income form relates money as a stock to income as a flow, the dimensional difference being allowed for by velocity, which has the units of the reciprocal of time. If velocity were a numerical constant over the cycle, either for contemporaneous money and income or for the variables separated by a fairly fixed time difference, or even if velocity were a highly regular function of a few variables, the quantity equation might be the most useful relation over the cycle—as indeed we have found it to be for longer secular movements. But even then, of course, *if* the rate of change of the stock of money were a good predictor of the movements in money, it would by that same token be a good predictor of movements in income. The consistency of the relation would offer a challenge to theory and an opportunity to policy, but, to repeat a point already made, the timing relations would not by themselves be decisive about the direction of influence.

We have accordingly placed heavier reliance on statistical and economic considerations than on purely dimensional ones.

The chief statistical consideration is the problem of allowing for trend. The availability of National Bureau of Economic Research reference cycle dates gives a general-purpose timing scale that obviates the necessity of choosing any single series as an index of that elusive concept "general business." The reference chronology can be used to explore the timing relation between another series and general business by estimating for that other series a set of dates to be regarded as comparable to reference cycle peaks and troughs. This is a fairly crude technique for estimating timing relations —I take it that this is the gravamen of item 2 in Culbertson's critique—and should preferably be supplemented by other techniques as we have in fact done to a limited extent (see below, Sec. C). But it is one of the few techniques currently available in anything like tested form; it is the only technique for which there is a large stock of comparable results for other series; and, by rendering it unnecessary to choose a particular series to represent general business, it not only saves much labor but, more important, permits comparable observations over a much longer period.

The technique is reasonably straightforward for a series that shows clearly marked ups and downs roughly comparable in duration to reference cycle phases. Consider, however, series like the total stock of housing or the total stock of money, which generally rise during both expansions and contractions in general business. This fact does not mean that either series is unrelated to the cycle, whether as cause or effect. But it does mean that the cyclical behavior of the series cannot be described in terms simply of ups and downs; and equally that the occasional turning points in either series are inadequate indicators of their cyclical timing.

The obvious statistical solution is to separate the cyclical behavior of such series from their secular behavior by allowing in one way or another for trend. The two most common ways of doing so are either to express the data in terms of deviations from a trend or to use first differences. The use of first differences, where it is applicable, has great advantages over the fitting of trends. True, first differences have the disadvantage of often yielding a rather erratic, choppy series with serial correlation of successive items. But they require no decision about the kind of trend to fit or the period to cover, the observations for any one period do not depend on the far distant observations for other periods that affect fitted trends, and the series can be extended backward or forward without either recomputing or extrapolating trends. It so happens that first differences of the logarithms of the stock of money (that is, percentage rates of change) display no significant trend. Hence statistical considerations on the whole recommend this device for describing the cyclical behavior of the money series.

Economic considerations reinforce the statistical, in respect both to the desirability of allowing for trend and to doing so by using percentage rates of change. A trend in the stock of money, almost whatever it might be, is unlikely to give rise to cyclical fluctuations if it is widely and correctly anticipated. Deviations from the expected longer period movement in the stock of money seem far more relevant for cyclical fluctuations than the stock of money itself. At the same time, there is no reason to expect a single long-time trend to prevail of the kind that one might approximate or extrapolate by curve-fitting. Throughout the period we have studied, the stock of money in the United States has been subject to control by political authorities, either by alteration of the monetary arrangements, or, more recently, by continuous discretionary control. Any trend is therefore a creation of the authorities. Nothing outside the political sphere prevents a shift from one trend to another or produces a return to an earlier trend after a departure, though, of course, both the effects of given monetary arrangements and the actions taken by discretionary authorities will be conditioned, if not determined, by contemporaneous and past economic developments. Hence, we must allow for a trend that can shift drastically from time to time. The use of first differences does so.

Still another set of economic considerations recommends the logarithmic first difference of the stock of money (percentage rate of change) as the relevant magnitude for cyclical analysis. Consider a hypothetical long-run moving equilibrium in which both output and the stock of money are rising at constant percentage rates, the rise being fully anticipated so that actual, expected, and desired stocks of money are equal. The result would tend to be a roughly constant percentage rate of change in prices, which might of course be zero or negative. The percentage rate of change in prices itself is the opportunity cost of holding money rather than goods, so a constant percentage rate of change in the stock of money corresponds to a constant opportunity cost of holding money rather than goods. An unanticipated change in the rate of change of the stock of money would then produce a deviation of the actual from the desired stock of money for two reasons: initially, it would make the actual stock deviate from the expected stock and therefore from the desired stock; subsequently, by altering the cost of holding money, it would change the desired stock itself. These discrepancies will set up adjustments that may very well be cyclical, involving overshooting and reversal. It is therefore theoretically appealing to regard the "normal" or secular monetary base around which cyclical fluctuations occur as described by a constant percentage rate of change in the stock of money and to regard changes in the percentage rate of change as the feature of monetary behavior that contributes to the generation of cycles.

B. The Meaning of "the" Lag

The selection of one or another feature of monetary behavior as most important for cyclical change does not settle the question how best to describe the cyclical timing relation between money and business. Strictly speaking, there is no such thing as *the* lag in the effect of monetary action. Suppose the effect on, say, national income of a single instantaneous monetary change could be isolated in full from the surrounding matrix. The effect would no doubt be found to begin immediately, rise to a crescendo, then decline gradually, and not disappear fully for an indefinite time. There is a distributed lag. When we refer to *the* lag, we mean something like the weighted average interval between the action and its effects; and when we refer to an "average" lag, we mean the average of such weighted averages for several episodes. And even this description is oversimplified. The effects may change sign after a time, the original effects setting up forces that tend to produce not merely a reversal but an overshooting, as, for example, when the feedback effects of business on money are in the opposite direction from the initial effects of money on business. Fortunately, perhaps, this connection is likely to be submerged by another: monetary changes are never single and instantaneous. They consist rather of a time sequence of changes, the effects rather of which accumulate, and which are themselves in part the accumulated effect of other changes in the economy rather than in any sense strictly autonomous. The concept of "lag" therefore becomes still more complex, referring to the timing relation between the resulting monetary series and a resulting series of effects. In principle, identification of the effects would require the determination of what national income, say, would have been in the absence of whatever changes in money are regarded as autonomous. Even then, a full description of timing relations might require an indefinitely large number of dimensions.

In practice, we evade the explicit isolation of the effects of autonomous monetary changes by the usual device of relying on the averaging out of the effects of other changes, which is to say, we take the average relation between the actual changes in money and in income as an estimate of the relation to be expected between an autonomous change in money and the resultant change in income. In practice, also, the problem of description is simplified because the observed time series on the money stock and on national income each has its own internal consistency and persistence, expressible statistically by its serial correlation function or its frequency spectrum. It is a fact that peaks in the rate of change of the stock of money tend to precede peaks in the deviation between the money stock and a smooth secular trend and these, in turn, tend to precede such peaks as occur in the money stock itself; it is a fact also that troughs in the rate of change of the money stock tend to precede troughs in the deviation from trend and these, in turn, tend to follow such troughs in the money stock as occur. No one of these characteristics alone is a full description of the money series, any more than one feature in a face is a full portrait. But also the regularities in the series may mean that a few such characteristics suffice to give an adequate description, just as the few lines of a sketch may convey an unmistakable likeness. Similar comments hold for national income or any other series intended to portray fluctuations in economic activity. Finally, while a full description of the interrelations between two series would require showing the links among all their features, the regularities in each may render a much more condensed description sufficient. It is simultaneously true that peaks in the rate of change of the money stock precede reference cycle peaks by sixteen months (on the average); that peaks in the deviation of the money stock from its trend do so by five months; that such absolute peaks as occur in the money stock precede reference cycle peaks by less than five months and may even lag; that peaks in the rate of change of income precede such peaks as occur in the stock of money; that they probably also precede peaks in the deviation of the money stock from its trend; that they probably follow peaks in the rate of change of money. I have not made detailed calculations for any but the first two items but those plus what we know about trends in money and income clearly imply the others. And note that there is no inconsistency between the view that changes in income are a consequence of monetary changes and the inclusion in this list of some comparisons in which the monetary feature follows rather than precedes the income feature.

What is true for description is true also for policy. If my conclusions about the independence and importance of money change are valid—conclusions not themselves based primarily on observed timing relations—then monetary policy actions that produce a peak in the rate of change of the stock of money can be expected on the average to be followed by a peak in general business some sixteen months later partly because these same actions and their consequences will also produce a peak in the deviation of the money stock from its trend some eleven months later. The timing of the peak in the rate of change is not a full description of the behavior of the money stock; or of the effects of monetary policy on the money stock; it is rather one summary measure of that behavior and of those effects that has been found to have a consistent relation with the subsequent course of business. Presumably, one reason for this consistent relation is because this feature of monetary behavior is consistently linked with other features, and one reason for variability in the relation is because these links are not rigid.

C. The Empirical Evidence

We have, in fact, made two sets of timing comparisons. In addition, experience has recently provided a most interesting bit of evidence.

1. The basic set of timing comparisons were made in connection with the National Bureau of Economic Research study on which I am collaborating with Anna J. Schwartz. It consists of two different timing comparisons.

a) One is the comparison to which Culbertson refers and the only one I have so far published, namely, between peaks and troughs in the percentage rate of change of the money stock and peaks and troughs in general business as dated by the National Bureau reference chronology. On the average of eighteen nonwar cycles since 1870, peaks in the rate of change of the stock of money precede reference peaks by sixteen months and troughs in the rate of change of the stock of money precede reference troughs by twelve months.

. . .

b) Because of the difficulty of dating peaks and troughs in so choppy and erratic a series as the rate of change of the stock of money, we have also made timing comparisons on a different basis. The rate of change series often seems to shift abruptly from one level to another. This suggests approximating it by a step function consisting of alternating high and low steps. We call the date at which the high step ends, the "step" peak, and the date at which the low step ends, the "step" trough. This procedure is equivalent to approximating the stock-of-money series itself by a series of connected semilogarithmic straight line segments. The dates of the kinks where two straight line segments meet are the step dates. For a series which can be fitted reasonably well in this way, it is perhaps intuitively obvious that the step dates approximate the dates at which deviations from a trend fitted to the stock of money reach their peaks and troughs. The step method, however, has the great advantage of requiring no fitting of trends.

The step dates necessarily come later than the dates of the turning points in the rate of change, since the date that marks the shift from a "high" rate of change to a "low" rate of change necessarily comes later than the date that marks the shift from a "rising" rate of change to a "falling" rate of change. Yet even so, the step dates on the average precede the reference dates by five months at peaks and four months at troughs.

. . .

2. Another set of timing comparisons are available as a by-product of a study by David Meiselman and me made for a different purpose, namely, to compare the relative stability of the investment multiplier and monetary velocity in the United States since 1896.* For the period before World War II our data are mostly annual and hence not very useful for the analysis of timing. For the period since World War II, we have computed from quarterly data correlations between the stock of money and consumption and the stock of money and income and various transformations of these variables, for various leads and lags. The results supplement the preceding findings

---

*See Part V, Selection 29—ed.

because they are based on correlations of time series rather than on a comparison of turning points. They are less significant because they are for a much shorter period of time and at that, one greatly affected in the earlier years by the heritage from the war, and because they do not sharply isolate cyclical movements from secular movements. On the whole, as we shall see, the results tend to confirm the preceding findings, so questions of the relative weight to be attached to the two sets are of no great practical importance.

a) The correlations that are most nearly comparable with the timing comparison 1(a) are between quarter-to-quarter percentage changes in the money stock and the percentage deviations of income and consumption from a trend. For 1948 through 1958, the correlations are highest when the rate of change of money is correlated with consumption or income three or four quarters later and decline smoothly as the lead is either shortened or lengthened. The correlation coefficients, though moderate in size, are clearly larger than could be expected from chance. The implied lead of nine to twelve months is somewhat shorter than the lead of twelve to sixteen months found in 1(a), but the difference is almost surely within the range to be expected from sampling fluctuations, so these results are highly consistent with those obtained from a comparison of timing points for a much longer period.

b) There is more of a choice in obtaining correlations comparable to the timing comparison 1(b) and the results are less clear cut. (i) Correlation of the stock of money with consumption or income, all in their original form, gives little if any information relevant to cyclical timing, since all three series are dominated by a sharp upward trend. The correlations are very high and remain high for widely varying leads or lags as is to be expected if the correlation is essentially between two trends. (ii) An alternative is to correlate percentage deviations of money from a trend with corresponding percentage deviations for consumption and income. Partly because of the difficulty of fitting a single satisfactory trend to the money stock, the correlations are extremely low for all timing relations. They are highest when money is correlated with consumption or income in the same quarter but even then are not higher than the value that would plausibly be attributed to chance alone. (iii) Another alternative is to correlate first differences of the stock of money with first differences of income or consumption. This is apparently the comparison Culbertson prefers. . . . These correlations too are not very satisfactory. For the postwar period as a whole (third quarter 1945 through 1958), they are rather low for money and consumption, but their highest value is statistically significant and is reached when money is correlated with consumption one quarter later; however, for money and income, the correlations are negative for all leads and lags. For the shorter period from 1948 through 1958, positive correlations are obtained for both consumption and income, though all are very low. The highest correlation is for money and consumption one quarter later and for money and income, two quarters later. If we neglect the puzzling negative correlations, these results show a lead for money of three to six months, which is highly consistent with the lead of four to five months found in 1(b).

• • •

39 THE LAG IN EFFECT OF MONETARY POLICY: REPLY

JOHN M. CULBERTSON

Although the method of estimating the delay involved in monetary policy actions suggested in John M. Culbertson's critique of Milton Friedman's position would lead to a shorter lag, Professor Culbertson himself might be overestimating the lag. The basis for this supposition lies in the fact that monetary variables alone are only one of a group of influences on economic activity and the further fact that actual changes in GNP or business conditions reflect the combined actions of all variables, monetary and nonmonetary alike. Thus economic activity may move in a direction opposite to that expected by a given monetary policy decision or more slowly than anticipated, not because of the monetary action but despite it. That being the case, the appropriate terminal date for measuring the impact of a monetary decision is the change in the output of a critical sector, such as the government-financed sector of the residential construction industry or the state and municipal investment market. Activity in these sensitive sectors is certain to vary prior to variations in output in less-sensitive areas and business conditions in general. The main contention of Professor Culbertson will be strengthened all the more by including this consideration.

Now that Friedman has revealed what lies behind his assertion that monetary policy operates with a long and variable lag, which he has used in supporting his monetary policy proposals, we can attempt a more definitive appraisal. The implications of the lag doctrine are extremely important for policy-planning, and although Friedman still does not face up to this they affect the whole body of existing theory and our view of how a market economy is governed.

Since Friedman's attack does not overturn the points that I made in my note, let me develop them and weigh Friedman's response, dealing with defects in Friedman's methodology. . . .

From John M. Culbertson, "The Lag in Effect of Monetary Policy: Reply," *Journal of Political Economy*, 69, 467–471. Reprinted by permission.

FRIEDMAN'S METHODOLOGICAL ERRORS

The required methodology is governed by the purpose of the analysis, which is here a quite definite one. We wish to determine, in general, under unspecified future conditions, what time interval can be expected to elapse between a monetary policy action and those proximate effects upon income that are the effective tool of stabilization policy. That is to say, we are seeking to estimate a causal relation, a relation that will hold in the future even though in many respects the future may be different from the past, and a relation of indicated direction, with causation running from our controlled or instrumental variable to the one that we seek to influence. When we have specified a causal relation and precisely defined what within the terms of the problem must be identified as the cause and the effect, we have defined the lag in effect, for it is the time interval between cause and effect.

The basic methodological criticisms of Friedman's argument can be summarized in two points: (1) Friedman's technique in inferring a causal lag from past data is fallacious in not adequately allowing for the role of causal relations other than the desired one. (2) Even apart from this, the arbitrary technique used to time the beginning and end points of the "lag" is erroneous as applied to the "lag" relevant to policy planning. Since the second point, although a simple one, decisively affects Friedman's lag measurement, let us consider it first, assuming for the time being that past income changes *are solely the result of exogenous money changes* and the only problem is measurement of the lag in effect. How, then, should the lag be measured?

Friedman's critics seem generally to have objected to his basing the lag estimate on a comparison of the inflection points in the *rate of change in money supply* with those in *absolute level of economic activity.* The grounds were that this introduces a spurious lag, since this criterion would find a "lag"—running in whichever direction suited the investigator—between two perfectly congruent series. The obvious comparisons that, whether or not valid on other grounds, at least avoid this bias, are those between, for example, either absolute peaks for both money and income or peak rates of increase for both money and income.

I suggested that the "lag" as measured in this second way would be much shorter. Friedman now gives us data that disclose just how completely his conclusions depend upon his peculiar measurement of the lag. If he compares, for example, the absolute peaks in the two series, his much-emphasized sixteen-month average lag shrinks down to a five-month lag! Probably a five-month "lag" is not far from what most students would have estimated and is in the range of the three to six month estimate of the lag (in my sense) that I hazarded as the basis for policy-planning best supported by present evidence. One possible reaction, then, is that this controversy is much ado about nothing. Put obscure methodological points aside, make one common-sense adjustment in Friedman's measurement to eliminate an obvious bias, and his findings no longer call for any surprise, nor for any revolution in government policy. Perhaps this is the most effective way to dispose of the policy-related aspect of the lag controversy.

But since Friedman concedes nothing to his critics on this crucial point, let us see what he offers in defense of his basis of comparison:

(1) He gives a discussion of "dimensional considerations," following which he conservatively concludes that these are only "suggestive," and "the crucial question is not arithmetic but substantive."

(2) Then, anent his "statistical considerations," he goes on to ask: "What relations are empirically stable and dependable? *What form of expressing variables yields the simplest and most easily handled relations?*" And he notes that, "The chief statistical consideration is the problem of allowing for trend" (italics mine). The substance of this second argument is that the comparison that Friedman uses offers a simple way of coping with the trend in money supply and thus is more convenient and less statistically onerous than its major competitor; that is why it was chosen.

(3) The "economic considerations" that Friedman invokes in this connection seem again statistical, substantially that it is appropriate to allow for trend in money supply and the comparison made offers an easy way of doing this.

Friedman's defense, then, is essentially one of statistical convenience. Its full absurdity in this connection can perhaps best be conveyed by an imaginary colloquy, which puts Friedman back on Capitol Hill:

Senator: Now, Professor Friedman, you tell us that your extensive empirical investiga-

tions have shown that we must reconstruct government stabilization policy because the effects of policy actions occur only after a long and variable lag.
Friedman: That is correct.
Senator: And now this lag that we must cope with, according to one method of measurement it averages only about five months, at downturns, which is not really surprising to us. But according to the other method, the one that you have chosen to use, it averages sixteen months, which is profoundly disturbing to our ideas and institutions. Please tell us now, just why was it that you chose to measure the lag in this second way?
Friedman: Because it is easier to measure in that way.

What *is* the proper starting point for measuring the lag from a historical series of unidirectional causation? It is that money behavior *controllable by government that is most immediately related causally to income change.* Clearly the government *can* control both the amount of, and the change in, the money supply. There is no basis here for choosing the inflection point that gives the longer lag.

But the decisive question is: What aspect of money change is, indeed, the causal agent? In general, we must decide this by reference to outside information, the general body of theoretical knowledge. Will an increase in income be caused by an increase in money or by an increase in the rate of increase of money (or decrease in the rate of decrease of money)? The burden of existing theory seems quite clear. We write an income equation of exchange that works tolerably well for rough purposes as $M = K \cdot GNP$. There seems to be no school of opinion holding that it should be $\Delta M = K \cdot GNP$. Corporate treasurers, bankers, and ordinary people seem to be concerned with maintaining their cash balances in some consistent relation to their expenditures, not with matching to their expenditures some *rate of change* in their cash. A world in which with a given income people would be equally satisfied with any money supply so long as it had a specified rate of change looks to me like a nonsense world. Existing theory strongly argues that the comparison yielding the shorter lag, rather than the one that Friedman has chosen, more closely corresponds to the true causal agent.

But if we now give up our assumption that income change is entirely caused by exogenous money change, then we must admit that no possible selection of arbitrary points in the historical series of changes in money and income can provide us a measure of the causal lag. On such assumptions, we must more carefully define our "cause" as a monetary policy action or a money change such as a policy action would bring about. Future monetary policy is an instrumental variable that we assume to be, in fact, controlled. Therefore, it is an exogenous variable to the analysis. By a monetary policy action what we must mean is the difference between a monetary policy *A* and a monetary policy *B,* although one of these may be a natural benchmark such as—in some defined sense—doing nothing. Just as in a medical experiment the "cause" is the fact that the patient was given medicine *A,* rather than a placebo, or in a physical experiment the cause is the fact that the gas is heated to temperature *A,* rather than held at *B,* the cause—the starting point for measurement of our lag—in monetary policy must be some departure in policy action.

The *effect,* the terminal point for measurement of our lag, must be defined as that effect, among the potentially infinitely numerous and extended consequences of the action, that is significant for the problem at hand. In our medical experiment, we may have a host of trivial effects, such as the grimace or conversation with which the patient receives the medicine, and an infinitely extended chain of events partially dependent upon our "cause," such as that the patient's speedier recovery caused him not to cancel a date with Mary, which caused him to marry Mary rather than Louise, which caused him to live in St. Louis rather than Superior, and to become the president of the family corporation rather than a school teacher. In some sense, all of these are "effects" of our "cause," but in such an analysis every event is the "effect" of a series of causes extending back to the beginning of time. Policy-planning and most research involves a species of partial analysis that attempts to dissect experience into limited causes and discrete effects.

So in our medical experiment the "effect" is defined as limited to some measure of progress in the current illness. For monetary policy planning, the "effect" also must be limited to the immediate consequences of action. The policy-maker does not, and should not, reason in this manner: "Now, if I buy an additional $100 million in government securities this month, considering the immediate effects upon income, the effects of the induced income change on future income through the multiplier, accelerator, psychological reactions, etc., the effect of all of this back upon income through future government policy (now seen as endogenous), and so on, what will be the total direct and indirect effect of my action from now until eternity, and at what future point must the weighted average of all of these effects be placed? If I want to increase income within the next six months, and this weighted average total effect does not occur for two years, or perhaps ten years, obviously my effort would be futile."

The policy-maker's effective instrument is the change in income directly and most immediately induced by his policy action. On the plausible assumption that the most substantial direct effects of the policy action upon income will be concentrated in this early period, the policy-maker can focus his attention on them and make his main question whether they will combat or accentuate economic fluctuations. Weighing the effect of this directly induced income change upon subsequent income change is a part of the problem of assessing the economic situation and the need for policy action, for the indirect effects of the policy action will be but one operative force not practically distinguishable from others at this remove. If the policy-maker buys some government securities because income is declining and the direct effects of this are felt during the decline, reducing its extent and hastening the upturn, policy is a success. If a year or two later economic expansion proceeds too rapidly, he can cope with this new problem by selling some securities.

Friedman essentially takes two different positions on defining the effects of policy, or the end point of the lag. In discussions of the lag concept he consistently espouses the lag in *total effects* with no cut-off point, including all direct and indirect effects. However, in all his lag measurements—even for individual policy episodes—he uses the subsequent cyclical turning point as the measure of "effect." This measure seems to bear no definable relation either to his conceptual total lag or to those limited "effects" with which the policy-maker is, indeed, concerned. It is bizarre to argue that, for example, in prosperity the effect of policy is measured by the occurrence of that event that policy is designed to avoid.

In summary, neither of the methods used by Friedman to time the beginning and end of the "lag" is valid.

• • •

40 A CRITIQUE OF PROFESSOR FRIEDMAN'S FINDINGS

JOHN H. KAREKEN
AND ROBERT M. SOLOW

How would Milton Friedman reply to the logic of Professors Kareken and Solow? Is he guilty of the poor reasoning attributed to him?

. . .

1. It is our view that Friedman's position is both empirically and logically untenable. That is to say, we claim two things. First: even given his general mode of approach, the data do not support the conclusion Friedman draws from them. Second: whatever the data say, the general mode of approach used by Friedman simply cannot bear the kind of interpretation he has placed on the results. There are yet other grounds on which one might reasonably object to (or at least desire to qualify) Friedman's methods and results. We will mention them later as possible hints for future research, but we have not pursued them.

2. We take up the logical point first. Its significance extends beyond the question of the lag pattern in monetary policy, since Friedman has used the length and reliability of his lag as strong evidence that in the mutual interaction between the monetary sphere and the level of economic activity the causal thrust is primarily from the former to the latter. Stripped to bare essentials, the Friedman . . . method is simply to plot a time series of some measure of the rate of change of the seasonally corrected stock of money. If this series is compared with the National Bureau reference dates for general cyclical peaks and troughs, it is found that with great uniformity the peaks and troughs of the cycles in the monetary change series precede the business cycle peaks and troughs in the manner described. Since (to what degree of approximation?) the stock of money and its rate of change are what the monetary authorities wish them to be, we may identify the cause to be the peak or trough in monetary changes and the long-delayed effect to be the corresponding peak or trough in business activity.

The unreliability of this line of argument is suggested by the following *reductio ad absurdum.* Imagine an economy buffeted by all kinds of cyclical forces, endogenous and exogenous. Suppose that by heroic (and perhaps even cyclical) variation in the money supply and its rate of change, the Federal Reserve manages deftly to counter all disturbing impulses and to stabilize the level of economic activity absolutely. Then an observer following the Friedman method would see peaks and troughs in monetary change accompanied by a steady level of aggregate activity. He would presumably conclude that monetary policy has no effects at all, which would be precisely the opposite of the truth.

This hypothetical example illustrates by an extreme case an important truth. One cannot deduce conclusions about the

---

effects of monetary policy or about their timing without making some hypothesis, explicit or implicit, about what the course of events would have been had the monetary authorities acted differently. Such conclusions are *ceteris paribus* statements, partial derivatives not total derivatives. There are rare occasions, cases of almost experimental control of extraneous factors, when it is safe (or at least irresistible) to make conclusions like this from a simple *ex post* record. But this is surely not one of those cases; there is no control of possible disturbances, and there is a long history of professional argument over the very point at issue. The Friedman argument is just about as sound logically as the claim that because interest rates tend to fall in recessions and private domestic investment does likewise, investment demand is necessarily positively related to interest rates.

We conclude therefore that as a matter of logic, the Friedman method cannot be interpreted as it has been. The observed pattern of peaks and troughs in the general business cycle and in the money supply and its increments is compatible with many hypotheses about why events turned out just so. For all we know, the cyclical peak occurring 16 months after a peak in the monetary series may have been fended off by monetary policy action for a year or more. There is no evading the necessity of beginning with some kind of model which permits one, for better or worse, to estimate the *ceteris paribus* effects of monetary policy.

3. But suppose we waive the methodological point and look at the empirical analysis itself. A question which must have occurred to many students immediately arises: why choose the *rate of change* of the money supply as the measured indicator of monetary policy, rather than the stock of money itself? The possibility must be considered that this choice stacks the cards in favor of a long monetary lead. Suppose that, apart from trends, the money supply and the level of activity move roughly simultaneously and that together they trace out fluctuations not too different from ordinary trigonometric oscillations. Then, as everyone knows, the rate of change in the stock of money will show an approximate quarter-cycle lead over business activity. And this is roughly what happens. The complaint can be made that this is an unnatural procedure, and that the equally unnatural procedure of plotting the rate of change of over-all activity against the stock of money would turn the lead into an equally long and erratic lag.

Against this criticism, Friedman has two replies, one based on expediency, the other on principle. The first is that the stock of money itself tends, because of its strong trend, to increase pretty much without interruption, business cycles showing themselves in a decreased rate of growth rather than in an absolute decline. If the data are to be analyzed by comparison at turning points, then obviously a monotonic series is useless, and it is natural to replace it by its rate of growth which does show well-marked cycles.

Secondly, this reply is reinforced by another consideration. A general belief that monetary factors influence aggregate activity does not entail any automatic conclusion as to whether the money stock, or its rate of change, or even some other characteristic, may be the natural time series to compare with the general state of business. So the changes in the money supply may well be the "right" series to use, and not merely the first difference of a more appropriate series.

Our own view is that only a play on words gets us into this purely verbal snare. From the policy point of view it is clearly immaterial whether we think in terms of M or changes in M. An agency which determines changes in M also determines M (except for an initial condition) and an agency which controls M also controls its rate of change. But it is not true, except in some irrelevant long-run sense, to say that the Federal Reserve controls either M or its rate of change.

What the Federal Reserve can do is buy and sell in the open market, set reserve requirements, and set the discount rate. A little less directly, . . . we may say that the authorities control the effective primary reserves of the commercial banks (or at least the part of them which does not arise at the discount window); and at one further remove we may say that the measure of monetary policy is the power of the banking system to carry earning assets. This is what the monetary authorities *do;* they do not move a pointer on a dial marked M or even ΔM. The appropriate lag, significant both for policy and for analytical purposes, seems to us to be that between particular *actions* of the monetary authorities and the consequent events in the economy at large.

4. But suppose we waive this point too, and agree to study the relations between M and/or ΔM and aggregate activity. How can we get around the absence of turning points in M, and somehow test the hypothesis that the lead of ΔM over general business is a mere reflection of an essentially simultaneous movement of M and general business? The simple observation seems never to have been made that instead of comparing the level of M and the level of economic activity we can compare the change in M with *the change* in economic activity. We have done this. . . . In summary [our results] overwhelmingly support the conclusion that the money supply itself and the level of aggregate output move more or less simultaneously over the business cycle, and that the lead of ΔM over aggregate output is a pure arithmetic artifact. From the observation of the last 40 years absolutely nothing can be inferred *by this method* about the causal interaction between the monetary sphere and the "real" sphere.

• • •

41 THE LENGTH OF THE LAG

THOMAS MAYER

Despite the strong conclusion arrived at by Professor Mayer concerning the existence of a long lag, the evidence in the following excerpt can be interpreted in a manner opposite to what he intends. First, however, it is necessary to reject the inside lag estimates of John H. Kareken and Robert M. Solow and Professor Mayer, and to substitute instead the 0- to 3-month computation of Dr. Willes as noted in the Introduction to this Part. Add to this short inside lag either the 3½-month outside lag in residential construction or the 1-month lag for inventories, as Professor Mayer found in his own studies, and we find that the total lag varies from 1 to 6½ months in order to reach 50 percent effectiveness in two key areas. Does not this finding suggest that monetary policy is quick-acting?

• • •

Although the authors themselves refer to their work as providing only "fragmentary evidence" and as "unfinished," the study prepared by Kareken and Solow for the Commission on Money and Credit is clearly one of the most important papers to emerge from the Commission's labors.* They summarize their results as follows:

> We believe our results do say something useful about those lags. For what they are worth, they do suggest that the two extreme positions on the flexibility of monetary policy are wrong. One polar view is that, while monetary policy is extremely powerful, it operates with a very long and irregular lag—of the order of magnitude of 18 months—and that this converts a powerful tool into a weapon much too dangerous to be used. The opposite view is that, while monetary policy is extremely powerful, it is also very quick-acting, easily reversed and delicately manipulated. Our conclusion is that it works neither so slowly as Friedman thinks, nor as quickly and surely as the Federal Reserve itself seems to believe . . . . Though the *full* results of policy changes on the flow of expenditures may be a long time coming, nevertheless the chain of effects is spread out over a fairly wide interval. This means that *some* effect comes reasonably quickly, and that the effects build up over time so that some substantial stabilizing power results after a lapse of time of the order of six or nine months.

In commenting on this paper Friedman averred that "some substantial stabilizing power," occurring with a six to nine months lag, "is in no way inconsistent with my own" conclusion. What Friedman appears not to have noticed is that Kareken and Solow's conclusion is inconsistent with *their own* evidence. The structure of the Kareken-Solow study is the following: they state their conclusion, as quoted above, in the summary at the start of their paper and then in the body provide estimates of the various component lags. However, they do not combine their component lags and do not refer back to their previously stated conclusion.

From Thomas Mayer, "The Lag in the Effect of Monetary Policy: Some Criticisms," *Western Economic Journal,* 5, 325–330. Reprinted by permission.

*See the previous selection—ed.

The first lag is time elapsing between the change in the relevant economic variable and the change in Federal Reserve policy, the so-called "inside lag." Kareken and Solow provide several measures of this lag using different variables as the signal the Federal Reserve should look at. Using National Bureau turning points the average lag is 8.5 months for a switch to an easy money policy, 3.0 months for a tight money policy; using the Federal Reserve index of industrial production yields an 8.0 months lag for an easy money policy and a 3.0 months lag for a tight policy; while using the unemployment rate gives a 10.0 months lag for an easy money policy and a 0.5 months lag for a tight policy. Once the Federal Reserve undertakes actions to change the gross reserve base there may be a lag until net reserves change, but Kareken and Solow state that this lag is negligible.

The next lag is from the change in reserves to the change in interest rates. Although Kareken and Solow use the bond rate as well as the rate on short-term bank loans in determining the impact on investment, they provide an estimate of the interest rate lag only for short-term bank loans. Their estimate is implausibly long. After six quarters (which is as far as their table goes) only about one-fifth of the effect on the interest rate has taken place. They are evidently concerned with the implausible magnitude of this lag since they qualify their conclusion by pointing to the possibility of prior changes in the availability of credit. But since Kareken and Solow do not provide any alternative estimate of the lag based on credit availability, we are left with the very long lag described above.

Once interest rates have changed, there is a lag until the induced change in investment occurs. Kareken and Solow analyze this lag for only three types of investment. First, there is what they refer to as "fixed investment." Actually their data refer only to, at most, producers' durable equipment, since the series they use are new orders for nonelectrical machinery and the new business equipment component of the index of industrial production. The lead times for producers' durable equipment (which accounts for only about one-third of gross fixed investment) can hardly be considered typical of the lead times of the other component of fixed investment, the various types of construction; I shall therefore refer to this sector as producers' durable equipment rather than as fixed investment. For this sector Kareken and Solow split the lag into two components, one going from the change in the bond rate to the change in new orders (as measured by the Department of Commerce series) and the other from the change in new orders to the change in production (as measured by the Federal Reserve's production index). The first of these lags is relatively short; it takes about 4 months until half the effect has been felt. The lag between the change in new orders and the change in production is longer. Kareken and Solow present three estimates. One shows the average lag to be 11 months, one gives it as 12 months and one as 15 months. Hence, the total lag from the change in the bond rate until the change in the output of producers' durable equipment is 14 to 18 months.

For the inventory sector Kareken and Solow show an average lag between the change in short-term bank interest rates and investment of about 8 or 9 months.

Finally there is residential construction. This sector, probably the most important for measuring the impact of monetary policy, receives short shrift:

> Unfortunately we did not have time to do an analogous study of residential construction. . . . The precise timing remains to be studied. But we can note here one bit of evidence—taken from VA and FHA records—which suggests that there is, on the average a lag of approximately 3.5 months between the decision to build a house and the beginning of construction. . . . Depending on how builders' orders and production of housing

materials are related, this could be an overestimate. Also, there is no doubt a lag—still to be determined—between Federal Reserve action and changes in building plans, so that this 3.5 month estimate should probably be taken as a minimum lag, considerably smaller than the total lag between Federal Reserve action and actual spending . . . .

Kareken and Solow do not mention an obvious lag, the lag between the start of construction and the average dollar spent for building labor.

It is difficult to compare these lags with Friedman's lag (from the specific money cycle turning points) of 18 months for the peaks and 12 months for the troughs, because Kareken and Solow omit many component lags. Only for inventories can the complete lag between Federal Reserve action and the change in output be put together. There is a lag of substantially more than 18 months until the short-term interest rate of banks changes, and then 8 or 9 months until half the effect of these higher interest rates takes place, so that the combined average lag is substantially more than *2 years.*

For producers' durable equipment the total lag cannot be calculated since we are not given the lag between Federal Reserve action and the change in the bond rate, the variable used in the equipment equation. If it is assumed that the bond rate reacts immediately, the total lag for this sector would be 14 to 18 months. But if one assumes that the lag for the bond rate is the same as, or greater than, that for the short-term interest rate of banks, the average lag becomes substantially more than 32 to 36 months.

Finally, there are three relevant lags in residential construction: the lag from the change in bank reserves to the decision to build, from the decision to the start of construction, and from the start of construction until the change in income. Kareken and Solow estimate only the lag from the decision to the start of construction. Given only this one lag, little can be said about the total lag for this sector.

To summarize, Kareken and Solow present complete lags for only one sector, inventories, and this lag is much longer than Friedman's lag. For another sector, producers' durable equipment, they give data for only two of the three lags, but these two lags alone are longer than Friedman's lag. For residential construction they present an estimate for only one of the three lags (which they find to be short) and give no information at all on the other two lags. Nor do they give any information on the weights they use to combine the lags of their three sectors. It is hard to see how they are able to combine them so that the total lag is less than Friedman's lag. Clearly, they should have criticized Friedman, not for overestimating, but for underestimating the lag.

The second part of Kareken and Solow's conclusion is that substantial effects of monetary policy occur within 6 to 9 months. Since the term "substantial effect" is hard to quantify, one cannot be clear if this statement is consistent with their evidence, but, in any case, this conclusion is subject to criticism on grounds of relevance. If interest rates and credit availability do have a powerful enough effect on income, the problem created by lags is *not* that the Federal Reserve cannot achieve a given effect in a short period of time. Even if only, say, 10 percent of the effect occurs within the first 6 months, the Federal Reserve could still achieve a sufficient effect within 6 months simply by adopting a policy whose ultimate effects are ten times as great as the effect it wants to achieve within 6 months. The obvious trouble with such a policy is that, after the 6-months period, the subsequent effects of the policy could be destabilizing. (Attempts to offset these effects by adopting a new and stronger monetary policy would lead to greater and greater fluctuations.)

The proper test is therefore not the absolute magnitude of the effect that can

Table 1. Number of Months Until 50 Percent of Effectiveness Is Reached[a]

	Kareken and Solow	Mayer
A. Inside lag	5¾[b]	6[c]
B. Credit market lag		
1. To change in net reserves	0	
2. To change in banks' short-term rates (Kareken and Solow) or credit conditions (Mayer)	18+[d]	½
C. Residential construction (from decision to build until start of construction)	3½	3
D. Producers' durable plant and equipment	14–18[e]	8½[f]
E. Inventories	8–9	1

[a]Average for expansionary and restrictive policies.
[b]Using National Bureau turning points as the criterion.
[c]Average for restrictive and expansionary policies. Includes the "policy period" lag, i.e., half the period over which the policy is applied.
[d]Mean lag is more than 18 months, since after 18 months only ⅕ of the effect has occurred.
[e]Figure actually is applicable only to producers' durable equipment.
[f]Manufacturers' plant and equipment sector combined with manufacturers' independent equipment sector by using "intermediate weights."
Sources: Kareken and Solow [see Selection 40], Mayer, "The Inflexibility of Monetary Policy," *Review of Economics and Statistics* 40, 358–374, and unpublished worksheets.

be achieved within 6 or 9 months, but rather whether the policy is stabilizing over the whole time for which it is effective. In a previous study* I attempted to measure just this thing and found that, given the lags I was using, a monetary policy of optimal size would have only quite limited ability to stabilize the index of industrial production, though it would do much better if one were to use the wholesale price index as a criterion instead of industrial production. I measured the lags for every sector used by Kareken and Solow as well as for a number of sectors they did not cover. Table 1 shows that there are two lags (the "inside lag" and the "decision to the start of construction lag" for residential construction) that are fairly similar in the two studies. The other lags, however, are much longer in the Kareken-Solow study. Their estimates are 1⅔ to 2 times as long as mine for producers' durable plant and equipment, 8 to 9 times as long for inventories, and more than 36 times as long for the credit market. This suggests that, if Kareken and Solow are right in their estimates, monetary policy would probably be destabilizing rather than stabilizing.

Admittedly these criticisms are in a way too severe, because Kareken and Solow continually stress the tentative nature of their findings and the precariousness of their estimates.

Kareken and Solow's statement of their conclusion as a contradiction of Friedman's results tends to obscure an important fact: all of the studies that have been made of the outside lag show a substantial lag.

• • •

*See sources for Table 1—ed.

42 CREDIT RATIONING, INTEREST RATE LAGS, AND MONETARY POLICY SPEED

DONALD P. TUCKER

The credit market lag, measured by the time required for the financial community to adjust to a shift in monetary policy, is the major source of discrepancy between the lag estimates of Thomas Mayer and Professors Kareken and Solow (see Table 1 in the previous selection). The following excerpt hints at one reason for this divergence. First note that Kareken and Solow calculate the credit market lag by considering movements in interest rates as indicating the reaction of financial institutions to a changed monetary stance. Mayer, on the other hand, relies on shifts in credit availability to signify central banking policy's effect on the markets. Donald P. Tucker demonstrates that when interest rates are sticky, measuring impact by interest rate movements overstates the length of the lag as compared with measurements based on changes in credit availability. Basic to this argument, of course, is the belief in interest rate inflexibility, which implies the absence of perfect competition in the credit markets. Only in industries characterized by imperfect competition can price be maintained in the face of external influences designed to raise price. The Introduction to the first section of Part II, as well as a number of articles within that section, asserts that the banking industry cannot be considered a perfectly competitive market, and so Professor Tucker's analysis is appropriate. A word of caution, however. It is difficult to be convinced that the explanation advanced here justifies the total discrepancy of 1½ years between the studies of Professor Mayer and Professors Kareken and Solow.

I. INTRODUCTION

Recent work on monetary policy speed has pointed to lags in the adjustment of production to changes in product demand and lags in the adjustment of interest rates on bank loans to changes in credit market conditions as two disequilibrium phenomena of some importance, and both types of lags have been supposed to reduce significantly the speed of monetary policy. This conclusion fails to consider the accelerating effects of the temporary credit rationing that will normally be associated with lags in interest rate adjustment in a period of monetary contraction. In this [article], a temporary credit rationing effect is embodied in a dynamic macroeconomic model with market clearing lags, and the speed with which this system adjusts to reductions in the money supply is studied. For certain ranges of parameter values, the impact of the credit rationing is strong enough to outweigh the direct delaying effect of the interest rate lag. The slower the rate at which the interest rate adjusts, in such cases, the more rapid the adjustment of income and employment.

The market for bank loans is generally regarded as highly imperfect, and this

From Donald P. Tucker, "Credit Rationing, Interest Rate Lags, and Monetary Policy Speed," *The Quarterly Journal of Economics,* February 1968, 54–59. Reprinted by permission.

imperfection manifests itself in two ways, it is argued.

First, banks are slow to adjust the interest rates they charge on loans when credit conditions change. These loan rates are administered prices, and they do not fluctuate freely from day to day as do the average market yields on widely traded debt instruments. Instead, a situation of excess demand or supply may persist for long periods of time in the bank loan market before loan rates are adjusted enough to clear the market. Certain empirical investigations, notably the interview study of Hodgman[1] and the econometric estimations of Kareken and Solow,* provide indirect evidence of this lag in credit-market adjustment.

Second, banks ration credit, at least some of the time. When borrowing demand at the prevailing rate on bank loans exceeds the quantity banks wish to lend, then the banks do not satisfy all the loan requests. Instead, some borrowers are given less than they requested, and some are given no loan at all. Although no direct quantitative measure of credit rationing has ever been obtained, to my knowledge, still it is widely believed to be a significant factor in times of credit tightness.

Since banks lie right in the middle of the causal chain through which monetary policy influences income and employment, these imperfections of the bank loan market should have a definite bearing on the outcome of monetary policy actions.

For example, one theoretical implication of credit rationing for the power of monetary policy has been explored extensively in the literature under the heading of the availability doctrine. Rationing provides a mechanism through which monetary policy may influence investment spending even if investors are completely insensitive to interest rate levels in making their spending plans. Increased monetary tightness imposed by the monetary authorities will cause a reduction in the flow of new lending to investors by increasing credit rationing. In consequence, the investors whose loan requests are denied will be forced to reduce their planned spending simply by lack of funds.

The recent study by Kareken and Solow on "Lags in Monetary Policy" points out another implication this credit market imperfection has for monetary policy. If investment depends on interest rates (their empirical results indicate it does), then the speed with which income and employment respond to monetary policy actions must depend on the speed with which interest rates respond. The rate on bank loans is only one of several relevant rates, but it is bound to have some importance to investors since bank lending to business is a significant component of sources of funds for business. Any sluggishness in the adjustment of this rate to changed credit conditions must have the effect of slowing down the impact of monetary policy actions on investment spending.

• • •

II. THE BASIC ARGUMENT

Note first that credit rationing and the interest rate adjustment lag are not independent phenomena but are merely two sides of the same adjustment process. The rationing arises only because of the interest rate lag.

Consider the effects of an open market sale by the monetary authorities. This transaction tends to reduce the supply of bank lending in two ways. It raises the rate of return on alternative assets (e.g., Treasury bills), initially increasing their attractiveness relative to loans from the banks' point of view. Also, it forces banks to sell some of their marketable securities to the public in order to meet

---

[1]D. R. Hodgman, *Commercial Bank Loan and Investment Policy* (Champaign, Ill.: University of Illinois, 1963), p. 29.

*See the two previous selections—ed.

minimum reserve requirements (assuming the reserve drain is not financed entirely by a reduction in excess reserves), thus giving banks an incentive to restore their secondary reserves by contracting their loan portfolios. In order to reduce the flow of new lending as they contract their loan portfolios, banks will have to ration credit for a while until the interest rate on loans rises sufficiently to reduce the quantity of lending demanded as well. Temporarily, at least, the bank loan market is not cleared.

Let Figure 1 represent the market for bank loans, and suppose the market is disturbed from an equilibrium position by a reduction in the supply schedule from *SS* to *S′S′*. At each possible interest rate, banks will supply less funds to the market than before. Furthermore, the prevailing interest rate is sticky, and initially banks do not change it at all. Under these circumstances, the quantity of lending falls immediately from q_0 to q_1 even though both the interest rate and the demand schedule remain unchanged. Credit is rationed.

Gradually banks respond to the excess demand by raising the interest rate, and as they do so, the quantity of lending increases. The market moves up the supply schedule *S′S′*, and the degree of credit

Figure 1 Supply Reduction in Lending Market

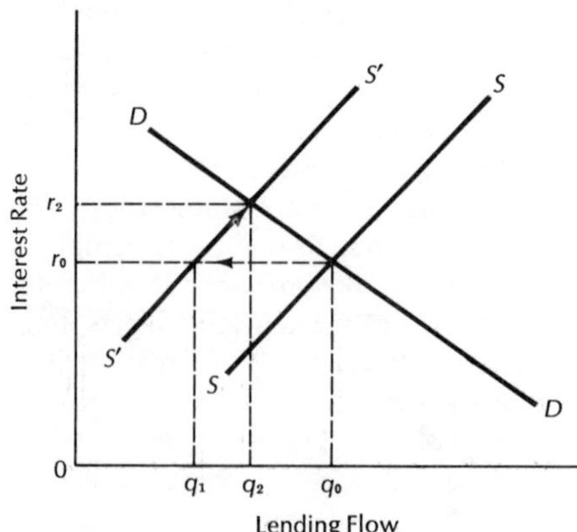

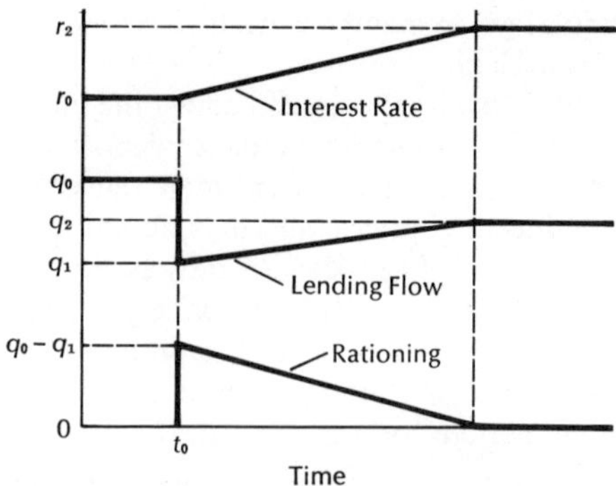

Figure 2 Responses to Supply Reduction in Lending Market

rationing, measured by the amount by which quantity demanded exceeds quantity supplied at each interest rate level, gradually declines. Equilibrium is eventually re-established at a new interest rate and quantity, r_2 and q_2, and the credit rationing disappears. Figure 2 shows the behavior through time of the three related variables after a reduction in the supply schedule for lending has occurred at time t_0.

Next, observe that there are two separate channels through which changes in credit market conditions will influence investment spending. Investment depends not only on interest rates, but also on the amount of credit rationing. Whatever the level of interest rates, investment spending must be lower the more extensive is credit rationing because some investors are forced by lack of funds to cancel investment plans they would like to carry out at prevailing interest rates.

When there is no lag in interest rate adjustments, then there can be no rationing, and only the first channel of influence will be operative. When there is a lag, by contrast, the influence transmitted through the first channel (interest rates) will be felt more gradually, and this tends to delay the response of investment. However, the lag is also accompanied by rationing, the full magnitude of which is felt immediately through the second channel, and this tends to accelerate the adjustment of investment. These two effects of the lag, the interest rate effect and the credit rationing effect, work against each other. Far from causing monetary policy to work more slowly on balance, lags in interest rate adjustment may actually cause the economy to respond more rapidly to monetary policy changes if this counterbalancing credit rationing effect is strong enough.

Suppose, for example, that the investment demand function has distributed lags both in its response to interest rate changes and in its response to credit rationing, but suppose its response to credit rationing is more prompt (inventory investment, for example, could respond promptly). Suppose, furthermore, that the strength of the investment response to credit rationing is equal to or greater than the ultimate impact of the interest rate change that follows. If there is no interest rate lag, then the speed with which investment adjusts will be governed entirely by the lags in the investment response to interest rate changes. But if the interest rate adjustment is delayed, then investment will initially face the full impact of credit rationing, to which it responds more rapidly (by assumption). The credit rationing may disappear before investment has adjusted very far, but during the short interval of credit rationing, it will move further toward equilibrium than it would have with instantaneous interest rate adjustment. Thus, because of credit rationing, an interest rate lag may speed up the impact of monetary policy.

As an alternative, suppose that there is a production adjustment lag. Production and employment respond only gradually when product demand changes, and at such times producers are faced with unplanned or unintended changes in their inventories. Not only is such a lag intuitively plausible, but it also finds empirical support in the work of Kareken and Solow. To be more specific, let the reduction in production in each period be proportional to the amount of excess supply. Suppose, furthermore, that the response of investment demand to a credit rationing gap is substantially stronger than its response to the corresponding interest rate change, and that the time patterns of the distributed lag coefficients in the investment demand function are about equal for credit rationing and for interest rate changes. Under these circumstances, the credit rationing gap associated with an interest rate lag will initially create a greater excess supply in the product market, and will thereby cause more rapid change in production and employment, than instantaneous complete adjustment of the interest rate could. Aside from the extreme case in which the credit rationing gap persists too long and causes the production level to overshoot its equilibrium, a slow interest rate adjustment should again lead to more rapid monetary policy impact.

• • •

the discriminatory impact of monetary policy

The central banking authorities can operate with two distinct classes of weapons found in their arsenal—general controls and selective controls. Selective controls find expression today only in the margin requirement, the percentage of a securities purchase that must be paid down in cash rather than borrowed. The Board of Governors can raise or lower this percentage as they see fit; since May 1970 it has stood at 65 percent. Other selective controls that now have only historical importance are the minimum down payment and maximum repayment period on consumer installment credit[1] and on real estate loans. These controls are aimed at specific sectors of the economy—the organized securities market, consumption (especially of durable consumer goods), and residential construction. A tightening of the monetary reins will affect activity adversely in these areas more directly, heavily, and immediately than in other economic sectors.

General controls—open market operations and reserve requirement and discount rate changes—act more broadly. By tightening or easing commercial bank reserve conditions, decreasing or increasing money supply, or raising or lowering interest rates, the monetary authorities can modify market conditions for all sectors of the economy. No one industry grouping is singled out for special attention.

Yet the nondiscriminatory nature of general controls is less clear than appears at the initial glance. In the first

---

[1]On December 24, 1969, President Nixon signed into law a bill which, among other things, granted the President the power to implement consumer credit controls. Mr. Nixon announced at that time that he did not contemplate use of these powers.

place, monetary policy works through the banking system, so that it is inherently discriminatory against this sector of the economy. Whether tight money brings increased profits to the banks by permitting them to raise their charges and fees or whether it lowers profits by forcing a reduction in the volume of business not offset by the increased rates has been to date a moot issue. Similarly, open market operations bring about price changes in government securities and thereby directly influence holders of governments—dealers, banks, and the nonbank public alike. As noted in relation to the even keel policy of the Federal Reserve (Selection 26) and in conjunction with the preference shown by the central bank for using open market operations rather than raising the reserve requirement when restraint is applied (Part VI, Introduction to the first section), the monetary authorities have demonstrated their willingness to cushion the difficulties, which are unavoidable side effects of their policy decisions, to the financial community.

In recent years attention has been focused on the discriminatory impact on the banking system of Regulation Q, which specifies maximum interest rates member banks may pay on various nondemand deposits. When the rates in the market on comparable assets exceed those payable by the commercial banks, depositors reduce their credit balances and switch to the higher-yielding substitutes. In 1964, for example, commercial banks were faced with a loss of time certificates of deposit (CDs), because the market yields were more favorable on alternative assets. Clearly, the existence of a legal maximum prevented the banks from competing effectively. In response to this loss of banking deposits, in late 1964 the Reserve Board relaxed the pressure and permitted a higher maximum rate on CDs. Banks raised their yields and fund flows were reversed. Again, in the first quarter of 1969, market rates, which averaged more than 6 percent for 3-month Treasury bills, were beyond the maximum interest rate on 91-day CDs, which was 6 percent on deposits of $100,000 or more. Is it surprising, then, that large commercial banks lost approximately $4 billion in such deposits over the 3-month interval?

The discriminatory impact of monetary policy is evident in other areas as well. But before entering into a fuller discussion, it is appropriate to digress for a moment on the meaning of discrimination.

Discrimination can arise, on the one hand, from the increased price of credit, and therefore from the reduced willingness of some borrowers to demand funds, while others continue to do so (Type A). Alternatively, discrimination can be said to exist when credit is scarce and some borrowers receive more favorable treatment than others do (Type B). These two meanings are graphically portrayed in Figure 1, a simple supply-and-demand diagram. When the supply of funds is reduced from S to S^1, along demand-for-funds curve D, interest rates rise from 7 percent to 8 percent. Whereas previously borrowers had obtained $200 billion, now only $150 billion will be available. Marginal borrowers who demand $50 billion at interest rates between 7 percent and 8 percent are cut off from the market. Type A discrimination—giving some access to credit and denying it to others—is created as a consequence of a shift in the central bank's policy that induces a reduction in lending potential. But the market, not the commercial bank administrators, decides who shall obtain the available funds. Indeed, it is the borrowers, who voluntarily reduce their demands, rather than the lenders, who turn down borrowers. Thus the point that monetary policy has differential effects in the present context must mean that such alternative policies as gov-

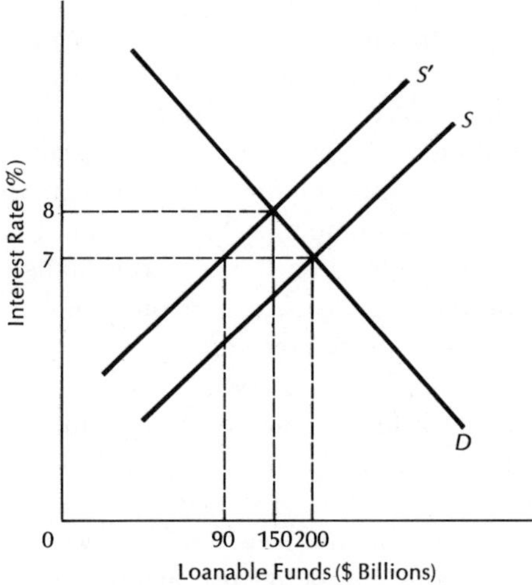

Figure 1 Types A and B Discrimination

ernment expenditure or tax measures would leave interest rates lower and therefore drive fewer borrowers from the market.

Type B discrimination stands in contrast to the interest-induced change in quantity demanded. In Type B, either because market adjustment is not instantaneous or because market control is exercised by the lenders or because of external, nonmarket considerations, a low rate is maintained, at least for some period of time. In Figure 1, when supply falls but a 7 percent interest rate is maintained, the quantity of loanable funds supplied falls by $110 billion, while the quantity of funds demanded remains at the previous level, $200 billion. The $90 billion of available credit must somehow be distributed among the $200 billion demanded, without price performing its usual allocating function. Rationing, then, must be accomplished by some other means, but whatever the method employed, some demanders—who are willing and able to pay the going rate—will be turned away just as others will be accommodated. The market may perform effectively here, too, with objective criteria other than price coming into play. It is also possible, however, that banks engage in some systematic differentiation even between borrowers who equally meet the objective criteria.

Picking up the main theme—discrimination in nonfinancial categories—it will be useful to classify these areas on the basis of Type A or Type B discrimination. Type A discrimination, you will recall, exists when the increase in interest rates forces some individuals or firms out of the market while others continue to demand credit. Borrowers who remove themselves from the market may do so for a number of reasons. A firm may have a strong liquid asset or profit position, and an increase in the loan interest rate leads it to substitute internal financing for external borrowing. In another instance, a firm may be unable to pass on the higher credit charges to its customers and, rather than absorb them itself, elects to reduce or delay its financing needs. The individual borrower who computes that his budget cannot absorb a higher interest levy also removes himself from the market. This situation occurs not infrequently in the case of consumer mortgage borrowing, because a one percentage point increase in the interest rate from 7 percent to 8 percent on a 30-year, $20,000 mortgage means an increased payment over the life of the mortgage of almost $5,000. Higher interest rates are also likely to reduce the demand for the more expensive consumer durables, financed on the installment plan. Another category involves the borrower whose demand is limited by institutional considerations. Many state and local governments are not permitted to exceed constitutionally specified maximum interest rates. As market rates rise beyond that maximum, such bodies must remove themselves from the market. (The demand curve for a borrower who is limited by a 6 percent interest rate maximum would be represented by a horizontal or perfectly elastic curve at 6 percent, extending for some finite distance and then turning downward.)

Discrimination from the supply side, or Type B discrimination, comes from the substitution of nonprice allocation for rationing by price. If the interest rate cannot or will not adjust, some of the other loan-allocation criteria increase in importance. Relative risk, past credit history, and the status of the customer, to mention just some of the more obvious criteria, receive a heavier weight in the decision-making machinery. The borrower with high profitability is a better risk than is the firm with low profits; the old, established customer is preferred over the newly opened business; the firm controlling its prices stands a better chance of repaying the bank than does the firm whose prices are subject to the vagaries of the marketplace. Thus systematic discrimination becomes commonplace, and although it is entirely rational from the lenders' points of view, it is arbitrary and unfair in the eyes of the rejected borrowers.

Related to Type B discrimination is the situation in which an externally fixed interest rate is imposed on the lender. The lender is prohibited by law from charging more than a specified rate, and as market rates rise, the fixed yield becomes increasingly unattractive. Consequently, lenders abandon this segment of the credit market and switch to more profitable forms instead. The market for mortgages guaranteed either by the Federal Housing Authority (FHA) or the Veterans Administration (VA) is a prime example of this phenomenon. In order to obtain a guarantee from either agency, the mortgage contract must meet the terms specified by the authorities, and a maximum interest rate is mandated. During periods of rising interest rates, however, such rates tend to be left behind by other market rates, and money for FHA and VA mortgages becomes ever more difficult to obtain. Consumers and unincorporated firms may also feel the squeeze as state usury laws prohibit lenders from exceeding a legal interest maximum. Thus some borrowers who are willing to pay the stated rate and may even be ready to exceed it find themselves unable to obtain credit.

Is there any evidence of a systematic bias, either Type A or B discrimination, against specific sectors of industry or specific groups? Two of the three articles in this section deal explicitly with the empirical evidence on this issue; the other article handles it implicitly. The opening selection, written by the members of the Commission on Money and Credit (CMC), discusses the results of their own experience and the conclusions of studies inspired by them. The focal point of the article concerns the aspect of the discrimination issue that has caught the most attention—big business versus small business. The CMC rejects the assertion that the credit needs of small business (relative to those of large business) are not adequately met because of the difference in size. Size per se does not elicit bias.

George L. Bach and C. J. Huizenga subject this very point to the test. The excerpt reprinted here not only lists their conclusions but details their methodology. Note their definition of discrimination—the difference between the allocation of credit in the absence of tight money and the distribution of loans under conditions of tight money. This broad conception includes both Types A and B discrimination. Second, note the assumption of "substantially identical . . . loan demand," necessary so that the authors can measure the decrease in credit caused by the shift in supply. Third, observe how Bach and Huizenga measure tightness—the looseness ratio. Their conclusion is that small business (again, relative to big business) is not adversely affected by tight money.

Their methodology has been attacked by Deane Carson.[2] Professor Carson does not take issue with their definition of discrimination but does wonder about the validity of assuming identical loan demand. Although Bach and Huizenga, in their defense, reject this criticism, no conclusive proof is marshaled to support their opinion.

The looseness ratio is also criticized by Professor Carson, primarily for not including other liquid assets in the numerator—specifically, long-term government securities in the less-than-a-year-to-maturity category—but also for not making a distinction in the denominator of the ratio between various types of deposits. (Can you see how this criticism may affect the validity of the Bach-Huizenga conclusions?) Although Carson can no more than presume that excluding these considerations led to a bias, Bach and Huizenga can safely presume otherwise.

In a more recent criticism of the Bach-Huizenga study, Professors Silber and Polakoff[3] reject the Bach-Huizenga definition of discrimination, arguing that Bach and Huizenga do not distinguish between bankers' bias and creditworthiness of the borrowers. The Bach-Huizenga definition appears the more relevant, but the interesting aspects of the Silber-Polakoff study lie in the model they construct and the conclusions they reach.

The previous studies have dealt with the credit extended by commercial banks. Commercial banks, however, are merely one source of credit to business firms. Other financial intermediaries serve the business sector as well. And trade credit—the credit extended by a supplier to his customers—also comes to the aid of firms in a bind. To be sure, the charges levied by lenders other than commercial banks are higher; in the extreme, Mafia credit frequently is so expensive that it often leads to loss of control over the firm. But it is not clear that trade credit is more expensive; indeed, delaying payment of a bill listed as "30 days Net"—full payment due in thirty days—by 60 days usually means a 2-month, interest-free loan. A. H. Meltzer, in a pathbreaking study of the relationship between trade credit and monetary policy,[4] concluded that between 1955 and 1957, the period of the Bach-Huizenga study, trade credit increased in such a way as "to have favored these [sic] firms against whom credit rationing is said to discriminate."

Thus, if one is to consider the whole range of credit sources available to small business, he will find it difficult to conclude that the needs of small business are sacri-

---

[2]D. Carson, "The Differential Effects of Tight Money: Comment," *American Economic Review*, 51, 1039–1042. See also the "Reply" by Professors Bach and Huizenga, *ibid.*, pp. 1042–1044.

[3]W. L. Silber and M. E. Polakoff, "The Differential Effects of Tight Money: An Econometric Study," *Journal of Finance*, 25, 83–97.

[4]A. H. Meltzer, "Mercantile Credit, Monetary Policy, and Size of Firms," *Review of Economics and Statistics*, 42, 429–437.

ficed even if the commercial banking industry is engaged in this form of discrimination.

What can be said concerning discrimination in other sectors, for example, FHA- or VA-financed housing? Few deny the existence of the differential impact. The issue here is what to do about it. No unique, generally accepted solution has been found.

Essentially the issue is one of equity versus efficiency. On the one hand, it seems quite unfair to make some sectors of the economy bear the brunt of a policy of monetary restraint. The injustice of central bank action is evident; it becomes intolerable when the sectors affected most harshly by the policy are not the causes of the malfunction that the policy is designed to correct. When an automobile boom causes inflation as seems to have been true in 1955, does it seem right to punish the housing industry? On the other hand, because monetary policy does affect some areas more quickly and more drastically than others, permitting these sectors to escape the impact of the control decision weakens monetary policy—it will be forced to work with a longer lag and will be weaker in the critical early months. Indeed, this dilemma has forced the central bank to raise the maximum permissible interest rate on time and savings deposits in commercial banks a number of times, as noted earlier. Although this action enables commercial banks to prevent losses to competitive institutions, the fact that they are able to maintain a larger deposit volume means *pari passu* an offset to a tight monetary policy. Similarly, in 1966, when the mortgage money was tightening up, an increase in the FHA- and VA-interest maximums simply encouraged home building, despite the economy's need for tighter money. David P. Eastburn, in the final selection in this Part, points out some of the ways of dealing with this dilemma. Consider his alternatives and judge for yourself the proper path to the solution.

We end this section with a note concerning coordination. The financial system is not entirely under the control of the monetary authorities, although the commercial banks controlling the majority of deposits are. The FDIC regulates nonmember, insured commercial banks, whereas the Federal Home Loan Bank Board supervises member savings and loans associations and some additional savings institutions. Moreover, Fannie Mae (formally, the Federal National Mortgage Association), which supports the secondary market in government-backed mortgages, operates independently as well. In order to deal effectively with the discriminatory-efficacy dilemma, coordination among these various agencies must be assured. In 1966 Congress made some contribution to this effort by authorizing the coordination of maximum interest rates payable on savings deposits by federally insured financial institutions. Although this is undoubtedly a move in the correct direction, the questions concerning centralization versus decentralization, raised in the second section of Part III, are equally relevant here.

43 THE DIFFERENTIAL EFFECTS OF MONETARY POLICY

COMMISSION ON MONEY AND CREDIT

Among the interesting points made in this selection is the *value judgment* that the impact of monetary policy on home building "has not been undesirable." This remark stands in clear contrast to the factual information given concerning the relative scarcity of credit to small business and to the conclusion that size alone does not lead to discrimination. Indeed, this conclusion is implicit in the facts and is acceptable insofar as the verifying statistics are correct. But the statement concerning residential construction cited earlier remains a matter of opinion. The CMC's opinion is clear. But it will not be shared by the potential buyer of a home who was counting on obtaining a mortgage on what to him were reasonable financing charges.

• • •

Another objection to the use of monetary measures for stabilization is that it is discriminatory in its application, with its restrictive effects falling particularly severely on investment in housing and on small business. Large businesses, which depend more on internal sources of financing and which have long-term relations with lending institutions, are held to be far less affected.

The available data which pertain mainly to the 1955–57 experience show that bank lending to large business increased relatively more during the cyclical upswing when money was tight than to small business. However, to a large extent the differences in the rates of growth of lending reflect cyclical differences in *demand* for credit. Industries in which large firms predominate were growing at a faster rate than industries with mainly small firms. In addition, small retail firms normally rely on trade credit more than on bank loans; and large corporations did increase their lending to small corporations and to noncorporate firms faster than their own sales increased.

Bank credit rationing did occur and was not uniform. But the criterion for rationing did not appear to be size of firm. The two criteria which prevailed for loans other than mortgage and consumer installment loans were credit-worthiness and the value to the bank of obtaining or retaining the borrower as a depositor. Banks tightened their credit standards and refused to make loans to marginal borrowers who might have been accommodated in an easy money period. They also shortened maturities on term loans. Customers with large compensating balances found it easier to obtain credit than those with small balances and equivalent credit ratings. Many banks reduced or were unwilling to expand credit lines to sales finance companies on that ground; however, these companies often obtained credit from nonbank sources. Similarly some types of construction loans were rationed, and promoters of new buildings sometimes had to pay high rates to obtain funds from nonbank sources. But because small banks, all of whose customers are small, were generally less loaned-up than large banks, small businesses with good credit ratings and good bank connections may have often had less difficulty in obtaining loans than some large businesses.

Firms with poor credit ratings and poor banking connections appear relatively more often in the category of small businesses. Firms with low credit ratings may have either inexperienced management or insufficient equity capital, frequently both. To the extent that well-managed firms have weak credit ratings, they often cannot get bank accommodation because they lack sufficient equity capital. The gap in the equity capital could be helped by a more realistic attitude on the part of the owners and by further development of specialized institutions, including small business investment corporations.

The operations of monetary policy have had a greater direct impact on the availability of mortgage credit for residential building than on any other major type of credit, in large measure because of the interest ceilings on low-down-payment mortgages insured or guaranteed by the federal government. Because mortgage lending rates are unlikely to move quickly enough to make mortgage loans fully competitive with bonds, the mortgage market would probably be more sensitive to credit restraint even without this feature. Moreover, interest charges are a large part of carrying costs on housing, and increasing costs cut demands for housing.

Because residential construction tends to move inversely with the business cycle, it tends to stabilize the economy as a whole. The residential construction industry has been destabilized by variations in monetary policy. It does not follow that residential construction would have been more stable if monetary policy had *not* been varied cyclically. Variations in *total* construction employment have followed general business cycle movements. The countercyclical behavior of residential construction only partially offset the cyclical variations in total construction. Taking all these factors into consideration, the Commission believes that the cyclical impact of monetary policy on residential construction has not been undesirable.

It is also claimed that monetary restraint affects adversely the distribution of income among individuals. This income distribution effect, however, is difficult to measure. On the assumption that employment will be the same if any of the following three measures is used, monetary restraint may be considered an alternative to outright inflation or as an alternative to control of demand by fiscal policy.

Clearly those who are net creditors will fare better with monetary restraint than with inflation. They avoid a reduction in the real value of their net assets, and they obtain a higher interest income. Who are the net creditors? Though the data available are neither accurate nor complete, apparently, on the average, persons with incomes below about $6,000 are net creditors, those in higher income groups are net debtors. These figures include the debt of corporations in which the individuals hold shares and further assume that their share of the debt of the federal government is proportionate to their federal tax payments. While the very low income families are net debtors, a small proportion, mainly retired persons, are net creditors. It is this group which loses most by unforeseen inflation and gains from higher interest rates.

At any level of government expenditures, a given level of demand may be achieved with a restrictive monetary policy and relatively low taxes or with an easier monetary policy and higher taxes. The use of restrictive monetary policy will tend to improve the position of net creditors and worsen the position of net debtors. How tax increases will affect them will depend on the character and composition of the increases. In general the Commission sees no reason to object to the use of monetary policy relative to tax policy on account of its differential impacts among sectors of the economy or size of business, or its direct income distribution effects.

. . .

44 THE DIFFERENTIAL EFFECTS OF TIGHT MONEY

GEORGE L. BACH AND C. J. HUIZENGA

Why can we not measure the differential impact of monetary policy by comparing the percentage increase of loans going to large businesses and the percentage obtained by small businesses? Is the sophisticated measuring rod used by the authors really necessary? Another question is: Could there be any relationship between the relative increases in interest rates noted in section V of this article and the credit supplied as found in section III? Finally, note the dating of the statistics in this selection. Although the data refer to happenings of more than a decade ago, they are still the most recent statistics.

Restrictive monetary policy is widely opposed because of its alleged undesirably discriminatory effects. Tight money, it is claimed, lets big borrowers go free while shutting off little ones. It restricts construction activity while letting investment in plant and equipment boom. Conversely, it restricts investment so sharply it induces recession. It runs up interest costs to those least able to pay. It penalizes new borrowers at the expense of old established customers. All these claims, and many more, have been urged upon Congress, by economists and by others, as powerful reasons against reliance on restrictive monetary policy to check moderate inflation.

Given substantially full employment, any restrictive policy is discriminatory in the sense that it changes the allocation of resources from what would have prevailed in the absence of the restriction. Assume full employment with excess demand (inflationary pressure) and some given allocation of resources. If monetary policy is now used to produce a smaller money supply than otherwise would have existed, a different allocation of resources may result. It is this shift in resources which is presumably meant when critics speak of the discriminatory (or differential) effects of tight money. We shall use the term in this sense.

The following pages describe an investigation of the "discriminatory" effects of tight money which isolates these effects by studying the differential lending-investing policies during the 1955–57 period of "tight" banks in contrast to those of "loose" banks which were otherwise substantially identical but where there was little or no pressure of tight money.

I. DESIGN OF STUDY

Identification of possible discriminatory effects of tight money during any period of credit restraint is difficult. In 1955–57, for example, we know that commercial bank lending to large borrowers rose much more than that to small borrowers. But this fact is not necessarily evidence that tight money led banks to discriminate against small borrowers. Instead, the observed results may have arisen largely from the demand side of markets rather

From G. L. Bach and C. J. Huizenga, "The Differential Effects of Tight Money," *American Economic Review,* 51, 52–59, 64–66, 70–72, 76–80. Reprinted by permission.

than from the supply side, and indeed there is much evidence that such was the case in that particular period. The problem is to devise a method of isolating the supply effects (that is, the discriminatory effects of tight money in restricting lending) as distinct from the effects of differing demands for credit.

To isolate the effects of tight money on the behavior of lenders, the following basic design was used. First a period was chosen when money was generally agreed to be tight and growing tighter—October 1955 to October 1957. Then a large sample of banks (about 1700) was chosen, large enough to permit stratification so that substantial numbers of banks in all major cells were presumably substantially identical in all respects (including potential loan demand) except for the differential impact of tight money upon them. Then the banks were divided into three subgroups—"tight," "medium," and "loose," depending on the degree of tightness induced in them by the over-all tightness of money. The tightest quartile of banks was placed in the tight group, the next two quartiles in the medium group, and the loosest quartile in the loose group. The loose banks, as is explained below, were selected so that it would be agreed that they were loose by almost any reasonable test—for example, they were not tight by standard tests at the beginning of the period, and they gained more deposits over the period than they increased their loans and investments.

Then the lending and investing behavior of these three groups of banks was compared over the period, with the presumption that the tight quartile would reflect the differential impact of tight money on the supply side, when compared with the loose quartile which apparently felt little if any pressure of tightness. This comparison between the tight and loose quartiles seems especially apt to isolate the differential effects of tight money, since loose banks were clearly quite loose and there is little evidence that they refused any borrowers because of shortage of lending power or for any reason other than failure of borrowers to meet general banking standards of credit-worthiness. In testing different hypotheses about possible discriminatory effects of tight money, banks were stratified by size and other major characteristics within each of the three tightness groupings, to assure comparability on factors other than tightness.

. . .

B. Measures of Bank Tightness

For explaining banker (lender) behavior, how tight a bank is depends on how tight the banker (the decision-maker) feels it is. One bank may be extremely tight for lending purposes, even though it has a large volume of excess reserves and liquid securities, *if* the banker believes that these reserves and securities are essential to the sound operation of the bank. Another bank may be loose for lending purposes, even though it has very small excess reserves and only a modest supply of liquid securities, *if* the banker feels that he nevertheless has more reserves and more securities than he needs for normal operating purposes (assuming that he is within standard examination regulations). Thus, standard measures like excess reserves and free reserves are not reliable measures of bank tightness for lending purposes.

. . .

This poses difficult problems of measuring the tightness of individual banks and of the banking system. We cannot peer into the banker's mind to see what makes him feel tight or loose. Indeed, the banker's own word is possibly not to be accepted. So we need to search for surrogate measures.

. . .

INDIVIDUAL BANKS. To test tight money hypotheses, we ranked all individual banks by degree of tightness as of October 1955, and by increase in tightness between October 1955 and October 1957. A more satisfactory measure than excess or free reserves appeared to be the ratio:

$$\frac{\text{excess reserves} - \text{borrowing} + \text{government bills and certificates}}{\text{deposits}}$$

We call this a looseness ratio, since an increase in the ratio means that the bank has become looser for lending purposes.

This ratio was used to rank individual banks as of October 1955. The ratio reflects the fact that banks consider short-term governments as secondary reserves, only slightly differentiated from actual reserves. Moreover, this ratio varies appreciably at individual banks with changes in economic conditions, at the same time that the ratio of excess reserves, or even free reserves, to deposits varies little for most banks. The ratio falls (indicates tightening) for the banking system as a whole and for most individual banks over the 1955–57 period, when we know that money was tightening for the system as a whole. On the other hand, the ratio has weaknesses. For example, it does not reflect the fact that interbank deposits provide a special source of liquidity to some banks; thus, most small country banks were probably relatively looser than the ratio shows. Neither is vault cash included. Nor are near-maturity securities other than bills and certificates. Most important, it does not include longer-term government securities, but there are convincing reasons for this exclusion.

• • •

To measure the *change* in tightness between October 1955 and October 1957 two tests were initially applied. First, all individual banks were ranked by the decrease in the looseness ratio between October 1955 and October 1957. Second, banks were ranked according to the percentage increase in their deposits over the period. For the individual bank, as distinguished from the banking system, it is primarily gain or loss of deposits which makes the bank looser or tighter for new lending and investing. Therefore, the simplest measure of whether an individual bank is growing looser or tighter is the extent to which it is gaining or losing deposits. Thus, all banks were ranked by percentage increase in deposits over the two-year period. Banks with the greatest loss of deposits showed the greatest increase in tightness, with others ranked in order of deposit gain.

Broadly, the rank-order results for individual banks were similar using these two methods over the 1955–57 period. However, the change-in-deposits method both seemed more significant in explaining individual bank lending-investment behavior and offered a more sharply discriminating measure as among individual banks. This is because changes in the tightness ratio were quite small for most banks, so that the individual bank ranking might be considerably influenced by small special circumstances, while differences in the rate of deposit growth were large. Thus, we decided to use the second measure alone—change in deposits between October 1955 and October 1957—as the criterion of the extent to which banks became tighter or looser.

To obtain the final tightness ranking of all individual banks, the ranking as of 1955 and the ranking by increase in tightness for the 1955–57 period were combined in the following way. First, banks were divided into the tightest and loosest halves on the basis of the looseness ratio as of October 1955. Then, all banks in the tightest half for 1955 were rank-ordered by the degree to which their tightness increased over the succeeding two years, as measured by relative deposit loss or gain. The tight group for the study (the tightest quartile) was then obtained by taking the 50 percent of the tight half as of 1955 which showed the greatest further increase in tightness by 1957. Similarly, the loosest half as of 1955 was rank-ordered by change in tightness, and the 50 percent showing the greatest increase in looseness was considered the loose group for the study. The remaining two inner quartiles were considered the medium group.

This test combines tightness as of the beginning of the period with change in tightness. In principle, there need be no relationship between these two measures. On the other hand, the purpose was to segregate at the two extremes banks which both were tight in absolute level and became tighter, from those that were clearly loose in absolute level and became looser. The procedure followed achieved this result. . . .

C. Hypotheses Investigated

Using this analytical approach, five general hypotheses were considered: (1) That tight money induced banks to shift from government securities to loans. (2) That tight money led banks to discriminate against small borrowers in lending to businesses. (3) That tight money led banks to differentiate in favor of particular industry groups among business borrowers. (4) That tight money was effective in checking loans especially to those firms which were primarily responsible for the 1955–57 investment and inventory boom. (5) That tight money led banks to raise interest charges especially to small borrowers and to particular industry groups against which they wished to discriminate.*

• • •

III. DISCRIMINATION BY SIZE OF BUSINESS BORROWER

One of the commonest objections to the use of tight money to check moderate inflation is that this policy discriminates against small businesses. During the 1955–57 period as shown in Table 1, loans to big businesses did indeed expand much more than those to small businesses. This does not, however, necessarily mean that tight money led to discrimination against small borrowers. Instead, the pattern of loans may have reflected differing demands from large and small borrowers, where the loan demands of credit-worthy large borrowers (as judged by commercial banking credit standards) rose more rapidly than those from credit-worthy small borrowers.

• • •

While the evidence generally fails to support the hypothesis that tight money leads banks to discriminate against small business borrowers, the argument has not been unmistakably refuted. We therefore conducted the following test of the hypothesis. The same groupings of banks into tight, medium, and loose were continued. To improve comparability banks were further divided into five different size-groups (based on volume of deposits). For this and all succeeding analyses of business loans, data include all commercial and industrial loans plus real estate loans to businesses at all member banks. The increase in loans to borrowers of different sizes was compared at tight, loose and medium banks, both for all banks combined and for banks in each of the five size-groups. If tight banks increased loans relatively more to large (compared to small) borrowers than did comparable loose banks, this test says that tight banks discriminated against small borrowers. Since the demand for loans was presumably substantially identical at tight and loose banks within bank size-groups and since loose banks were not restrained significantly by tight money, the analysis presumes that any such discrimination by tight banks would be attributable to tight money.

Table 2, for example, shows that at medium-sized banks loans to borrowers of all sizes rose more at loose than at tight banks, with the behavior of medium banks intermediate. We might say that tight banks discriminated against borrowers of all sizes, but they surely did not

*In this abridgment, only items 2 and 5 are presented. The methods used for the remaining categories are substantially the same, and the conclusions may be found in the final section—ed.

Table 1. Bank Loans to Businesses[a]

Asset Size of Borrower[b] (000's omitted)	Percent Increase in Loans, October 1955–October 1957
All borrowers	*31.9*
Less than $50	− 3.0
$50 to $250	16.7
$250 to $1,000	24.8
$1,000 to $5,000	21.3
$5,000 to $25,000	24.7
$25,000 to $100,000	51.1
$100,000 or more	66.4

[a]Reproduced from [*Financing Small Business.* Report to the Committees on Banking and Currency and the Select Committees on Banking and Currency, 85th Cong., 2nd sess., by the Federal Reserve System, Parts 1 and 2 (Washington, D.C., 1958), p. 37]. Data cover commercial and industrial loans at all member banks, plus real estate loans to businesses.

[b]As of October 1955.

Table 2. Increase in Loans to Business Borrowers at Medium-Sized Banks, October 1955–October 1957[a]

Assets of Borrower (000's omitted)	Percent Increase in Loans at:		
	Loose Banks	*Medium Banks*	*Tight Banks*
Under $50	21	−11	−13
$50–250	76	10	5
$250–1,000	72	25	25
$1,000–5,000	72	50	30
$5,000–25,000	90	49	30
$25,000–100,000	266	104	14
$100,000 and over	25	30	22

[a]Commercial and industrial loans plus real estate loans to businesses at all member banks with total deposits of $100–500 million as of October 1955.

discriminate especially against small borrowers. On the contrary, compared to loose banks, they discriminated especially against most *large* borrowers. That is, loose banks increased their loans to large borrowers by percentages far in excess of the increases of loans to small borrowers, while tight banks increased their loans to large borrowers only somewhat more than to small borrowers. Since borrower loan-demand was presumably substantially identical at loose, medium, and tight banks, this evidence appears, at least for these medium-sized banks, clearly to reject the hypothesis that tight money led banks to discriminate especially against small borrowers.*

. . .

In summary, the size-of-borrower data reject the hypothesis that tight money led banks to discriminate substantially against small borrowers in favor of large. Only at banks in the $500–$1,000 million deposit size-group are the data consistent with this hypothesis of substantial discrimination; for the banking system as a whole and for all other size-groups of banks, either the differential behavior at tight and loose banks was slight or it was in favor of small borrowers. Crudely, the data suggest that bankers tended under tight money, as would have been expected, to meet their strongest credit-worthy loan demands while in the main adhering to their regular criteria of credit-

*The remainder of this section presents data on percentage increases in loans to different-sized borrowers by tight, medium, and loose banks and by deposit size. Table 2 is representative of the data omitted—ed.

worthiness; and that in so far as limited discrimination occurred on other bases, bankers may well have tended to care especially for their best customers—at large banks especially larger businesses and at small banks especially smaller businesses. But this last sentence is based more on the "feel" of the data and on interviews with bankers than on rigorous analysis of the data; and the central fact of lack of substantial lender discrimination by size of borrower is the one that emerges from the data.

• • •

V. INTEREST RATES

Small businesses generally pay higher interest rates at banks than do large businesses, primarily reflecting differences in size of loan. Small businesses usually borrow small amounts, and investigation charges, servicing charges, and related expenses bulk relatively much larger than on the large loans customarily obtained by large businesses. Large businesses often pay lower interest rates on comparable size loans than do small businesses, but the differences are small and probably reflect mainly differences in risk and in loan-administration costs.

Table 3 shows interest rates paid by borrowers of different sizes in 1955, in 1957, and the net increase over the two-year period. In both 1955 and 1957, the average interest rate paid varied inversely with the size of borrower. But as interest rates rose with tight money over the two-year period, rates to large borrowers were increased considerably more than rates to small borrowers. Over the two years, the spread between average rates to the largest and smallest borrowers declined from 2.5 to 2.1 percent. While the average rate on all new loans rose from 4.2 to 5 percent, that on loans to large borrowers rose nearly twice as much absolutely, and even more relatively, as that on loans to small borrowers. During the period, moreover, bank requirements that borrowers maintain compensating balances also became more widespread. Since these requirements apply primarily to large borrowers it is probable that differences in effective interest rates narrowed even more than the data in Table 3 indicate.

This greater increase in rates to large borrowers probably reflected, at least in part, the fact that small borrowers by 1955 were already paying rates near the customary or legal upper limits for non-consumer loans at many banks. These legal limits are as low as 6 percent in eleven states, including New York, New Jersey and Pennsylvania, and range up to 15 percent in others. Thus as interest rates rose, rates to large borrowers could be increased without violating the customary or legal upper limit, while rates to small borrowers could be raised little or

Table 3. Interest Rates on Business Loans, by Size of Borrower[a]

Asset Size of Borrower (000's omitted)	Average Interest Rate (Percent Per Annum)		
	1955	1957	Absolute Increase
All borrowers	*4.2*	*5.0*	*.8*
Under $50	5.8	6.5	.7
$50 to $250	5.1	5.7	.6
$250 to $1,000	4.6	5.4	.8
$1,000 to $5,000	4.1	5.1	1.0
$5,000 to $25,000	3.7	4.8	1.1
$25,000 to $100,000	3.4	4.5	1.1
$100,000 and over	3.3	4.4	1.1

[a]Size of borrower as of October 1955. Rates are average rates charged by reporting banks over the July–October period for 1955 and 1957. More detailed data, for loans at different size banks, are presented by the Federal Reserve in [*ibid.*, pp. 388–389].

not at all. In any case, for the banking system as a whole, it is clear that interest rates to small borrowers rose less than those to large borrowers. In the aggregate tight money did not lead to discrimination in interest costs against small borrowers.

• • •

In summary, therefore, there is little evidence of much differential interest rate behavior at tight and loose banks during the period of increasingly tight money. This finding is consistent with the hypothesis that the pattern of interest rates at banks is set by general market forces, and that banks generally follow a policy of price leadership in establishing interest rates, rather than using them as a device to discriminate among borrowers. The hypothesis that tight money raised interest costs especially to small borrowers is clearly rejected by the data.

VI. CONCLUSION

What is the significance of these findings for the use of restrictive monetary policy in the future? Tight money in 1955–57 apparently led those commercial banks which felt its impact to alter their asset portfolios significantly; they shifted to obtain funds to increase loans to profitable borrowers, especially business firms, even at the cost of liquidating government securities on a declining market. Discrimination amongst borrowers was apparently largely on traditional banking standards of credit-worthiness and goodness of borrowers, with differing changes in loans to various borrower groups reflecting primarily differences in loan demands, rather than discrimination by lenders on other grounds, once standards of credit-worthiness were met. Widespread criticisms of tight money as unfairly discriminating against small borrowers, both in availability of loans and interest costs, are not supported by the data.

On the other hand, the fact that increasingly tight banks continued to increase loans to good business customers, whose demand for money reflected partly heavy investment outlays and inventory carrying costs, meant that tight money did not act to deter especially these prime movers in the investment boom. Thus, although tight money in 1955–57 may have led to little "unfair" discrimination against particular borrower groups, it did permit funds to go extensively to the same borrowers who would have obtained them in the absence of tight money. Whether the marginal borrowers shut out by tight money would have contributed significantly to either undesirable investment or inflation cannot be told from these data. Probably at least as much (more, on the objective evidence) of the marginal credit shut off was to large as to small firms, but no comparable generalization as to industry is possible from these data.

Over all, tight money in 1955–57 appears not to have changed greatly the allocation of bank credit among major classes of business borrowers from what it would have been with looser money, certainly not by size of firm and only moderately by industry—partly because money was not tight enough to limit seriously loans to credit-worthy customers at a substantial proportion of all banks. Tight money's main effect was apparently to hold down the total volume of credit while inducing credit rationing at tight banks mainly in response to relative strength of demand among "good" bank customers. Whether one evaluates this conclusion as strengthening or weakening the case for restrictive monetary policy may depend largely on his taste for direct controls as against market forces. Tight money helped to restrict total spending and keep the price level down while doing relatively little directly to reallocate resources—the traditional objective of general monetary policy. It apparently did not especially check the industries at the core of the investment boom.

45 UNEVEN IMPACTS OF MONETARY POLICY: WHAT TO DO ABOUT THEM?

DAVID P. EASTBURN

The year 1966 will be known in monetary and banking circles as the year of the "crunch." Severe restraints on the expansion of credit were imposed by the Federal Reserve, interest rates skyrocketed, and borrowers found it difficult to obtain all the credit they needed. To be sure, not all borrowers found it equally hard; some segments of the economy were hit harder than others. Housing was hit especially heavily; the shortage of mortgage credit has been blamed for the 25 percent drop in spending on residential construction. In the wake of this fall in spending, construction materials suppliers and the producers of home furnishings were hit by a reduction in demand. Business borrowers, on the other hand, found credit less scarce, although they had to face steeper terms. Dr. Eastburn wrote his article with the experience of the crunch fresh in everyone's mind. One word of caution: before concluding that the addition of new selective controls would increase the efficiency of discretionary policy, remember that in order to apply the controls effectively, the authorities must correctly identify the causes of the malfunction in the economy. With the art of forecasting at today's levels, to ask for such a diagnosis may be expecting too much of the central bankers.

Events of the past year [i.e., 1966—ed.] have demonstrated that monetary policy can have strongly uneven impacts. No one is particularly happy about this fact, least of all the Federal Reserve. For not only do these impacts raise obvious questions of equity, but they produce economic and political repercussions that make the Fed's job more difficult. If monetary policy is to be of maximum effectiveness in the future, serious consideration will have to be given to the unevenness of its impacts.

Three approaches might be explored:

1. Tolerate the uneven impacts
2. Remove market imperfections that help produce them
3. Deal with them selectively

From David P. Eastburn, "Uneven Impacts of Monetary Policy: What to Do About Them?" Federal Reserve Bank of Philadelphia, *Business Review*, January 1967, p. 2, 21–23.

Which of these approaches one takes depends to a great extent on his philosophy of monetary policy—the degree to which he would have it intervene in the market place to influence the allocation of resources.

1. *Tolerate them.* This is not simply a do-nothing position reflecting a callous disregard for the problem or for the human consequences of it. In its finest sense, this approach involves a careful calculation of costs and benefits.

Those who would take this approach believe that uneven impacts are a price for letting the market place work. They have no question about the trade-off. Although they might wish the market would allocate credit more evenly, they argue that intervention runs the risk of doing an even worse job and severely damaging the economy in the process. The market works remarkably well considering all the impediments that have been put in its way. Despite our efforts to learn more about the monetary system, we could not possibly know better than the market.

Nor do those who take this approach necessarily overlook the drift of public sentiment *toward* intervention in markets. They feel the public is misguided in attempting to provide special supports for certain parts of the economy and trying to channel resources in one direction rather than another. If special support is deemed politically or socially appropriate for some particular part of the economy, say housing, this is better provided directly by means such as subsidies, rather than through monetary policy. Theirs is the purest form of non-interventionist philosophy of monetary policy.

2. *Remove market imperfections.* Since the market is not completely free and perfect, another approach would remove some of the imperfections which help produce uneven impacts.

Examples suggested by recent events naturally tend to cluster in markets for mortgages and savings. Some have proposed that usury laws be changed to permit rates on mortgages to compete with those on alternative investments. Others have suggested that creation of a secondary market would improve the liquidity of conventional mortgages and make them more attractive. Still others have even raised the possibility that rates on outstanding mortgages could fluctuate as rates on other instruments move up and down. Proposals such as these are designed to alter the market mechanism so as to improve the competitiveness of mortgages.

Another field for action is in rates on time and savings deposits. Experience of the past year has reinforced the view of many that ceilings on such deposits impair the free flow of funds and should be removed. But the past year also has demonstrated the severe disruption of relationships among savings institutions that can ensue from a freer flow of time and savings funds. It is much more painful to *remove* market imperfections to open up competition than simply to *immobilize* imperfections to preserve the *status quo.*

So even though this approach may be designed to make the market better able to do its job without producing severely uneven impacts, it is not so simple as it might seem. Who is willing to face the disruption of existing institutional patterns that can ensue from removing impediments to a free flow of funds?

3. *Deal selectively.* This third approach has been the one most often used. In fact, a review of Federal Reserve history suggests that the selective approach to monetary policy has tended to recur whenever general instruments of policy have been under great pressure. For purposes of illustration:

"Direct action" in the late 1920's; designed to deal selectively with the problem of credit flowing into the stock market.

Margin requirements; imposed in 1934 to deal with the same problem.

Moral suasion; use of official pronouncements from time to time throughout the past fifty years to encourage or discourage the flow of credit in certain directions.

Regulations W and X; for the purpose of restraining the expansion of consumer and real-estate credit.

"Operation Twist"; designed in the early 1960's to influence the structure of rates in order to resolve conflicting objectives of domestic and international policy.

The September 1, 1966 letter from the Federal Reserve System to member banks; intended to induce banks to curtail business lending in return for longer accommodation at the discount window.*

The case for a selective approach rests firmly on the fact that monetary policy does impinge on the economy selectively. Although general instruments of policy

*See headnote to selection 36—ed.

purport only to regulate the total supply of credit and not various uses of credit, they do in fact affect some uses more than others.

This being the case, why not employ existing instruments of policy, or design new ones, to influence uses of credit in a *desired* manner? In rebuttal to those who say that this would interfere with the free market, proponents of the selective approach reply that operations of the market place are not sacred. In the first place, the market may not take into consideration the public's social priorities. And secondly, experience tells us that the market frequently permits imbalances to arise: consumer credit may be so plentiful as to produce a boom in consumer durables; credit to business may be so readily available as to encourage overinvestment.

Monetary policy long since has been accepted as a way of preventing extremes —booms and busts—in over-all economic activity. Shouldn't the next evolutionary step be to influence *parts* of the economy that produce these over-all extremes? We'll never know as much as we'd like about how the economy works, and policy always will require human judgment, so mistakes will be made. But surely, over time, we should learn more and make fewer mistakes. Hopefully this has been happening in monetary policy up to now.

Which of these approaches will be taken probably will depend on which has the least disadvantages. Of the three, the selective approach departs most drastically from a philosophy of nonintervention in the market place. Removing impediments to competition—the second approach—would help the market work more freely but would require drastic changes in existing institutional relationships. To take the first approach—tolerating the uneven impacts—would run against the mainstream of public sentiment. The public seems intolerant of the market place if it frustrates their social or economic priorities. The public may be misguided in this attitude, but in a democratic society the public is always "right." If this continues to be the nature of public sentiment, some action will be needed to deal with uneven impacts of policy.

Perhaps the best approach is a combination of the three. Free markets offer the unquestioned advantage of allocating funds according to demands. The fact that markets generally are relatively free in our economy goes a long way toward explaining the rapid growth and high standard of living we have enjoyed. To the extent possible, therefore, freedom of markets is a desirable base from which to start.

This requires action to remove some market imperfections and impediments to the free flow of funds. However, it is unrealistic to think that this approach can go very far without running into strong opposition. A selective approach may be needed to do the rest of the job.

If this is so, some forward planning may be required. In ordinary circumstances, the impacts of monetary policy are even enough that an over-all approach presents no problem. But in exceptional periods of restraint, the selective approach has tended to be an *ad hoc* expedient. Perhaps careful consideration of the advantages and disadvantages of the selective approach—including such troublesome aspects as the administrative burden and exposure of policy to pressure groups—would place us in better position to deal with uneven impacts in the future.

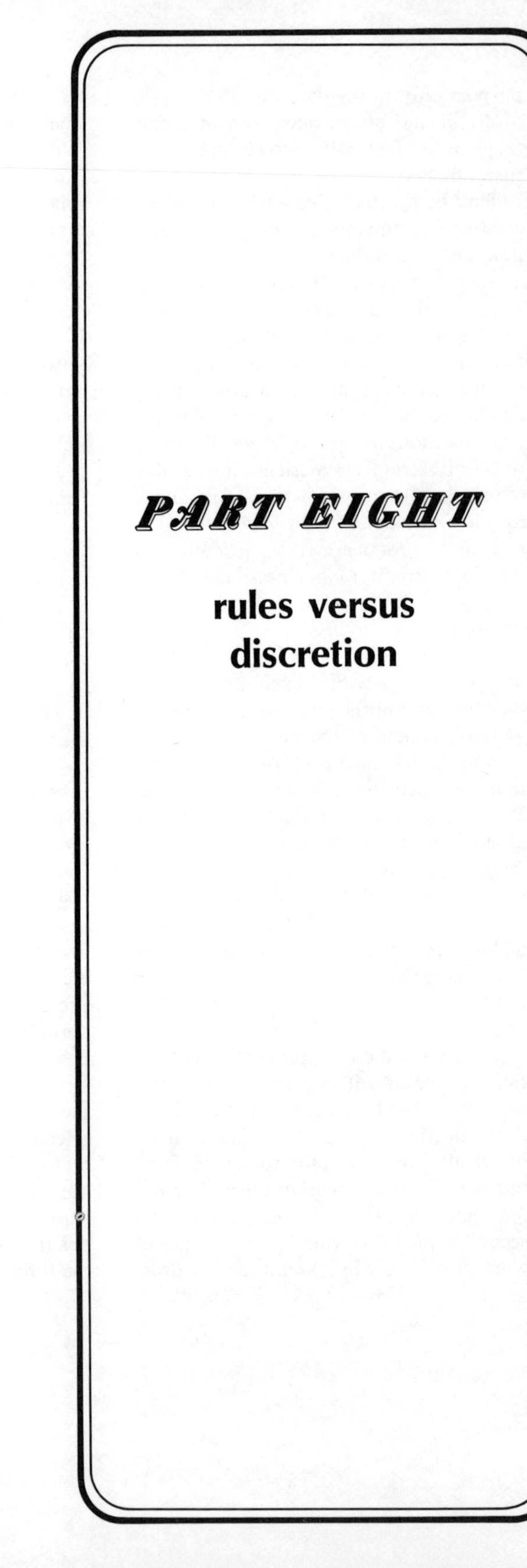

PART EIGHT

rules versus discretion

What is the optimal form of governmental intervention in the monetary system? Is the present practice whereby the supply of money is controlled by the central bank authorities the best? Or, alternatively, should central bank discretion be eliminated and a mechanistic formula be substituted? This is what the "rules versus discretion" controversy is all about.

To a slight degree, differing philosophies of government color the views of the disputants. Those who oppose discretion are concerned with limiting the powers of government and subscribe to a conservative political philosophy. "The government that governs least governs best" is at the center of this viewpoint. The corollary to this dictum states that where a clear-cut need for government action is evident, the powers of those charged with implementing policy should extend no further than is necessary. Just as the competitive market economy disperses economic power, so too should political influence be atomized. Control by individuals is anathema, and rules are preferred to discretion whenever feasible.

Opposed to this outlook, which takes a pessimistic view of human nature, is the belief that government is not a necessary evil but is a prerequisite for the stability and progress of society. Checks and balances, rather than rules, ensure against the usurpation of power by any single man or by a small caucus. As long as those left to conduct the policy are responsible to an elective authority, the democratic principle is maintained.

It is not for an economist to debate the validity or merits of these two philosophies of government. Moreover, it is not really necessary. When one comes to discuss the specific issues where the implications of the philosophies are relevant, it becomes apparent that differences in policy recommendations stem less from ideological grounds than from pragmatic concerns.

That specific, practical evaluations and not philosophies matter in the rule versus discretion debate is clearly evident in the controversy over the monetary rule. The rule that has gained widespread attention today is that the money supply should be increased by a constant rate day by day and year by year. Whether that rate is 3 percent or 4 percent or some other percentage is a secondary consideration; that money supply is to increase automatically is of the utmost importance. The authors of the selections in this Part clash over the workability of the rule and the historical record of discretion; ideological arguments will be found in the first selection only, and even there they play a minor role.

The monetary rule controversy can be understood best if we consider what the proponents of the rule must achieve to establish their case. Essentially, those supporting the rule must fulfill three conditions in order to prove the validity of their proposal. First, they must demonstrate that discretionary monetary policy has been unsuccessful, that its historical record has been poor. Second, they must show convincingly that the poor record is a direct consequence of discretion rather than a result of causes unrelated to the exercise of monetary policy by the central bankers. If this is not the case—if, for example, the ineffectiveness of past monetary policy was a result of an inadequate control mechanism—the logical conclusion is to equip the authorities with suitable armaments rather than dismiss them for incompetence. Reform within, not replacement of, the present system is called for. Third, a positive case must be made for the rule. Unless the rule is demonstrably superior to the present system, no matter how poor the latter may be, it can never be considered a suitable replacement.

Milton Friedman takes each of these three points in turn and declares in favor of the rule. His critique of monetary policy is brief, and the interested reader may wish to supplement it by referring to Friedman's monumental *A Monetary History of the United States, 1867–1960,* written with Anna J. Schwartz. Edward S. Shaw contributes a different dimension to the issue, demonstrating what he conceives to be the advantages of the rule, although his main topic is, in fact, the benefits of stable prices. Professors Friedman and Shaw assign the highest priority to the goal of price level stability. Accompanying this value judgment is the further belief that controlling money supply mechanically is the only way to achieve stable prices.

Those opposed to the rule do so for a number of reasons. First, they have no faith in mechanistic controls over the money supply under present institutional conditions. Moreover, should the institutional structure be reformed by eliminating the ability of commercial banks to vary the money supply, for example, the link connecting money and prices will still be more complex than that imagined by the proponents of the rule. Velocity is not stable; the quantity theory of money is denied. These points and some additional arguments are made by Daniel Ahearn in the third selection. Essentially, his article focuses on the technical difficulties surrounding the implementation of the rule. In other words, he attacks the rule's advocates for not meeting the third condition cited earlier—to demonstrate that the rule is superior to discretion.

Nor is the case against discretion as strong as Milton Friedman contends. Few economists accept the Friedman contention that the responsibility for the Great Depression of the 1930s rests primarily on the monetary authorities or that they are solely to blame for other episodes of less dramatic impact. Indeed, a different reading of history, although it would not absolve the Federal Reserve entirely, would reduce the cogency of the criticism. The British scholar Thomas Wilson, for example, attributes the depth of the depression to a "declining demand for houses and a serious exhaustion of investment opportunities" coming on top of a "fall in the rate of consumption."[1] It is doubtful that any action by the Federal Reserve could have prevented or even inhibited the snowballing effect of this structural weakness. Remember, too, that at this time the monetary authorities could not lower bank reserve requirements and thereby ease the pressures on the banks; this power was given to them only after the crash.

These points lead to two further observations. The first has to do with the relevance of past history for the present. On the one hand, the institutional framework has changed markedly since the middle of the 1930s and especially after the Banking Act of 1935. Just one example will suffice. Federal Reserve officers today have far greater flexibility in their choice of monetary weapons. The difficulties of discretion attributable to inadequate armament in the third and fourth decades of this century are not likely to be repeated. In addition, as with most of us who learn by experience, early errors of the Federal Reserve, reflected in its history, probably will not recur. Such mistakes can be ascribed to the infancy and adolescence of the Federal Reserve System; in its adulthood, they must decline. Thus we should be wary in projecting past monetary history into the future.

The second implication of the early period concerns the changing objectives of monetary policy. In 1914 the Federal Reserve was charged with the task of accommodating business; in the third decade of the century price stability and maintenance of the international value of the dollar were of prime importance; in the depression years of the 1930s, expansion of the sluggish economy was a major concern; in the fifth decade, war finance headed the list of priorities. Thus the Federal Reserve has found itself responding flexibly to the changing demands of the economy and society. Indeed, the Employment Act of 1946 declares that the policy of the federal government—and this declaration surely encompasses the Federal Reserve, too—is to promote maximum production, employment, and purchasing power. Consequently, a policy designed with a single objective—price stability—implicitly forsakes other goals of society, claps the authority in a rigid mold, and eliminates the flexibility that makes for adaptation. (The implicit assumption underlying this statement is the inability to achieve other goals unless some degree of price stability is sacrificed. How valid is this assumption? See Part IX on inflation.) Moreover, evaluating past history with price stability as the criterion leads to false impressions in judging the efficacy of discretion. The appropriate test for measuring the effectiveness of discretionary policy is not whether prices have remained stable but whether the Federal Reserve was able to move toward its objectives *as it had defined them*. Thus the fact that government financing during the war years 1941–1945 was successful and that the interest rate pattern was maintained as the central bank wished it to be indicates the effectiveness of discretionary monetary policy.

---

[1]Thomas Wilson, *Fluctuations in Income and Employment: with Special Reference to Recent American Experience and Post-War Prospects* (New York: Pitman, 1948).

In short, those who oppose the rule and the practicability of monetary rules in general find absurd the belief that fallible men can devise infallible rules. Moreover, they do not agree that the record of discretionary monetary policy is as poor as some economists believe or as incapable of improvement.

As was true in many issues already investigated, logical analysis alone is insufficient to resolve controversies. Empirical studies can prove valuable aids in these instances. The final selection consists of an excerpt from Franco Modigliani's article on rules versus discretion. This tour de force concludes in favor of discretion and is a study that must be considered seriously.

In the last few years, the rule has been adopted by a number of Congressional leaders, and dissatisfaction with monetary policies has encouraged others to support it. Whether the rule is being advocated sincerely or as a ploy to swing the Federal Reserve around to a less restrictive monetary policy is difficult to ascertain. The Joint Economic Committee has recommended that the money supply grow at an annual rate of no less than 2 percent or more than 6 percent. Congress as a whole has not reacted to this suggestion, and apparently neither has the Federal Reserve. The problem falls in another area; it will be wise to keep a close watch on future developments there.

46 WHAT IS TO BE OUR INTERNAL MONETARY POLICY?

MILTON FRIEDMAN

The money supply rule is spelled out most clearly in the following excerpt from Professor Friedman's brief but perceptive *A Program for Monetary Stability*. That the rule is an integral part of his book is important, for two circumstances under which the rule might be introduced can be clearly envisaged. One possibility is to order the Federal Reserve to increase the money supply by a constant percentage, while leaving the present institutions and monetary framework unaltered. In this instance, both practical and theoretical difficulties abound, many of which are indicated in Daniel Ahearn's article. Alternatively, and this is surely the implication of the aforementioned monograph, the whole institutional framework could be altered, with the constant growth of money supply rule among the reforms to be implemented. Then Friedman's case becomes more convincing, although its practical chances of being legislated into effect recede proportionally. In the event that the reform is to be all-pervasive, one critic has noted impishly that the proper title of the book ought to have been "A Program for Monetary Sterility."

• • •

In a celebrated article on "Rules versus Authorities in Monetary Policy,"* Henry Simons contrasted sharply two ways of answering this question: one, by specifying a general goal and then giving monetary authorities wide powers to use at their discretion in promoting it; the other, by assigning specific responsibilities to monetary authorities to be carried out in accordance with rules specified in advance and known to all. As Simons made clear, the contrast is not complete. The general goal alone limits somewhat the discretion of the authorities and the powers assigned to them do so to an even greater extent; and reasonable rules are hardly capable of being written that do not leave some measure of discretion. Yet the contrast is nonetheless both marked and important.

In practice, we have relied almost wholly on authorities. . . . We have done so not by intention but because the change in the role of the gold standard brought about by World War I loosened so greatly what the authors of the Federal Reserve Act had expected to be the effective "rule" limiting the discretion of the monetary authorities. In the absence of the strait-jacket of a rigid gold standard, "accommodating commerce and business," to quote the original Federal Reserve Act, imposed hardly any restrictions on the discretion of the authorities.

Relying so largely on the discretion of authorities in so important an area of policy is highly objectionable on political

From Milton Friedman, *A Program for Monetary Stability* (New York: Fordham University Press, 1960), pp. 84–86, 88–94, 98–99.

*Henry Simons, "Rules versus Authorities in Monetary Policy," *Journal of Political Economy*, 44, 1–30, reprinted in F. A. Lutz and L. W. Mints (eds.), *Readings in Monetary Theory* (Homewood, Ill.: Richard D. Irwin, 1951), pp. 337–368—ed.

grounds in a free society. Experience has demonstrated that it has also had unfortunate monetary consequences. It has meant continual and unpredictable shifts in the immediate guides to policy and in the content of policy as the persons and attitudes dominating the authorities have changed—from the "real bills" emphasis of the early 1920's to the offsetting of inventory speculation of the mid-20's to the restraint of stock market speculation of the late '20's to the sensitivity to external pressures and timidity in face of internal drains of the early '30's, to the bond-support policies of the '40's, to the sensitivity to cyclical movements and reliance on "announcement effects" of the '50's. It has meant continual exposure of the authorities to political and economic pressures and to the deceptive effects of short-lived tides of events and opinions. The role of the monetary authorities is to provide a stable monetary background, to go counter to or at least not reinforce the ever shifting tides of current opinion and events. This is the justification for their alleged "independence." Yet the vagueness of their responsibilities and the wide range of their discretion has left them no means other than "wisdom" and personal perspective of withstanding contemporaneous pressures and has denied them the bulwark that clearly assigned responsibilities and definite rules would have provided.

Reliance on discretion in pursuing general goals has meant also the absence of any satisfactory criteria for judging performance. This has made it nearly impossible to assess responsibility for success or failure and has greatly enhanced the difficulty of learning by experience. The Reserve System, or even monetary authorities more broadly defined, have not been the sole agencies responsible for the general goals that they have sought to promote, and that have become the current translation of "sound credit conditions and the accommodation of commerce, industry, and agriculture"—such general goals as economic stability, full employment, price stability, growth. These goals are to be approached through the joint actions of many public and private agencies, of which monetary authorities are only one. Success or failure in achieving them cannot be attributed to monetary policy alone, and hence cannot be a criterion of performance. An amusing dividend from reading *Annual Reports* of the Federal Reserve System *seriatim* is the sharp cyclical pattern that emerges in the potency attributed to monetary forces and policy. In years of prosperity, monetary policy is a potent instrument, the skillful handling of which deserves credit for the favorable course of events; in years of adversity, other forces are the important sources of economic change, monetary policy has little leeway, and only the skillful handling of the exceedingly limited powers available prevented conditions from being even worse.

The granting of wide and important responsibilities that are neither limited by clearly defined rules for guiding policy nor subject to test by external criteria of performance is a serious defect of our present monetary arrangements. It renders monetary policy a potential source of uncertainty and instability. It also gives greater power to the men in charge for good or ill, greater "flexibility" to meet problems as they arise, to use the phrase that the Reserve System likes to emphasize. . . . Experience suggests that eliminating the danger of instability and uncertainty of policy is far more urgent than preserving "flexibility." The major need in reforming our present control of monetary policy is, therefore, to provide more definite guides to policy and more satisfactory criteria of performance.

• • •

A satisfactory policy guide or rule should be connected more directly with the means available to the monetary authority than is the price level. We will, I believe, further the ultimate end of achieving a reasonably stable price level better by specifying the role of the monetary authorities in terms of magnitudes they effectively control and for whose behavior they can properly be held responsible than by instructing them solely to do the right thing at the right time when there is no clear and accepted criterion even after the event whether they have done so. In this as in so many human activities what seems the long way round may be the short way home.

The most important magnitude that the monetary authorities can effectively control and for which they have primary responsibility is the stock of money. Under present circumstances, even the stock of money is not directly controlled by the System. The System controls directly its own earning assets. . . . The total of high-powered money is affected in addition by such factors as gold flows, changes in Treasury balances, and the like; and the total money stock for any given total of high-powered money is affected by the ratio of high-powered money to deposits that banks choose to hold and the ratio of currency to deposits that the public chooses to hold. These slips between control of earning assets and of the stock of money would be largely eliminated by the reforms proposed in the preceding chapters.* These reforms would make changes in the earning assets of the Reserve System essentially identical with changes in the money supply and thereby give the System direct control over the money supply. But even under present circumstances, the links between Reserve action and the money supply are sufficiently close, the effects occur sufficiently rapidly, and the connections are sufficiently well understood, so that reasonably close control over the money supply is feasible, given the will. I do not mean to say that the process would not involve much trial and some error but only that the errors need not be cumulative and could be corrected fairly promptly. The process involves technical problems of considerable complexity, but they are of a kind with which the System has much experience and for which the System has trained personnel.

The stock of money therefore seems to me the relevant magnitude in terms of which to formulate monetary rules and the behavior of which should be a criterion of policy performance. The question remains, what behavior of the stock of money should we seek to achieve either by instructing the monetary authorities to do so, or by designing a system under which the desired pattern would be produced automatically?

• • •

The [simplest] rule is that the stock of money be increased at a fixed rate year-in and year-out without any variation in the rate of increase to meet cyclical needs. This rule could be adopted by the Reserve System itself. Alternatively, Congress could instruct the Reserve System to follow it. If it were adopted without any other changes in our monetary arrangements, the Reserve System would have much discretion in the precise techniques used to increase the stock of money and it could achieve the objective only with an appreciable though not large margin of error—perhaps one-half to one percentage point. If the other changes I have recommended were made, the area of discretion would be narrowed radically and so would the margin of error.

To make the rule specific, we need (1) to define the stock of money to which it refers, (2) to state what the fixed rate of increase should be or how it should be determined, (3) to state what if any allowance should be made for intra-year or seasonal movements.

(1) I have heretofore used the term "the stock of money" as if it were self-evident. Of course it is not. There is a continuum of assets possessing in various degrees the qualities we attribute to the ideal construct of "money" and hence there is no unique way to draw a line

*The major reform suggested is a 100 percent reserve requirement on all commercial bank deposits—ed.

separating "money" from "near-monies"; for different purposes or at different times it may be appropriate to draw this line at different points on the continuum. In our own research we have found the most useful concept to be one that includes currency held by the public plus adjusted demand deposits plus time deposits in commercial banks but excludes time deposits in mutual savings banks, shares in savings and loan associations, and the like. The Reserve System has generally used the term "money" more narrowly, to include only currency and demand deposits, and many economists have used it more broadly, to include also time deposits in mutual savings banks. I am inclined myself to favor the concept we have used because it seems to be somewhat more closely related empirically to income and other economic magnitudes than the other concepts and because it does not require classifying the deposit liabilities of individual institutions in terms of bookkeeping categories that permit much variation. But the evidence for this concept is certainly far from conclusive.* More important, I do not believe it is vital which particular concept is chosen as long as first, it is at least as broad as currency plus adjusted demand deposits; second, a definite and clear-cut choice is made; and, third, the rate of increase chosen is adapted to the concept. The possible candidates for inclusion have had different secular rates of growth and are likely to continue to do so. They do not however vary radically with respect to one another over short periods and they would vary even less if some of my earlier suggestions were adopted, in particular, payment of interest on reserve balances with the Federal Reserve, and abolition of the present prohibition on the payment of interest on demand deposits and ceiling on the interest on time deposits.

(2) The rate of increase should be chosen so that on the average it could be expected to correspond with a roughly stable long-run level of final product prices. For the concept of money just recommended, namely, currency plus all commercial bank deposits, this would have required a rate of growth of slightly over 4% per year on the average of the past 90 years—something over 3% to allow for growth in output and 1% to allow for a secular decrease in velocity, which is to say for the increase in the stock of money per unit of output that the public has wished to hold as its real per capita income rose. To judge from this evidence, a rate of increase of 3 to 5% per year might be expected to correspond with a roughly stable price level for this particular concept of money. Since time deposits have grown in the past decade relative to demand deposits, and non-commercial bank time deposits relative to commercial, a somewhat lower rate of increase might be appropriate if a narrower definition were adopted, a somewhat higher rate, if a broader definition were adopted.

As with the definition, the particular rate of increase adopted seems to me less important than the adoption of a fixed rate provided only that the rate is somewhere in the range suggested and that it is adapted to the definition of money. A rate that turned out to be somewhat too high would mean a mild secular price rise, a rate that turned out to be somewhat too low, a mild secular price fall. Neither, it seems to me, would be serious. What is seriously disturbing to economic stability are rapid and sizable fluctuations in prices, not mild and steady secular movements in either direction. A fixed rate of increase in the stock of money would almost certainly rule out such rapid and sizable fluctuations, though it would not rule out mild cyclical or secular fluctuations, and it would give a firm basis for long range planning on the part of the public.

(3) I find the treatment of intra-year movements more puzzling. We now take for granted a seasonal movement in the

---

*See Selections 2 and 4, and 29—ed.

stock of money and tend to assimilate it to other seasonal movements. Yet there is a crucial difference. The seasonal movement in the stock of money is a quasi-deliberate act of policy, not a product of climatic or similar circumstances. One initial objective of the Reserve System was to reduce seasonal fluctuations in interest rates. It has accomplished this objective by widening seasonal movements in the stock of money. I see no objection to seasonal variation in the stock of money, provided it is regular so that the public can adapt to it. On the other hand, neither do I see any objection to seasonal fluctuations in short-term interest rates. While the kind of pegging involved in eliminating seasonal fluctuations in interest rates has some special justifications, it is by no means free from the defects of other kinds of pegging. Moreover, there is no way to determine at all precisely what seasonal movement is required in the stock of money to eliminate a seasonal in interest rates. The actual seasonal that has been introduced into the stock of money has been sizable and has varied considerably from year to year. Hence, the proposal, which at first sight seems attractive, to apply a regular rate of increase to the seasonally adjusted stock of money, would involve introducing an essentially arbitrary element into the behavior of the stock of money—there is no seasonal to adjust until a decision is made what seasonal to introduce. My own tentative conclusion is that it would be preferable to dispense with seasonal adjustments and to adopt the rule that the actual stock of money should grow month by month at the predetermined rate. To avoid misunderstanding, let me note explicitly that this would be consistent with seasonal movements in currency and deposits separately, as long as they offset one another.

The proposal to increase the money stock at a fixed rate month-in and month-out is certainly simple. It is likely to strike many of you as also simple-minded. Surely, you will say, it is easy to do better. Surely, it would be better to "lean against the wind," in the expressive phrase of a Federal Reserve chairman, rather than to stand straight upright whichever way the wind is blowing. Some of my previous comments perhaps suggest that the matter is not so simple. We seldom in fact know which way the economic wind is blowing until several months after the event, yet to be effective, we need to know which way the wind is going to be blowing when the measures we take now will be effective, itself a variable date that may be a half year or a year or two years from now. Leaning today against next year's wind is hardly an easy task in the present state of meteorology.

Analogies aside, the historical record gives little basis for supposing that it is an easy task to do better than the simple rule I have suggested. Since at least the early 1920's, our monetary authorities have been trying to do just that; they have been trying to use monetary policy as an instrument for promoting stability. On the whole, the persons in charge of monetary policy have been as able, public spirited, and farsighted a group as one could reasonably hope to have in such positions, though of course there have been some exceptions in both directions, and they have been served by a research staff that has numbered some of our leading monetary scholars and has maintained a high standard of technical excellence. Yet over this period as a whole, I doubt that many, if any, informed students of monetary affairs would disagree with the judgment that the actual behavior of the money stock has clearly been decidedly worse than the behavior that would have been produced by the simple rule—and this is true even if we leave out the wartime periods when the simple rule would almost surely have been departed from and perhaps rightly so.

The simple rule would have avoided the excessive expansion of the stock of money from 1919 to 1920 and the sharp contraction thereafter, the fairly mild but steady deflationary pressure of the later 1920's, the collapse of the stock of money from 1929 to 1933, the rather rapid rise thereafter, and the sharp decline in the course of the 1937–38 recession. In the period since World War II, the simple rule would have produced a lower rate of growth in the stock of money until the end of 1946 than was in fact realized, almost the same rate of growth during 1947, a faster rate of growth from sometime in 1947 to the end of 1949, which is to say, throughout the closing phases of the 1946–48 expansion and the whole of the 1948–49 contraction. The simple rule would have produced about the same rate of growth in the stock of money as was realized on the average from 1950 to early or mid-1953; a higher rate from then to mid-1954, or throughout most of the 1953–54 recession; about the same rate as was experienced from mid-1954 to mid-1955; a somewhat higher rate from then until the end of 1957; especially in the last half of 1957, after the 1957–58 contraction got under way; a lower rate than experienced in the first half of 1958, and about the same as the rate actually experienced from then to mid-1959.

The striking improvements in the behavior of the stock of money that would have been produced by the simple rule are for the inter-war period and for the major fluctuations of that period. It is these that make me so confident that informed students would render a nearly unanimous verdict in favor of the simple rule for the period as a whole. But, rule or no rule, changes in the monetary structure—notably federal insurance of bank deposits, the altered asset structure of banks, and the altered role of gold—and changes in the attitudes of the monetary authorities—notably their heightened sensitivity to contractions—render a repetition of major mistakes like those made during the inter-war period highly unlikely. It is nearly inconceivable that the monetary authorities would now permit the money stock to decline by one-third, as it did from 1929–33, or even by nearly 4% in 10 months, as it did in 1937. It is no doubt a merit of the rule that it provides insurance against such major mistakes but it may plausibly be argued that other factors have already provided adequate insurance—though I would be tempted to add that new mistakes are legion and insurance against major mistakes differing in kind from those in the past, in particular against unduly large increases in the money supply, is well worth while.

For the period since World War II, the contrast is not nearly so clear or sharp. The monetary authorities have followed a policy that has produced a behavior of the money supply very close to its hypothetical behavior under the rule, far closer than between the wars. In consequence, a finer criterion of performance is required to judge the desirability or undesirability of such discrepancies as there are, and this is true also for the milder discrepancies in the earlier period. My own judgment is that even for these, the rule would have produced clearly superior results, but I cannot be so sure that this judgment would be widely shared as I am for the period as a whole.

• • •

In summing up this discussion of the appropriate behavior of the money stock, I am tempted to paraphrase what Colin Clark once wrote about the case for free trade. Like other academicians, I am accustomed to being met with the refrain, "It's all right in theory but it won't work in practice." Aside from the questionable logic of the remark in general, in this instance almost the reverse of what is intended is true. There is little to be said in theory for the rule that the money supply should grow at a constant rate. The case for it is entirely that it would work in practice. There are persuasive theoretical grounds for desiring to vary the rate of growth to offset other factors. The difficulty is that, in practice, we do not know when to do so and by how much. In practice, therefore, deviations from the simple rule have been destabilizing rather than the reverse.

I should like to emphasize that I do not regard steady growth in the money stock as the be-all and end-all of monetary policy for all time. It is a rule that has much to recommend it in the present state of our knowledge. It would avoid the major mistakes that have marred our past record. It would assure long-run stability in the purchasing power of the dollar. But I should hope that as we operated under it we would accumulate more evidence and learn to understand more fully the workings of the monetary mechanism. As we did so, we could perhaps devise still better rules for controlling the stock of money that could command widespread professional support and public understanding.

• • •

47 THE POSITIVE CASE FOR AUTOMATIC MONETARY CONTROL

EDWARD S. SHAW

Professor Shaw advocates that the supply of money grow in line with its demand, thereby assuring that prices remain stable. Although few economists will reject this theorem, they hesitate to adopt the implications drawn by the author from what he calls the Demand Standard, namely, that the money supply should be increased by a constant percentage. Can you explain the crux of this dispute? Note, too, that even if one were to agree with Shaw, technical difficulties might make the ideal far from realizable in practice. One question should be asked: Which price index is going to be stabilized? For those of you who find the Shavian arguments unconvincing, work out rebuttals for his "rejoinders."

• • •

The case for automatic control does not rest solely on disillusionment with discretionary control. There are six principal ways in which continuous and stable growth in money can increase the probability of growth in real output at a relatively high rate with minimal perturbations.

1. Stable growth in money lays the foundation for a solvent and efficient payments mechanism. In recurrent inflation, bank capital is sharply reduced relative to bank assets and deposits. Each deflation undermines bank capital through deterioration in asset quality. Our own banking system is propped upright, at public expense, by various devices that are presumed to be adequate substitutes for private investment in banking. Each of these devices has originated during violent movements in the money supply.

2. Stable growth in money supplied and demanded removes one hazard of private or governmental economic planning. That is uncertainty about the length of the monetary yardstick that planners use to measure prospective costs and revenues. Our own monetary system provides us with a yardstick, the value of the dollar, that has been shrinking for sixty years. Steady shrinkage at a constant rate is tolerable and certainly not as damaging to the planning process as shrinkage by fits and starts. Our yardstick has been rubberized, stretching out in each deflation and snapping back in each bout we have with inflation.

3. Stable growth in money avoids the inflations that distort the form of real capital accumulation, and it relieves the economic system of the interruptions in capital formation that result when deflation is applied as the remedy for inflation. Deflation does not undo damage done by inflation: it compounds the damage. During inflation savings are used wastefully on capital projects that are made to seem worthwhile by advancing prices. During deflation savings are destroyed by underemployment of men and resources. Savings misapplied or lost are never recoverable.

From Edward S. Shaw, "Money Supply and Stable Economic Growth," in N. H. Jacoby (ed.), *United States Monetary Policy* (New York: Praeger, 1964), pp. 66–71.

4. Stable growth in money and stability in the price level create a favorable environment for flexible individual prices and price relationships. General price deflation results in specific price rigidities, usually in the form of price floors. It invites combination in restraint of price adjustments downward. General price inflation produces its own crop of controlled or administered prices. The controls may be ceilings imposed by buyers or escalators dictated by sellers. Flexibility of the price level promotes rigidity of price relationships. Since a private-enterprise society relies upon flexible price relationships to allocate resources and guide demands, flexible price levels reduce its growth potential.

5. Stable growth of money and stability in the price level diminish social conflict. Deflation in the last century was politically and socially divisive. Inflation in this century has helped to cleave the population into pressure groups. Any pronounced swing in the price level incites an organized March on Washington and concessions to noisy claimants for special advantage. When price levels are on the move, rational competition of the market place loses out to passionate competition for political leverage.

6. Steady growth in money contributes to development of orderly financial arrangements throughout the community. Deflation creates its distinctive pattern of debt, financial assets, and financial institutions. Inflation gives rise to a different pattern. Debtors are affected by a consideration that should not occur to them—the chance of windfall gain by inflation, of windfall loss by deflation. Creditors pick and choose their financial assets not solely according to debtors' real productivity but also according to debtors' vulnerability to unstable price levels. Loanable funds are allocated inefficiently among borrowers through a financial mechanism that is unduly intricate and expensive.

Stable growth in money minimizes financial distractions in the growth process. Stop-and-go growth in money, dignified as "monetary management," is a nervous tic in the economic system that diverts to finance attention and resources that should be spent on real aspects of development. Money is at its best when it is unobtrusive, its supply increasing according to a firm rule that is known to everyone.

AN INNING FOR THE OPPOSITION

It is not too partisan to say much less about the con's of automatic money than about the pro's. The principle of "look-Ma-no-hands" in money management has been debated so often that the critics have their brief well in hand. I shall tip off a few of their points simply to warn readers that there are two sides of the issue.

Objection 1

There is no one infallible rule of monetary growth. Since any single standard will not do, we must entrust our monetary fate to authority. It will deduce, in frequent conclave of its experts, the community's need for money and turn the money tap to just the right volume. Money is a mystery, and the layman should delegate its management to the expert.

Rejoinder

There is no expert in money management. Neither of our money-management teams, the Treasury or the Board, has earned the accolade of public confidence. Both teams have *expertise* in credit-management, but that is a different matter.

No one can measure the community's "need for money"—the quantity demanded at a stable price level in a growing economy—on a day-to-day or even month-to-month basis. There is no clear channel of communication from public to monetary authority that reports growth in demand for money . . . so that growth in supply can be in continuous balance with it. The balance of supply with demand for *money* is not improved when it is the practice of the authority to study demand for the wrong thing—for *credit*.

Objection 2

The first half-century of our experiences with discretionary management has not been a fair test. It has been distorted by two world wars and their aftermath of crisis and disaster. The Treasury and the Board have done remarkably well under the circumstances. In a tranquil world the Federal Reserve Act would be an effective charter for sound money.

Rejoinder

Peace and tranquility are not on the horizon of the next half-century. It is just as well to take the pessimistic stand that temptations to misuse the monetary system will not diminish. There will be occasions when the Treasury will want to borrow cheaply in disregard of monetary stability. There will be occasions when the Board will think it wise to disillusion the inflationary expectations that Treasury policy has generated.

If there were clear sailing ahead, discretionary management would be good enough. With trouble in prospect, it is more important to put monetary control on automatic pilot so that mistakes in policy will not aggravate our misfortunes. When inflationary forces are rampant, we will not want them intensified by monetary expansion in behalf of cheap credit for the Treasury. When deflation is the hazard, we will not want it accelerated by the Board's precautions against the next inflation. In rough weather the wheel of the monetary system should be lashed down.

Objection 3

A growing economy has a changing pattern of credit requirements. Legitimate demands for credit rise and fall, and they come from different sectors of the community in an unpredictable rotation. There must be a flexible program of credit control, and a central management of credit that is alert to satisfy legitimate demands while discouraging speculation, to segregate credit of high quality from credit of low quality, to smooth out discontinuities on credit markets, and to encourage development of credit facilities.

Rejoinder

Granted that credit management by the banking system is an important resource-allocation function in the United States economy, the linkage of money with credit is an historical accident. Credit is one of various possible uses for the purchasing power that the monetary system commands as it increases the money supply. Whatever the use may be, disposing of the monetary system's purchasing power is incidental to the process of creating money.

The Credit Standard of money management, written into the Federal Reserve Act and administered by Treasury and Board, is a built-in destabilizer of economic activity. The community's demands upon the monetary system for credit grow quantitatively and improve qualitatively in each cyclic boom. They shrink in volume and deteriorate in quality during each cyclic relapse. The effect of linking the money supply to the cyclic yo-yo of credit demand is to intensify cycles.

Real growth is measured in terms of goods. It is not measured in terms of credit. In guiding real growth, monetary expansion should have the direct impact on markets for goods that fiscal policy has. Monetary policy is not committed by any Law of Nature to work its effects upon goods only after a detour through the markets for credit. Monetary policy yields perverse results on markets for goods when the impression develops, as it has in this country, that the credit detour is the end of the line for monetary policy.

In earlier phases of American economic growth, credit markets were embryonic. Then the banking system necessarily wore two hats, as supplier of money and as supplier of credit. Now the credit markets have matured, and there are efficient channels outside of the banking system for the flow of funds from saving to investment in real capital. Now the monetary system can attend to its essential function of supplying money.

Objection 4

The Demand Standard is provincial. It would isolate the American economy from world markets, raising a domestic rule of monetary growth to a pedestal above the principle of international economic cooperation. In view of this country's responsibility for stable growth internationally, self-interest in monetary policy is a luxury we cannot afford.

Rejoinder

American monetary policy has not abided by the rules of an international standard since 1914. The national gold stock has been a buffer between money here and money abroad. On the record the Credit Standard has been autarchic.

Sawtooth growth in the money supply of this country indicates our immaturity as London's successor to the role of international central bank. If a stable dollar is to be the anchor of a stable pound, peso, franc, yen, or piastre, rates of growth in the supply of dollars must vary no more between such extremes as *plus* 20 per cent and *minus* 10 per cent. Under our present rules of monetary management, we are announcing that we do not choose to run for the job that was London's for a century. Under an automatic rule, there would be less incentive for our allies to work out their own regional monetary coalitions.

. . .

48 AUTOMATIC INCREASES IN THE MONEY SUPPLY: SOME PROBLEMS

DANIEL AHEARN

Dr. Ahearn's article lists some objections to adopting the Friedman-Shaw rule. Additional questions were raised in the Introduction to this Part. Here are a few more. Which price index ought to be stabilized? Can we be certain that trends of money and prices, predicated upon discretionary policy and providing the data upon which the rule is based, will not be altered once the rule is installed? Will not the rule, too, require some experimentation, and is this not another name for discretion?

• • •

In the opinion of its advocates, an automatic annual increase in the money supply at approximately the long-term rate of increase in real production would provide more stable money conditions than have prevailed under discretionary policies in the past, would stabilize expectations by creating a climate of certainty as to what future money conditions would be, and would evade the problems posed for discretionary monetary policy by lags between the time monetary actions are taken and the time they have effect on the economy. But such a plan would also involve a number of difficulties.

QUESTION OF DEFINITION OF MONEY SUPPLY

One problem is to ensure that the quantity which is to be increased every year is in fact what the economy is using as money. The crux of the difficulty is the artificiality of any legal definition. The moneyness of assets is a fluid and shifting quality, depending on business habits and institutions which themselves shift over time. At any point of time there is a question as to what should be included in a definition of the money supply, as a glance at any money and banking textbook will indicate. It can reasonably be asked whether the money supply should also include commercial bank time deposits, savings bank deposits, savings and loan shares, and perhaps some or even all U.S. Government securities. The major problem is that a fixed rule freezes the definition over time even though the economy may be gradually attributing greater moneyness to an asset not regulated. Thus, if a fixed rule had in the early 1800s fixed a regular percentage increase in the supply of banknotes—the major component of the money supply at the time—the rule would have become largely irrelevant with the emergence of demand deposits as the major type of money. It is no answer to say that in the event of such institutional shifts the rule could be changed, for this merely admits discretion by the back door. It is the strength of a discretionary monetary policy that it can take account of the changing moneyness of financial assets and the development of

---

From Daniel Ahearn, *Federal Reserve Policy Reappraised, 1951–1959* (New York: Columbia University Press, 1963), pp. 225–231.

new financial institutions and practices insofar as they affect the role of money.

DIFFICULTIES OF ENSURING STEADY MONEY GROWTH RATE

There is also the troublesome fact that proposing a steady percentage growth in the money supply, however defined, does not achieve it. To be sure, Friedman has implied that the Federal Reserve has finger-tip control over the money supply: "There is no doubt that if it wanted to, it [the Federal Reserve] has both the formal power and the actual technical capacity to control the total stock of money with a time lag measured in weeks and to a degree of precision measured in tenths of 1 percent."[1] But this is mistaken, as is apparent from the lags between changes in bank reserve positions (which the Federal Reserve can influence immediately) and the total money supply. The difficulty is that the money supply hinges on the willingness of banks to lend or invest excess reserves, the willingness of business and individuals to borrow, the asset preferences of individuals and nonbank institutions—all of which are subject to only imperfect control by the Federal Reserve.

Difficulties of control might be particularly acute in recession or depression. For one thing, it is entirely possible for the Federal Reserve to be supplying excess reserves to the banks and for the banks to be using the new reserves to create new deposits in payment for Government securities without achieving expansion in the money supply at the desired rate because business and individuals were repaying loans, and thus extinguishing their deposit balances. In a serious depression, as during the 1930s, the banks might not even be willing to invest the excess reserve balances supplied to them by the central bank so these could pile up without affecting the money supply.

In ordinary circumstances, the difficulties might be less dramatic but nevertheless could pose problems for a policy committed to a 4 percent annual increase in money supply. For example, suppose that the money supply began to rise more than 4 percent a year because of increased loan demands. Since there are constantly small jiggles in the money supply, the authorities would be likely to wait to see whether the trend was *really* moving away from 4 percent. By the time they acted, the money supply might be moving up considerably faster than 4 percent a year. Apart from the initial delay, their action would take effect with some lags, as we have seen. In fact, the restrictive impact on the money supply might take effect months later when conditions had changed and private repayments of loans were decreasing the money supply. Thus, perversity in the money supply could reappear, even under the 4 percent automatic increase rate.

. . .

These, of course, are only hypothetical objections to the "automatic increase" rule and only actual experience with central bank operation under such a rule could give a definitive answer as to its practicability. This analysis, however, does suggest that the mere adoption of such a rule would not preclude some difficulty in effectively enforcing steady annual growth in the money supply.

STABILITY IN EXPECTATIONS AND MONETARY GROWTH

Even if a steady planned growth in the money supply were achieved, stable expectations on the part of the public and the business community would not necessarily follow. Expectations depend on many things beside the money supply. Specifically, if prices rose steadily even though money growth was doing no more than keeping pace with growth in

---

[1]U.S. Congress, Joint Committee, *Employment, Growth, and Price Levels: Hearings* (Washington, D.C.: G.P.O., 1959), Part 4, p. 609.

physical production, it is strongly probable that inflationary expectations would result. On the other hand, if private production fell sharply and remained sluggish, despite a 4 percent increase in money supply, expectations probably would be affected adversely, despite the continued steady growth in money supply. Indeed, sharp shifts in any important variables might be expected to be reflected in business and consumer expectations.

It might be argued that sharp changes in nonmonetary variables would be unlikely in an environment of stable monetary growth. But it would seem overoptimistic to maintain that a steadily rising trend for money supply would ensure stability in other major economic variables. Moreover, a steadily rising money supply does not necessarily mean a steadily rising flow of expenditure; changes in the rate of use or velocity of money could still provide a monetary stimulus to instability.

COMPATIBILITY OF THE RULE WITH ECONOMIC NEEDS

A discretionary monetary policy has one cardinal virtue: it enables the monetary authorities to take account of changing economic circumstances. It is extraordinarily difficult to devise an arbitrary rule which in essence endeavors in advance to provide for all the kinds of instability and problems that may arise in the distant future. And if the rule does encounter unanticipated circumstances, it may prevent badly needed action. For example, if a major depression so increased liquidity preferences as to create an enormous demand for money, it would seem ridiculous to deny the satisfaction of this demand, which presumably would have to be met before economic recovery could get underway, simply because of a rule which had been designed for completely different circumstances. Yet Shaw has vigorously shut the door on exceptions to such a rule, saying, "When the nominal supply of money is growing at a stable rate, a serious recession would itself generate a very large increase in *real* money [money balances deflated by a price index]."*

The problem is that price rigidity might prevent any substantial price decline in recession, preventing a large increase in *real* money balances. Even if real money balances did rise, and thus supplemented the 4 percent increase in nominal money balances added by the rule, the recession might still persist and perhaps even worsen. If this happened, it seems dubious that an a priori rule should prevent action that might be helpful.

Application of the rule also would not have been appropriate from 1945 to 1951, a prosperous period in which the money supply rose about 3 percent a year. On Friedman's or Shaw's reckoning this is somewhat less than would be called for by the automatic rule. Yet 1945–1951 were years of fairly rapid inflation. Of course, even if the money supply had been held to a lower rate of growth, or no growth at all, the economy's accumulated store of liquid assets and current incomes could still have financed excessive demands for goods which had been unavailable in the war years and were still in short supply. Thus inflation probably still would have been a problem. But it seems plausible that a reduced creation of new money would have had some desirable effects.

It seems difficult to escape the conclusion that central banking by preordained rule would not permit adjustment to changing circumstances. In a world which is in a state of flux, this is a serious disadvantage.

PROBABILITY OF ABANDONMENT IN DIFFICULT CIRCUMSTANCES

If economic or political exigencies were to require monetary action different from

---

*See the previous article—ed.

that prescribed by a fixed rule, it is hard to believe that the rule would not give way. The worst experience with discretionary control of the money supply came during the Great Depression and during World Wars I and II; these were national emergencies. Such periods of stress, in which the Government and the people are concerned about the survival of the nation, are the very times in which an arbitrary rule would be brushed aside if it seemed an impediment to needed action. Thus the proposed automaticity would have broken down at the very time it was needed. As Warren Smith has said: "like the gold standard, it would be a 'fair weather' rule, and fair weather would be unlikely to last very long."[2]

PROBLEM OF TIME LAGS

Time lags might well be almost as much of a problem for a monetary policy administered by reference to a fixed rule as for a discretionary policy. The fixed rule policy eliminates the necessity for the central bank to recognize turns in business and accordingly shortens the "recognition" lag, that is, the period between the need for action and the central bank's awareness of a need for action. But the fixed rule would not at all affect the lag between the time actions are taken and the time they have effect on the economy, and this lag is the main reason, according to Friedman, that discretionary monetary policy has been destabilizing. Friedman said:

> Monetary and fiscal policy is rather like a water tap that you turn on now and that then only starts to run 6, 9, 12, 16 months from now. It is because of this long lag in the reaction to policy that you have this tendency for policy in fact to have an effect opposite to that intended.[3]

This sort of lag would be troublesome for any monetary actions, discretionary or automatic. It might be said that since all money-supply changes under the automatic rule would be at the same rate, for example, 4 percent a year, lags in their impact would be irrelevant; whenever they took effect, their impact would be the same. But what matters for the economy is not simply the amount of money created but the money conditions created by the interaction of the 4 percent increase in money supply and the incremental demand for money and these vary considerably. In prosperous periods demand for money could outrun a 4 percent increase in supply and create tight money conditions; in recessions, easy money could result from the fact that the incremental demand for money fell short of the 4 percent rise in supply. Just as with discretionary policy, lags could mean that tight money had its effect in the following recession, while easy money took effect in a prosperous period.

Thus, so far as lags are concerned, there is little to be gained from replacement of discretionary control over the money supply by a rule calling for an automatic 4 percent annual increase in money supply.

• • •

---

[2]Friedman, *op. cit.,* p. 165.

[3]Friedman, *op. cit.,* p. 165.

49 SOME EMPIRICAL TESTS OF MONETARY MANAGEMENT AND OF RULES VERSUS DISCRETION

FRANCO MODIGLIANI

In order to test the effectiveness of the constant growth in money supply rule, a starting point must be chosen. After all, 3 percent growth does not begin at zero. This choice is a complex one, however, for if the initial period is one in which money supply was abnormally high or, alternatively, abnormally low, a bias is built right into the test. In the first case, money supply in future periods is apt to be too expansive, whereas the reverse is true in the latter instance. Franco Modigliani avoids this problem by considering each period anew, so that for each period he implicitly asks, How effective would a 3 percent per annum increase in money supply be if the rule were initiated today? The result is then contrasted to discretionary behavior. But, as the author is quick to point out, the result does not test accurately the Friedman rule, which requires a constant rate over all periods from some initial (but unspecified) beginning point. Also note that Professor Modigliani avoids the lag issue by implicitly assuming that a change in the money supply during a given period is related to an output change in that very same period. How great a bias this introduces into the test depends on one's conclusions regarding the length of the lag.

I. PURPOSE OF THE ARTICLE

The purpose of this [article] is to suggest some empirical tests designed to establish how well a monetary authority has managed the money supply and to compare its performance with what might have happened if the money supply had been managed according to some well-defined "automatic rules." Such a comparison is obviously relevant to the continuing debate over "rules versus discretion" in monetary management; in addition, it provides some gauge of the difficulty of the task of properly managing the money supply. The method outlined is then applied to the United States for the period for which the required data are available, namely, from 1947 to 1962.

In the tests presented here I propose to score the performance of the monetary authority (hereinafter referred to as "the Authority") or of any given rule, with reference to the basic domestic goal of *full employment with price stability* and without any regard to, or allowance for, other goals that the Authority may have been pursuing, such as supporting the price of government bonds, stabilizing interest rates, protecting the gold stock, creating an orderly environment, or what have you. Knowledge of such other goals will, however, be relevant in interpreting the record of performance and in assessing the cost in terms of price stability and full employment which has been paid in the pursuit of other goals.

One further feature of the test procedure is that it implicitly holds monetary management solely responsible for failure to achieve the stated domestic goal. I am

From Franco Modigliani, "Some Empirical Tests of Monetary Management and of Rules Versus Discretion," *Journal of Political Economy*, 72, 3, 211–214, 216–223, 242–244. Reprinted by permission.

of course fully aware that there exist tools of economic stabilization besides monetary management, chiefly fiscal policy. But this recognition does not logically invalidate my procedure, at least as long as the fiscal authority is not in a position to change money supply contrary to the desires of the monetary authority. Now, under present American institutions, the federal government cannot by and large directly affect the money supply except to the extent of changing its own cash balance (which is not included in the money supply). Such changes have been generally minor in the period under consideration and, in any event, it was always within the power of the Authority to offset them, if it so desired. Thus my approach amounts to regarding fiscal policy as a datum among the many data shaping the problem with which monetary management must cope.

II. OUTLINE OF THE APPROACH

1. Definition and Measurement of the "Target Money Supply"

The approach I propose consists in developing a measure of the appropriate or "target" money supply for each period and then comparing this target with the actual supply in the period, in scoring the Authority, or with the supply resulting from a stated rule, in scoring the rule.

Since the explicitly postulated goal is *full employment with price stability,* I propose to define the "target" money supply $\mathbf{M}_t$ as *the stock of means of payments that would have been needed in period "t" to transact a full employment income, "$\mathbf{X}_t$," at the target price level for the period, "$\mathbf{P}_t$."*

The above definition of the target supply can be restated symbolically as

$$\mathbf{M}_t=\mathbf{X}_t\mathbf{P}_t/\mathbf{m}_t=\mathbf{Y}_t/\mathbf{m}_t, \qquad (1)$$

where

$$\mathbf{Y}=\mathbf{X}_t\mathbf{P}_t \qquad (2)$$

denotes the target money income or target aggregate demand and

$$\mathbf{m}_t=\mathbf{Y}_t/\mathbf{M}_t \qquad (3)$$

is the ratio of target income to the money supply needed to achieve that income. Since the ratio of income to the stock of means of payments is customarily referred to as the "velocity of circulation," one may think of $\mathbf{m}_t$ as the velocity that would have prevailed in period *t* if the target money supply had in fact been provided.

The main analytical problem in implementing the tests consists in finding empirical approximations to the three variables appearing on the right-hand side of equation (1), namely, **X, P,** and **m,** and in selecting a suitable time unit for the analysis. . . .

Consider first the target real income $\mathbf{X}_t$. We may think of this quantity as the level of real income achievable with a rate of utilization of the labor force as high as seems realistically feasible, with due consideration to the definition of employment and labor force underlying the available data. Accordingly I propose to define the target rate of utilization of the labor force in period *t* as the rate actually prevailing in that period or 96 percent, whichever is larger. Next, I propose to estimate target real income by relying on the assumption that real income is roughly proportional to employment, at least within the moderate range of fluctuations of the employment rate characteristic of the postwar period. These considerations lead to the following operational approximation of $\mathbf{X}_t$, denoted hereafter by $\mathfrak{X}_t$.

Let X_t denote real gross national product (GNP) in period *t,* and e_t denote the (average) rate of utilization of the labor force in that period (the ratio of employment to labor force). Then

$$\mathfrak{X}_t=\text{Empirical estimate of } \mathbf{X}_t=X_tU_t \quad \text{(A1)}$$

$$U_t=\begin{cases}1, \text{ if } e_t \text{ is 0.96 or higher}\\ 0.96/e_t \text{ if } e_t \text{ is less than 0.96.}\end{cases}$$

In order to define the target price level $\mathbf{P}_t$, we need to give precise content to the rather vague notion of "stabilizing the price level." We propose to define this notion operationally by identifying the target price level in period t with the level ruling at the opening of the period, denoted by $P_{t'}$. Thus

$$\mathbf{P}_t = P_{t'} . \qquad \text{(A2)}$$

This assumption implies that in short run —more precisely within a "period"—the Authority should refuse to support and validate wage and price increases above the opening price level, even though this policy might lead to less than full employment in that period. At the same time, if prices have nonetheless changed in the period—whether through cost push and sellers' inflation or from errors in the money supply—then the newly reached price level should be accepted as a *fait accompli*. It would become the new line to be held in the following period, no attempt being made at rolling prices back up or down.

Which measure of the "price level" should be stabilized? In line with the above definition of $\mathbf{X}_t$ and $\mathbf{Y}_t$ it seems natural to choose the implicit GNP deflator. One might well argue that a more relevant price level is that of consumption goods; fortunately this issue can be bypassed since the short-run movements of the two indexes have been sufficiently similar over the relevant period, so that the result of the test would be substantially the same, whichever price index was used.

Since the implicit GNP deflator is only available on a quarterly basis, one arrives at the following operational approximation:

$\mathfrak{P}_t \equiv$ Empirical estimate of $\mathbf{P}_t = P_t$
$=$ implicit GNP deflator for the latest quarter preceding period t. (A2′)

Expressions (A1) and (A2) imply the following operational measure of target income or aggregate demand:

$\mathfrak{Y}_t \equiv$ Empirical estimate of $\mathbf{Y}_t$

$$= \mathfrak{X}_t \mathfrak{P}_t = X_t U_t P_{t'} .$$

There remains the challenging problem of estimating the target-income velocity m_t. Here I propose to rely on the assumption that m_t can be approximated by the actual velocity in period t. Hence

$\mathfrak{m}_t \equiv$ Empirical estimate of $\mathbf{m}_t$

$$= m_t = Y_t / M_t . \qquad \text{(A3)}$$

This is no doubt a rather heroic assumption, though it may not be too serious as long as M_t is reasonably close to $\mathbf{M}_t$. As will presently be seen (cf. Table 1, col. [3]), in the period covered by the tests the estimated difference between these two quantities remained within 3 percent, with but a single exception. Furthermore, . . . some allowance can be made for likely biases resulting from this assumption.

Substitution of equations (A1), (A2), and (A3) into equation (1) yields the empirical estimate of the target money supply $\mathfrak{M}_t$:

$\mathfrak{M}_t =$ Empirical estimate of $\mathbf{M}_t$

$$= \mathfrak{Y}_t / \mathfrak{m}_t = \frac{\mathfrak{Y}_t}{Y_t} M_t = \frac{X_t U_t P_{t'}}{Y_t} M_t . \qquad (4)$$

One can now readily score the performance of the money. Authority in any period t by computing the relative error in the money supply $E[M]_t$, defined as

$E[M]_t \equiv$ Empirical estimate of

$$\frac{M_t - \mathbf{M}_t}{\mathbf{M}_t} = \frac{M_t - \mathfrak{M}_t}{\mathfrak{M}_t} = \frac{Y_t - \mathfrak{Y}_t}{\mathfrak{Y}_t} \equiv E[Y]_t . \qquad (5)$$

A positive value for $E[M]$ indicates an excessive money supply, or excessively loose monetary policy for that period, while a negative value indicates an insufficient supply or excessively tight policy.

The one issue that still needs to be settled before one can proceed to the computations of $E[M]_t$ is the choice of the length of the interval t. It is obvious that if a very short interval, say, less than a quarter, is chosen, all the variables, and in particular the money supply, and income velocity, will be subject to erratic movements, and the measures will also be rather erratic. On the other hand as the interval is lengthened the problem arises that underlying conditions may be changing and that average behavior over the entire period may convey little interesting information. These considerations suggest that one quarter and one year are probably the minimum and maximum limits for a meaningful test. In the tests presented here I have compromised on two quarters as the unit of analysis, though the procedure could be readily applied to periods of different duration. Accordingly values of $E[M]_t$ have been computed for the 31 half-yearly periods spanning the interval from the second half of 1947 to the end of 1962. These values are tabulated in column (3) of Table 1.

• • •

Table 1. Test of Monetary Management and Comparison with Simple Rule*[a]
(Percent)

Periods and Years	Error in M $(M_t-\mathfrak{M}_t/\mathfrak{M}_t)$ $=(Y_t-\mathfrak{Y}_t/\mathfrak{Y}_t)$ (3)	Target Change in M $(\mathfrak{M}_t-M_{t'}/M_{t'})$ (4)	Actual Change in M $(M_t-M_{t'}/M_{t'})$ (5)	Error of 3 Percent Rule Applied to M $E[M^r]$ (6)
Subperiod I (Pre-accord):				
1947-II	2.8	−1.8	1.0	2.9
1948-I	2.6	−2.9	−0.3	4.2
1948-II	1.7	−1.8	−0.1	3.0
1949-I	−2.2	1.7	−0.5	−0.5
1949-II	−3.7	3.4	−0.3	−2.2
1950-I	−2.0	3.7	1.7	−2.5
Summary measures:				
$\Sigma E/6$	−0.13			0.81
$\Sigma\|E\|/6$	2.50			2.55
$\sqrt{\Sigma E^2/6}$	2.58			2.80
Correct signals				2/6
Wrong signals				3/6
Subperiod II (Korean War):				
1950-II	2.9	−1.4	1.5	2.6
1951-I	4.1	−2.5	1.6	3.7
1951-II	1.0	1.2	2.2	−0.1
Subperiod III (Post-accord):				
1952-I	0.1	1.6	1.7	−0.5
1952-II	1.0	0.5	1.5	0.6
1953-I	−0.2	1.1	0.9	0.0
1953-II	0.4	−0.3	0.1	1.4
1954-I	−0.9	1.3	0.4	−0.2
1954-II	−1.5	3.0	1.5	−1.8
1955-I	−0.1	1.5	1.6	−0.4
1955-II	0.6	−0.1	0.5	1.2
1956-I	1.3	−0.8	0.5	1.9

(Continued)

Table 1. Test of Monetary Management and Comparison wih Simple Rule*[a] (Continued)
(Percent)

Periods and Years	Error in M $(M_t - \mathfrak{M}_t/\mathfrak{M}_t)$ $= (Y_t - \mathfrak{Y}_t/\mathfrak{Y}_t)$ (3)	Target Change in M $(\mathfrak{M}_t - M_{t'}/M_{t'})$ (4)	Actual Change in M $(M_t - M_{t'}/M_{t'})$ (5)	Error of 3 Percent Rule Applied to M $E[M^r]$ (6)
1956-II	1.3	−1.2	0.1	2.3
1957-I	1.2	−0.9	0.3	2.1
1957-II	0.7	−1.0	−0.3	2.2
1958-I	−2.2	2.7	0.5	−1.6
1958-II	−2.7	4.3	1.6	−3.1
1959-I	−0.9	2.2	1.3	−1.0
1959-II	−1.0	0.9	−0.1	0.2
1960-I	−0.8	−0.4	−1.2	(1.5)
Summary measures:				
$\Sigma E/17$	−0.22			0.29
$\Sigma \lvert E \rvert/17$	1.00			1.29
$\sqrt{\Sigma E^2/17}$	1.20			1.56
Correct signals				4/17
Wrong signals				11/17
Subperiod IV (Gold problem):				
1960-II	−1.6	1.9	0.3	−0.8
1961-I	−2.6	3.5	0.9	−2.3
1961-II	−2.3	3.2	0.9	−2.0
1962-I	−1.1	1.7	0.6	−0.6
1962-II	−1.1	1.4	0.3	−0.3
Summary measures:				
$\Sigma E/5$	−1.74			−1.20
$\Sigma \lvert E \rvert/5$	1.74			1.20
$\sqrt{\Sigma E^2/5}$	1.84			1.44
Correct signals				5/5
Wrong signals				0/5
All periods (excluding Korean War):				
Summary measures:				
$\Sigma E/28$	−0.47			0.13
$\Sigma \lvert E \rvert/28$	1.45			1.55
$\sqrt{\Sigma E^2/28}$	1.70			1.87
Correct signals				11/28
Wrong signals				14/28

*Columns 1, 2 and 7–9 have been omitted—ed.
[a]For definition of symbols see text. . . .

III. PERFORMANCE OF THE MONEY AUTHORITY AND COMPARISON WITH A SIMPLE RULE

1. Explanation of Table 1

. . . Table 1 contains a number of . . . columns, three of which are of concern at this point as they are designed to throw light on the sources of the error shown in column (3). Column (4) shows the "target change" in money supply or the percentage increment over the average supply of the previous quarter needed to achieve the target level in period t: This increment is given by $(\mathfrak{M}_t - M_{t'})/M_{t'}$. By relating the figures of column (4) to those of column (3) one can see whether there is any systematic tendency for excesses or insufficiencies in the money supply to be related to the direction and size of the required change. Column (5) shows the actual change in the money supply in the period, $(M_t - M_{t'})/M_{t'}$. When the entry in this column has the same sign as that of column (4) this indicates that the actual change was in the direction called for and conversely.

The figures of column (4) are also useful in gauging the difficulty of the task facing the Authority in its endeavor to keep the money supply on the "target" track. If the figures in this column turned out to be very nearly the same, period after period, this task would clearly be a relatively easy one that could be accomplished by a routine behavior and could be easily embodied in a mechanical rule of expansion. If, on the other hand, these figures are found to fluctuate widely from period to period, this must be taken as a prima facie indication that the task of correctly managing the money supply is a complex one.

Some further light on this issue can also be gathered from the figures of column (6), which show the error in the money supply that would have resulted in each period had the Authority chosen to pursue a passive policy of mechanically "stabilizing" the money supply.

In an economy in which labor force and productivity, and hence full employment income, were roughly constant, such a passive policy would consist in maintaining a constant supply of means of payments. If, on the other hand, full-employment output follows a reasonably stable long-term trend, this policy might be identified with one of changing the money supply according to the indicated long-term trend. Such a policy will be recognized as bearing a close resemblance to the type of "rule" of monetary management advocated by Friedman and others.

The money supply that would have resulted in each period from increasing M at the rate of g percent per year will be denoted hereafter by $M^r(g, M)_t$ . . . In calculating $M^r(g, M)$, g was assigned the value of 3 percent per year—this being the rate most commonly suggested by proponents of management by rule—and the average money supply of the latest quarter preceding period t, $M_{t'}$ has been used as the base to which the factor $(1+g)$ is applied. Since a rate of expansion of 3 percent per year implies that the average supply for a given half-year period should be approximately 1⅛ percent above the average supply of the previous quarter, one arrives at the operational formula

$$M^r(0.03, M)_t = (1.01125) M_{t'}. \quad (7)$$

Values of $M^r(0.03, M)$ are not shown separately in the table. Instead column (6) shows the percentage error, or deviation of $M^r(0.03, M)$ from the target supply $\mathfrak{M}_t$, that is,

$$E[M^r(0.03, M)]_t = \frac{M^r(0.03, M)_t - \mathfrak{M}_t}{\mathfrak{M}_t}$$

Note that this error is (approximately) equal to the difference between the percentage change in M called for by the rule, which is 1⅛ percent, or approximately 1.1 percent, and the target change which is shown in column (4). Thus for 1947-I it appears from column (4) that the change required to bring about the target supply was a contraction of 1.8 percent; hence the error resulting from the rule is $1.1 - (-1.8) = 2.9$, which is the figure appearing in column (6).

In interpreting the figures of column (6) it must be recognized that there is one important difference between the $M^r(g, M)$-rule and the type of rule advocated by Friedman. His rule calls for a *steady expansion* of the money supply at a rate of g percent per year whereas the value $M^r(g, M)_t$ at each point of time is obtained by applying the growth factor to the *actual money supply outstanding at the beginning of the period.* Clearly this historical supply will in general differ from the supply that would have existed had the rule been followed *throughout*. For this reason the figures of column (6) cannot be taken as an exact test of a pure Friedman-type rule; indeed it is doubtful that such a test can ever be performed from historical data. Nonetheless, our tests of the $M^r(g, M)$ rule . . . are useful for a number of reasons. In the first place these rules can be regarded as "calibrating devices" for measuring the performance of the Authority in the same spirit as "naïve" forecasts are useful in testing the accuracy of actual forecasts. In other words, by comparing the entries of column (6) with those of column (3) one can test whether, in any given period, the Authority performed any better than if it had adopted a passive policy of adjusting the supply according to the long-run trend. In the second place, . . . the performance of my rules, together with other evidence, can be used to provide an upper bound to the quality of performance of strict Friedman-type rules.

• • •

2. The Choice of Subperiods for the Analysis

If one is interested not only in scoring the performance of the Authority but also in understanding the major forces that impinge on that performance, it seems useful to divide the entire postwar era into four subperiods, in each of which the Authority was presumably acting under somewhat different constraints. In the first period, labeled "Pre-accord," and extending from 1947-II to 1950-I, the Authority's freedom of action was seriously curtailed by the commitment to support the market for government securities at, or near, the low level of interest rates inherited from the war period. The second period, labeled "Korean War," includes the span from 1950-II to 1951-II and corresponds to the acute phase of the conflict. It is of rather limited interest for present purposes, since the overriding preoccupation of the Authority was presumably not domestic stability but support of the war effort. The remaining "Post-accord" years from 1952-I to 1962-II have been further subdivided into two parts in recognition of the fact that, somewhere around the turn of the decade, the Authority became very much preoccupied with the so-called gold problem and the need to support the interest rate structure—at least at its short end—in order to minimize short-term capital outflows. Unfortunately, it is hard to pinpoint the date at which this concern became important. In the table I have chosen the second half of 1960 as a reasonable approximation, though others may prefer to place the dividing line somewhat earlier and the basic information provided in the table will enable them to do so quite readily. Thus, Period III extends from 1952-I to 1960-I and is labeled "Post-accord." It is in many respects the most interesting and critical period for the purpose of assessing the *ability* of the Authority to manage money successfully in the pursuit of full employment and price stability, for it represents the only sizable stretch of years in which there were no apparent important constraints distracting it from this goal. The remaining five observations, from 1960-II to 1962-II, constitute the fourth, "Gold problem," period.

We now proceed to an examination of the record for each subperiod and for the period as a whole.

3. Analysis of the Record

a) PERIOD I ("PRE-ACCORD"), 1947–50. In this period the record of the Authority does not appear too favorable. First, comparison of columns (4) and (5) shows that the money supply was adjusted in the *wrong direction* in three out of the six periods: in 1947-I the supply was permitted to expand when a contraction was called for, while in 1949-I and 1949-II the supply was contracted when an expansion was called for. In the remaining three periods when the change was in the right direction, its magnitude was substantially smaller than required. As a result, as can be seen from column (3), the supply was appreciably too large in each of the first three periods when a contraction was required and appreciably too small in the last three periods in which an expansion was appropriate. A summary impression for the entire period can be gathered from the averages shown in the table at the end of each subperiod, although, as pointed out earlier, these averages must be interpreted with extreme caution in view of the likely and varying biases affecting each figure. The simple arithmetic average $\langle E \rangle_{\mathrm{av}}$ is close to zero, indicating that on the whole the excesses and deficiencies nearly balanced out. However, the average absolute error, $\langle |E| \rangle_{\mathrm{av}}$, a far more relevant figure, shows that, on the average, the actual money supply was 2.5 percent off.

Note that this relatively poor record cannot be fully accounted for by the absence of an "accord," since half the errors arise from an excessively *tight* policy. A useful clue can perhaps be found from the figures of column (4); they reveal that in this early postwar period tracking the target money supply called for sharp and widely varying changes in the money supply, ranging all the way from -2.9 to 3.7 percent. It is therefore not surprising to find, from the figures of column (6), that reliance on the passive rule $M^r(0.03, M)$ would have led on the whole to even *poorer* results. Such a policy would again have called for a change in the *wrong* direction in half of the six periods and would have led to an even larger excess in the money supply in each of the first three periods and to an even greater deficiency in the last. Only in 1949-I and 1949-II, or in two periods out of six, did the use of discretion lead to a worse outcome than a passive policy. For the period as a whole the average absolute error under such a policy, some 2.55 percent, is even greater than that of column (3).

b) PERIOD II ("KOREAN WAR"), 1950-II TO 1951-II. In this period the money supply was uniformly excessive and by amounts larger than would have resulted from a passive policy. However, in view of the circumstances, it would seem wise to disregard this episode altogether.

c) PERIOD III ("POST-ACCORD"), 1952-I TO 1960-I. In this critical period, which includes seventeen observations, the record of the money authority is rather favorable. In every one of the ten periods in which an expansion of the money supply was called for, there actually was an expansion, except for 1959-II when there was essentially no change. In the two periods in which little change was called for (1953-II and 1955-II) there actually was little change. In four of the remaining five periods in which a significant contraction was called for the supply actually contracted or changed very little. Thus the direction of change was missed conspicuously in only one period (1956-I) out of seventeen. But while the direction of change was generally correct, there was again a tendency for the magnitude to be smaller than called for. As a result the supply was significantly excessive in seven periods, including six of the seven instances in which a contraction was required, and was significantly deficient in seven, all but one of which called for expansion, though only two of the errors exceed 2 percent. In the remaining three periods M was within 0.02 percent of the estimated target. The average absolute error for the entire subperiod turns out to be only about 1 percent, though the target change again varied widely from -1.2 to 4.3 percent.

The rather impressive quality of this over-all performance is further confirmed by comparing it with the outcome of the passive rule. In the first place the rule would have led to the wrong direction of change in seven instances instead of one. Second, in twelve cases out of seventeen the error in column (6) is larger than that in column (3); and in only three of the remaining five cases did the rule perform distinctly better, 1954-I, 1958-I, and 1959-II. For the entire period the average absolute error for the "rule" is nearly 30 percent larger than that for the actual money supply.

d) PERIOD IV ("GOLD PROBLEM"), 1960-II TO 1962-II. The record for this period requires little comment. In each of the five periods an expansion of the money supply was called for and the supply was expanded, but a good deal less than called for. Thus, monetary management appears consistently much too restrictive by our criterion, the average deficiency (and average absolute error) amounting to at least 1¾ percent and probably substantially more in view of the downward bias of the measure. By contrast the rule performs approximately as well as in the previous period, outscoring the Authority in every period and leading to an average absolute error about 30 percent lower.

e) THE POSTWAR PERIOD AS A WHOLE. Taking the period as a whole—excepting only the Korean War years—one still finds that discretionary policy outperformed the rule, though by a rather slender margin; it did better in somewhat over half of the periods (16 of 28) and the average error in the money supply, though rather discouragingly high at 1.45 percent, is still somewhat lower than that resulting from the rule, 1.55 percent.

Though the period as a whole is quite relevant in judging the effectiveness of the rule and of the Authority, it is only of limited relevance if one is interested in assessing the *ability* of the Authority to use discretion to advantage in the pursuit of economic stability. It seems fairly evident, in fact, that the overexpansive policy of the first three periods resulted at least in part from the obligation to support the government bond market. Indeed, under the circumstances the increase in the money supply was contained within remarkably narrow limits. Similarly, there can be little doubt that the overtight policy of the Authority since 1960 did not stem primarily from its inability to foresee and offset shifts in the underlying conditions, but from its fear that an easier policy would have affected unfavorably the United States gold and short term liability position—though the acceptance of this policy may have been fostered by an over-all deflationary bias. When the record is examined closely for the critical period in which the Authority was presumably free to concentrate on domestic stability, namely, 1952 to 1960-I, plus possibly the last three observations of Period I, the evidence distinctly supports the use of discretion over the mechanical rule.

The conclusion is reinforced by a close examination of the circumstances surrounding the three relatively minor recessions that marred this period, beginning respectively at the turn of 1948, in the middle of 1953, and in the middle of 1957. It is apparent from column (3) that both in 1948-II and 1957-I the money supply was distinctly excessive, at least in terms of our measure. Hence these contractions could not be readily attributed to an overrestrictive monetary policy. And if anyone held the view that these episodes represented a reaction to an overexpansive policy, this would only weaken the case for a passive policy, for in both 1948-II and 1957-I the rule would have led to an even greater excess in M, while in 1953-I there was essentially no difference between M and M^r. In fact, throughout the postwar period the only contraction that might be attributed with some justification to an overtightness that would have been avoided by relying on a passive policy is that beginning in the middle of 1960. It appears that in 1960-I, as well as in 1959-II, the money supply was appreciably short of the target, and that the rule would have led to a larger supply in both periods.

• • •

CONCLUSIONS—RULES OR DISCRETION?

What inferences can one draw from this record with respect to the longstanding debate on "Rules versus Discretion"? Clearly, from the point of view of assessing the *ability* of the Authority to use discretion to advantage, the relevant portion of the record is that pertaining to the critical period 1952 to 1960-I. This record appears favorable to discretionary policy, at least in comparison with any of the commonly advocated type of rules or even with the more flexible variants tested,* *as long as the Authority makes use of its discretion in the pursuit of the stated goals.* Yet, the experience of the two subperiods when discretionary policy was outperformed by a host of simple rules is certainly not irrelevant to the debate, even if it be agreed that in these periods the Authority was not primarily concerned with full employment and price stability. For one of the possible objections to discretion is precisely that it may be used to serve other goals, or, in other words, that under the present setup discretion is not limited to the *means* but extends to the *goals.* It is of course conceivable that, at times, other goals should in fact be given priority over the goals of full employment and price stability. But one might well argue that the obligation to adhere to a rule designed to serve those goals, until exceptions are explicitly authorized, would serve to focus attention on the existence of conflicts and lay open to public debate the ranking of these goals and the search for alternatives.

While there is some merit in these arguments, they do not seem to me to justify in the least the conclusion that monetary management should be entrusted to some mechanical rule. As I see it, the inference to be drawn from the tests is rather that (1) on the whole the evidence supports the use of discretion over a rule, but that (2) there is room for some limitations in the use of discretion, particularly in the form of spelling out more precisely the goals to which the discretionary powers should be directed, and the procedures by which these goals are to be changed.

To advocate for the Authority a large measure of discretion in the pursuit of well-defined and appropriately established goals is not to deny that certain rules may be useful as a guide in choosing a course of action, especially if they have both sound theoretical underpinning and solid empirical support. . . . But no mechanical rule can be relied upon at all times. Indeed, the tests show how fruitless is the search for some chimerical collection of assets, means of payments or not, whose pseudo-velocity is sufficiently stable in the short run so that monetary policy can be encapsulated in the mechanical prescription of watching that collection and seeing to it that it expands at some stated rate. My labor has failed to uncover any such collection, and I am prepared to predict with considerable confidence that further search will prove no more successful. . . . At best, therefore, rules can provide only a rough guide for monetary management. But their function cannot, and should not, be to prevent the Authority from utilizing any other relevant information, or to relieve it from bearing the responsibility for the outcome.

---

*The more sophisticated rules have been omitted from this excerpt—ed.

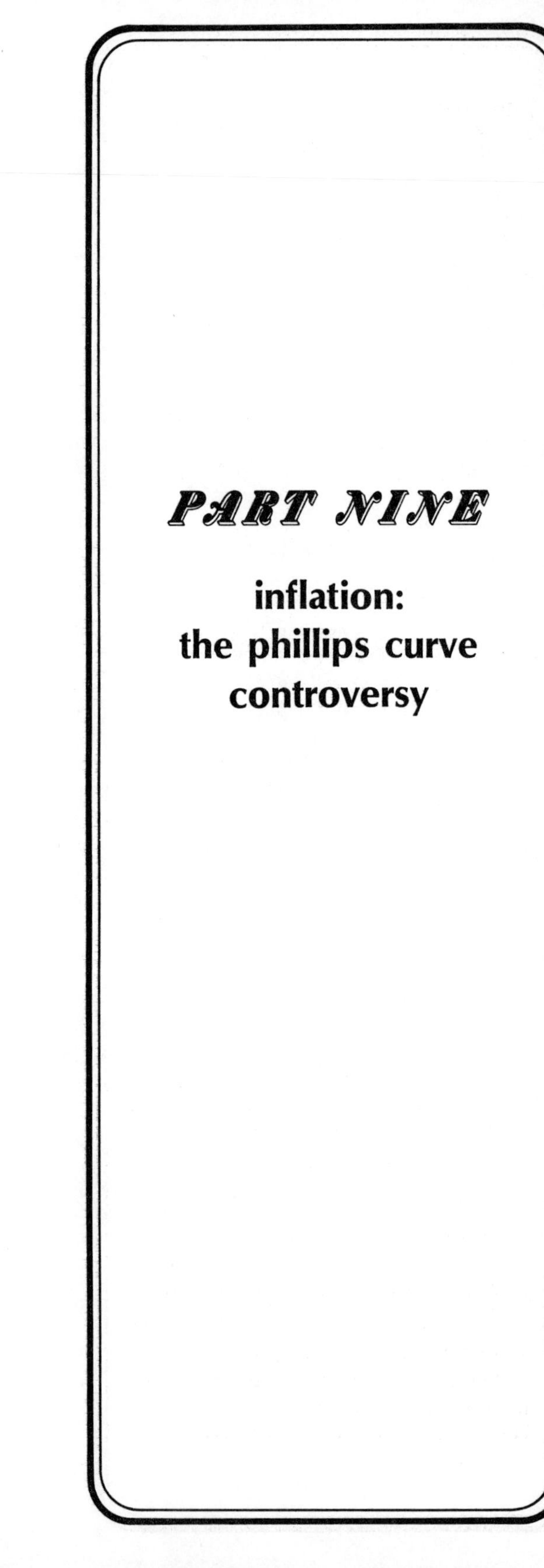

PART NINE

inflation: the phillips curve controversy

The inflation that characterized 1968—a 4.7 point increase in the consumer price index (CPI) and a rise of 4.6 percentage points in the more comprehensive GNP deflator—continued into 1969. During the first half of 1969, the CPI showed a further increase, rising from 123.7 in December 1968 to 127.6 by the following June. The broader GNP deflator mirrored this upward sweep; in the second quarter of 1969 the deflator stood at 127.3, whereas half a year earlier it had reached only 123.5. Public concern was aroused, and certainly the "Democratic" inflation contributed to the Republican victory in the November 1968 Presidential election. Yet inflation has not been a stranger to American economic and political life. A survey of the GNP deflator for the years since the late 1930s will demonstrate that it failed to move upward in only one year.

The major newsworthy feature of the current inflation, of course, lies not in its presence but in its strength. Whereas prices rose less than 2 percent annually in the 1956–1965 period, they escalated rapidly after 1966. The annual percentage increase in the deflator for each year since 1965 has been as follows:

1965/66	2.7
1966/67	3.2
1967/68	4.0
1968/69	4.7
1969 II/1970 II	5.3

What caused the inflation that has manifested itself in the United States economy for more than a decade? Is there a single explanation for the earlier creeping inflation and for the strong inflation of the second half of the surging sixties?

Before any attempt is made to answer these questions, another must be asked: What do we mean by inflation? Two separate aspects of this question deserve consideration. First, does an upward movement of a price index such as the CPI or the GNP deflator accurately represent what is commonly thought of as inflation? Second, even if price index measures are accurate, is any general price increase to be deemed "inflationary"?

Price indexes are, and for technical reasons must be, based on samples. Not all the manifold goods and services that constitute a modern economy can be included, nor can the variety of prices charged for each individual commodity be surveyed. Moreover, the weights by which the importance of each entry is measured are subject to change, but continuous surveys designed to detect these changes are not presently feasible. Errors can creep in at each stage of the index calculation. Statisticians are well aware of these problems and other difficulties as well. The best that the users of the indexes can assume is a mutual canceling of the errors, so that year-to-year comparisons are valid. A more serious problem is encountered when the issue of quality changes is considered. A rise in the price of a good should not be considered inflationary if that price rise is warranted by quality improvements. Unfortunately, no one has yet devised a satisfactory method of measuring quality, so it is impossible to allocate a price increase into its noninflationary quality component and its inflationary nonquality share. Estimates of qualitative improvements in goods and services range from 1 percent to 2 percent a year for the aggregate economy. When taken at the upper limit of 2 percent, such improvements eliminate entirely the inflation of the 1950s; at the lower limit they reduce it to within the ranges of statistical error of the indexes.

Turn now to a still more basic question by assuming away the issue of index number accuracy. Will a rise in an accurate index lead to the unalterable conclusion of inflation? Some economists would indeed agree that "general price increases" and "inflation" are synonymous. Others prefer to distinguish between inflation and "reflation," the latter term referring to a price increase that follows a fall in the general price level during the preceding contraction phase of the business cycle. Pragmatic considerations support this distinction; inflation typically connotes the need for anti-inflationary measures, whereas reflation does not. According to the latter view, then, the word "inflation" is utilized only to describe a general rise in prices that is unacceptable to the public. This subjective definition occasions a number of difficulties, not the least of which is the inability to detect when reflation is transformed into inflation. On the other hand, the numerical precision of the first definition is illusory; subjective appraisal creeps in when public policy decisions are inevitable. The economists who consider any general price rise as inflationary do disagree over the minimal rate of inflation that must be imminent before disinflationary countermeasures are taken. Some would object to even a 1 percent per annum inflation, but others would call in the monetary and fiscal weapons only if the rate of price increase exceeded 4 percent annually. Semantics aside, the essential question is not "What is inflation?" but "How much inflation can the economy tolerate before repressive action should be initiated?" The answer to this question depends on the weight given to the virtues of price stability as opposed to the costs of imposing a disinflationary policy.

From discussing the meaning of inflation we proceed to its causes. A number of distinct theories of inflation can be identified. When the capacity output of the producers of goods and services has been reached and demand is still not met, excess demand or demand-pull inflation is present. Although the quantity theorists attribute this price rise to an increase in the quantity of money and the Keynesians direct their focus on the rise in consumer, investment, or government expenditures, both schools agree that excessive demand is the culprit, because it rises faster than output can be supplied.

A second common cause of inflation is known as "cost-push." The argument here rests essentially on the assumption of imperfect competition and asserts that the power of unions and/or managements enables them to increase prices, often in the face of relatively weak demand conditions. The "demand-shift" hypothesis synthesizes demand-pull and cost-push. Increased demand in one sector of the economy exerts pressure on other sectors. This reaction may be direct, as occurs when the price rise originates in an input used by other sectors. It may also be indirect, as would be the case when input suppliers, such as laborers in other sectors, demand concessions similar to those obtained in the excess-demand industry. A "bottleneck" theory of inflation is also tenable. As demand increases, uneven income elasticities lead to greater pressures in some sectors of the economy than in others, and although ultimately the bottlenecks can be expanded and the flow of goods freed, temporarily at least prices will rise. At the same time, because of downward rigidities, other prices and wages do not fall.

All these theories of inflation are plausible; they certainly are not mutually exclusive. The inflation immediately following World War II was of the demand-pull variety; the post-1966 inflation has had similar overtones. On the other hand, general demand pressure is a less than plausible explanation for the creeping price rise of the mid-1950s and early 1960s, and cost-push or demand-shift provide acceptable alternatives. Unfortunately, rarely can causal relations be distinguished from the available statistics.

Whatever the cause, policy makers would like to avoid inflation, because it arbitrarily redistributes income as well as distorts resource allocation from its noninflationary path. But inhibiting inflation through the common monetary and fiscal tools causes no fewer difficulties than it resolves. Unemployment is one of the unasked for side effects of anti-inflationary actions. Less inflation is purchased at the cost of higher unemployment; conversely, only with a greater degree of inflation can unemployment be reduced. Neither alternative is pleasant to contemplate; the policy makers must select or "trade off" between them.

The existence of the inflation-unemployment trade-off (or the Phillips curve, for short) has been the subject of theoretical controversy and the object of attempts at empirical verification. Roger W. Spencer demonstrates in the opening article of this Part that in essence, the controversy depends on the time horizon focused on by the policy makers. No one denies the existence of a trade-off in the short run; whether or not this dilemma resolves itself in the long run is another question. It is well for policy makers to remember Lord Keynes's well-known dictum: "In the long run, we are all dead."

Both sides of the dispute agree that it is desirable to keep the Phillips curve from shifting upward and still more beneficial if the curve can be shifted downward. Solutions aimed at reducing the dilemma can be divided into those that increase market efficiency without directly modifying the labor-management power structure and those designed to reduce the impact of imperfectly competitive market conditions.

The first group comprises such measures as improving the job-availability information system, facilitating worker retraining and relocation, and enabling firms to increase their efficiency through technical and even financial aid. Much can be accomplished in the way of increasing the unimpeded movement of capital and labor. Indeed, most of the programs mentioned here have been implemented, although not always for the express purpose of resolving the Phillips curve dilemma.

Insofar as the inflation-unemployment trade-off results from the existence and use of economic power, measures to reduce both undesired manifestations simultaneously must be directed at restraining such power or preventing its abuse. Strengthening antitrust policy and eliminating legislation whose impact works to stifle competition —such as resale price maintenance laws—is one of the routes along which the attack can be directed. A second path, now common to many Western governments, is the initiation of an "incomes policy," involving the exercise of centralized direction of wage and price decisions. The wage-price guideposts, which are the subject of the second selection, became the incomes policy of the Kennedy-Johnson administrations. The guideposts were initially voluntary or noncoercive, and they were directed at big business and the labor giants alike. Both business and labor were expected to restrain prices and wages by limiting increases in their incomes to the 3.2 percent historical increase in productivity. This incomes policy was surely a far step from the wage-price freeze authorized by the British government in August 1966, which lasted until the following August.

The ultimate objective of the guideposts is clear—restraining the use of inflation-generating market power. Have the guideposts achieved their goal? Can they work? The answers are not clear-cut. Arthur F. Burns flatly states, "No." More important still, in the view of Professor Burns, are the expensive side effects created by the existence of the guideposts. For details, see the final selection in this Part.

The challenge posed by Burns has been met by proponents of the guideposts. Their rebuttal proceeds as follows:

1. The guideposts were never meant to be rigid rules applicable to every price and wage contract. Instead, their function was educational; they were designed to teach the public and the direct participants in the wage-price-setting process how prices ought to be set if cost-push inflation was to be avoided.

2. Rather than restrict competition, the guideposts outline how competitive firms operating in a competitive economy would react to changing demands.

3. They have worked in the desired direction, and aside from the 1962 steel price confrontation, relations with the business and labor communities have not deteriorated.

4. Finally, other alternatives, such as more vigorous antitrust enforcement, do not preclude an incomes policy. Voluntary self-enforcement accompanied by occasional governmental intervention is far more consistent with the American ethic than is any other form of control.

John Sheahan's concluding paragraphs on the guideposts are worth citing:

> The guideposts, in sum, represent an intelligent gamble to achieve an important national objective. They have served at the very least to direct attention toward the issues involved in

trying to link problems in individual markets to those of economic growth, to the efficiency of the productive systems as a whole, and to the distribution of income. It is no accident that they came in on the heels of a major improvement in the ability to use monetary and fiscal policy to prevent major depressions—an improvement which in turn makes price stability harder to achieve.

The guideposts were not a sufficient solution to this new problem; they are not satisfactory as they stand. They are a promising move in a direction which yielded some gain and created some new problems. Those problems must now be faced more explicitly, with clearer criteria, a recognition of past mistakes, respect for the healthy foundations of a flexible economic system, and a continuing sense that further improvement is not only desirable, but also possible.[1]

As this Introduction is being written, the debate over an incomes policy is being renewed. The apparent failure of the tight monetary and fiscal policies to contain the continuing inflation in early 1970—the GNP deflator rose by more than 6 percent in the first quarter of 1970—coupled with the marked rise in unemployment—the unemployment rate rose from 3.5 percent in December, 1969, to 4.8 percent in April, 1970—has led to demands ranging from a wage-price freeze to Presidential "jawboning." Time alone will tell what policies will be adopted, if any.

In closing, a word of caution must be added. Those who would persist in restraining inflation by monetary and fiscal policy, notwithstanding the higher unemployment level, must realize that unemployment does not hit all groups equally. The first to feel the hardships of the government's disinflationary policy is likely to be the marginal worker—the unskilled, the young, and the nonwhite. Can we afford to increase the poverty of the already poor, the already disadvantaged, the already discriminated against, in order to reduce the degree of inflation? These issues extend beyond the economic; they are sociological, political, and ethical, too.

More broadly put, the focus in this Part centers on the inflation-unemployment dilemma. Although a book of readings on monetary economics must be selective and can choose to ignore other trade-offs, the economist, the politician, and the citizen cannot avoid them. Inflation-poverty; inflation-economic growth; unemployment-balance-of-payments deficit—these are some of the other dilemmas that make their presence felt, although obviously not simultaneously. Wise and compassionate policies are needed to resolve the problems; measures must be devised that will make trade-offs unnecessary. A mature nation surely can react positively.

---

[1]*Have Guideposts Helped to Stabilize the Economy?* Brookings Research Report 75 (Washington, D.C.: The Brookings Institution, 1967).

50 THE RELATION BETWEEN PRICES AND EMPLOYMENT: TWO VIEWS

ROGER W. SPENCER

A quantitative measure of the unemployment-inflation trade-off is a prerequisite for informed policy making. It is not enough to state that the cost of less inflation is more unemployment; the authorities must know how much more. As Dr. Spencer points out here, the fact that economists are far from agreement regarding the exact values of the short-run trade-off indicates the absence of one critical element in the decision-making process. Other missing elements can be mentioned. The Phillips curve may not be symmetrical even in the short run. Thus a .5 percent decrease in unemployment accompanied by, say, a 1.5 percent rate of inflation does not assure anyone that a decrease in the rate of inflation by 1.5 percent will not lead to a 1 percent increase in unemployment. Recent data have been generated from decreasing unemployment and increasing inflation; we have no data to assure us of reversibility. Another point is that the Phillips curve is used in aggregate analysis; yet the policy maker is also very much interested in the disaggregate—for example, in the composition of the unemployed. Finally, as with many quantitative studies, a Phillips curve based on past data may be irrelevant in the future.

Despite all these hesitations, decisions must be made, even on the basis of inadequate data. In the interim, economists are busy working to improve our understanding of the challenge, qualitatively and quantitatively.

Monetary and fiscal authorities are currently confronted with the task of simultaneously slowing price increases and maintaining employment growth. Policies directed toward the achievement of both objectives are affected by the policymakers' understanding of the underlying factors influencing prices and employment (or unemployment). Two principal views on this issue have emerged in the past decade. One stresses the short-run "trade-off" between prices and unemployment, and the other emphasizes the absence of a stable long-run relationship between varying rates of anticipated price changes and the level of unemployment. The short-run, for purposes of this analysis, is a period in which the relevant economic factors do not fully adjust to expectations, while the long-run is a period in which the values of actual and anticipated variables coincide.

This article discusses these two views of the relation between prices and employment without delving excessively into the theoretical complexities of the relation. For expositional purposes, the two views are discussed separately, because the literature tends to be divided into these two groups. The purpose of the article, however, is to demonstrate that the differences between the two views stem primarily from the emphasis on short-run vs. long-run considerations rather than from diametrically opposing

From Roger W. Spencer, "The Relation Between Prices and Employment: Two Views," Federal Reserve Bank of St. Louis, *Review,* 51, No. 3 (March 1969), 15–21.

theories or models. Whether the short run or the long run is emphasized has substantially different implications for stabilization policy. These different implications are discussed in the concluding section of the article.

THE SHORT-RUN TRADE-OFF VIEW

High levels of unemployment in this country have generally been associated with slowly changing price levels, while low levels of unemployment have usually been accompanied by rapidly rising prices. These observed relationships have prompted attempts to explain price variations through changes in unemployment relative to the labor force. The Trade-Off View does not focus on unemployment as a determinant of prices directly, however. It holds that unemployment and the rate of change of unemployment influence money wages, and wage changes, in turn, bring about changes in the level of prices.

A. W. Phillips' study of the relation between wages and unemployment in England is generally considered the point of departure for most recent investigations into the trade-off controversy.[1] Phillips constructed a "trade-off curve" between the unemployment rate and wage changes, which indicated that wages in Great Britain rose rapidly when unemployment was declining and slowly when unemployment was rising. The "Phillips curve" was drawn to reflect a relationship between wages and unemployment, but other analysts have maintained that a similar relationship holds between prices and unemployment. They have assumed or observed that the factors which influence wages similarly influence other prices, or that wages are a principal independent determinant of prices.

Those analysts who follow Phillips in stressing a trade-off between wages or other prices and unemployment have found several factors besides employment pressures which apparently determine wage changes. Factors most often included in this group are profits, productivity, and the cost-of-living. Employment pressures, however, remain the primary explanatory variable.

Factors Influencing Wage-Price Changes

The unemployment rate reflects the state of the demand for labor, a demand which is derived from the demand for goods and services. In a period of rising labor demand, employers attempt to attract workers from one another, thus bidding up wage rates. Additional labor may be obtained by attracting, through higher pay, such "secondary" or "reserve" workers as housewives, students, retired persons, or those already holding one job. The ability of workers to obtain large wage gains may be increased in periods of rising demand for goods and services when employers are especially anxious to avoid strikes. Profits are usually higher and inventories are often at lower levels when demand is high; consequently, employers probably exhibit less resistance to wage demands at such times.

A state of falling demand for goods and services and labor is reflected in a higher unemployment rate. According to Phillips, ". . . it appears that workers are reluctant to offer their services at less than the prevailing rates when the demand for labour is low and unemployment is high so that wage rates fall only very slowly."

Changes in both profits and consumer prices are positively associated with changes in wages in the Trade-Off View. Workers often use high earnings reports and cost-of-living advances to improve their bargaining position. Some

---

[1]A. W. Phillips, "The Relationship Between Unemployment and the Rate of Change of Money Wage Rates in the United Kingdom, 1861–1957," *Economica,* Vol. XXV (November 1958), pp. 283–299.

labor groups have cost-of-living escalator clauses written into their wage contracts.

No general agreement relating productivity and wage changes can be found among those who favor the Trade-Off View. Statistical studies have produced conflicting results. Analysts have found insignificant, significantly positive, and significantly negative relationships between productivity and wage changes. Consequently, for purposes of analysis, productivity is generally assumed to increase at some constant rate. Analysts then can focus on the effects of changes in other variables, particularly unemployment, on wage rates.

Most observers who emphasize the Trade-Off View relate money (nominal) wage changes to the above explanatory variables through regression analysis. If all but one of the explanatory factors are held constant, a relationship between one variable—usually the unemployment rate—and wages can be depicted graphically. The resulting curve slopes downward from left to right, and is usually shaped similar to the rounded "L" determined by Phillips. (See Figures 1 and 2.) The nonlinear shape suggests the existence of a critical high-employment range. According to Levy, "That price inflation, rather than reduced unemployment, is the main result of any expansionary policy after the economy has reached a *critical* high employment range, is a basic inference from traditional economics which is rarely questioned."[2]

The critical high-employment range may be defined as that range in which the number of employment vacancies are approximately equal to the number of workers seeking employment. By this definition, excess demand in the labor market exists when the number of vacancies exceeds the number of job seekers, and there is an excess supply of labor when the number of workers seeking employment exceeds the number of vacancies. Excess demand causes wage rates to rise rapidly in the former case, and excess supply in the latter case tends to slow the rate of wage increase. Labor demand and supply factors may vary from sector to sector, but there is some evidence that a close tie exists between the "... aggregate unemployment rate and unemployment among various subgroups in the population."

The Stability of the Phillips Curve

An issue of particular importance to policymakers is the stability of the prices (wages)-employment relationship. Most Trade-Off View studies, by holding constant those factors other than unemployment which determine wages, do not stress fluctuations within a Phillips curve, shifts of the curve itself, or changes in the critical high-employment range. These studies, which rely heavily on regression analysis, often imply that the economy is operating on a single curve, and stabilization actions directed toward guiding the economy to some point off the curve may prove unsuccessful. Such studies, strictly interpreted, indicate that the Phillips curve is a stable relationship. This implication is refuted by Michael Levy, who found that "during the post-war years, the basic (Phillips curve) relationship for the U.S. economy between wage rate advances on the one hand, and the unemployment rate, the corporate profit rate, and cost-of-living increases on the other, has been highly unstable." [Italics omitted]

Although the relationship may be technically unstable, a plotting of the wage and price changes and the unemployment rate reveals that Phillips' hypothesis—regarding the association of declining unemployment with rapidly rising wages (prices), and rising unemployment with slowly changing wages (prices)—has been generally observable over the past sixteen years. A simple correlation be-

---

[2]Michael E. Levy, "Full Employment Without Inflation," *The Conference Board Record,* Vol. IV (November 1967).

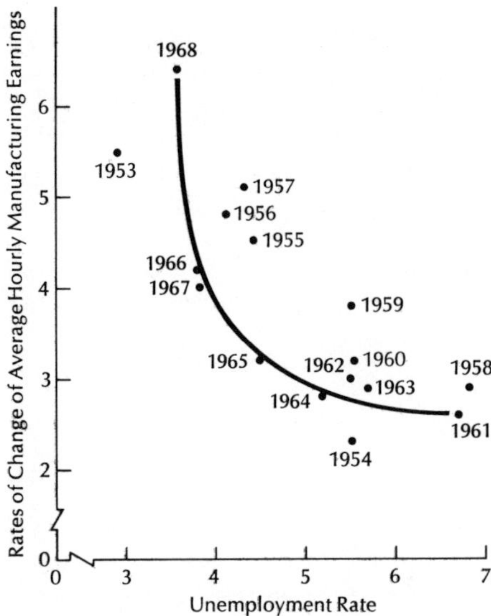

Figure 1 Rates of Change of Manufacturing Wages and Rates of Labor Unemployment
Curve has been arbitrarily fitted to 1961–1968 data. Data shown are in percentages.

tween two variables, as given here by a plotting of points on a two-dimensional graph, does not demonstrate causality, however. The relationship between the rate of change of manufacturing wages and the unemployment rate for the 1953–1968 period is plotted in Figure 1. The curve, which is similar in shape to the curve determined by Phillips, has been arbitrarily drawn to fit the data from 1961 to 1968, a period of uninterrupted economic expansion. The shape of the curve would be altered to some extent if fitted to the 1953–1960 period. For the sixteen-year period, the curve would be shifted slightly to the right.

Graphical trade-off analysis usually focuses on the wages-unemployment relationship, but it has also been extended to the prices-unemployment relationship as has been done in Figure 2. The overall fit for the sixteen-year period would not be as satisfactory as in the previous chart, but there is a close parallel for the past eight years. In some earlier years, sharp price increases occurred at varying rates of unemployment. Unemployment averaged slightly above 4 percent of the labor force in the 1955 to 1957 period, more than 5 percent from 1959 to 1960, and a little less than 4 percent in the 1965 to 1968 period. This evidence suggests that the critical high-employment range has varied, perhaps reflecting the changing nature of the labor force in particular and the economy in general.

Phillips curves derived from regression analysis are based on rather specific assumptions, and the shape can vary substantially when minor modifications of the behavioral assumptions are made, as illustrated by the two following examples. A basic curve derived by George Perry relating consumer prices and unemployment was constructed from an equation in which prices were allowed to respond freely to market pressures. By assuming instead that half of the price increases were autonomous, Perry found that the curve, fairly steeply sloped in the first instance, became relatively flat. In fact, the slope of the curve was less than half of that calculated originally.[3]

[3]G. L. Perry, *Unemployment, Money Wage Rates, and Inflation* (Cambridge, Mass.: The M.I.T. Press, 1966), p. 68.

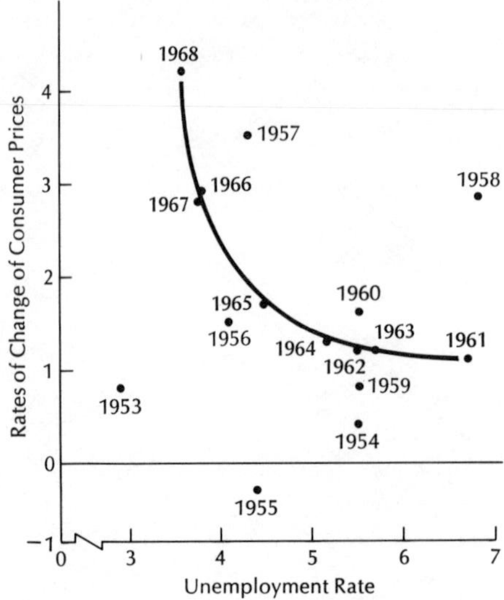

Figure 2 Rates of Change of Consumer Prices and Rates of Labor Unemployment
Curve has been arbitrarily fitted to 1961–1968 data. Data shown are in percentages.

Ronald Bodkin[4] determined a near-horizontal linear relation between wages and unemployment. Rees and Hamilton,[5] utilizing the same data and nearly the same assumptions as Bodkin, found a much steeper curve. Their results precipitated the remark:

> Our final caution is that we have been astounded by how many very different Phillips curves can be constructed on reasonable assumptions from the same body of data. The nature of the relationship between wage changes and unemployment is highly sensitive to the exact choice of the other variables that enter the regression and to the forms of all the variables. For this reason, the authors of Phillips curves would do well to label them conspicuously *"Unstable. Apply with extreme care."*

This conclusion implies that the usefulness of such statements as "... 4 percent unemployment is consistent with a 2 percent rate of inflation if profit rates are at 11.6 percent . . ." is limited by the validity of the assumptions which underlie the model.

Characteristics of the Trade-Off View

The chief characteristics of the Trade-Off View might be summarized as:

1. The relation between money wages and unemployment is stressed, rather than the prices-unemployment relation.

2. Money wage changes are assumed to be a primary, if not the primary, determinant of changes in prices of final goods; consequently, changes in prices of final goods follow wage changes.

3. The relevant variables are specified in nominal rather than real (or price-deflated) terms.

4. The basic relationships are established by the use of regression analysis using observed data.

---

[4] R. G. Bodkin, *The Wage-Price-Productivity Nexus* (Philadelphia: University of Pennsylvania Press, 1966), p. 279.

[5] Albert Rees and Mary T. Hamilton, "The Wage-Price-Productivity Perplex," *Journal of Political Economy*, 75, 70.

5. The relation between rates of wage or price changes and the unemployment rate may be represented by a line which curves downward on a graph from left to right.

6. The rationale behind movements along the Phillips curve, rather than shifts of the curve itself, is stressed. The policymakers attempt to attain the point on the curve which seems least undesirable.

7. The time units and period covered by the analysis are specified in terms of months, quarters, or years. Phrases such as "the length of time required for the factors to reach their long-run values" are not found in the Trade-Off View.

THE LONG-RUN EQUILIBRIUM VIEW

The Long-Run Equilibrium View considers the trade-offs between wages or prices and unemployment as transitory phenomena, and that no such trade-off exists after factors have completely adjusted to the trend of spending growth. In the short-run there can be a discrepancy between expectations and actual price or wage changes, but not in the long-run. After the discrepancies between expected and actual values have worked themselves out, the only relevant magnitudes are "real," or price-deflated ones.

To illustrate the view, consider the following hypothesized sequence of events in the upswing of a business cycle, beginning with an initial condition of significant unemployment. Monetary or fiscal actions may start an upturn of business activity. Spending occurs in anticipation of a continuation of the price levels which had prevailed in the downswing. Employers begin actively seeking workers to accommodate the rising demand, but wages increase only moderately since a large number of unemployed are seeking jobs. Output and employment rise more rapidly than wages or prices. The remainder of the scenario is outlined by Milton Friedman:

> Because selling prices of products typically respond to an unanticipated rise in nominal demand faster than prices of factors of production, real wages received have gone down —though real wages anticipated by employees went up, since employees implicitly evaluated the wages offered at the earlier price level. Indeed, the simultaneous fall *ex post* in real wages to employers and rise *ex ante* in real wages to employees is what enabled employment to increase. [The non-technical reader may wish to substitute "anticipated" for *"ex ante"* and "actual" for *"ex post."*] But the decline *ex post* in real wages will soon come to affect anticipations. Employees will start to reckon on rising prices of the things they buy and to demand higher nominal wages for the future. "Market" unemployment is below the "natural" level. There is an excess demand for labor so real wages will tend to rise toward their initial level.[6]

As real wages approach their original level, employers are no longer motivated to hire workers as rapidly or bid up wages so much as in the earlier portion of the upswing. Moreover, rising wages may encourage employers to utilize more labor-saving equipment and relatively fewer workers. As the growth of demand for labor slows, the unemployment rate declines to its "natural" level. Economic units come to anticipate the rate of inflation, and are no longer misled by increases in money income—the so-called "money illusion." The unexpected price increases which accompanied the original expansion of total demand and production caused a temporary reduction of unemployment below the long-run equilibrium level. Only accelerating inflation —a situation in which actual price rises continue to exceed anticipated rise—can keep the actual unemployment rate below the "natural" rate.

Inflation has not been allowed to rise uncontrolled for sustained periods in this country, so little empirical evidence can

---

[6]Milton Friedman, "The Role of Monetary Policy," *The American Economic Review,* Vol. LVIII (March 1968), p. 10.

be amassed to support the contentions that no permanent trade-off exists. In other countries such as Brazil, however, it has been found that sustained inflation does not generate continuous employment gains; in fact, recessions and high unemployment rates have occurred as secular inflation continued. Unanticipated price increases have, in those countries as well as in the United States, generated increased temporary employment, just as unanticipated declines in the rate of price increase have caused temporary rise in unemployment. But if inflation is "fully and instantaneously discounted, the Phillips curve becomes a vertical line over the point of 'equilibrium unemployment.' This is the rate of unemployment where wage increases equal productivity gains plus changes in income shares. The unemployment-price stability trade-off is gone." In other words, there is no particular rate of price change related to a particular rate of unemployment when the price changes are fully anticipated. Unemployment shifts to its equilibrium value and is consistent with any rate of change of prices. A low rate of unemployment can no longer be "traded-off" against rapidly rising prices, nor can a high unemployment rate be "traded-off" against slowly changing prices.

Costs of Information

A modified version of the Long-Run Equilibrium View is framed in terms of costs of obtaining information about job opportunities. When the demand for labor is low, the costs to a worker of discovering the state of labor demand are relatively high because employers are not actively seeking workers by publicizing extensive lists of vacancies. Employers are not as likely to absorb job training and transfer costs as they are when aggregate demand is rising. When labor demand rises and employers begin bidding up wage rates to attract additional labor, the costs of information, training and transferring are lowered to employees. The lower costs mean that employees will not have to search as long for acceptable employment, and the shorter the search time, the lower the rate of unemployment. Rising wages are accompanied by a declining unemployment rate.

A reversal of stimulative policies will generate declining demand for labor. Some workers will accept smaller wage increases or reduced wages, but others will prefer to leave their jobs to seek employment at their former money wage rates. They expect prices and wages will remain at their earlier, higher levels. Prices and output will have fallen, however, and the high real wage rate will have stimulated employers to lower the quantity of labor demanded, thereby raising search costs to those workers who leave their jobs to seek employment elsewhere. Higher search costs and lower money wage rates will be accompanied by rising unemployment. When workers realize that demand and price increases have slowed, they will be willing to accept the lower money wage rates and unemployment will stabilize at the "natural" level. For the stabilization to occur, however, no money illusion can exist. Anticipated wage (or price) changes must equal actual wage (or price) changes.

The costs-of-information approach combines the two factors determining the equilibrium rate of unemployment—the structure of real wage rates as determined by labor demand and supply, and "imperfections" within the labor market. Bottlenecks, labor and product market monopolies, positive costs of information, training and transfers create "imperfections" in the labor market. In other words, all markets are not cleared instantaneously and without cost. At any point in time the degree of the so-called "imperfection" within the labor market will vary, depending on transactions and information costs; correspondingly, the "natural" rate of unemployment will vary.

Enactment of policies oriented toward eliminating or reducing market imperfections (adjustment costs) will cause the short-run Phillips curve to shift to the left and down. Policies which increase these costs move the short-run Phillips curve upward and to the right. Different forces are at work at different times, causing the curve to shift frequently. Expectations of higher prices will cause the curve to shift upward, and expectations of lower prices move the curve in the opposite direction. The optimal stabilization policies, therefore, would be those which would reduce market adjustment costs and expectations of higher prices. Enactment of such policies would at first move the short-run Phillips curve to the left and downward, and in time, as expectations are fully realized, cause the curve to become a vertical line over the "natural" rate of unemployment.

A hypothetical, long-run relationship between prices and unemployment is presented in Figure 3. Point *D* represents the "natural," or equilibrium rate of unemployment before market imperfections or adjustment costs are reduced. Curve *A* represents one of many possible short-run Phillips curves that exist before price changes are fully anticipated. After the rate of inflation becomes fully discounted, the unemployment rate will shift from some point beneath curve *A* to point *D*, regardless of whether prices are rising at some slow rate, *X*, or a rapid rate, *Z*. The shift may occur along any of an infinite number of Phillips curves. The vertical line above point *D* indicates that no economic units—workers or employers, sellers or consumers, borrowers or lenders—are surprised by price changes. If programs to reduce labor and product market imperfections are implemented, vertical line *B* will shift, after a transitory period, to the left. Vertical line *C* represents the new long-run relationship between prices and employment above point *E*.

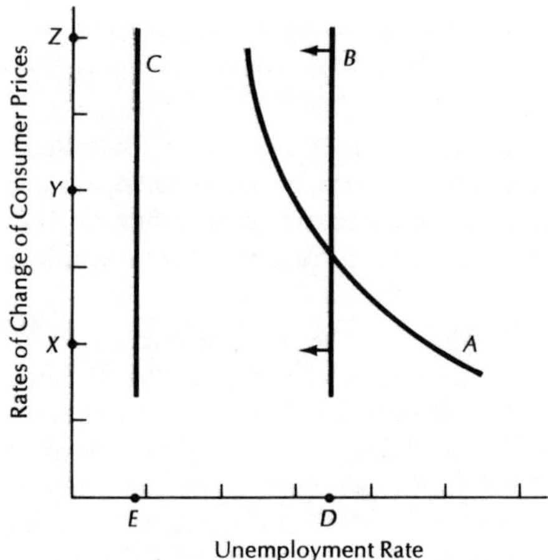

Figure 3 Hypothetical Relationships Between Prices and Unemployment

Curve *A* is a short-run prices-unemployment relationship. Vertical line *B* is the long-run relationship between prices (fully anticipated regardless of the rate of change) and the "natural" rate of unemployment, *D*, before reduction of market "imperfections." Vertical line *C* is a similar long-run relationship between prices and unemployment after assumed reduction of labor and product market imperfections.

Characteristics of the Long-Run Equilibrium View

The principal characteristics of the Long-Run Equilibrium View might be summarized as:

1. The relationship between all prices and unemployment is emphasized, rather than the wages-unemployment relation.

2. Changes in selling prices usually precede changes in the prices of productive agents.

3. The relevant economic factors are specified in real rather than nominal terms.

4. Because of the lack of data on accelerating inflations, expectations of price changes, and the "natural" rate of unem-

ployment, the analysis is generally accomplished through abstract reasoning rather than empirical testing.

5. The relation between the long-run rate of price or wage changes and the unemployment rate is a vertical line over the equilibrium rate of unemployment.

6. The long-run relationship and reasons for observed shifts of the Phillips curve are stressed. The authorities do not have to choose as a target some fixed relationship between prices and unemployment on a Phillips curve, but can attempt to move the economy off a short-run curve. In the long-run, they can seek any trend in prices desired without a sacrifice in terms of foregone employment or production.

7. The time period of the analysis is not specified. In the long-run, the actual values of the relevant economic variables equal the expected values, while in the short-run, they do not.

POLICY IMPLICATIONS OF THE TWO VIEWS

Unemployment declined from 5.2 percent of the labor force in 1964 to 3.5 percent in 1968. The annual rate of increase in consumer prices rose from 1.3 percent to 4.2 percent for corresponding years. These data indicate, according to the Trade-Off View, that stabilization authorities must decide to accept either high rates of price increases in order to maintain low unemployment rates, or adopt deflationary measures and accept relatively high levels of unemployment. Only significant reductions of imperfections within the product and labor markets could prevent employment declines in the face of deflationary policies.

Proponents of the Long-Run Equilibrium View point out that even in the absence of structural improvements, monetary and fiscal policies need not be limited by a short-run trade-off between prices and employment. Continuation of expansionary developments will generate either (1) a high, steady rate of inflation which will eventually become fully anticipated and confer no net additional employment benefits (unemployment will gradually return to its "natural" rate), or (2) an accelerating rate of inflation which will permit unemployment to remain below the "natural" rate. Neither expansionary policy alternative appears economically or politically desirable. Deflationary actions would produce increased unemployment (as expectations of price changes are slowly revised) but only temporarily, according to the Equilibrium View. As soon as a new price trend becomes stabilized and fully anticipated, nominal and real wages will coincide, and unemployment will fall to its "natural" rate. An inflationary policy is neither a necessary nor a sufficient condition for the attainment of high levels of employment. Since price expectations seem to change only slowly, actions to reduce the rate of inflation should probably be applied gradually to minimize the transition cost in terms of reduced output and increased unemployment.

Both views recognize the merits of structural measures in complementing monetary and fiscal actions. Policies which reduce the costs of obtaining employment information, improve labor mobility and skills, and eliminate product and labor market monopolies will lower the optimal level of unemployment. Adoption of such policies would improve the short-run dilemma faced by monetary and fiscal authorities and enable them to shift their long-run unemployment target to a lower level.

51 GUIDEPOSTS FOR NONINFLATIONARY WAGE AND PRICE BEHAVIOR

COUNCIL OF ECONOMIC ADVISERS

In a decentralized economic system, each party, after considering various alternatives, acts on the one that yields it the most favorable outcome. Presumably, many such independent decisions culminate in the welfare optimum for the whole economy. But such thinking disregards the interdependence of many economic units; the result is that an individual unit takes action only after it has estimated how another unit will react. For example, if a labor union anticipates either a 4 percent increase in prices next year or an equivalent increase in wages of workers in other unions, it will be acting most rationally if its negotiators insist on at least a 4 percent wage boost. If this inflationary psychology pervades other unions as well and management too, a 4 percent increase in wages and prices will be realized. But the economic condition of no individual union member is improved permanently by this step; the members would have been no worse off with stable wages and prices. The guideposts can be interpreted as the government's attempt to drive this point home. They are based on the belief that if all parties adhere to a uniform set of rules, then, through implicit cooperation, none will turn out to be losers.

• • •

There are important segments of the economy where firms are large or employees well-organized, or both. In these sectors, private parties may exercise considerable discretion over the terms of wage bargains and price decisions. Thus, at least in the short run, there is considerable room for the exercise of private power and a parallel need for the assumption of private responsibility.

Individual wage and price decisions assume national importance when they involve large numbers of workers and large amounts of output directly, or when they are regarded by large segments of the economy as setting a pattern. Because such decisions affect the progress of the whole economy, there is legitimate reason for public interest in their content and consequences. An informed public, aware of the significance of major wage bargains and price decisions, and equipped to judge for itself their compatibility with the national interest, can help to create an atmosphere in which the parties to such decisions will exercise their powers responsibly.

How is the public to judge whether a particular wage-price decision is in the national interest? No simple test exists, and it is not possible to set out systematically all of the many considerations which bear on such a judgment. However, since the question is of prime importance to the strength and progress of the American economy, it deserves widespread public discussion and clarification of the issues. What follows is intended as a contribution to such a discussion.

Mandatory controls in peacetime over the outcomes of wage negotiations and over individual price decisions are nei-

From *Economic Report of the President, 1962* (Washington, D.C.: U.S. Government Printing Office, 1962), pp. 185–190.

ther desirable in the American tradition nor practical in a diffuse and decentralized continental economy. Free collective bargaining is the vehicle for the achievement of contractual agreements on wages, fringes, and working conditions, as well as on the "web of rules" by which a large segment of industry governs the performance of work and the distribution of rewards. Similarly, final price decisions lie—and should continue to lie—in the hands of individual firms. It is, however, both desirable and practical that discretionary decisions on wages and prices recognize the national interest in the results. The guideposts suggested here as aids to public understanding are not concerned primarily with the relation of employers and employees to each other, but rather with their joint relation to the rest of the economy.

WAGES, PRICES, AND PRODUCTIVITY

If all prices remain stable, all hourly labor costs may increase as fast as economy-wide productivity without, for that reason alone, changing the relative share of labor and nonlabor incomes in total output. At the same time, each kind of income increases steadily in absolute amount. If hourly labor costs increase at a slower rate than productivity, the share of nonlabor incomes will grow or prices will fall, or both. Conversely, if hourly labor costs increase more rapidly than productivity, the share of labor incomes in the total product will increase or prices will rise, or both. It is this relationship among long-run economy-wide productivity, wages, and prices which makes the rate of productivity change an important benchmark for noninflationary wage and price behavior.

Productivity is a *guide* rather than a *rule* for appraising wage and price behavior for several reasons. First, there are a number of problems involved in measuring productivity change, and a number of alternative measures are available. Second, there is nothing immutable in fact or in justice about the distribution of the total product between labor and nonlabor incomes. Third, the pattern of wages and prices among industries is and should be responsive to forces other than changes in productivity.

ALTERNATIVE MEASURES OF PRODUCTIVITY

If the rate of growth of productivity over time is to serve as a useful benchmark for wage and price behavior, there must be some meeting of minds about the appropriate methods of measuring the trend rate of increase in productivity, both for industry as a whole and for individual industries. This is a large and complex subject and there is much still to be learned. The most that can be done at present is to give some indication of orders of magnitude, and of the range within which most plausible measures are likely to fall.

. . .

THE SHARE OF LABOR INCOME

The proportions in which labor and nonlabor incomes share the product of industry have not been immutable throughout American history, nor can they be expected to stand forever where they are today. It is desirable that labor and management should bargain explicitly about the distribution of the income of particular firms or industries. It is, however, undesirable that they should bargain implicitly about the general price level. Excessive wage settlements which are paid for through price increases in major industries put direct pressure on the general price level and produce spillover and imitative effects throughout the economy. Such settlements may fail to redistribute income within the industry involved; rather they redistribute income between that industry and other segments of the economy through the mechanism of inflation.

PRICES AND WAGES IN INDIVIDUAL INDUSTRIES

What are the guideposts which may be used in judging whether a particular price or wage decision may be inflationary? The desired objective is a stable price level, within which particular prices rise, fall, or remain stable in response to economic pressures. Hence, price stability within any particular industry is not necessarily a correct guide to price and wage decisions in that industry. It is possible, however, to describe in broad outline a set of guides which, if followed, would preserve over-all price stability while still allowing sufficient flexibility to accommodate objectives of efficiency and equity. These are not arbitrary guides. They describe—briefly and no doubt incompletely—how prices and wage rates would behave in a smoothly functioning competitive economy operating near full employment. Nor do they constitute a mechanical formula for determining whether a particular price or wage decision is inflationary. They will serve their purpose if they suggest to the interested public a useful way of approaching the appraisal of such a decision.

If, as a point of departure, we assume no change in the relative shares of labor and nonlabor incomes in a particular industry, then a general guide may be advanced for noninflationary wage behavior, and another for noninflationary price behavior. Both guides, as will be seen, are only first approximations.

The general guide for noninflationary wage behavior is that the rate of increase in wage rates (including fringe benefits) in each industry be equal to the trend rate of over-all productivity increase. General acceptance of this guide would maintain stability of labor cost per unit of output for the economy as a whole—though not of course for individual industries.

The general guide for noninflationary price behavior calls for price reduction if the industry's rate of productivity increase exceeds the over-all rate—for this would mean declining unit labor costs; it calls for an appropriate increase in price if the opposite relationship prevails; and it calls for stable prices if the two rates of productivity increase are equal.

These are advanced as general guideposts. To reconcile them with objectives of equity and efficiency, specific modifications must be made to adapt them to the circumstances of particular industries. If all of these modifications are made, each in the specific circumstances to which it applies, they are consistent with stability of the general price level. Public judgments about the effects on the price level of particular wage or price decisions should take into account the modifications as well as the general guides. The most important modifications are the following:

1. Wage rate increases would exceed the general guide rate in an industry which would otherwise be unable to attract sufficient labor; or in which wage rates are exceptionally low compared with the range of wages earned elsewhere by similar labor, because the bargaining position of workers has been weak in particular local labor markets.

2. Wage rate increases would fall short of the general guide rate in an industry which could not provide jobs for its entire labor force even in times of generally full employment; or in which wage rates are exceptionally high compared with the range of wages earned elsewhere by similar labor, because the bargaining position of workers has been especially strong.

3. Prices would rise more rapidly, or fall more slowly, than indicated by the general guide rate in an industry in which the level of profits was insufficient to attract the capital required to finance a

needed expansion in capacity; or in which costs other than labor costs had risen.

4. Prices would rise more slowly, or fall more rapidly, than indicated by the general guide in an industry in which the relation of productive capacity to full employment demand shows the desirability of an outflow of capital from the industry; or in which costs other than labor costs have fallen; or in which excessive market power has resulted in rates of profit substantially higher than those earned elsewhere on investments of comparable risk.

It is a measure of the difficulty of the problem that even these complex guideposts leave out of account several important considerations. Although output per man-hour rises mainly in response to improvements in the quantity and quality of capital goods with which employees are equipped, employees are often able to improve their performance by means within their own control. It is obviously in the public interest that incentives be preserved which would reward employees for such efforts.

Also, in connection with the use of measures of over-all productivity gain as benchmarks for wage increases, it must be borne in mind that average hourly labor costs often change through the process of up- or down-grading, shifts between wage and salaried employment, and other forces. Such changes may either add to or subtract from the increment which is available for wage increases under the over-all productivity guide.

Finally, it must be reiterated that collective bargaining within an industry over the division of the proceeds between labor and nonlabor income is not necessarily disruptive of over-all price stability. The relative shares can change within the bounds of noninflationary price behavior. But when a disagreement between management and labor is resolved by passing the bill to the rest of the economy, the bill is paid in depreciated currency to the ultimate advantage of no one.

It is no accident that productivity is the central guidepost for wage settlements. Ultimately, it is rising output per man hour which must yield the ingredients of a rising standard of living. Growth in productivity makes it possible for real wages and real profits to rise side by side.

• • •

52 WAGES AND PRICES BY FORMULA?

ARTHUR F. BURNS

The crux of the debate between economists who sympathize with the guideposts and those who oppose them—Federal Reserve Chairman Burns belongs to the latter group—lies in the degree of competitiveness in the American economy. That big business and big labor characterize the economic landscape is not denied. The central question is, Does size connote power? The Kennedy-Johnson economists who promulgated the guideposts felt that the giants did exercise market power; frequently they were united, albeit only implicitly, against the powerless consumer. The responsibility of the federal government therefore became to restrain this inevitable exercise of power. Burns places more confidence in the competitive forces facing business and labor and requiring them to circumscribe their actions.

A second issue of dispute lies in a more technical question, Are the guideposts designed in a technically proper manner? See if you can distinguish these separate lines of criticism in the following selection.

• • •

TROUBLESOME CONSEQUENCES

As every economist knows, there are only two ways of raising the real earnings of labor. They can be raised by (1) increasing output per man-hour of work or (2) enlarging the share of total income that accrues to wage and salary workers.

Of these two sources, the first is basic, and it has always been vastly more important in our country than the second. The guidelines have the great merit of calling attention to this fact. Taking the economy as a whole, it is the cost of labor that dominates production costs. If the cost of labor per unit of output rises, business firms will ordinarily seek to protect their profit margins by raising prices. But a rise in wage rates, using this term broadly so as to include fringe benefits, need not involve a rise in production costs. It will do that only if the rise in the hourly wage rate is proportionately greater than the increase in output per man-hour. Therefore, if the average percentage increase in wage rate across the nation merely equals the average percentage increase in output per man-hour, the general level of prices could remain stable without reducing the fraction of the nation's output accruing to stockholders and other income claimants.

By expressing this basic truth, the guideposts have helped to direct the attention of thoughtful citizens to ways of raising output per man-hour—ways such as investing in more and better tools of production, improving the education and skills of workers, improving the quality of management, and eliminating featherbedding and restrictive trading practices.

Public enlightenment, however, has been an incidental aspect of the guideposts. Being a tool of policy, they point

From Arthur F. Burns, "Wages and Prices by Formula?" *Harvard Business Review*, 43, No. 2 (March–April 1965), 58–64.

to a course of action. Their essential purpose is to curb inflation—or, more precisely, to permit monetary and fiscal policies to stimulate production and employment without stirring up inflationary pressures from trade unions or corporations. And if the guidelines for prices and wages were generally observed, it is indeed true that the existing links between the flow of money to markets, on the one hand, and the flow of goods and services to purchasers, on the other, would be broken. In such a world the levels of wages and prices would be governed by formula, and they would no longer reflect the changing forces of market demand and market supply—as they now do.

If the policy of the guideposts became fully effective, it would therefore change drastically the workings of our commodity and labor markets, and thereby modify—for better or worse—the character of our economic system.

Practical Effects

Let us try to visualize a little more definitely how the guideposts, if they were generally and fully respected, would work out in practice.

Statistical records stretching back into the nineteenth century demonstrate that, although the over-all productivity of our economy occasionally declines, its trend has been steadily upward. If this continues to be true, as we may reasonably suppose, general observance of the guidelines will result in higher wages every year, regardless of the stage of the business cycle or the level of unemployment or the state of the balance of payments. The rise of wages will be the same, on the average, in years of recession as in years of prosperity; but in any given recession the rise of wages could easily be larger than in the preceding years of prosperity. Furthermore, the average wage will tend to rise in any given year by the same percentage in every firm, regardless of its profitability or the state of the market for different kinds of labor.

However, general observance of the guidepost for prices will not freeze individual prices or the relations among them. What it would tend to freeze is (1) the general level of prices and (2) the ratio of individual prices to unit labor costs of production. The tendency of the price-cost ratio to remain constant will be stronger in some industries than in others. Strictly speaking, the guidepost for prices specifies merely that the ratio of price to unit labor cost of production should not rise; it does not argue against a decline of the price-cost ratio. Hence, firms or industries experiencing a weak demand for their products or keen foreign competition may need to be content with prices that decline relative to their unit labor costs. On the other hand, firms or industries that are favored in the marketplace would be unable to raise prices relative to their unit labor costs even if their incoming orders were many times as large as their production. Nor would they be able to raise prices to compensate for increases in costs of production other than those of labor.

The broad effect of these tendencies would be to keep more or less constant the percentage share of the national income—or of national output—going to labor. Changes in the use of capital relative to the use of labor, whether upward or downward, could still have a large influence on the size of the national income but not on the proportion of income accruing to labor. Unless major shifts occurred in the occupational or industrial distribution of employment, any fluctuation in labor's percentage share of the national income would be due primarily to the discrepancy between the movement of over-all productivity in a particular year and the corresponding trend increase. Nonlabor income, in the aggregate, would also tend to be a constant percentage of the national income.

It is well to bear in mind, however, that since profits are only a fraction of nonlabor income, the share of profits in the total national income could either rise or decline. In the postwar period, the amount paid by corporations on account of excises, customs duties, property taxes, licensing fees, and other indirect taxes has risen more rapidly than their net output. If this trend continues, the income share of investors in the corporate sector will tend to undergo a persistent decline, while that of labor will tend to remain constant.

Throttling of Competition

In the hypothetical economy that I have sketched, monopolies—whether of business or labor—would no longer have the power to push up the price level. Put more precisely, if trade unions and business firms complied voluntarily with the guidelines, they would relinquish any market power that they have not yet used or that they might gain in the future. This is worth noting, but it is not the main point.

The *fundamental* point of the preceding analysis is that general observance of the guideposts would throttle the forces of competition no less effectively than those of monopoly. The point is important because, unlike much of the rest of the world, the rivalry among U.S. business firms is very keen. Even in industries where a few corporations dominate the market—as in the case of automobiles, steel, and aluminum—each corporation competes actively against the others in its industry, against rival products of other industries, and against foreign suppliers. Competition in labor markets is also stronger than casual references to labor monopoly may suggest. After all, only a little over a fourth of the population working for wages or salaries is unionized, and many of the trade unions are weak. By and large, it is competition—not monopoly—that has vast sweep and power in our everyday life. Since free competitive markets would virtually cease to exist in an economy that observed the guidelines, this transformation of the economy merits serious reflection.

To be sure, compliance with the guidelines would be voluntary in the economy we are considering. That, however, may not mean much. For when economic freedom is not exercised, it is no longer a part of life. As far as I can see, an economy in which wages and prices are set voluntarily according to a formula suggested by the government would be almost indistinguishable from an economy in which wages and prices are directly fixed by governmental authorities. In either case—

—the movement of resources toward uses that are favored by the buying public would be impeded;
—the tendency to economize on the use of what happens to be especially scarce, whether it be materials or labor or equipment, would be weakened;
—since prices will no longer tend to equate demand and supply in individual markets, some form of rationing would need to be practiced.

In all likelihood, therefore, a shift from our present market economy to one of voluntary compliance with the guidelines would adversely affect efficiency. It would also adversely affect the rate of economic growth and the rate of improvement of the general standard of living.

It is true, of course, that controlled economies can and do escape complete rigidity. The exigencies of life do not permit their authorities to be blind to considerations of efficiency or social harmony, so that price and wage edicts have to be modified here and there. Black markets tend to develop, and—despite their unsavory character—they often perform a useful function in facilitating production. Moreover, managers gradually become skillful in "gray practices," such as reclassifying labor in order to escape the wage restraints or modifying products in order to escape the price restraints. Our hypothetical economy of voluntary compliance would also have its safety valve; that is to say, the guidelines would be modified in "a relatively few cases" in the interest of equity or efficiency. However, gray or black markets, which impart some fluidity and resilience to authoritarian economies, could not exist in the economy of voluntary compliance that we have been considering here.

ARE THE GUIDES WORKABLE?

This theoretical sketch of how our economy would work if the guidelines were generally and fully observed has blinked institutional factors—such as the adjustments caused by the disappearance of auction markets, the new role of trade unions, and so on. Moreover, our theoretical sketch has tacitly assumed that voluntary compliance with the guidelines is merely a matter of will. Life is not that simple. Even if everyone responded to the government's plea for "cooperation" and sought faithfully to act in accordance with the guidelines, it would frequently be difficult or actually impossible to do so.

There is, first of all, a vast gap in our statistical arsenal. To comply with the guideline for *wages,* businessmen would need to know the trend increase of the over-all output of the nation per manhour. Once this highly complex magnitude had been estimated by the government, it would presumably be subjected to outside review, revised if need be, and accompanied by a specification of the boundaries of the year (if a year be the interval) to which it would apply. All firms dealing with labor, except those newly established, would then know what wage adjustment was expected of them.

Compliance with the *price* guideline would be infinitely harder. For this purpose, every company would need to know the trend increase in the productivity of its own industry and how this increase compares with the trend increase of overall productivity of the economy. Such information is not generally available, nor is it readily usable.

Applying the Indexes

The productivity indexes now being published, besides being often out of date, lump together a great variety of products. In time, more detailed and more current indexes of productivity will doubtless be constructed, but there are limits to what is statistically feasible. Even if measures of this type become available for each of a thousand or ten thousand industries, much confusion or perplexity will still remain:

Should a manufacturer of bricks, for example, be guided in his pricing by an index of productivity for the stone, clay, and glass group or by an index confined to brick manufacture?

If the latter, is the pertinent index a nationwide measure, one confined to his region, or perhaps to his locality or plant?

How should a manufacturing firm proceed when its output is not standardized or when it makes a hundred different items, instead of just one product?

If the appropriate index is not available, as may long remain the case for many firms, especially in the service trades, what is the best "proxy" for it?

Will the judgment of a company's management on such issues, even if made entirely in good faith, be acceptable to others—such as its trade union, the Council of Economic Advisers, or the general public—who also seek only what is right?

Better statistics on productivity will reduce these difficulties; however, they cannot possibly remove them.

Changes in Work Force

Another puzzling problem would be posed by changes in the composition of labor that is used in industry. Consider, for example, the case of a company that has recently decided to employ more skilled workers of different sorts and less unskilled labor:

> Since skilled labor is compensated at a higher rate, the average wage per hour that is paid by the company to its workers will go up, quite apart from any wage increase that may be needed for the individual grades of labor. Let us now suppose that the wage guidepost calls for an increase of, say, 3%. Then the company's employees will naturally expect an increase of this size in their individual rates of pay.
>
> But may not the company's personnel executive, who has become steeped in the mathematics of the guidelines, properly insist that the average wage has already gone up this much or more on account of the more intensive use of skilled labor and that no increase of wage rates is therefore warranted by the government's guideline? Will the trade union's representative grasp this statistical subtlety? Will he not argue that the guideline requires an increase of 3%, that other organizations are putting through such increases, and that simple justice requires that the same be done by this company?
>
> Suppose that the personnel executive perseveres and finally convinces the union's representative. Will the latter, in turn, be able to persuade the company's employees? Can we even be sure that the company's board of directors will be convinced by the argument of its personnel officer?

In view of modern trends that emphasize the use of higher skills, this sort of difficulty would be bound to occur frequently in an economy of voluntary compliance.

Other Pitfalls and Puzzles

A related puzzle with which businessmen would need to grapple arises from changes in the composition of output. Suppose that a firm has two plants, that each of them makes a unique product, that the output per man-hour is constant in each plant, but that the two plants differ in efficiency. If the wage guidepost calls for a 3% increase in wages, it might appear, since no improvement of productivity has occurred in either plant, that a corresponding increase in the price of each of the two products is justified by the guideline for prices. But are price advances really proper if the firm has shifted some workers from the less efficient to the more efficient of its two plants and thereby raised the output per man-hour of the entire firm as much as or more than the trend increase of national productivity? In that event, does the guidepost for prices require that the productivity of each plant be taken separately or that the two be taken in combination?

Another problem that businessmen and trade-union leaders would need to face is whether the modifications of the guideposts that the Council of Economic Advisers has officially sanctioned apply in a particular case. In assuming, as I have, a general willingness to comply with the guidelines, I have not meant to abstract from human nature entirely. Since the modifications suggested by the Council are phrased in very general terms, men acting in good faith may feel that their situation is precisely the kind of rare case that permits some departure from the guidelines. But will business managers and labor leaders always or even frequently agree in their interpretation of what modifications are permissible? In any event, is it not likely that the modifications will turn out to be numerous, rather than, as now intended by the Administration, relatively few?

In view of these and many other problems that are bound to arise in practice, the guidelines would prove unworkable over a very large segment of industry, even if everyone sought conscientiously to observe them. To deal with this critical difficulty, a new governmental apparatus might need to be established; its function would be to spell out detailed rules and to interpret them in individual cases. Although there is no way of telling just how such an agency would work, it seems reasonable to expect that not a few of its clarifying rules and interpretations would be arbitrary, that its advisory rulings would at times involve considerable delay and thereby cause some economic trouble, and that the rulings themselves would have at least some inflationary bias. These factors inevitably cast a cloud over the preceding analysis of how an economy of voluntary compliance would function, but they hardly make the prospect more inviting.

SPECTER OF CONTROLS

I have as yet said nothing about the aspect of guidepost policy that has aroused the most skepticism—namely, the likelihood of general observance on a voluntary basis. In recent years unemployment has been fairly large, and many industries have had sufficient capacity to increase output readily. Under such conditions, upward pressure on prices cannot be great. Even so, the guidelines have been sharply criticized or defied by powerful segments of the business and labor community. The critical test of the inhibiting power of the guidelines will come, of course, when both labor and commodity markets become appreciably tighter—and this test may come soon. If the recent wage settlement in the automobile industry is at all indicative, expectations of a high degree of compliance with the guidelines are hardly warranted. Similar experiments in other countries also suggest that general price stability will not long be maintained through voluntary restraint.

But once the government in power has committed itself to a policy, it may become difficult to move off in a new direction. A strong commitment to the policy of the guidelines inevitably means that any extensive private defiance would, besides frustrating the government's anti-inflation policy, injure its prestige. There is always a possibility, therefore, that failure to comply voluntarily with the guidelines will be followed by some coercive measure. This might initially take the form, as has frequently been proposed, of a review by a governmental board of the facts surrounding the price or wage changes that are being contemplated. The thought behind proposals of this nature is that once the facts are clearly developed, the force of public opinion will ordinarily suffice to ensure "responsible" action by corporations and trade unions.

No one can be sure whether this expectation will be fulfilled. But if it is, the governmental review board will have virtually become an agency for fixing prices and wages. If, on the other hand, the board's reports were flouted with any frequency, the next step might well be outright price and wage fixing by the government. It would seem, therefore, that from whatever angle we examine the guidelines, direct controls pop up dangerously around the corner.

Incipient Realities

This danger must not be dismissed as an illusion. Although the guidelines are still in their infancy, they have already hardened. . . . Nor has the evolution of the Administration's thinking concerning the guidelines been confined to a literary plane. In April 1962, only three months after the announcement of the guidelines, the Administration moved sternly to force the leading steel companies to cancel the price increases that they had just posted. This interference with the workings of a private market had no clear sanction in law, and it caused consternation in business circles. Fortunately, a crisis was avoided by a prompt and concerted effort of the Administration, in which President Kennedy himself took the leading part, to restore business confidence.

Since then, the government has been more cautious. But it has continued to espouse the need for moderation in the matter of wages and prices, and now and then has even gently rattled its sword. Early in 1964 President Johnson requested the Council to reaffirm the guideposts. He emphasized his commitment to this policy by adding that he would "keep a close watch on price and wage developments, with the aid of an early warning system which is being set up." Last summer, when intimations of a rise in the price of steel appeared in the press, the President lost no time in declaring that such action would "strongly conflict with our national interest in price stability."

TOWARD SOUNDER POLICIES

As this account of recent history suggests, the guidepost policy may, under the pressure of events, move our nation's economy in an authoritarian direction. The danger may not yet be large, in view of prevailing political attitudes, but it could become serious in a time of trouble or emergency. And this is not the only risk, as I shall presently note. However, the fact that many citizens both within and outside government favor the guidelines must also be considered, for it means that they see smaller risks or larger advantages in this policy than I do.

It may readily be granted that the guidepost policy has the meritorious objective of blunting the power of monopolists to push up the price level. This is the feature of the policy that its proponents often stress. Indeed, they are apt to argue that it matters little in practice whether or not the bulk of the economic community pays any attention to the guidelines—as long as the major corporations and trade unions do so.

But if the guidelines are circumscribed in this fashion, they are still subject to the criticism of interfering with the competitive forces of the markets in which many major corporations actually operate. Moreover, the absence of a precise indication of what firms, industries, or trade unions are covered by the guidelines can create a mood of uncertainty that will militate against compliance. Not least important, the effectiveness of the guidelines in curbing inflation becomes doubtful when their application is restricted. For the very limitation on wage and price increases in the guideline sector of the economy would facilitate increases in the uncovered sector whenever an expansive economic policy generated a monetary demand that grew faster than the supply of goods and services.

Another argument frequently advanced in favor of the guideposts is that if they were in fact respected on a sufficient scale, then profit margins would tend to be maintained and the chances of prolonging the current business expansion would therefore be improved. This consideration is bound to count in men's thinking at a time when our nation is striving to reduce unemployment and to spread prosperity.

We must not, however, become so absorbed in today's problems that we overlook those that will haunt us in a later day. If the guidelines may stretch out the expansion now by helping to maintain the relatively high profit margins of prosperity, may they not at some later time stretch out contraction by serving to maintain the low profit margins of recession?

Let me add, also, that I recognize that the guideline policy was adopted by the Administration only after it had given serious consideration to alternatives. The thought of its economists apparently is that, in general:

> Monetary and fiscal tools must be used to promote expansion as long as the economy is not operating at full employment.
>
> Other devices must therefore be employed (in the absence of full employment) to prevent inflation.
>
> Policies aiming to increase competition or to improve productivity cannot accomplish much in the short run or cannot be pushed hard for political reasons.
>
> Direct controls of wages and prices cannot and should not be seriously considered under peace-time conditions.

Consequently, there is only one major way left for curbing immediate inflation—namely, through devices of exhortation.

And the guidelines for wages and prices are merely a promising specific application of the technique of exhortation.

Locus of Responsibility

Space will not permit me to unravel this complicated argument, but I at least want to suggest why I think it may be faulty. Once the government looks to trade unions and business firms to stave off inflation, there is a danger that it will not discharge adequately its own traditional responsibility of controlling the money supply and of maintaining an environment of competition. In the past our own and other governments have often found it convenient to blame profiteers, corporations, or trade unions for a rising price level. Only rarely have they pointed the finger of blame at their own policies—such as flooding the economy with newly created currency or bank deposits.

To the extent that the government relies on private compliance with its guidelines for prices and wages, it may more easily be tempted to push an expansive monetary and fiscal policy beyond prudent limits. Besides, it may fail to resist strongly enough the political pressure for higher minimum wages, larger trade union immunities, higher farm price supports, higher import duties, more import quotas, larger stockpiling programs, and other protective measures that serve either to raise prices or to prevent them from falling.

One of the major needs of our times is to give less heed to special interest groups and to reassert the paramount interest of consumers in vigorous competition. The political obstacles to reducing artificial props for prices are undoubtedly formidable. However, reforms of this type—supplemented by more stringent antitrust laws, effective enforcement of these laws, and reasonable steps to curb featherbedding—are likely to contribute more to the maintenance of reasonable stability in the general price level than will the guidelines for wages and prices on which we have recently come to rely.

Guidelines for Government

Another major need of our times is for better guidelines to aid the government itself in formulating and carrying out its economic policies. The widespread tendency of attributing most existing unemployment to a deficiency of aggregate demand is an oversimplification. Thus:

When the amount of unemployment is larger than the number of job vacancies at existing wages, the aggregate demand for labor *is* clearly insufficient to provide employment for everyone who is able, willing, and seeking to work. At such a time, a deficiency of aggregate demand exists, and a governmental policy that relies on monetary and fiscal devices to expand demand is, in principle, well suited to the nation's needs.

When the number of vacant jobs is equal to or larger than the number of the unemployed, however, there is *no* deficiency of aggregate demand. A government that is seriously concerned about inflation will not pursue an expansive monetary and fiscal policy at such a time, and—instead of lecturing the private community on the need for moderation—will itself lead the nation in a policy of restraint. This does not mean its concern about unemployment will cease but, rather, that it will direct its policy measures toward better matching of the men and women who seek work with the jobs that need to be filled.

A sensible guideline for monetary and fiscal policy is, therefore, not the volume or rate of unemployment as such, but the relation between the number of the unemployed and the number of job vacancies. As yet, such a guideline is merely a theorist's dream because statistics on job vacancies hardly exist in our country. There are grounds for hoping, however, that this condition will be corrected in another few years, so that we will become better equipped for promoting our national goals.

The problem of achieving and maintaining prosperity without inflation in a free society is a very difficult one. We must be willing as a people to seek out and to explore new ways of meeting this critical challenge of our times. But we also must remain mindful of the lessons of past experience—particularly, the need for prudent control of the money supply and the need for maintaining and enhancing the forces of competition. The progress that we make will depend heavily on the economic understanding of citizens and the intensity of their interest in public policies.

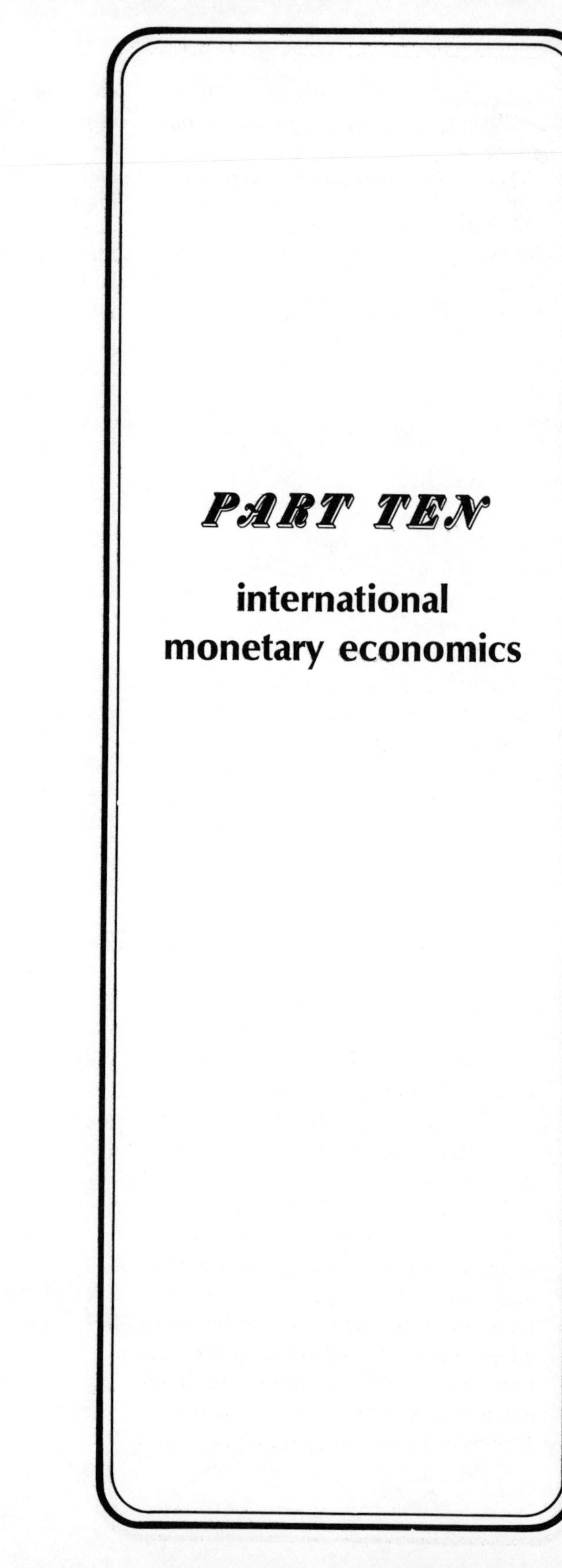

PART TEN

international monetary economics

During the first two weeks of May 1969, the international community witnessed a new crisis. Anticipating an upward revaluation of the West German mark, speculators sold other foreign currencies, notably dollars, British pounds, and French francs, in order to buy marks and thereby profit from the expected increase in the mark's value. For if the mark were revalued from 25 cents to 27 cents, marks bought at the lower price could be sold subsequently at the higher price.

Currency speculation has always manifested itself in international finance, and under the present system of fixed exchange rates, which themselves can be but rarely are changed, the game is one of "Heads I win, tails I don't lose." In the event that the mark was revalued, speculators stood to gain moderately; the presumed revaluation was 6 percent to 10 percent; if the mark's price held fast, the loss consisted only of a small interest rate payment on borrowed funds plus minor transactions charges. Moreover, the speculating game has a special clause that often dictates its outcome. It says that if enough speculators concur on a "heads" verdict, heads indeed will turn up; speculation reaps its own reward. This certainly was the case. On October 26, 1969, Germany revalued the mark from 25 cents to 27.32 cents.

A far less comfortable position is experienced by countries facing or thought to face devaluation. The need for a reduction in the external value of a nation's currency is evidenced by one or more of the following: (1) a continuing deficit in its payments position; (2) a fall in the exchange rate below its official par value and often to the support level, which, according to International Monetary Fund regulations, is 1 percent below the official rate; and

(3) a steady loss of gold and/or foreign exchange reserves. A persistent drain of reserves leads ultimately to the elimination of the nation's entire stock of reserve assets. But no government can permit the nation to become internationally insolvent; the financing of temporary payments deficits necessitates a certain amount of reserves. Measures will have to be taken to preserve the vanishing stock of the nation's foreign exchange before it is depleted. The standard remedy, of course, is devaluation. Speculators, aware of the inevitability of devaluation, sell the devaluation-prone currency while the crisis is brewing and expect to reap the gain when they buy back the devalued currency at its new and lower price.

The speculative assault against the pound sterling in 1964 fits this description. A substantial drain of British reserves early in the year was accompanied by a depreciating pound, which dropped from its peg at $2.80 to $2.7875 by July. By November, the Bank of England was dipping deeply into its reserve coffer, and the exchange rate had depreciated further, to $2.7825. Matters turned progressively worse, and notwithstanding pronouncements and measures taken by British officials, the loss of confidence in the stability of the $2.80 par value of the pound intensified. It has been estimated that on November 24, Britain was losing reserves at a rate of $1 million per minute, a rate destined to eliminate all of England's reserves in only five days. John Brooks will pick up the story from here; we shall note only the importance of international cooperation. Cooperative action by the world's leading central bankers successfully trimmed the wind from the sails of the speculators. The international central banking community scraped up $3 billion to tide over the pound. Such mutual assistance is not a recent phenomenon. As early as 1961 the central bankers had established a network of "swaps." (In a swap, central banks exchange domestic funds for foreign funds for short intervals; this device enables them to withstand, at least initially, speculative attacks.) In a world where cooperation is so difficult to obtain, the success of the central bankers represents a triumphant demonstration of what can be done.

The fact that the success of the 1964 defense of the pound was short-lived is already history. On November 18, 1967, the pound was devalued by 14.3 percent, from $2.80 to $2.40. In 1968 the French franc came under attack, and France, too, received substantial international support as she lost almost a third of her reserve funds in the six months following May. But on August 8, 1969, the franc was devalued from 20.255 cents a franc to 18.004 cents. The mark episode is only a recent incident in what is apparently an ever-increasing nervousness experienced by holders and traders of foreign currency, a circumstance capitalized on by speculators. Speculative activity intensifies but rarely creates the basic conditions for currency revaluation, and, although the effects of this type of gambling cannot be ignored, the cure ought to be directed to the disease and not the side effects. The layman, of course, cannot help being confused by the waves of crises, as well as by the actions of the major governments to straighten out the system. Art Buchwald's humorous column hits to the heart of this confusion.

The instability now pervading the international financial system may be attributed to two related issues—the absence of a properly functioning adjustment mechanism and the lack of adequate international liquidity. There is little need to review here the provisions of the Bretton Woods accord signed in 1944 and the role of the International Monetary Fund (IMF), established at that time. It will suffice to note that among the major objectives of the IMF's "Articles of Agreement" was the maintenance of stable exchange rates and the provision of additional international liquidity. Because the par values, as established initially, were not expected to be permanent—the alignment would be thrown out of kilter soon after economic trends within the IMF member nations differed—arrangements were made for controlled modifications in the exchange rates. The system is known as the "adjustable peg." Conceptually this adjustment mechanism should work; unfortunately, as the various crises have demonstrated so obviously, practice has differed from theory.

How is the adjustment mechanism to be reformed? Four proposals can be distinguished.

1. Retain the adjustable peg, and introduce minor modifications on an *ad hoc* basis as needed.
2. Revamp the system entirely by removing the peg and permitting exchange rates to "float" (or be "freely flexible") in response to the forces of supply and demand for foreign exchange.
3. Retain the peg but permit greater responsiveness to the market by enlarging the current 2 percent band surrounding the peg to, say, 10 percent. This proposal is known as the "widened band."
4. Introduce a "crawling peg," or a "gliding parity," a self-adjusting mechanism that would obviate the need for major exchange-rate adjustments.

Each of these methods has its advocates, and each raises serious issues, some economic in nature and some political. George W. McKenzie reviews the four alternatives and adds a fifth alternative, which combines numbers 3 and 4. Three points deserve to be emphasized in this context. First, under the present system, a "fundamental disequilibrium," necessitating a change in the external value of the currency, is difficult to identify. Moreover, even if a persistent imbalance can be recognized as a fundamental disequilibrium, the exact degree of exchange-rate adjustment needed to restore equilibrium is hardly known in advance. Under the last three proposals, and especially if numbers 2 or 4 are implemented, these questions will be less troublesome or eliminated entirely, because the exchange rate will be permitted, more or less, to find its own level. Second, a comment is in order concerning the likelihood of reform on a systematic basis. Chances do seem favorable; even such staid, conservative publications as the *Wall Street Journal* and England's *The Economist* have expressed dissatisfaction with the present system; in November 1968 the British weekly entitled its lead editorial "It's Better to Float," and in May 1969 added that "The Time to Float" is now. The alliance between some spokesmen of the financial community and many academic economists (the latter have long been dissatisfied with the present mechanism) as well as the interest expressed at high levels of the American government, suggest that some sort of reform is imminent. One can anticipate that the reform is unlikely to involve a drastic change from the present system, as is implied by the second proposal. Reforms 3 and 4 are the most likely candidates.

Finally, any reform proposal cannot ignore the political climate at home. One and perhaps the major objection to West Germany's appreciating the mark was the fear of domestic political repercussions. In one demonstration in Bonn, a placard reading "D-Mark Revaluation—Betrayal of the German Worker" was displayed, and an opinion poll found that the electorate was almost unanimously against an upward adjustment of the exchange rate. To be sure, the public may have misunderstood the benefits of revaluation, but this likelihood makes their opinions no less crucial for the men who represent them. Devaluation, too, can lead to internal pressures and dissent, especially for a nation that depends heavily on imports. The devaluation-induced rise in import prices increases the cost of living; it may also bring in its wake a bout of inflation, which may nullify the devaluation. It is naïve to believe that a country loath to adjust its currency under the present international financial system would accept the same undesirable outcome under revamped international financial arrangements. In essence, the reforms are designed to impose discipline on a nation's external balance, an imposition that often runs contrary to its own social and economic goals. Of course, a nation, like an individual, cannot eat its cake and have it; deficit nations especially cannot expect to be consistently bailed out by surplus nations. Some form of discipline may be necessary. But whether discipline should be exercised through exchange-rate adjustments is not at all clear. Selective measures, including border taxes and controls on disruptive capital flows, might be more desirable for the deficit nation than the general depreciation implied by the reform proposals. Indeed, aside from the political objectives achievable the selective-control way, certain economic goals may be more easily reached as well. Devaluation, for example, may lead to the stifling of economic growth as investment imports fall while consumption is hardly affected; selective controls would permit the authorities to choose which imports ought to be discouraged.

It would not be premature to state that the relative merits of the proposed alternative systems are not fully understood. The first step, of course, is to ask the proper questions. Many of them are found in the fourth selection, taken from the recent study of George N. Halm, *Toward Limited Exchange-Rate Flexibility*. Some of the questions are theoretical, others are practical; all are germane. Unfortunately, there is little empirical evidence that can be marshaled in support of any of the reform proposals, because neither the wider band nor the crawling peg has been tried. In recent years, Canada has experimented with a floating exchange rate, but the conclusions regarding its efficacy and its relevance are still being debated. Thus, while questions abound, answers are scarce.

Earlier, mention was made of a second issue concerning the world of international finance—the liquidity problem. In fact, two issues can be distinguished: (1) Is the existing stock of international reserves allocated properly? (2) Is the reserve stock sufficient to enable world trade and capital flows to expand at a rapid pace? The first question involves essentially the distribution of the world's total reserves. The problem becomes manifest when a temporary disequilibrium in a nation's payments balance has to be paid off in reserves, but sufficient reserves are not at hand to cover the deficit. This situation may be either a seasonal occurrence or the result of a speculative run. Inadequate reserves introduce additional uncertainties into the financial scene and make exchange-rate adjustments more imminent. The swap network and other manifestations of central bank cooperation have reduced the severity of this problem, because their very essence involves the shifting of reserves from nations who do not need them immediately to those who do. The previously mentioned reform of the present adjustment mechanism would reduce still further the need for stocks of temporary liquidity.

It is obvious, however, that more efficient means of reallocating reserves cannot solve problems arising from a global dearth of international liquidity. The background for the creation of a new type of international liquidity, designed to supplement the present stock of reserves, is presented in the final selection. Thomas E. Davis proceeds to explain how the Special Drawing Rights, popularly referred to as "paper gold," would in fact increase international liquidity.

Finally, it must be pointed out that with the creation of SDRs ($9.5 billion, which is roughly 12 percent of international liquid reserves as of the end of 1969, will be created between 1970 and 1972) dissipation of the pressure surrounding reform of the adjustment mechanism is to be anticipated. Because each IMF member nation will be allotted newly created reserves, it will be able to resist foreign currency drains more easily. Thus, a given par value is maintainable for a longer period of time in the hope either that the outflow will be reversed or that additional SDRs will become available.

One can only marvel at the rapid pace of restructuring on the international economic scene. Gold, which held a prominent place in the international picture, is no longer a major source of new reserves. Speculative runs on gold in the middle of March 1968 led the world's major central bankers to terminate sales of gold to private holders. In addition, they declared their unwillingness to purchase new gold, because future additions to liquidity would be provided by SDRs. To be sure, the agreement reached with the Union of South Africa in December 1969 requires that the IMF purchase gold; however, the conditions are such that substantial gold purchases are unlikely. Most economists will welcome the virtual disappearance of gold as a monetary asset; it is clearly an anachronism. Why waste scarce capital and labor resources to remove a metal from the earth, which, soon after being mined, will be relegated to subterranean depositories? The SDRs, on the other hand, are book entries, analogous to banking deposits, with close to zero production costs. The supplanting of gold by "paper gold" as a source of international reserves thus permits economizing on scarce resources and constitutes a cost-saving without a corresponding loss in utility.

What, then, is to be gold's role in the world economy? The answer is quite clear; barring the some $40 billion held by the central banks, it is a metal with certain jewelry and industrial uses—and the price of newly mined gold will be determined hereafter primarily by its private demand and supply.

In Part I it was pointed out that the essence of money was its acceptability. In domestic affairs, the existence of private checking deposits and government fiat currency has demonstrated that a monetary economy can function without a gold base. The SDR is simply the culmination of the historical development of money. International money, too, will be abstract, and as times goes by, gold will leave only a vestigial trace on the monetary affairs of the world community.

53 IN DEFENSE OF STERLING

JOHN BROOKS

Central bank cooperation dates back to the roaring twenties, when Lord Norman, Governor of the Bank of England, Benjamin Strong, President of the Federal Reserve Bank of New York, and their French and German counterparts kept regular contact with one another during a period when transatlantic communications were, by contemporary standards, primitive. The joint meetings and understandings which often led to combined operations, were resented by many as an infringement of national sovereignty by a small caucus of international bankers, responsible only to a code of their own. Today, although central bankers still meet—and now they meet regularly at the monthly conference of the Bank for International Settlements in Switzerland—major policy decisions are not made without consulting with and at times obtaining permission from their respective governments. This practice will be evident to the reader of the following selection. Note, too, that despite the major technological advances in the communications field, no guarantee can be given that person-to-person contacts will be established quickly, as the frantic attempts to reach Dr. Holtrop demonstrate. Indeed, despite the fact that cooperation has worked amazingly well in the past, it is not difficult to imagine how the episode described by Brooks could have concluded less happily. Would not a formal stand-by mechanism, oriented to crisis as well as noncrisis situations, be preferable to the ad hockery displayed here? Or what about a rule? Or a free market?

Down on Liberty Street, Coombs* slept fitfully until he was awakened by the clock radio in his room at about three-thirty New York time—that is to say, eight-thirty London time and nine-thirty farther east on the European Continent. A series of foreign-exchange crises involving Europe had so accustomed him to the time differential that he was inclined to think in terms of the European day, referring casually to 8 a.m. in New York as "lunchtime," and 9 a.m. as "midafternoon." So when he got up it was, in his terms, "morning," despite the stars that were shining over Liberty Street. Coombs got dressed, went to his office on the tenth floor, where he had some breakfast provided by the bank's regular night kitchen staff, and began placing telephone calls to the various leading central banks of the non-Communist world. All the calls were put through by one telephone operator, who handles the Federal Reserve Bank's switchboard during off hours, and all of them were eligible for a special government-emergency priority that the bank's officers are entitled to claim, but on this occasion it did not have to be used, because at four-fifteen, when Coombs began his telephoning, the transatlantic circuits were almost entirely clear.

From John Brooks, *Business Adventures* (New York: Weybright & Talley, 1968), pp. 353–354, 357–364, 367.

*Charles A. Coombs is Vice-President of the Federal Reserve Bank of New York in charge of the Reserve System's foreign exchange operations—ed.

The calls were made essentially to lay the groundwork for what was to come. The morning news from the Bank of England, obtained in one of the first calls from Liberty Street, was that conditions were unchanged from the previous day: the speculative attack on the pound was continuing unabated, and the Bank of England was sustaining the pound's price at $2.7860 by throwing still more of its reserves on the market. Coombs had reason to believe that when the New York foreign-exchange market opened, some five hours later, vast additional quantities of pounds would be thrown on the market on this side of the Atlantic, and more British dollars and gold would have to be spent. He conveyed this alarming intelligence to his counterparts at such institutions as the Deutsche Bundesbank, in Frankfurt; the Banque de France, in Paris; the Banca d'Italia, in Rome; and the Bank of Japan, in Tokyo. (In the last case, the officers had to be reached at their homes, for the fourteen-hour time difference made it already past 6 p.m. in the Orient.) Then, coming to the crux of the matter, Coombs informed the representatives of the various banks that they were soon to be asked, in behalf of the Bank of England, for a loan far bigger than any they had ever been asked for before. "Without going into specific figures, I tried to make the point that it was a crisis of the first magnitude, which many of them still didn't realize," Coombs has said. An officer of the Bundesbank, who knew as much about the extent of the crisis as anyone outside London, Washington, and New York, has said that in Frankfurt they were "mentally prepared"—or "braced" might be a better word—for the huge touch that was about to be put on them, but that right up to the time of Coombs' call they had been hoping the speculative attack on the pound would subside of its own accord, and even after the call they had no idea how much they might be asked for. In any event, as soon as Coombs was off the wire the Bundesbank's governor called a board of managers' meeting, and, as things turned out, the meeting was to remain in session all day long.

Still, all this was preparatory. Actual requests, in specific amounts, had to be made by the head of one central bank of the head of another. At the time Coombs was making his softening-up calls, the head of the Federal Reserve Bank was in the bank's limousine, somewhere between New Canaan and Liberty Street, and the bank's limousine, in flagrant nonconformity with the James Bond style of high-level international dealings, was not equipped with a telephone.

Hayes, the man being awaited, had been president of the Federal Reserve Bank of New York for a little over eight years. . . . When he arrived at his desk at about five-thirty, Hayes' first act was to punch Coombs' button on his interoffice phone and get the foreign-department chief's latest appraisal of the situation. He learned that, as he had expected, the Bank of England's sickening dollar drain was continuing unabated. Worse than that, though; Coombs said his contacts with local bankers who were also on emergency early-morning vigil (men in the foreign departments of the huge commercial banks like the Chase Manhattan and the First National City) indicated that overnight there had accumulated a fantastic pile of orders to unload pounds on the New York market as soon as it opened. The Bank of England, already almost inundated, could expect a new tidal wave from New York to hit in four hours. The need for haste thus became even more urgent. Hayes and Coombs agreed that the project of putting together an international package of credits to Britain should be announced as soon as possible after the New York opening—perhaps as early as ten o'clock. So that the bank would have a single center for all its foreign communications, Hayes decided to forsake his own office—a spacious one with panelled walls and comfortable chairs grouped around a fireplace—and let Coombs' quarters, down the hall, which were much smaller and more austere but more efficiently arranged, serve as the command post. Once there, he picked up one of three telephones and asked the operator to get him Lord Cromer, at the Bank of England. When the connection was made, the two men—the key figures in the proposed rescue operation—reviewed their plans a final time, checking the sums they had tentatively decided to ask of each central bank and agreeing on who would call whom first.

• • •

Beginning at about six o'clock that morning, Hayes [grabbed] the phone, right along with Lord Cromer. One after another, the leading central bankers of the world—among them President Karl Blessing, of the Deutsche Bundesbank; Dr. Guido Carli, of the Bank of Italy; Governor Jacques Brunet, of the Bank of France; Dr. Walter Schwegler, of the Swiss National Bank; and Governor Per Åsbrink, of the Swedish Riksbank—picked up *their* phones and discovered, some of them with considerable surprise, the degree of gravity that the sterling crisis had reached in the past day, the fact that the United States had committed itself to a short-term loan of one billion dollars, and that they were being asked to dig deep into their own nations' reserves to help tide sterling over. Some first heard all this from Hayes, some from Lord Cromer; in either case, they heard it not from a casual or official acquaintance but from a fellow-member of that esoteric fraternity the Basel club. Hayes, whose position as representative of the one country that had already pledged a huge sum cast him almost automatically as the leader of the operation, was careful to make it clear in each of his calls that his part in the proceedings was to put the weight of the Federal Reserve behind a request that formally came from the Bank of England. "The pound's situation is critical, and I understand the Bank of England is requesting a credit line of two hundred and fifty million dollars from you," he would say, in his calm way, to one Continental central-bank governor or another. "I'm sure you understand that this is a situation where we all have to stand together." . . . In those cases in which he was on particularly close terms with his Continental counterpart, he spoke more informally, using a central-bankers' jargon in which the conventional numerical unit is a million dollars. Hayes would say smoothly in such cases, "Do you think you can come in for, say, a hundred and fifty?" Regardless of the degree of formality of the approach Hayes made, the first response, he says, was generally cageyness, not unmixed with shock. "Is it really as bad as all that, Al? We were still hoping that the pound would recover on its own" is the kind of thing he recalls having heard several times. When Hayes assured them that it was indeed as bad as all that, and that the pound would certainly not recover on its own, the usual response was something like "We'll have to see what we can do and then call you back." Some of the Continental central bankers have said that what impressed them most about Hayes' first call was not so much what he said as when he said it. Realizing that it was still well before dawn in New York, and knowing Hayes' addiction to what are commonly thought of as bankers' hours, these Europeans perceived that things must be grave the moment they heard his voice. As soon as Hayes had broken the ice at each Continental bank, Coombs would take over and get down to details with his counterparts.

The first round of calls left Hayes, Lord Cromer, and their associates on Liberty and Threadneedle Streets relatively hopeful. Not one bank had given them a flat no—not even, to their delight, the Bank of France, although French policy had already begun moving sharply away from coöperation with Britain and the United States in monetary matters, among others. Furthermore, several governors had surprised them by suggesting that their countries' subscriptions to the loan might actually be bigger than those suggested. With this encouragement, Hayes and Lord Cromer decided to raise their sights. They had originally been aiming for credits of two and a half billion dollars; now, on reconsideration, they saw that there was a chance for three billion. "We decided to up the ante a little here and there," Hayes says. "There was no way of knowing precisely what sum would be the least that would do the job of turning the tide. We knew we would be relying to a large extent on the psychological effect of our announcement—assuming we would be able to make the announcement. Three seemed to us a good round figure."

But difficulties lay ahead, and the biggest difficulty, it became clear as the return calls from the various banks began to come in, was to get the thing done quickly. The hardest point to convey, Hayes and Coombs found, was that each passing minute meant a further loss of a million dollars or more to the British reserves, and that if normal channels were followed the loans would unquestionably come too late to avert devaluation of the pound. Some of the central banks were required by law to consult their governments before making a commitment and some were not, but even those that were not insisted on doing so, as a courtesy; this took time, especially since more than one Finance Minister, unaware that he was being sought to approve an enormous loan on an instant's notice, with little evidence of the necessity for it beyond the assurance of Lord Cromer and Hayes, was temporarily unavailable. (One happened to be engaged in debate in his country's parliament.) And even in cases where the Finance Minister was at hand, he was sometimes reluctant to act in such a shotgun way. Governments move more deliberately in money matters than central bankers do. Some of the Finance Ministers said, in effect, that upon proper submission of a balance sheet of the Bank of England, along with a formal written application for the emergency credit, they would gladly consider the matter. Furthermore, some of the central banks themselves showed a maddening inclination to stand on ceremony. The foreign-exchange chief of one bank is said to have replied to the request by saying, "Well, isn't this convenient! We happen to have a board meeting scheduled for tomorrow. We'll take the matter up then and afterward get in touch with you." The reply of Coombs, who happened to be the man on the wire in New York, is not recorded in substance, but its manner is reported to have been uncharacteristically vehement. Even Hayes' celebrated imperturbability was shaken a time or two, or so those who were present have said; his tone remained as calm and even as ever, but its volume rose far above the usual level.

The problems that the Continental central banks faced in meeting the challenge are well exemplified by the situation at the richest and most powerful of them, the Deutsche Bundesbank. Its board of managers was already sitting in emergency session as a result of Coombs' early call when another New York call—this one from Hayes to President Blessing—gave the Bundesbank its first indication of exactly how much it was being asked to put up. The amounts the various central banks were asked for that morning have never been made public, but, on the basis of what *has* become known, it is reasonable to assume that the Bundesbank was asked for half a billion dollars—the highest quota of the lot, and certainly the largest sum that any central bank other than the Federal Reserve had ever been called upon to supply to another on a few hours' notice. Hard on the heels of Hayes' call conveying this jarring information, Blessing heard from Lord Cromer, in London, who confirmed everything that Hayes had said about the seriousness of the crisis and repeated the request. Wincing a bit, perhaps, the Bundesbank managers agreed in principle that the thing had to be done. But right there their problems began. Proper procedure must be adhered to, Blessing and his aides decided. Before taking any action, they must consult with their economic partners in the European Common Market and the Bank for International Settlements, and the key man to be consulted, since he was then serving as president of the Bank for International Settlements, was Dr. Marius W. Holtrop, governor of the Bank of the Netherlands, which, of course, was also being asked to contribute. A rush person-to-person call was put through from Frankfurt to Amsterdam. Dr. Holtrop, the Bundesbank managers were informed, wasn't in Amsterdam; by chance, he had taken a train that morning to The Hague to meet his country's Finance Minister for consultation on other matters. For the Bank of the Netherlands to make any such important commitment without the knowledge of its governor was out of the question, and, similarly, the Bank of Belgium, a nation whose monetary policies are linked inextricably with the Netherlands', was reluctant to act until Amsterdam had given its O.K. So for an hour or more, as millions of dollars continued to drain out of the Bank of England and the world monetary order stood in jeopardy, the whole rescue operation was hung up while Dr. Holtrop, crossing the Dutch lowlands by train, or perhaps already in The Hague and tied up in a traffic jam, could not be found.

All this, of course, meant agonizing frustration in New York. As morning began here at last, Hayes' and Coombs' campaign got a boost from Washington. The leading government monetary authorities—Martin at the Federal Reserve Board, Dillon and Roosa at the Treasury—had been intimately involved in the previous day's planning for the rescue, and of course part of the planning had been the decision to let the New York bank, as the Federal Reserve System's and the Treasury's normal operating arm in international monetary dealings, serve as campaign headquarters. So the members of the Washington contingent had slept at home and come to their offices at the normal hour. Now, having learned from Hayes of the difficulties that were developing, Martin, Dillon, and Roosa pitched in with transatlantic calls of their own to emphasize the extent of America's concern over the matter. But no number of calls from anywhere could hold back the clock—or, for that matter, find Dr. Holtrop—and Hayes and Coombs finally had to abandon their idea of having a credit bundle ready in time for an announcement to the world at or near 10 a.m. in New York. And there were other reasons, too, for a fading of the early hopes. As the New York markets opened, the extent of the alarm that had spread around the financial world overnight was only too clearly revealed. The bank's foreign-exchange trading desk, on the seventh floor, reported that the assault on the pound at the New York opening had been fully as terrifying as they had expected, and that the atmosphere in the local exchange market had reached a state not far from panic. From the bank's securities department came an alarming report that the market for United States government bonds was coming under the heaviest pressure in years, reflecting an ominous lack of confidence in the dollar on the part of bond traders. This intelligence served as a grim reminder to Hayes and Coombs of something they knew already—that a fall of the pound in relation to the dollar could quite possibly be followed, in a kind of chain reaction, by a forced devaluation of the dollar in relation to gold, which might cause monetary chaos everywhere. If Hayes and Coombs had been permitting themselves any moments of idle reverie in which to picture themselves simply as good Samaritans, this was just the news to bring them back to reality. And then word arrived that the wild tales flying around Wall Street showed signs of crystallizing into a single tale, demoralizingly credible because it was so specific. The British government, it was being said, would announce a sterling devaluation at around noon New York time. Here was something that could be authoritatively refuted, at least in respect to timing, since Britain would obviously not devalue while the credit negotiations were under way. Torn between the desire to quell a destructive rumor and the need to keep the negotiations secret until they were concluded, Hayes compromised. He had one of his associates call a few key Wall Street bankers and traders to say, as emphatically as possible, that the latest devaluation rumor was, to his firm knowledge, false. "Can you be more specific?" the associate was asked, and he replied, because there was nothing else he could reply, "No, I can't."

This unsupported word was something, but it was not enough; the foreign-exchange and bond markets were only momentarily reassured. There were times that morning, Hayes and Coombs now admit, when they put down their telephones, looked at each other across the table in Coombs' office, and wordlessly exchanged the thought: It isn't going to be done in time. But—in the best tradition of melodrama, which sometimes seems to survive stubbornly in nature at a time when it is dead in art—just when things looked darkest, good news began to arrive. Dr. Holtrop had been tracked down in a restaurant in The Hague, where he was having lunch with the Netherlands' Minister of Finance, Dr. J. W. Witteveen; moreover, Dr. Holtrop had endorsed the rescue operation, and as for the matter of consulting his government, *that* was no problem, since the responsible representative of his government was sitting across the table from him. The chief obstacle was thus overcome, and after Dr. Holtrop had been reached the difficulties began narrowing down to annoyances like the necessity for continually apologizing to the Japanese for routing them out of bed as midnight arrived and passed in Tokyo. The tide had turned. Before noon in New York, Hayes and Coombs, and Lord Cromer and his deputies in London as well, knew that they had agreement in principle from ten Continental central banks—those in West Germany, Italy, France, the Netherlands, Belgium, Switzerland, Canada, Sweden, Austria, and Japan—and also from the Bank for International Settlements.

• • •

Apparently, the secrecy of the operation had been successfully preserved and the announcement struck the New York foreign-exchange market all of a heap, because the reaction was as swift and as electric as anyone could have wished. Speculators against the pound decided instantly and with no hesitation that their game was up. Immediately after the announcement, the Federal Reserve Bank put in a bid for pounds at $2.7868—a figure slightly above the level at which the pound had been forcibly maintained all day by the Bank of England. So great was the rush of speculators to get free of their speculative positions by buying pounds that the Federal Reserve Bank found very few pounds for sale at that price. Around two-fifteen, there were a strange and heartening few minutes in which no sterling was available in New York at *any* price. Pounds were eventually offered for sale again at a higher price, and were immediately gobbled up, and thus the price went on climbing all afternoon, to a closing of just above $2.79.

Triumph! The pound was out of immediate danger; the thing had worked.

• • •

54 MONEY QUIZ: YOU CAN EARN HIGH MARKS EXPOUNDING FRANC FACTS

ART BUCHWALD

Perhaps with the departure of President de Gaulle from the international political scene, a source of American-French discord will be eliminated. But so will a butt for Mr. Buchwald's incisive wit.

Now that everyone understands the world monetary crisis, we're going to give you your final quiz:

1. If I have five French francs and you have three West German deutschemarks, what will we have all together?

A. One of the damnedest money messes since World War II.

2. If I want to sell my French francs for German marks at 10 per cent less than they're officially quoted, what currency will hurt the most?

A. The British pound.

3. Why?

A. Because it's tied to the American dollar.

4. When the American dollar gets in serious trouble, what country sells its dollar and demands gold, to make it go down further?

A. France.

5. When the French franc gets in trouble, what country agrees to go to its rescue and shore it up with its own gold?

A. The United States.

6. Why?

A. Because of the British pound.

7. When the British pound gets into trouble, who is the first person to demand that it be devalued?

A. President Charles de Gaulle.

8. When the French franc gets in trouble, who is the last person to agree to its devaluation?

A. President Charles de Gaulle.

9. Why?

A. Because of the West German mark.

10. What has the German mark got to do with the French franc?

A. The West German mark is undervalued, because the Germans don't have enough inflation. The French franc is overvalued, because the French have too much inflation.

11. What is the solution?

A. The British have to tighten their belts.

12. What happens to all the gold that is supposed to support world currencies?

A. It's bought by the Swiss for people who have numbered accounts in Zurich.

13. When they buy the gold, what happens to the currencies?

A. Except for the Swiss franc and the German mark, they go down.

14. Why?

A. Because everyone is afraid of the British pound.

15. What can France do to restore confidence in the French franc?

A. Attack the American dollar.

---

16. How can they do this?

A. By using the money we've loaned them to preserve their franc.

17. Why would we allow this?

A. To preserve the British pound.

18. Who will President de Gaulle blame if his reforms don't work?

A. The United States.

19. Who will get the credit if de Gaulle can pull it off?

A. That's a stupid question.

20. What can the average American do until the money crisis blows over?

A. Take an Englishman to lunch.

55 INTERNATIONAL MONETARY REFORM AND THE "CRAWLING PEG"

GEORGE W. McKENZIE

One of the major reasons that Professor McKenzie lists for rejecting the present system of fixed exchange rates is its implications for the effectiveness of domestic monetary policy. He claims that an anti-inflationary monetary policy is self-defeating because it generates expansion-inducing international capital flows. After reading this author's explanation of the mechanism, consider the following questions. First, must a tight monetary policy increase domestic interest rates by a magnitude sufficient to induce large-scale capital inflows? Second, even if domestic interest rates do rise sufficiently and capital inflows are encouraged thereby, will not the exchange rate rise (remember that under the present international monetary system, a narrow band around the par value within which the exchange rate can fluctuate does exist) and thus weaken the incentive offered by the increased interest rates? Third, cannot the monetary authorities indefinitely sterilize the inflow of foreign exchange by such measures as a 100 percent reserve requirement against foreign funds? These questions suggest that McKenzie's arguments are less compelling than they appear to be.*

In order for the world economy to function smoothly, it is necessary that the international monetary system meet three basic tests:

1. It should provide an environment in which each participating country can pursue its own domestic goals, such as full-employment, reasonable price stability, economic growth, and social justice.

2. It should be conducive to stability and growth in international trade and capital investments.

3. It should operate without the imposition of direct controls on international transactions, since these controls reduce the benefits of international specialization.

Over the past decade, there has been continuous and growing concern by many economists and Government officials that the framework of the International Monetary Fund (IMF), as developed at Bretton Woods in 1944, is unable to meet these three goals and, hence, should be modified. To most casual observers, the events of the past two years seem to support this concern. An air of uncertainty and skepticism surrounds the Bretton Woods System, which has experienced the British devaluation, the increase in the free market price of gold, the imposition of restrictions on domestic activity in France and the United Kingdom, and a proliferation of controls on international transactions.

This article proposes that the basic philosophy underlying the International Monetary Fund is *workable,* but that to

From George W. McKenzie, "International Monetary Reform and the 'Crawling Peg,'" Federal Reserve Bank of St. Louis, *Review,* February 1969, pp. 15–23.

*A general rebuttal and counterrebuttal that discuss the issues can be found in the July 1969 *Review* of the Federal Reserve Bank of St. Louis, 51, No. 7, 21–31.

be satisfactorily implemented, certain reforms in its operation are needed. In particular, a "crawling peg" exchange rate system should be substituted for the current "adjustable peg" mechanism.

The national representatives who drafted the IMF's Articles of Agreement generally believed that reasonably stable exchange rates were necessary for the growth of international transactions. While they hoped that rates could remain pegged for extended periods of time, they also recognized that some countries might want to adjust their exchange rates if they were experiencing serious international payments imbalances. Hence, the "adjustable peg" concept was created.

In practice, the "peg" has been adjusted only infrequently by industrial countries and often only as a last resort. Thus an important policy instrument for dealing with international payments difficulties has not been utilized. In contrast, under a "crawling peg" system, exchange rates would vary but only on the basis of a predetermined formula agreed upon by the members of the IMF. Such an international monetary arrangement would have the following advantages:

1. Exchange rate flexibility would increase the effectiveness of monetary policy in achieving domestic goals.

2. By spreading exchange rate adjustments over long periods, the "crawling peg" system would avoid the periodic exchange crises and uncertainty of the present system.

3. The incentive for countries to impose controls on international transactions would be reduced. Indeed, a prerequisite for the successful operation of the "crawling peg" is a reduction in such controls.

Thus the "crawling peg" meets the three basic tests of a satisfactory international monetary system. Before examining the "crawling peg" in detail, the present system and the sources of its weakness are discussed.

THE BRETTON WOODS SYSTEM

Because exchange rates are pegged under the Bretton Woods System, a gap may develop between the *demand* for foreign exchange by a country's citizens to purchase goods, services, and financial items abroad and the *supply* of foreign exchange generated by sales of such items to foreigners. If the country's officials consider the imbalance to be *temporary,* they may fill the gap by allowing a net change in their country's international reserves, consisting of (a) gold, (b) foreign exchange, and (c) its position vis-à-vis the IMF. In addition, countries may arrange to obtain loans from one or more countries.

International reserves exist in order to enable countries to withstand such temporary payments deficits. However, since the deficit country has a limited stock of reserves, its ability to rely on them to bridge a continuing gap between its international payments and receipts is also limited. Supplemental loans from trading partners may be sought but are usually contingent upon some form of positive balance-of-payments adjustment. In addition, the surplus countries, while initially welcoming reserve accumulation as an indicator of their strength in the world economy, eventually may want to limit their build-up and hence will put pressure on the deficit country to take remedial action. Thus countries experiencing prolonged deficits under the present system eventually must undertake severe measures of adjustment. These usually take the form of either policies of exchange rate adjustments, aimed at switching spending from foreign to domestic goods, or policies aimed at reducing aggregate expenditure and hence spending abroad. Although in extreme circumstances a deficit country is permitted, under the IMF Articles of Agreement, to impose controls on international transactions in order to correct a deficit, this course generally encounters opposition.

The "Adjustable Peg"

Because changes in exchange rate par values are discretionary, and their timing and magnitude are extremely difficult for officials to determine, exchange rates tend to be altered only as a last resort under the "adjustable peg" system. As an alternative, industrial countries have developed a complex network of credit facilities and supplements to existing reserve assets that enable them to postpone exchange rate changes in the hope that either the situation will correct itself, or that suitable domestic policies can be implemented.

Therefore, when they do occur, exchange rate adjustments are usually relatively large in magnitude, and concentrate within a short period a large burden on the import and export sectors of the initiating country and its trading partners. On the other hand, failure to undertake such adjustments may be equally costly. If a country's payments deficit is due to costs and prices rising faster at home than abroad, domestic export- and import-competing industries will find business dwindling.

The prospect of large periodic exchange rate adjustments can lead to a considerable loss of confidence in the currencies of the countries involved. Suppose that country X has experienced prolonged balance-of-payments deficits and the expectation is that its officials will fail to prevent new deficits. Many people, speculating that the only way for X to solve its problems is through devaluation, will convert assets denominated in X's currency into gold or assets denominated in some other currency which is expected to maintain its value. In addition, speculators will sell X's currency in the forward exchange market in the hope of being able to buy it back later at a lower price.

These pressures make the price of X's currency in the forward market expensive relative to the spot price, or current price, and thus make hedging quite costly. An X importer who must deliver a certain amount of foreign exchange in the future may discover that the premium he has to pay to buy foreign exchange in the forward market is prohibitive. However, if X does devalue he then finds that his bill is higher in terms of his own currency.

This example indicates that considerable uncertainty can be generated under the present "adjustable peg" system. The difficulty lies not in the fact that exchange rate adjustments are possible, but that they are postponed so long that even the dullest speculator knows that some change must be made. When an exchange rate adjustment is anticipated, speculators are in a position to make large profits with relatively little risk. In fact, speculative capital movements, in anticipation of an exchange rate adjustment, may actually force a change upon a country which had no fundamental economic reason for the adjustment.

An alternative to altering exchange rates is a policy which entails a slower rate of relative price adjustment: countries with deficits could allow wages to increase at a slower rate than productivity increases. As a result, costs would decline and this would enable the country to improve its international price competitiveness. Conversely, a country experiencing a surplus in its balance of payments might allow its wages to increase at a rate higher than productivity increases, thereby reducing its competitiveness. Such policies, however, would be difficult to administer and would probably meet political resistance. Not only would it be difficult to control wages, but there are also problems in measuring productivity changes. In addition, the period of adjustment could be extremely long, and a country with insufficient reserves might be forced to seek an alternate and more costly remedy.

The Fixed Exchange Rate and Domestic Economic Policy

Not only does the present fixed exchange rate system prevent smooth balance-of-payments adjustments: it also severely frustrates the application of domestic stabilization policies.

To understand this weakness, consider the hypothetical situation in which a country, such as Italy, is experiencing inflation but has no balance-of--payments deficit or surplus. In an attempt to control rising prices, the Italian Central Bank decides to sell government securities in the open market. This reduces the level of demand deposits and hence the funds available to commercial banks. Interest rates and security yields rise. The yield differentials that emerge between Italian and foreign securities induce arbitrage, that is, investors sell their foreign assets and purchase Italian securities. In addition, Italians borrow funds in countries where interest costs are lower. This capital inflow creates a surplus in Italy's balance of payments. As economic activity slows, imports decline and hence the surplus grows.

In order to maintain the exchange rate at its pegged level, the Italian Central Bank then enters the exchange markets to purchase the "excess" supply of foreign exchange. The impact of this operation is identical to one where the central bank purchases government securities in the open market, that is, there is an increase in the money supply. This will tend to offset the effect of the original restrictive monetary policy. Economic activity will be stimulated to return to its original level and hence imports will increase. As interest rates and security yields return to their original levels the capital inflow will be reduced, returning the balance of payments to its previous state. Thus the goal of slowing the rate of inflation through monetary policy will be thwarted by the goal of maintaining the pegged exchange rate, as [Figure 1] shows.

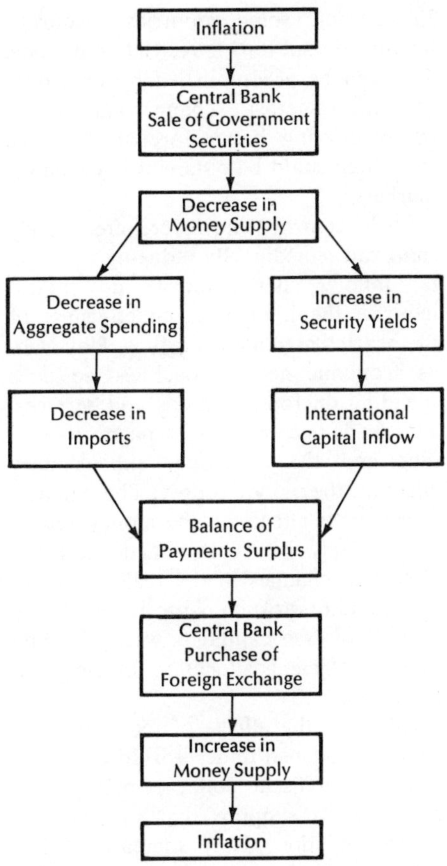

Figure 1

With this view in mind, foreign officials have sought to increase the effectiveness of monetary policy by placing controls on the foreign operations of their country's banking institutions. Such controls, designed to prevent capital inflows during periods of restrictive monetary policy, include:

1. Limits or ceilings on the expansion of credit by banks. This reduces the incentive to borrow in general.

2. Higher reserve requirements against bank liabilities to foreigners than against liabilities to its own citizens. This reduces banks' incentive to borrow abroad.

3. Quantitative limits on net foreign liabilities.

4. Requirements that a bank's spot foreign assets and liabilities should be equal.

5. Prohibiting interest payments on deposits owned by foreigners.

In addition, some countries encourage lending abroad during restrictive periods. This can be accomplished by providing guarantees against exchange rate changes or by offering better foreign exchange rates than could be obtained in exchange markets.

Such controls, however, are merely short-run remedies. By reducing the capital inflow, such controls do indeed increase the immediate effectiveness of the restrictive monetary policy. However, as economic activity declines, so does spending on foreign goods and services. This leads once again to a payments surplus and the offsetting, expansionary effect on the money supply. The balance-of-payments effects on the money supply have merely been postponed until the impact of changes in the real sector are felt. In addition such controls reduce the benefits of free capital flows by leading to an inefficient allocation of financial resources.

Although the effects of monetary policy are weakened under a fixed exchange rate system, fiscal policy remains effective. Let us suppose that in order to reduce inflation, Italy increases taxes, thereby reducing government financing operations. As a consequence of this decline in government financing operations, security prices rise and yields fall. This leads to a capital outflow and hence a deterioration in the balance of payments. However, as domestic economic activity slows because of the reduction in disposable income, imports will decline and this will tend to offset the deterioration in the capital account. Thus balance-of-payments equilibrium will be restored, the net effect on the money supply will be zero, and hence the slowdown in economic activity will be preserved. This sequence of events can be seen [in Figure 2].

The drawback of fiscal policy is its implementation. As with monetary policy, there is a time lag between the actual change in economic conditions and recognition of the need for policy response. Fiscal policy measures, however, are subject to an additional lag between recognition and actual legislation of measures. Frequently this lag arises from political considerations. For example, no one likes an increase in taxes.

In reality, the responses of the real and financial sectors to changes in interest rates and aggregate spending will take time. In addition, there are tariff and quota restrictions on international trade and various impediments to the free flow of capital, which may prevent the process from working itself out.

In addition, there may be a conflict of policy aims in the short run. In situations when there is (a) unemployment and a balance-of-payments surplus or (b) inflation and a deficit, policies which change the level of aggregate spending will be consistent with the achievement of both internal and external balance. However, when there is (a) unemployment and a payments deficit, or (b) inflation and a surplus, it becomes difficult for officials to achieve both domestic and international goals. Policies which reduce spending and eliminate a balance-of-payments deficit will only increase unemployment.

Figure 2

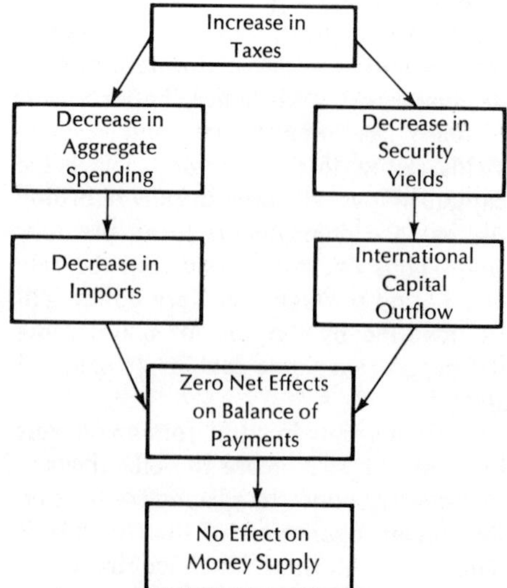

Similarly, attempts to reduce a payments surplus by stimulating spending when there is inflation lead to more, not less, inflation. Resolving this conflict is not easy since it involves weighing the value of domestic, social, and political goals against the costs of international payments imbalances.

DOMESTIC AND INTERNATIONAL STABILIZATION AND THE "CRAWLING PEG"

Many economists have argued that the best method to avoid the dilemma posed by the present international monetary system is to allow greater flexibility in exchange rates. This could be achieved by either or both of the following modifications:

1. Introduce flexibility in the parity exchange rate so that it might "crawl" over time.
2. Widen the band in which exchange rates fluctuate around the parity level. (At present, the band is one percent on either side of the parity.)

The "Crawling Peg"

The basic idea behind a "crawling peg" system is that there exists an exchange rate which equilibrates the international supply and demand for a particular currency. However, the possibility that political or economic uncertainties might generate undesirable fluctuations in the supply and demand over short periods suggests that the movement of the exchange rate should be restrained. To accomplish this, countries would continue to hold the foreign exchange market rate within a predetermined range during any business day by sale and purchase of international reserves. However, the parity rate would be allowed to change from day to day by small amounts.

The actual formula for changing the parity exchange rate or peg would have to be determined by the members of the IMF. However, there are at least two possibilities. James Meade[1] has suggested that the peg be allowed to "crawl" not more than one-sixth of one percent in any one month, with the timing of such changes subject to the discretion of government officials. Such a plan would thus not impinge upon the sovereignty of individual countries. Nevertheless, international co-operation would still have to be maintained in order to avoid the possibility of countries undertaking mutually conflicting actions, such as beggar-my-neighbor policies.

An alternative is for the IMF to adopt a plan such that the peg's "crawl" is automatic. For instance, today's parity rate might be a moving average of exchange rates over a certain previous period of time. (The rate would be allowed to move freely within a band around the "crawling peg.") If the trend in a country's exchange rate was up, then its parity rate would crawl up as well. Such a system eliminates the possibility of human error that would exist under the discretionary "crawling peg." On the other hand, it assumes that the operation of the foreign exchange market will bring desirable results. The ultimate choice between these two alternatives would depend on the results of carefully weighing the political and economic feasibility of each.

A Wider Band

In the previous discussion we assumed that there existed around the parity level a band in which exchange rates were free to vary without official intervention. The width of the band might remain at two percent, as it is today, or it might be

---

[1]James E. Meade, "The International Monetary Mechanism," *The Three Banks Review*, September, 1964.

broadened perhaps to ten percent. Under the automatic version of the "crawling peg," this band would play an important role, since past exchange rate movements within it would determine today's parity. Should the exchange rate threaten to move outside the limits prescribed by the band, officials would be obliged to intervene in the foreign exchange markets.

Any proposal designed *solely* to widen the band of variation around an inflexible parity is unsatisfactory since it provides no guarantee that the long-run equilibrium exchange rate will fall within the band. It should be emphasized that the "crawling peg" proposal is designed to allow exchange rates to seek their equilibrium levels while limiting undesirable short-run fluctuations.

Freely Flexible Exchange Rates

An extreme plan for greater exchange rate flexibility would eliminate the concepts of "peg" or "band" and allow rates to fluctuate freely. This proposal is countered by those who argue that potentially wide fluctuations will lead to increased risk and hence restrict the growth of international trade and investment activities. Milton Friedman points out, however, that intelligent speculators will tend to move the exchange rate toward its equilibrium value.[2]

Consider a situation in which interest rates are roughly equivalent in the United States and the United Kingdom and the price of pound sterling is expected to fall. Speculators will then sell pounds in the forward exchange market in the hope of later buying pounds at a lower price. As this forward selling develops, the forward price of pounds falls.

Arbitragers seeking to take advantage of the spread between the spot and forward rates will then sell spot pounds, thus driving down the spot exchange rate. Simultaneously, they will buy pounds in the forward market, thus moderating the fall in the forward rate caused by the speculative pressures.

The operations of arbitragers and speculators may help to move the exchange rate toward its ultimate equilibrium. However, there is no guarantee that they will always possess sufficient foresight to avoid adversely affecting the stability of international transactions by under- or over-shooting the long term equilibrium exchange rate. In fact, this question can only be answered empirically. . . . Canada, with a flexible rate between 1950 and 1962, experienced a growing level of international trade and investment activity. In addition, there is evidence that speculation did not cause any destabilizing exchange rate fluctuations.

It would seem desirable to guard against the unknown risks of flexible exchange rates by adopting the "crawling peg" constraint on the spot rate. Under this system, the difference between spot and forward exchange rates would be kept within reasonable bounds by arbitrage. This spread is an important consideration for international traders and investors who may desire to hedge their transactions. If the cost of hedging is high, there will be good reason for the growth of international transactions to be slowed.

Again, suppose that the price of pound sterling is expected to fall and that interest rates are roughly equal in the United States and United Kingdom. Individuals would realize that the spot rate cannot fall by more than a predetermined amount under the "crawling peg" system. Any divergence of the forward rate by more than this would induce arbitrage, that is, there is an incentive to buy pounds forward with the knowledge that they can be re-sold at a price higher than the current forward rate. The forward rate would thus be kept within reasonable bounds by the increased demand generated by such operations.

---

[2]M. Friedman, "The Case for Flexible Exchange Rates," in M. Friedman (ed.), *Essays in Positive Economics* (Chicago: University of Chicago Press, 1953), pp. 157–203.

Implications for Monetary Policy

One of the implications of the "crawling peg" is that it would *increase* the effectiveness of domestic monetary policy in the short run.

Let us again consider a situation where Italy is experiencing inflation and its central bank seeks to restrain economic activity by selling Government securities on the open market. As interest rates rise, investors will find Italian assets more attractive. There will be an increase in demand for lire, and the exchange rate will tend to appreciate. As a result, as the lira appreciates over time, Italy's exports will decrease and Italians will substitute imports for domestically produced goods. This tends to reinforce, rather than to weaken, the effects of the original decrease in the money supply. Because there is no balance-of-payments deficit or surplus, there is no offsetting monetary effect. Consider [Figure 3].

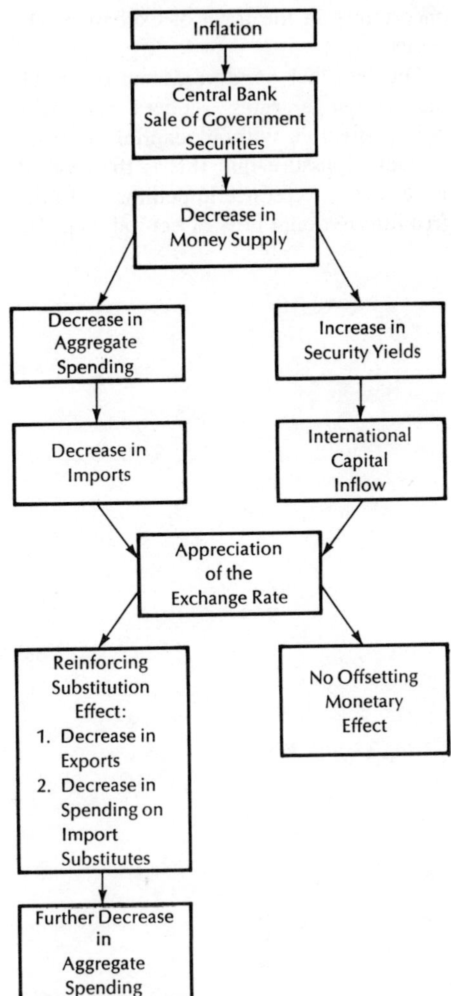

Figure 3

It should be emphasized that the continued effectiveness of monetary policy in achieving domestic aims hinges upon the degree of exchange rate variability that the members of the IMF deem to be acceptable. If the peg is allowed to "crawl" at a slow rate, monetary policy will be almost as ineffective as under a fixed exchange rate system. If, however, the range of potential variability is reasonably wide, then monetary policy can be expected to have an influence on domestic economic activity within a relatively short period. This will have the added benefit of reducing the capital controls required to increase the effectiveness of monetary policy under the present system.

• • •

CONCLUSIONS

If the industrialized nations of the world are going to place heavy reliance on monetary actions to achieve domestic goals, then under a pegged exchange rate system these actions may be considerably weakened unless controls on capital movements are imposed. This involves costs: not only are such restrictions incompatible with the goal of international currency convertibility, but by raising "barriers" to entry into international capital markets, these restrictions bring about an inefficient allocation of resources throughout the world. In addition, the present pegged exchange rate system is not conducive to international adjustment, but instead fosters periodic uncertainty in the form of exchange rate crises.

On the other hand, a system of crawling exchange rates renders monetary policy effective without capital controls. In fact, to assure that this is the case, it is necessary to reduce impediments to the free international flow of capital. Equally important is that this system enables long run balance-of-payments adjustments through greater exchange rate flexibility. The increased flexibility does not mean instability, however, for the exchange rate will be free to vary, or "crawl," only within bounds predetermined by the IMF.

56 QUESTIONS FOR DISCUSSION

GEORGE N. HALM

Two distinct categories of questions characterize the series of queries raised by Professor Halm. The first has to do with transitional problems as the world economy evolves from present international arrangements to a newer system, whatever form that may take. The second group is concerned with an evaluation of each reform program per se and is therefore post-transitional. Also included in this second category are technical questions aimed at understanding the exact form that the new plan is to possess, because many details within each general category of reform are yet to be ironed out.

To avoid confusion and to permit comparability, note that when Halm uses the term "gliding parity," he refers to the reform more commonly called the crawling peg.

. . .

The introduction of a system of limited exchange-rate flexibility requires the thorough discussion of many questions. Vague fears must be dispelled, transition difficulties overcome, and choices made between several versions of limited flexibility. The cost of experimenting can be reduced if the whole problem is viewed from several angles before practical work begins.

THE LACKING ADJUSTMENT MECHANISM

If the present system has been working adequately, why the repeated international monetary crises, the disalignment of exchange rates, and the introduction of exchange restrictions? Whatever the reasons, can we hope to eliminate the causes of external imbalance while maintaining rigid exchange rates? How long can we shore up the present system by *ad hoc* arrangements? Would the introduction of Special Drawing Rights eliminate the major weakness of the present system—the absence of a functioning adjustment mechanism?

FIXED EXCHANGE RATES

Why should we be justified in violating the basic principles of the market economy in the foreign-exchange market? Why should this important market not perform the function of equilibrating demand and supply? Why should it be immune to the known dangers of price control? Can fixed exchange rates have their claimed disciplinary effect on national monetary policy (1) if full employment is the primary concern of national economic policy, (2) if international liquidity reserves are very large, (3) if the financing of balance-of-payments defi-

---

From George N. Halm, *Toward Limited Exchange-Rate Flexibility*, Essays in International Finance No. 73 (March 1969), pp. 24–27; reprinted by permission of International Finance Section, Princeton University.

cits is guaranteed for the country whose money serves as intervention currency, (4) if the parities can be changed in the case of "fundamental" disequilibrium? If monetary discipline cannot be relied upon, can the desired results be achieved by an incomes policy?

FREELY FLUCTUATING EXCHANGE RATES

If price signals are needed in the foreign-exchange market, are the presently permitted margins sufficient? Precisely, why should freely fluctuating exchange rates lead to (1) wide price variations, (2) self-aggravating speculation, (3) destruction of monetary discipline, (4) competitive exchange depreciation? How do reserve losses and exchange-rate variations compare as signals on which to orient responsible monetary behavior? Why must it be taken for granted that international monetary cooperation will cease to operate as soon as exchange rates are permitted to fluctuate?

THE BAND PROPOSAL

Could a wider band for permissible exchange-rate variations combine the discipline of a fixed parity with sufficient flexibility inside the band? Would the argument for a widened band still hold if the parity were permitted to glide? How much would the band have to be widened to provide an adjustment mechanism for international trade? Would a band of a total width of 10 percent have avoided the imbalances of the last 10 years? Would the width of the band needed for trade adjustment be compatible with confidence in the international payments system? Assuming that exchange rates have become disaligned under the present system, would the introduction of a wider band have to be preceded by a general realignment of parities or should the width of the band be so generous that existing deviations of parities can be absorbed without exhausting the newly permitted flexibility? Would it be desirable to begin with a modest widening of the band, for example, a doubling of the presently permitted range, and then to continue to broaden the band as experience and confidence is gained? Would private speculation tend to be equilibrating or disequilibrating? How effective and how expensive would hedging operations be? Must we assume that private and social costs connected with greater exchange-rate flexibility will be greater than those of the present system? Should exchange-rate variations between fixed support points be completely free or should the monetary authorities be permitted to intervene even before the support points have been reached? How could surplus countries be induced to let their currencies appreciate?

THE GLIDING PARITY

Should parity adjustments be permitted under carefully defined circumstances, provided that these adjustments are very small and frequent? Under which conditions should these adjustments be permitted? Should they be quasi-automatic or depend on permission by the IMF? Can an adjustment formula be found precise enough to permit measurements whose exactness matches the smallness of the permitted changes or are these small and frequent changes only meant to give the quality of gradualness to contemplated large parity adjustments? How can disequilibrating speculation be avoided in a gliding-parity system? Can speculative capital flows be prevented by artificial interest-rate differentials? Are these differentials compatible with the desired freedom for domestic monetary policy? Can domestic economic policy rely exclusively on fiscal instruments so that the monetary instruments are available for the achievement of external balance?

Should the monetary authorities intervene so as to make the direction and degree of parity changes less obvious? Could a gliding-parity formula be precise enough to serve international monetary cooperation, yet vague enough to prevent anticipation of parity changes by private speculators?

THE MOVABLE BAND

Should widened band and gliding parity be combined in a movable band? Would a movable band seriously weaken the guidance of monetary policy that is to be gained from fixed support points? Should the widened band be considered a first step toward limited exchange-rate flexibility and the gliding parity be introduced, as a second step, when the exchange rates get stuck at the support points? How can surplus countries be induced to let their parities glide upward when the formula demands?

WIDENED BAND, GLIDING PARITY, AND THE DOLLAR

How can widened band and/or gliding parity be introduced into the present international payments system? How would the dollar in its role as reserve, transaction, and intervention currency be affected? Could a widened or a movable band be introduced while gold convertibility of the dollar at $35 an ounce of gold is maintained? Assuming that the dollar as intervention and reserve currency cannot move as much and as freely as other currencies, could the United States be satisfied with one-half the width of the band that is enjoyed by other countries? Would the automatic borrowing rights enjoyed by the United States compensate for this restriction? Would the introduction of a widened or a movable band reduce or increase the need for international liquidity reserves? What changes in the Articles of Agreement of the IMF would be implied?

57 THE NEW INTERNATIONAL MONETARY PLAN IN PERSPECTIVE

THOMAS E. DAVIS

This article was published originally in February 1968. By October 1969, the required number of IMF member nations had accepted the amendment concerning SDRs as proposed by the IMF's Board of Governors in April 1968, and $3.5 billion was allocated in 1970. (The United States received $866,880,000 of the initial distribution.)

It must be pointed out that the creation of SDRs was not the only means of increasing international liquidity. Appreciating gold is one alternative, and had been strongly recommended by a number of French political leaders and economists. Other suggestions included increasing the number of reserve currencies by including the mark, the French franc, and some other European currencies. Why were these other plans dropped in favor of the SDRs? Should they have been eliminated?

Recent developments in international finance, highlighted by the devaluation of the British pound and speculative activity in the London gold market, have created considerable public interest in the future viability of the international monetary system. Policy-makers, of course, have been vitally interested in this issue for a number of years. In fact, more than four years ago, officials here and abroad undertook a series of intensive studies designed to appraise the outlook for the functioning of the international monetary system and to assess its probable future needs. These studies generally agreed that the present system, based on fixed exchange rates and the established price of gold, has proved its value as a foundation on which to build for the future. Moreover, it was agreed that due to increasingly close cooperation between central banks and the development of extensive official short-term credit facilities, the present system has demonstrated a great capacity to adapt to changing circumstances and to meet successfully conditions of periodic strain.

Despite the past success of the present system, officials and academicians alike also have agreed that the system is confronted by certain actual or potential problems. Customarily, these problems are grouped under three main headings: (1) insufficient effectiveness in the balance of payments adjustment process, (2) the risk of potential instability resulting from a change of confidence in, and a subsequent shift between, existing international reserve assets, and (3) the problem of assuring an adequate long-run supply of international reserve assets consistent with a desirable and noninflationary economic growth rate in the world economy.

In recognition of these three problems, continuous official efforts have been made during the past four years to explore and develop mutually acceptable methods to improve the international

From Thomas E. Davis, "The New International Monetary Plan in Perspective," Federal Reserve Bank of Kansas City, *Monthly Review*, February 1968, pp. 11–17.

monetary system. As a result, considerable progress has been made in clarifying the issues and responsibilities involved in both the balance of payments adjustment problem and the "confidence" problem.

The most notable accomplishment, however, has been directed toward the problem of assuring an adequate long-run supply of international reserves. This accomplishment occurred at the annual meeting of the International Monetary Fund (IMF) held in Rio de Janeiro, Brazil, in September 1967, when a resolution was unanimously adopted to proceed with a plan to establish, within the Fund, machinery for the creation of a new international reserve facility. This facility, which is to take the form of special drawing rights (SDR's), is intended to meet the need, as and when it arises, for a supplement to existing international reserve assets. As specified in the approved resolution, the plan for the new facility is to be formally incorporated into a proposed amendment to the Fund's Articles of Agreement, which in turn is to be submitted for approval to the Fund's Board of Governors no later than March 31, 1968. Upon approval by the Fund's Board of Governors, the proposed amendment will be submitted to the 107 member countries of the IMF for their ratification—a process which will require an 80 percent majority of the voting power of IMF members and which is expected to be completed before the end of 1969. After ratification, the Fund will be able to activate the plan provided 85 percent of the weighted votes of the Fund members support the creation of special drawing rights.

In view of the widespread interest in the plan for creating special drawing rights, this article discusses the major factors underlying the need for supplementing existing international reserve assets, and reviews and comments on some of the principal features of the proposed plan.

THE NEED FOR A RESERVE SUPPLEMENT

Under the present international monetary system, international reserves consist of the aggregate stock of assets and facilities which are unconditionally available to national monetary authorities to support the par value of their currencies in foreign exchange markets when their external payments are in deficit. Traditionally, reserves comprise countries' official holdings of gold and convertible foreign exchange, primarily dollars and sterling. In recent years, as countries have recognized that their reserve positions with the IMF serve the function of reserves, total international reserves have come to be considered as the sum of gold, foreign exchange, and IMF reserve positions held officially by all countries.

It is widely recognized today that an adequate supply of international reserves is indispensable to the proper functioning of the international monetary system. Reserves provide the means by which a country can finance a temporary balance of payments deficit without resorting to undesirable measures designed to correct the deficit, such as deflationary domestic policies or restrictions on international trade and payments. Thus, an adequate supply of reserves not only affords a country more time in which it can implement desirable corrective policies when faced with an external deficit, but also serves as a basis for keeping trade and payments free from restrictions and for maintaining confidence in currencies in general.

Due to the importance of an adequate reserve supply, monetary authorities continually have been aware of the need to assure a satisfactory growth rate in the stock of international reserves. During the postwar period and throughout most of the 1950's, however, the growth in international reserves did not present a major problem. Reserves in the world outside the United States grew quite rapidly during the period without deliberate reserve action. Facilitating this growth were the moderate balance of payments deficits experienced by the United States, as well as the steady increase in the amount of gold produced and accumulated as part of official gold stocks. Often cited as evidence of the adequacy of reserves during this period is the dismantling of European trade restrictions and the introduction of widespread currency convertibility in 1958.

In recent years, monetary authorities have become increasingly concerned about the future adequacy of international reserves. In fact, a growing consensus has developed that the future supply of reserves emanating from existing sources is not likely to keep pace with the growing long-run need for reserves. This consensus is based partly on the expectation that, at the established price of gold, the future growth in the stock of monetary gold will not be sufficient to meet legitimate reserve needs. It also is based on the expectation that future reserve growth is not likely to be met by increased U.S. dollar holdings to the same extent as in the past. Since the expected shortfall in future reserve growth provides the underlying rationale for the need to create a reserve supplement, further consideration is given below to the factors affecting both the need for and the supply of international reserves.

The expectation that the need for international reserves will increase over the long run generally is supported by two reasons. First, the long-run growth in world trade is likely to be accompanied by larger absolute swings in external payments imbalances, which in turn will require a larger stock of reserves with which to finance the imbalances. It should be emphasized, however, that no direct proportionality exists between the growth in world trade and payments and the need for reserves. This is because the need for reserves is related to the magnitude of payments imbalances, which while undoubtedly influenced by the growth of trade, can also be significantly affected by many other factors, such as the speed and efficiency of the balance of payments adjustment process and the equilibrating nature of international capital flows. Thus, while a qualitative assessment of future reserve needs can justifiably be based on the expected growth of world trade and payments, no satisfactory quantitative projection can be made on this basis alone. Second, as a matter of policy most countries today wish to see an increase in their international reserves over time, whereas no country is prepared to accept a long-run decline in its reserves. The United States, during most of the 1950's, was a notable exception to this latter statement. The striving of countries to accumulate reserves over the long run is attributed partly to their expectations of larger future payments imbalances, partly to their desire to assure their own financial and political independence, and partly to their desire to be able to meet future payments deficits without turning to unpleasant domestic corrective measures and restrictive international policies.

The expectation that the supply of international reserves will not be adequate to meet the secular increase in the need for reserves is related generally to the recent deceleration in the growth rate of reserves. As evidence of this deceleration, aggregate monetary reserves grew at an annual rate of only 2.0 percent in 1966, which was considerably less than the average annual growth rate of 2.5 percent between the end of 1950 and 1965, and markedly below the average growth rate of 3.5 percent during the six-year period 1960–65. Moreover, during the first half of 1967, monetary reserves actually declined at an annual rate of 1.7 percent. Thus, at the end of June 1967, monetary reserves totaled $71,020 million, or just slightly above the level reached at the end of 1965.

The factors contributing to the recent deceleration in the growth of international reserves generally are thought to be those which will continue to limit the future growth of reserves. These factors

Table 1. International Reserve Assets
In millions of U.S. dollars

	1950	1960	1964	1965	1966	Mid-1967
Gold held officially by countries	33,755	38,030	40,845	41,850	40,905	40,535
Total official gold holdings*	35,300	40,505	43,015	43,225	43,185	42,975
Foreign exchange	13,290	18,670	23,510	23,025	24,385	24,590
U.S. dollars	4,890	11,088	15,771	15,849	14,965	16,308
Other Reserve Currencies†	8,400	7,582	7,739	7,176	9,420	8,282
Reserve Positions in IMF	1,671	3,570	4,155	5,376	6,330	5,897
IMF Gold Holdings	1,494	2,439	2,179	1,869	2,652	2,669
IMF Net Reserve Creation‡	177	1,131	1,976	3,507	3,678	3,228
Total	48,715	60,270	68,505	70,250	71,620	71,020

*Includes gold held by countries and international organizations.

†Includes British pounds sterling plus a residual item including official monetary liabilities of countries other than the United States and United Kingdom.

‡Equals Reserve Positions in IMF, minus IMF Gold Holdings.

SOURCE: International Financial Statistics.

are best understood by reviewing the recent and prospective developments in each of the three components of monetary reserves, i.e., gold, foreign exchange, and reserve positions in the IMF.

Gold available for official reserves constitutes a residual remaining after new gold production in noncommunist countries and sales of gold by the Soviet Union have met the private absorption of gold for industrial, artistic, and professional uses and for hoarding and speculation. During the 15 years prior to 1966, official gold holdings of countries and international financial institutions rose at an average annual rate of $528 million, as private demand was less than the total amount of new gold supplied. In 1966, however, official holdings dropped $40 million, as private demand exceeded the amount of new gold supplied. In addition, throughout the first half of 1967, private demand continued to exceed the supply of new gold, so that official holdings dropped $210 million to a level of $42,975 million, or to just about the same level that prevailed at the end of 1964. Projections based on these developments—a steady and rapid increase in the private demand for gold combined with a slow rise in production—indicate that official gold holdings are unlikely to increase in the future at a desirable rate; unless, of course, supplemented by large Soviet gold sales. Indeed, if official holdings are sold to meet a rise in private demand in excess of new gold production, official holdings may tend to decline. For these reasons, it is generally thought that new additions to official gold holdings cannot be relied upon as a dependable source of future reserve growth.

Until recently, official holdings of foreign exchange have constituted one of the most rapidly growing components of international reserves. For example, between the end of 1950 and 1964 foreign exchange holdings grew at an average annual rate of $730 million, and during the five-year period 1960 through 1964, the annual increase averaged as much as $1,458 million. This growth in foreign exchange holdings was primarily in U.S. dollar liabilities, which was a consequence of the U.S. balance of payments deficits. While the U.S. deficits have continued since 1964, total U.S. dollar liabilities have risen only moderately above the level reached at the end of 1964, because the United States has financed its deficits mainly by drawing down its gold stock as well as its reserve position in the IMF. Total foreign exchange holdings also have risen only moderately since the end of 1964, increasing by $1,080 million to a level of $24,590 million at the end of June 1967. Moreover, most of this increase has reflected either temporary factors such as central bank currency swaps, or special transactions like the transfer into British reserves in 1966 of assets formerly held as dollar securities by the British government. Thus, the recent slowdown in the growth of "ordinary" foreign exchange holdings, and the general realization that a further growth in U.S. dollar liabilities is likely to exert increasing pressure on U.S. gold reserves, are the primary reasons why it is considered unwise to depend on new additions to foreign exchange holdings as a major source of future reserve growth.

A reserve position in the IMF represents the amount that a member country may obtain, or draw, essentially automatically from the Fund, whenever the country is experiencing a balance of payments deficit. In recent years, IMF reserve positions have been the most rapidly growing component of international reserves, rising from $4,155 million at the end of 1964 to $5,897 million in mid-1967. The major factors accounting for this increase were the large drawings on the Fund in 1965, particularly by the United Kingdom, and the net payment of gold to the Fund in 1966 in connection with the 25 percent increase in Fund quotas. In assessing the net contribution of this rise in Fund reserve positions to aggregate monetary reserves, it is necessary, of course, to omit the rise in Fund gold holdings. This is because a rise in Fund gold holdings involves an equivalent decrease in member countries' gold reserves. On this basis, net reserve creation by the Fund still has increased substantially in recent years, rising by $1,252 million from the end of 1964 to mid-1967. Nonetheless, since net reserve creation by the Fund reflects essentially medium-term credits extended to member countries by the Fund, the subsequent repayment of these credits will tend to cancel these temporary additions to international reserves; unless, of course, drawings increase at a rate not offset by repayments. Thus, under present arrangements, reserve positions in the IMF may not provide the basis for regular or permanent additions to the aggregate stock of international reserves.

In view of these factors, indicating that the supply of international reserves from traditional sources is unlikely to meet future needs, monetary authorities have found it advisable to establish a plan to provide for a permanent supplement to existing reserve assets. The major aspects of this plan are summarized in the following section.

THE PLAN FOR A RESERVE SUPPLEMENT

The plan to establish a supplementary reserve asset is basically quite simple in substance, but appropriately contains certain detailed provisions governing the activation, allocation, and use of the new asset. In essence, the plan would create a new international reserve asset in the form of special drawing rights (SDR's), which would be transferable among participating countries, and would be backed by a commitment of participating countries to accept them in exchange for convertible currencies. These SDR's would appear as book entries in a Special Drawing Account at the IMF and would be denominated in units of account equivalent to the gold value of one U.S. dollar. SDR's also would be guaranteed in terms of gold, and would carry a moderate rate of interest [1½ percent annually—ed.]. It should be emphasized, however, that the value of the new reserve facility would rest fundamentally on the obligation of participants to accept it, in much the same way as the value of domestic fiduciary money derives from its status as legal tender.

Activation and Allocation of SDR's

The activation of the plan to create SDR's is to depend upon a widely recognized global need for reserve creation. Procedurally, the Managing Director of the IMF, after having satisfied himself that there is a need to supplement reserves, will undertake consultations to ascertain that there is broad support among the participants for the creation of SDR's in the amount he proposes. If the Executive Directors of the Fund agree with his proposal, it must then be approved by the Fund's Board of Governors by an 85 percent majority of the voting power of the participating countries.

Since SDR's are intended to assure an adequate long-run growth rate in total reserves, the amount created usually will not vary from year to year in response to the payments positions or reserve needs of individual countries. Rather, the amount to be created normally will be for a specific period ahead—initially a five-year period*—during which SDR's will be allocated at designated intervals. Underlying this principle is the belief that not only should SDR's be created on the basis of global reserve needs but that, given the present state of knowledge and institutional arrangements, it is neither feasible nor desirable to make short-term changes in the volume of world reserves to meet cyclical swings in international economic activity. In the case of unexpected major developments, however, there are provisions for changing the rate of issue within the specified period.

The allocation of SDR's will be made to all participating countries in proportion to their IMF quotas. For example, if a decision is made to create $1 billion of SDR's per year for five years, the United States, which currently has 24.6 percent of total Fund quotas, would receive $246 million of the SDR's created each year—for a total of $1,230 million over the five-year period. Receiving an allocation of SDR's simply means that in each of the five years the Fund would credit the United States on the books of the Special Drawing Account with $246 million of SDR's.

*In fact, 3 years—ed.

The Use of SDR's

Since the plan calls for the establishment of a new and untried reserve asset, the most extensive provisions of the plan are directed toward the use of this asset. Generally, these provisions set forth rules on participating countries' eligibility to use and receive SDR's, their obligation to accept SDR's, and if necessary, their obligation to partially reconstitute the amount actually used. The major points in each of these provisions are summarized below.

Each participating country is entitled to use its SDR's to acquire an equivalent amount of convertible currencies only for balance of payments needs or in the light of developments in its total reserves. A country's exercise of this right is not subject to prior challenge, nor is it contingent on the adoption of appropriate policies designed to restore balance of payments equilibrium. In this latter sense, SDR's are unconditionally available—unlike the present credit facilities of the IMF, which are conditional in nature. There is, however, a proviso attached to the unconditional use of SDR's. This proviso stipulates that no country should use SDR's merely to change the composition of its reserve assets. In the event that a country fails to observe this proviso, the Fund may direct transfers of SDR's to that country to offset such misuse.

Each participating country is obligated to accept SDR's, and to provide in exchange an equivalent amount of convertible currency up to an amount where its total holdings, including its allocations, are equal to three times its cumulative allocations. Put more simply, a country's acceptance obligation is always the difference between its actual holdings and three times its cumulative allocations. For example, if a country's initial allocations were $100 million and it used none of its SDR's, its acceptance obligation would be $200 million; and if it had transferred all of its initial allocations to other countries, its acceptance obligation would be $300 million. A country could, of course, accept and hold SDR's in excess of this amount.

The acceptance obligation, as indicated earlier, is the foundation of the plan since it provides the fundamental backing for the new asset. This obligation makes unnecessary a pool of currencies like those used to back the present IMF credit facilities. Thus, great care was taken to make the obligations large enough to assure any participant that its holdings would be fully usable.

Countries likely to receive a transfer of SDR's will normally be those with strong balance of payments or reserve positions. To assure this normal flow, the Fund, in its capacity as intermediary, will try to guide the transfer of SDR's to these countries in a manner designed to maintain over time an equal ratio in their holdings of SDR's to their total reserves. This rule is complemented by a special provision permitting a reserve currency country, such as the United States, that wants to buy balances of its own currency held by another country, to direct its transfer specifically to that country, provided the latter agrees. Regardless of how the transfers are arranged, whether directly between participants or indirectly through the Fund, they all are to be recorded in the Fund's Special Drawing Account by a debit to the account of the user and a credit to the account of the receiver.

Participating countries that use SDR's will incur an obligation to reconstitute, or restore, their position, depending on the amount and duration of use. The rules for reconstitution specify that over a five-year period a country's average net use is not to exceed 70 per cent of its average cumulative allocation. A country could, of course, exceed the 70 per cent use rate during the period, but would be obligated to restore its position at the end of the period. The primary purpose of the reconstitution obligation is to prevent a country from financing persistent external deficits by the exclusive use of SDR's. However, to the extent that the balance of payments adjustment process works effectively, reconstitution will tend to work automatically through the usual process of a country moving from a deficit to a surplus position, and so becoming eligible to receive SDR's.

The reconstitution provision, to be sure, may impose a repayment obligation on part of a country's use of SDR's, but it does not significantly impair the quality of the asset. Indeed, that portion which is not required to be repaid, i.e., 70 per cent of the cumulative allocations, will constitute a stock of unconditionally available reserve assets and will be a permanent addition to the total supply of international reserves.

CONCLUSION

The plan to establish a new international reserve facility in the form of special drawing rights represents a major accomplishment in the continuing official effort to assure the future viability of the international monetary system. The plan provides a workable mechanism through which international reserves can be expanded on a permanent basis in accordance with the needs of the world economy, rather than being dependent—as in the past—on the uncertain by-product of such forces as the supply and private absorption of gold, the external payments position of reserve currency countries, and the decisions of participating countries concerning the composition of their reserves.

SELECTED BIBLIOGRAPHY

Following is a brief list of books and articles rather than a comprehensive bibliography that few will read. Note that bibliographical references found elsewhere in this text are not repeated here.

PART I THE CONTROVERSY OVER THE DEFINITION OF MONEY

Cacy, J. A. "Alternative Approaches to the Analysis of the Financial Structure," Federal Reserve Bank of Kansas City, *Monthly Review,* March 1968, pp. 3–9.

Chetty, V. K. "On Measuring the Nearness of Near-Moneys," *American Economic Review,* 59, 270–281. (Econometric)

Friedman, M., and A. J. Schwartz. *Monetary Statistics of the United States: Estimates, Sources, Methods.* New York: National Bureau of Economics Research, 1970.

Meltzer, Allan H. "Money, Intermediation, and Growth," *Journal of Economic Literature,* 7, 27–40. (Bibliographic)

PART II ISSUES IN COMMERCIAL BANKING

Portfolio Analysis and Its Implications

Jessup, Paul F. (ed.). *Innovations in Bank Management: Selection Readings.* New York: Holt, Rinehart & Winston, 1969, pp. 5–60 and 360–383. (A number of short articles)

Tobin, James. "Commercial Banks as Creators of 'Money,' " in Deane Carson (ed.), *Banking and Monetary Studies.* Homewood, Illinois: Richard D. Irwin, 1963.

Bank Size and The Structure of the Banking Industry

Administrator of National Banks, *Studies in Banking Competition and Bank Structure: Articles Reprinted from the National Banking Review.* Washington, D.C., 1966. (Articles of varying difficulty)

Fischer, Gerald C. *American Banking Structure.* New York: Columbia University Press, 1968.

Mote, L. R. "Competition in Banking," Federal Reserve Bank of Chicago, *Business Conditions,* January and February 1967. Reprinted in Jessup, *op cit.,* pp. 421–443.

PART III THE STRUCTURE OF THE FEDERAL RESERVE SYSTEM

Federal Reserve Independence

Clifford, A. J. *The Independence of the Federal Reserve System.* Philadelphia: University of Pennsylvania Press, 1965.

The Bank Supervision Controversy

U.S. Congress, House of Representatives, Committee on Banking and Currency, Subcommittee on Bank Supervision and Insurance, *Consolidation of Bank Examining and Supervisory Functions: Hearings.* Washington, D.C.: Government Printing Office, 1965. (Choose from among the testimonies)

PART IV THE MONEY MARKET AND THE FEDERAL RESERVE

Friedman, M. "The Euro-Dollar Market: Some First Principles," *The Morgan Guaranty Survey,* October 1969, pp. 4–14.

Heebner, A. G. *Negotiable Certificates of Deposits: The Development of a Money Market Instrument.* New York: New York University, Institute of Finance, Graduate School of Business, 1969.

Klopstock, F. "Money Creation in the Euro-Dollar Market—A Note on Professor Friedman's Views," Federal Reserve Bank of New York, *Monthly Review,* 52, No. 1, pp. 12–15.

Robinson, R. I. *Money and Capital Markets.* New York: McGraw-Hill, 1964.

PART V KEYNES VERSUS THE QUANTITY THEORY: THEORETICAL AND EMPIRICAL STUDIES

American Economic Review, 55, 693–792. (A debate on the Friedman-Meiselman analysis and conclusions—highly sophisticated econometrics)

Kaminow, Ira. "The Myth of Fiscal Policy: The Monetarist View," Federal Reserve Bank of Philadelphia, *Business Review,* December 1969, pp. 10–18.

PART VI THE TOOLS OF MONETARY POLICY

Reserve Requirements and Open Market Operations

Bain, A. D. "Monetary Control Through Open-Market Operations and Reserve-Requirement Variations," *Economic Journal,* 74, 137–146.

Grossman, Herschel I. "The Reserve Base, Reserve Requirements, and the Equilibrium Rate of Interest," *Quarterly Journal of Economics,* 81, 312–320.

Discounting and the Discount Rate

Anderson, C. J. "Evolution of the Role and Functioning of the Discount Mechanism," and D. M. Jones, "A Review of Recent Academic Literature on the Discount Mechanism." Both are part of the series, *Fundamental Reappraisal of the Discount Mechanism.* Washington, D.C.: Board of Governors of the Federal Reserve System, 1966.

Garvy, G. "The Discount Mechanism in the United States," Banca Nazionale del Lavoro, *Quarterly Review,* 87, 311–332.

PART VII PROBLEMS OF MONETARY POLICY

Lags

Willes, M. H. "Lags in Monetary and Fiscal Policy," Federal Reserve Bank of Philadelphia, *Business Conditions,* March 1968, pp. 3–10. (Survey)

The Discriminatory Impact of Monetary Policy

McGouldrick, P. F., and J. E. Petersen. "Monetary Restraint and Borrowing and Capital Spending by Large State and Local Governments in 1966," *Federal Reserve Bulletin,* 54, 552–581.

PART VIII RULES VERSUS DISCRETION

Friedman, M., and W. Heller. *Monetary Versus Fiscal Policy: A Dialogue.* New York: Norton, 1969.

Struble, F. M., and J. A. Cacy. "The Money Supply Rule and Countercyclical Monetary Policy," Federal Reserve Bank of Kansas City, *Monthly Review,* June–July 1968, pp. 3–9.

PART IX INFLATION: THE PHILLIPS CURVE CONTROVERSY

"Problems of Achieving and Maintaining a Stable Price Level," *American Economic Review,* 50, 177–222. (A series of articles on the Phillips curve)

Shultz, G. P., and R. Z. Aliber (eds.). *Guidelines: Informal Controls and the Market Place.* Chicago: University of Chicago Press, 1966, pp. 17–66. (A debate between M. Friedman and R. M. Solow)

PART X INTERNATIONAL MONETARY ECONOMICS

Federal Reserve Bank of Boston. *The International Adjustment Mechanism.* Boston: 1969. (Papers and discussions by leading economists.)

Meade, J. E. "Exchange-Rate Flexibility," *Three Banks Review,* 70, 3–27.

BIOGRAPHICAL NOTES

Daniel Ahearn is presently Vice President and Economist of Wellington Management Company, a mutual fund management firm in Boston. This Columbia Ph.D. previously held positions in the banking industry and with the federal government.

Joseph Aschheim is a Professor of Economics at George Washington University in Washington, D.C. Author of *Techniques of Monetary Control* and of a new textbook in macroeconomics, Professor Aschheim has served as a consultant to numerous governmental organizations. He received his Ph.D. from Harvard University.

George L. Bach is the Frank E. Buck Professor of Economics at Stanford University, to which he came after a distinguished career at the Carnegie Institute of Technology. Professor Bach is the author of one of the most popular elementary economics texts and has written extensively in the field of monetary economics.

George J. Benston is a Professor of Finance and Accounting at the University of Rochester. He received his doctorate from the University of Chicago, where his interest in the cost aspects of banking operations was nurtured. Dr. Benston is also a C.P.A. and has written on finance and accounting topics.

John Brooks is a staff writer on economic and financial topics for *The New Yorker*. He has written numerous popular books on economics, his most recent being *Once in Golconda*, a description of Wall Street activities during 1920s and 1930s.

Art Buchwald is the nationally syndicated columnist-satirist of the *Washington Post*.

Arthur F. Burns was appointed Chairman of the Board of Governors of the Federal Reserve System in 1970. His distinguished career includes service as Chairman of the Council of Economic Advisers (1953–1956), President of the renowned National Bureau of Economic Research (1956–1966), and John Bates Clark Professor of Economics at Columbia University.

The Commission on Money and Credit was an ad hoc private group, organized in the 1950s to examine the monetary structure and policies in the United States. Its membership comprised recognized leaders of the business, labor, academic, and financial communities.

The Council of Economic Advisers is a group of three economists, appointed by the President of the United States to serve as his chief economists. The Council was mandated by the Employment Act of 1946.

John M. Culbertson served as an economist for the Board of Governors of the Federal Reserve System from 1950 to 1957. He moved from there to the University of Wisconsin, where he is now a Professor of Economics. Professor Culbertson's research interests and publications lie in the general area of macroeconomic policy.

Thomas E. Davis became Research Officer and Economist at the Federal Reserve Bank of Kansas City in 1968 soon after joining the Bank's staff. He previously worked at the New York Fed as an international economist. Dr. Davis received his Ph.D. from the University of Michigan.

Fred C. DeLong is a practicing banker who, since 1966, has been the Senior Vice President at Pittsburgh's Mellon National Bank and Trust Company. He has been associated with Mellon professionally since 1937.

David P. Eastburn was elected President of the Federal Reserve Bank of Philadelphia in 1970, culminating a climb to the top that began in 1942, when he joined the Philadelphia Fed as a member of the research staff. Dr. Eastburn received his Ph.D. from the University of Pennsylvania.

The Federal Open Market Committee is composed of the seven-man Board of Governors of the Federal Reserve System and five of the twelve Presidents of the Federal Reserve Banks. Their primary responsibility is to decide the posture of open market operations.

James G. Fortson has written widely in the field of applied agricultural economics. He is an Assistant Professor in the School of Forest Resources and Director of the Administrative Data Processing Division of the University of Georgia.

Milton Friedman is the Paul Snowden Russell Distinguished Service Professor of Economics at the University of Chicago, a member of the research staff of the National Bureau of Economic Research, a past President of the American Economic Association, and author of numerous books and articles on monetary economics.

Carter H. Golembe is the President of his own consulting firm, Carter H. Golembe Associates, Inc., in Washington, D.C., and specializes in advising financial institutions. Dr. Golembe, who holds a Ph.D. from Columbia University and an LL.B. from George Washington University, has written extensively on bank structure and regulation.

Stuart I. Greenbaum began his career with the Federal Reserve Bank of Kansas City and moved to academic life in 1967, when he became an Associate Professor of Economics at the University of Kentucky. He has focused his research interests on various aspects of the banking industry.

John G. Gurley has been a Professor of Economics at Stanford University since 1961, having come there from the senior staff of Washington's renowned Brookings Institution. He also served as editor of the *American Economic Review* from 1962 to 1968.

Warren J. Gustus has divided his professional career among the business, academic, and government worlds. He left the Vice Presidency of a business consulting firm in 1966 to become Economic Advisor to the President of the Federal Reserve Bank of Philadelphia.

Jack M. Guttentag spent eight years at the Federal Reserve Bank of New York, where he rose to the position of Chief of the Domestic Research Division. He left the New York Fed to join the Department of Finance at the Wharton School of Finance and Commerce of the University of Pennsylvania and has been a Professor of Finance there since 1967.

George N. Halm came to the United States from Germany in 1937 and joined the faculty of Tufts University as a Professor of Economics. He has remained at Tufts but is now at the Fletcher School of Law and Diplomacy. Professor Halm has written primarily in the area of international finance and is the author of texts in comparative economic systems and money and banking.

Edward S. Herman is a Professor of Finance at the Wharton School of Commerce and Finance of the University of Pennsylvania. His recent major publications have been in the area of financial intermediaries. Professor Herman received his Ph.D. from the Berkeley campus of the University of California.

Clarence J. Huizenga is Director of the Unified M.B.A. Program at the Stanford Graduate School of Business in Palo Alto, California. His research interests lie in the area of consumer credit.

John H. Kareken is Professor of Economics at the University of Minnesota and an economic adviser to the Federal Reserve Bank of Minneapolis. Professor Kareken, who received his Ph.D. from the Massachusetts Institute of Technology (M.I.T.), spent some time in Washington as an economist for various governmental bodies.

Fred H. Klopstock is the Manager of the International Research Division of the Federal Reserve Bank of New York. The major writings of this Berlin University Ph.D. recipient have been in the area of international finance.

Thomas Mayer has written a best-selling work on monetary policy as well as numerous articles on monetary economics. Currently Professor of Economics at the Davis campus of the University of California, he received his doctorate from Columbia University.

George W. McKenzie received his Ph.D. from the University of California at Berkeley in 1967 and currently is an Assistant Professor of Economics at Washington University in St. Louis. His main interests lie in the fields of econometrics and international finance.

William McC. Martin, Jr., spent twenty years (1951–1970) as Chairman of the Board of Governors of the Federal Reserve System. Before that he served for a short period as Assistant Secretary of the Treasury, and, when only 32, was elected President of the New York Stock Exchange.

Paul Meek has been an Assistant Vice President of the Federal Reserve Bank of New York since 1966, with major responsibility in the area of open market operations. Dr. Meek joined the Bank in 1956 after a brief stay with the United States Operations Mission to Indonesia. His doctorate was granted by the University of Virginia.

David I. Meiselman has been engaged in research on the term structure of interest rates since his graduate days at the University of Chicago. After receiving his doctorate there, he became a Senior Economist in the Office of the Comptroller of the Currency. He is now the F. R. Bigelow Professor of Economics at Macalester College in St. Paul, Minnesota.

George W. Mitchell is a Governor of the Federal Reserve System, having been appointed to the Board of Governors by President Kennedy in 1961. Prior to that time he served as a Vice President of the Federal Reserve Bank of Chicago.

Franco Modigliani holds doctorates in jurisprudence (Rome, 1939), social science (New School, 1944), and law (Chicago, 1957). This prolific writer has been a Professor of Economics and Finance at M.I.T. since 1962.

George R. Morrison left the academic world in 1967 to join the First National City Bank of New York. He migrated westward soon after and is currently an Associate Professor of Economics at the San Diego branch of the University of California. He received his Ph.D. from the University of Chicago.

Murray E. Polakoff is Vice Dean and Professor of Finance at New York University's Graduate School of Business Administration. He has also taught at the University of Texas and the University of Rochester. His primary research interest lies in the realm of monetary policy.

Jonas Prager, who edited this anthology, is an Associate Professor of Economics at New York University. He served as a Visiting Senior Economist for the Bank of Israel for two years and will return to Israel as a Fulbright-Hays scholar in 1971.

Richard A. Radford received his B.A. in Economics from Cambridge in 1946. Since 1947, he has been on the staff of the International Monetary Fund. His famous article is based on his experience as a prisoner of war in Italy and Germany from 1942 to 1945.

Lawrence S. Ritter is Professor of Finance and Chairman of the Finance Department at the Graduate School of Business Administration of New York University. Professor Ritter was elected to the presidency of the American Finance Association for 1970–71. Aside from his numerous writings on monetary economics, Ritter has also authored a book on baseball.

Denis H. Robertson became Sir Denis in 1953 in recognition of his outstanding stature as an economist. He was educated at Cambridge, by John Maynard Keynes among others, and later became a colleague and critic of his mentor. Sir Denis held professorships in economics at the London School of Economics and at Cambridge. This master of *Alice in Wonderland* died in 1963.

Roland I. Robinson was a member of the Board of Governors of the Federal Reserve System from 1934 to 1946 and again from 1956 to 1961. Author of a well-known text on banking, he is currently a Professor of Economics at Michigan State University.

Robert H. Scott received his doctorate from Harvard University. He has been a Professor of Business Economics at the University of Washington in Seattle since 1961 and has written widely on a range of macroeconomic subjects.

Edward S. Shaw received his A.B., M.A., and Ph.D. from Stanford University, where he has spent the major part of his academic career. Professor Shaw has written numerous books and articles on monetary economics and is now a Professor of Economics at Stanford.

Warren L. Smith left his position as Professor of Economics at the University of Michigan in 1968 to serve as a member of President Johnson's Council of Economic Advisers. An expert on monetary policy, Professor Smith returned to Michigan in 1969.

Robert M. Solow was awarded the American Economic Association's prestigious John Bates Clark Medal in 1961 in recognition of his outstanding abilities. He became a Professor of Economics at M.I.T. in 1958 and has written widely on general economic theory.

Roger W. Spencer joined the Federal Reserve Bank of St. Louis as a business economist in 1968. He received his Ph.D. from the University of Virginia, and has also taught in various universities.

Robert W. Stone is a Senior Vice President of New York's Irving Trust Company. From 1962 to 1965, he was the Manager of the Federal Reserve's Open Market Account and a Vice President of the Federal Reserve Bank of New York.

Frederick M. Struble served as a financial economist for the Federal Reserve Bank of Kansas City from 1962 to 1969, when he joined the research staff of the Board of Governors of the Federal Reserve System. He received his Ph.D. from the University of Colorado.

Richard H. Timberlake has been a Professor of Finance at the University of Georgia since 1964. In addition to numerous articles on monetary history, Professor Timberlake has written a popular text on money and banking.

James Tobin chairs the Department of Economics at Yale University, where he is also a Professor of Economics. He left Yale briefly in 1961–1962 to serve as a member of the Council of Economic Advisers under President Kennedy. In 1955 Professor Tobin was awarded the John Bates Clark Medal of the American Economic Association in recognition of his achievements as an economist.

Donald P. Tucker joined the research staff of the Board of Governors of the Federal Reserve System in 1970, after a stint with Washington's Urban Institute and the University of Chicago. He received his Ph.D. from M. I. T.